HANDBOOK OF SUSTAINABLE DEVELOPMENT

Handbook of Sustainable Development

Edited by

Giles Atkinson

Senior Lecturer in Environmental Policy, Department of Geography and Environment and Deputy Director, Centre for Environmental Policy and Governance (CEPG), London School of Economics and Political Science, UK

Simon Dietz

Lecturer in Environmental Policy, Department of Geography and Environment and Centre for Environmental Policy and Governance (CEPG), London School of Economics and Political Science, UK

Eric Neumayer

Professor of Environment and Development, Department of Geography and Environment and Centre for Environmental Policy and Governance (CEPG), London School of Economics and Political Science, UK

Edward Elgar
Cheltenham, UK • Northampton, MA, USA

Published by
Edward Elgar Publishing Limited
Glensanda House
Montpellier Parade
Cheltenham
Glos GL50 1UA
UK

Edward Elgar Publishing, Inc.
William Pratt House
9 Dewey Court
Northampton
Massachusetts 01060
USA

A catalogue record for this book
is available from the British Library

Library of Congress Cataloguing in Publication Data

Handbook of sustainable development/edited by Giles Atkinson, Simon Dietz,
    Eric Neumayer.
        p. cm. — (Elgar original reference)
    Includes bibliographical references and index.
    1. Sustainable development. I. Atkinson, Giles, 1969– . II. Dietz, Simon,
    1979– . III. Neumayer, Eric, 1970– . IV. Series.
    HC79.E5H3186   2006
    338.9'27—dc22   2006014312

ISBN 978 1 84376 577 6 (cased)

Printed and bound in Great Britain by MPG Books Ltd, Bodmin, Cornwall

Contents

PART VII   THE INTERNATIONAL DIMENSION

Contributors

W. Neil Adger, Tyndall Centre for Climate Change Research, School of Environmental Sciences, University of East Anglia, Norwich, UK.

Julian Agyeman, Department of Urban and Environmental Policy and Planning, Tufts University, Medford, MA, USA.

Giles Atkinson, Department of Geography and Environment and Centre for Environmental Policy and Governance (CEPG), London School of Economics and Political Science, London, UK.

Richard M. Auty, Department of Geography, Lancaster University, Lancaster, UK.

Jan Bebbington, Centre for Social and Environmental Accounting Research, University of St Andrews, St Andrews, UK.

Katharine Bolt, World Conservation Monitoring Centre (WCMC), Cambridge, UK.

Camilla Bretteville Froyn, Center for International Climate and Environmental Research – Oslo (CICERO), Norway.

Matthew A. Cole, Department of Economics, University of Birmingham, Birmingham, UK.

Simon Dietz, Department of Geography and Environment and Centre for Environmental Policy and Governance (CEPG), London School of Economics and Political Science, London, UK.

Timothy J. Foxon, Cambridge Centre for Climate Change Mitigation Research (4CMR), Department of Land Economy, University of Cambridge, UK.

Kevin P. Gallagher, Department of International Relations, Boston University, Boston, MA, USA.

Rob Gray, Centre for Social and Environmental Accounting Research, University of St Andrews, St Andrews, UK.

Clive Hamilton, The Australia Institute, Canberra, Australia.

Kirk Hamilton, Environment Department, The World Bank, Washington, DC, USA.

Geoffrey Heal, Graduate School of Business, Columbia University, New York, USA.

Cameron Hepburn, St Hugh's College, Environmental Change Institute, and Department of Economics, University of Oxford, Oxford, UK.

Tim Jackson, Centre for Environmental Strategy, University of Surrey, Guildford, UK.

Bengt Kriström, Department of Forest Economics, Swedish University of Agricultural Sciences (SLU) – Umeå, Umeå, Sweden.

Glenn-Marie Lange, The Earth Institute at Colombia University, New York, USA.

Ramón López, Department of Agricultural and Resource Economics, University of Maryland at College Park, MD, USA.

Geoffrey McNicoll, Population Council, New York, USA.

Ian Moffatt, School of Biological and Environmental Sciences, University of Stirling, Stirling, UK.

Eric Neumayer, Department of Geography and Environment and Centre for Environmental Policy and Governance (CEPG), London School of Economics and Political Science, London, UK.

Bryan G. Norton, School of Public Policy, Georgia Institute of Technology, Atlanta, GA, USA.

The late **David Pearce**, formerly Department of Economics, University College London, London, UK.

Alan Randall, Department of Agricultural, Environmental and Development Economics, The Ohio State University, Columbus, Ohio, USA.

Giovanni Ruta, Environment Department, The World Bank, Washington, DC, USA.

Yvonne Rydin, Bartlett School of Planning, University College London, London, UK.

Clement A. Tisdell, School of Economics, The University of Queensland, Brisbane, Australia.

Jeroen C.J.M. van den Bergh, Faculty of Economics and Business Administration and Institute for Environmental Studies, Free University, Amsterdam, The Netherlands.

John Vogler, School of Politics, International Relations and Philosophy (SPIRE), Keele University, Keele, UK.

Alexandra Winkels, School of Development Studies, University of East Anglia, Norwich, UK.

Preface

This book has, at its heart, a concern with taking stock, twenty years on from the influential Brundtland Report (WCED, 1987), of the concept of sustainable development and its implications for the conduct of public policy. There is little doubt about the prominence of the term 'sustainable development' in contemporary debates about environmental and resources policy specifically and development policy more generally. Indeed, if anything the term itself has suffered from overuse alternatively as a panacea for all modern ills or as a meaningless catch-all theme to which all policy challenges (no matter of what complexion) are somehow inextricably linked. Nor is there consensus about what sustainable development is, which has led to another source of criticism.

All this has led some critics to dismiss the concept altogether as one further example of the triumph of rhetoric over substance. Such criticisms are understandable but ultimately undeserved and, in reflecting within these pages on what sustainable development is, how it can be achieved and how it can be measured, it is the aim of this volume to provide ample demonstration of this. What we can conclude from the contributions that follow is that while sustainable development does indeed imply a broad research and policy agenda (both in terms of its scale and its scope), it is also an agenda that is far more coherent than might appear to be the case at first glance. Much of this coherency stems from a shared concern about the development path that developed and developing countries (as well as the world as a whole) are on. For us, as others, this is the essential difference between saying that some action is 'undesirable' and saying that it is 'unsustainable'. That is, undesirable actions may warrant the attentions of policy makers but are not necessarily the domain of concern about sustainable development.

That said, the evolving literature, coming as it does from a variety of disciplinary perspectives, contains a wide range of topics and policy challenges to study and respond to. We have not shied away from this diversity – of subject matter and approach – here. So, in initially mapping out the structure of this volume, we were immediately faced with the challenge of choosing what should be included. Some topics on our initial wish-list, without mentioning these by name, may have ended up being excluded for entirely pragmatic reasons usually to do with the availability of authors. We are hopeful, however, that no central topic has failed to make it into the finished volume because of these reasons. More generally, we sought to be comprehensive, yet not encyclopaedic, and to reflect the contributions that different intellectual disciplines and policy foci have brought to the fore without pretending that we could do justice to all. While making such judgements was no easy feat, we have found the process of putting together this volume to be an illuminating experience.

In particular, we have been delighted to have such high quality contributions from current *and*, just as significantly, future research leaders in such a wide variety of fields. We, therefore, hope that the final volume provides a broad but accessible snap-shot of the sustainable development literature that many from a variety of disciplinary or policy backgrounds will find of interest. While at least some of the concepts and ideas in these chapters have been around for considerably longer than the Brundtland Report, we find it hard to escape the conclusion that this literature has come a long way in a relatively short space of time. That there is surely much more to come in the future makes working in this field all the more worthwhile.

Sadly, during the latter stages of preparing this volume for submission for publication, one of our contributors, David Pearce, passed away suddenly. Those working in this field owe much to David who made huge contributions, most significantly in 1989 with the seminal *Blueprint for a Green Economy* (or *Blueprint 1* or just *Blueprint* as it is also commonly known). While there is an undercurrent, in the sustainability literature, of 'who said what, first' with regards to key concepts, it is fair to say that so much of what is now the received wisdom originated in *Blueprint*. David continued to make a number of important contributions to this debate over the ensuing years. We are proud to be able to include one of his last writings on the topic of sustainable development here and we humbly dedicate this volume to David's memory.

GA
SD
EN

Acknowledgements

We would to thank, first and foremost, the authors who have contributed to this volume both through their cooperation and willingness to observe deadlines and make revisions and their delivery of high quality and accessible chapters. We would also like to express our appreciation to all at Edward Elgar Publishing, particularly Edward Elgar and Dymphna Evans, for the faith they have shown in this endeavour, as well as this book's production editor, Caroline Cornish.

We thank the following for permission to reprint or use material.

University of Chicago Press for the use of Figure 2.1 in Chapter 2. This originally appeared in Norton, B. (2005), *Sustainability: A Philosophy of Adaptive Ecosystem Management*, Chicago: University of Chicago Press.

Chapters 3 and 18 by Giovanni Ruta and Kirk Hamilton and by Kirk Hamilton and Katharine Bolt respectively appear by kind permission of The World Bank.

1 Introduction

Giles Atkinson, Simon Dietz and Eric Neumayer

A handbook of sustainable development

The demand that countries pursue policies aimed at achieving 'sustainable development' or 'sustainability' has become a clarion call for many over the past two decades. A number of key events can lay claim to establishing this principle in the policy landscape. Among these are the publication of the Brundtland Report (WCED, 1987), the Earth Summit in 1992 and, more recently, the World Summit in 2002. Yet a moment's reflection makes it clear that formidable challenges confront policy makers who have publicly stated their commitment to the goal of sustainable development, not least in determining what it is exactly they have signed up to. To this end, a huge amount of literature has been generated and, as we near the twentieth anniversary of the seminal Brundtland Report, it seems timely to provide an account of the considerable progress that has been made in fleshing out these issues. This is the primary purpose of the current volume.

We undertake this task with just a little trepidation. Some might argue that, as sustainable development appears to be such a complex concept, bringing disparate contributions together under one umbrella – moreover in the form of a 'handbook' – is a fool's errand. Others might argue that, while such an account is worthwhile, we have made important omissions. Mindful of both points, we offer the following response. We agree it would be quite wrong to claim there is a unified theory of sustainable development. Indeed, it became clear very early on that interest in sustainable development was drawn from a broad church. For example, the Brundtland Report viewed sustainable development as serving many different (and possibly competing) goals: economic development, a better environment and a particular concern for human well-being both now and in the future. In fact, the debate has become far broader since then. We have deliberately sought to reflect this diversity rather than impose a narrow and rigid (but ultimately misleading) interpretation of the issues. While we do not claim to have been exhaustive, we are confident nonetheless there is a comprehensive and coherent story about sustainable development permeating this volume. It is the objective of this introductory chapter to summarize what we understand this story to be.

Sustainable development: what does it mean and how is it to be achieved?
We begin by asking whether sustainable development can be defined in relatively succinct terms. A number of definitions can be found in the contributions to this volume. Several authors cite the famous Brundtland Report definition – 'development that meets the needs of the present generation without compromising the ability of future generations to meet their own needs' (WCED, 1987, p. 43). Some have adopted this definition or offered a slight change in emphasis. Others have added further requirements or provisos about particular actions that meeting this stated goal might necessitate. At the heart of each definition is a common concern about the way in which the fruits of development are shared across generations. Such distributive concerns have a distinctly philosophical flavour, so it is appropriate that this volume begins with Bryan Norton's critical discussion of the ethical dimension underpinning sustainable development (Chapter 2). For Norton, an understanding of the ethics of sustainable development is essentially an anthropocentric endeavour. In other words, what is of interest is human well-being and how to sustain that well-being over time. Tension occurs when there is, in Norton's words, 'competition' between the well-being of, or opportunities faced by, current and future people. Much of this volume is concerned with the reasons why such tensions might arise and how they might be resolved. Recognition of the responsibility that present generations have over impacts on the future – the basic tenet of sustainability – is best served, Norton argues, by an avowedly pragmatic philosophy based on learning about which novel rules for managing the resource base can be made to work in practice (rather than rely on an abstract ethical theory).

On the basis that there exists a broadly accepted ethical position that we, as the current generation, have obligations to the future, it follows we should ask what these are and whether current behaviour is consistent with making good on these duties. Addressing these issues requires that we seek to understand the means available to society to generate future well-being or opportunities, namely its resources or resource base. This resource base, as Giovanni Ruta and Kirk Hamilton set out in Chapter 3, consists of an array of stocks of wealth. It includes produced capital and human resources as well as natural resources (such as energy resources, land and biological resources) and environmental resources (such as clean air and water). The terminology here, from economics, is that these latter resources can be thought of as assets; part of natural wealth or capital. The 'capital approach' has now become ubiquitous in much of the sustainability literature and can be traced back to seminal contributions such as Pearce et al. (1989). There are at least two reasons for the widespread use of this approach. First, it has an intuitive appeal, insofar as entreaties to manage these resources sensibly chime with popular notions of 'not eating into one's capital' or 'not selling the family silver'. Second, while this capital or wealth-based approach has proven useful in working out core theoretical notions of sustainability, it also leads to some specific and insightful analytical implications. For example, Ruta and Hamilton discuss a recent study by the World Bank (2006), which provides estimates of, and policy implications relating to, a range of components of natural wealth across countries.

To reiterate, a core element of sustainability is the appropriate manage-ment of a broadly construed portfolio of capital and wealth, including natural and environmental resources, by the current generation. Although the capital approach does not require particular assumptions to be made about the relative importance of different assets, such speculation is inevitable. Indeed, it is the source of one of the great sustainability debates, the answer to which in no small part determines the likely extent of sacri-fice required by the present generation in adjusting and adapting behaviour. Understandably this debate, characterized in terms of whether develop-ment should be weakly sustainable or strongly sustainable,[1] cuts across a number of chapters in this volume. For *weak sustainability*, there is no special place for the environment as such. Put another way, it is the 'overall' portfolio of wealth bequeathed to the future that matters. As long as the real value of this portfolio is held constant it matters little that its con-stituent parts change over the development path. *Strong sustainability*, by contrast, requires that the environment is accorded explicit and special pro-tection. There are a number of variants on this position. Most generally, it requires that 'natural wealth' should (in some way) be preserved intact through specific conservation rules. Strong sustainability should hence rep-resent the greater policy challenge, because current human actions would be significantly more constrained (as certain development paths would be effectively 'off-limits').

The practical implication of this distinction is thus a matter of some importance. But, while a great deal of actual development policy seems to be implicitly predicated on weak sustainability,[2] within the academic litera-ture there is arguably some consensus over the position that the 'real' world corresponds neither to one polar extreme nor the other. For example, Jeroen van den Bergh reminds us in Chapter 4 that the theory underlying weak sustainability was developed in the context of an economy dependent on a non-renewable resource such as oil. By following the 'Hartwick' rule (or sometimes the 'Hartwick–Solow' rule: Hartwick, 1977; Solow, 1986), sustainable development could be achieved by 'covering off' the liquidation of a finite resource with investment in other forms of wealth. The question being asked here is: are countries saving enough for the future? Later in this volume (Chapter 18) it is shown how for developing countries that are highly dependent on exhaustible resources as a share of economic activity this focus can yield valuable predictions about development prospects. Can such (Hartwick) rules be extended across *all* natural wealth? The answer is that we simply do not know and so this argument would require an extraordinarily large leap of faith. At the same time, it seems overly cautious to claim *all* natural wealth must be conserved in its entirety. Not surprisingly, it is difficult in practice to find proponents for either extreme position.

In reality then there are likely to be far more complementarities between the two approaches than are commonly given credit.[3] At least three lines of reasoning are worth bearing in mind with regards to this point. In any given year about 10–30 countries are not saving enough to cover their depletion of natural resources in the World Bank savings database.[4] So even by a so-called weak sustainability criterion a clear signal is provided that a very real problem for the development prospects of these countries exists. Second, so long as it is not being argued that all natural assets must be conserved (and typically it is not) then there is a guiding role for key insights from both approaches (Pearce et al., 1996). For example, more moderate interpretations of strong sustainability tend to argue there are certain *critical* resources that are both crucial for human development and have no substitutes. That is, not all of nature is critical. For those critical assets which absolutely must be conserved (at some level), some (physical) indication is clearly needed about the extent of conservation. However, we would still need to know whether (or not) enough is being saved for the future and this will entail assessing changes in total wealth including what is happening to the 'rest' of nature that is deemed to be 'usable'. Third, as argued in a later chapter (Chapter 18), central to stronger notions of sustainability is the sense that development paths will take countries dangerously close to (or beyond) important environmental thresholds. Yet even though a savings analysis (often thought to be synonymous with weaker approaches) might be reckoned to have little to say here, a more considered response would be that relevance depends not on the existence of thresholds but on the nature or character of that threshold. While this is very much a technical detail, which roughly speaking depends on whether the harmful impacts on approaching a threshold are knowable or entail a 'nasty surprise', its practical implications are no less important for that.[5]

There is a challenging research agenda here: that is, how much of nature 'should' be conserved and how many (and what type of) threshold problems are there in practice? Central to this challenge is the conviction that the notion of a critical resource provides the basis for consensus in an otherwise seemingly intractable debate between weak and strong approaches. Hence, much of the middle-ground in discussions about sustainable development could well centre on identifying critical assets, understanding how they function and managing these resources accordingly. In other words, the conflict between weak and strong sustainability would largely dissolve if it could be determined which assets were critical. Unfortunately, the problem with this otherwise pragmatic standpoint is that there exists considerable uncertainty about which natural assets are critical. Hence there is corresponding uncertainty about the location of this middle-ground.

Recourse to evidence would be one clear way through this impasse. However, those who over a decade ago (for example Pearce et al., 1994) expected a body of empirical evidence to emerge on the issue of substitutability might be disappointed by progress. Most welcome then is recent work (World Bank, 2006, discussed in Chapter 3) that has built on earlier contributions such as Berndt and Field (1981) in quantifying the degree of substitutability between commercial natural resources and other forms of wealth. While this provides valuable information on the ability to maintain economic production in the face of declining natural resource stocks, it is unlikely that such direct evidence will be as straightforward to uncover for broader classes of natural assets affecting human well-being directly or perhaps indirectly (as subtle and intangible inputs to production). This is simply a reflection of the complexity of understanding the physical world in which we live. However, there are signs of progress in understanding the implications of, say, ecological processes for human well-being. For example, more than any other single school of thought, ecological economics has been explicitly premised on exactly this objective. Moreover, as van den Bergh notes in Chapter 4, the challenge of sustainable development has evolved to occupy a central place in an otherwise eclectic array of policy concerns and analytical perspectives.

Chapter 5 offers a prominent illustration of this advance in the knowledge of ecological systems. Neil Adger outlines how progress in understanding the concept of resilience has contributed to this process. As Adger explains, resilience is central to sustaining ecosystem functions in the face of external pressures and perturbations. Unsurprisingly, complexities abound. Early speculation about the relationship between diversity and resilience (for example Common and Perrings, 1992) has given way to insights with less straightforward implications for conservation management. However, the central message broadly persists that a loss of resilience is a threat to sustainability, and resilience – and thus the future provision of ecosystem services – is being compromised by unrelenting human pressure on the environment. As an illustration, Adger notes that this negative process is epitomized by the ongoing diminution of the world's living coral reefs. The reward for human development of policies that preserve or enhance resilience – perhaps at some reference level – is a more stable environment for continued use of ecological services.

The broad thrust of policy decision-rules intended to deal with threats to sustainable development, in a world with critical resources, is explored in detail by Alan Randall in Chapter 6. In the spirit of our earlier discussion of the 'middle-ground', his is a two-tier approach involving a combination of safe minimum standards (SMS) for critical resources and standard cost–benefit rules (markets augmented by public policies that pass cost–benefit tests). With regard to the latter, Randall situates this economic approach within a broad array of considerations: cost–benefit thinking subject to moral constraints rather than allowing the economist's notion of (social) efficiency to trump all else. Thus threats to sustainability, perhaps brought about by the likely loss of a critical resource, could justify a strict conservation rule (although this can be overridden if its costs are 'intolerable'). There is no single or unifying rationale for observing SMS. Instead, Randall presents a simple but compelling case that it is an approach that commands broad consensus. As such, this is a testable criterion, which is clearly a desirable attribute for making costly but uncertain decisions in democratic societies.

Intergenerational equity: discounting, population and technological change
In the SMS framework previously discussed, cost–benefit analysis (CBA) has a place unless there is a sustainability threat. One reason for this demarcation is that such threats might be characterized by a combination of uncertainty and possibly (irreversible) large losses in well-being. Nor is CBA well-equipped to deal with contemporary environmental problems which are characterized by impacts that could be felt 100 to 200 years from now (and beyond). That is, conventional ways of discounting future costs and benefits in economic appraisal typically give very low weight to these distant concerns. Such observations about the 'tyranny of discounting' draw on long-standing concerns. In Chapter 7, Cameron Hepburn brings us up-to-date with the discounting debate, noting interesting developments that reassert the relevance of cost–benefit approaches in understanding the social worth of policies affecting the far-off future. Thus, while Hepburn outlines a number of alternative approaches to discounting (which go beyond overly simple prescriptions not to discount at all), just as interesting are recent developments in the theory and practice of discounting, which provide powerful arguments for using *declining* discount rates to appraise public policies with impacts in the distant future. While this introduces well-known problems into decision-making, these disadvantages must be weighed carefully against the advantages of making economic appraisals more sensitive to preferences for environmental outcomes in the far-off future.

In many countries and for the world as a whole, any development path must sustain well-being or opportunities over a considerably larger population than currently prevails. In turn, population growth may further threaten sustainability as human populations place added pressure on natural assets. In Chapter 8, Geoffrey McNicoll sets out this integral part of the sustainable development story, which itself has roots in historical debates about the relationship between population and development. Recent interventions have, in McNicoll's view, generated more heat than light, focusing on elusive (and perhaps even futile) questions about 'how many people the world can support' and arriving at extreme prognoses whereby population levels can increase without limit (for example Simon, 1981) or resource constraints result in dramatic population collapse or collapse in living standards (for example Meadows et al., 1972). McNicoll shows that, away from such extreme debate, there is a wealth of useful analyses, which neither dismisses the possibility that population change increases pressure on natural assets nor blithely assumes this relationship can be straightforwardly disentangled from other factors. Indeed, the population–environment nexus is unlikely to be carved in stone. As with so many other issues in the sustainable development area, it is mediated to a large extent by institutions and policy regimes. Put another way, bad policies or poor institutional arrangements can exacerbate the environmental impacts of population pressure. A key question then is what is the appropriate balance of policy between, on the one hand, interventions aiming to influence migration and fertility decisions directly and, on the other hand, efforts to create or strengthen institutions?

Against concern about the consequences of population growth lie questions about the ability of technological change to deliver sustainable development. McNicoll reminds us that analogous questions have been an active source of debate in the economic growth literature. Such issues are obviously highly relevant to concerns about sustainability, for the claim that current behaviour is unsustainable implies possibly strong judgements about how well-being or opportunities will be generated in the (far-off) future. Historical examples abound where similar concerns about impending sustainability threats have been rendered obsolete by technological advances. Moreover, as Chapter 8 points out, much of modern growth theory has been predicated on the primacy of technological change in driving economic development. A timely reminder of the relevance of these discussions was made by Weitzman and Löfgren (1997). They presented the theory and illustrative calculations (for the US) behind the claim that even a moderate but predictable flow of technological change might mean that, not only would such productivity advances play a significant role in determining prospects for sustainable development, this could play the decisive role.

The proposition that technological change can be relied on to take care of the future is somewhat out of kilter with the more cautious approach generally advocated by those concerned about sustainable development. The substance of this caution stems from two main considerations. First, contemporary sustainability threats often relate to the loss of natural assets that are tangibly different to those referred to in any number of reassuring historical examples. Ultimately, history will prove the protagonists in such debates right or wrong but, in terms of decision-making in the here and now, there is mounting suspicion that losses of critical assets could entail substantial losses in well-being comparable or greater in magnitude to those increases attributable to technological improvements. Until practical data exist to evaluate this claim directly, fundamental questions relate to how decision-making should proceed in light of uncertainty. Second, a reliable stream of technological improvement requires a policy climate conducive to innovation effort (Aghion and Howitt, 1998). This is an important point, because new knowledge must be created. One primary way of doing so is through inputs to the research and development (R&D) sector, but this is a costly process influenced by a variety of incentives.[6]

The second point has prompted researchers to seek a deeper understanding not only of the process of knowledge creation but also of how new innovations diffuse into production (and consumption) processes. In terms of sustainability, there is particular concern about the direction of technological change. That is, it could be argued innovation has shown a long-term tendency towards greener technologies that drive the material or energy intensity of economic production downwards (see also Chapter 15). Does it follow that this decoupling is simply a spontaneous by-product of innovative activity? In Chapter 9, Timothy Foxon outlines explanations of how innovations come on-stream and how cleaner technologies in particular are adopted. There are important lessons to be learned from, in effect, 'backward engineering' the actual adoption of new technologies and so understanding the technical and economic circumstances under which change occurred. In doing so, examples are uncovered of existing technologies that have become 'locked-in', even though possibly 'superior' technologies exist. Understanding the reasons for such phenomena is also important. A prominent environmental example is the pervasiveness of carbon-based technologies in modern economies. Proponents of the lock-in notion argue that both economic processes and policy institutions, which otherwise might be harnessed to foster change, can become constrained to serving the status quo. International experience appears to be varied.

Sustainable development is concerned with development prospects along a path stretching into the far-off future. It is entirely plausible, and indeed to be expected, that technological change will intervene to change the nature of this path. This issue therefore merits serious consideration in discussions about threats to sustainability. Yet, neither should it be used to 'stop the conversation' about obligations of the current generation to the future. While technological change might alter the nature of these obligations, challenging questions arise from consideration of what policy regimes can best harness innovation as one means of sustaining development.

Intragenerational equity and the social dimension

Sustainable development has always been about more than just a sophisticated articulation of concern for future generations. Another prominent theme has been intragenerational equity, that is, the distribution of income, environmental burdens and other relevant factors within the currently existing generation. This tradition owes much to the Brundtland Commission, for which concern about future generations was only part of the story: concern for poverty in the present generation was also important, indeed for the WCED arguably the highest priority. Explanations vary as to why present generation inequities might make development unsustainable. Perhaps it is a logical consequence of concern for *inter*generational equity (for example Solow, 1992). Others have put forward mechanisms whereby a development path is unsustainable, because there are disparities in well-being or opportunities *within* the current generation. A few have simply asserted that greater intragenerational equity is intrinsically desirable and by hook or by crook must be relevant to sustainable development. All of this suggests policy makers follow a more specific requirement to prohibit not only current development that comes at the expense of the future, but also increases in current well-being that further broaden the gap between, say, rich and poor. Three chapters in this volume outline the case for integrating intragenerational equity within the sustainable development story.

In Chapter 10, Geoffrey Heal and Bengt Kriström assess recent efforts by economists to build current distributive considerations into analyses of sustainable development. What this involves is moving beyond highly aggregated assessments of whether the current generation is overusing its resource base. Heal and Kriström attribute this to a welcome resurgence in economic interest around distributive issues in cost–benefit analysis and policy appraisal more generally. Given that an important element of any sustainable development strategy will be strengthening environmental policies, Kriström uses these public policy interventions to illustrate frameworks for analysing distributive impacts. This raises an array of interesting issues. First, there are questions surrounding how best to understand and quantify distributive impacts across households, firms and so on within, say, the national economy. Second, there are questions regarding the main lessons emerging from this analysis. For Heal and Kriström, the key message is that environmental policy creates winners and losers.[7] While there is mixed evidence about the socioeconomic characteristics of those who fall in each category, the fact remains that those charged with designing and implementing environmental and sustainable development policies cannot escape making hard choices. In order to ensure that such policies are socially acceptable, identifying the potential obstacles that undesirable distributive impacts represent is crucial.

In Chapter 11, Julian Agyeman reminds us that concern for social justice in the here and now has always been at the heart of the environmental justice movement. Indeed, it is arguable that some of the credit for the recent emergence of *environmental* equity concerns in economic analysis (for example Serret and Johnstone, 2005) must go to this movement. It began as a grassroots campaign, originating outside of (and sometimes in opposition to) the mainstream environmental movement in the US. In this respect, it has evolved in parallel rather than together with the sustainable development debate. However, as Agyeman notes, environmental justice proponents have identified much in common with the sustainability agenda. Emphasis is placed on the burden of pollution and how that burden is distributed across communities with different socio-economic characteristics. Within the US, particular interest has surrounded the incidence of these environmental inequities by ethnic origin. In each example the implication is that an unequal distribution of some environmental burden along a socio-economic axis is unjust. In turn, policy should strive for a more equal distribution, although how this might be achieved depends on a proper understanding of the dynamic process whereby environmental burdens and risks are assigned (see also Chapter 10).

International disparities – in terms, say, of how global environmental burdens are distributed – might also be characterized as environmental justice problems. Another perspective which relates the link between (especially international) disparities in living standards and differences in human 'vulnerability' to environmental and other stresses has rapidly become part of the vocabulary of sustainable development as noted in Chapter 12 by Neil Adger and Alexandra Winkels. For example, there is concern about how vulnerable certain groups are when exposed to climate-related risks. The emphasis on vulnerability predicts that those living in chronic poverty, without access to the resources necessary to live a decent life, are those least able to cope or adapt. In this context, links are forged with key contributions from the poverty literature, notably the writings of Amartya Sen (1981, 1984). Since the social pillar of sustainability plausibly demands we work to minimize poverty worldwide, Adger and Winkels argue the vulnerability perspective constitutes a valuable analytical tool, offering a multidimensional explanation of how the distribution of resources in society presses those least fortunate into unsustainable livelihoods and vice versa. In this way, not only is vulnerability reduction a legitimate sustainable development goal, because it is instrumental in reducing poverty, it can also contribute to fostering sustainable livelihoods among those sections of society least capable of pursuing them. All other things being equal, this could contribute to the attainment of sustainable development goals society-wide.

Growth, consumption and natural wealth
An important connection between recent attempts to understand the determinants of poor economic performance and the measurement of sustainability is the finding of a negative and significant relationship between natural resource abundance and economic growth. This is the so-called 'resource curse hypothesis' or 'paradox of plenty'. It is a paradox, because common sense suggests resource-rich countries have distinct long-term economic advantages over (otherwise similar) resource-poor countries. As Richard Auty shows in Chapter 13, the fact that a large number of countries in the former category appear not to have benefited in this way has led to considerable effort being expended in seeking to understand why the resource curse arises and, more importantly, whether it can be avoided. Perhaps the most convincing of recent arguments are those which focus on the political economy of resource-rich countries. As Auty points out, there is likely to be a vicious circle at work here. Resource windfalls, for example, encourage rent-seeking among interest groups and permit governments to prolong 'bad' policies. While notable examples of sound resource management do exist, transforming countries that habitually dissipate resource rents is far from easy.

Another important node for research into the economic, social and environmental performance of developing countries is the classical process of structural change, whereby the importance of the (rural) primary sector in a national economy decreases at the expense of the (urban) manufacturing and service sectors. As Ramón López explains in Chapter 14, structural change has been a pervasive trend in modern economic development, be it in countries that have performed well over the past few decades (for example in Far East Asia) or in countries that have failed to satisfy development expectations (for example many Latin American and sub-Saharan African countries). López thus draws a distinction between structural change with positive outcomes – in terms of decreasing pressure on natural assets and increasing living standards – and structural change with negative outcomes, whereby the rural poor simply become the urban poor. Hence the understanding of how 'benign structural change' comes about as opposed to 'perverse structural change' has an important role to play in fostering sustainability in developing countries. López argues that, while benign structural change is 'pulled along' by labour demand from the increasingly productive urban non-primary sector, perverse structural change is pushed by the depletion and degradation of rural natural assets and/or by the disenfranchisement of the rural poor. The rural labour force migrates to urban areas as a consequence, but in many cases the necessary investment and productivity improvements in the non-primary sector have yet to be made. Crucially, López portrays the latter process as the result of policy failure, itself the result of an institutional bias against the rural poor. In this respect, the similarities with Chapter 13 could not be clearer.

Among certain schools of thought, it is almost an article of faith that economic growth results in greater resource use and environmental degradation. Yet cross-country empirical studies in the early 1990s seemingly showed that, for certain pollutants, as the economy grows, so environmental quality first deteriorates, but then actually improves. This is the so-called Environmental Kuznets Curve (EKC). Matthew Cole, in Chapter 15, reviews the evidence from EKC studies for local and global pollutants. While these studies have seen their fair share of criticism on a variety of grounds, Cole notes that recent developments in the literature have sought to provide a more thorough explanation of the process of economic change driving the EKC (where it exists). At least two interesting implications emerge. First, a combination of environmental effects accompany economic growth that work in opposite directions. Certain effects diminish environmental quality (for example scale effects) while other effects enhance it (for example technical effects). Second, initial conclusions that countries might simply grow out of their environmental problems were – as many had suspected – far too simplistic. The environment-growth paths described by EKCs often reflect policies which, even if facilitated by rising incomes, do not arise automatically.

Raising consumption is one objective of development policy around the world. For a large number of countries, where poverty is widespread, this is a necessity. In wealthier countries, in some quarters, there has been a fair degree of soul-searching about the desirability of progress driven by ever-increasing consumption. For example, where the environmental effects of growth appear to be less than benign (for example carbon dioxide emissions), there is arguably a clear mandate for the study of how consumption can be made 'sustainable' or at least to have less damaging by-products. Tim Jackson takes up this task in Chapter 16. In fact, the consequences of consumption practices for sustainable development are not confined to environmental effects, as the consumption choices we make affect social equity and well-being more broadly. Despite the potentially fundamental questions such a focus could raise, Jackson explains that much of the recent sustainable consumption literature, especially (and without any great surprise) at the political level, has shied away from them, restricting itself to an incremental shift in consumption towards 'greener' products. Yet Jackson argues this reticence might constitute a missed opportunity. Not only does it conflate the issues of production and consumption, the inability to engage with *how much* we consume in absolute terms runs the risk of ignoring scale effects. He asks: what is the true purpose of consumption? In doing so, he outlines a number of theories as to why ever-increasing material consumption may actually be something of a social pathology. All this leaves a question mark over the degree to which much of this consumption is actually making people in the world's richest nations any happier. While such accounts pose tremendous challenges to established theories – sustainable development theories included – there are a number of useful and immediate policy implications, not least the futility of naive appeals to 'stop consuming so much'.

Progress in measuring sustainable development
Consumption, economic growth and environmental degradation impact sustainable development in complex and often apparently contradictory ways. The question is: how do we know whether overall we are on a sustainable development path? If the rhetoric of policy makers committed to sustainable development is to be judged against the reality of performance, then the means must be found to measure and monitor sustainable development. Put another way, in the absence of such information we cannot even broach the question of whether development is sustainable. A number of chapters in this volume examine a variety of proposals that respond to this measurement challenge. Broadly speaking, they fall into one of two camps. First, there are those approaches seeking to adjust or extend the existing economic or national accounts to better reflect resource depletion and environmental degradation. These activities are typically labelled 'green national accounting' or 'resource and environmental accounting'. Second, there are approaches that have sought to construct (sometimes highly aggregated) physical environmental indicators. Common to both approaches is the overarching conviction that development cannot be sustainable if policy makers continue to rely on the same narrow set of economic indicators used to guide the short-term management of the macroeconomy, most notably Gross Domestic Product (GDP). Chapters 17 and 18 draw on the activities of two international organizations with a key role to play in the pursuit of sustainable development: the United Nations and the World Bank. The approaches taken by both institutions fall within the ambit of green national accounting, but there are important

contrasts in terms of methods and emphasis, most notably about whether we need an analogously powerful accounting aggregate or indicator to rival GDP.

Glenn-Marie Lange provides a critical appraisal, in Chapter 17, of the United Nations System of Environmental and Economic Accounting (SEEA) (UN et al., 2003). This system is designed as an adjunct to – not a replacement for – the conventional System of National Accounts. Clearly, this falls short of the more radical plea to overhaul the national accounts. It takes the more conservative (but in all likelihood correct) view that satellite accounts best permit experimentation and nurture of novel and worthwhile proposals, without compromising uses associated with the conventional accounting framework. In terms of uptake across countries, the SEEA appears to have been a qualified success. Lange reports that a number of countries (but by no means all) have been busy in the implementation of a wide range of accounting activities based on this framework. This includes asset accounts (natural resource balances), flow accounts for materials, energy and pollution, environmental protection expenditures and, finally, green alternatives to GDP. In other respects, Lange offers cause for both optimism and pessimism. On the one hand, a number of countries are increasingly exploring the policy implications of resource and environmental accounts. This is a welcome development. In the past, there was a suspicion that many official green accounting programmes were initiated with very little discussion of end-uses (Hamilton et al., 1994). As Lange shows, the strength of a number of accounting activities covered by the SEEA framework lies precisely in the detailed policy questions they can address. On the other hand, the SEEA provides little leadership on the major debates about competing methods, particularly with regard to the valuation of resource stocks and their depletion and degradation. This embedded ambiguity could well limit the uptake of these frameworks and necessitate a search for leadership elsewhere.

By contrast, Kirk Hamilton and Katharine Bolt describe the singular approach taken by the World Bank in adopting genuine saving (or adjusted net saving) as its primary indicator of sustainability (Chapter 18). As described in this chapter, postponing consumption (for example by saving out of income or through investing in human resources) boosts a country's (genuine) saving rate, while (net) depletion of natural assets (for example mining or harvesting commercial natural resources or emitting pollutants such as carbon dioxide and particulate matter) shrinks it. Sustainability requires that countries avoid negative genuine saving rates at the very least. As Hamilton and Bolt note, the proposition that we should be interested in saving rates (and changes in wealth per capita in the presence of population growth), as one important piece of the puzzle for measuring sustainable development, has survived rigorous scrutiny by economic growth theorists. Scrutiny outside the economic domain has identified genuine saving's commitment to *weak* sustainability, which, in line with our previous discussion, may be insufficiently demanding where critical natural assets are concerned. Even if the analysis is confined to weak sustainability, empirical findings to date suggest many countries find it hard to achieve positive genuine saving. Moreover, Hamilton and Bolt note that empirical evidence suggests that genuine saving is a reasonably strong predictor of future consumption. In other words, this indicator can provide important signals for policy. As reported in Chapter 18, had countries such as Venezuela and Nigeria followed the standard Hartwick rule or maintained genuine saving at some modest and constant rate, they would be considerably better off than is actually the case.

Beyond the province of green national accounting, a wide array of indicators has been proposed. Efforts to measure sustainable economic well-being led to the construction of an Index of Sustainable Economic Welfare (ISEW: Daly et al., 1989), also known by various names, including the Genuine Progress Indicator (GPI: Cobb et al., 1995). The ISEW aims to provide a 'better' measure of current and future well-being than GDP. Although this aim is shared with the environmental and resource accounting literature, the two traditions engage little beyond this.[8] In Chapter 19, Clive Hamilton notes that many ISEW studies claim striking findings to the effect that the measured level of well-being increases at first (from its level in the initial study year; typically 1950), before declining at some point (usually around the 1970s or 1980s), sometimes steeply. At face value, this indicates that, while well-being per capita initially rose, it has been declining for some time, in some cases precipitously. Thus ISEW studies can be viewed as a bold attempt to construct national welfare accounts in a world where relevant shadow prices assume that environmental change is very costly indeed. ISEW/GPI studies thus appear to reveal *dis*-saving on a massive and unsustainable scale. While there are substantial suspicions, discussed by Clive Hamilton, that the findings of these studies are largely an artefact of the particular methods used by practitioners, it is interesting to note the burgeoning 'mainstream' respectability of the notion that people living in modern advanced economies are no more happy despite evidence of economic progress (especially in the literature on happiness and its determinants: see, for example, Layard, 2005).

Numerous indicators purporting to measure sustainability now exist. Indeed, to cover all of these would command a volume in itself. This is in marked contrast to the early 1990s, when there was growing recognition of the need to monitor progress towards sustainability goals, but few practical indicators existed. Put this way, considerable progress has been made in constructing practical indicators over the past 10 years or so. The genuine saving and ISEW/GPI indicators are but two examples. In Chapter 20, Ian Moffatt outlines and assesses three further indicators, in this case focusing on physical environmental pressures: material flows, environmental space and ecological footprints. In fact, the search for sustainability indicators has become something of a mini-industry in the literature on sustainable development. So too has criticism of these indicators. Much of this criticism needs to be taken in context: it is often the case that an indicator is useful in one domain and less useful in another. For example, there is no doubting the success of ecological footprints as a rhetorical device. The analogy of a footprint – describing how biophysical limits might nominally bind on economic activity – graphically illustrates the notion of 'living beyond our means'. Whether decision-makers should base policy directly on this information is another matter. By contrast, resource and environmental accounting, described in Chapter 17, can be extremely useful in guiding policy but it is unlikely to interest, much less excite, a broader audience. Other indicators might be made more useful if methodological problems (or, in some cases, errors) can be addressed. Take the case of 'material flows': highly aggregated indicators of the mass of material dragged through the economic system and the residuals that are the by-products of this activity. It is hard to take anything positive from an indicator that simply adds, say, tonnes of residuals together regardless of the harm those materials cause in the receptor environment. However, once one starts distinguishing between more and less harmful materials, in a meaningful way, then material flow accounting could represent a more useful measurement tool.

How then might policy makers make sense of the array of sustainability indicators now available? A reasonable expectation is that, over time, many of these indicators will wither on the vine. It is to be hoped that those that survive this process are the most useful, and proper scrutiny of indicators is one way in which this outcome can be achieved. This search for measures of sustainable development is unlikely to result in one indicator able to 'out-compete' all rivals. It is not credible that a single indicator is able to describe all relevant aspects of the development path. Thus, a better picture of whether countries are developing sustainably will require a judicious mix of indicators. With regard to the indicators that might be included in this portfolio, that crucial debate is still in its infancy.

Sustainable development at different scales
Such is the apparent appeal of sustainable development, the term 'sustainable' is now prefixed to numerous and disparate policy objectives. Within the academic literature, it has been variously asked how regions, local

districts (for example cities), economic sectors and corporations can be 'sustainable'. Much of this makes eminent sense even if sustainable development were solely a macro-goal, as there would be legitimate questions about how, for example, the households and corporations that comprise this society might contribute to the macro-objective. Yet, as the authors of a number of chapters in this volume demonstrate, adopting these more disaggregated approaches to understanding sustainable development might also yield additional insights.

The quest for local or urban sustainability has been understood not just as a contribution to some broader societal objective, but also as an agenda in its own right. As Yvonne Rydin explains in Chapter 21, much of the impetus for this was supplied by Agenda 21 in 1992, which provided a powerful focus for interest in local sustainability. This local perspective has led to ambitious policy aims. For example, it has been argued that, as 'global' environmental problems have their roots in ultimately local behaviour, this places an onus on tackling such problems at local levels. While this does not diminish the need for international co-operation to sustain meaningful outcomes on global problems such as climate change (where each locality's contribution, in isolation, is to say the least marginal: see Chapter 24), an intriguing example, cited by Rydin, shows how co-ordinated efforts across US cities have sought to bypass federal government reticence over climate change mitigation. One interpretation of this could be that policy makers at local tiers of decision-making provide a better reflection of their citizens' preferences than at higher tiers, the latter perhaps being all too influenced by various interest groups and special pleading. In a related vein, a distinctive feature of the local sustainability agenda has been the identification of an enhanced role for meaningful public participation in (local) decision-making.

At first blush, the idea that a particular economic sector should be 'sustainable' might be treated with derision. The economic fortunes of most sectors can be expected to 'wax and wane' over plausible development paths. Indeed, sectors such as mining clearly involve inherently unsustainable activities, although this does not in itself remove the justification for such projects. Whether there is a justification for sustaining particular sectors depends on the sector in question and what is meant by 'sustainable'. For example, some would argue the entire notion of sustaining a sector 'in perpetuity' makes little sense. Rather it is the contribution of that sector to sustainable development in some wider sense that is of real interest. However, as Clement Tisdell points out in Chapter 22, both perspectives are likely to be relevant in the case of agriculture. It is highly desirable for the *global* agricultural system to be sustainable in terms of fulfilling the nutritional needs of the world's population both now and in the future.

Certain countries may well place a premium on food security and this might further motivate concerns about sustainable agriculture within nations. While, as Tisdell notes, concern over food production failing to keep pace with demand is hardly new, contemporary issues have added some novel twists to the story. Thus it may be that the resource base on which future agricultural productivity depends is being 'homogenized', with a reliance on ever higher yielding but ultimately less resilient genetic materials (see also Chapter 5). While this drive towards uniformity in agricultural systems serves to increase food output, it might well come at the expense of sustainability.

An increasing number of corporate entities have affirmed their apparent support for sustainability through, for example, the medium of dedicated environmental or (increasingly) sustainability reports. However, Rob Gray and Jan Bebbington argue forcefully in Chapter 23 that the notion of corporate sustainability might not be as helpful as it first appears. Indeed, they argue that there is a danger this term has been captured by those in the corporate world who seek to dress up almost any action as being somehow commensurate with pursuing sustainability. At the very least, this suggests the need for a rigorous evaluation of corporate environmental or sustainability reports in the same way that corporate financial accounts are scrutinized and verified. Taking a step back, it would be a surprise (albeit a pleasant one) if, merely by shining a light on corporate activities, a sufficient number of these entities would spontaneously fall in line with society's broader environmental or sustainable development objectives. Pressures to produce reports (even those that are a true and fair reflection of environmental performance) are unlikely to change incentives sufficiently. In other words, such actions are highly unlikely to be an adequate substitute for environmental and sustainable development policy.

The international dimension

A characteristic of many natural assets that cannot be ignored is that they are not just shared across generations but also across national boundaries. The list is large and includes 'open access' resources over which there is no ownership (for example the global atmosphere and the oceans) as well as those resources owned by a sovereign state that nevertheless provide ecological services across borders (for example forests and biological resources). Inevitably, better management of these assets necessitates that hugely complex issues of international co-operation are successfully brokered. In Chapter 24, Camilla Bretteville Froyn provides compelling arguments, drawn from applications of game theory and public choice theory, that agreement between countries on managing international environmental resources cannot be presumed and that actual co-operation will almost always be circumvented by what is within the art of the – politically – possible. This does not imply meaningful and sustainable agreement is unattainable, but, in the absence of strong and credible international governance, a number of rather exacting conditions must be fulfilled. Among these conditions is the balancing of distributive considerations, both in terms of dividing the gains from co-operation among parties and in terms of the outcomes of internal conflicts among likely winners and losers within each negotiating country. Perhaps the single major challenge is to re-orientate perceptions and incentives such that co-operation is unanimously seen as the best way forward in the face of competing domestic and international interests.

Given the undoubted and growing influence of international trade on the fortunes of the world economy and its constituent countries and regions, it was always likely that issues surrounding the impact of trade on the environment and sustainable development would loom large. Indeed, few issues have been so controversial, a point that is reflected in the range of extreme positions held. For some, trade and globalization are inherently unsustainable, arguably an unhelpful approach to what is essentially an empirical question.[9] At the other extreme lie those who argue unfettered trade can serve many goals (economic, environmental and so on), thus being of universal benefit. In Chapter 25, Kevin Gallagher provides an overview of some of these controversies and, in doing so, outlines an array of candidate pathways whereby trade either benefits or harms the economy and environment. Interestingly, the empirical evidence continues to be mixed. In fact, recent studies have sought to make sense of this apparently frustrating finding, observing that trade openness is far from the only determinant of development prospects and that the direction and extent of its impact is inextricably linked to other policy variables (such as the strength of domestic environmental policy). However, a further concern that arises is whether the understandable desire of the World Trade Organization (WTO) to remove trade barriers in the guise of environmental protection punishes 'bad' and 'good' environmental actions in equal measure. Similarly, anxiety surrounds the prospect that international environmental agreements containing trade restrictions will fall foul of WTO rules, which is somewhat ironic given that, in certain prominent cases, these provisions have arguably been crucial in sustaining a meaningful agreement (Barrett, 2003). While these concerns have yet to manifest themselves in practice, a number of commentators have called for a counterweight World Environmental Organization.

In Chapter 26, John Vogler traces the recent historical evolution of international forums that have helped shape the contemporary politics of sustainable development. He charts the shift in this political debate from a primary emphasis on environmental issues at the 1972 Stockholm Conference, through a shared focus on environmental, social and economic development at the Rio de Janeiro Earth Summit in 1992, to arguably a primary emphasis on poverty alleviation at the Johannesburg World Summit in 2002. This does not necessarily mean environmental protection has been effectively sidelined, of interest mainly in its capacity to alleviate poverty. Rather, it would appear that what began as a call to protect the environment in the service of human development has become a more specific call to *prioritize* improvements in the well-being of the very worst-off now and in the future. It is likely, of course, that this change in emphasis will result in different environmental priorities (see also Chapter 11). Vogler draws the general conclusion that the principle of sustainable development has become firmly embedded in the international political system. However, he argues this offers cause for both 'hope' and 'despair'. On the one hand, it is clear from any analysis that regional and national self-interest has played a major role in the international politics of sustainable development, often throwing up more obstacles than opportunities. On the other hand, the 'institutionalization' of sustainable development – through which it has acquired a momentum all of its own – might help to shape and alter national perspectives of self-interest, thus facilitating deeper agreement and action than might otherwise have prevailed.

A major source of friction in international discussions on sustainable development surrounds the question of whether the programme requires additional and substantial financing. Accepting this is the case, there is doubt over whether the necessary international transfer of funds will be forthcoming. However, it would quite wrong to abandon all hope that this challenge can be met, as argued by the late David Pearce in Chapter 27. Given David's important and influential contributions to the understanding of sustainable development, it is fitting that we leave him the last word in this volume. Towards what sadly turned out to be the end of his life, David became interested in how the substantial financial flows that need to be levered to secure sustainable development can be motivated by eminently sensible economic arguments. His source of inspiration, as outlined in Chapter 27, was the notion of a Coasian bargain (Coase, 1960), whereby a 'polluter' has a property right underpinning their current (unsustainable) behaviour – perhaps because a threatened biological resource is sovereign property – such that it is in the interests of the 'sufferer' (or beneficiary of conservation) to pay the polluter to change their behaviour. As the chapter points out, overcoming well-known obstacles to these Coasian bargains remains a challenge, but if these can be navigated then it motivates possibly substantial financial flows linked to payments for environmental services: so-called market creation initiatives. The current vernacular is that these created markets can be 'pro-poor', thus ticking two boxes *vis-à-vis* concern about sustainable development. Similarly, the development of novel financial instruments to deal with environmental threats – such as climate-related risks – offers at least a cautious note of optimism to the effect that financial expertise can be harnessed to deliver sustainable development.

Concluding remarks

Almost two decades after the publication of the Brundtland Report (WCED, 1987), the debate on what is sustainable development, how to measure progress towards it and how to put sustainable development into practice has come a remarkably long way. This volume is in many ways an exercise in account-taking of what has been achieved, on which aspects consensus has emerged and what remaining challenges lie ahead. Much more is known now than 20 years ago, and there is general agreement on a great deal of the fundamentals of sustainable development. That said, as this volume illustrates, there are many areas of continued disagreement. This suggests that there is much more to be learned and that the study of sustainable development will continue to be a thriving area of research. To reiterate the sentiments we outlined at the outset of this chapter, while this volume cannot, and indeed could not feasibly, do justice to all aspects of sustainable development, we believe that the contributors have covered a wide range of the most important topics in this expansive field. Our hope is that readers will enjoy these excellent contributions as much as we have in the course of assembling this volume.

Notes

1. While there is some debate about when exactly this terminology entered the literature, the main ideas can be found in Pearce et al. (1989), as well as Daly (1994).
2. The intellectual case for this position is set out in, for example, Solow (1992) as well as Chapter 3 of this volume.
3. Thanks are due to Kirk Hamilton for helpful discussion relating to these points.
4. These countries thus have a 'negative genuine saving rate': this concept is explained in more detail later in this chapter.
5. Hamilton and Bolt (in Chapter 18) note that if we are facing a threshold problem, then the saving analysis will signal unsustainability as long as the marginal damage curve is smooth as the threshold is approached. So if the threshold is one arising from clearing forest land, what this means is that as the forested area declines to the critical or threshold amount, arbitrarily large losses in well-being are associated with deforestation of a further hectare. However, if the marginal damage curve is kinked and becomes vertical at the threshold, then the saving analysis does not forewarn us of a problem. In the forest example, this means that while all seems well before the threshold, an unpleasant surprise awaits around the corner if deforestation continues.
6. For some countries it is possible to adopt existing, more advanced and perhaps cleaner technologies from more technologically advanced countries (see, for a recent discussion, Perkins and Neumayer, 2005).
7. While at the margins so-called 'win–win' options may exist, the pervasiveness of these easy options can be seriously questioned.

8. It is notable that genuine saving approaches have been concerned as much with fleshing out the theoretical properties of the link between saving and sustainability as with practical issues about measurement. By contrast, for example, the ISEW and other similar approaches have been measurement-driven with little reference to theory. Clearly, measurement is a pressing aim given that current systems of economic indicators do not clearly signal that an economy is on or off an unsustainable path. However, there is also a critically important role for conceptual work which formally examines the properties of indicators and their measurement, not just on optimal development paths but also, more importantly, for 'real world' economies which diverge substantially from optimality (see, for example, Dasgupta and Mäler, 2000).
9. Chapter 20 notes that prominent indicators have been produced which rest heavily on this assumption.

References

Aghion, P. and P. Howitt (1998), *Endogenous Growth Theory*, Cambridge, MA: MIT Press.
Barrett, S. (2003), *Environment and Statecraft*, Cambridge: Cambridge University Press.
Berndt, E.R. and B.C. Field (eds) (1981), *Modeling and Measuring Natural Resource Substitution*, Cambridge, MA: MIT Press.
Coase, R.H. (1960), 'The problem of social cost', *Journal of Law and Economics*, **3**: 1–44.
Cobb, C., T. Halstead and J. Rowe (1995), *The Genuine Progress Indicator: Summary of Data and Methodology*, San Francisco: Redefining Progress.
Common, M. and C. Perrings (1992), 'Towards an ecological economics of sustainability', *Ecological Economics*, **6**: 7–34.
Daly, H.E. (1994), 'Operationalizing sustainable development by investing in natural capital', in A. Jansson, M. Hammer, C. Folke and R. Costanza (eds), *Investing in Natural Capital: The Ecological Economics Approach to Sustainability*, Washington, DC: Island Press, pp. 22–37.
Daly, H.E., J.B. Cobb and C.W. Cobb (1989), *For the Common Good: Redirecting the Economy towards Community, the Environment, and a Sustainable Future*, Boston: Beacon Press.
Dasgupta, P. and K.-G. Mäler (2000), 'Net national product, wealth and social well-being.' *Environment and Development Economics*, **5**: 69–93.
Hamilton, K., D.W. Pearce, G. Atkinson, A. Gomez-Lobo and C. Young (1994), 'The policy implications of natural resource and environmental accounting', Working Paper, University College London and University of East Anglia, Norwich, Centre for Social and Economic Research on the Global Environment.
Hartwick, J.M. (1977), 'Intergenerational equity and the investing of rents of exhaustible resources', *American Economic Review*, **67**(5): 972–4.
Layard, R. (2005), *Happiness: Lessons from a New Science*, London: Allen Lane.
Meadows, D.H., D.L. Meadows and J. Randers (1972), *The Limits to Growth: A Report for the Club of Rome's Project on the Predicament of Mankind*, New York: Universe Books.
Pearce, D.W. (2003), *Conceptual Framework for Analysing the Distributive Impacts of Environmental Policies*, OECD Environment Directorate Workshop on the Distribution of Benefits and Costs of Environmental Policies, 4–5 March, Paris.
Pearce, D.W., G. Atkinson and R. Dubourg (1994), 'The economics of sustainable development', *Annual Review of Energy and the Environment*, **19**: 457–74.
Pearce, D.W., K. Hamilton and G. Atkinson (1996), 'Measuring sustainable development: progress on indicators', *Environment and Development Economics*, **1**(1): 85–101.
Pearce, D.W., A. Markandya and E.B. Barbier (1989), *Blueprint for a Green Economy*, London: Earthscan.
Perkins, R. and E. Neumayer (2005), 'International technological diffusion, latecomer advantage and economic globalization: a multi-technology analysis', *Annals of the American Association of Geographers*, **95**: 789–808.
Sen, A. (1981), *Poverty and Famines: an Essay on Entitlements and Famines*, Oxford: Clarendon.
Sen, A. (1984), *Resources, Values and Development*, Oxford: Blackwell.

Serret, Y. and N. Johnstone (eds) (2005), *The Distributional Effects of Environmental Policy*, Cheltenham, UK and Northampton, MA, USA: Edward Elgar and Paris: OECD.

Simon, J.S. (1981), *The Ultimate Resource*, Princeton: Princeton University Press.

Solow, R.M. (1986), 'On the intergenerational allocation of natural resources', *Scandinavian Journal of Economics*, **88**(1): 141–49.

Solow, R.M. (1992), *An Almost Practical Step Toward Sustainability*, Washington, DC: Resources for the Future.

United Nations, European Commission, International Monetary Fund, Organisation for Economic Co-operation and Development and World Bank (2003), 'Integrated Environmental and Economic Accounting 2003', *Handbook of National Accounting, Studies in Methods*, New York: United Nations.

WCED (World Commission on Environment and Development) (1987), *Our Common Future*, Oxford: Oxford University Press.

Weitzman, M. and K.G. Lofgren (1997), 'On the welfare significance of green accounting as taught by parable', *Journal of Environmental Economics and Management*, **32**(2): 139–53.

World Bank (2006), *Where is the Wealth of Nations?*, Washington DC: World Bank.

PART I

FUNDAMENTALS OF SUSTAINABLE DEVELOPMENT

2 Ethics and sustainable development: an adaptive approach to environmental choice*

Bryan G. Norton

1. Introduction

Most writing on environmental ethics concerns the dichotomy between humans and non-humans, and much of the work in the field has been motivated by the effort to escape 'anthropocentrism' with respect to environmental *values*. Resulting debates about whether to extend 'moral considerability' to various elements of non-human nature have been, to say the least, inconclusive, and writings in this vein have had no discernible impact on the development of sustainability theory or on public policy more generally (Goodpaster, 1978). In this contribution, a new approach to re-conceptualizing our responsibilities toward nature is proposed, an approach that begins with a re-examination of spatio-temporal scaling in the conceptualization of environmental problems and human responses to them. Before turning in the following sections to a description of this emerging approach to management – sometimes called 'adaptive management' – I will in this introductory section briefly summarize the current situation in environmental ethics.

Discussions in the field of environmental ethics, which emerged as a separate sub-field of ethics in the early 1970s, have, as just noted, turned on defining and explaining key dichotomies (Norton, 2005). This trend originated in the publication, by the historian Lynn White, Jr, of an influential essay (1967), 'The historical roots of our ecologic crisis', in which he declared that Christianity 'is the most anthropocentric religion the world has seen', setting the stage for a spate of responses by ethicists who questioned the longstanding ethical divide between humans and non-humans.[1] Environmental ethicists have, accordingly, focused on the dualisms of modernism: humans vs non-humans, moral exclusivism – the view that all and only humans have intrinsic value, and the underlying dichotomy between matter and spirit. From 1970 until the early 1990s, these dichotomous formulations dominated environmental ethics as the question of where to draw the crucial line between those beings that are morally considerable and those that are morally irrelevant seemed so seminal a question that the field could not proceed without some resolution of it, and yet discussions of 'intrinsic' or 'inherent' value shed little light on practical questions about what to do.

Worse, emphasis on these dichotomies created an irresolvable conflict with environmental economists, blocking any integration of philosophical and economic discourse (Norton and Minteer, 2002). Because economists insist that all values are values of human beings (consumers), they are in ontological disagreement with environmental ethicists, who wish to shift the line of moral consideration to include non-humans and their interests.

The debate over intrinsic value could of course be brought to bear upon questions of sustainable development, as it seems reasonable for a non-anthropocentrist, who attributes intrinsic value to some non-humans, to advocate sustainable use of 'resources' for all intrinsically valuable beings. As the debates have actually evolved, however, this has not been a nexus of active discussion – the debate about sustainable development has been staged at the edges of mainstream, environmental economics and of the emerging competitor, ecological economics, both of which count human values only. Environmental ethicists, rejecting this exclusivism, have argued indiscriminately against all attempts to assess the economic and instrumental uses of the material world only for the satisfaction of human needs and demands. Thus, by objecting to the economic framework of analysis (because it is anthropocentric), environmental ethicists have been at cross purposes with both sides in the debate about how to define sustainable development.

By the 1990s, a few philosophers began to see that this unfortunate stalemate between economic approaches and environmental philosophy rested mainly on ideological commitments and a priori theories, theories that for non-empirical reasons attempt to force all environmental value into a single valuational currency. No empirical evidence can be brought to bear upon whether nature has intrinsic value, and commitments to valuing objects as consumable items with a price are likewise based on a priori assumptions. Worse, the categorical nature of the debate has encouraged all-or-nothing answers to complex management problems, and a conceptual polarization that leads to direct oppositions and an inability to frame questions as open to compromise.

If one instead adopts pluralism, accepting the fact that humans value nature in many ways, and considers these values to range along a continuum from purely selfish uses to spiritual and less instrumental uses, it is unclear – and not really very important – where to 'separate' one kind of value from another (Stone, 1987; Norton, 2005). If we think of natural objects as having many kinds of value, arguments about why we should protect nature slide into the background and the focus moves to protecting as many of the values of nature as possible, for the longest time that is foreseeable. Of course there will be disagreements about priorities and immediate objectives, but if policies are devised to protect as much of nature as possible for the use and enjoyment of humans for as long into the future as possible, then it is perhaps not crucial whether those values preserved are counted in one theoretical framework or another.

The viewpoint advanced here is referred to as *environmental pragmatism*, which is advanced as a philosophy of environmental action that begins with real-world problems, not with abstract, theory-dependent questions regarding what kind of value nature has (Light and Katz, 1996; Norton, 2005). Environmental pragmatism can be seen as a third way in environmental ethics: it bypasses the theoretically grounded questions of environmental ethics and focuses on learning our way out of uncertainty in particular situations. If the 'true' value of natural systems is unknown today, this is all the more reason to save them for the future, where their full and true value may be learned.

Further, pragmatism complements the search for sustainable development because it is a forward-looking philosophy, defining truth as that which will prevail, within the community of inquirers, in the long run. This feature makes it a natural complement to the theory of sustainable development and acts as the unifying thread in the justification of preservation efforts at all scales: this forward-looking sense of responsibility and commitment to learning our way to sustainability can be thought of as pragmatism's contribution to the theory of sustainable development (Lee, 1993; Norton, 1999; Norton, 2005).

In the remainder of this chapter, I will propose one approach to a new environmental philosophy, a philosophy that is more geared to learning to be sustainable than in defining what kind of good nature has. This philosophy emphasizes social learning and community adaptation, and it derives its method more from the epistemology of pragmatism than from theoretical ethics.

2. Adaptive management

To introduce the adaptive management approach, I will briefly explain how it rests on three intellectual pillars, and then propose a more explicit definition of adaptive management before undertaking to elaborate the theory by discussing each of these pillars in more detail.

I.   *A Commitment to a Unified Method: Naturalism*. Attempts to separate factual from value content in the process of deliberation are rejected; there is only one method for evaluating human assertions, including assertions with all kinds of mixes of descriptive and prescriptive content, and that is the method of experience – active experimentation when possible, and careful observation otherwise. The scientific method is embraced as the best approach to evaluating hypotheses about cause and effect, but also about what is valuable to individuals and cultures.

II. *A Relationship between Values and Boundaries.* The values of people who care about the environment are expressed in the ways they (a) 'bound' the natural system associated with a given problem, and (b) the choices they make in focusing on physical dynamics they use to 'model' those problems.

III. *A New Approach to Scaling and Environmental Problems.* Building on this idea, scalar choices in modeling environmental problems, if made a topic for open public discussion, might provide insight into the temporal and spatial 'horizons' over which impacts will be measured, and processes of change monitored. In policy, they direct the formation of effective administrative strategies for addressing problems; scientifically, careful attention to the dimensions and models developed in response to environmental problems might clarify problem formulation and illuminate public discourse.

This approach to management is often referred to as 'adaptive management' in North America,[2] but it is practiced elsewhere in varied forms and with different names. Adaptive management, which can be understood as a search for a locally anchored conception of sustainability and sustainable management, sets out to use science and social learning as tools to achieve cooperation in the pursuit of management goals (Walters, 1986; Lee, 1993; Gunderson et al., 1995; Gunderson and Holling, 2002; Norton, 2005). In the United States, the ideas were first articulated by the scientific and philosophical forester, Aldo Leopold, who emphasized the importance of multi-scalar adaptation in his essay, 'Thinking like a mountain', and who advocated scientific management throughout his career.[3]

Three characteristics can be taken to define a process of adaptive management:

- Experimentalism: adaptive managers respond to uncertainty by undertaking reversible actions and studying outcomes to reduce uncertainty at the next decision point.
- Multi-Scalar Modeling: adaptive managers model environmental problems within multi-scaled ('hierarchical') space–time systems.
- Place-Orientation: adaptive managers address environmental problems from a 'place' which means problems are embedded in a local context of natural systems but also of political forces.

By profession, most adaptive managers are ecologists and most discussions to date have emphasized learning our way out of scientific uncertainty; these ecologists have paid less attention to developing appropriate processes for *evaluating environmental change* and for setting intelligent *goals* for environmental management. Here, we will incorporate the ideas of these ecologists and expand them to include learning about social values as an integral part of the adaptive management process.

3. Naturalism: the method of experience

As noted above, much discussion in environmental ethics has centered on the debate between anthropocentrists and non-anthropocentrists, between those who limit moral considerability to humans and those who extend human considerability into the non-human world. Unfortunately, environmental ethicists have not paid as much attention to another controversial dichotomy, that between 'facts' and 'values' – between descriptive and prescriptive language. Analytic philosophers have been very cautious about mixing facts and values in argumentation, a trend initiated by David Hume, who promulgated 'Hume's Law', which is usually taken to deny the possibility of deducing an 'ought' proposition from any body of 'is' propositions. Recently, two prominent environmental ethicists have argued, adopting arguments reminiscent of Hume, for forsaking science and descriptive studies and concentrating on 'intrinsic values' in the effort to protect natural systems, processes and elements.

In particular, J. Baird Callicott (2002) and Mark Sagoff (2004) have both argued that environmentalists should play down instrumental arguments for saving species and biodiversity, basing their main arguments on the 'intrinsic value' of nature. Sagoff says: 'indeed environmental policy is most characterized by the opposition between instrumental values and aesthetic and moral judgments and convictions.' (2004, p. 20). He goes on to argue that 'Environmental controversies . . . turn on the discovery and acceptance of moral and aesthetic judgments as facts.' (p. 39). Unfortunately, he describes no means to separate fact from fiction in assertions that this or that has intrinsic value and explicitly claims that scientific arguments have no bearing on defending environmental values or goals.

Callicott (2002) joins Sagoff in sharply separating science from ethics and instrumental uses from non-instrumental appreciation: 'We subjects value objects in one or both of at least two ways – instrumentally or intrinsically – between which there is no middle term.' (p. 16). Callicott goes on to emphasize the subjective source of these intrinsic values:

> All value, in short, is of subjective provenance. And I hold that intrinsic value should be defined negatively, in contradistinction to instrumental value, as the

value of something that is left over when all its instrumental value has been sub-tracted ('intrinsic value' and 'noninstrumental value' are two names for one and the same thing).

Emphasizing the personal and the subjective nature of intrinsic valuings, he says: 'Indeed, it is logically possible to value intrinsically anything under the sun – an old worn-out shoe, for example.' (Callicott, 2004, p. 10). Callicott and Sagoff, then, have called for a strategy of emphasizing intrin-sic values over instrumental uses of nature in arguing for the protection of nature. In doing so, they rely on a sharp dichotomy between descriptive and prescriptive discourse, and on sharply separating instrumental reasons for protecting nature from non-instrumental reasons. These non-natural qual-ities are, apparently, apprehended through intuition or created by emo-tional affects, and they seem ill-suited to provide inter-subjectively valid or convincing reasons for environmental action.

A more realistic – and less theory-driven – view of the relation between factual and evaluative discourse is advocated by B.A.O. Williams (1985), who argued persuasively that, in ordinary discourse, fact-discourse and value-discourse are inseparable; when philosophers separate them, they do so on the basis of a specialized theory, such as logical positivism. In the ordinary discourse in which citizens discuss and evaluate their environ-ment, these discourses are inseparable; to insist on partitioning policy dis-course into fact-discourse (positivistic science) and value-discourse is to artificialize that discourse. There is an alternative, of course. Following pragmatists such as C.S. Peirce and John Dewey, one can advocate a prag-matic epistemology for environmental science and policy discourse, a dis-course conducted so as to maximize social learning among participants (Dewey, 1927; 1966; Lee, 1993). This epistemology insists upon a single method – the method of experience – and this method applies equally to factual claims and evaluative ones. Following Dewey, assertions that some-thing or some process is *valued* are taken as a hypothesis that that thing or process is *valuable*. Pursuing that value, and acting upon associated values, provides communities with experience that can support or undermine the claim that the thing or process is indeed valuable.

Non-naturalism thus construes environmental values in ways that are not easily related to scientifically measurable indicators. If the public and policy makers are going to support environmental actions, it will be neces-sary to cite values and to explain and justify environmentally motivated actions, but it is difficult to see how one would link 'non-natural' qualities of nature with empirically measurable indicators. Insistence upon a sharp separation of facts from values, means from ends, and instrumental from non-instrumental values makes connections between ecological change and social values more abstract, theoretical and tenuous. It makes the integration of the discourses of environmental science and environmental value virtually impossible. Worse, it estranges values from management science, creating a situation in which managers must look outside the adaptive process for indications of social value; they must *either* turn to economists' measurements of consumers' unconsidered preferences, *or* they can ask environmental ethicists to divine the nature of nature's non-natural qualities.

So, rejecting non-naturalism, the first pillar of my proposed approach is a form of methodological naturalism. This method, while not expecting *deductions* from facts to values, relies on the open-ended, public process of challenging beliefs and values with contrary experience. From these challenges, we expect attitudes, values and beliefs to change – but the changes cannot be justified by deductive arguments flowing one way from facts to values. The changes needed to support a new conservation consciousness are usually reorganizations and re-conceptualizations of facts, not deductions from value-neutral facts. The specific means by which assertions of value are connected will be through the development and refinement of measurable indicators that reflect values articulated by the stakeholders who represent multiple positions within the community. Pluralism is operationalized in process as communities participate in choosing multiple indicators, as will be discussed in the next two sections.

4.   Values and bounding

While one need not challenge Hume's Law to see a non-deductive connection between factual information and values, two assumptions that Hume made in formulating his law should be challenged. By stating the law as a prohibition against deriving 'ought' sentences from 'is' sentences, Hume implied that fact-discourse and evaluative discourse could be sharply separated, and that the difference would announce itself syntactically via the evident copula. In real discourse, they are all mixed together in ordinary speech; to separate them artificializes normal discourse in important ways.

This argument, however, raises an inevitable question: How, exactly, *do* values manifest themselves in scientific, descriptive literature, which claims to be 'value-free' and is apparently 'scrubbed' of evaluative language before publication in scientific journals? In order to answer this question, it is useful to follow Funtowicz and Ravetz (1990; 1995) in distinguishing between 'curiosity-driven' (discipline-driven) science and 'mission-oriented' (problem-driven) science. Authors who place their research in disciplinary journals succeed, to varying degrees, in purging evidence of values from their scientific papers. Adaptive management, however, is an active, mission-oriented science and, as Funtowicz and Ravetz argue, it often takes place in contexts where stakeholders have different perspectives and interests. In these contexts, scientific models and reports that are taken to bear on management decisions will, in effect, be 'peer reviewed' not only by appropriate disciplinary scientists, but also by scientists in different fields, and by interested laypersons. This places a transparency requirement on scientific discourse: if science is to be advanced as a guide to controversial policies, then that science must be explainable – and explained – in ordinary speech that requires no scientific credentials to understand.

When attention shifts from disciplinary science to mission-oriented science, values slip back into the discourse, because participants are proposing and evaluating policies from their own perspective, given their own models of the problems. So, if we want to find values implicit in scientific work, we should look closely at the discourse of management science. The values and interests of participants are coded into the choices they make to 'model' the problem – to bound the problem spatially, to form a temporal horizon, and to describe a function of the system that is considered problematic. These values are often embedded in the choices individuals and groups make when they choose/develop a 'mental model' of the problem they are addressing.

A historical example may help to illustrate what is claimed here. Chesapeake Bay, on the East Coast of the US, is among the most productive – and loved – bodies of water in the world. The Bay is the mouth of the Susqhehanna River, and many other tributaries that drain a huge portion of the Northeastern United States. By the 1970s there were multiple danger signals that the Bay was becoming polluted, even if it was unclear what was driving the widespread changes in Bay functioning, especially the increasing turbidity and consequent die-back of the vast underwater grass flats that formed the base of the Bay's food-web. Until the 1970s, when the US Environmental Protection Agency (EPA) undertook a detailed scientific study, pollution issues had mostly centered around toxic and point source pollution problems, including polluting industries and inadequate sewage treatment in a densely packed area of residences, agriculture and industry. It was learned that, while environmental monitors were paying attention to small-scale, local variables, a large-scale variable associated with a larger-scale dynamic – one driven by the total input of nutrients into the bay from its tributaries – posed a slower-moving, but more profound threat to bay health. Agricultural and residential run-off of nitrogen and phosphorous was causing increased turbidity, reducing submerged aquatic vegetation beds, and causing algal blooms and anoxia in deep waters. The rich farmlands of Pennsylvania, the Piedmont, and the coastal plain all drain into the Chesapeake. To save the Chesapeake, it would be necessary to gain the co-operation of countless upstream users of the waters that eventually enter the bay, a monumental task, since Pennsylvania and the District of Columbia, situated upstream on tributaries, have no coastline on the Bay and no direct stake in its protection.

Nevertheless, against all odds, the larger Bay community – enabled by the EPA study and countless private research efforts – succeeded in transforming the public consciousness to think of the Bay as an organic, connected watershed. Tom Horton, an environmental journalist and activist said it best when, at the height of this period of intense social learning, he wrote: 'We are throwing out our old maps of the bay. They are outdated not because of shoaling or erosion or political boundary shifts, but because the public needs a radically new perception of North America's greatest estuary' (Horton, 1987, pp. 7–8). He pointed out that, as the problem with bay water quality expanded beyond point-source pollution, to include non-point sources, residents of the area had to change their mental model of the processes of pollution; and they had to address activities throughout the watershed, adopting a model that includes all the lands contributing run-off to the bay.

What is important to learn from this analysis is that the 'transformation' of the Bay from an estuary into a watershed occurred in a context of mission-oriented science and it was as much a process of transformation of public consciousness as it was a change in scientific understanding. It was a dramatic change in perspective that was driven by values – an outpouring of love and commitments not to let the Bay become more unhealthy. In order to address the problem of Bay water quality, it was necessary to create a new 'model' of what was going wrong. The shift in models led to a public campaign, driven by the deep and varied values residents felt toward the Bay, which was marked, for example, by the outstanding success of the Chesapeake Bay Foundation, a private foundation that advocates, educates and supports science to guide Bay management. So, we have here an example of a value-driven re-mapping of a complex natural system, how it works, and how pollution is being delivered into it. We can say that a new 'cultural model' was formed (Kempton et al., 1995; Kempton and Falk, 2000; Paolisso, 2002), and Chesapeake Bay management, while not perfect, of course, has been a model of cross-state co-operation as serious steps have been taken throughout the watershed to reduce non-point-source as well as point-source pollution.

How should we interpret this transformation? A scientific finding that the Bay was threatened by processes outside its currently conceived boundaries, interacting with the strength of the love for the Bay as a 'place', created a new model that more accurately represented the problems of the Bay, and also expanded the sense of responsibility of residents and users of the Bay. The public understanding embraced the larger system, and they shifted their attention to addressing non-point-source pollution problems throughout the watershed. One could correctly argue that it was values – the love felt for the Bay – that was driving the acceptance of these models; it would be just as correct, however, to say that it was the scientific studies that analyzed the problem as watershed-sized that enveloped and embodied that love in a new ecophysical model of the Bay and its problems.

Residents and officials of the Bay area, upon being convinced that the Bay's health was threatened, and that a large part of the problem came from the larger-scale watershed system, shifted to a larger perspective on Bay health, a perspective that is more aligned with a scientific understanding of the problem faced. This shift in perspective, however, is not just scientific: it expresses a deep and varied set of social values that residents and stakeholders feel toward the Bay. And, when Horton describes the change in hydrological and cartographic terms, the underlying truth is that the shift to a watershed-sized model was the expression of an implicit value, a sense of caring for the health of the Bay as a part of one's way of life. The love and respect residents had for the Bay, once the nature of the threat was better understood, expressed itself in a ready embrace of the Bay as a watershed. Their local valuings came to express a community consensus in goals and values, transforming a local consciousness into a regional consciousness and sense of responsibility. Through social learning, the residents of the area discovered how to 'think like a watershed', and began living in a larger 'place' than before.

Social values are imputed to environmental and ecological systems implicitly in the process of developing 'models' – either cultural or scientific – of the problem that needs addressing. These models, if they are similar across all participants in public deliberations, can be very helpful in developing common understandings and in undertaking experimental actions. If they are very different, communication may be difficult, and environmental problems remain recalcitrant, dividing communities and undermining co-operative and experimental action. In many cases, communities are paralyzed because they have not had the kind of social learning experience that took place in the Chesapeake region, and co-operative action to address pressing and perceived problems are gridlocked. Differing values and interests – according to the hypothesis of this Part – thus inform and shape the models that participants use to understand environmental problems in their areas. Diversity of perspective and differences about value are thus key aspects of difficulties in deciding what, exactly, is the problem to be addressed.

5. Scaling and environmental problem formulation
Environmental disputes are so difficult, among other reasons, because it is so difficult to provide a definitive problem formulation. This feature was

well explained by Rittel and Webber (1973), who distinguished 'benign' and 'wicked' problems. Benign problems, they said, have determinate answers and when the solution is found, the problem is uncontroversially 'solved'. Mathematics and some areas of science exemplify benign problems. Wicked problems, on the other hand, resist unified problem formulation; there is controversy regarding what models to use and what data are important. Rittel and Webber suggest that wicked problems, because they are perceived differently by different interest groups with different values and goals, have no determinate solution because there is no agreement on the problem formulation. They can be 'resolved' by finding a temporary balance among competing interests and social goals, but as the situation changes, the problem changes and becomes more open-ended. Rittel and Webber explicitly mention that wicked problems have a way of coming back in new forms; as society addresses one symptom or set of symptoms, new symptoms appear, sometimes as unintended effects of treatments of the original problem.

Most environmental problems are wicked problems; they affect multiple values, and they impact different elements of the community differently, encouraging the development of multiple models of understanding and remedy. While resistance to unified problem formulation is endemic to wicked problems, and requires iterative negotiations to find even temporary resolutions and agreements on actions, one aspect of wicked problems – the temporal open-endedness which often attends wicked problems and brings them back in more virulent form as larger and larger systems are affected – may be susceptible to clarification through modeling. Ecologists have introduced 'hierarchy theory' (HT), as a set of conventions to clarify space–time relations in complex systems (Allen and Starr, 1982; Holling, 1992; Norton, 2005). HT can be characterized by two axioms (which happen to coincide with the second and third key characteristics of Adaptive Management listed in the 'Introduction'). HT encompasses a set of models of ecological systems that are characterized by two constraints on observer and system behavior: (i) The system is conceived as composed of nested subsystems, such that any subsystem is smaller (by at least one order of magnitude) than the system of which it is a component, and (ii) all observations of the system are taken from a particular perspective within the physical hierarchy. A major addition, encouraged by environmental pragmatism, is to expand (ii) to (ii'): All observations *and evaluations* orient from a particular perspective within the physical hierarchy. An effect of this innovation is to make environmental values, evaluation and social learning about values endogenous to the broader, adaptive management process.

This conceptual apparatus allows us to see human decision-makers as located within layered subsystems and supersystems, with the smallest subsystems being the fastest-changing, and the larger systems changing more slowly. These larger, slower-changing systems provide the environment for adaptation by subsystems (including organisms and places – composed of individuals and cultures). This convention allows us to associate temporal 'horizons' with changing features of landscapes as is illustrated in the famous metaphor used by Aldo Leopold, a forester and wildlife manager. Leopold set out to remove predators from the Forest Service ranges he managed in the Southwestern US. When the deer starved for lack of browse, he regretted his decision to extirpate wolves, chiding himself for not yet having learned to 'think like a mountain' (Leopold, 1949). He had not yet, that is, understood the role of the targeted species in the broader system. When he came to understand that role, he accepted responsibilities for the long-term consequences of his decisions, and advocated wolf protection in wilderness areas.

Leopold's account parallels the above case of Chesapeake Bay. In both cases, human activities – intended to improve the lot of human consumers of nature's bounty – threatened larger-scale dynamics. Thinking like a mountain – or a watershed – requires accepting responsibility for the impacts one's decisions will have on subsequent generations. Accepting this responsibility is inseparable from adopting a larger ecophysical model of the system under management. At this point in time, armed with some knowledge of changing systems and how to model them, we begin to accept moral responsibility for actions that were once thought to be morally neutral. In both cases, accepting moral responsibility – and a sense of caring – were inseparable from adopting a changing causal model of what has happened to deer populations on Leopold's metaphoric mountain, and to submerged aquatic vegetation in the Chesapeake. Chesapeake Watershed residents, busily plying their trades and tending their lawns, discovered that the ways in which they were pursuing their economic well-being could turn the Chesapeake into an anaerobic slime pond. In both cases the total impacts of individual actions to improve individual well-being turn out to reduce the ratio of opportunities to constraints faced by subsequent generations.

Using this framework of actions embedded within nested, hierarchical systems, it is possible to articulate a new approach to evaluating changes in human-dominated systems. Human management of the environment takes place within environmental systems as they are embedded in larger and larger – and progressively slower-changing – supersystems. Each generation is concerned for its short-term well-being (personal survival), but also must be concerned to leave a viable range of choices for subsequent generations. Given our expanding knowledge of our impacts on the larger and normally slower-changing systems that form our environment, it seems reasonable also to accept responsibility for activities that can change the range of choices that will be open to posterity.

A concept of sustainability nicely 'falls out' from this conception of adaptive management, in that a 'schematic definition' of sustainability can be constructed on the axioms of adaptive management, provided only that prior generations accept responsibility for their impacts on the choice sets of subsequent generations. Given this rather sparse set of assumptions and hypothetical premises, it is possible to provide a simple and elegant definition of *sustainability*, or rather what might better be called a definitional schema for sustainability definitions (Norton, 2005). Because of the place-based emphasis of adaptive management and the recognition of pervasive uncertainty, there is only so much that one can say about what is sustainable at the very general level of a universal definition. Speaking at this level of general theory, sustainability is best thought of as a cluster of variables; local communities can fill in the blanks, so to speak, to form a set of criteria and goals that reflect their needs and values. While local determination must play a key role in the details, adaptive management, and its associated definitional schema, makes evident the *structure* and *internal relationships* that are essential to more specific, locally applicable definitions of sustainable policies.

The two principles of hierarchy theory, when embodied in models, place individual actors in a world that is encountered as a mixture of opportunities and constraints; some of the chooser's choices result in survival: the chooser lives to choose again. If the chooser survives and has offspring, the offspring will also choose in the face of similar but changing environmental conditions. Some choices of others lead to death with no offspring. Other choices lead to continuation and to offspring who will face a similar, but possibly a changing array of possibilities and limitations. This is the basic structure of an evolution-through-selection model that interprets the environment of a chooser as a mixture of opportunities and constraints; it contextualizes the 'game' of adaptation and survival and can be represented as in Figure 2.1A.

Community-level success, in other words, requires success on two levels: at least some individuals from each generation must be sufficiently adapted to the environment to survive and reproduce *and*, for the population to survive over many generations, the collective actions of the population must be appropriate for (adaptive to) its environment. Since humans are necessarily social animals (because of the long period of helpless infancy of individuals), individual survival depends also on reasonable levels of stability in the 'ecological background' and in the cultural context, the stage on which individuals act. Successful cultures develop specific adaptations appropriate to their place, adaptation to the cycles and constancies of background systems that usually change more slowly than individual behaviors. This simple

A. At a Given Time   The Environment

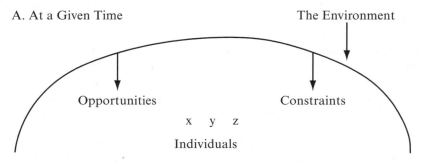

Individuals face their environment as a complex mix
of *opportunities* and *constraints* as they *adapt* to their
environment at any given time

B. The Cross-Scale Dynamic across Time

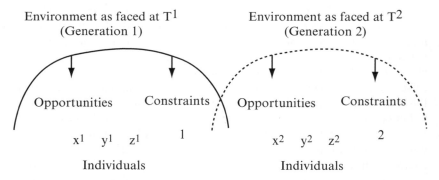

Choices made by members of an earlier generation can
change the mix of opportunities and constraints faced by
subsequent generations, limiting the latter's choices in
their attempt to adapt

Source: Norton (2005, p. 97).

Figure 2.1   Schematic definition for sustainability

model, if given a temporal expression, represents the relationship between
individuals who live in an earlier generation and those who live later, and the
possibility that later generations might face opportunities limited by the collective choices of their predecessors is represented in Figure 2.1B.

From this simple framework, a schematic definition of sustainability emerges: individuals in earlier generations alter their environment, using up some resources, leaving others. If all individuals in the earlier generations over-consume, and if they do not create new opportunities, then they will have changed the environment that subsequent generations encounter, making survival more difficult. A set of behaviors is thus understood as sustainable if and only if its practice in generation m will not reduce the ratio of opportunities to constraints that will be encountered by individuals in subsequent generations n, o, p.

Although the model has a 'flat', schematic character, it could also be given a richer, normative-moral interpretation, as is hinted at by use of the terms *opportunities* and *constraints*. If we stipulate that the actors are human individuals, then the simple model provides a representation of intergenerational impacts of decisions regarding resources; our little model can thus be enriched to allow a normative interpretation or analogue. If we accept that having a range of choices is good for free human individuals, we can see the structure, in skeletal form, of the normative theory of sustainability. An action or a policy is not sustainable if it will reduce the ratio of opportunities to constraints in the future.

Each generation stands in this asymmetric relationship to subsequent ones: choices made today could, in principle, reduce the range of free choices available to subsequent generations. Thus it makes sense to recognize impacts that play out on multiple, distinct scales. If it is agreed that maintaining a constant or expanding set of choices for the future is good, and that imposing crushing constraints on future people is bad, our little model has the potential to represent, and relate to each other, the short- and long-term impacts of choices *and* to allow either a physical, descriptive interpretation or a normative one.

This schematic definition, understood within the general model of adaptive management, captures two of our most important basic intuitions about sustainability: (1) that sustainability, incorporating a multi-scalar and multi-criteria analysis, refers to a relationship between generations existing at different times – a relationship having to do with the physical existence of important opportunities – and (2) that this relationship has an important *normative* dimension, a dimension that cannot be captured by economic measures alone, but one that involves important questions of intergenerational equity. Thus we can tentatively put adaptive management – complete with a schematic definition of sustainability – forward as a useful and comprehensive approach to environmental science and management. Adaptive management, in this context, encompasses the experimental search for better understanding, better goals, and better decisions.

6. Conclusions

It has been claimed that, *provided a community accepts responsibility for its impacts on the future and the set of choices (adaptations) available to future people*, a plausible definition of sustainability results. Next it is necessary to show how multi-scalar evaluation of impacts of actions can be correlated with a pluralistic approach to environmental values. If it is recognized that some actions – or aggregations of actions – of individuals threaten a valued aspect of the environment on a multi-generational time scale, there arises a competition between the 'good' of current individuals (consumption and increased individual welfare) and the 'good' of future people (who we can expect to want to face a broad array of opportunities to adapt to their environment as they see fit). Further, if we accept that (following Hierarchy Theory) these goods are associated with different social and ecological dynamics, which unfold at different scales, it may be possible to identify public policies that protect both kinds of goods; or, it may be possible to find an acceptable balance among the values if they turn out to be competing (Norton, 2005).

In a pluralistic value system – if it is embedded in a multi-scalar system – some human values can be associated with faster ('economic') processes of production and consumption. Protection of native vegetation and improving bay water quality, on the other hand, are associated with a large-scaled system and with values that, because they unfold at different scales and are supported by different processes, need not compete with economic values in real multi-scaled systems. It becomes conceivable to find win–win policies that provide adequate increments of individual welfare, but which do so in a way that does not destroy options open for future choosers.

Multi-scalar thinking, an emphasis on experience, and a forward-looking, pragmatic, problem-oriented attitude have been argued to be adequate to adaptive management processes, even though the goal of 'sustainable development' is not yet clearly defined. By recognizing that we can learn from experience, and by developing multiple criteria associated with different scales, it is possible for a community – much as the Chesapeake community did – to learn itself into a new set of indicators, a new set of concerns, and a whole new understanding of their place and the space around that place. If environmental ethics is to contribute to pursuit of sustainable development, that contribution seems more likely to come from the pragmatic line of analysis, functioning as a 'philosophy' of adaptive management, than from sterile discussions of which elements of nature have intrinsic value and moral considerability.

Notes

* Some of the research for this paper was supported by the Human Social Dynamics program of the National Science Foundation (NSF Award 0433165).
1. For a detailed account of the impact of White's paper on the history of environmental ethics, see Norton (2005, Section 5.3).
2. Holling (1978). A note on terminology: perhaps the closest analogue to adaptive management in Europe is 'Ecological Modernization', which shares some tenets with adaptive management, but also differs in emphasis. See Hajer (1995).
3. Leopold (1949). Leopold's pleas for careful science in management are too numerous to mention here. I have recently made the case that Leopold was the first 'adaptive manager', even though the term was not in use in his time. See Norton (2005).

References

Allen, T.F.H. and T.B. Starr (1982), *Hierarchy: Perspectives for Ecological Complexity*, Illinois: University of Chicago Press.
Callicott, J. Baird (2002), 'The pragmatic power and promise of theoretical environmental ethics', *Environmental Values*, **11**: 3–25.
Dewey, John (1927), *The Public and its Problems*, Athens, Ohio: Swallow Press, Ohio University Press.
Dewey, John (1966), *Logic: The Theory of Inquiry*, New York: Holt, Rhinehart, Winston.
Funtowicz, Sylvio and J.R. Ravetz (1990), *Uncertainty and Quality in Science for Policy*, Dordrecht, The Netherlands: Kluwer Academic Publishers.
Funtowicz, Sylvio and J.R. Ravetz (1995), 'Science for a post-normal age', in L. Westra and J. Lemons (eds), *Perspectives on Ecological Integrity*, Dordrecht, The Netherlands: Kluwer Academic Publishers, pp. 146–61.
Goodpaster, Kenneth (1978), 'On being morally considerable', *Journal of Philosophy*, **75**: 308–25.
Gunderson, L.H. and C.S. Holling (2002), *Panarchy: Understanding Transformations in Human and Natural Systems*, Washington, DC: Island Press.
Gunderson, L.H., C.S. Holling and S.S. Light (1995), *Barriers and Bridges to the Renewal of Ecosystems and Institutions*, New York: Columbia University Press.
Hajer, Maarten A. (1995), *The Politics of Environmental Discourse: Ecological Modernization and the Policy Process*, Oxford, UK: Clarendon, Oxford University Press.
Holling, C.S. (1978), *Adaptive Environmental Assessment and Management*, London: John Wiley.
Holling, C.S. (1992), 'Cross-scale morphology, geometry, and dynamics of ecosystems', *Ecological Monographs*, **62**: 447–502.
Horton, Tom (1987), *Bay Country*, Baltimore, MD: Johns Hopkins University Press.
Kempton, Willett and J. Falk (2000), 'Cultural models of Pfisteria: toward cultivating more appropriate risk perceptions', *Coastal Management*, **28**(4): 273–85.
Kempton, Willett, J.S. Boster and J.A. Hartley (1995), *Environmental Values in American Culture*, Cambridge, MA: MIT Press.
Lee, Kai (1993), *Compass and Gyroscope: Integrating Science and Politics for the Environment*, Washington, DC: Island Press.
Leopold, Aldo (1949), *A Sand County Almanac and Sketches Here and There*, Oxford, UK: Oxford University Press.
Light, A. and E. Katz (1996), *Environmental Pragmatism*, London: Routledge.
Norton, Bryan (2005), *Sustainability: A Philosophy of Adaptive Ecosystem Management*, Chicago, IL: University of Chicago Press.
Norton, Bryan (1999), 'Pragmatism, adaptive management, and sustainability', *Environmental Values*, **8**: 451–66.
Norton, Bryan and Ben A. Minteer (2002), 'From environmental ethics to environmental public philosophy: ethicists and economists, 1973–2010', in Tom Tietenberg and Henk Folmer (eds), *The International Yearbook of Environmental and Resource Economics 2002/2003*, Cheltenham, UK and Brookfield, MA, USA: Edward Elgar, pp. 373–407.

Paolisso, M. (2002), 'Blue crabs and controversy on the Chesapeake Bay: A cultural model for understanding watermen's reasoning about blue crab management', *Human Organization*, **61**(3): 226–39.

Rittel, H.W.J. and M.M. Webber (1973), 'Dilemmas in a general theory of planning', *Policy Sciences*, **4**: 155–69.

Sagoff, Mark (2004), *Price, Principle, and the Environment*, New York: Cambridge University Press.

Stone, Christopher (1987), *Earth and Other Ethics: The Case for Moral Pluralism*, New York: Harper & Row.

Walters, C. (1986), *Adaptive Management of Renewable Resources*, New York: McMillan.

White, Lynn (1967), 'The historical roots of our ecologic crisis', *Science*, **155**: 1203–07.

Williams, Bernard A.O. (1985), *Ethics and the Limits of Philosophy*, Cambridge, MA: Harvard University Press.

3   The capital approach to sustainability
Giovanni Ruta and Kirk Hamilton

1.   Introduction[1]

It is a matter of fact that sustainability has been adopted by many scientists, prime ministers and citizens alike as a goal for the world we would like to live in, and yet that its measurement is largely non-existent. The purpose of the chapter is to approach the measurement challenge the way an economist would: if sustainability means leaving future generations with at least as many opportunities as we have today, then the way to achieve this is by passing on to future generations a level of capital that is at least as high as ours today.

The measurement of sustainability can then be likened to an accounting exercise in that the object being measured is capital, very much the same way a firm would report the value of buildings, machinery and trademarks in its books at the end of each year. But when we start thinking about a country's capital, produced assets – such as buildings and machines – are not enough to describe the complex set of elements which form the base for the production of well-being. The chapter starts by establishing the conceptual link between sustainability and wealth. Next, the methods and tools underpinning the wealth estimates are explained followed by a presentation of the main highlights from recent findings on wealth estimation. This discussion draws on the results published by World Bank (2006a) which presents estimates of 'total' capital, or wealth, for nearly 120 countries. A further section is devoted to the components of intangible capital: a major determinant of wealth. Finally, the policy implications of the capital approach to sustainability are presented.

2.   Sustainability, wealth and well-being

Most people will agree that sustainable development is something that is desirable, like happiness, yet few will be able to pinpoint its practical implications. A myriad of definitions have been proposed but it has not been easy to find one that simultaneously satisfies economists, ecologists, sociologists, philosophers and policy makers. The problem in part relates to uncertainty about the object of sustainability, rather than the idea itself. What is it that ought to be sustained?

Natural scientists and ecologists will typically respond to the question above by stating that it is the capacity of the ecosystem that needs to be sustained. Concepts such as diversity and resilience become then useful in addressing the complex measurement issues. An ecologically based measure of sustainability is especially important in those cases in which the natural resource is critical to survival. The ozone layer and the oceans truly provide services that can hardly be thought of as replaceable. A world economy that depletes the ozone layer cannot be considered sustainable. More generally, however, identifying sustainable development with a halt on all ecosystem transformation would probably come at prohibitive costs for the economy.

A more comprehensive approach would identify sustainable development with the maintenance of a non-declining level of a number of ecological, social and economic indicators. While appealing, a problem with this approach is that it is difficult to make claims about sustainability when some indicators increase while others decrease. Would a society be sustainable if equity is enhanced while natural resources are lost? In this chapter, we argue that what needs to be sustained should be a comprehensive object. In particular, we argue that the concept of social well-being should be the starting point. One may even emphasize that well-being, or utility, is simply the result of the different elements of what constitutes development, including a clean environment, income and social relations.

The question of 'what' should be sustained will automatically lead to concerns about measurement. And measuring well-being is indeed a non-trivial matter. Yet, this is where economics makes a crucial contribution. It turns out that, if properly measured, capital or wealth constitute an appropriate measure of social welfare. Following the lead of the Brundtland Commission, the issue was clearly put by Pearce et al. (1989) who argued that sustainable well-being is possible if the next generation inherits 'a stock of wealth . . . no less than the stock inherited by the previous generation' (p. 34). Wealth, or capital assets, becomes the object of the sustainable development paradigm.

From well-being to wealth

A myopic approach to sustainability will typically consider well-being as approximated by income. To have sustained well-being, the quantity of goods and services produced in an economy should not decline from one year to the next. A defendant of this proposal might point to the fact that, by and large, higher income leads to higher well-being. Moreover, growth of income is important to address social goals such as poverty alleviation. Income measures, however, do not say much about sustainability. Higher income does not necessarily mean higher sustainability, in the same way as a higher fishery catch does not necessarily mean a bigger fish stock.

The fact that income, or for that matter consumption, does not have a direct welfare connotation was highlighted in a seminal paper by Samuelson (1961).

Assume you observe two countries, A and B. Both countries produce the same level of income but while A consumes it all, B saves a part of its income and invests it into productive capital. Citizen A is consuming more than citizen B but given country B's saving effort, B will soon be able to generate a higher level of income and increase its consumption possibilities. In order to compare well-being between the two countries, current income provides a misleading signal: while starting from the same level of income, B will soon be able to produce more, owing to its saving effort. Current consumption similarly provides a misleading signal. The choice has to be made 'in the space of all present and future consumption . . . the only valid approximation to a measure of welfare comes from computing *wealth-like* magnitudes not income magnitudes' (Samuelson, 1961, pp. 50, 57).

Irving Fisher (1906) provided the original insight that current wealth equals the present value of future consumption.[2] For the relationship between current and future consumption and wealth to hold, one should however make sure that, in the latter, all assets that are needed for the generation of well-being are included. Fisher (1906) identified three types of assets: immovable wealth, comprising of land and the fixed structures upon it, movable assets, or commodities, and human beings. As we shall see, these assets remain of interest although terminology has changed and more categories have been added to this list.

From wealth to sustainability

If wealth is the correct measure of well-being, sustainability can be expressed in terms of changes in wealth. A major strength of the capital approach to sustainability is the fact that it provides a simple and forward-looking guide to policy makers.

Consider the following definition of sustainability: a development path is sustainable if social well-being, that is, the present value of current and future consumption, does not decline at any point along the path:[3]

$$V_{t+1} \geq V_t \text{ for } t > 0 \qquad (3.1)$$

Given that social welfare equals wealth, a simple sustainability test requires that wealth does not decline over time. In other words, the level of net saving, adjusted to take into account the net changes in natural and human capital, should be positive for the economy to be sustainable.

The strength of this definition of sustainability is that it provides a forward-looking guide to policy. Decision makers at time t do not usually know what utility or well-being will look like far in the future. But they don't need to. To achieve sustainability, the only thing the committed policy maker should worry about is that *current* net saving be positive.

In making this claim, we implicitly adopt a paradigm which allows for the possibility of replacing natural capital with produced capital. This approach has the weakness of not being able to account for irreplaceable assets such as biodiversity hot-spots and the oceans' regulating function over the global climate. Low substitutability critically hinders sustainability. Substitutability refers to the extent to which an asset, for example natural resources, can be replaced by another asset, for example man-made capital, in the production process. If substitutability is low, that is, the elasticity of substitution between man-made capital and exhaustible natural resources is less than one, sustainability is not possible in the absence of technical progress (Dasgupta and Heal, 1979).

Pearce and Atkinson (1993) and Pearce et al. (1996) have highlighted the advantages and limits of the so-called 'weak sustainability' rule. While undermined by the existence of irreplaceable and unique assets, weak sustainability has the non-trivial advantage of being easy to apply and still provide a strong signal: 'even on a weak sustainability rule many countries are unlikely to pass a sustainability test' (Pearce and Atkinson, 1993, p. 105). Hamilton and Clemens (1999) calculated the first country-wide genuine saving rates for developing countries, showing that the greatest wealth dissipation is taking place in many of the poorest countries in the world. Chapter 18 deals explicitly with the theory and practice of genuine saving. For present purposes, it suffices to say that genuine saving measures the true rate of saving of an economy, after accounting for the depletion of natural resources, investments in human capital and damages from (certain) pollutants.

The advantage of measurability

The capital approach to sustainability provides an answer to the measurability dilemma. Measurement requires that our computation of wealth (a) be comprehensive and (b) use the right prices. Comprehensiveness means that not only should produced capital be counted as wealth but also natural resources, human capital and social capital should be accounted for. The next section describes the estimation issues. While substantial progress has been made in the measurement of natural capital, many assets are left outside due to the lack of data. Groundwater and fishery stocks, for example, are not included in the measures of natural wealth presented in this chapter. Human and social capital is still very hard to measure. The approach here is to compute it as the difference between total wealth and the sum of the tangible components of wealth (produced capital and natural capital).

Proper accounting prices are required to measure the individual components of wealth. This is not difficult for marketed, produced goods. It is, however, a challenge when it comes to non-marketed items, for which prices are not directly observable. Asset prices are intimately related to the scarcity of the asset. If an economy is running out of clean water, citizens will usually have to pay higher prices for potable water. As many environmental and natural resources are provided at no charge, the market price is usually a bad signal of their scarcity and modelled accounting prices need to be estimated.

Knowing the composition of wealth helps inform policy making
The wealth estimates not only provide a measure of well-being, they also provide useful insight into the composition of capital assets in an economy. Policies to foster sustainability depend on the relative endowments of resources a country has available for the generation of well-being. Economic management for sustainability can be equated to a process of portfolio management, in which economic decisions entail the transformation of one resource into another.

Forested areas can be transformed into cropland; oil rents can be invested in school facilities. Sustainability is not about keeping this or that asset intact, but rather about keeping the system's ability to produce well-being. Sustainable development in an oil country, such as Venezuela, will mean investing resource rents in human or physical capital.[4] Development need not only entail the transformation of natural capital in other assets. In a resource-poor, rural based economy such as Ethiopia, sustainable development means keeping, and possibly increasing, the land's capacity to produce an economic surplus, which only then can be invested in other assets. In biodiversity-rich countries, such as Peru, sustainability will entail managing pristine areas so as to maximize revenues from sustainable forestry, tourism and bioprospecting research.

Knowing the basis of a society's welfare is a desirable objective. The next task is to understand how concrete estimates of total wealth can be obtained.

3. The architecture of the wealth estimates
Broadly speaking, total wealth is composed of produced capital, natural capital and intangible capital, where the latter is an aggregate including human, social and institutional capital. Rather than summing up these three components, the estimation proceeds by first estimating total wealth, then produced capital and natural capital and finally calculating intangible capital as the difference between total wealth and the sum of produced and natural capital (Table 3.1).

Estimating total wealth
To measure total wealth, and in line with Fisher (1906), Hamilton and Hartwick (2005) show that the current value of wealth, composed of

Table 3.1   Estimating wealth in four steps

	(1) Total capital	(2) Produced capital	(3) Natural capital	(4) = (1)−(2)−(3) Intangible capital
Method used	Present Value of consumption	Perpetual Inventory Method	Present Value of rents Opportunity cost	Difference
Assets included	By definition, all assets that contribute to national consumption	Machinery, equipment and infrastructure Urban land	Sub-soil assets Forest resources (timber and non-timber) Crop and pasture land Protected areas	Human capital Governance Institutional effectiveness All other assets not measured in column (2) and (3)

man-made, human and natural capital, is in fact equal to the present value of future consumption:

$$W_t = \int_t^\infty C(s)e^{-r(s-t)}ds \qquad (3.2)$$

Where $C(s)$ is consumption at time s, and r is the discount rate.

Yet, future consumption is unknown. It can be shown that if consumption grows at a constant rate, equation (3.2) conveniently reduces to a function of current consumption and the rate of time preference only. The problem is then one of estimating a level of current consumption that can be increased sustainably over time. For this reason, in computing the initial level of consumptions, the following issues are considered:

- *The volatility of consumption.* To solve this problem, a three-year average of consumption is used.
- *Negative rates of genuine or adjusted net saving.* When genuine saving is negative, countries are consuming natural resources and jeopardizing the prospects for future consumption. In order to correct for unsustainable levels of consumption, negative genuine saving is subtracted from consumption.

Produced capital
The aggregate for produced capital includes physical capital – that is, equipment, machinery and structures – and urban land.

There are a number of estimation methods available for the calculation of physical capital stocks. Some of them, such as the derivation of capital stocks from insurance values or accounting values or from direct surveys, entail enormous expenditures and face problems of limited availability and adequacy of the data. Other estimation procedures, such as the perpetual inventory method (PIM) are cheaper and more easily implementable since they only require investment data and information on the assets service life and depreciation pattern. Here, the following PIM formula was used to compute the value of machinery, equipment and structures:

$$K_t = \sum_{i=0}^{19} I_{t-i}(1 - \alpha)^i \tag{3.3}$$

where I is the value of investment in constant prices and $\alpha = 0.05$ is a geometric depreciation rate.[5]

Urban land was valued as a fixed proportion of the value of physical capital. This is a fallback for the more palatable and data intensive option of using country-specific proportions. A constant proportion equal to 24 per cent is then assumed.[6]

Natural capital
Natural capital is the sum of non-renewable resources (including energy resources such as oil, natural gas and coal, and mineral resources), cropland, pasture land, forested areas (including areas used for timber extraction and non-timber forest products) and protected areas.

The PIM is not useful in valuing natural capital, given that most natural resources are accumulated over a very long time span. The present value method is used in most cases. This method consists of computing the present value of a given natural resource net rents over the life span of the resource. When data on rents (or benefits) is not available, the opportunity cost method is used instead.

- *Sub-soil assets.* Estimating future rents for sub-soil assets is subject to a high level of uncertainty. Here the simplifying assumption that rents grow at a constant rate is used. Moreover, an average life of a mine is assumed to be 20 years (this may vary from country to country though and from one resource to the other).
- *Timber resources.* The predominant economic use of forests has been as a source of timber. Timber wealth is calculated as the net present value of rents from roundwood production. The estimation then requires data on roundwood production, unit rents and the time to exhaustion of the forest (if unsustainably managed). Notice that the use of rents to value capital implicitly assumes that the timber value

of a forest is given by the currently exploitable timber, rather than the volume of the resource itself.

- *Non-timber forest products.* Average world values (from Lampietti and Dixon, 1995) are applied to a share of the country's forest.
- *Cropland.* Given the lack of data on land prices, land values are computed on the basis of the present value of land rents, assuming that the products of the land are sold at world prices. The return to land is computed as the difference between the market value of output crops and crop-specific production costs. Nine representative crops are selected based mainly on their production significance in terms of sowing area, production volume and revenue. The nine representative crops considered are: maize, rice, wheat, banana, grapes, apples, oranges, soybean and coffee. A country's overall land rent is calculated as a weighted average (weighted by sowing areas) of rents from the crop categories. A projected growth in production (land areas are assumed to stay constant) is assumed based on Rosengrant et al. (1995).
- *Pasture land.* The returns to pasture land are assumed to be a fixed proportion of the value of output. On average, costs of production are 55 per cent of revenues, and therefore returns to pasture land are assumed to be 45 per cent of output value. Value of output is based on the production of beef, lamb, milk and wool valued at international prices. As is the case for cropland, this rental share of output values is applied to country-specific outputs of pasture land valued at world prices. A projected growth in production is assumed also in this case (Rosengrant et al., 1995).
- *Protected areas.* Values are obtained using, as a proxy, the lower of the unit values of cropland and pasture land; an imperfect and conservative measure of the opportunity cost of protecting land areas. Precise estimations are very difficult to undertake and country-specific data are sparse.

Intangible capital

Even after accounting for produced capital and a large set of natural resource assets, the wealth estimates show that most countries' wealth is captured by what we call 'intangible capital'. By definition, intangible capital captures all those assets that are unaccounted for in the wealth estimates. It includes assets such as the skills and know-how embodied in the labour force: human capital. It also encompasses social capital; that is, the amount of trust among people in a society and their ability to work together for common purposes. Finally, it includes those elements of governance that boost the productivity of the economy. For example, if an economy has a very efficient judicial system, clear property rights and an effective government, the effects will be picked up in the form of higher total wealth and thus will increase the 'intangible capital' residual.

The intangible capital residual also includes other assets which, for lack of data coverage, could not be accounted for in the wealth estimates. The main omissions include coastal and marine resources, such as fisheries, and the net depletion of renewable natural resources such as underground water and environmental services.

4. The highlights of the capital estimates

Country-specific estimates of total capital are presented in World Bank (2006a). Table 3.2 summarizes the results by region, income group and for the world as a whole. High energy and mineral exporters are treated as a separate group. The relative distribution of assets in these countries is such that the aggregates would tend to overestimate the role of natural capital – particularly sub-soil – in the groups such countries are in.

A quick glance at Table 3.2 reveals the following.

Firstly, the average world citizen 'owns' a total wealth of nearly US$96 000. The number becomes US$90 000 if oil exporters are included. This level of wealth is comparable to the one for Brazil (US$90 000), Libya (US$89 000) or Croatia (US$91 000).

Second, total wealth in high income countries is several times higher than in low income countries (column 2). This fact is only partially due to the use of nominal exchange rates as opposed to purchasing power parity (PPP) exchange rates typically used to compare welfare between high income and developing countries.

Third, natural capital is higher in value in high income countries than in low income countries (column 3 and Figure 3.1). This evidence contradicts a common perception that high income countries have 'used up' their natural resources.

Fourth, the share of natural capital in total wealth decreases with income (column 6 and Figure 3.2). The world's poorest countries – particularly in South and East Asia – depend heavily on natural resources. Development cannot be pursued without maintaining an ever watchful eye on how natural resources are managed.

Lastly, intangible capital – an aggregate including human capital, the quality of institutions and governance – constitutes the preponderant form of wealth, an insight that goes back to the very origins of modern economic thinking (columns 5 and 8).

Points three and four above are particularly relevant from the perspective of sustainability. Natural resource abundance is also a characteristic of wealthy economies. What we are observing is better management of

Table 3.2 Estimates of total wealth and its components by region and income group in 2000 (US$ per capita and %)

Group	Dollars per capita				Percent share of total wealth		
	Total Wealth	Natural Capital	Prod. Capital	Intang. Capital	Natural Capital	Prod. Capital	Intang. Capital
Lat. Am. and Carib.	69 145	7 018	10 677	51 451	10%	15%	74%
Sub-Saharan Africa	13 631	1 816	1 628	10 187	13%	12%	75%
South Asia	6 906	1 749	1 115	4 043	25%	16%	59%
East Asia and Pacif.	11 958	2 511	3 189	6 258	21%	27%	52%
Mid. East and N. Africa	23 920	2 764	4 075	17 080	12%	17%	71%
Eur. and Central Asia	41 964	3 795	8 446	29 722	9%	20%	71%
Low Income	7 532	1 925	1 174	4 434	26%	16%	59%
Lower Middle Income	22 674	2 970	4 187	15 517	13%	18%	68%
Upper Middle Income	76 538	8 706	16 831	51 001	11%	22%	67%
High Income OECD	439 063	9 531	76 193	353 339	2%	17%	80%
World (excl. oil)	*95 860*	*4 011*	*16 850*	*74 998*	*1%*	*17%*	*82%*
Oil countries	22 952	12 656	7 937	2 359	55%	35%	10%
World	90 210	4 681	16 160	69 369	5%	18%	77%

Source: World Bank (2006a).

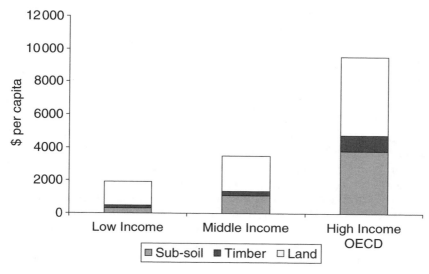

Source: World Bank (2006a).

Figure 3.1 Value of natural capital per capita by income group

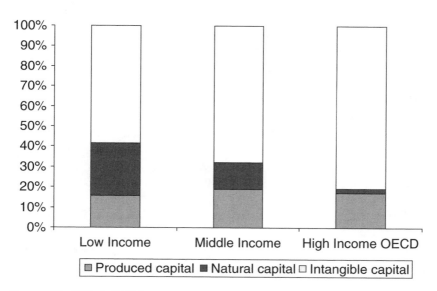

Source: World Bank (2006a).

Figure 3.2 Wealth composition by income group

resources such as agricultural land (resulting in higher yields) and forests (resulting in timber rents that are sustained over time).

Yet, low income countries are more dependent (in terms of relative share) than high income countries on natural resources. This provides useful information. What we are observing is low levels of diversification and low levels of intangible assets such as education and efficient institutions. Given the importance of natural capital on the wealth of poor countries, one should look at the individual sub-components (Table 3.3).

If one excludes large resource exporting countries, which constitute a group by themselves, land resources (columns 5–7 in Table 3.3) are very important in low income countries, with a value of 75 per cent, followed by sub-soil assets (column 2), with 17 per cent. In middle income countries land resources account for 61 per cent of natural capital, while sub-soil assets account for 31 per cent of the total.

The importance of land resources (that is, cropland, pasture land and protected areas) decreases with the level of income. This fact is partly the effect of using international prices for agricultural products, a procedure that overestimates the value of land in countries with subsistence agricultural production. However, the results also suggest a potential poverty–land dependence trap in low income countries. Countries in which

Table 3.3   Estimates of the components of natural capital by income group as a percentage of the total in 2000

Income Group	Sub-soil assets	Timber resources	NTFR	PA	Crop land	Pasture land	Natural capital
Low Income	17%	6%	2%	6%	59%	10%	100%
Lower Middle Income	24%	5%	4%	4%	52%	11%	100%
Upper Middle Income	55%	3%	2%	4%	23%	13%	100%
Middle Income	31%	5%	3%	4%	45%	12%	100%
High Income Non-OECD	1%	0%	0%	33%	44%	22%	100%
High Income OECD	40%	8%	2%	13%	21%	16%	100%
World (excl. oil)	*32%*	*6%*	*3%*	*8%*	*37%*	*13%*	*100%*
Oil countries	75%	2%	4%	5%	10%	5%	100%
World	41%	5%	3%	7%	32%	12%	100%

Source: World Bank (2006a).

land resources account for more than one third of total wealth – such as Niger, Burundi, Moldova to name a few – all belong to the low income country group.

By contrast, high dependence on sub-soil assets is not necessarily a characteristic of low income countries. Countries which are rich in mineral and energy resources may be found in each of the income groups. Rents from sub-soil assets can be key in raising countries out of poverty, but do not represent a sufficient condition: high rents require efficient management in order to achieve poverty reduction (see Chapters 13 and 14).

5. Understanding intangible capital

Given its role in the wealth numbers, one should look more closely at the intangible capital component. Regression analysis can help us pinpoint its major determinants. Three factors – average years of schooling per capita, rule of law, and remittances received per capita – explain 89 per cent of the total variation in the residual across countries.[7] Figure 3.3 shows the relative importance of each factor, with rule of law accounting for 57 per cent and schooling accounting for 36 per cent of intangible capital.

Table 3.4 reports the marginal returns, measured at the mean, to unit increases in the three factors for each level of income. Increasing the average stock of schooling by one year per person, increases total wealth per capita by nearly $840 in poor countries,[8] nearly $2000 in middle income countries and over $16000 in high income countries. A one-point increase in the rule of law index (on a 100 point scale) boosts total wealth by over $100 in poor countries, over $400 in middle income countries, and nearly $3000 in high income countries. Larger stocks of produced capital – usually at higher income levels – will also boost the returns to education and governance. This helps to explain the wide ranges in marginal returns as countries get richer.

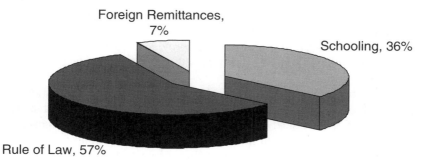

Source: World Bank (2006a).

Figure 3.3 Factors explaining the intangible capital residual

Table 3.4   *Variation in intangible capital due to a unit variation in the explanatory variables, by income group*

	Marginal returns to schooling	Marginal returns to rule of law	Marginal returns to foreign remittances
Low Income	838	111	29
Lower Middle Income	1 721	362	27
Upper Middle Income	2 398	481	110
High Income OECD	16 430	2 973	306

Notes: Figures represent the increase in the intangible capital residual associated with a 1-unit increase in the given factor.

Source: World Bank (2006a).

The analysis of intangible capital provides useful insight for policy makers. Education expenditure can obviously play a role, but these expenditures have to be effective in actually creating human capital. Investing in rule of law is clearly complex – an efficient judicial system for example calls not only for competitive salaries but also for competent institutions that can be trusted by citizens and entrepreneurs alike. The returns to doing so, however, are potentially very large.

6.   The capital approach to sustainability: implications

A key contribution of the economic debate of sustainability is that it sets the ground for measurement. Hartwick (1977) demonstrated that under some stringent conditions, non-declining real wealth implies non-declining consumption. More in general, non-declining real wealth is associated with non-declining social welfare. The bottom line is that comprehensive measures of wealth and its changes appear as meaningful indicators to track sustainable development. Saving, in particular, constitutes a significant measure of sustainability and one that provides useful insight for policy making. Chapter 18 analyzes thoroughly the theory and evidence related to genuine saving.

By looking at comprehensive wealth, the objective is to understand the potential for the creation of well-being in a country. This approach revives the ideas of the classical economists, who identified not only man-made capital but also labour and natural resources as determinants of production. From the numbers, it is evident that the components of wealth vary widely across regions and according to level of income. Managing each component of the portfolio and transforming efficiently one type of asset into another is germane to a country's development policy.

Implications for policy makers

Economic decisions are usually the domain of finance and economy ministers and seldom take into account environmental concerns. The capital approach to sustainability expands the responsibilities of economic management to include the management of natural resources, human capital and institutions. The wealth estimates indicate that the development process entails a diminishing dependence on natural resources while increasing the reliance on human skills and the country's social and institutional infrastructure. Notice that this need not occur at the expense of environmental degradation. While less important in relative terms, natural resources are larger in absolute terms in richer countries.

Managing development in the poorest countries requires the recognition of the role of natural resources as a source of subsistence. In aggregate, natural capital represents a quarter of wealth in low income countries. Throughout the world, many rural households depend on the services of forest ecosystems, fisheries and agricultural land for subsistence. These resources are typically renewable, and the management challenge essentially entails sustainability in use. Institutions and social arrangements that foster conservation include the clear definition of property rights and the control of corruption and poaching. On a positive note, there must be policies geared toward increasing the productivity of assets, so as to allow growing income and consequently higher savings to finance investment.

In resource-rich countries, natural resources are a fundamental source of development finance. Fiscal policies should be geared toward capturing resource rents. Examples include energy royalties, taxes on tourism revenues, underground water tariffs. Public expenditure should give priority to high return investments, as opposed to the more commonly observed excessive public consumption expenditure (see Chapters 13 and 14). This may prove difficult with fiscal shocks, typical of oil countries, and low absorptive capacity. In the short term, investment in financial assets may be a better option compared to an unsustainable increase in current expenditures. Botswana, for example, has been able to manage diamond revenues successfully through a strict budget balance rule.

Investment in man-made, human capital and reliable institutions is crucial. Governments should invest in education, an efficient judicial system and rule of law and policies aiming at attracting remittances.

Implications for economists and statisticians

Good decision-making requires good information. The wealth estimates discussed in this chapter constitute a contribution to this work on 'greening' the national accounts. Including monetary estimation of natural capital in a country's macroeconomic balance sheet is important in representing the actual sources of welfare for the country. The economic valuation of environment and natural resources is the basic building block of a comprehensive accounting system. Valuation can usefully inform monitoring and enforcement, decision-making through cost–benefit analysis and fiscal policies.

Asset prices have to reflect the social worth of capital, which in turn reflects its social scarcity. Moreover, achieving sustainability critically depends on the substitutability of man-made capital and natural resources. The substitutability issue is also a measurement problem. Valuing total wealth as the sum of produced, natural and human capital relies on the assumption that assets are substitutable. It must be possible to deplete one resource and substitute it with other assets, for our assumed 'weakly' sustainable world to hold. If assets are irreplaceable, while being essential for the production of well-being, physical measures must complement monetary measures of capital.

7.   Summing up

The discussion in this chapter was motivated by the need to adopt a pragmatic measure of current generations' bequest of opportunities to future generations. A narrow definition of 'opportunities' – associated with capital – was identified. Wealth per capita, measured as the sum of all assets that allow the production of well-being, was thus our measure of 'opportunities'. To the extent that future generations are left with a level of *total* wealth per capita at least as high as today's wealth, then we are on a sustainable path, at least from a weak sustainability perspective.

Where is the wealth of nations? The estimates of comprehensive wealth and its components go beyond a simple sustainability test and provide insights about what constitutes a country's base for producing well-being. By and large, wealth is about intangible assets. Intangible does not mean indefinable. In fact, a very strong association between education attainment, governance and institutions on one side and intangible capital on the other is found. A society investing in skilled workers, trusted institutions and efficient government is building the very basis of welfare creation. These sorts of intangible assets explain the high level of wealth of countries in Europe, North America and East Asia.

How about natural capital? The wealth estimates suggest the importance of natural resources management in maintaining wealth in the poorest countries in the world. For the average citizen of Ethiopia, natural capital – particularly crop land – constitutes more than 40 per cent of available assets. Depleting forest resources and degrading agricultural soils will impair the prospect for poverty alleviation. Sustainability here not only requires investing resource rents into some form of capital. Within a subsistence economy, it means managing natural assets so as to provide the basis for income. Mineral deposits, once discovered, can only be depleted. Sustainability here means investing resource rents in some form of capital. The Hartwick rule for sustainability has, however, been neglected by many resource-rich countries, leading to consumption levels that are unsustainable, explaining economic downturns.

Finally, to measure sustainability truly, the focus has to be on changes in wealth. The wealth estimates provide an insightful vision of the world and its prospects for generating welfare. Any sensible sustainability test should, however, look at the change in capital rather than at the stock. Chapter 18 introduces genuine saving – that is, the annual change in total real wealth – as a measure of sustainability. Breaking down total wealth into its components is a major step forward in the analysis of country-level endowments and welfare generation possibilities. The estimates made available here contribute to this work even if data constraints limit our ability to measure some assets in a comprehensive way. This work has just begun.

Notes

1. The opinions expressed are those of the authors.
2. Fisher's argument was motivated by the need to find a measure of comprehensive wealth. This led to the intuition that the value of an asset is the capitalization of the stream of future services expected to be produced by that asset.
3. Alternatively, one may adopt a definition in terms of non-declining utility or well-being (as in Pezzey, 1989). Dasgupta (2001) argues that expression (3.1), while less ambitious, has more practical force.
4. A large portion of the literature on sustainability has concentrated on the conditions to achieve sustainability in the presence of exhaustible natural resources. Hartwick (1977) defined a particular saving rule and finds that as a result, a constant level of consumption can be achieved, even in the presence of finite resources and fixed technology, provided substitutability is high enough. Hartwick's saving rule is crucial in that it provides a simple guide for policy in resource-rich countries.
5. Expression (3.3) implicitly assumes a 'One-Hoss-Shay' retirement pattern: capital stock after depreciation is unproductive and exits the production process after 20 years.
6. The estimation of the value of urban land is based on Canada's detailed national balance sheet information. Urban land is estimated to be 33 per cent of the value of structures, which in turn is estimated to be 72 per cent of the total value of physical capital.
7. The specified model represents the residual as a function of domestic human capital, as captured by the per capita years of schooling of the working population, human capital abroad, as captured by the amount of remittances by workers outside the country, and governance/social capital, expressed here as a rule of law index. We considered a simple Cobb–Douglas function:

   $$R = A S^\alpha F^\beta L^\gamma$$

   where S is years of schooling per worker, F is remittances from abroad and L is the rule of law index. There is also a set of income group dummies that take into account differences linked to income levels.
8. In comparison, low income countries spend nearly US$51 per student in primary school (World Bank, 2006b).

References

Dasgupta, P. (2001), *Human Well-Being and the Natural Environment*, Oxford: Oxford University Press.

Dasgupta, P. and G.M. Heal (1979), *Economic Theory and Exhaustible Resources*, Cambridge: Cambridge University Press.

Fisher, I. (1906), *The Nature of Capital and Income*, New York: Macmillan.

Hamilton, K. and M. Clemens (1999), 'Genuine savings rates in developing countries', *The World Bank Economic Review*, **13**(2): 333–56.

Hamilton, K. and J.M. Hartwick (2005), 'Investing exhaustible resource rents and the path of consumption', *Canadian Journal of Economics*, **38**(2): 615–21.

Hartwick, John M. (1977), 'Intergenerational equity and the investing of rents from exhaustible resources', *American Economic Review*, **66**: 972–4.

Lampietti, J. and J. Dixon (1995), 'To see the forest for the trees: a guide to non-timber forest benefits', Environment Department Papers, No. 13, Washington DC: World Bank.

Pearce, D.W. and G. Atkinson (1993), 'Capital theory and the measurement of sustainable development: an indicator of weak sustainability', *Ecological Economics*, **8**(2): 103–8.

Pearce, D.W., K. Hamilton and G. Atkinson (1996), 'Measuring sustainable development: progress on indicators', *Environment and Development Economics*, **1**: 85–101.

Pearce, D.W., A. Markandya and E. Barbier (1989), *Blueprint for a Green Economy*, London: Earthscan.

Pezzey, J. (1989), 'Economic analysis of sustainable growth and sustainable Development', Environment Department Working Paper 15, Washington, DC: World Bank.

Rosengrant, M.W., M. Agcaoili-Sombilla and N.D. Perez (1995), 'Global food projections to 2020: implications for investment', Food, Agriculture, and the Environment Discussion paper 5, International Food Policy Research Institute, Washington DC.

Samuelson, P. (1961), 'The evaluation of "Social Income": Capital Formation and Wealth', in F.A. Lutz and D.C. Hague (eds), *The Theory of Capital*, New York: St Martin's Press.

Smith, Adam (1776)[1977], *An Inquiry into the Nature and Causes of the Wealth of Nations*, Chicago: University of Chicago Press.

World Bank (2006a), *Where is the Wealth of Nations?*, Washington DC: The World Bank.

World Bank (2006b), *World Development Indicators 2006*, Washington, DC: World Bank.

4 Sustainable development in ecological economics

Jeroen C.J.M. van den Bergh

1. Introduction

The notions of 'sustainable development' and 'sustainability' are interpreted in various ways. This has become most clear perhaps in the field of ecological economics, where different disciplines have offered particular perspectives on these notions. Ecological economics (EE) was founded at the end of the 1980s. It integrates elements of economics and ecology, as well as of thermodynamics, ethics, and a number of other natural and social sciences to provide for an integrated and biophysical perspective on environment–economy interactions. EE expresses the view that the economy is a subsystem of a larger local and global ecosystem that limits physical growth of the economy. At the same time, it is critical of the dominant paradigm of (environmental and resource) economics, characterized by rational agents and equilibrium thinking. Instead, EE is characterized by the use of physical (material, energy, chemical, biological) indicators and comprehensive, multidisciplinary systems analysis. Both features are consistent with the fact that (un)sustainable development, generally seen as an important dimension of performance of the overall systems level, occupies a central position in the study of EE.

All intellectual founders and antecedents of EE have written extensively about sustainable development, even if not using this particular terminology. For example, H.E. Daly proposed the idea of a 'steady state economy', associated with the objective to minimize the use of materials and energy 'throughput' in the economy (Daly, 1991). In addition, he has suggested the Index of Sustainable Economic Welfare (ISEW: see also Chapter 19) as a sustainable welfare indicator (Daly and Cobb, 1989). K.E. Boulding proposed the opposition between the 'cowboy economy' and the 'spaceship economy' (Boulding, 1966). The spaceship metaphor can be seen as a precursor to the modern view on sustainability from a global environmental perspective. Finally, C.S. Holling (1973, 1986) has originated the notion of resilience (Chapter 5), which has proven to be a fruitful and distinctive way of thinking about sustainable development.

This chapter tries to provide a broad sketch of ideas, approaches and policy angles that ecological economics has offered in the study of sustainable development. The result is the following structure. Section 2 discusses the distinctive character of ecological economics approaches to sustainable development as compared with mainstream economics. Section 3 then examines the well-known opposition between strong and weak sustainability. Section 4 addresses the sustainability of open systems, involving issues like spatial sustainability and sustainable trade. Section 5 deals with measurement of, and models for, sustainable development. Section 6 discusses policies specifically oriented towards sustainability. Section 7 concludes.

2.   Ecological versus environmental economics

An important distinction between ecological economics (EE) and environmental and resource economics (ERE) relates to scale versus allocation. ERE studies optimal allocation or efficiency of using scarce resources. Consistent with this idea is the objective to optimize social welfare and thus strive towards an optimal level of external costs. Daly (for example, 1992) argues that ERE has, however, neglected the issue of optimal physical scale or size of the economy. Consistent with this neglect, ERE tends to regard sustainable development as identical to sustainable growth. EE, on the other hand, sees sustainable development more in line with the older notions of development and structural change. Not surprisingly, history, institutional context and poverty receive much more attention in EE discussions and analyses of the concept. Somewhat related is the fact that ERE, or at least many of its proponents, does not seem to take physical limits to growth as seriously as supporters of EE. This might have to do with optimism about both the inventiveness of humans (technical progress and problem-solving in general) as well as about the stability of nature and environmental systems to withstand pressure caused by humans. Possibly, EE generally assumes a longer time horizon than ERE. In this sense, the different approaches to sustainable development – optimistic versus precautionary – bear a strong relationship with the different positions in the growth debate (van den Bergh and de Mooij, 1999).

The main goals and criteria for evaluating developments, policies and projects differ between EE and ERE. The dominant criterion of ERE is efficiency (or sometimes a more limited version, such as costs-effectiveness). EE is best characterized by a 'precautionary principle' linked to environmental sustainability, with much attention for 'small-probability–large-impact' combinations. This precautionary principle is closely related to a concern for instability of ecosystems, loss of biodiversity, and environmental ethical considerations ('biocentric ethics'). Efficiency is in EE of secondary concern. Furthermore, whereas in ERE distribution and equity are secondary criteria, 'distribution' is often in EE considered a more important criterion. In line with this, EE emphasizes (basic) needs, North–South welfare differences, and the complex link between poverty and environment. In addition, a recent emphasis in the literature is that it is impossible to analyse distribution and efficiency perfectly separately, as the latter depends on the former (Martinez-Alier and O'Connor, 1999). One argument here is that preferences are interdependent and income distribution affects individual well-being. Subjective welfare studies show that relative rather than absolute income is an important factor of happiness (Tversky and Simonson, 2000; Brekke and Howarth, 2002; van Praag and Ferrer-i-Carbonell, 2004).

3. Strong versus weak sustainability

Sustainability and sustainable development have been defined, interpreted and analysed in various ways (see Pezzey, 1989, 1993; Toman et al., 1995). Beckerman (1994) has argued that these notions serve no purpose as they are already captured in the concept of intergenerational welfare optimization. Responses by Common, Daly, El Serafy and Jacobs in *Environmental Values* vol. 4 (1995, issues 1 and 2) and vol. 5 (1996, issue 1) oppose this view. In particular, the opposition between strong and weak sustainability has received much attention in the literature (Ayres et al., 2001).

Weak sustainability

Weak sustainability has been defined using notions like 'economic capital' and 'natural capital' (Cabeza-Gutés, 1996). Economic capital comprises machines, labour and knowledge. Natural capital covers resources, environment and nature. Weak sustainability is defined as maintaining 'total capital', defined as the 'sum' of the two types of capital. Evidently, under this goal the substitution of natural capital by economic capital is allowed for. The methodological aspects of this approach are most clearly expressed in economic growth theory (Solow, 1974, 1986; Hartwick, 1977). This theory translates weak sustainability into intergenerational equity (Toman et al., 1995). Sustainability is usually interpreted as a constraint on economic growth, namely non-decreasing welfare. This is quite a strict criterion, as any temporary decrease in welfare implies an unsustainable development. Pezzey (1989) has referred to 'sustainedness' in this respect, since such a pattern can be assessed only after the fact. As a weaker alternative criterion, Pezzey (1993) proposes 'survivability', according to which a reduction in welfare is allowed as long as the level of consumption exceeds some subsistence level.

In the general economic case, social welfare is a function of utility, which is difficult to operationalize. In practice, simple models often equate utility to (aggregate) consumption, defined as gross output less investment. This gives rise to 'Hicksian sustainability', or non-decreasing consumption, which is equivalent to 'Hartwick–Solow sustainability' defined in terms of maintaining the total capital stock of society.

Strong sustainability
Strong sustainability, on the other hand, requires that every type of capital – economic and natural – is maintained separately, or that even, at a lower level of disaggregation, capital stocks are maintained. Various motivations for strong sustainability exist:

- Natural resources are considered as essential inputs in economic production, consumption or welfare that cannot be substituted for by manufactured or human capital. Life support functions of nature and environment are often mentioned here.
- Acknowledgement of environmental integrity and 'rights of nature' (bioethics).
- Risk aversion in combination with irreversible changes in natural capital. In this context the terms stability, resilience, (bio)diversity and ecosystem health (Costanza et al., 1992) are often mentioned.

Within EE frequently a particular type of (un)sustainability is pointed out, namely the stability and resilience of ecosystems. Stability is defined at the level of biological populations. This means that variables return to equilibrium values after perturbation. Resilience (resistance to change, or robustness) is defined at the system level and refers to the maintenance of organization or structure and functions of a system in the face of stress (see Chapter 12). Perrings (1998) mentions two alternative approaches to resilience: one is directed at the time necessary for a disturbed system to return to its original state (Pimm, 1984); the other is directed at the intensity of disturbance that a system can absorb before moving to another state (Holling, 1973). In line with the latter interpretation resilience has been phrased 'Holling sustainability', as opposed to weak 'Solow–Hartwick sustainability' (Common and Perrings, 1992). The comparison shows that EE studies pay much attention to the sensitivity of ecosystems at a micro level, often in applied studies, whereas ERE extends economic growth theory with environmental variables, emphasizing determinism and coarse long-term trends in a macro approach that lacks micro detail. From this perspective EE and ERE approaches to sustainability can give rise to complementary as well as contradictory insights.

'Very strong' sustainability, as supported by the Deep Ecology movement and those who believe in the 'right-to-life' of other species, would then imply that every component or subsystem of the natural environment, every species, and every physical stock must be preserved. A compromise version of strong sustainability focuses on preserving ecosystems and environmental assets that are critical for life-support or unique and irreplaceable. The ozone layer is an example of the first; songbirds or coral reefs might be an example of the second. Another way of formulating such a compromise is that a minimum amount of certain environmental assets should be maintained, based on the idea that these assets are partly complementary to economic assets and partly substitutable by the latter.

How to judge or resolve the opposition?

The opposition between strong and weak sustainability is ultimately a question about the substitutability between the products and services of the market economy and the environment, or the substitution of natural by produced capital (including human capital or knowledge). This has often been discussed in the context of production processes (see the special issue of *Ecological Economics*, vol. 22(3) (1997) on the contributions of Nicholas Georgescu-Roegen to ecological economics). However, the distinction also applies to consumption and individual welfare. This is most clearly expressed in the notion of lexicographic preference orderings, which is consistent with the Maslow pyramid (Stern, 1997). It denies universal substitutability. This is consistent with findings in experiments and stated preference valuation (Spash and Hanley, 1995; Gowdy, 1997).

A problem with the weak sustainability approach as formalized in growth theory with environment or resources is that this was formulated explicitly for non-renewable resources, not for complex biological systems. Moreover, the tools of growth theory – deterministic dynamic optimization models with one dynamic equation describing the environment – are too rough to incorporate scientific facts of complex evolutionary (irreversible) living systems. Therefore, growth theory cannot offer a complete, and perhaps not even a relevant, perspective on sustainability.

Resilience can be considered as a global, structural stability concept, based on the idea that multiple locally stable ecosystem equilibria can exist. Sustainability can thus be directly related to resilience. In line with this, weak sustainability can cause extreme sensitivity to either natural disturbances (for example, diseases in the case of agriculture focusing on only a few crops: see Chapter 22) or economic disturbances (international financial markets as in the case of the small Pacific island nation of Nauru: Gowdy and McDaniel, 1999). Such extreme sensitivity or lack of resilience of regional systems in the face of external factors is a telling argument against weak sustainability. Traditional economic models with environment and resources do, however, not address resilience, fluctuations and cycles. Business cycle theories might be useful in this respect (Young, 1996). Indeed, one may wonder why other types of dynamic macroeconomics – apart from growth theory – have seen so little application in environmental economics, for example, to address questions related to the interaction between sustainability and unemployment. Finally, it is very likely that the truth is in between weak and strong sustainability. Perfect substitutability is not realistic, but neither is maintenance of all individual environmental stocks and biological populations.

4.   Spatial sustainability and sustainable trade

When talking about sustainability, scale and openness of a system are important. Openness means that the system may affect other systems and be affected from outside, either by other regions or by the global system. A relevant question about sustainability in an open (regional/national) system context is whether trade can substitute for nature at the local level. The international dimension of environmental problems and policy has received much attention over the last decade. Nevertheless, this has predominantly concerned attention for international trade with traditional economic welfare- or externality-based models. Dynamic issues of regional sustainability and its counterpart sustainable trade have hardly received attention. As a result, much is known about the efficiency of trade but not about its sustainability. This would require some merger of dynamic theories (including possibly growth theories), trade theories, resources and externalities. The result is a very complex system.

Countries with a history of resource depletion and ecosystem damage may look sustainable. Indeed, numerical results in Pearce and Atkinson (1995) show that this is the case for the Netherlands and Japan, both of which have hardly any forest land. This hints at the problem of sustainability of open regions or countries, which evidently can surpass local sustainability limits by engaging in international trade.

Daly and Cobb (1989) have expressed the opinion that insights from traditional comparative advantage theory have less relevance these days as the assumption of immobile capital flows no longer holds. They conclude, referring to statements by J.M. Keynes, that production of products should, whenever feasible, take place in the home country. An additional argument for this view is that sustainability at a regional scale can be better controlled in an autarchic than an open region.

In order to 'measure' regional unsustainability, Wackernagel and Rees (1996) have formulated the 'ecological footprint' (EF: see also Chapter 20) and applied it to countries (as well as other spatial units). They conclude that many countries, in particular small ones, use directly and indirectly more surface area than is available inside their national boundaries. Evidently, this is compensated by international trade. Wackernagel and Rees try to argue on the basis of the EF that autarchy is to be preferred to a trading region. Van den Bergh and Verbruggen (1999) criticize the EF indicator and applications:

- The EF is an example of 'false concreteness': the resulting land area is hypothetical and too crude a measure of various types of environmental pressure.
- The EF method does not distinguish between sustainable and unsustainable land use, notably in agriculture.
- Aggregation of different environmental problems occurs through an implicit weighting that lacks any motivation.
- CO_2 emissions due to burning fossil fuels are translated, on the basis of an arbitrary 'sustainability scenario' (forestation to capture CO_2), into hypothetical seizure of land.

Comparing the EF of countries with their available land area implies that national consumption should remain within boundaries defined by national production opportunities, which represents a normative and arbitrary *ex ante* anti-trade bias. Relatively small or densely populated countries (in terms of available land area) need, for evident reasons, to trade a large part of their national income. Spatial scales indeed correlate strongly with the proportion of trade in consumption. For illustration: cities trade 100 per cent of their consumption, and the world as a whole is autarchic. Use of the EF thus seems to suggest that we should get rid of cities, but this neglects agglomeration effects and comparative advantages.

An adequate approach to assess spatial sustainability and sustainable trade should not start from any biases but instead allow the question to be addressed of whether concentration of people in space is desirable from a global sustainability perspective. Positive externalities of concentration (for example, agglomeration effects) and of trade (comparative advantages) should be taken into account and traded off against negative environmental externalities (Grazi et al. 2007). In addition, the various negative impacts of trade in social and political dimensions, such as weakening community structures and preventing individual human perception of ecological impacts of consumptive decisions, should be taken into account. On the other hand, attention needs to be given to the negative consequences of reducing international trade, such as destabilizing international agreements, trade wars and less diffusion of knowledge and technology.

5. Measurement and models

Many studies have developed indicators for sustainable development. As a result, different approaches are available. These can be classified as follows:

- Ecological (for example, biodiversity) versus physical (material or energy) indicators.
- Stock (capital) versus flow indicators.
- Source versus effect indicators.
- Monetary versus other indicators.
- Sustainability versus progress indicators (green and sustainable GDP measures, ISEW, GPI).

Indicators suffer from two main problems. First, often they aggregate information in a way that does not give rise to useful indicators from either a social welfare or environmental sustainability perspective (Ebert and Welsch, 2004). Secondly, they often represent a supply side perspective, suggesting value theories much in the spirit of the Marxian labour value theory. EE has produced several of these, such as energy indicators (energy value theory), ecological footprints (land value theory), and MIPS (material value theory). Economists are critical of such theories, as since Marshall it is widely agreed that values represent relative scarcity, which is the result of an interaction of demand and supply. This is not to say that one market dimension cannot sometimes dominate. For example, basic needs may become unsatisfied once absolute supply limits have been reached.

Models of sustainable development come in various types. Simple models from population biology (ecology) have been incorporated in economic models of renewable resources, which perhaps can be seen as the most simple approaches to the sustainability problem. Specific models have been developed for the analysis of fisheries, forestry and water management. EE has tried to move beyond such models by including advanced insights from ecology (see Folke, 1999). Resulting studies deal with one or more of four levels: biological populations (multispecies), ecosystems, biophysical processes (for example, hydrology, climate change), and coevolution of economic and environmental systems.

A particular model of interest here is the 'four box model' for terrestrial ecosystems as proposed by Holling (1986). It depicts ecosystems and their changes in a two-dimensional diagram with the axes 'stored capital' (biomass) and 'connectedness' (complexity of the food web). Ecosystems can repeatedly move through four phases: 'exploitation', 'conservation', 'release' and 'reorganization'. The 'release' phase can be initiated by forest fires, storms and outbreak of diseases. Such dynamics of ecosystems have given rise to questions about their stability and resilience. In the above-mentioned 'four-box model', management aimed at artificially prolonging a certain phase, notably 'conservation', can in fact reduce the resilience of the system. For example, checking small forest fires, which leave seeds intact, tends to result in an accumulation of forest biomass. This in turn will increase the probability of the occurrence of a large forest fire, going along with very high temperatures, which can destroy plant seeds and thus prevent the 'reorganization' phase from occurring successfully.

A range of other economic–ecological models exists, focusing on ecosystem management and integrated systems ranging from regions to the globe (Costanza et al., 1993; Rotmans and de Vries, 1997; van den Bergh et al., 2004). Integrated ecological–economic modelling has been practised since at least the early 1970s. One can be modestly optimistic about the feasibility of formal linking of economic and ecological models, but it requires significant financial and human resource investments. Such investments have been undertaken in some areas of application, notably in the area of climate change and policy, but less so in the area of ecosystem management modelling.

Costanza et al. (1997, p. xxii) state that the integration of economics and ecology is hampered by the lack of space in economic theories and models. Although it is true that mainstream economics has largely assumed away space and spatial externalities between economic agents, the statement neglects the large area of spatial economics. This covers regional, urban and transport economics as well as spatial informatics – mainly the application of geographical information systems (GIS). GIS applications are nowadays often considered an essential input to integrated spatial models, because they allow the capturing of interactions between economic and ecological phenomena at a detailed spatial scale. It is not beforehand clear, however, that using a high spatial resolution will always be fruitful. Whereas many ecological and hydrological processes are amenable to a grid-based description, most economic processes operate at higher scales. This explains, for instance, why a method like 'cellular automata' has been more popular in landscape ecology than in spatial economics (Engelen et al., 1995).

Simultaneous changes in the economy and the environment are sometimes referred to as coevolution. Strictly, this notion means that variation in either subsystem depends on the other subsystem (Norgaard, 1984; Faber and Proops, 1990; van den Bergh, 2004a). Coevolution thus reflects mutual selection of economic and environmental systems that creates a unique historical development. In this sense EE is close in spirit to evolutionary economics, which is characterized by concepts like diversity, selection, innovation, path dependence, and lock-in (Mulder and van den Bergh, 2001). The evolutionary perspective suggests that systems are adaptive and coincidental rather than optimal. Some of these notions can and have been translated into evolutionary, notably multi-agent models (van den Bergh, 2004b; Janssen, 2002). Such models depend on boundedly rational agents, which in fact can be seen as a response to the critique of EE on the rational-agent assumption that underlies much of traditional environmental economics.

Finally, within EE modelling of sustainable development attention is given to describing structural change. In this context 'industrial ecology' and 'industrial metabolism' are relevant areas of research (Graedel and Allenby, 2003; van den Bergh and Janssen, 2005). They combine environmental science, economics and analysis of technologies to realize a minimal environmental pressure caused by substance and material flows. Important strategies studied include 'dematerialization', recycling and reuse, waste management and enhancing durability of products. This is what Herman Daly would associate with keeping constant or reducing resource throughput.

6. Sustainability policy

Can one distinguish between sustainability policies and other environmental policies? One view is that the former include all environmental regulation since this will affect the degree of (un)sustainability. Another view is that certain policies or instruments are specifically focused on long term sustainability issues. A few examples are as follows. First, if it is recognized that a transition from the current unsustainable system to a sustainable one is prevented by the lock-in of certain technologies, notably fossil fuel-based, then un-locking policy is needed. Price corrections are clearly insufficient as increasing returns to scale play a dominant role. Stimulating diversity, for example, through subsidies, support of niche markets and public R&D are important elements of un-locking policy (Unruh, 2002).

Second, policies for sustainable development can include theoretical insights such as investment rules that stimulate constant total capital (Hartwick, 1977) and intergenerational transfers to compensate for environmental changes (Howarth and Norgaard, 1995). Both fit the weak sustainability approach, as substitution of natural capital is allowed for. Costanza (1994) in addition mentions three instruments. First, a natural capital depreciation tax would stimulate consumption in a more sustainable direction. The result would be a shift from use of (and investment in) non-renewable to renewable resources. Second, a 'precautionary polluter pays principle' could stimulate caution in making decisions with much uncertainty about the occurrence and size of environmental damage. Third, a system of ecological tariffs as countervailing duties would allow countries or trading blocs to apply strict policies (including the previous suggestions) so as to make sure that producers would not be stimulated to move overseas. The result would be that ecological costs would be reflected in prices of both domestically produced and imported products.

A number of instruments have been proposed to address the uncertainty and complexity surrounding ecosystems and sustainability. The notion of 'safe minimum standards' (Ciriacy-Wantrup 1952) points to the fact that efficiency means exploring the borders, whereas in many circumstances – characterized by a large degree of uncertainty – it would be better to take account of safety margins (see Chapter 6). A flexible instrument to do this is an 'environmental bond' (Perrings, 1989; Costanza and Perrings, 1990). An investment or project that is surrounded by much uncertainty concerning environmental consequences is complemented by an insurance bond with a value equal to the maximum expected environmental damage. This bond functions as a deposit that is completely or partly refunded (with interest) depending on the amount of environmental damage that has resulted from the respective investment project. If environmental damages are nil the entire deposit is returned; in cases of actual or threatening negative environmental effects the deposit serves to compensate or prevent damage. This instrument can, among others, be applied to land reclamation, investment in infrastructure, transport and treatment of hazardous (toxic, nuclear) substances, and location of agriculture and industrial activities near sensitive nature areas. As a consequence of environmental bonds, the (expected) private costs of such activities will increase, causing investors to decide more conservatively, and so take account of environmental risks associated with their activities and investment projects.

Economists traditionally analyse uncertainty by defining 'states of the world' with associated probabilities, and maximizing an expected benefit function. Fundamental or complete uncertainty, that is surprises, implies a different approach, namely 'adaptive management' (see Chapter 2). This is based on the idea that management of complex and uncontrollable systems requires an interaction between experimental research, monitoring, learning processes and policy choices, with the objective to learn from disturbances. This recipe has been applied to problems of fisheries, agriculture (ecological alternatives for pesticides) and forestry. Adaptive management also covers an interaction between various disciplines, experts and 'stakeholders' (Holling, 1978; Walters, 1986; and Gunderson et al., 1995). Similar advice follows from an evolutionary perspective (Rammel and van den Bergh, 2003).

A number of studies in the field of EE have examined the environmental policy implications of alternative theories of economic behaviour, which stress bounded rationality of economic agents, both consumers and producers (van den Bergh et al., 2000; Brekke and Howarth, 2002). Alternative theories or elements thereof include 'satisficing', lexicographic preferences, relative welfare, habits and routines, imitation, reciprocity, myopia, changing and endogenous preferences, and various models of behaviour under uncertainty. Some insights relevant to sustainability policy are as follows. First, policies aimed at changing consumer preferences make sense when sovereign preferences are inconsistent with long-run goals of sustainability

(Norton et al., 1998). Second, a 'hierarchy of needs' perspective relates to the notion of strong sustainability in that it emphasizes uniqueness and non-substitutability of goods and services provided by nature (Stern, 1997; Blamey and Common, 1999). It suggests that individuals may be unwilling to make a trade-off between economic and environmental goods or services. Finally, policy under uncertainty should reckon with strategies like imitation and pursuit of wealth, and aim at increasing or maintaining diversity of knowledge, technology and behaviour (Roe, 1996).

7.   Conclusions and future research
This chapter has covered a broad spectrum of issues related to sustainability and sustainable development. Ecological economics offers a distinctive approach to sustainability, which includes much attention for ecosystem resilience. The opposition between weak and strong sustainability is somewhat artificial, as the realistic or inevitable approach lies somewhere in between. Ecological economists nevertheless often tend to move in the direction of strong sustainability. Whereas global sustainability and sustainable development have received an enormous amount of attention, spatial sustainability and sustainable trade are grossly neglected issues. The large and growing amount of literature on international trade and environment adopts essentially a static perspective. The analysis of spatial sustainability requires an integration of insights and approaches from growth theory, international trade theory, resource economics and ecology. No one has yet succeeded in doing this and it seems likely that analytical approaches will fall short. In the area of sustainability policy various concrete suggestions offered by ecological economics were discussed. More theoretical and empirical research seems needed into which sustainability policies match the various types of bounded rationality that characterize the behaviour of economic agents.

References
Ayres, R.U., J.C.J.M. van den Bergh and J.M. Gowdy (2001), 'Strong versus weak sustainability: economics, natural sciences and "consilience"', *Environmental Ethics*, **23**(1): 155–68.
Beckerman, W. (1994), 'Sustainable development: is it a useful concept?', *Environmental Values*, **3**: 191–209.
Blamey, R.K. and M.S. Common (1999), 'Valuation and ethics in environmental economics', in J.C.J.M. van den Bergh (ed.), *Handbook of Environmental and Resource Economics*, Cheltenham, UK and Northampton, MA, USA: Edward Elgar, pp. 809–23.
Boulding, K.E. (1966), 'The economics of the coming spaceship earth', in H. Jarret (ed.), *Environmental Quality in a Growing Economy*, Baltimore: Johns Hopkins University Press.
Brekke, K.A. and R.B. Howarth (2002), *Status, Growth, and the Environment: Goods as Symbols in Applied Welfare Economics*, Cheltenham, UK and Northampton, MA, USA: Edward Elgar.
Cabeza-Gutés, M. (1996), 'The concept of weak sustainability', *Ecological Economics*, **17**: 147–56.

Ciriacy-Wantrup, S.V. (1952), *Resource Conservation: Economics and Policies*, Berkeley: University of California Press.
Common, M. and C. Perrings (1992), 'Towards an ecological economics of sustainability', *Ecological Economics*, **6**: 7–34.
Costanza, R. (1994), 'Three general policies to achieve sustainability', in A. Jansson et al. (eds), *Investing in Natural Capital: the Ecological Economics Approach to Sustainability*, Washington, DC: Island, pp. 392–407.
Costanza, R. and C.H. Perrings (1990), 'A flexible assurance bonding system for improved environmental management', *Ecological Economics*, **2**: 57–76.
Costanza, R., B. Norton and B.J. Haskell (eds) (1992), *Ecosystem Health: New Goals for Environmental Management*, Washington DC, USA: Island Press.
Costanza, R., C. Perrings and C.J. Cleveland (eds) (1997), *The Development of Ecological Economics*, Cheltenham, UK and Northampton, MA, USA: Edward Elgar.
Costanza, R., L. Wainger, C. Folke and K.-G. Mäler (1993), 'Modeling complex ecological economic systems', *BioScience*, **43**: 545–55.
Daly, H.E. (1991), *Steady-State Economics*, 2nd edn, Washington DC: Island Press.
Daly, H.E. (1992), 'Allocation, distribution, and scale: towards an economics that is efficient, just and sustainable', *Ecological Economics*, **6**: 185–93.
Daly, H.E. and W. Cobb (1989), *For the Common Good: Redirecting the Economy Toward Community, the Environment and a Sustainable Future*, Boston: Beacon Press.
Ebert, U. and H. Welsch (2004), 'Meaningful environmental indices: a social choice approach', *Journal of Environmental Economics and Management*, **47**: 270–83.
Engelen, G., R. White, I. Uljee and P. Drazan (1995), 'Using cellular automata for integrated modelling of socio-environmental systems', *Environmental Monitoring and Assessment*, **34**: 203–14.
Faber, M. and J.L.R. Proops (1990), *Evolution, Time, Production and the Environment*, Heidelberg: Springer-Verlag.
Folke, C. (1999), 'Ecological principles and environmental economic analysis', in J.C.J.M. van den Bergh (ed.), *Handbook of Environmental and Resource Economics*, Cheltenham, UK and Northampton, MA, USA: Edward Elgar, pp. 895–911.
Gowdy, J. (1997), 'The value of biodiversity: markets, society and ecosystems', *Land Economics*, **73**: 25–41.
Gowdy, J.M. and C. McDaniel (1999), 'The physical destruction of Nauru: an example of weak sustainability', *Land Economics*, **75**: 333–8.
Graedel, T.E. and B.R. Allenby (2003), *Industrial Ecology*, 2nd edn (1st edn 1995), Prentice Hall, Upper Saddle River, NJ: Pearson Education.
Grazi, F., J.C.J.M. van den Bergh and P. Rietveld (2007), 'Welfare economics versus ecological footprint: modelling agglomeration, externalities and trade', *Environmental and Resource Economics*, forthcoming.
Gunderson, L.H., C.S. Holling and S.S. Light (eds) (1995), *Barriers and Bridges to the Renewal of Ecosystems and Institutions*, New York: Columbia University Press.
Hartwick, J. (1977), 'Intergenerational equity and the investing of rents from exhaustible resources', *American Economic Review*, **67**: 972–4.
Holling, C.S. (1973), 'Resilience and stability of ecological systems', *Annual Review of Ecological Systems*, **4**: 1–24.
Holling, C.S. (ed.) (1978), *Adaptive Environmental Assessment and Management*, New York: Wiley.
Holling, C.S. (1986), 'The resilience of terrestrial ecosystems: local surprise and global change', in W.C. Clark and R.E. Munn (eds), *Sustainable Development of the Biosphere*, Cambridge: Cambridge University Press.
Howarth, R.B. and R.B. Norgaard (1995), 'Intergenerational choices under global environmental change', in D. Bromley (ed.), *Handbook of Environmental Economics*, Oxford: Blackwell.
Janssen, M.A. (2002), *Complexity and Ecosystem Management: The Theory and Practice of Multi-Agent Systems*, Cheltenham, UK and Northampton, MA, USA: Edward Elgar.
Martinez-Alier, J. and M. O'Connor (1999), 'Distributional issues: an overview', in J.C.J.M. van den Bergh (ed.), *Handbook of Environmental and Resource Economics*, Cheltenham, UK and Northampton, MA, USA: Edward Elgar, pp. 380–92.

Mulder, P. and J.C.J.M. van den Bergh (2001), 'Evolutionary economic theories of sustainable development', *Growth and Change*, **32**(4): 110–34.

Norgaard, R.B. (1984), 'Coevolutionary development potential', *Land Economics*, **60**: 160–73.

Norton, B., R. Costanza and R.C. Bishop (1998), 'The evolution of preferences. Why "sovereign" preferences may not lead to sustainable policies and what to do about it', *Ecological Economics*, **24**: 193–211.

Pearce, D. and G. Atkinson (1995), 'Measuring sustainable development', in D.W. Bromley (ed.), *The Handbook of Environmental Economics*, Oxford: Blackwell.

Perrings, C. (1989), 'Environmental bonds and environmental research in innovative activities', *Ecological Economics*, **1**: 95–115.

Perrings, C. (1998), 'Resilience in the dynamics of economy–environment systems', *Environmental and Resource Economics*, **11**: 503–20.

Pezzey, J. (1989), 'Economic analysis of sustainable growth and sustainable development', Environmental Department Working paper no. 15, Environmental Department, The World Bank, reprinted as J. Pezzey, 'Sustainable development concepts: an economic analysis', World Bank Environment Paper 2 (1992).

Pezzey, J. (1993), 'Sustainability: an interdisciplinary guide', *Environmental Values*, **1**: 321–62.

Pimm, S.L. (1984), 'The complexity and stability of ecosystems', *Nature*, **307**: 321–6.

Rammel, C. and J.C.J.M. van den Bergh (2003), 'Evolutionary policies for sustainable development: adaptive flexibility and risk minimising', *Ecological Economics*, **47**(2): 121–33.

Roe, E.M. (1996), 'Sustainable development and Girardian economics', *Ecological Economics*, **16**: 87–93.

Rotmans, J. and H.J.M. de Vries (1997), *Perspectives on Global Change: the TARGETS Approach*, Cambridge, UK: Cambridge University Press.

Solow, R.M. (1974), 'Intergenerational equity and exhaustible resources', *Review of Economic Studies*, **41** (Symposium Issue): 29–45.

Solow, R.M. (1986), 'On the intergenerational allocation of natural resources', *Scandinavian Journal of Economics*, **88**: 141–90.

Spash, C. and N. Hanley (1995), 'Preferences, information and biodiversity preservation', *Ecological Economics*, **12**: 191–208.

Stern, D. (1997), 'Limits to substitution and irreversibility in production and consumption: a neoclassical interpretation of ecological economics', *Ecological Economics*, **22**: 197–215.

Toman, M.A., J. Pezzey and J. Krautkraemer (1995), 'Neoclassical economic growth theory and "sustainability"', in D.W. Bromley (ed.), *Handbook of Environmental Economics*, Oxford: Blackwell.

Tversky, A. and I. Simonson (2000), 'Context-dependent preferences', in D. Kahneman and A. Tversky (eds), *Choices, Values and Frames*, Cambridge: Cambridge University Press, pp. 518–27.

Unruh, G.C. (2002), 'Escaping carbon lock-in', *Energy Policy*, **30**: 317–25.

van den Bergh, J.C.J.M. (2004a), 'Evolutionary thinking in environmental economics: retrospect and prospect', in J. Foster and W. Hölzl (eds), *Applied Evolutionary Economics and Complex Systems*, Cheltenham, UK and Northampton, MA, USA: Edward Elgar, pp. 239–75.

van den Bergh, J.C.J.M. (2004b), 'Evolutionary modelling', in J. Proops and P. Safonov (eds), *Modelling in Ecological Economics*, Cheltenham, UK and Northampton, MA, USA: Edward Elgar, pp. 9–35.

van den Bergh, J.C.J.M., A. Barendregt and A. Gilbert (2004), *Spatial Ecological–Economic Analysis for Wetland Management: Modelling and Scenario Evaluation of Land-Use*, Cambridge, UK: Cambridge University Press.

van den Bergh, J.C.J.M., A. Ferrer-i-Carbonell and G. Munda (2000), 'Alternative models of individual behaviour and implications for environmental policy', *Ecological Economics*, **32**(1): 43–61.

van den Bergh, J.C.J.M. and R.A. de Mooij (1999), 'An assessment of the growth debate', in J.C.J.M. van den Bergh (ed.), *Handbook of Environmental Resources*, Cheltenham, UK and Northampton, MA, USA: Edward Elgar, pp. 643–55.

van den Bergh, J.C.J.M. and M.A. Janssen (eds), (2005), *Economics of Industrial Ecology: Use of Materials, Structural Change and Spatial Scales*, Cambridge, MA, USA: MIT Press.

van den Bergh, J.C.J.M. and H. Verbruggen (1999), 'Spatial sustainability, trade and indicators: an evaluation of the "ecological footprint"', *Ecological Economics*, **29**(1): 63–74.

van Praag, B.M.S. and A. Ferrer-i-Carbonell (2004), *Happiness Quantified: A Satisfaction Calculus Approach*, Oxford: Oxford University Press.

Young, C.E.F. (1996), 'Effective demand and "weak" sustainability: a macroeconomic model', in J.C.J.M van den Bergh and J. van der Straaten (eds), *Economy and Ecosystems in Change: Analytical and Historical Approaches*, Cheltenham, UK and Northampton, MA, USA: Edward Elgar.

Wackernagel, M. and W. Rees (1996), *Our Ecological Footprint: Reducing Human Impact on the Earth*, Gabriola Island, BC and Philadelphia, PA: New Society Publishers.

Walters, C. (1986), *Adaptive Management of Renewable Resources*, New York: Macmillan.

5 Ecological and social resilience
W. Neil Adger

1. Introduction

The world needs to be resilient to change. Sustaining life, sustaining well-being and sustaining the environment into the future increasingly means adapting to new circumstances and potentially unpredictable perturbations and challenges. New technologies for example have unforeseen consequences while demographic and cultural changes bring about new challenges for sustainable living. Setting single goals and universal prescriptions for sustainable development across the world seems increasingly unrealistic and potentially counter-productive. In these circumstances, a new emphasis on building resilience, and recognition of the linkages between elements of society and the ecosystems on which they depend, seems a sensible contribution to sustainable development. But understanding what the resilience of a social–ecological system might be, and the identification of the mechanisms which link the wider environment with human well-being, are far from trivial.

Resilience is a property of a system. In ecological sciences, resilience relates to the properties of ecosystems at different scales, rather than populations. There has been a significant evolution of the concept of resilience in ecology over the past decade in terms of its measurement and in terms of understanding how resilience interacts with other system properties such as diversity and stability. It has been demonstrated empirically that resilience is an essential factor underlying the sustainability of natural resources and ecosystem services (Gunderson and Holling, 2002). Resilience therefore is defined in relation to changes in ecosystems which are in turn related to human use and pressure on the natural world. To link resilience with sustainable development, it is therefore necessary to define the resilience of the actual interaction between humans and nature: the resilience of social-ecological systems is a central objective of sustainability. A social-ecological system in this context is, for example, a natural resource and its resource users. Examples of social-ecological systems are a fishery, a managed forest ecosystem, and the interaction of the carbon economy with global atmospheric sinks and climate (Gunderson and Pritchard, 2002).

Social elements of these coupled systems include the well-being and the governance of access and regulation to the resources in question. The resilience of a social-ecological system is made up of a number of elements: the amount of disturbance a system can absorb and still retain the same characteristics and controls on function and structure; the degree to which a system is capable of self-organization; and the ability to build and increase the capacity for learning and adaptation (Carpenter et al., 2001; Berkes et al., 2003).

The ultimate goal of sustainable development is to promote use of the environment and resources to meet the needs of present society without compromising the future. What then does knowledge of resilience contribute to meeting such goals? First, resilient social-ecological systems have within them the ability to absorb shocks and hence maintain ecosystems and governance structures maintaining options for future users. Resilient systems can, in other words, cope, adapt or reorganize without sacrificing the provision of ecosystem services. Second, a loss of resilience in social-ecological systems is often associated with irreversible change, the creation of vulnerabilities for marginalized elements of society, and the reduction of flows of ecosystem services. Even actions and strategies which are apparently rational in the short run can reduce resilience. Hence building resilience is compatible with sustainable development and indeed provides a superior framework for analysing sustainability in the context of irreversibility, surprise and non-marginal change. The chapter outlines examples of where management of resources for resilience brings about benefits for sustainability, including adapting to climate change and managing the consequences of disasters. It proceeds by examining how resilience is currently understood across the natural and social sciences, explains elements of social resilience, and discusses hypotheses concerning how they interact with ecological resilience thereby explaining how resilience is a component of sustainable development.

2. Ecological resilience

The resilience of an ecological system relates to the functioning of the system, rather than the stability of its component populations, or even the ability to maintain a steady ecological state. Ecosystems have diverse properties which ecologists have sought to measure – these form the basis of normative statements about sustainability and sustainable utilization of ecosystems (Holling and Meffe, 1996). Many tropical terrestrial ecosystems, for example, have stable and diverse populations but are relatively low in resilience. Similar ecosystems in temperate regions with apparently low diversity can exhibit greater resilience.

Different ecosystem types, from terrestrial and marine environments, display a number of common features (following Holling et al., 1995; Gunderson, 2000; Gunderson and Holling, 2002). First, change in most ecosystems is not gradual but rather is triggered by external perturbations, and is episodic. Second, spatial attributes in ecosystems are not uniform but are skewed in their distribution and patchy at different scales 'from the leaf, to the landscape, to the planet' (Holling et al., 1995, p. 49), with the implication that scaling up of management solutions cannot simply be aggregated across scales. What works for a single location will not work for a whole eco-region. Finally, ecosystems often have more than one equilibrium: the functions which control ecosystems promote stability, but other destabilizing influences, such as physiological reaction to pathogens create diversity and resilience. These attributes lead to a range of implications for understanding resilience and for management.

From declining fish stocks in the Pacific, through to land use change in the Sahel, ecosystems have been shown to be subject to periodic shifts into states which are often less desirable for, but are often triggered by, human use (Scheffer et al., 2001). Figure 5.1 documents examples of shifts in human-used ecosystems from one stable state to another across a number of ecosystem types. These shifts are often triggered by single events such as a tropical storm impacting on coral reefs or through fires and their impact on forest ecosystems. Sometimes they are caused by longer-term events such as the removal of one predator from an ecological system.

In Figure 5.1, the initial state is in column 1 and shows that, in relation to the two major state variables for each ecosystem (x and y axis), there may be more than one equilibrium position. For the ecosystems highlighted, from coral reefs to lake ecosystems, human action has reduced the capacity of ecosystems to cope with perturbations. The causes may be the over-exploitation of an important species (for example over-grazing of grasses, over-harvesting of fishes) or chronic stress such as pollution and nutrient loading. Over time the probability increases that the ecosystem will flip into the states represented in column 4 of Figure 5.1, which tend to be simplified, 'weedy' ecosystems characterized by lower levels of ecosystem services (Folke et al., 2004). The undesirable states in column 4, such as algae-dominated reefs, also tend to be difficult to reverse, because they tend to be caused by changes in so-called 'slow' variables such as land use, nutrient stocks and reduction in long-lived organisms (Folke et al., 2004).

Within the ecological sciences there is a continued focus on the relationship between diversity (the common focus of conservation practice) and resilience. The links between diversity of species and the stability of ecosystems now appear to be more widely accepted (Folke et al., 2004). An emerging new area is that of the diversity of response within ecosystems to external perturbations – this is the observation that different species providing the same function within ecosystems have different mechanisms for retaining the resilience of the system (Elmqvist et al., 2003). This raises

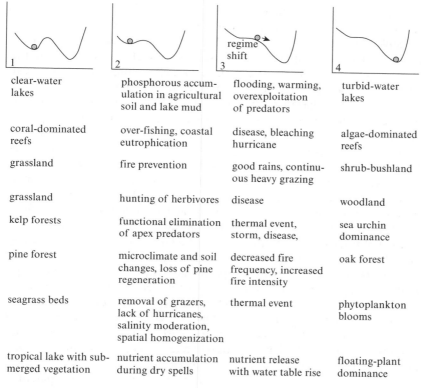

clear-water lakes	phosphorous accumulation in agricultural soil and lake mud	flooding, warming, overexploitation of predators	turbid-water lakes
coral-dominated reefs	over-fishing, coastal eutrophication	disease, bleaching hurricane	algae-dominated reefs
grassland	fire prevention	good rains, continuous heavy grazing	shrub-bushland
grassland	hunting of herbivores	disease	woodland
kelp forests	functional elimination of apex predators	thermal event, storm, disease,	sea urchin dominance
pine forest	microclimate and soil changes, loss of pine regeneration	decreased fire frequency, increased fire intensity	oak forest
seagrass beds	removal of grazers, lack of hurricanes, salinity moderation, spatial homogenization	thermal event	phytoplankton blooms
tropical lake with submerged vegetation	nutrient accumulation during dry spells	nutrient release with water table rise	floating-plant dominance

Source: Folke et al. (2004).

Figure 5.1 *Changes in the states of eight ecosystems from high resilience states (1) to low resilience states (4) via causal mechanisms (2) and triggers (3)*

the possibility that response diversity increases the likelihood for renewal and reorganization to the desired states in column 1 in Figure 5.1. Response diversity is an inherent characteristic of ecological populations, however, and cannot easily be managed by human action.

The case of coral reefs provides a good example of the nature of resilience of ecosystems and interactions with human use. Periodic natural disturbance has been shown to be an important element promoting the diversity and resilience of coral reef ecosystems (Nyström et al., 2000). But coral reef resilience is reduced through chronic stress as a result of human activities on land: for example through agricultural pollution or poorly treated sewage, and through over-fishing (Jackson et al., 2001). Observations throughout the tropics, and particularly in the Caribbean, demonstrate that many sites only have half the live coral cover of three decades previously (for example Gardner et al., 2003). Resilience is being reduced through inappropriate fisheries management, as well as through indirect mechanisms such as land development or clearance, as well as through natural events such as hurricane damage or freshwater sediment inputs.

Nyström and colleagues (2000) outline the ecological pathways of these changes highlighted in Figure 5.1. Coral reefs once dominated by hard corals, attractive to reef fishes and as nurseries for many commercial species as well as for tourism, have changed state in a number of locations in the Caribbean to systems dominated by fleshy algae. The triggers for these changes are often natural, but the chronic stresses are human. Over-fishing of key reef species and nutrient loading into coastal areas from agriculture and sewage present one set of stresses – algae can multiply and smother coral growth. The coral reefs of the Caribbean in some cases persisted since the role of fish species in keeping algae at bay was taken over by sea urchins. But ultimately the chronic stress on coral reefs resulted in a change in state when 99 per cent of sea urchins in particular locations were wiped out by a novel pathogen. These phase shifts in coral reefs have been observed in other areas, for example as a result of persistent or high El Niño events which increase sea surface temperatures beyond the thermal stress limits of corals. In all instances of phase shifts, ecological theories are not good predictors of whether systems will return to previous states (Hughes et al., 2005).

Phase shifts and stresses to environmental systems are also apparent in the arena of climate change (human-induced as well as natural). The present global 'experiment', of perturbing the world's climate system by increasing global concentrations of carbon dioxide and other greenhouse gases, could bring about many unknowable and irreversible phase shifts in ecological, physical and ultimately human systems. Such phase shifts and threshold effects in climate change are increasingly referred to as abrupt or rapid climate change. Examples include significant warming (that is more than 6°C) of the earth's atmosphere because of positive feedbacks in the carbon cycle; melting of the West Antarctic Ice Sheet leading to 5–7 metres of sea level rise; or collapse of the thermohaline circulation of the Atlantic Ocean (Alley et al., 2003).

But, as Hulme (2003) points out, these possible abrupt changes in climate are different in their characteristics – they may be abrupt in the sense of being an unexpected change in the direction of a trend, abrupt because of the rate of change, or abrupt because some threshold has been exceeded. There are, of course, precedents for localized abrupt climatic changes in human history (Diamond, 2004). Hulme (2003) argues that the Sahelian dry period from the 1960s to the 1980s, when precipitation fell by 30 per cent in most areas, represented a directional change from the previous decades which were steadily wetter. Clearly the anticipated phase shifts in climate are difficult for societies to adapt to and represent a major perturbation to social-ecological resilience. This is particularly so when social resilience is dependent on decisions that lock the technologies and societies into inflexible patterns of resource use. If decisions on building irrigation schemes and dams are based on the mean river flows from a wet period, as was the case in East African river systems (Conway, 2005), this leads to loss of resilience when a phase shift occurs.

In summary, the resilience of ecological (and physical) systems is increasingly understood to be reliant on mechanisms associated with diversity and with slowly changing environmental variables. Resilience promotes both the production of socially useful ecosystem services and provides a stable environment for human use of these services. Loss of resilience is, from a human perspective, undesirable.

3. Social elements of resilience

A key component of the emergent resilience analysis in ecology is the recognition that ecosystems do not exist in isolation from the human world. The stability and resilience, as well as the value and cultural significance, of most of the world's ecosystems are therefore intimately bound up in their human use. As the examples of environmental change above show, human use of natural systems reduces resilience at many scales. But from the traditional societies of hunters and gatherers, to the subsistence and commercial use of the world's farmlands, human use has the potential to be both sustainable and resilient. This section examines the economic arguments for resilience and the determinants of social dimensions of resilience.

But many processes of economic development are not sustainable or resilient, including the reliance on fossil fuels and the fetishism of consumption. Economic growth, involving unsustainable resource use or use of the environment causing chronic stress on ecosystems, creates vulnerabilities and makes society more sensitive to shocks. In economic terms, ecological resilience itself is therefore important for human well-being for three reasons (Arrow et al., 1995). First, as outlined above, discontinuous change in ecosystem functions is associated with a loss of productivity and of ecosystem services. Second, the irreversible (or reversible only at significant resource costs: Mäler, 2000) impacts of a loss of resilience affect the portfolio of options for future use. Hence losing resilience reduces positive option values attached to the environment. Third, Arrow et al. (1995) argue that loss of resilience and more to unfamiliar states (column 4 in Figure 5.1) increases the uncertainties associated with environmental interactions.

In other words, dealing with unfamiliar and undesirable states has added costs, and hence entails a loss of welfare.

These economic reasons for preserving ecological resilience are, however, only part of the story. Sustainable development brings a normative domain to the relationship between ecological resilience and society. Sustainable development necessarily relates to human values: what is desirable, what is undesirable, and for whom. Thus the stable ecological states in column 4 in Figure 5.1 may be ecologically poor and unproductive from a human-use perspective and hence unsustainable (see Norton, 1995). As Levin et al. (1998) point out, 'resilience makes no distinctions, preserving ecologically or socially undesirable situations as well as desirable ones' (p. 225). A social-ecological resilience compatible with sustainability needs to consider societal demands for ecosystem services, equity, vulnerability in the distribution of resources, and the governance of resources.

Resilience in social-ecological systems includes the ability for positive adaptation despite adversity and hence involves human agency. The social elements of resilience are therefore bound up with the ability of groups or communities to adapt in the face of external social, political or environmental stresses and disturbances (Adger, 2000) and highlight the necessity of collective action. If formal and informal institutions themselves are resilient, they can promote wider resilience. Institutions (including modes of socialized behaviour as well as more formal structures of governance or law) can be persistent, sustainable and resilient depending on a range of parameters. The persistence of institutions of governance depends, for example, on legitimacy and on selecting environmental risks which resonate with the institutions' agenda. Thus the resilience of institutions is based on their historical evolution and their inclusivity or exclusivity and how effective they are in 'oiling the wheels' of society. Resilient communities are promoted through integrating features of social organization such as trust, norms and networks. The cultural context of institutional adaptation, and indeed the differing conceptions of human environment interactions within different knowledge systems, is central to the resilience of institutions. These cultural contexts and local technical knowledge tend to be overlooked in considering equity and economic efficiency aspects of the sustainable use of natural resources (Gadgil et al., 2003). Hence the resilience of communities is not simply a matter of the economic relations between them, but is determined, as with social capital, by their inclusivity and degree of trust.

The nature of social resilience can be inferred from perturbations and coping with change. Adger (2000) hypothesizes that social resilience is a function of resource dependency. The more resource-dependent a society, the more tightly coupled it is to the ecosystem functions and services on which it depends. Fishing communities depend on the abundance and migration patterns of fish stocks, as well as the integrity of habitats, the regularity of ocean currents, and the competition for fish from other fishing communities as well as natural predators. Hence fishing communities are resource-dependent. But they can maintain and build resilience through promoting diversity in livelihoods or even migrating with fish stocks (Adger et al., 2002). Resource dependency is the reliance on a narrow range of resources leading to social and economic stresses within economic and ecological systems. So, for example, the dependence of economies on mineral or renewable resources depends on how much of the economy is reliant on their mineral production; how volatile the world markets are in these commodities; and how much boom and bust there is in these commodities. Auty (1998 and Chapter 13) argues that resource endowments of minerals and high dependency ratios partly explain trajectories of development and the ultimate destiny of resource-dependent societies. The preoccupation with capturing the benefits of resource endowments during boom times in oil-rich or forest-rich countries impedes the creation of economic linkages, land reform and diversification of the economies (see discussion in Vincent, 1992; Neumayer, 2005). Dependency, whether on sub-soil or on living resources, brings its own set of problems and does not necessarily promote resilience.

The direct dependence of communities on ecosystems is an influence on their social resilience and ability to cope with shocks, particularly for food security and coping with hazards. Resilience can be undermined by high variability and exploitative relationships in the market system or natural or induced disturbance in the environmental system. Resilience therefore depends on the diversity of the ecosystem as well as the institutional rules that govern social-ecological systems.

4. Sustainability, resilience and adaptive management

Can resilience be enhanced to promote sustainable development? Action to promote resilience implies management based on the recognition of the dynamics and patchiness outlined above, and on the recognition of values and dynamics of institutions that create and constrain human use. Promoting resilience is therefore directly dependent on the recognition of community engagement in resource management – particularly in areas where communities rely on ecosystem health for their own well-being or livelihoods – as a means of preserving ecosystem integrity. It is also dependent on the recognition of different worldviews and knowledge systems that can, without reference to standard science, formulate successful knowledge of functions of the environment and successful institutions to manage these functions (Berkes, 1999).

Integrated conservation and development approaches that include collaborative resource management would appear to be central to reducing vulnerability and increasing resilience to improve the well-being of those societies and ecosystems dependent on natural resources. In many situations, where full knowledge about a system does not exist and optimum productivity is not an obtainable goal, an iterative management process that is informed and evolves through an ongoing learning process is about the best that can be achieved. Adaptive management (see also Chapter 2) not only pursues the goal of greater ecological stability, but also that of more flexible institutions for resource management (Olsson et al., 2004).

Promoting resilience requires flexibility and adaptation in decision-making on resource use and conservation. Hence it is argued that adaptive management of resources can improve the resilience of people and the environment and reduce vulnerability (Olsson et al., 2004). Under such an approach, an evolving management process for social as well as ecological systems is developed through iterative and learning processes. So can adaptive management ensure the resilience of social systems over time in the face of external stresses and perturbations? Clearly individuals and communities have been adapting to change throughout history. Societies have coped with climate variability through adopting new technologies, adapting their locations or moving their settlements (Diamond, 2004).

Not all adaptations are sustainable and there is recent historical evidence that large-scale, systematic changes in regional climate have had profoundly negative consequences for many societies in the past. But collective response and institutional resilience remain the dominant factor in sustaining adaptation. When faced with contemporary climatic perturbations in the Canadian Arctic, the Inuvialuit people of Sachs Harbour have been making short-term adjustments to their resource management (Berkes and Jolly, 2001). Their adaptations include switching hunted species and changing the timing and methods of hunting. Flexibility within cultural traditions and networks makes other forms of adaptation possible for this community, such as food-sharing networks and intercommunity trade. Newly evolving co-management institutions are creating linkages across scales (local, regional, national and international) and hence transmitting local concerns to a wider audience and also being able to draw on the same wider community for assistance and advice. In a globalizing world, networks and learning opportunities cross traditional scales – engagement and exchange are both local and global processes at the same time (Berkes, 2002).

The autonomy that allows recognition of different forms of knowledge is important. Olsson and Folke (2001) examine the local knowledge of ecosystem processes for a coastal crayfish fishery in Sweden and argue that the collective management of this resource involves institutions at diverse scales. They find that local-level institutions for direct management (harvesting strategies and seasonal patterns, for example) have been self-organizing, have created spaces for evolutionary re-organization, and give precedence to knowledgeable individuals. These institutional characteristics, they argue, provide evidence both of the importance of local knowledge at the ecosystems scale, and that evolution of institutions takes place through strategies of adaptive management as they move to higher and deeper levels of knowledge.

Adaptive management requires, at its core, retaining flexibility in the relationship between social resilience, changing property rights and institutional evolution. Coastal districts in Vietnam, for example, are impacted seasonally by landfall typhoons and coastal storms. Although fishing, farming and other activities have evolved to cope with this risk over the millennia, the radical redirection of the economy during the 1990s towards individual responsibility and private property and away from central planning diminished the resilience of many systems and resources, from upland forests to coastal communities reliant on aquaculture (Adger et al., 2001).

Social-ecological resilience is important in the context of vulnerability to disasters. Changing resilience over time directly affects the ability to cope with perturbations, to recover and to adapt. Following the 2004 Asian tsunami, there is emerging evidence that those areas in South and South East Asia where ecosystems such as mangroves had previously been lost were those that suffered the greatest impact. Importantly, traditional resource management institutions have played an important part in post-disaster recovery and rebuilding the resilience of communities (Adger et al., 2005). Coping with extreme weather events such as hurricanes also tests social and ecological resilience. The Cayman Islands, for example, has implemented adaptation actions at national and community levels but suffered significant impacts from Hurricane Ivan in 2004. Tompkins (2005) found that social learning, a diversity of adaptations, and the promotion of strong local social cohesion and mechanisms for collective action have all enhanced resilience and continue to guide planning for future climate change. In Trinidad and Tobago, networks associated with present day coral reef management also play a key role in disaster preparedness and in building resilience (Tompkins and Adger, 2004).

There is growing evidence and experience of adaptive management building resilience, from traditional environmental management systems through to government-led collective action and experimentation with new institutional arrangements. A key lesson for adaptive management is that the nature of relationships between community members is critical, as is access to, and participation in, the wider decision-making process.

5. Conclusions

Resilience constitutes a radical critique of the traditional objectives of resource management. It is required because of the failure of institutions, ecological science, or economic policies to reverse the unsustainable management of resources or to reduce the large-scale environmental consequences of resource use. Resilience involves recognizing the dynamics of systems and functions that ecosystems play in protecting and facilitating human society and in promoting the robustness or resilience of ecological systems. But at the same time, flexibility and resilience are important characteristics of societies where environmental and societal risks permeate decision-making. The promotion of resilience of social-ecological systems is therefore a normative and ethical issue, not simply a descriptive theory of a natural state of the world. Global economic interests, property rights abuses, and asymmetric access to power and information combine to create conditions where environments become critical, and populations become vulnerable.

As vulnerability is lowered and criticality reduced, so resilience increases. But in an ecological sense, resilience relates to the functioning of the system, rather than the stability of the component populations. Resilience is the key to sustainability in the wider sense. Resilience, in both its social and ecological manifestations, is an important criterion for the sustainability of development and resource use, since all human welfare is ultimately dependent on the biosphere and its sometimes surprising nature.

References

Adger, W.N. (2000), 'Social and ecological resilience: are they related?', *Progress in Human Geography*, **24**, 347–64.

Adger, W.N., P.M. Kelly and N.H. Ninh (eds) (2001), *Living with Environmental Change: Social Resilience, Adaptation and Vulnerability in Vietnam*, London: Routledge.

Adger, W.N., T.P. Hughes, C. Folke, S. Carpenter and J. Rockström (2005), 'Resilience of coastal social-ecological systems to disasters', *Science*, **309**(5737): 1036–9.

Adger, W.N., P.M. Kelly, A. Winkels, L.Q. Huy and C. Locke (2002), 'Migration, remittances, livelihood trajectories and social resilience', *Ambio*, **31**, 358–66.

Alley, R.B., J. Marotzke, W.D. Nordhaus, J.T. Overpeck, D.M. Peteet, R.A., Jr. Pielke, R.T. Pierrehumbert, P.B. Rhines, T.F. Stocker, L.D. Talley and J.M. Wallace (2003), 'Abrupt climate change', *Science*, **299**, 2005–10.

Arrow, K., B. Bolin, R. Costanza, P. Dasgupta, C. Folke, C.S. Holling, B.O. Jansson, S. Levin, K.-G. Mäler, C. Perrings and D. Pimentel (1995), 'Economic growth, carrying capacity and the environment', *Science*, **268**, 520–21.

Auty, R.M. (1998), 'Social sustainability in mineral-driven development', *Journal of International Development*, **10**, 487–500.

Berkes, F. (1999), *Sacred Ecology*, Philadelphia: Taylor and Francis.

Berkes, F. (2002), 'Cross-scale institutional linkages for commons management: perspectives from the bottom up', in E. Ostrom, T. Dietz, N. Dolsak, P.C. Stern, S. Stonich and E.U. Weber (eds), *The Drama of the Commons*, Washington DC: National Academy Press, pp. 293–321.

Berkes, F. and D. Jolly (2001), 'Adapting to climate change: social-ecological resilience in a Canadian Western Arctic community', *Conservation Ecology*, **5**(2): 18, (online) www.consecol.org/Journal/vol5/iss2/.

Berkes, F., J. Colding and C. Folke (eds) (2003), *Navigating Social-Ecological Systems: Building Resilience for Complexity and Change*, Cambridge: Cambridge University Press.

Carpenter, S., B. Walker, J.M. Anderies and N. Abel (2001), 'From metaphor to measurement: resilience of what to what?', *Ecosystems*, **4**, 765–81.

Conway, D. (2005), 'From headwater tributaries to international river: observing and adapting to climate variability and change in the Nile basin', *Global Environmental Change*, **15**, 99–114.

Diamond, J. (2004), *Collapse: How Societies Choose to Fail or to Succeed*, New York: Viking.

Elmqvist, T., C. Folke, M. Nystrom, G. Peterson, J. Bengtsson, B. Walker and, J. Norberg (2003), 'Response diversity, ecosystem change, and resilience', *Frontiers in Ecology and the Environment*, **1**, 488–94.

Folke, C., S. Carpenter, B. Walker, M. Scheffer, T. Elmqvist, L. Gunderson and C.S. Holling (2004), 'Regime shifts, resilience, and biodiversity in ecosystem management', *Annual Review of Ecology Evolution and Systematics*, **35**, 557–81.

Gadgil, M., P. Olsson, F. Berkes and C. Folke (2003), 'Exploring the role of local ecological knowledge in ecosystem management: three case studies', in F. Berkes, J. Colding and C. Folke (eds), *Navigating Social-Ecological Systems: Building Resilience for Complexity and Change*, Cambridge: Cambridge University Press, pp.189–209.

Gardner, T.A., I.M. Cote, J.A. Gill, A. Grant and A.R. Watkinson (2003), 'Long-term region-wide declines in Caribbean corals', *Science*, **301**, 958–60.

Gunderson, L.H. (2000), 'Ecological resilience: in theory and application', *Annual Review of Ecology and Systematics*, **31**, 425–39.

Gunderson, L.H. and C.S. Holling (eds) (2002), *Panarchy: Understanding Transformations in Human and Natural Systems*, Washington DC: Island Press.

Gunderson, L.H. and L. Pritchard Jr (eds) (2002), *Resilience and the Behaviour of Large-Scale Systems*, SCOPE Vol. **60**, Washington DC: Island Press.

Holling, C.S., D.W. Schindler, B.W. Walker and J. Roughgarden (1995), 'Biodiversity in the functioning of ecosystems: an ecological synthesis', in C. Perrings, K.-G. Mäler, C. Folke, C.S. Holling and B.O. Jansson (eds), *Biodiversity Loss: Economic and Ecological Issues*, Cambridge: Cambridge University Press, pp. 44–83.

Holling, C.S. and G.K. Meffe (1996), 'Command and control and the pathology of natural resource management', *Conservation Biology*, **10**, 328–37.

Hughes, T.P., D.R. Bellwood, C. Folke, R.S. Steneck and J. Wilson (2005), 'New paradigms for supporting the resilience of marine ecosystems', *Trends in Ecology and Evolution*, **20**, 380–86.

Hulme, M. (2003), 'Abrupt climate change: can society cope?', *Philosophical Transactions of the Royal Society (A)*, **361**, 2001–21.

Jackson, J.B.C., M.X. Kirby, W.H. Berger, K.A. Bjorndal, L.W. Botsford, B.J. Bourque, R.H. Bradbury, R. Cooke, J. Erlandson, J.A. Estes, T.P. Hughes, S. Kidwell, C.B. Lange, H.S. Lenihan, J.M. Pandolfi, C.H. Peterson, R.S. Steneck, M.J. Tegner and R.R. Warner (2001), 'Historical overfishing and the recent collapse of coastal ecosystems', *Science*, **293**, 629–38.

Levin, S., S. Barrett, S. Aniyar, W. Baumol, C. Bliss, B. Bolin, P. Dasgupta, P. Ehrlich, C. Folke, I.M. Gren, C.S. Holling, A.M. Jansson, B.O. Jansson, K.-G. Mäler, D. Martin, C. Perrings and E. Sheshinski (1998), 'Resilience in natural and socioeconomic systems' *Environment and Development Economics*, **3**, 222–35.

Mäler, K.-G. (2000), 'Development, ecological resources and their management: a study of complex systems dynamics', *European Economic Review*, **44**, 645–65.

Neumayer, E. (2005), 'Does high indebtedness increase resource exploitation?', *Environment and Development Economics*, **10**, 127–41.

Norton, B. (1995), 'Resilience and options', *Ecological Economics*, **15**, 133–6.

Nyström, M., C. Folke and F. Moberg (2000), 'Coral reef disturbance and resilience in a human-dominated environment', *Trends in Ecology and Evolution*, **15**, 413–17.

Olsson, P. and C. Folke (2001), 'Local ecological knowledge and institutional dynamics for ecosystem management: a study of crayfish management in the Lake Racken watershed, Sweden', *Ecosystems*, **4**, 85–104.

Olsson, P., C. Folke and F. Berkes (2004), 'Adaptive co-management for building resilience in social-ecological systems', *Environmental Management*, **34**, 75–90.

Scheffer, M., S. Carpenter, J.A. Foley, C. Folke and B. Walker (2001), 'Catastrophic shifts in ecosystems', *Nature*, **413**, 591–6.

Tompkins, E.L. (2005), 'Planning for climate change in small islands: Insights from national hurricane preparedness in the Cayman Islands', *Global Environmental Change*, **15**, 139–49.

Tompkins, E.L. and W.N. Adger (2004), 'Does adaptive management of natural resources enhance resilience to climate change?', *Ecology and Society*, **9**(2), 10, www.ecologyandsociety.org/vol9/iss 2/art10.

Vincent, J.R. (1992), 'The tropical timber trade and sustainable development', *Science*, **256**, 1651–5.

6 Benefit–cost analysis and a safe minimum standard of conservation
Alan Randall

1. Introduction[1]

The Brundtland Commission definition of sustainability – meet(ing) the needs of the present without compromising the ability of future generations to meet their own needs (World Commission on Environment and Development, 1987) – would be satisfied by any arrangement that succeeds in maintaining welfare for the indefinite future. The goal of sustaining welfare can be met, in principle, by arrangements that allow great scope for substitution in production and consumption and rely, as time unfolds, on continuing technological progress and accumulation of capital to compensate for population growth and depletion of natural resources (Solow, 1974). Life may well be different in the future, just as life today is different from just a few generations ago, but it will be at least as satisfying. That is the promise of approaches that seek to sustain welfare – weak sustainability, the Hartwick rule, and green accounting (see Chapters 3, 17 and 18).

The idea that welfare is what should be sustained accords well with post-industrial-revolution human experience in the well-off countries. Our production systems and consumption bundles keep changing and the old ways of doing things disappear apace, but it all seems to be making us better-off. Those concerned with sustainability could hardly take seriously a weaker form of sustainability. After all, weak sustainability places a lot of faith in technology, substitutability of capital for natural resources, and the ability of markets to transmit the right incentives. Many economists agree that sustaining welfare is the appropriate goal, but tend to assume that well-functioning markets will attain it automatically. That is, they agree with the weak sustainability goal, but question the need for explicit weak sustainability policies.

Among the environmental community and the public at large, more demanding commitments to sustainability have their dedicated promoters. Strong sustainability – roughly, the commitment to compensate for depletion of exhaustible resources by augmenting economically-equivalent capital and/or renewable resources, and to limit the use of renewable resources to a sustainable level ('cut a tree, plant a tree') – offers an alternative to weak sustainability, one that assumes much less about the substitutability of capital for natural resources (see Chapter 4). There are also sustainability concepts that are less global, and more particular and local. The goal may be to sustain particular natural resources for reasons that are prudential (they might be essential for human welfare), or aesthetic (they are much appreciated for their contribution to human satisfaction, or perhaps for their own sake). Respect for, and attachment to, place may motivate local sustainability concepts that are related only remotely to worries about the world running out of something essential for human welfare.

Here, I do not propose to argue for or against any particular concept of sustainability. Instead, I simply assert that there is a certain commonsense appeal to the notion that sustaining welfare is a reasonable business-as-usual goal, but that attention to particular resources makes sense when there are plausible threats of resource crises. I argue below that people who find this a commonsense sort of approach will find much to like about a policy framework that, for business-as-usual resource allocation decisions, relies on markets supported by public actions that pass a benefit–cost filter, but invokes a safe minimum standard (SMS) of conservation principle for guidance when crises loom regarding particular natural resources.

In what follows, I summarize the moral arguments for attending to benefits and costs for business-as-usual decisions, and argue for explicit morally-justified constraints to deal with exceptional threats. The SMS is proposed as one such constraint to deal with threatened resource crises, and it is shown that this conception of the SMS has clear implications for SMS design, providing an internally consistent specification of the intolerable cost clause and endorsing early warning and implementation of SMS policies. Then, some key implications for doing benefit–cost analysis (BCA)[2] and implementing the SMS are highlighted. Finally, I discuss ways of embedding the SMS in policy processes, and offer some concluding comments.

2.   The search for ethical justifications

Benefits and costs are morally considerable
We begin with a search for convincing reasons why the public decision process ought to be concerned with benefits and costs. One way to frame the question is: are there good reasons to believe that a benign and conscientious public decision-maker has a duty to consult an account of benefits and costs (Copp, 1985; Randall, 1999)? The traditional epistemological approach to ethics suggests that good reasons should be founded in a theory of right action, allowing us to conclude that benefits and costs are serious considerations in the search for right action.

When called upon to defend the systematic use of BCA in public decision processes, economists are likely to start talking about the need to impose a market-like efficiency on the activities of government (for example,

Arrow et al., 1996). BCA can be defended as an instrument for accomplishing just that, but the fundamental question remains: why impose a market-like efficiency on the activities of government? We need convincing arguments why market efficiency is good in its own domain, and why it should be emulated in the government domain. As I argued in 1999 (Randall, 1999, pp. 251–2), the efficiency approach to right action is problematic, even if we concede the considerable instrumental virtues of efficiency.

A more promising avenue (I believe) is to argue that BCA provides an acceptable account of preference satisfaction, and preference satisfaction matters ethically. In the extreme, consider welfarism: the goodness of an individual life is exactly the level of satisfaction of the individual's preferences, and the goodness of a society is a matter only of the level of satisfaction of its members.[3] From these premises, economists have developed, invoking various assumptions and restrictions as necessary and convenient, the whole apparatus of welfare change measurement, of which BCA is the direct practical implementation.

Welfarism is a particular kind of axiology, the theory that goodness is a matter of value (Vallentyne, 1987): particular in that it confines considerations of value to consequences alone, and considers only welfare when valuing consequences. And axiology is particular among moral theories, being just one of the foundational ethics in the western tradition. The others are Kantianism, which defines right action as that which is obedient to moral duties derived ultimately from a set of universal moral principles; and contractarianism, in which right action respects the rights of individuals. Both of these theories are deontological, because the justification of Kantian moral imperatives and of individual rights requires appeal ultimately to some asserted principle. It is now generally conceded (Williams, 1985) that the epistemological moral theories, axiological and deontological, all are wrong (or at least seriously incomplete) about some things that matter morally. By casting welfarism as a particular kind of axiology, we give it legitimacy as a moral theory, but at the cost of conceding that it too is wrong (or at least seriously incomplete) about some things.

Benefits and costs cannot count for everything   Hubin (1994) asks us to consider *benefit cost moral theory* (BCMT): the theory that right action is whatever maximizes the excess of benefits over costs, as economists understand the terms benefit and costs. Note that BCMT is founded in welfarism, but implemented according to rules of welfare measurement that weight individual preferences by endowments thus emulating the market, but introducing the morally-unsettling property that the preferences of the well-off count for more. It is hard to imagine a single supporter of such a moral theory, among philosophers or the public at large. Instead, we would find unanimity that such a moral theory is inadequate, and an enormous diversity of reasons as to exactly why.

Value pluralism   Given the inadequacy of the epistemological moral theories, it seems unlikely that any one will defeat the others decisively (Williams, 1985). This existential value pluralism suggests that the task of the thoughtful moral agent in the policy arena is, then, to find principles that can command broad agreement and serve to guide society toward consensus on particular real world policy resolutions. Taylor (1989) points out that value pluralism is not just morally-inarticulate relativism; it is a search for principles that provide moral guidance for action.[4]

Benefits and costs must count for something   The failure of BCMT is hardly an argument that BC considerations are morally irrelevant. Hubin offers the analogy of *democratic moral theory*: right action is whatever commands a plurality of the eligible votes. This too is a thoroughly unacceptable moral theory. Nevertheless, democratic institutions flourish in a wide variety of circumstances, and good reasons can be found for a society taking seriously the wishes of its citizens expressed through the ballot. So, the gross inadequacy of democratic moral theory serves to justify not abandoning democratic procedures but nesting them within a framework of constitutional restraints, and all of this embedded in a public life where moral and ethical issues are discussed openly and vigorously.

It turns out that one cannot imagine a plausible moral theory in which the level of satisfaction of individual preferences counts for nothing at all (Hubin, 1994).[5] Examining a broad array of contending moral theories, it turns out that preference satisfaction counts for something, in each of them. Clearly, benefits and costs, among other concerns, are morally considerable.

Public roles for benefit and cost information   To this point, we have concluded that a society of thoughtful moral agents would agree to take seriously an account of benefits and costs, within some more complete set of principles. At this point, the interesting questions are about what else, beyond preference satisfaction, might one want to consider, and in what manner might one want to take account of those things. One approach treats benefit and cost information as simply one kind of decision-relevant information.

Benefit–cost analysis to inform decisions, rather than to decide issues   Suppose that respect for benefits and costs is one of a set of principles that together provide a framework for public decisions. The notion that benefits and costs cannot always be decisive in public policy, but should nevertheless play some role, is congenial to many economists (for example, Arrow et al., 1996, p. 221). But there are at least two kinds of problems with this approach. First, it leaves unanswered the question of exactly what role. Are there particular situations and circumstances in which an account of preference satisfaction should be ignored entirely, and others in which it should be decisive? How should an account of preference satisfaction be weighted relative to other kinds of information? Can the answers to these questions be principled, or must they always be circumstantial? Second, it opens the door to 'fixing' BCA – if other considerations matter, that must be because BCA gets it wrong in some systematic ways, so why not try to fix these problems.[6] If the one true moral theory is ever-elusive, then it follows that the perfect decision criterion is impossible, which renders foolish the project of perfecting BCA.

A benefit–cost decision rule subject to constraints   An alternative approach would be to endorse a benefit–cost decision rule for those issues where no overriding moral concerns are threatened.[7] Benefits and costs could then be decisive within some broad domain, while that domain is itself bounded by constraints reflecting rights that ought to be respected and moral principles that ought to be taken seriously.[8] This would implement the commonsense notion that preference satisfaction is perfectly fine so long as it doesn't threaten any concerns that are more important.

The general form of such constraints might be: *don't do anything disgusting*. The basic idea is that a pluralistic society would agree to be bound by a general-form constraint to eschew actions that violate obvious limits on decent public policy. This kind of constraint is in principle broad enough to take seriously the objections to unrestrained pursuit of preference satisfaction that might be made from a wide range of philosophical perspectives. Examples of such constraints might include: don't violate the rights that other people and perhaps other entities might reasonably be believed to hold; be obedient to the duties that arise from universal moral principles, or that could reasonably be derived therefrom; don't impose inordinate risks upon the future, in pursuit of immediate but modest benefit; and, don't sacrifice important intrinsic values in the service of mere instrumental ends. In each of these cases, the domain within which pursuit of preference satisfaction is permitted would be bounded by non-utilitarian constraints; and these constraints themselves would be determined by serious moral agents in pluralistic processes.

A safe minimum standard of conservation is a commonsense precaution
The safe minimum standard of conservation was proposed by Ciriacy-Wantrup (1968) and defended by Bishop (1978) as a rational response to

uncertainty about the workings of environmental systems. Given the intuitive plausibility of carelessly exploiting a resource beyond the limits of its resilience, society should pre-commit to preserving a sufficient stock of the renewable resource to ensure its survival.

Economists raised two kinds of objections to the SMS as a utilitarian response to uncertainty.[9] First, in order to adopt an SMS constraint voluntarily, a rational utilitarian would need to have sharply discontinuous preferences. Second, Bishop's (1978) attempt to show that a risk-averse utilitarian would rationally adopt an SMS constraint – formally, the SMS is the maximin solution – failed. Writing with Ready, Bishop (Ready and Bishop, 1991) conceded that game theory did not support his earlier attempt at a utilitarian justification of a discrete interruption of business-as-usual when the SMS constraint was reached. The quest for an internally consistent utilitarian justification of the SMS remains elusive.[10]

Farmer and Randall (1998) take a very different approach. Rather than attempting to derive the SMS constraint from any particular epistemological moral theory, they argue from existential moral pluralism that the SMS is best framed as a decision heuristic adopted for good reason: a sharp break from business-as-usual that – given the fear of possible disastrous consequences from anthropogenic modification of environmental systems about which we know so little – could earn the allegiance of moral agents operating from a variety of principles. Three principled intuitions that we would expect to be honored widely – the existence of future humans is valued; the welfare of future humans is valued; and moral agents should resolve these intergenerational concerns in the context of their intragenerational obligations to each other – provide substantial justification for this kind of SMS.

3.   Implications for implementation

I have offered justifications for adopting a policy framework that, for business-as-usual resource allocation decisions, relies on markets supported by public actions that pass a benefit–cost filter, but invokes a safe minimum standard of conservation principle for guidance when crises loom regarding particular natural resources. It follows that the practical implementation of these decision tools should serve effectively the purposes that justify them.

Implications for doing BCA

The reasons for agreeing to take benefits and costs seriously in the policy process are reasons why preference satisfaction matters morally. It follows that BCA should provide an acceptable account of preference satisfaction.

In the Appendix, a stylized BCA framework is provided that enables us to identify the essential characteristics of the benefit–cost criterion. The underlying value system is homocentric, instrumentalist and welfarist. The environment is regarded as a resource, an instrument for serving human purposes. Humans do the valuing, and value at the household level derives exclusively from the satisfaction of human preferences. Value is aggregated across households according to the potential Pareto-improvement (PPI) criterion, which is consistent with Benthamite utilitarianism. Since voluntary exchange and contractarian political processes honor the actual Pareto-improvement (PI) criterion, the PPI can be interpreted, albeit with important caveats, in market and contractarian terms.

Proposals are evaluated according to the 'with and without' principle, which requires that both baseline and with-project conditions be projected into the distant future. Benefits and costs are discounted to reflect the opportunity cost of capital, and expressed in present value terms. While the BCA model is presented in deterministic terms, uncertainty about future conditions can be recognized by expressing the valuations in *ex ante* expected value terms.

Hubin argues that BCA does in fact provide an acceptable account of preference satisfaction. Its main weakness in this respect, the endowment-weighting of preferences, stems directly from its reaching out to market institutions, efficiency logic, and contractarian epistemological ethics; and it can be argued that these accommodations gain, as well as lose, legitimacy for BCA.

If BC analysts wish to claim, based on the justifications provided here, that the public has a duty to take BCA seriously, then the analysts themselves have a duty to implement the PPI valuation framework rigorously and carefully. The result would be BCAs that depart from customary practice – to the extent that customary practice retains some remnants of BCA's roots in financial feasibility analysis – in several ways. Less attention would be paid to market prices and demands, while more attention would be paid to public preferences for public goods and the non-market values those preferences imply, and to willingness-to-sell as the appropriate measure of costs. We found, much earlier in this essay, that a claimed need to impose a market-like efficiency on the activities of government provides an implausible justification for taking benefits and costs seriously. Now, we find that a sounder justification for BCA entails an obligation on the part of the analyst to pay more than customary attention to preferences and less than customary attention to market outcomes.

Implications for implementing the SMS
Farmer and Randall (1998) argue that the SMS constraint makes most sense when cast transparently as a discrete interruption of business-as-usual, imposed to act upon firm, and often non-utilitarian, intuitions that to permit

threatened destruction of a unique renewable resource would be foolish and (perhaps) morally wrong. The justification for this discrete switch has implications for the construction and implementation of the Farmer–Randall (FR) SMS. For illustrative purposes, we assume a renewable natural resource with a logistic regeneration function (Figure 6.1).[11] With deterministic regeneration, S_{min} represents the minimum resource carried forward in order to avoid resource exhaustion. The Ciriacy–Wantrup SMS addresses the stochastic nature of regeneration – it is *safe* in the sense that it carries forward a sustainable stock of the resource even in the worst-case regeneration scenario. The FR SMS – designed to respect the heuristics that moral agents value future humans and their welfare, but resolve these intergenerational concerns in the context of their intragenerational obligations to each other – is set at SMS*, which provides for an essential harvest, D_{min}.

The essential harvest concept is most powerful in the case of an essential resource, where it has moral and practical implications for public choice. Moral theories encounter serious difficulties in dealing with intergenerational problems, but one thing seems clear: no serious moral theory demands that a generation decimate itself for the benefit of future generations. The SMS, in the multigenerational context, can be effective only if each succeeding generation reaffirms the SMS commitment. Not only that, but each current generation in its turn would abide by the SMS only if it confidently expected succeeding generations to do the same – otherwise, in the end, little is gained by current sacrifice. Moral and practical reasoning

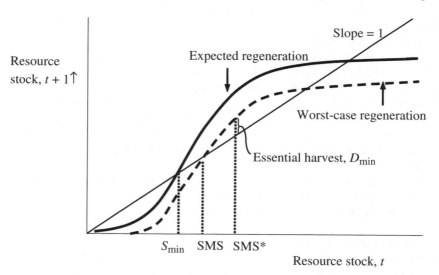

Figure 6.1   The safe minimum standard of conservation

lead to the same conclusion – in the case of an essential resource, the SMS must be set at SMS* to allow for essential harvest by each succeeding generation. The FR SMS emphasizes early warning and early implementation of conservation policies that require relatively modest sacrifices on the part of society. Since unilateral withdrawal from any intertemporal obligation is always a possibility, conservationists have a strong interest in keeping the costs of conservation tolerably low.

Many SMS proponents envision using an SMS to ensure preservation of unique and valued natural resources (often biotic), whether or not they are strictly essential to human welfare. For the case of an inessential renewable resource, practical reasoning reaffirms the logic of the essential resource case. Imagine that some minimal harvest or use of the resource enjoys strong political support (in the extreme, is politically essential). Then an SMS* policy is recommended for practical reasons – again, conservationists have a strong interest in keeping the costs of conservation tolerably low.[12] Moral reasoning is murkier in this case, because moral theories differ as to what obligations humans may have toward unique and much-appreciated entities that are ultimately inessential to welfare.

Defining the intolerable cost   The standard rendition of the SMS policy prescription contains an escape clause: the SMS should be maintained unless the costs of so doing are intolerably high (Bishop, 1978). At the outset, the 'intolerable cost' clause was tacked on to the SMS, ad hoc. More recent authors have offered quite different analyses aimed at bringing the intolerable cost *inside* the SMS framework. Rolfe (1995) proposes an SMS for risk-averse utilitarians, in which the limits of tolerable cost are defined by willingness to pay for risk reduction.[13] Randall and Farmer (1995) call on the concept of essential harvest, D_{min}, to define both SMS* and the intolerable cost – any SMS obligation requiring that a generation forgo the essential harvest is *ipso facto* intolerable.

4.   Embedding SMS in policy and management – what is needed?
It has become commonplace to characterize support for the SMS among environmental economists as wide but shallow. Yet Berrens (2001) argues that the SMS is attracting much more than cursory attention in the literature, in resource/environmental economics textbooks,[14] in laws with rather sweeping application (the US Endangered Species Act, ESA),[15] and in limited local policy applications. A very broad-brush review suggests that the ESA has evolved, via amendments and conventions adopted to guide application, much along the lines of the SMS. To relieve 'excessive' economic burdens, land can be excluded from the designated critical habitat, or a species may be exempted from protection, provisions that parallel the

intolerable cost escape clause in SMS.[16] Nevertheless, the ESA fails to capture an essential feature of the FR SMS, the early-warning trigger designed to keep the costs of conservation tolerably low – and it might be argued that the much lamented 'train wreck' collisions of interests that make ESA so controversial are the inevitable result of this omission.

There is a modest amount of literature on local implementation of SMS procedures. Berrens reports, favorably and with only modest reservations, on several local applications of ESA. Woodward and Bishop (1997) argue that procedures drawing on the SMS and precautionary principle traditions make sense when policy makers face a wide divergence of beliefs among the experts they consult. Farmer (2001) reports a case where stakeholder convention processes were much improved by restructuring them around SMS concepts. Woodward and Bishop (2003) develop criteria for sustainability-constrained sector-level planning.

Implementation of a serious SMS-based policy requires that society monitor the landscape for indicators that warn of a particular risk of a resource crisis and, when the alarm is sounded, take seriously the call for avoidance/mitigation measures beyond those justified by ordinary welfare considerations. That much is agreed by most SMS proponents. But what comes next? The answer depends on what status we accord the SMS. It could be argued that the SMS, to be effective, must be codified into statute law (as happened, roughly, with ESA) or even constitutional law, or at least incorporated in administrative rules. An alternative view (Michael Farmer, personal communication) is captured in the idea of 'principles that guide'. On-the-ground policy practitioners should be bound (by law or regulation) to certain broad-brush principles and encouraged to interpret these principles in practice via some kind of serious policy dialogue. This stands in contrast to formal technocratic planning procedures on the one hand, and abdication to stakeholder-consensus processes on the other.

5.   Concluding comments

This chapter has elucidated the moral foundations of benefit–cost analysis and argued that it provides commonsense guidance for business-as-usual policy. While some economics textbooks argue that, in an ideal economy, resource crises are impossible, a mainstream economics literature has arisen that takes sustainability issues seriously indeed (Pezzey and Toman, 2002). However, BCA (even the extended BCA that includes non-market and passive use values, and incorporates risk-aversion into the value estimation procedures) – by conflating uncertainty and gross ignorance of how natural systems work with ordinary risk – provides an unconvincing response to sustainability threats. The safe minimum standard of conservation was proposed by Ciriacy-Wantrup to address this perceived deficiency in business-as-usual economic thinking.

Some commentators have expressed concern that the SMS is fundamentally inconsistent: the SMS exception, as a break from business-as-usual cannot be justified by whatever justifies business-as-usual. But this insistence on internal consistency seems out of step with recent developments in philosophy. The search for the one epistemological moral theory that defeats all others seems hopeless, and much current thinking in ethics is aimed at finding robust principled ways to translate diverse moral sentiments among ethically inclined persons so that a rule deemed moral is at least possible.

Many economists have assumed unquestioningly that a credible SMS must be a utilitarian SMS. Thus, Rolfe proposes an SMS that is little more than extended BCA – at best a warning flag raised in information-poor situations to remind the analysts to bend over backwards to give uncertainty and non-use values their due.[17] Others (Bishop, Ready and Bishop) invoke extreme risk-aversion in the quest for a utilitarian SMS.

The Farmer–Randall SMS proposed and defended here is a substantive SMS that calls for an explicit policy switch made for good reasons. It is motivated not just by uncertainty in the real world, but also by ambiguity concerning what we as a society care about, especially when the distant future is at issue. This substantive SMS is guided by principles adopted by serious moral agents in the absence of a complete and convincing epistemological moral theory. From this perspective, the economists' impulse to retreat into more familiar moral territory (for example, front-loading a lot of risk aversion into a BCA) should be resisted – it simply does not take principles very seriously.

The BCA subject to SMS framework proposed and defended here would honor weak sustainability for business-as-usual circumstances, but reserve a strong sustainability instrument targeted to particular, credible threats of resource exhaustion. As such, it respects the modern experience of technical progress and increasing welfare even as substitution in production and consumption proceeds apace, and the reasonable instinct for caution as we continue to push at the frontiers of what can be known about our planet's capacity to support future welfare.

Appendix: a stylized BCA framework

Consider a complex environment E producing a vector of services $S(t)$ through time. The output of services is determined by the attributes $A(t)$ of the environment and the human-controlled factors $X(t)$ applied:

$$S(t) = f[A(t), X(t)]. \qquad (A6.1)$$

The attributes of the environment are themselves the result of interaction between nature and human activity. Where $N(t)$ refers to a vector of natural-systems factors,

$$A(t) = g[N(t), X(t)]. \qquad (A6.2)$$

This completes the production for environmental services. But the economist should never underestimate the effort and multidisciplinary expertise required for developing quantitative projections of $S(t)$ over the long time-horizon relevant for conservation issues.

Each household $h = 1, \ldots, H$, gains utility from consuming/using/enjoying environmental services and ordinary commodities Z. Thus,

$$U_h(t) = U_h[S_h(t), Z_h(t)] \qquad (A6.3)$$

By minimizing expenditures subject to the constraint that household utility be maintained at the baseline level, household valuations for environmental services, $V_h[S_h(t)]$, can be obtained. The value of E, viewed as an asset, is the present value of the services it provides:

$$PV(E) = \sum_{h=1}^{H} \int_{t_0}^{\infty} V_h[S_h(t)]e^{-rt}dt \qquad (A6.4)$$

where r is the inflation-free discount rate.

Now, consider a project Δ that would change $[X(t)]$ to $X^{\Delta}(t)$, thereby changing E to some with-project state E^{Δ} at some cost C^{Δ}. Environmental attributes would be changed to $A^{\Delta}(t)$ and environmental services to $S^{\Delta}(t)$. The net present value of the project would be

$$PV(\Delta) = PV(E^{\Delta} - C^{\Delta} - E). \qquad (A6.5)$$

Notes

1. Once again, I am grateful to Michael Farmer – who has contributed in many ways to all of my writings since 1991 on these topics, in several cases as my co-author – for stimulating discussions, helpful suggestions, and incisive comments.
2. Or cost–benefit analysis (CBA) as it tends to be known in Europe.
3. This definition follows Sen (1989). According to Kagan (1998), current usage among philosophers defines welfarism more narrowly, that is, as evaluating welfare by the Benthamite utilitarian welfare function, and thus ignoring distributional concerns.
4. Taylor emphasizes the search for principles capturing and generalizing prior moral intuitions that transcend and precede moral theories – principles that (he argues) routinely go under-valued in standard moral epistemology, but are forced to the front by value pluralism.
5. Randall and Farmer (1995) have considered the two ethical theories that contend for the allegiance of mainstream economists, consequentialism and contractarianism, and the

major alternative, Kantianism. They show that, while each of these ethical theories has different ways of taking preference satisfaction into consideration, each of them does consider preference satisfaction in some way. Even a thoughtful Kantian would concur that there exists a broad domain of human concerns where happiness may be pursued without violating moral strictures; and, within that domain, more preference satisfaction is better than less.

6. There is a long history of proposed 'fixes', for example, various tweaks to introduce into the BC calculations risk aversion and sensitivity to distributional considerations.

7. There are many reasons for such an endorsement. It would: respect preferences, while leaving them subordinate to principles; accommodate a non-trivial range of individual autonomy; encourage decisions that would increase the 'size of the game' while minimizing waste and unproductive rent-seeking; and (Farmer and Randall, 2005) reinforce politically-liberal values as opposed to technocracy and elitism.

8. The idea of a zone of autonomy, surrounded by constraints that both reinforce and limit it, is embedded in the concept of constitutional democracy. To free individuals for the pursuit of happiness, constraints securing some well-defined set of human rights seem essential. If the beneficence of reasonably free markets is to be enjoyed, a set of secure property rights is also necessary. People acting together to govern themselves need also to establish a framework of laws, statutes, regulations and policies, to legitimize and also to limit the role of activist government.

9. A third objection, which I merely mention here, invokes the standard textbook discussion of resource extraction/harvest to deny the problem that the SMS is intended to fix – arguing that in an ideal economy the resource crisis is self-correcting because impending scarcity will induce higher prices that encourage conservation and substitution.

10. In a recent working paper, Margolis and Naevdal (2004) argue that the SMS can in fact be derived rigorously as a utilitarian maximin strategy for biological resource systems characterized by threshold phenomena.

11. Logistic regeneration, while useful for illustrative purposes, is ecologically naive. Recently, economists have examined the implications, for SMS-type policies, of more ecologically-sound models of population viability (Bulte and van Kooten, 2001).

12. Berrens, McKee and Farmer (1999) examine two endangered species cases, concluding that local distributional concerns loom large in determining whether the economic consequences of preservation actions are politically intolerable. This insight suggests that designers of SMS-based policy may be able to expand the scope of politically acceptable costs by consciously addressing distributional issues.

13. My objections to Rolfe's approach are principled: it does not take uncertainty and gross ignorance about the way the world works seriously enough. Unsurprisingly, the empirical record on utilitarian justifications for SMS policies is mixed. While Solomon, Corey-Luse and Halvorsen (2004) argue for SMS protections for Florida manatees on the grounds that benefits far exceed costs, Bulte and van Kooten (2000) argue that SMS policies should be considered for minke whales and ancient temperate rainforests, *because* utilitarian calculations provide little support for preservation.

14. A current survey would substantially expand Berrens' list of well-regarded textbooks that take the SMS seriously.

15. Margolis and Naevdal (2004), whose SMS pays close attention to thresholds, argue that the common regulatory practice of 'capping' air and water pollution (that is, setting enforceable upper limits on pollution) owes much to SMS thinking.

16. Under ESA as amended, these decisions are made by a cabinet-level Endangered Species Committee, a provision that (Berrens notes) is consistent with Randall's (1991) notion that, to avoid conflation of SMS with a risk-averse BC test, invoking the intolerable cost clause should require an extraordinary decision process.

17. See also Farrow (2004), who makes a similar argument concerning the precautionary principle.

References

Arrow, K.J., M.L. Cropper, G.C. Eads, R.W. Hahn, L.B. Lave, R.G. Noll, P.R. Portney, M. Russell, R. Schmalensee, V.K. Smith and R.N. Stavins (1996), 'Is there a role for benefit–cost analysis in environmental, health, and safety regulation?', *Science*, **272**(5259): 221–2.

Berrens, R.P. (2001), 'The safe minimum standard of conservation and endangered species: a review', *Environmental Conservation*, **28**(2): 104–16.

Berrens, R.P., M. McKee and M.C. Farmer (1999), 'Incorporating distributional considerations in the safe minimum standard approach: endangered species and local impacts', *Ecological Economics*, **30**(3): 461–74.

Bishop, R.C. (1978), 'Endangered species and uncertainty: the economics of a safe minimum standard', *American Journal of Agricultural Economics*, **60**(1): 10–18.

Bulte, E.H. and G.C. van Kooten (2000), 'Economic science, endangered species, and biodiversity loss', *Conservation Biology*, **14**(1): 113–19.

Bulte, E.H. and G.C. van Kooten (2001), 'Harvesting and conserving a species when numbers are low: population viability and gambler's ruin in bioeconomic models', *Ecological Economics*, **37**(1): 87–100.

Ciriacy-Wantrup, S.V. (1968), *Resource Conservation: Economics and Policies*, 3rd edn, Berkeley, CA: University of California, Division of Agricultural Science.

Copp, D. (1985), 'Morality, reason, and management science: the rationale of cost–benefit analysis', in E. Paul, J. Paul and F. Miller (eds), *Ethics and Economics*, Oxford: Blackwell, pp. 128–51.

Farmer, M.C. (2001), 'Getting the safe minimum standard to work in the real world: a case study in moral pragmatism', *Ecological Economics*, **38**(2): 209–26.

Farmer, M.C. and A. Randall (1998), 'The rationality of a safe minimum standard of conservation', *Land Economics*, **74**: 287–302.

Farmer, M.C. and A. Randall (2005), 'Making value compromises in an efficient economy: efficiency as value dialogue', in J.L. Innes, G.M. Hickey and H.F. Hoen (eds), *Forestry and Environmental Change: Socioeconomic and Political Dimensions*, International Union of Forest Research Organizations series, Wallingford, UK: CABI, pp. 31–52.

Farrow, S. (2004), 'Using risk assessment, benefit–cost analysis, and real options to implement a precautionary principle', *Risk Analysis*, **34**(3): 727–35.

Hubin, D.C. (1994), 'The moral justification of benefit/cost analysis', *Economics and Philosophy*, **10**: 169–94.

Kagan, S. (1998), *Normative Ethics*, Boulder, CO: Westview Press.

Margolis, M. and E. Naevdal (2004), 'Safe minimum standards in dynamic resource problems – conditions for living on the edge of uncertainty', Discussion paper 04-03, Resources for the Future, Inc., Washington DC, February.

Pezzey, J. and M. Toman (2002), 'Progress and problems in the economics of sustainability', in T. Tietenberg and H. Folmer (eds), *International Yearbook of Environmental and Resource Economics 2002/2003*, Cheltenham, UK, and Northampton, MA, USA: Edward Elgar, pp. 165–232.

Randall, A. (1991), 'The economic value of biodiversity', *Ambio-A Journal of the Human Environment*, **20**(2): 64–8.

Randall, A. (1999), 'Taking benefits and costs seriously', in H. Folmer and T. Tietenberg (eds), *The International Yearbook of Environmental and Resource Economics 1999/2000*, Cheltenham, UK, and Northampton, MA, USA: Edward Elgar, pp. 250–72.

Randall, A. and M.C. Farmer (1995), 'Benefits, costs, and a safe minimum standard of conservation', in D. Bromley (ed.), *Handbook of Environmental Economics*, Oxford, UK and Cambridge MA: Blackwell, pp. 26–44.

Ready, R.C. and R.C. Bishop (1991), 'Endangered species and the safe minimum standard', *American Journal of Agricultural Economics*, **73**(2), May: 309–12.

Rolfe, J. (1995), 'Ulysses revisited – a closer look at the safe minimum standard of conservation', *Australian Journal of Agricultural Economics*, **39**: 55–70.

Sen, A. (1989), *On Ethics and Economics*, New York: Basil Blackwell.

Solomon, B.D., C.M. Corey-Luse and K.E. Halvorsen (2004), 'The Florida manatee and eco-tourism: toward a safe minimum standard', *Ecological Economics*, **50**(1–2): 101–15.
Solow, R.M. (1974), 'Intergenerational equity and exhaustible resources', *Review of Economic Studies: Symposium on the Economics of Exhaustible Resources*, **41**: 29–45.
Taylor, C.R. (1989), *Sources of the Self: the Making of Modern Identity*, Cambridge, MA: Harvard University Press.
Vallentyne, P. (1987), 'The teleological/deontological distinction', *Journal of Value Inquiry*, **21**: 21–32.
Williams, B. (1985), *Ethics and the Limits of Philosophy*, Cambridge, MA: Harvard University Press.
Woodward, R.T. and R.C. Bishop (1997), 'How to decide when experts disagree: Uncertainty-based choice rules in environmental policy', *Land Economics*, **73**(4): 492–507.
Woodward, R.T. and R.C. Bishop (2003), 'Sector-level decisions in a sustainability-constrained economy', *Land Economics*, **79**: 1–14.
World Commission on Environment and Development (1987), *Our Common Future*, New York: Oxford University Press.

PART II

INTERGENERATIONAL EQUITY

7 Valuing the far-off future: discounting and its alternatives
Cameron Hepburn

1. Introduction

The challenges of climate change, biodiversity protection, declining fish stocks and nuclear waste management mean that policy makers now have to take important decisions with impacts decades, if not centuries, into the future. The way we value the future is crucial in determining what action to take in response to such challenges.

Whenever economists think about intertemporal decisions, whether concerning trade-offs between today and tomorrow or between the present generation and our distant descendants, we reach almost instinctively for the discount rate. This instinct is not without good reason – the practice of discounting, embedded in social cost–benefit analysis, has served us extremely well in formulating policy over the short to medium term. For longer term decisions, however, results from this trusty tool can appear increasingly contrary to intergenerational equity and sustainable development. In response, some have advocated jettisoning the tool altogether and turning to alternative methods of valuing the future. Others take the view that these long term challenges bring trade-offs between intergenerational efficiency and equity into sharp focus and it is no surprise that social cost–benefit analysis, which generally ignores distributional considerations, supports efficient but unsustainable projects. They conclude that the tool is functioning properly, but must be employed in a framework that guarantees intergenerational equity. A third hypothesis is that although the tool works correctly for short term decisions, it needs repairing and refinement for long term decisions. In particular, if future economic conditions are assumed to be uncertain – a reasonable assumption when looking decades or centuries into the future – using a constant discount rate is approximately correct over shorter time periods (up to about 30 years), but is increasingly incorrect thereafter. The more accurate procedure is to employ a declining discount rate over time.

This chapter reviews social discounting (section 2), addresses the arguments for and against a zero discount rate (section 3), outlines the research on declining social discount rates (section 4), and considers some alternatives to discounting in social decision-making (section 5).

2. Exponential discounting and its implications

Cost–benefit analysis, efficiency and equity
Economics has a long tradition of separating efficiency from equity, and social cost–benefit analysis is no exception, where the Kaldor–Hicks criterion is relied upon to justify projects that are efficient.[1] Distributional effects are ignored, which is argued to be legitimate when the decision-maker also controls the tax system and can redistribute income to achieve equity. In practice, of course, the distributional effects of some projects are important, and cost–benefit analysis and should be employed as a *guide* for decision-making rather than a substitute for judgement (Lind, 1982). It can be a very useful guide because, when done properly, it focuses our attention on the valuation of the most important impacts of a decision.

For intergenerational investments, distributional effects are often especially important because there is no intergenerational tax system available to redistribute wealth (Lind, 1995; 1999). Although economic instruments can create wealth transfers between generations (such as certain changes to tax law and fiscal policy), there is no guarantee that the transfer will reach the intended recipient when there are many intervening generations. Drèze and Stern (1990) note that 'hypothetical transfers of the Hicks–Kaldor variety . . . are not relevant when such transfers will not take place'. In such circumstances, explicit consideration of intergenerational equity appears to be necessary.

Estimating the social discount rate
In social cost–benefit analysis, the social discount function, $D(t)$, is used to convert flows of future cost and benefits into their present equivalents. If the net present value of the investment exceeds zero, the project is efficient. The social discount rate, $s(t)$, measures the annual rate of decline in the discount function, $D(t)$. In continuous time, the two are connected by the equation:

$$D(t) = \exp\left[-\int_0^t s(\tau)d\tau \right] \tag{7.1}$$

A constant social discount rate implies that the discount function declines exponentially, $D(t) = \exp(-st)$.[2]

As practitioners know, the value of the social discount rate is often critical in determining whether projects pass social cost–benefit analysis. As a result, spirited debates have erupted in the past over its correct conceptual foundation. Happily, the debate was largely resolved at a 1977 conference, where Lind (1982, p. 89) reported that the recommended approach is to 'equate the social rate of discount with the social rate of time preference as determined by consumption rates of interest and estimated on the basis of the returns on market instruments that are available to investors'. Under this approach, the social discount rate, for a given utility function, can be expressed by the well-known accounting relation:

$$s = \delta + \eta g \tag{7.2}$$

where δ is the utility discount rate (or the rate of pure time preference), η is the elasticity of marginal utility and g is the rate of growth of consumption per capita. Even if the utility discount rate δ is zero, the social discount rate is positive when consumption growth, g, is positive and $\eta > 0$. Equation (7.2) shows that in general, the appropriate social discount rate is *not* constant over time, but is a function of the expected future consumption path.

The discounting dilemma
In recent years, debates about the correct foundation for the social discount rate have been replaced by controversy over discounting and intergenerational equity. To see that evaluation of long term investments is extremely sensitive to the discount rate, observe that the present value of £100 in 100 years' time is £37 at a 1 per cent discount rate, £5.2 at 3 per cent, £2 at 4 per cent and only 12p at 7 per cent. Because small changes in the discount rate have large impacts on long-term policy outcomes, arguments about the 'correct' number have intensified. For instance, the marginal damage from emissions of carbon dioxide is estimated by the FUND model (Tol, 2005) to be \$58/tC at a 0 per cent utility discount rate, \$11/tC at a 1 per cent utility discount rate, with damages of -\$2.3/tC (i.e. net *benefits*) at a 3 per cent utility discount rate. Indeed, exponential discounting at moderate discount rates implies that costs and benefits in the far future are effectively irrelevant. While this might be entirely appropriate for individuals (who will no longer be alive), many people would argue that this is an unsatisfactory basis for public policy.

3. Zero discounting
Given these difficulties, some people find it tempting to suggest that we should simply not discount the cash flows in social cost–benefit analysis. But not discounting amounts to using a social discount rate of $s = 0$ per cent, which is extremely dubious given our experience to date with positive consumption growth: $g > 0$ in equation (7.2). In contrast, a credible argument for employing a zero *utility* discount rate ($\delta = 0$) can be advanced,

based upon the ethical position that the weight placed upon a person's utility should not be reduced simply because they live in the future.

Indeed, this ethical position is adopted by Stern et al. (2006) and supported by a string of eminent scholars, including Ramsey (1928), Pigou (1932), Harrod (1948) and Solow (1974), and even Koopmans (1965) expressed an 'ethical preference for neutrality as between the welfare of different generations'. Broome (1992) provides a coherent argument for zero discounting based on the presumption of impartiality found both in the utilitarian tradition (Sidgwick, 1907; Harsanyi, 1977) and also in Rawls (1971), who concluded that 'there is no reason for the parties [in the original position] to give any weight to mere position in time.'[3]

However, not all philosophers and economists accept the presumption of impartiality. Beckerman and Hepburn (2007) stress that reasonable minds may differ; Arrow (1999), for instance, prefers the notion of agent-relative ethics advanced by Scheffler (1982). Even if one does accept a *presumption* of impartiality and zero discounting, there are four counter-arguments that might overturn this presumption: the 'no optimum' argument, the 'excessive sacrifice' argument, the 'risk of extinction' argument, and the 'political acceptability' argument. We examine all four.

First, Koopmans (1960, 1965) demonstrated that in an infinite horizon model, there is no optimum if a zero rate of time preference is employed. Consider a unit of investment today that yields a tiny but perpetual stream of consumption. Each unit investment causes a finite loss of utility today, but generates a small gain in utility to an infinite number of generations. It follows that no matter how low current consumption, further reductions in consumption are justified by the infinite benefit provided to future generations. The logical implication of zero discounting is the impoverishment of the current generation. Furthermore, the same logic applies to every generation, so that each successive generation would find itself being impoverished in order to further the well-being of the next.[4] Broome (1992), however, counters that humanity will not exist forever.[5] Furthermore, Asheim et al. (2001) demonstrate that zero utility discounting (or 'equity', as they term it) does not rule out the existence of an optimum under certain reasonable technologies.[6]

Second, even if we suppose a finite but large number of future generations, a zero discount rate is argued to require excessive sacrifice by the current generation, in the form of extremely high savings rates. Arrow (1999) concludes that the ethical requirement to treat all generations alike imposes morally unacceptable and excessively high savings rates on each generation. But Parfit (1984) has argued that the excessive sacrifice problem is not a reason to reject zero utility discounting. Rather, it should be resolved by employing a utility function with a minimum level of well-being below which no generation should fall.[7] Asheim and Buchholz (2003) point out that the 'excessive sacrifice' argument can be circumvented, under plausible technologies, by a utility function which is more concave.

Third, each generation has a non-zero probability of extinction. Suppose that the risk of extinction follows a Poisson process such that the conditional probability of extinction at any given time is constant. Yaari (1965) demonstrated that this is equivalent to a model with an infinite time horizon where utility is discounted at the (constant) Poisson rate. As such, accounting for the risk of extinction is mathematically identical to positive utility discounting. While admitting the strength of this argument, Broome (1992) asserts that extinction risk and the pure rate of time preference 'should be accounted for separately'. But extinction risk is clearly not project-specific, so it would be accounted for in the same way across all projects (except projects aimed at reducing an extinction risk). Irrespective of how this is done, the mathematical effect is the same – the well-being of future generations is effectively discounted. Hence Dasgupta and Heal (1979) argue that 'one might find it ethically feasible to discount future utilities as positive rates, not because one is myopic, but because there is a positive chance that future generations will not exist'. Given that the risk of human extinction is probably (and hopefully) quite low, the appropriate utility discount rate would be very small.[8]

Finally, Harvey (1994) rejects zero utility discounting on the basis that it is so obviously incompatible with the time preference of most people that its use in public policy would be illegitimate. While the significance of revealed preferences is debatable (Beckerman and Hepburn, 2007), Harvey is surely correct when he states that the notion that events in ten thousand years are as important as those occurring now simply does not pass 'the laugh test'.

In summary, the 'no optimum' argument and the 'excessive sacrifice' argument for positive time preference are refutable. In contrast, the 'risk of extinction' argument provides a sound conceptual basis for a positive utility discount rate. This might be backed up at a practical level by the 'political acceptability' argument, or by the more fundamental view that impartiality is not a compelling ethical standpoint. Overall, the arguments for a small positive utility discount rate appear persuasive. Zero discounting is not intellectually compelling.

4. Declining discount rates

Over recent years, several persuasive theoretical reasons have been advanced to justify a social discount rate that declines as time passes.[9] Declining discount rates are appealing to people concerned about intergenerational equity, but perhaps more importantly, they are likely to be *necessary* for achieving intergenerational efficiency. Groom et al. (2005) provide a detailed review of the case for declining discount rates. This section provides an overview of the main arguments.

Evidence on individual time preference

Evidence from experiments over the last couple of decades suggests that humans use a declining discount rate, in the form of a 'hyperbolic discounting' function, in making intertemporal choices.[10] In these experiments, people typically choose between different rewards (for example, money, durable goods, sweets or relief from noise) with different delays, so that an implicit discount function can be constructed.[11] The resulting discount functions suggest that humans employ a higher discount rate for consumption trade-offs in the present than for trade-offs in the future. While other interpretations, such as similarity relations (Rubinstein, 2003) and sub-additive discounting (Read, 2001), are possible, the evidence for hyperbolic discounting is relatively strong.

Pearce et al. (2003) present the argument that if people's preferences count, and these behavioural results reveal underlying preferences, then declining discount rates ought to be integrated into social policy formulation. Pearce et al. recognize, however, that the assumptions in this chain of reasoning might be disputed. First, as hyperbolic discounting provides an explanation for procrastination, drug addiction, undersaving, and organizational failure, the argument that behaviour reflects preferences is weakened. Second, Pearce et al. and Beckerman and Hepburn (2007) stress that Hume would resist concluding that the government *should* discount the future hyperbolically because individual citizens *do*. The recent literature on 'optimal paternalism' suggests, amongst other things, that governments may be justified in intervening not only to correct externalities, but also to correct 'internalities' – behaviour that is damaging to the actor.[12] Whether or not one supports a paternalistic role for government, one might question the wisdom of adopting a schedule of discount rates that explains procrastination, addiction and potentially the unforeseen collapses in renewable resource stocks (Hepburn, 2003).

Pessimism about the future

Equation (7.2) makes it clear that the consumption rate of interest – and thus also the social rate of time preference in a representative agent economy – is a function of consumption growth. If consumption growth, g, will fall in the future, and the utility discount rate, δ, and the elasticity of marginal utility, η, are constant, it follows from equation (7.2) that the social discount rate also declines through time. Furthermore, if decreases in the *level* of consumption are expected – so that consumption growth is negative – the appropriate social rate of time preference could be negative. Declines in the level of consumption are impossible in an optimal growth model in an idealized economy with productive capital. For the social discount rate to be negative, either capital must be unproductive, or a distortion, such as an environmental externality, must have driven a wedge between the market return to capital and the consumption rate of interest (Weitzman, 1994).

Uncertainty

It is an understatement to say that we can have little confidence in economic forecasts several decades into the future. In the face of such uncertainty, the most appropriate response is to incorporate it into our economic models. Suppose that the future comprises two equally likely states with social discount rate either 2 per cent or 6 per cent. Discount *factors* corresponding to these two *rates* are shown in Table 7.1. The average of those discount factors is called the 'certainty-equivalent discount factor', and working backwards from this we can find the 'certainty-equivalent discount rate', which starts at 4 per cent and declines asymptotically to 2 per cent as time passes.[13] In this uncertain world, a project is efficient if it passes social cost–benefit analysis using the certainty-equivalent discount rate, which declines through time.

The two key assumptions in this example are that the discount rate is uncertain and *persistent*, so that the expected discount rate in one period is correlated with the discount rate the period before. If these two assumptions hold, intergenerational efficiency requires a declining social discount rate (Weitzman, 1998, 2001).

The particular shape of the decline is determined by the specification of uncertainty in the economy. Newell and Pizer (2003) use data on past US interest rates to estimate a reduced-form time series process which is then employed to forecast future rates. The level of uncertainty and persistence in their forecasts is high enough to generate a relatively rapid decline in the certainty-equivalent discount rate with significant policy implications. While econometric tests reported in Groom et al. (2006) suggest that Newell and Pizer (2003) should have employed a state-space or regime-shifting model instead, their key conclusion remains intact – the certainty-equivalent discount rate declines at a rate that is significant for the appraisal of long term projects.

Table 7.1   Numerical example of a declining certainty-equivalent discount rate

Time (years from present)	1	10	50	100	200	400
Discount factor for 2% rate	0.98	0.82	0.37	0.14	0.02	0.00
Discount factor for 6% rate	0.94	0.56	0.05	0.00	0.00	0.00
Certainty-equivalent discount factor	0.96	0.69	0.21	0.07	0.01	0.00
Certainty-equivalent (average) discount rate	4.0%	3.8%	3.1%	2.7%	2.4%	2.2%

Gollier (2001, 2002a, 2002b) provides an even more solidly grounded justification for declining discount rates by specifying an underlying utility function and analysing an optimal growth model. He demonstrates that a similar result can hold, for certain types of utility functions. Under uncertainty, the social discount rate in equation (7.2) needs to be modified to account for an additional prudence effect:

$$s = \delta + \eta g - \frac{1}{2} \eta P \, \text{var}(g) \tag{7.3}$$

where P is the measure of relative prudence introduced by Kimball (1990). This prudence effect leads to 'precautionary saving', reducing the discount rate. Moreover, if there is no risk of recession and people have decreasing relative risk aversion, the optimal social discount rate is declining over time.

These two sets of results show that employing a declining social discount rate is *necessary* for intergenerational efficiency (Weitzman, 1998) and also for intergenerational optimality under relatively plausible utility functions (Gollier, 2002a, b). The theory in this section provides a compelling reason for employing declining discount rates in social cost–benefit analysis.

Inter-generational equity
Not only are declining social discount rates necessary for efficiency, it turns out that they are also necessary for some specifications of intergenerational equity. Chichilnisky (1996, 1997) introduces two axioms for sustainable development requiring that the ranking of consumption paths be sensitive to consumption in both the present and the very long run. Sensitivity to the present means that rankings are not solely determined by the 'tails' of the consumption stream. Sensitivity to the future means that there is no date after which consumption is irrelevant to the rankings. These axioms lead to the following criterion:

$$U = \alpha \int_0^\infty u(c(t)) \Delta(t) dt + (1 - \alpha) \lim_{t \to \infty} u(c(t)) \tag{7.4}$$

where $\Delta(t)$ is the utility discount function, and $0 < \alpha < 1$ is the weight placed on the integral part. Heal (2003) notes that the Chilchilnisky criterion has no solution under standard exponential discounting, where $\Delta(t) = \exp(-\delta t)$. It makes sense to initially maximize the integral part, before switching to maximizing the asymptotic path. This refuses to yield a solution, however, because it is always optimal to delay the switching point as this increases the integral part with no reduction in the asymptotic part. Interestingly, however, equation (7.4) does have a solution provided that the utility discount rate, δ, declines over time, asymptotically approaching zero.

In short, a declining utility discount rate is necessary for a solution satisfying Chichilnisky's axioms of sustainable development.

Li and Löfgren (2000) propose a similar model which examines a society of two individuals, a utilitarian and a conservationist. The implication of this model is similarly that the utility discount rate must decline along the optimal path.

Conclusions on declining discount rates
Incorporating uncertainty into social cost–benefit analysis leads to the conclusion that a declining social discount rate is necessary for efficient decision-making. Indeed, it was on this basis that the United Kingdom government has incorporated declining social discount rates in its most recent HM Treasury (2003) Green Book, which contains the official guidance on government project and policy appraisal. Pessimistic future projections and, to a lesser extent, the evidence from individual behaviour could further support that conclusion. Finally, the fact that declining discount rates also emerge from specifications of intergenerational equity employed by Chilchilnisky (1996, 1997) and Li and Löfgren (2000), suggests that they are an ideal way to navigate between the demands of intertemporal efficiency and the concerns of intergenerational equity.

5.   Alternatives to discounting
Although declining discount rates provide an appealing solution to the dual problems of intergenerational efficiency and equity, there are other possible solutions. Schelling (1995) proposes an alternative based around ignoring discount rates and specifying a richer utility function. Kopp and Portney (1999) and Page (2003) suggest using voting mechanisms. Finally, discounting reflects a consequentialist ethical position, so alternatives based upon deontological ethics are considered.

Schelling's utility function approach
Schelling (1995) argues that investments for people in the far-distant future should not be evaluated using the conventional discounted cash flow framework. Instead, such investments should be considered much like foreign aid. For instance, investment now to reduce future greenhouse gas emissions should not be viewed as saving, but rather as a transfer of consumption from ourselves to people living in the distant future, which is similar to making sacrifices now for the benefit of our contemporaries who are distant from us geographically or culturally. The only difference is that the transfer mechanism is no longer the 'leaky bucket' of Okun (1975), but rather an 'incubation bucket', where the gift multiplies in transit. Given that people are generally unwilling to make sacrifices for the benefit of richer

people distant in geography or culture, we should not expect such sacrifices for richer people distant in time.

In other words, the 'utility function approach', as Schelling (1995) calls it, would drop the use of a discount rate, and instead present policy makers with a menu of investments and a calculation of the utility increase in each world region (and time period) for each investment. This approach has the merit of insisting on transparency in the weights placed on consumption flows at each point in time and space, which is to be welcomed. However, debate would focus on the appropriate utility function to employ to value consumption increases in different regions at different times. Ultimately, in addition to reflecting marginal utilities at different points in time and space, the weights would probably also have to reflect the human tendency to discount for unfamiliarity along temporal, spatial and cultural dimensions.

Voting mechanisms

Many scholars have argued that although discounting is appropriate for short term policy evaluation, it is stretched to breaking point by complex long term challenges such as climate change. For instance, global climate policy is likely to have non-marginal effects on the economy, implying that conventional consumption discounting is inappropriate. Consumption discounting rests on the assumption that the project or policy being evaluated is a small perturbation on the business as usual path. If the project is non-marginal, then the consumption discounting 'short cut' is inapplicable, and a full welfare comparison of different paths is necessary instead.[14]

Of course, conducting a full welfare comparison involves a certain amount of complexity. Alternatives to the welfare economics approach include the use of mock referenda, proposed by Kopp and Portney (1999), where a random sample of the population would be presented with a detailed description of the likely effects – across time and space – of the policy being implemented or not. The description would include all relevant information, such as the full costs of the policy and even the likelihood of other countries taking relevant action. Respondents would then vote for or against the policy. By varying the estimate of the costs for different respondents, a willingness to pay locus for the policy would be determined.

Their approach has the appeal of valuing the future by asking citizens directly, rather than by examining their behaviour or by reference to particular moral judgements. Problems with this approach, as Kopp and Portney (1999) note, include the usual possible biases in stated preference surveys and the difficulty of providing adequate information for an appropriate decision on such a complex topic.

Page (2003) also proposes that voting should be considered as an alternative to discounted cash flow analysis for important long term public decisions. In contrast to cost–benefit analysis, with its emphasis on achieving efficiency, he notes that voting mechanisms (with one-person-one-vote) are more likely to produce fair outcomes.

One difficulty with both proposals is that the people affected by the policy – future human beings – remain disenfranchised, just as they are on current markets. Unlike Kopp and Portney, Page tackles this problem by proposing to extend voting rights hypothetically to unborn future generations. Under the (unrealistic) assumption that there will be an infinite number of future generations, he concludes that intergenerational voting amounts to an application of the von Weizsäcker (1965) overtaking criterion. This leads to a dictatorship of the future, so 'safeguards' protecting the interests of the present would be needed which, Page argues, would be easy to construct given the position of power of the present generation.

The challenge with this proposal is to make it operational. Without safeguards, the implication is that the present should impoverish itself for future generations. As such the safeguards would in fact constitute the crux of this proposal. Determining the appropriate safeguards amounts to asking how the interests of the present and the future should be balanced, and this appears to lead us back to where we started, or to employing a different ethical approach altogether.

Deontological approaches

Sen (1982) argues that the welfare economic framework is insufficiently robust to deal with questions of intergenerational equity because it fails to incorporate concepts of liberty, rights and entitlements as ends in themselves. He considers an episode of torture, where the person tortured (the 'heretic') is worse off and the torturer (the 'inquisitor') is better off after the torture. Further, suppose that although the inquisitor is better off, he is still worse off than the heretic. Then the torture is justified under a utilitarian or Rawlsian social welfare function. Sen (1982) contends that society may want to grant the heretic a right to personal liberty that cannot be violated merely to achieve a net gain in utility or an improvement for the worst-off individual. He adds that an analogy between pollution and torture is 'not absurd', and that perhaps the liberty of future generations is unacceptably compromised by the present generation's insouciance about pollution.

If the consequentialist foundations of cost–benefit analysis are deemed inadequate, discounted cash flow analysis must be rejected where it generates results that contravene the rights of future generations. Howarth (2003) lends support for this position, arguing that although cost–benefit analysis is useful to identify potential welfare improvements, it is trumped by the moral duty to ensure that opportunities are sustained from generation to generation. Page (1997) similarly argues that we have a duty – analogous to a constitutional requirement – to ensure that intergenerational equity is satisfied before efficiency is considered.

Pigou (1932) agreed that such duties existed, describing the government as the 'trustee for unborn generations'. But Schwartz (1978) and Parfit (1983) question whether the notion of a duty to posterity is well-defined, on the grounds that decisions today not only determine the welfare but also the identities of future humans. Every person born, whether wealthy or impoverished, should simply be grateful that, by our actions, we have chosen them from the set of potential persons. Howarth (2003) answers that, at a minimum, we owe well-defined duties to the newly born, thus creating duties for at least an expected lifetime.

Assuming a duty to posterity is conceptually possible, the final step is to specify the content of the duty. Howarth (2003) reviews several different formulations of the duty, which ultimately appear to amount to a duty to ensure either weak or strong sustainability. As such, deontological approaches comprise the claim that intergenerational equity is captured by a (well-defined) duty of sustainability to future generations, and that this duty trumps considerations of efficiency. While these approaches do not reject the use of discounting, they subjugate efficiency considerations to those of rights and/or equity. This is not inconsistent with the view expressed in section 2 above that cost–benefit analysis is a guide for decision-making rather than a substitute for judgement (Lind, 1982).

6. Conclusion

This chapter has explained why discounting occupies such an important and controversial place in long-term policy decisions. While intertemporal trade-offs will always be important, the developments reported in this chapter provide reason to hope that discounting may eventually become less controversial. Arguments for a zero social discount rate need not be taken seriously unless they are based upon extremely pessimistic future economic projections. Arguments for a zero utility discount rate are more plausible, but not necessarily convincing. Indeed, there is a good case for employing a positive, but very low, utility discount rate to reflect extinction risk.

Furthermore, the fact that declining social discount rates are necessary for efficiency reduces the degree of conflict between intergenerational equity and efficiency. Economists detest inefficiency, and it is surely only a matter of time before other governments adopt efficient (declining) social discount rates. If so, the discounting controversies of the future will concern the particular specification of economic uncertainty and the precise shape of the decline, rather than the particular (constant) discount rate.

Finally, even if declining discount rates reduce the tension between intergenerational equity and efficiency, they do not eliminate it. Discounting and cost–benefit analysis provide a useful guide to potential welfare improve-ments, but unless infallible mechanisms for intergenerational transfers become available, project-specific considerations of intergenerational equity will continue to be important. The ethical arguments, consequen-tialist and deontological, outlined in this chapter provide some guidance. Ultimately, however, the appropriate trade-off between equity and efficiency, intergenerationally or otherwise, raises fundamental issues in philosophy. Consensus is unlikely, if not impossible. At least the clarifica-tion that efficient discount rates should be declining reduces the domain of disagreement.

Notes

1. Recall that a change passes the Kaldor (1939) criterion if the gainers could compensate the losers, and the Hicks (1940) criterion if the losers could not pay the gainers to prevent the change. Compensation is not actually required.
2. The discrete time analogue of the discount function is the discount *factor*, given by: $D(t) = 1/(1+s)^t$.
3. Broome disagrees with Rawls, but on the grounds that Rawls confuses impartiality with generation neutrality.
4. Dasgupta and Heal (1979, pp. 267–8) provide an equivalent example. In an exhaustible resources model with zero discounting, whatever the current rate of extraction, it is always better to lower it.
5. Broom in fact asserts that 'the earth will not exist for ever', but this is not really the point. It is the existence of humanity – on earth or otherwise – that is important in an anthro-pocentric welfare function.
6. The technologies must be 'immediately productive', meaning that there are negative transfer costs to the future if the future is worse off than the present, and 'eventually pro-ductive', meaning that there exists a feasible and efficient path with constant utility. A one-sector increasing and concave production function, for instance, satisfies these two requirements.
7. As Dasgupta et al. (1999) point out, this type of constraint does not admit trade-offs between competing goals. Such constraints are therefore frowned upon by economists. If the goals are not competing, the shadow price of the constraint is zero; if they are competing the shadow price is positive.
8. Stern et al. (2006) accept this argument and apply a utility discount rate of 0.1 per cent to account for extinction risk.
9. Some of these proposals are considered in section 5.
10. Interestingly, evidence suggests that some animals do likewise. Green and Myerson (1996) and Mazur (1987) provide summaries of evidence on the behaviour of birds.
11. See, for instance, Thaler (1981), Cropper et al. (1994), Kirby (1997), Harris and Laibson (2001) and the reviews by Frederick et al. (2002) and Ainslie (1992).
12. Recent work on sin taxes by O'Donoghue and Rabin (2003) provides an example of this type of approach. See also Feldstein (1964), who asks whether the government should act in the best interests of the public, or do what the public wants.
13. The certainty-equivalent average discount rate is given by $s_c(t) = (1/D_c(t))^{1/t} - 1$, where $D_c(t)$ is the certainty-equivalent discount factor.
14. This is the approach adopted in Stern et al. (2006). Further background is in Hepburn (2006).

References

Ainslie, G. (1992), *Picoeconomics*, Cambridge: Cambridge University Press.

Arrow, K. (1999), 'Discounting, morality, and gaming', in P.R. Portney and J.P. Weyant (eds), *Discounting and Intergenerational Equity*, Washington, DC: Resources for the Future, pp. 13–21.

Asheim, G.B. and W. Buchholz (2003), 'The malleability of undiscounted utilitarianism as a criterion of intergenerational justice', *Economica*, **70**: 405–22.

Asheim, G.B., W. Buchholz and B. Tungodden (2001), 'Justifying sustainability', *Journal of Environmental Economics and Management*, **41**(3): 252–68.

Beckerman, W. and C. Hepburn (2007), 'Ethics of the discount rate in the *Stern Review on the Economics of Climate Change*', *World Economics*, **8**(1), forthcoming.

Broome, J. (1992), *Counting the Cost of Global Warming*, Cambridge: White Horse Press.

Broome, J. (1999), *Ethics out of Economics*, Cambridge: Cambridge University Press.

Chichilnisky, G. (1996), 'An axiomatic approach to sustainable development', *Social Choice and Welfare*, **13**: 231–57.

Chichilnisky, G. (1997), 'What is sustainable development?', *Land Economics*, **73**: 467–91.

Cropper, M.L., S.K. Aydede and P.R. Portney (1994), 'Preferences for life saving programs: how the public discounts time and age', *Journal of Risk and Uncertainty*, **8**: 243–65.

Dasgupta, P.S. and G.M. Heal (1979), *Economic Theory and Exhaustible Resources*, Cambridge: Cambridge University Press.

Dasgupta, P.S., K.-G. Mäler and S. Barrett (1999), 'Intergenerational equity, social discount rates and global warming', in P.R. Portney and J.P. Weyant (eds), *Discounting and Intergenerational Equity*, Washington, DC: Resources for the Future, pp. 51–78.

Drèze, J. and N. Stern (1990), 'Policy reform, shadow prices, and market prices', *Journal of Public Economics*, **42**(1): 1–45.

Feldstein, M.S. (1964), 'The social time preference discount rate in cost benefit analysis', *Economic Journal*, **74**(294): 360–79.

Frederick, S., G. Loewenstein and T. O'Donoghue (2002), 'Time discounting and time preference: a critical review', *Journal of Economic Literature*, **40**(2): 351–401.

Gollier, C. (2001), *The Economics of Risk and Time*, Cambridge, MA: MIT Press.

Gollier, C. (2002a), 'Time horizon and the discount rate', *Journal of Economic Theory*, **107**(2): 463–73.

Gollier, C. (2002b), 'Discounting an uncertain future', *Journal of Public Economics*, **85**: 149–66.

Green, L. and J. Myerson (1996), 'Exponential versus hyperbolic discounting of delayed outcomes: risk and waiting time', *American Zoologist*, **36**: 496–505.

Groom, B., C. Hepburn, P. Koundouri and D.W. Pearce (2005), 'Discounting the future: The long and short of it', *Environment and Resource Economics*, **31**(1): 445–93.

Groom, B., P. Koundouri, E. Panopoulou and T. Pantelidis (2006), 'Discounting the distant future: how much does model selection affect the certainly equivalent rate?', *Journal of Applied Econometrics* forthcoming.

Harris, C. and D. Laibson (2001), 'Dynamic choices of hyperbolic consumers', *Econometrica*, **69**(4): 935–57.

Harrod, R.F. (1948), *Towards a Dynamic Economics*, London: Macmillan.

Harsanyi, J.C. (1977), *Rational Behavior and Bargaining Equilibrium in Games and Social Situations*, Cambridge: Cambridge University Press.

Harvey, C.M. (1994), 'The reasonableness of non-constant discounting', *Journal of Public Economics*, **53**: 31–51.

Heal, G. (1998), *Valuing the Future: Economic Theory and Sustainability*, New York: Columbia University Press.

Heal, G.M. (2003), 'Intertemporal welfare economics and the environment', in K.-G. Mäler and J. Vincent (eds), *Handbook of Environmental Economics*, Amsterdam: North Holland.

Hepburn, C. (2003), 'Resource collapse and hyperbolic discounting', Oxford University Department of Economics, Discussion Paper 159.

Hepburn, C. (2006), 'Discounting climate change damages: working note for the Stern review', Oxford University, mimeo, October.

Hicks, J.R. (1940), 'The valuation of the social income', *Economica*, **7**: 105–24.

HM Treasury (2003), *The Green Book: Appraisal and Evaluation in Central Government*, London: HM Treasury.

Howarth, R.B. (2003), 'Discounting and sustainability: towards reconciliation', *International Journal of Sustainable Development*, **6**: 87–97.

Kaldor, N. (1939), 'Welfare propositions of economics and interpersonal comparisons of utility', *Economic Journal*, **49**: 549–52.

Kimball, M.S. (1990), 'Precautionary saving in the small and in the large', *Econometrica*, **58**: 53–73.

Kirby, K.N. (1997), 'Bidding on the future: evidence against normative discounting of delayed rewards', *Journal of Experimental Psychology*, **126**: 54–70.

Koopmans, T.C. (1960), 'Stationary ordinal utility and impatience', *Econometrica*, **28**(2): 287–309.

Koopmans, T.C. (1965), 'On the concept of optimal economic growth', *Pontificae Academiae Scientiarum Scripta Varia*, **28**: 225–300.

Kopp, R.J. and P.R. Portney (1999), 'Mock referenda for intergenerational discounting', in P.R. Portney and J.P. Weyant (eds), *Discounting and Intergenerational Equity*, Washington, DC: Resources for the Future, pp. 87–98.

Li, C.Z. and K.G. Löfgren (2000), 'Renewable resources and economic sustainability: a dynamic analysis with heterogeneous time preferences', *Journal of Environmental Economics and Management*, **40**: 236–50.

Lind, R.C. (1982), 'A primer on the major issues relating to the discount rate for evaluating national energy options', in R.C. Lind (ed.), *Discounting for Time and Risk in Energy Policy*, Washington, DC: Resources for the Future, pp. 21–94.

Lind, R.C. (1995), 'Intergenerational equity, discounting and the role of cost-benefit analysis in evaluating global climate policy', *Energy Policy*, **23**: 379–89.

Lind, R.C. (1999), 'Analysis for intergenerational decisionmaking', in P.R. Portney and J.P. Weyant (eds), *Discounting and Intergenerational Equity*, Washington, DC: Resources for the Future, pp. 173–80.

Mazur, J.E. (1987), 'An adjusting procedure for studying delayed reinforcement', in H. Rachlin (ed.), *Quantitative Analyses of Behavior: the Effect of Delay and of Intervening Events on Reinforcement Value*, Hillsdale, NJ: Lawrence Erlbaum Associates, pp. 55–73.

Newell, R. and W. Pizer (2003), 'Discounting the benefits of climate change mitigation: how much do uncertain rates increase valuations?', *Journal of Environmental Economics and Management*, **46**(1): 53–71.

O'Donoghue, T. and M. Rabin (2003), 'Studying optimal paternalism, illustrated by a model of sin taxes', *American Economic Review*, **93**: 186–91.

Okun, A. (1975), *Equality and Efficiency: The Big Trade-off*, Washington: The Brookings Institution.

Page, T. (1997), 'On the problem of achieving efficiency and equity intergenerationally', *Land Economics*, **73**(4): 580–96.

Page, T. (2003), 'Balancing efficiency and equity in long-run decision-making', *International Journal of Sustainable Development*, **6**: 70–86.

Parfit, D. (1983), 'Energy policy and the further future: the identity problem', in D. MacLean and P.G. Brown (eds), *Energy and the Future*, Totowa, NJ: Rowman and Littlefield.

Parfit, D. (1984), *Reasons and Persons'*, Oxford: Oxford University Press.

Pearce, D.W. (2003), 'The social cost of carbon and its policy implications', *Oxford Review of Economic Policy*, **19**(3): 362–84.

Pearce, D.W., A. Markandya and E.B. Barbier (1989), *Blueprint for a Green Economy*, London: Earthscan.

Pearce, D.W., B. Groom, C. Hepburn and C. Koundouri (2003), 'Valuing the future: Recent advances in social discounting', *World Economics*, **4**: 121–41.

Pigou, A.C. (1932), *The Economics of Welfare*, London: Macmillan, 4th edn (1st edn 1920).

Ramsey, F.P. (1928), 'A mathematical theory of saving', *Economic Journal*, **38**: 543–59.

Rawls, J. (1971), *A Theory of Justice*, Oxford: Oxford University Press.

Read, D. (2001), 'Is time-discounting hyperbolic or subadditive?', *Journal of Risk and Uncertainty*, **23**: 5–32.

Rubinstein, A. (2003), 'Is it "economics and psychology"?: The case of hyperbolic discounting', *International Economic Review*, **44**: 1207–16.

Scheffler, S. (1982), *The Rejection of Consequentialism'*, Oxford: Clarendon Press.

Schelling, T. (1995), 'Intergenerational discounting', *Energy Policy*, **23**: 395–401.

Schwartz, T. (1978), 'Obligations to posterity', in R.I. Sikora and B. Barry (eds), *Obligations to Future Generations*, Philadelphia: Temple University Press.

Sen, A.K. (1982), 'Approaches to the choice of discount rate for social benefit-cost analysis', in R.C. Lind (ed.), *Discounting for Time and Risk in Energy Policy*, Washington, DC: Resources for the Future, pp. 325–53.

Sidgwick, H. (1907), *The Methods of Ethics*, London: Macmillan, 7th edn.

Solow, R. (1974), 'The economics of resources of the resources of economics', *American Economic Review*, **64**(2): 1–14.

Sozou, P.D. (1998), 'On hyperbolic discounting and uncertain hazard rates', *Proceedings of the Royal Society of London (Series B)*, **265**: 2015–20.

Stern, N.H., S. Peters, V. Bakhshi, A. Bowen, C. Cameron, S. Catovsky, D. Crane, S. Cruickshank, S. Dietz, N. Edmonson, S.-L. Garbett, L. Hamid, G. Hoffman, D. Ingram, B. Jones, N. Patmore, H. Radcliffe, R. Sathiyarajah, M. Stock, C. Taylor, T. Vernon, H. Wanjie and D. Zenghelis (2006), *Stern Review. The Economics of Climate Change*, Cambridge: Cambridge University Press..

Strotz, R. (1956), 'Myopia and inconsistency in dynamic utility maximisation', *Review of Economic Studies*, **23**: 165–80.

Thaler, R.H. (1981), 'Some empirical evidence on dynamic inconsistency', *Economic Letters*, **8**: 201–07.

Tol, R.S.J. (1999), 'Time discounting and optimal control of climate change – an application of FUND', *Climatic Change*, **41**: 351–62.

Tol, R.S.J. (2005), 'The marginal damage costs of carbon dioxide emissions: an assessment of the uncertainties', *Energy Policy*, **33**: 2064–74.

von Weizsäcker, C.C. (1965), 'Existence of optimal programs of accumulation for an infinite horizon', *Review of Economic Studies*, **32**: 85–104.

Weitzman, M. (1994), 'On the "environmental" discount rate', *Journal of Environmental Economics and Management*, **26**: 200–209.

Weitzman, M. (1998), 'Why the far distant future should be discounted at its lowest possible rate', *Journal of Environmental Economics and Management*, **36**: 201–208.

Weitzman, M. (2001), 'Gamma discounting', *American Economic Review*, **91**(1): 261–71.

Yaari, M.E. (1965), 'Uncertain lifetime, life insurance, and the theory of the consumer', *Review of Economic Studies*, **32**(2): 137–50.

8 Population and sustainability
Geoffrey McNicoll

1. Introduction

Problems of sustainability can arise at almost any scale of human activity that draws on natural resources or environmental amenity. In some regions minuscule numbers of hunter-gatherers are thought to have hunted Pleistocene megafauna to extinction; complex pre-industrial societies have disappeared, unable to adapt to ecological changes – not least, evidence suggests, changes they themselves wrought (Burney and Flannery, 2005; Janssen and Scheffer, 2004). But modern economic development has brought with it sustainability problems of potentially far greater magnitude – a result not only of the technological capabilities at hand but of the demographic realities of much larger populations and an accelerated pace of change.

A simple picture of those modern realities is seen in Figure 8.1. It charts a staggered series of population expansions in major world regions since the beginning of the industrial era, attributable to lowered mortality resulting from nutritional improvements, the spread of medical and public health services, and advances in education and income. In each of the regions population growth slows and eventually halts as fertility also drops, completing the pattern known as the demographic transition. The population trajectories shown for the 21st century are forecasts, of course, but moderately secure ones, given improving economic conditions and absent major unforeseen calamities. Worldwide, the medium UN projections foresee world population increasing from its 2005 level of 6.5 billion to a peak of about 9 billion around 2075. Very low fertility, if it persists, will lead to actual declines in population size – an all but certain near-term prospect in Europe and a plausible prospect by mid-century in East Asia.

Historically, the increase in population over the course of a country's demographic transition was typically around three- to five-fold, with the pace of change seldom much above 1 per cent per year; in the transitions still underway the increases may end up more like ten-fold or even greater and growth rates have peaked well above 2 per cent per year. In both situations the size changes are accompanied by shifts in age composition – from populations in which half are aged below 20 years to ones with half over 50 – and in concentration, from predominantly rural to overwhelmingly urban.

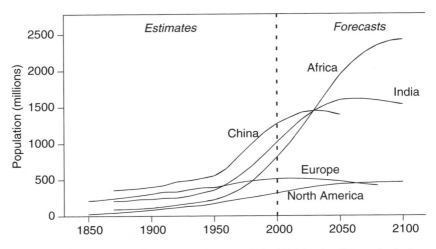

Source: Maddison (2003) and United Nations Population Division (medium projection).

*Figure 8.1   Population growth in selected countries and regions,
1850–2100 (estimates and forecasts)*

The lagged onset and uneven pace of the transitions across regions generate striking regional differences in population characteristics at any given time. Many population–environment and population–resource issues are thus geographically delimited; for others, however, the scale of environmental spillovers, migration flows and international trade may require an interregional or global perspective. This chapter reviews the implications of these various features of modern demographic change for sustainable development – gauged in terms of their effects both on the development process and on its outcomes (human well-being and environmental conditions).

The discussion need not be narrowed at the outset by specifying just what sustainable development sustains. The conventional polar choices are the wherewithal needed to assure the welfare of future generations – a generalized notion of capital – and that part of it that is not human-made – what is now usually termed natural capital. Conservation of the former, allowing substitutability among forms of capital, is weak sustainability, and conservation of the latter is strong sustainability. (See, for example, Chapters 3, 4 and 6 of this volume on these concepts and the problems associated with them.) I take as a premise, however, that sustainable development is a topic of interest and importance to the extent that substitutability of natural capital with other kinds of capital in the processes yielding human well-being is less than perfect.

2.   Population and resources in the theory of economic growth

For the classical economists, fixity of land was a self-evident resource constraint on the agrarian economies of their day. The course of economic growth was simply described. With expanding (man-made) capital and labour, an initial period of increasing returns (derived from scale economies and division of labour) gave way over time to diminishing returns, eventually yielding a stationary state. To Adam Smith and many others, that notional end point was a bleak prospect: profit rates dropped toward zero, population growth tailed off, and wages fell to subsistence levels. A very different, more hopeful, vision of stationarity, still in the classical tradition, was set out by J.S. Mill in a famous chapter of his *Principles of Political Economy* (1848): population and capital would again have ceased to grow, but earlier in the process and through individual or social choice rather than necessity. Productivity, however, could continue to increase. Gains in well-being would come also from the earlier halting of population growth, and consequent lower population–resource ratios. A similarly optimistic depiction of a future stationary state – with the 'economic problem' solved and human energies diverted to other pursuits – was later drawn by Keynes (1932).

As technological change increasingly came to be seen as the driver of economic growth, and as urban industrialization distanced most economic activity from the land, theorists of economic growth lost interest in natural resources. With a focus only on capital, labour and technology, and with constant rates of population growth, savings and technological change, the models yielded steady-state growth paths in which output expanded indefinitely along with capital and labour. More elaborate formulations distinguished among different sectors of the economy. In dualistic growth models, for example, a low-productivity, resource-based agricultural sector provided labour and investment to a dynamic but resource-free modern sector, which eventually dominated the economy (see also Chapter 14). With recognition of non-linearities associated with local increasing returns and other self-reinforcing mechanisms in the economy, there could be more than one equilibrium growth path, with the actual outcome sensitive to initial conditions or to perhaps fortuitous events along the way (see, for example, Becker et al., 1990; Foley, 2000).

Although it typically did not do so, this neoclassical modelling tradition was no less able than its classical forebears to take account of resource constraints. (See Lee, 1991, on this point.) Renewable resources would simply add another reproducible form of capital as a factor of production. Non-renewable resources, assuming they were not fully substitutable by other factors and not indefinitely extendable through technological advances, would be inconsistent with any steady-state outcome that entailed positive population growth. Requiring population growth, in the long term, to come to an end is not, of course, a radical demand to make of the theory.

While the actual role of population and resources in economic development is an empirical issue, a lot of the debate on the matter has been based on modelling exercises little more complicated than these. Much of it takes the form of window dressing, tracing out over time the implications of a priori, if often implicit, assumptions about that role. A single assumed functional form or relationship – an investment function, a scale effect, presence (or absence) of a resource constraint – after some initial period comes to dominate the model's behaviour. Familiar examples can be drawn from two models occupying polar positions in the resources debate of the 1970s and 1980s: the model underpinning Julian Simon's *The Ultimate Resource* (1981) and that supporting the Club of Rome's *Limits to Growth* scenarios (Meadows et al., 2004). In Simon's case, the existence of resource constraints on the economy is simply denied. Positive feedbacks from a larger population stimulate inventiveness, production and investment, and favour indefinite continuation of at least moderate population growth, leading both to economic prosperity and to vastly expanded numbers of people. (The discussion of the model's output ignores that latter expansion by being couched only in per capita values – see Simon, 1977.) For the Meadows team, negative feedback loops working through food production crises and adverse health effects of pollution lead to dramatic population collapses – made even sharper when lagged effects are introduced. Such models, heroically aggregated, are better seen as rhetorical devices, buttresses to qualitative argument, rather than serious efforts at simulation. Their output may point to parts of the formulation that it is important to get right, but it does not help in getting it right. While their authors were persuaded that they were accurately portraying the qualitative evidence about population and resources, as they respectively read it, the models in themselves merely dramatized their differences.

More focused models can achieve more, if at a lower level of ambition. The demonstration of 'trap' situations involving local environmental degradation is a case in point – see Dasgupta (1993). As an example, the PEDA (Population–Environment–Development–Agriculture) model developed by Lutz et al. (2002) describes the interactions among population growth, education, land degradation, agricultural production and food insecurity. It permits simulation of the vicious circle in which illiteracy, land degradation and hunger can perpetuate themselves, and points to the conditions required for that cycle to be broken. While still quite stylized, it is cast at a level that permits testing of its behaviour against actual experience, supporting its value for policy experiment.

3.   Optimal population trajectories

Since population change is in some measure a matter of social choice, it can notionally be regarded as a policy variable in a modelling exercise. Varying it over its feasible range then allows it to be optimized for a specified welfare function. The concept of an optimum population size for some designated territory – at which, other things equal, per capita economic well-being (or some other welfare criterion) was maximized – followed as a simple consequence of diminishing returns to labour. A small literature on the subject begins with Edwin Cannan in the late nineteenth century (see Robbins, 1927) and peters out with Alfred Sauvy (1952–54) in the mid-twentieth.

This is distinct, of course, from the investigation of human 'carrying capacity' – such as the question of how many people the earth can support. At a subsistence level of consumption some of these numbers are extravagant indeed – Cohen (1995) assembles many of them – but the maximization involved, although in a sense it is concerned with the issue of sustainability, has closer ties to the economics of animal husbandry than to human welfare. (The technological contingency of such calculations is well indicated by the estimate, due to Smil (1991) that fully one-third of the present human population would not exist were it not for the food derived from synthetic nitrogenous fertilizer – a product of the Haber-Bosch process for nitrogen fixation developed only in the early 20th century.) If it is assumed that present-day rich-country consumption patterns are to be replicated worldwide, carrying capacity plummets: for Pimentel et al. (1999) the earth's long-term sustainability calls for a population less than half its present level.

The question of optimal size also arises for the populations of cities. The urban 'built environment', after all, is the immediate environment of half the human population. Beyond some size, scale diseconomies deriving from pollution, congestion and other negative externalities affecting health or livability may eventually outweigh economies of agglomeration (see, for example, Mills and de Ferranti, 1971; Tolley, 1974). But other dimensions of the built environment, including its aesthetic qualities, would equally warrant attention in a welfare criterion. Singling out the relationship of population size to the subjective welfare of the average inhabitant, among all the other contributors to urban well-being, seems of limited value. Not surprisingly, like the broader topic of optimum population, this too has not proven a fruitful area of research.

What might be of more interest is the optimal *path* of population change over time. The age-structure dynamics of population growth are analogous to the vintage dynamics of capital stock, though with more limited scope for policy influence. For specified welfare criteria, optimal population trajectories can be derived to show how resource-constrained stationarity should be approached (see Pitchford, 1974; Arthur and McNicoll, 1977; Zimmerman, 1989).

Abstract theorizing of this kind is a means of playing with ideas rather than deriving actual policies. Nonetheless, just such an optimization exercise, part static and part dynamic, lay behind the introduction in 1979 of China's radical one-child-per-family policy. The background, recounted by Greenhalgh (2005), was the belated conviction on the part of China's leadership in the 1970s that the country's population growth was damaging its development prospects and the consequent recasting of the problem, as they saw it, from being one for social scientists and political ideologues to one for systems engineers and limits-to-growth theorists. The latter experts were at hand in the persons of a group of engineers and scientists (led by a missile engineer, Song Jian), who became the principals in promoting the new technocratic approach. They investigated both the static optimum – the target population size – and alternative trajectories that would lead toward it. On the former, as they summarized it: 'We have done studies based on likely economic development trends, nutritional requirements, freshwater resources, and environmental and ecological equilibrium, and we conclude that 700 million seems to be China's optimum population in the long run' (Song et al., 1985, p. 214). They then solved the optimal control problem of how fertility should evolve to reach the target population over the next century if the peak population was not to exceed 1.2 billion, there were pre-set constraints on the acceptable lower bound of fertility and upper bound of old-age dependency, and there was to be a smooth transition to the target population while minimizing the total person-years lived in excess of 700 million per year. The resulting policy called for fertility to be quickly brought down to its lower bound, held there for 50 years or so (yielding, after a time, negative population growth), then allowed to rise back to replacement level. While various minimum fertility levels were considered, one child per family was argued to be the best. The human costs of attaining such a trajectory (involving 'a lot of unpleasantness in the enforcement of the program' and the social and economic problems of the ensuing rapid population ageing were held to be unavoidable in making up for the 'dogged stubbornness of the 1950s' when Maoist pronatalism prevailed (Song et al., 1985, p. 267).

For both countries and cities, the specification of a welfare criterion to be optimized requires decisions on the ingredients of well-being and on how its distribution over the population and over time is to be valued. The inherent arbitrariness of that exercise explains the lack of enthusiasm for the concept of an optimum as a formal construct – though the idea may hold some political potency. Changes in trade and technology – either of which can transform economies of scale – erode what little meaning there is in a static optimum population for a country or locality. A fortiori, the inherent unpredictability of those trends, along with the many unknowns in future environmental change, vitiates the usefulness of more ambitious modelling over time – modelling that has necessarily to assume known dynamics.

4. Exhaustible resources and environmental services

Past worries about rapid or continued population growth have often been linked to the idea that a country – or the world – is running out of some supposedly critical natural resource (see Demeny, 1989 for an historical perspective). There have been numerous candidates for those resources in the past. Mostly, such claims have turned out to be greatly overstated; almost always they neglect or underplay the scope for societal adaptation through technological and social change. A classic case was the concern in 19th century Britain that its industry would be crippled as coal supplies were mined out (Jevons, 1865). The widely-publicized wagers between economist Julian Simon and biologist Paul Ehrlich on whether stocks of selected mineral resources were approaching exhaustion, to be signalled by steadily rising prices, were all won by Simon as prices fell over the specified period (Simon, 1996, pp. 35–6). A prominent historian of China titled a study of that country's environmental history: 'three thousand years of unsustainable development' (Elvin, 1993).

Moreover, even if we would accept, contra Simon in *The Ultimate Resource*, that stocks of many resources are indeed finite and exhaustible, it does not follow that the link to population should necessarily be of much consequence. For many resources, indeed, the pace of approach to exhaustion might be at most marginally affected by feasible changes in population growth. As put bluntly in a 1986 panel report from the US National Research Council,

> slower population growth delay[s] the time at which a particular stage of resource depletion is reached, [but] has no necessary or even probable effect on the number of people who will live under a particular stage of resource depletion. . . [T]he rate of population growth has no effect on the number of persons who are able to use a resource, although it does, of course, advance the date at which exhaustion occurs . . . Unless one is more concerned with the welfare of people born in the distant future than those born in the immediate future, there is little reason to be concerned about the rate at which population growth is depleting the stock of exhaustible resources (US National Research Council, 1986: 15).

But that judgement is altogether too dismissive of the problem as a whole. 'Mining' a resource that would be potentially renewable, such as a fishery or an aquifer, or degrading land through erosion or salination may be a population-related effect. (The resources allowed as potential sources of concern by the NRC panel were fuelwood, forest land, and fish; many would add access to fresh water.) These are cases where the concept of a sustainable yield is straightforward enough, but constructing and maintaining the institutional conditions required to safeguard that yield are demanding. Far from a society simply using up one resource and moving on to other things – presumably having replaced that part of its natural capital by other resources or by other forms of capital – the outcome may amount to an effectively irreversible loss in welfare.

The shift in focus here is from physical 'stuff', epitomized by stocks of minerals in the ground, to environmental services that humans draw upon. Environmental services encompass not only provision of food and fuel but also climate regulation, pollination, soil formation and retention, nutrient cycling, and much else. And they include direct environmental effects on well-being through recreation and aesthetic enjoyment. A massive study of time trends in the use of these services, judged against sustainable levels, is the Millennium Ecosystem Assessment. In its first report (2005), the Assessment finds that most of the services it examined are being degraded or drawn on at unsustainable rates. Dryland regions, covering two-fifths of the world's land surface and containing one-third of the world population, are especially affected.

But to what extent can this degradation be linked to population change rather than to economic growth or to the numerous factors that might lead to irresponsible patterns of consumption? People's numbers, but also their proclivities to consume and their exploitative abilities, can all be factors in degrading environmental services. In stylized form, this proposition is conveyed in the familiar Ehrlich–Holdren 'IPAT' identity: *Impact = Population × Affluence × Technology* (Ehrlich and Holdren, 1972). 'Impact' here indicates a persisting rather than transitory environmental effect. It is an external intrusion into an ecosystem which tends to reduce its capacity to provide environmental services. An example of an environmental impact is a country's carbon dioxide emissions, which degrade the environmental service provided by the atmosphere in regulating heat radiation from the earth's surface. The $P \times A \times T$ decomposition in that case would be population times per capita GDP times the 'carbon intensity' of the economy. At a given level of affluence and carbon intensity, emissions rise in proportion to population.

Interpreted as a causal relationship rather than as an identity, the $I = PAT$ equation is commonly used to emphasize the responsibility for environmental damage on the part, jointly, of population size, a high-consumption lifestyle, and environmentally-destructive technology, each amplifying the others. Implicitly, it asserts that these factors can together be seen as the main human causes of degradation. The categorization should not, of course, be taken for granted. In particular, social organizational and behavioural factors would often warrant separate scrutiny as causes of degradation rather than being subsumed within A and T.

If P, A and T were independent of each other, the multiplicative relationship would be equivalent to an additive relationship among growth rates. In the carbon case, the growth rate of emissions would equal the sum of the growth rates of the three components. However, P, A and T are not in fact independent of each other. For any defined population and environment, they are variables in a complex economic, demographic and socio-cultural system. Each also has major distributional dimensions and is a function of time. Consumption – or any other measure of human welfare – is an output of this system; environmental effects, both intended and unintended, are outputs as well. And even at the global level the system is not autonomous: it is influenced by 'natural' changes in the environment and by environmental feedbacks from human activity.

Because of the dependency among P, A and T, the Ehrlich–Holdren formula cannot resolve disputes on the relative contributions of factors responsible for environmental degradation. For this task, Preston (1994) has proposed looking at the variances of the growth rates of I, P, A and T over different regions or countries. Writing these as σ^2_P, and so on, the additive relationship among growth rates implies the following relationship among variances and covariances:

$$\sigma^2_I = \sigma^2_P + \sigma^2_A + \sigma^2_T + 2 \operatorname{cov}_{PA} + 2 \operatorname{cov}_{PT} + 2 \operatorname{cov}_{AT}$$

The covariance terms are the interaction effects. If each is relatively small in a given case, there is a simple decomposition of the impact variance into the variance imputed to each factor. Otherwise, the one or more significant interaction terms can be explicitly noted.

In Preston's analysis of carbon emission data for major world regions over 1980–90, used as an illustration, population growth makes a minor contribution to the total variance; the major contributors are the growth of A and T, with a substantial offsetting effect from the interaction of A and T. Given the 50 per cent or so increase in global population projected for this century, the future role of population growth in carbon emissions is nonetheless of some importance. Detailed studies of this relationship include Bongaarts (1992), Meyerson (1998), and O'Neill et al. (2001). Important too, of course, are the demographic consequences of any resulting climate change, such as those working through shifts in food production, disease patterns and sea levels.

Specification of a more general functional relationship, $I = f(P, A, T)$, permits calculation of impact elasticities with respect to the three factors, rather than implicitly assuming elasticities of 1. At the country level there is some evidence that the population elasticity is indeed close to 1 for carbon emissions but may be higher for some other pollutants (see Cole and Neumayer, 2004).

Complicating any estimation of population–environment relationships is the non-linearity of environmental systems. The Millennium Ecosystem Assessment, mentioned above, warns of an increasing likelihood of 'non-linear changes in ecosystems (including accelerating, abrupt, and potentially irreversible changes), with important consequences for human well-being' (2005, p. 11). Holling (1986) notes that ecosystems may be resilient under the pressure of human activity until a point is reached at which there is sharp discontinuous change. Kasperson et al. (1995) identify a series of thresholds in nature–society trajectories as human activity in a region intensifies beyond sustainability: first a threshold of impoverishment, then endangerment, and finally criticality – the stage at which human wealth and well-being in the region enter an irreparable decline. The working out of the process is detailed in particular settings: criticality is exemplified by the Aral Sea basin. More dramatic historical cases are described by Diamond (2005). Curtailing growth in human numbers may not be a sufficient change to deflect those outcomes, nor may it even be necessary in some circumstances (as discussed below), but population increase has usually been an exacerbating factor.

5.   Institutional mediation

Most important links between population and environmental services are institutionally contingent. Under some institutional arrangements – for example, a strong management regime, well-defined property rights, or effective community norms and sanctions – population growth in a region need not adversely affect the local environment. Access to a limited resource can be rationed or governed in some other way so that it is not overused. Or the institutional forms may be such that the population growth itself is prevented – by negative feedbacks halting natural increase (an apparent condition found often in hunter-gatherer societies) or by diverting the growth elsewhere, through migration. If this institutional mediation ultimately proves inadequate to the task, the limits on the environmental services being drawn on would be exceeded and degradation would ensue. This can happen well short of those limits if economic or political change undermines a management regime or erodes norms and sanctions. Excessive deforestation can often be traced to such institutional breakdowns (or to ill-considered efforts at institutional reform) rather than to population growth itself. In other cases, a resource may have been so abundant that no management or sanctions were needed: that is a setting where the familiar 'tragedy of the commons' may unfold as the number of claimants to the resource or their exploitative abilities increases (see Hardin, 1968).

An appreciable amount of literature now exists on these issues of institutional design, both theoretical and empirical, and ranging in scale from local common-pool resources such as irrigation water or community forests to the global environment (see, for example, Ostrom, 1990; Baden and Noonan, 1998). Small common-pool resource systems receive most attention: a favourite example is the experience of Swiss alpine villages, where social regulation limiting overgrazing has been maintained for many generations. Larger systems usually show less symmetry in participant involvement and participant stakes: benefits can be appropriated by favoured insiders, costs shed to outsiders. Judgement of sustainability in such cases may depend on where a system's boundaries are placed, and whether those cost-shedding options can be curtailed (see McNicoll, 2002).

Physical spillover effects of human activity beyond the location of that activity, such as downwind acid rain from industrial plants or downstream flooding caused by watershed destruction, present relatively straightforward technical problems for design of a governance regime. The greater difficulties are likely to be political. These can be formidable even within a country, a fortiori where the environmental effects involve degradation of a global commons. Population change here raises added complications. Thus, in negotiating a regulatory regime to limit global carbon emissions, anticipated population growth in a country can be treated either as a foreordained factor to be accommodated by the international community – occasioning a response analogous to political redistricting in a parliamentary democracy – or treated wholly as a domestic matter (an outcome of social policy) that should not affect assignment of emission quotas.

Adverse effects of human activity can also be transferred from one region to another through the normal economic relationships among societies, notably through trade. A poorer society may be more willing to incur environmental damage in return for economic gain, or be less able to prevent it. The concept of a community's 'ecological footprint' was developed to account for such displaced effects by translating them back into material terms, calculating the total area required to sustain each community's population and level of consumption (see Wackernagel and Rees, 1996, and, for criticism, Neumayer, 2003; see also Chapter 20). An implicit presumption of environmental autarky would disallow rich countries buying renewable resources from poor countries; notionally, if implausibly, they could maintain their consumption by somehow reducing their population.

6.   Population ageing and population decline

As noted earlier, the age composition of populations that emerge from the transition to low mortality and fertility are heavily weighted toward the elderly, and after transitional effects on the age distribution have worked themselves out, actual declines in population numbers are likely. For example, if fertility were to stay at the current European average of around 1.4 lifetime births per woman (0.65 births below the replacement level), each generation will be about one-third smaller than its predecessor. Change of that magnitude could not be offset by any politically feasible level of immigration.

After the ecological damage associated with industrialization it might be expected that the ending of the demographic transition would have positive effects on sustainability. There are fewer additional people, or even fewer people in total, and those there are will mostly live compactly in cities and have the milder and perhaps more environmentally-friendly consumption habits of the elderly. There may be scope for ecological recovery. In Europe, for instance, the evidence suggests a strong expansion in forested area is occurring as land drops out of use for cultivation and grazing (Waggoner and Ausubel, 2001). The so-called environmental Kuznets curve (see Chapter 15) – the posited inverted-U relationship between income and degradation – gives additional grounds for environmental optimism since post-transition societies are likely to be prosperous. But there are countervailing trends as well. Household size tends to diminish, for example, and small households, especially in sprawling suburbs, are less efficient energy users (see O'Neill and Chen, 2002). Moreover, ecosystem maintenance increasingly calls for active intervention rather than simply halting damage. Mere neglect does not necessarily yield restoration. Many human-transformed landscapes that have valued productive or amenity qualities similarly require continuing maintenance. Expectations of strengthened environmentalism around the world may not be borne out – preferences, after all, tend to adapt to realities – and even a strong environmental ethic is powerless in the face of irreversibilities.

Population decline, of course, can come about for reasons other than post-transition demographic maturity: from wars or civil violence and natural disasters, and (a potentially larger demographic threat) from epidemic disease (see Smil, 2005). These events too have implications for sustainability, at least locally. Their effect is magnified to the degree they do harm to the productive base of the economy (including its natural resource base) and to the social institutions that maintain the coherence of a society over time.

7. Conclusions and research directions

Much of the research that would shed light on demographic aspects of sustainability is best covered under the general heading of sustainable development. This is largely true for the long-run changes that constitute the demographic transition. To a considerable degree the transition is neither an autonomous process nor policy-led, but a by-product of economic and cultural change, and it is this latter that should be the research focus. For example, in studies of rainforest destruction – a standard illustration of adverse demographic-cum-development impact on the environment – a basic characteristic of the system is precisely its demographic openness. Demographic 'pressure' supposedly leads to land clearing for pioneer settlement, but a broader research perspective would investigate the economic incentives favouring that kind of settlement over, say, cityward migration (Brazil's rural population in 2005 was one-third smaller than its 1970 peak). As to policy influence, migration and fertility might be seen as potential candidates to be demographic control variables in a population–economy–environment system, but even if they technically lie within a government's policy space, aside from cross-border movement most governments have very limited if any direct purchase over them.

While there may thus be less content in population and sustainability than first appears, an important research agenda remains. A critical subject, signalled above, is the design of governing institutions for population–economy–environment systems, able to ensure sustainable resource use. Those institutions are of interest at a range of system levels – local, national and international – and are likely to entail intricate combinations of pricing and rationing systems and means of enforcement. At the local level, and possibly at other levels too, governing institutions might seek to include measures aiming at the social control of population growth.

A less elusive but similarly important research area concerns demographic effects on consumption. How resource- and energy-intensive will the consumption future be, given what we know about the course of population levels and composition? How do we assess substitutability in consumption – say, between 'real' and 'virtual' environmental amenity? And, well beyond the demographic dimension but still informed by it, are we, in confronting sustainability problems, dealing with time-limited effects of a population peaking later this century (with an additional 2–3 billion people added to the world total) but then dropping, allowing some measure of ecological recovery, or are we entering a new, destabilized environmental era in which sustainability in any but the weakest sense is continually out of reach?

References

Arthur, W. Brian and Geoffrey McNicoll (1977), 'Optimal growth with age dependence: a theory of population policy', *Review of Economic Studies*, **44**(1): 111–23.

Baden, John A. and Douglas S. Noonan (eds) (1998), *Managing the Commons*, 2nd edn, Bloomington, IN: Indiana University Press.

Becker, Gary S., Kevin M. Murphy and Robert Tamura (1990), 'Human capital, fertility, and economic growth', *Journal of Political Economy*, **98**: S12–S37.

Bongaarts, John (1992), 'Population growth and global warming', *Population and Development Review*, **18**: 299–319.

Burney, D.A. and T.F. Flannery (2005), 'Fifty millennia of catastrophic extinctions after human contact', *Trends in Ecology & Evolution*, **20**: 395–401.

Cohen, Joel (1995), *How Many People Can the Earth Support?*, New York: Norton.

Cole, Matthew A. and Eric Neumayer (2004), 'Examining the impact of demographic factors on air pollution', *Population and Environment*, **26**: 5–21.

Dasgupta, Partha (1993), *An Inquiry into Well-Being and Destitution*, Oxford: Clarendon Press.

Demeny, Paul (1989), 'Demography and the limits to growth', in Michael S. Teitelbaum and Jay M. Winter (eds), *Population and Resources in Western Intellectual Traditions*. Supplement to *Population and Development Review*, New York: Population Council.

Diamond, Jared (2005), *Collapse: How Societies Choose to Fail or Succeed*, New York: Penguin.

Ehrlich, Paul R. and John P. Holdren (1972), 'One-dimensional ecology', *Bulletin of the Atomic Scientists*, **28**(June): 16–27.

Elvin, Mark (1993), 'Three thousand years of unsustainable development: China's environment from archaic times to the present', *East Asian History*, (Canberra) No. 6.

Foley, Duncan K. (2000), 'Stabilization of human populations through economic increasing returns', *Economic Letters*, **68**: 309–17.

Greenhalgh, Susan (2005), 'Missile science, population science: the origins of China's one-child policy', *China Quarterly*, No. 182: 253–76.

Hardin, Garrett S. (1968), 'The tragedy of the commons', *Science*, **162**: 1243–48.

Holling, C.S. (1986), 'The resilience of terrestrial ecosystems: local surprise and global change', in William C. Clark and R.E. Munn (eds), *Sustainable Development of the Biosphere*, Cambridge: Cambridge University Press.

Janssen, Marco A. and Marten Scheffer (2004), 'Overexploitation of renewable resources by ancient societies and the role of sunk-cost effects', *Ecology and Society*, **9**(1): 6, www.ecologyandsociety.org/vol9/iss 1/art6/.

Jevons, W. Stanley (1865), *The Coal Question: An Enquiry Concerning the Progress of the Nation, and the Probable Exhaustion of Our Coal-mines*, London: Macmillan.

Kasperson, Jeanne X., Roger E. Kasperson and B.L. Turner II (eds) (1995), *Regions at Risk: Comparisons of Threatened Environments*, Tokyo: United Nations University Press.

Keynes, John Maynard (1932), 'Economic possibilities for our grandchildren', in J.M. Keynes, *Essays in Persuasion*, London: Macmillan.

Lee, Ronald D. (1991), 'Comment: the second tragedy of the commons', in Kingsley Davis and Mikhail S. Bernstam (eds), *Resources, Environment, and Population*, New York: Oxford University Press.

Lutz, Wolfgang, Alexia Prskawetz and Warren Sanderson (eds) (2002), *Population and Environment: Methods of Analysis*, Supplement to *Population and Development Review*, New York: Population Council.

Lutz, Wolfgang, et al. (2002), 'Population, natural resources, and food security: lessons from comparing full and reduced-form models', in W. Lutz, A. Prskawetz and W. Sanderson (eds) (2002), *Population and Environment: Methods of Analysis*, New York: Population Council.

Maddison, Angus (2003), *The World Economy: Historical Statistics*, Paris: Organisation for Economic Co-operation and Development.

McNicoll, Geoffrey (2002), 'Managing population–environment systems: problems of institutional design', in W. Lutz, A. Prskawetz and W. Sanderson (eds) (2002), *Population and Environment: Methods of Analysis*, New York: Population Council, pp. 144–64.

Meadows, Donella, Jorgen Randers and Dennis Meadows (2004), *The Limits to Growth: The 30-year Update*, White River Junction, VT: Chelsea Green.

Meyerson, Frederick A.B. (1998), 'Population, carbon emissions, and global warming: the forgotten relationship at Kyoto', *Population and Development Review*, **24**: 115–30.

Mill, John Stuart (1848), *Principles of Political Economy*, London: Parker.

Millennium Ecosystem Assessment (2005), *Ecosystems and Human Well-Being: Synthesis*, New York: Island Press.

Mills, Edwin S. and David M. de Ferranti (1971), 'Market choices and optimum city size', *American Economic Review*, **61**(Papers & Proceedings): 340–45.

Neumayer, Eric (2003), *Weak versus Strong Sustainability: Exploring the Limits of Two Opposing Paradigms*, 2nd edn, Cheltenham, UK and Northampton, MA, USA: Edward Elgar.

O'Neill, Brian C. and Belinda S. Chen (2002), 'Demographic determinants of household energy use in the United States', in W. Lutz, A. Prskawetz and W. Sanderson (eds) (2002), *Population and Environment: Methods of Analysis*, New York: Population Council, pp. 53–8.

O'Neill, Brian C., F. Landis MacKellar and Wolfgang Lutz (2001), *Population and Climate Change*, Cambridge: Cambridge University Press.

Ostrom, Elinor (1990), *Governing the Commons: The Evolution of Institutions for Collective Action*, Cambridge: Cambridge University Press.

Pimental, David, et al. (1999), 'Will limits of the Earth's resources control human numbers?', *Environment, Development and Sustainability*, **1**: 19–39.

Pitchford, J.D. (1974), *Population in Economic Growth*, New York: Elsevier.

Preston, Samuel H. (1994), *Population and Environment: From Rio to Cairo*, Liège: International Union for the Scientific Study of Population.

Robbins, Lionel (1927), 'The optimum theory of population', in T.E. Gregory and Hugh Dalton (eds), *London Essays in Economics in Honour of Edwin Cannan*, London: Routledge.

Sauvy, Alfred (1952–54), *Théorie Générale de la Population*, Paris: Presses Universitaires de France, 2 vols (translated as *General Theory of Population*, New York: Basic Books, 1969).

Simon, Julian L. (1977), *The Economics of Population Growth*, Princeton: Princeton University Press.

Simon, Julian S. (1981), 2nd edn 1996, *The Ultimate Resource*, Princeton: Princeton University Press.

Smil, Vaclav (1991), 'Population growth and nitrogen: an exploration of a critical existential link', *Population and Development Review*, **17**: 569–601.

Smil, Vaclav (2005), 'The next 50 years: fatal discontinuities', *Population and Development Review*, **31**: 201–36.

Song, Jian, Chi-Hsien Tuan and Jing-Yuan Yu (1985), *Population Control in China: Theory and Applications*, New York: Praeger.

Tolley, George S. (1974), 'The welfare economics of city bigness', *Journal of Urban Economics*, **1**: 324–45.

US National Research Council (1986), *Population Growth and Economic Development: Policy Questions*, Washington, DC: National Academy Press.

Wackenagel, Mathis and William E. Rees (1996), *Our Ecological Footprint: Reducing Human Impact on the Earth'*, Philadelphia: New Society Publishers.

Waggoner, Paul E. and Jesse H. Ausubel (2001), 'How much will feeding more and wealthier people encroach on forests?', *Population and Development Review*, **27**: 239–57.

Zimmermann, Klaus F. (ed.) (1989), *Economic Theory of Optimal Population*, Berlin: Springer-Verlag.

9 Technological lock-in and the role of innovation
Timothy J. Foxon

1. Sustainability and the need for technological innovation[1]

Despite increases in our understanding of the issues raised by the challenge of environmental, social and economic sustainability, movement has been frustratingly slow towards achieving levels of resource use and waste production that are within appropriate environmental limits and provide socially acceptable levels of economic prosperity and social justice.

As first described by Ehrlich and Holdren (1971), environmental impact (I) of a nation or region may be usefully decomposed into three factors: population (P), average consumption per capita, which depends on affluence (A), and environmental impact per unit of consumption, which depends on technology (T), in the equation (identity) $I = P \times A \times T$. Limiting growth in environmental impact and eventually reducing it to a level within the earth's ecological footprint (Chapter 20) will require progress on all three of these factors. Chapter 8 discussed issues relating to stabilizing population levels, and Chapter 16 addresses social and economic issues relating to moving towards sustainable patterns of consumption. This chapter discusses the challenge of technological innovation required to achieve radical reductions in average environmental impact per unit of consumption.

Section 2 argues that individual technologies, and their development, are best understood as part of wider technological and innovation systems. Section 3 examines how increasing returns to the adoption of technologies may give rise to 'lock-in' of incumbent technologies, preventing the adoption of potentially superior alternatives. Section 4 examines how similar types of increasing returns apply to institutional frameworks of social rules and constraints. Section 5 brings these two ideas together, arguing that technological systems co-evolve with institutional systems. This may give rise to lock-in of current techno-institutional systems, such as high carbon energy systems, creating barriers to the innovation and adoption of more sustainable systems. Section 6 examines the challenge for policy makers of promoting innovation for a transition to more sustainable socio-economic systems. Finally, Section 7 provides some conclusions and assesses the implications for future research and policy needs.

2. Understanding technological systems

The view that individual technologies, and the way they develop, are best understood as part of wider technological and innovation systems was significantly developed by studies in the late 1980s and early 1990s. In his seminal work on development of different electricity systems, Hughes (1983) showed the extent to which such large technical systems embody both technical and social factors. Similarly, Carlsson and Stankiewicz (1991) examined the 'dynamic knowledge and competence networks' making up technological systems. These approaches enable both stability and change in technological systems to be investigated within a common analytical framework. Related work examined the processes of innovation from a systems perspective. Rather than being categorized as a one-way, linear flow from R&D to new products, innovation is seen as a process of matching technical possibilities to market opportunities, involving multiple interactions and types of learning (Freeman and Soete, 1997). An *innovation system* may be defined as 'the elements and relationships which interact in the production, diffusion and use of new, and economically-useful, knowledge' (Lundvall, 1992). Early work focused on national systems of innovation, following the pioneering study of the Japanese economy by Freeman (1988). In a major multi-country study, Nelson (1993) and collaborators compared the national innovation systems of 15 countries, finding that the differences between them reflected different institutional arrangements, including: systems of university research and training and industrial R&D; financial institutions; management skills; public infrastructure; and national monetary, fiscal and trade policies. Innovation is the principal source of economic growth (Mokyr, 2002) and a key source of new employment opportunities and skills, as well as providing potential for realizing environmental benefits (see recent reviews by Kemp, 1997; Ruttan, 2001; Grubler et al., 2002 and Foxon, 2003).

The systems approach emphasizes the role of uncertainty and cognitive limits to firms' or individuals' ability to gather and process information for their decision-making, known as 'bounded rationality' (Simon, 1955; 1959). Innovation is necessarily characterized by uncertainty about future markets, technology potential and policy and regulatory environments, and so firms' expectations of the future have a crucial influence on their present decision-making. Expectations are often implicitly or explicitly shared between firms in the same industry, giving rise to trajectories of technological development which can resemble self-fulfilling prophecies (Dosi, 1982; MacKenzie, 1992).[2]

3. Technological lock-in

The view outlined above suggests that the development of technologies both influences and is influenced by the social, economic and cultural setting in which they develop (Rip and Kemp, 1998; Kemp, 2000). This leads to the idea that the successful innovation and take-up of a new technology depends on the path of its development – so-called 'path dependency' (David, 1985), including the particular characteristics of initial markets, the institutional and regulatory factors governing its introduction and the expectations of consumers. Of particular interest is the extent to which such factors favour incumbent technologies against newcomers. Arthur examined increasing returns to adoption, that is positive feedbacks which mean that the more a technology is adopted, the more likely it is to be further adopted. He argued that these can lead to 'lock-in' of incumbent technologies, preventing the take-up of potentially superior alternatives (Arthur, 1989).

Arthur (1994) identified four major classes of increasing returns: *scale economies*, *learning effects*, *adaptive expectations* and *network economies*, which all contribute to this positive feedback that favours existing technologies. The first of these, *scale economies*, occurs when unit costs decline with increasing output. For example, when a technology has large set-up or fixed costs because of indivisibilities, unit production costs decline as they are spread over increasing production volume. Thus, an existing technology often has significant 'sunk costs' from earlier investments, and so, if these are still yielding benefits, incentives to invest in alternative technologies to garner these benefits will be diminished. *Learning effects* act to improve products or reduce their cost as specialized skills and knowledge accumulate through production and market experience. This idea was first formulated as 'learning-by-doing' (Arrow, 1962), and learning curves have been empirically demonstrated for a number of technologies, showing unit costs declining with cumulative production (IEA, 2000). *Adaptive expectations* arise as increasing adoption reduces uncertainty and both users and producers become increasingly confident about quality, performance and longevity of the current technology. This means that there be may a lack of 'market pull' for alternatives. *Network* or *co-ordination effects* occur when advantages accrue to agents adopting the same technologies as others (see also Katz and Shapiro, 1985). This effect is clear, for example, in telecommunications technologies; for example the more that others have a mobile phone or fax machine, the more it is in your advantage to have one (which is compatible). Similarly, infrastructures develop based on the attributes of existing technologies, creating a barrier to the adoption of alternative technologies with different attributes.

Arthur (1989) showed that, in a simple model of two competing technologies, these effects can amplify small, essentially random, initial variations in market share, resulting in one technology achieving complete market dominance at the expense of the other – referred to as technological 'lock-in'.

He speculated that, once lock-in is achieved, this can prevent the take-up of potentially superior alternatives. David and others performed a series of historical studies, which showed the plausibility of arguments of path dependence and lock-in. The most well-known is the example of the QWERTY keyboard layout (David, 1985), which was originally designed to slow down typists to prevent the jamming of early mechanical typewriters, and has now achieved almost universal dominance, at the expense of arguably superior designs. Another example is the 'light water' nuclear reactor design, which was originally designed for submarine propulsion, but, following political pressure for rapid peaceful use of nuclear technology, was adopted for the first nuclear power stations and rapidly became the standard design in the US (Cowan, 1990). Specific historical examples of path dependence have been criticized, particularly QWERTY (Liebowitz and Margolis, 1995), as has the failure to explain how 'lock-in' is eventually broken, but the empirical evidence strongly supports the original theoretical argument (David, 1997).

4.   Institutional lock-in

As described in section 2, the systems approach emphasizes that individual technologies are not only supported by the wider technological system of which they are part, but also by the institutional framework of social rules and conventions that reinforces that technological system. To better understand the development of such frameworks, insights may be drawn from work in institutional economics, which is currently undergoing a renaissance (Schmid, 2004).

Institutions may be defined as any form of constraint that human beings devise to shape human interaction (Hodgson, 1988). These include formal constraints, such as legislation, economic rules and contracts, and informal constraints, such as social conventions and codes of behaviour. There has been much interest in the study of how institutions evolve over time, and how this creates drivers and barriers for social change, and influences economic performance. North (1990) argues that all the features identified by Arthur as creating increasing returns to the adoption of technologies can also be applied to institutions. New institutions often entail *high set-up* or *fixed costs*. There are significant *learning effects* for organizations that arise because of the opportunities provided by the institutional framework. There are *co-ordination effects*, directly via contracts with other organizations and indirectly by induced investment, and through the informal constraints generated. *Adaptive expectations* occur because increased prevalence of contracting based on a specific institutional framework reduces uncertainty about the continuation of that framework. In summary, North argues, 'the interdependent web of an institutional matrix produces massive increasing returns' (North, 1990, p. 95).

Building on this work, Pierson (2000) argues that political institutions are particularly prone to increasing returns, because of four factors: the central role of *collective action*; the *high density* of institutions; the possibilities for using political authority to enhance *asymmetries of power*; and the *complexity and opacity* of politics. Collective action follows from the fact that, in politics, the consequences of an individual or organization's actions are highly dependent on the actions of others. This means that institutions usually have high start-up costs and are subject to adaptive expectations. Furthermore, because formal institutions and public policies place extensive, legally binding constraints on behaviour, they are subject to learning, co-ordination and expectation effects, and so become difficult to change, once implemented. The allocation of political power to particular actors is also a source of positive feedback. When actors are in a position to impose rules on others, they may use this authority to generate changes in the rules (both formal institutions and public policies) so as to enhance their own power. Finally, the complexity of the goals of politics, as well as the loose and diffuse links between actions and outcomes, make politics inherently ambiguous and mistakes difficult to rectify. These four factors create path dependency and lock-in of particular political institutions, such as regulatory frameworks. This helps to explain significant features of institutional development: specific patterns of timing and sequence matter; a wide range of social outcomes may be possible; large consequences may result from relatively small or contingent events; particular courses of action, once introduced, can be almost impossible to reverse; and, consequently, political development is punctuated by critical moments or junctures that shape the basic contours of social life.

5.   Co-evolution of technological and institutional systems

The above ideas of systems thinking and increasing returns to both technologies and institutions may be combined, by analysing the process of co-evolution of technological and institutional systems (Unruh, 2000; Nelson and Sampat, 2001). As modern technological systems are deeply embedded in institutional structures, the above factors leading to institutional lock-in can interact with and reinforce the drivers of technological lock-in.

Unruh (2000, 2002) suggests that modern technological systems, such as the carbon-based energy system, have undergone a process of technological and institutional co-evolution, driven by path-dependent increasing returns to scale. He introduces the term 'techno-institutional complex' (TIC), composed of technological systems and the public and private institutions that govern their diffusion and use, and which become 'inter-linked, feeding off one another in a self-referential system' (Unruh, 2000, p. 825).

In particular, he describes how these techno-institutional complexes create persistent incentive structures that strongly influence system evolution and stability. Building on the work of Arthur (1989, 1994), he shows how the positive feedbacks of increasing returns both to technologies and to their supporting institutions can create rapid expansion in the early stages of development of technology systems. However, once a stable techno-institutional system is in place, it acquires a stability and resistance to change. In evolutionary language, the selection environment highly favours changes which represent only incremental changes to the current system, but strongly discourages radical changes which would fundamentally alter the system. Thus, a system which has benefited from a long period of increasing returns, such as the carbon-based energy system, may become 'locked-in', preventing the development and take-up of alternative technologies, such as low carbon, renewable energy sources. The work of Pierson (2000) on increasing returns to political institutions, discussed in Section 4, is particularly relevant here. Actors, such as those with large investments in current market-leading technologies, who benefit from the current institutional framework (including formal rules and public policies) will act to try to maintain that framework, thus contributing to the lock-in of the current technological system.

Unruh uses the general example of the electricity generation TIC, and we can apply his example to the particular case of the UK electricity system. In this case, institutional factors, driven by the desire to satisfy increasing electricity demand and a regulatory framework based on increasing competition and reducing unit prices to the consumer, fed back into the expansion of the technological system. In the UK, institutional change (liberalization of electricity markets) led to the so-called 'dash for gas' in the 1990s – a rapid expansion of power stations using gas turbines. These were smaller and quicker to build than coal or nuclear power stations, thus generating quicker profits in the newly-liberalized market. The availability of gas turbines was partly the result of this technology being transferred from the aerospace industry, where it had already benefited from a long period of investment (and state support) and increasing returns. This technological change reinforced the institutional drivers to meet increasing electricity demands by expanding generation capacity, rather than, for example, creating stronger incentives for energy efficiency measures. Such insights were employed in a recent study of current UK innovation systems for new and renewable energy technologies (ICEPT/E4Tech, 2003; Foxon et al., 2005a). There it was argued that institutional barriers are leading to systems failures preventing the successful innovation and take-up of a wider range of renewable technologies.

6.   Promoting innovation for a transition to more sustainable socio-economic systems

We conclude by examining some of the implications of this systems view of technological change and innovation for policy making aiming to promote a transition to more sustainable socio-economic systems. As we have argued, individual technologies are not only supported by the wider technological system of which they are part, but also the institutional framework of social rules and conventions that reinforces that technological system. This can lead to the lock-in of existing techno-institutional systems, such as the high carbon fossil-fuel based energy system. Of course, lock-in of systems does not last for ever, and analysis of examples of historical change may usefully increase understanding of how radical systems change occurs.

A useful framework for understanding how the wider technological system constrains the evolution of technologies is provided by the work on technological transitions by Kemp (1994) and Geels (2002). Kemp (1994) proposed three explanatory levels: *technological niches, socio-technical regimes* and *landscapes*. The basic idea is that each higher level has a greater degree of stability and resistance to change, due to interactions and linkages between the elements forming that configuration. Higher levels then impose constraints on the direction of change of lower levels, reinforcing *technological trajectories* (Dosi, 1982).

The idea of a *socio-technical regime* reflects the interaction between the actors and institutions involved in creating and reinforcing a particular technological system. As described by Rip and Kemp (1998): 'A socio-technical regime is the rule-set or grammar embedded in a complex of engineering practices; production process technologies; product characteristics, skills and procedures; ways of handling relevant artefacts and persons; ways of defining problems; all of them embedded in institutions and infrastructures.' This definition makes it clear that a regime consists in large part of the prevailing set of routines used by the actors in a particular area of technology.

A *landscape* represents the broader political, social and cultural values and institutions that form the deep structural relationships of a society. As such, landscapes are even more resistant to change than regimes.

In this picture of the innovation process, whereas the existing regime generates incremental innovation, radical innovations are generated in *niches*. As a regime will usually not be totally homogeneous, niches occur, providing spaces that are at least partially insulated from 'normal' market selection in the regime: for example, specialized sectors of the market or locations where a slightly different institutional rule-set applies. Such niches can act as 'incubation rooms' for radical novelties (Schot, 1998).

Niches provide locations for learning processes to occur, and space to build up the social networks that support innovations, such as supply chains and user–producer relationships. The idea of promoting shifts to more sustainable regimes through the deliberate creation and support of niches, so-called '*strategic niche management*' has been put forward by Kemp and colleagues (Kemp et al., 1998). This idea, that radical change comes from actors outside the current mainstream, echoes work on 'disruptive innovation' in the management literature (Utterback, 1994; Christensen, 1997). Based on a number of historical case studies, this argues that firms that are successful within an existing technological regime typically pursue only incremental innovation within this regime, responding to the perceived demands of their customers. They may then fail to recognize the potential of a new innovation to create new markets, which may grow and eventually replace those for the existing mainstream technology.

Geels (2002, 2005) examined a number of technological transitions, for example that from sailing ships to steamships, using the three-level *niche, regime, landscape* model introduced above (see also Elzen et al., 2004). He argued that novelties typically emerge in niches, which are embedded in, but partially isolated from, existing regimes and landscapes. For example, transatlantic passenger transport formed a key niche for the new steamship system. If these niches grow successfully, and their development is reinforced by changes happening more slowly at the regime level, then it is possible that a regime shift will occur. Geels argues that regime shifts, and ultimately *transitions* to new socio-technological landscapes, may occur through a process of niche-cumulation. In this case, radical innovations are used in a number of market niches, which gradually grow and coalesce to form a new regime.

Building on this work, Kemp and Rotmans (2005) proposed the concept of transition management. This combines the formation of a vision and strategic goals for the long-term development of a technology area, with transition paths towards these goals and steps forward, termed *experiments*, that seek to develop and grow niches for more sustainable technological alternatives. The transition approach was adopted in the Fourth Netherlands Environmental Policy Plan, and the Dutch Ministry of Economic Affairs (2004) is now applying it to innovation in energy policy. The Ministry argues that this involves a new form of concerted action between market and government, based on:

- *Relationships built on mutual trust*: Stakeholders want to be able to rely on a policy line not being changed unexpectedly once adopted, through commitment to the direction taken, the approach and the main roads formulated. The government places trust in market players by offering them 'experimentation space'.

- *Partnership*: Government, market and society are partners in the process of setting policy aims, creating opportunities and undertaking transition experiments, for example through ministries setting up 'one stop shops' for advice and problem solving.
- *Brokerage*: The government facilitates the building of networks and coalitions between actors in transition paths.
- *Leadership*: Stakeholders require the government to declare itself clearly in favour of a long-term agenda of sustainability and innovation that is set for a long time, and to tailor current policy to it.

In investigating some of the implications of the above ideas for policy making to promote more sustainable innovation, a couple of case studies (of UK low carbon energy innovation and of EC policy-making processes that support alternative energy sources in vehicles) and a review of similar policy analyses in Europe (Rennings et al., 2003) and the US (Alic et al., 2003) are worth considering. Foxon et al. (2005b) outlines five guiding principles for sustainable innovation policy based on the findings of these studies.

The first guiding principle argues for the development of a *sustainable innovation policy regime* that brings together appropriate strands of current innovation and environmental policy and regulatory regimes, and is situated between high-level aspirations (for example promoting sustainable development) and specific sectoral policy measures (for example a tax on non-recyclable materials in automobiles). This would require the creation of a *long-term, stable and consistent strategic framework* to promote a transition to more sustainable systems, seeking to apply the lessons that might be gleaned from experience with the Dutch Government's current 'Transition Approach'.

The second guiding principle proposes applying approaches based on *systems thinking and practice*, in order to engage with the complexity and systemic interactions of innovation systems and policy-making processes. This type of systems thinking can inform policy processes, through the concept of 'systems failures' as a rationale for public policy intervention (Edquist, 1994; 2001; Smith, 2000), and through the identification and use of 'techno-economic' and 'policy' windows of opportunity (Nill, 2003; 2004; Sartorius and Zundel, 2005). It also suggests the value of promoting a diversity of options to overcome lock-in of current systems, through the support of niches in which learning can occur, the development of a skills base, the creation of knowledge networks, and improved expectations of future market opportunities.

The third guiding principle advances the *procedural and institutional basis* for the delivery of sustainable innovation policy, while acknowledging the constraints of time pressure, risk-aversion and lack of reward for innovation faced by real policy processes. Here, government and industry play complementary roles in promoting sustainable innovation, with government setting public policy objectives informed by stakeholder consultation and rigorous analysis, and industry providing the technical knowledge, resources and entrepreneurial spirit to generate innovation. Public–private institutional structures, reflecting these complementary roles, could be directed at specific sectoral tasks for the implementation of sustainable innovation, and involve a targeted effort to stimulate and engage sustainable innovation 'incubators'.

The fourth guiding principle promotes the development of a *more integrated mix of policy processes, measures and instruments* that would cohere synergistically to promote sustainable innovation. Processes and criteria for improvement could include: applying sustainability indicators and sustainable innovation criteria; balancing benefits and costs of likely economic, environmental and social impacts; using a dedicated risk assessment tool; assessing instruments in terms of factors relevant to the innovation process; and applying growing knowledge about which instruments work well or poorly together, including in terms of overlapping, sequential implementation or replacement (Porter and van der Linde, 1995; Gunningham and Grabowsky, 1998; Makuch, 2003a; 2003b).

The fifth guiding principle is that *policy learning* should be embedded in the sustainable innovation policy process. This suggests the value of providing a highly responsive way to modulate the evolutionary paths of sustainable technological systems and to mitigate the unintended harmful consequences of policies. This would involve monitoring and evaluation of policy implementation, and the review of policy impacts on sustainable innovation systems.

7. Conclusions and ways forward

This chapter has reviewed issues relating to the role of technological change and innovation in moving societies towards greater sustainability. Though the importance of technologies in helping to provide sustainable solutions is often promoted by commentators from all parts of the political spectrum, policy measures to promote such innovation have frequently failed to recognize the complexity and systemic nature of innovation processes. As we have seen, increasing returns to adoption in both technological systems and in supporting institutional systems may lead to lock-in, creating barriers to the innovation and deployment of technological alternatives.

This emerging understanding of innovation systems and how past technological transitions have occurred could provide insight into approaches for promoting radical innovation for greater sustainability, for example, through the support of niches and a diversity of options. However, efforts to steer or modulate such a transition will also require significant institutional change in many countries. For example, the UK policy style has been based largely on centralized decision-making processes and heavy emphasis on the use of market-based instruments without addressing other institutional and knowledge factors relating to the creation of markets for new technologies. This contrasts with a policy style of more decentralized and public–private collaborative decision-making, which has enabled the Netherlands to become a leader in practising and learning how a technology transition for sustainability could be promoted. Further practical experience and analysis will be needed for the implementation of the above ideas and principles for promoting sustainable innovation to overcome technological and institutional lock-in.

Notes

1. I would like to thank Peter Pearson, Zen Makuch and Macarena Mata for fruitful interactions in the course of work leading up to this chapter and to the UK Economic and Social Research Council (ESRC)'s Sustainable Technologies Programme for support of that work.
2. The most well-known example is 'Moore's law', that the number of components on state-of-the-art microchips, and so the computing power, will double every 12–18 months. This widely known 'law', formulated in 1964, has held remarkably well from the first transistor in 1959 to present day chips, and may have guided the efforts of innovators in the semiconductor industry. See: www.intel.com/research/silicon/mooreslaw.htm

References

Alic, J., D. Mowery and E. Rubin (2003), *U.S. Technology and Innovation Policies: Lessons for Climate Change*, Pew Center on Global Climate Change.
Arrow, K. (1962), 'The economic implications of learning by doing', *Review of Economic Studies*, **29**: 155–73.
Arthur, W.B. (1989), 'Competing technologies, increasing returns, and lock-in by historical events', *The Economic Journal*, **99**: 116–31.
Arthur, W.B. (1994), *Increasing Returns and Path Dependence in the Economy*, Ann Arbor: University of Michigan Press.
Carlsson, B. and R. Stankiewicz (1991), 'On the nature, function and composition of technological systems', *Journal of Evolutionary Economics*, **1**: 93–118.
Christensen, C. (1997), *The Innovator's Dilemma: When New Technologies Cause Great Firms to Fail*, Boston: Harvard Business School Press.
Cowan, R. (1990), 'Nuclear power reactors: a study in technological lock-in', *Journal of Economic History*, **50**: 801–14.
David, P. (1985), 'Clio and the economics of QWERTY', *American Economic Review*, **75**: 332–7.
David, P. (1997), 'Path dependence and the quest for historical economics: One more chorus in the ballad of QWERTY', *Discussion Papers in Economic and Social History*, Number 20, University of Oxford.
Dosi, G. (1982), 'Technological paradigms and technological trajectories', *Research Policy*, **11**: 147–62.
Edquist, C. (1994), 'Technology policy: the interaction between governments and markets', in G. Aichholzer and G. Schienstock (eds), *Technology Policy: Towards an Integration of Social and Ecological Concerns*, Berlin: Walter de Gruyter.
Edquist, C. (2001), 'Innovation policy – a systemic approach', in D. Archibugi and B-A. Lundvall (eds), *The Globalizing Learning Economy*, Oxford: Oxford University Press.

Ehrlich, P. and J. Holdren (1971), 'Impact of population growth', *Science*, **171**: 1212–17.

Elzen, B., F. Geels and K. Green (eds) (2004), *System Innovation and the Transition to Sustainability: Theory, Evidence and Policy*, Cheltenham, UK and Northampton, MA, USA: Edward Elgar.

Foxon, T.J. (2003), *Inducing Innovation for a Low-carbon Future: Drivers, Barriers, and Policies*, London: The Carbon Trust, also available at www.thecarbontrust.co.uk/Publications/publicationdetail.htm?productid=CT-2003-07.

Foxon, T.J. and R. Kemp (2007), 'Innovation impacts of environmental policies', in D. Marinova, D. Annandale and J. Phillimore (eds), *International Handbook on Environment and Technology Management*, Cheltenham, UK and Northampton, MA, USA: Edward Elgar, pp. 119–39.

Foxon, T.J., R. Gross, A. Chase, J. Howes, A. Arnall and D. Anderson (2005a), 'The UK innovation systems for new and renewable energy technologies', *Energy Policy*, **33**(16): 2123–37.

Foxon, T.J., P. Pearson, Z. Makuch and M. Mata (2005b), 'Transforming policy processes to promote sustainable innovation: some guiding principles', *Report for policy-makers*, March 2005, Imperial College London, available at www.sustainabletechnologies.ac.uk/PDF/project%20reports/SI_policy_guidance_final_version.pdf.

Freeman, C. (1988), 'Japan: a new national system of innovation?', in G. Dosi, C. Freeman, R. Nelson, G. Silverberg and L. Soete (1988), *Technical Change and Economic Theory*, London: Pinter Publishers.

Freeman, C. and L. Soete (1997), *The Economics of Industrial Innovation*, 3rd edn, London: Pinter.

Geels, F. (2002), 'Technological transitions as evolutionary reconfiguration processes: a multi-level perspective and a case-study', *Research Policy*, **31**: 1257–74.

Geels, F. (2005), *Technological Transitions and System Innovations: A Co-evolutionary and Socio-Technical Analysis*, Cheltenham, UK and Northampton, MA, USA: Edward Elgar.

Grubler, A., N. Nakicenovic and W.D. Nordhaus (2002), *Technological Change and the Environment*, RFF Press, Resources for the Future, Washington DC and International Institute for Applied Systems Analysis (IIASA), Laxenburg, Vienna.

Gunningham, N. and P. Grabosky (1998), *Smart Regulation. Designing Environmental Policy*, Oxford: Clarendon Press.

Hodgson, G. (1988), *Economics and Institutions*, Cambridge: Polity Press.

Hughes, T. (1983), *Networks of Power*, Baltimore: Johns Hopkins University Press.

ICEPT & E4Tech (2003), 'The UK innovation systems for new and renewable energy technologies', Report for UK DTI, June 2003, www.dti.gov.uk/files/file22069.pdf.

International Energy Agency (IEA) (2000), *Experience Curves for Energy Technology Policy*, Paris: OECD.

Katz, M. and C. Shapiro (1985), 'Network externalities, competition and compatibility', *American Economic Review*, **75**(3): 424–40.

Kemp, R. (1994), 'Technology and the transition to environmental sustainability: the problem of technological regime shifts', *Futures*, **26**: 1023–46.

Kemp, R. (1997), *Environmental Policy and Technical Change: A Comparison of the Technological Impact of Policy Instruments*, Cheltenham, UK and Northampton, MA, USA: Edward Elgar.

Kemp, R. (2000), 'Technology and environmental policy – innovation effects of past policies and suggestions for improvement', *Paper for OECD Workshop on Innovation and Environment*, 19 June, Paris.

Kemp, R. and J. Rotmans (2005), 'The management of the co-evolution of technical, environmental and social systems', in Matthias Weber and Jens Hemmelskamp (eds), *Towards Environmental Innovation Systems*, Berlin: Springer Verlag.

Kemp, R., J.W. Schot and R. Hoogma (1998), 'Regime shifts to sustainability through processes of niche formation: the approach of strategic niche management', *Technology Analysis and Strategic Management*, **10**: 175–96.

Liebowitz, S.J. and S.E. Margolis (1995), 'Path dependence, lock in, and history', *Journal of Law, Economics and Organisation*, **11**: 205–26.

Lundvall, B-A. (ed.) (1992), *National Systems of Innovation: Towards a Theory of Innovation and Interactive Learning*, London: Pinter Publishers.

MacKenzie, D. (1992), 'Economic and sociological explanations of technological change', in R. Coombs, P. Saviotti and V. Walsh (eds), *Technological Change and Company Strategies: Economic and Sociological Perspectives*, Academic Press, (re-printed in D. MacKenzie (1996), *Knowing Machines: Essays on Technical Change*, Cambridge, Mass: MIT Press).

Makuch, Z. (2003a), 'Smart regulation and the revised batteries directive: the future of voluntary agreements', *European Environmental Law Review*, August/September, **12**(8/9): 225–56.

Makuch, Z. (2003b), 'Smart regulation and the revised batteries directive: legislated taxation systems and collection schemes', *European Environmental Law Review*, **12**(10): 257–88.

Ministry of Economic Affairs (The Netherlands) (2004), 'Innovation in Energy Policy – energy transition: state of affairs and way ahead', available at www.energietransitie.nl.

Mokyr, J. (2002), 'Innovation in an historical perspective: tales of technology and evolution', in B. Steil, D. Victor and R. Nelson (eds), *Technological Innovation and Economic Performance*, Princeton: Princeton Univeristy Press.

Nelson, R. (1993), *National Innovation Systems: A comparative analysis*, New York: Oxford University Press.

Nelson, R. and B. Sampat (2001), 'Making sense of institutions as a factor shaping economic performance', *Journal of Economic Behaviour & Organization*, **44**: 31–54.

Nill, J. (2003), 'Windows of sustainability opportunities – determinants of techno-economic time windows and conditions under which environmental innovation policy can utilise them', *Paper for the DRUID PhD Winter 2003 Conference*, Aalborg, Denmark, January.

Nill, J. (2004), 'Time strategies of transitions and the transformed role of subsidies as environmental innovation policy instrument', in K. Jacob, M. Binder and A. Wieczorek (eds), *Proceedings of the 2003 Berlin Conference on the Human Dimensions of Global Environmental Change*, Environmental Policy Research Centre: Berlin, pp. 295–307, www.fu-berlin.de/ffu/akumwelt/bc2003/proceedings/295%20-%20307%20nill.pdf.

North, D.C. (1990), *Institutions, Institutional Change and Economic Performance*, Cambridge: Cambridge University Press.

Pierson, P. (2000), 'Increasing returns, path dependence, and the study of politics', *American Political Science Review*, **94**(2): 251–67.

Porter, M. and C. van der Linde (1995), 'Green and competitive: ending the stalemate', *Harvard Business Review*, **73**(5): 120–34.

Rennings, K., R. Kemp, M. Bartolomeo, J. Hemmelskamp and D. Hitchens (2003), *Blueprints for an Integration of Science, Technology and Environmental Policy (BLUEPRINT)*, Final Report of 5th Framework Strata project, available at www.insme.info/documenti/blueprint.pdf.

Rip, A. and R. Kemp (1998), 'Technological change', in S. Rayner and E.L. Malone (eds), *Human Choices and Climate Change, Vol. 2*, Columbus, Ohio: Battelle Press.

Ruttan, V.W. (2001), *Technology, Growth and Development: An Induced Innovation, Perspective*, New York: Oxford University Press.

Sartorius, C. and S. Zundel (eds) (2005), *Time Strategies, Innovation and Environmental Policy*, Cheltenham, UK and Northampton, MA, USA: Edward Elgar.

Schmid, A. (2004), *Conflict and Cooperation: Institutional and Behavioral Economics*, Oxford: Blackwell Publishing.

Schot, J. (1998), 'The usefulness of evolutionary models for explaining innovation: the case of the Netherlands in the nineteenth century', *History of Technology*, **14**: 173–200.

Simon, H.A. (1955), 'A behavioral model of rational choice', *Quarterly Journal of Economics*, **69**: 1–18.

Simon, H.A. (1959), 'Theories of decision making in economics', *American Economic Review*, **49**: 258–83.

Smith, K. (2000), 'Innovation as a systemic phenomenon: Rethinking the role of policy', *Enterprise & Innovation Management Studies*, **1**(1): 73–102.

Unruh, G.C. (2000), 'Understanding carbon lock in', *Energy Policy*, **28**: 817–30.

Unruh, G.C. (2002), 'Escaping carbon lock in', *Energy Policy*, **30**: 317–25.

Utterback, J.M. (1994), *Mastering the Dynamics of Innovation: How Companies can Seize Opportunities in the Face of Technological Change*, Boston: Harvard Business School Press.

PART III

INTERGENERATIONAL EQUITY AND THE SOCIAL DIMENSION

10 Distribution, sustainability and environmental policy
Geoffrey Heal and Bengt Kriström

1. Introduction[1]

The purpose of environmental policy is to change consumption and production patterns in ways that enhance welfare, broadly interpreted. Policy change will, inevitably, create 'winners' and 'losers' among the economy's households and firms. Indeed, the daily drama of environmental policy typically involves making hard choices rather than implementing 'win–win' policies. In any realistic setting environmental policy imposes *both* gains and losses. How to weigh together such gains and losses in practice remains a subtle and difficult issue that has been handled rather cavalierly in the modern environmental economics literature. Or so we will argue.

Nevertheless, interest in distributional issues is re-appearing in our field for several reasons. A direct reason for being concerned with environmental policy and distribution is that an understanding of distributional impacts allows the shaping of policy packages that are more likely to be accepted by the public. Policy makers may also be more likely to accept, for example, incentive-based instruments if distributional issues are given serious attention. Hourcade (2001, p. 1) discusses the practical difficulties of implementing the Kyoto protocol, observing that

> finishing the 'Kyoto business' reveals additional fundamental difficulties stemming from the fact that the 'cap and trade' approach was too often interpreted as an 'open sesame' solution. This would be the case if the world was an homogenous 'tabula rasa' as in the simple models for first year economics students. But it is increasingly clear that the real world is full of complexities in the form of sectoral heterogeneities and country specifics.

Thus, if we shed light on how environmental policy maps into consequences for different households, firms, sectors, countries and even different generations, we obtain a richer basis for making decisions.

But perhaps the most pertinent reasons for an economist to give more attention to equity issues are to be found at the conceptual level. Economists have routinely relied on the possibility of separating efficiency and equity. This separation rests on assumptions that are likely to be violated when market failures such as externalities, information asymmetries and

155

public goods enter the analysis. McGuire and Aaron (1969) argued that the separation is often not possible when dealing with publicly funded public goods. Stiglitz's (1995) analysis of information failures and Brown and Heal's (1979) paper on increasing returns to scale are contributions with the same basic message; the separation between efficiency and equity rests on assumptions that need to be scrutinized. An important lesson from modern economic theory on market failures is that we really need to study efficiency and equity together.

When the separation theorem does not hold, *who* wins and *who* loses from a certain policy change becomes important, if not critical, in applied welfare analysis. The Kaldor–Hicks criterion, widely used in cost–benefit analysis, is based on sums of benefits and costs. A positive net sum of benefits and costs suggests that potential compensation is possible and that the change makes the total cake bigger. In a sense this criterion holds the essence of the separation idea; the cake is made larger and compensations potentially exist to take care of any distributional problem. We will discuss this idea in more detail below.

There are also a number of interesting other developments in economics and econometrics that highlight the need for careful scrutiny of equity issues. For example, endogenous growth theory sheds light on why economic growth may depend on the distribution of income under certain market failures, see for example Perotti (1996). Because there are complex connections between sustainability and economic growth, a scrutiny of distributional issues is not without interest for environmental economists. An extension of recent work on the environment–growth nexus adds the distribution of power; are environmental problems less severe in more equal and more democratic countries? See for example Boyce (2002) for a summary of this work.

Furthermore, in the literature on assessing the benefits and costs of public programs, distributional information has been given a more prominent place. Carneiro, Hansen and Heckman (2002, p. 1) observe that 'modern welfare economics emphasizes the importance of accounting for the impact of public policy on distribution of outcomes'.

There may well be other reasons to explain why distributional issues are now returning to the frontlines of research in environmental economics (and in other areas of economics as well, see for example Atkinson and Bourguignon, 1998). Suffice it to note here that a recent OECD volume edited by Serret and Johnstone (2006) contains a useful summary of recent relevant work. To be sure, there is a very substantial amount of literature on environmental equity, involving for example siting issues, but because this literature is mainly outside economics we shall sidestep it here (see Chapter 11).

If we accept the position that it is of interest to study equity per se in environmental economics, the natural next step is to ask what economics has to offer in this regard. While economics provides a crisp and useful working definition of an efficient environmental policy, it cannot claim to offer a final resolution to just what a 'fair' environmental policy entails. Rather, it offers a structured way of thinking about distributional issues and suggests ways of disentangling them empirically. Our goal, as well as our space here, is limited and we shall be content with beginning a discussion of a conceptual framework for thinking about sustainability and distribution.[2] We will also try to summarize some salient insights from the empirical literature.

Section 2 discusses the intergenerational dimension of the problem in terms of sustainable welfare measurement. We then turn to the intragenerational issues in section 3. We use a three-layer perspective (individual agent, individual market, sector/general equilibrium). Section 4 gives a brief overview of empirics. Section 5 concludes.

2. Inter-generational equity

The current literature on dynamic welfare measurement is mainly based on representative agent models, to permit sharp focus on the intergenerational issues. It also provides a useful starting point for pinning down the sustainability concept.[3] If we want to shed empirical light on distributional issues in an intertemporal world, the question is: what should we measure? The answer to this question is not independent of social objectives; what should we maximize? In turn, this boils down to pinning down a particular view about how resources should be distributed among different generations. Mostly, the results have been obtained within a utilitarian framework, where a weighted sum of utilities is maximized.

A key concept is the state valuation function which measures the present value of all future welfare on an optimal path. We can think of this as a kind of generalized (but not observable) measure of wealth. It provides a natural candidate for a sustainability index; if the sum of welfare is nondecreasing over time on an efficient but not necessarily optimal path, development can be defined as sustainable.

One important forerunner to this literature was Samuelson (1961), who suggested that wealth-like measures were more useful than income measures, in assessing the (long-run) prosperity of the economy. As is well-known the discussion about the merits of wealth as a measure of prosperity dates back to contributions by Fisher, Lindahl and Hicks.

There are two alternative measures of wealth, the value of capital stocks at shadow prices and the present value of all future consumption. Samuelson (1961) discussed the latter but found no way of operationalizing this idea. Recently, Heal and Kriström (2005a) showed that this wealth measure is closely linked to the sum of welfare and its change over time. Furthermore, the change of the sum of all future utilities over time can be measured by (comprehensive) net investment. This is the genuine savings concept that the World Bank has promoted over the last years (see Chapters 3 and 18 for more discussion). It is impossible here to go into any detail about the properties of these measures, let alone the underlying assumptions. Asheim (forthcoming) provides a detailed taxonomy of assumptions and results, to which the interested reader is referred for a concise summary. Heal and Kriström (2005b) presents a literature review.

In short, by looking at comprehensive measures of how our capital stocks are changing over time, we obtain potentially useful information about the long-run prosperity of the economy and its sustainability. Such measures shed some light on intergenerational equity and tell us something about whether or not we are currently 'over-using' our resource base. At present, empirical studies have mostly focused on aggregate data and therefore only address the question of whether the economy as a whole is 'over-using' its resource base. We next add the intragenerational dimension of the problem.

3. Intra-generational equity

Because, as noted, the literature on dynamic welfare measurement is primarily based on the representative agent framework it has little to say about intragenerational distribution. One way of extending the standard Ramsey model is to introduce a social welfare function, as in Aronsson and Löfgren (1999). If social welfare is optimally distributed within each generation at each point in time, we are back to the standard results of the representative agent model. The reason is that society is indifferent to a small redistribution of individual utilities in the vicinity of the social optimum.

Whether a policy is regressive or progressive, affects a certain ethnic group disproportionally or hampers children in other ways than adults, is of little interest in an idealized society at the global optimum. Costless transfers are, in a sense, available, so that 'winners' can compensate 'losers' across and within generations. Loosely speaking, this is why an increase of a comprehensive income measure, such as 'green NNP', may be a sign-preserving measure of social welfare change, even when taking distributional issues into account.

However, Aronsson and Löfgren (1999) shows that if the economy is far away from the social welfare optimum, 'green NNP' is not a sign-preserving measure of welfare. From the static case we know that a policy is welfare-improving if the weighted sum of compensating (equivalent) variation is positive, see for example Johansson (1993). The weights are social weights indicating the relative social value of giving one unit of welfare to a particular household or household group. The Kaldor–Hicks compensation criteria provide sign-preserving measures of social welfare only when the weights are assumed to be equal or, in other words, when income is distributed optimally. An excellent account of the debate around social weights in cost–benefit analysis and the connection to the Kaldor–Hicks criterion can be found in Persky (2001).

The upshot of all this is that it is useful to have a framework within which we can shed light on the impacts of environmental policy at a detailed level. We describe such a framework in what follows.

We begin by examining impacts of environmental policy at the household/firm level. We then examine how a subset of households and firms interact in one particular market and proceed to analyse the interaction of a subset of markets in a given sector. Finally, we end at the level of the economy, in which all markets interact. This framework, developed in more detail in Kriström (2006) and followed closely below, focuses mostly on an increasingly complex interaction between markets and agents. We shall end by sketching one possible way of including connections between ecological and economic systems in a dynamic general equilibrium setting.

The individual household and firm

We begin with the household and first look at costs and very briefly comment on the benefits of environmental policy. We focus on environmental policy, even though it is clear that the distributional impacts of natural resources policy may be very important. A useful framework for analysing the distributional impacts of resource policy is developed in Rose et al. (1998).

To a first-order approximation, one could define the cost of, for example, an environmental tax by looking at the price change only; one multiplies the gross price change with the current consumption level or with the post-change level. This first is an upper bound, because households invariably are price-responsive and cut their consumption. A lower bound on the cost can be obtained by taking the consumption level after adjustment and multiplying this with the price change. This is an underestimate of the true economic cost, because it assumes that the household attaches no value to the consumption that gets lost in the adjustment. The upper and lower bound calculated in the way suggested will always bound the true economic cost, which is the loss in consumer surplus.

To fix ideas, consider the many ways in which a household may be affected by changes of aspiration levels in environmental policy.

- *The price of a 'directly linked' good is affected.* For example, a carbon tax will raise the price of fossil fuels. Thus, transportation and heating costs are directly affected. These will, in turn, vary across households in several dimensions, including preferences, income, the prices of other goods, regionally and so on.

- *Prices of other goods change.* The household will also be affected as the relative prices of other goods are affected, following market adjustments.
- *Income from work.* Increased stringency of environmental policy may lead to significant losses of income, at least in the short-run, as some firms are shut down.
- *Other income may be affected.* Because households are owners of all firms, profits affect household income. In addition, income from certain natural assets may also be affected by natural resource policies, for example changes in forestry laws or zoning restrictions.
- *Households may be compensated.* Household net income depends on the structure of the prevailing tax system. Revenues from environmental taxes and permit auctions must, in one way or another, be returned to the economy. Several options have been scrutinized, for example reduced payroll taxes, reduced VAT and lump-sum returns. Each choice maps into different distributional consequences. A quantitative regulation provides no income and therefore no way of returning to the economy what is basically a scarcity rent.
- *Environmental benefits.* These are valued differently by different households, depending on preferences, income and prices of various goods and services.

In a complete study, the benefits and the costs would be analyzed in an integrated way and the incidence of net benefits would be the focal point. There seems to exist a fairly widespread belief that environmental policy is regressive, in the sense that lower income households shoulder a disproportionate share of the burden. Whether or not this regressivity is amplified if we allow for market repercussions will be discussed below.

Even if the question of regressivity appears straightforward, we must pin down an answer to the question of just what we should measure. As noted, we can study consumer surplus measures as well as more general wealth-based measures (although they are typically aggregated to the economy as a whole). Alternatively, one could focus on how environmental quality per se is distributed, an intensive line of inquiry in the literature on environmental equity (see Martinez-Alier, 2002).

But suppose that we are interested in whether or not the costs of environmental policy are regressively distributed across the income dimension. We then need to decide upon a measure of income, a remarkably subtle issue, the reason being that there are many concepts of income, including, but not limited to: full income (wage plus value of leisure), Hicksian income, gross or net wage income, lifetime vs 'instantaneous' income and so on and so forth. In so far as the results are independent of the concept of income chosen, there is not much to be said.

However, there is some empirical evidence suggesting that a policy measure is regressive if we use 'instantaneous' income (say, yearly income), but neutral if we use lifetime income. Poterba (1991) shows that taxes on gasoline appear much less regressive when taken as a percentage of total consumption expenditures (this is the proxy for lifetime income).[4] However, Smith (1992, p. 250) finds that the distinction between annual income and lifetime income makes little difference for UK data, in distributional analysis of energy and carbon taxation.[5] In short, conclusions about the distributional impacts of environmental policy are not necessarily robust towards the concept of income used. This conclusion is borne out by experience from the literature on the burden of taxation which suggests that 'The choice of income measure clearly affects both the estimated distribution of taxes by income class and the effect of reform proposals.'[6]

Furthermore, a comprehensive appraisal of regressivity/progressivity necessitates that we also take into account repercussions at various degrees of complexity, from the single market up to the whole economy, ideally within a framework that includes ecology–economy interactions. We shall take these up in turn, but let us first discuss impacts at the level of the firm in this first stage of our triple-stage analysis.

Individual firms

Environmental policy affects the firm through prices on inputs and outputs, but may also affect technology, depending on the specifics of regulation. In some cases, environmental regulations include the level of production. From a distributional perspective there is a difference between a regulatory measure and an incentive-based instrument at the level of the firm. Without environmental policy, the firm will expand emissions until the marginal benefit is zero; the firm is provided one input for free. A regulation of emissions is a constraint on the use of this free input.

One can take the view that the tax cum regulation discussion is simply a debate about how the scarcity rent should be distributed. The rent can be distributed to households via the tax or remain with the firm's owners under a regulation. Intuitively, there could be a difference between these two cases over the long run. If the rent is captured by firms rather than taxed away, this will attract resources to the regulated sector (relative to the tax case), such that one can expect a larger number of firms in the long run under a regulatory scheme, see Spulber (1985). Some have therefore argued that consumers benefit from regulation since one expects relatively higher output and therefore lower prices; see Hochman and Zilberman (1978) and Dewees (1983).[7] Note, however, that these resources are 'stolen away' from other parts of the economy. If the argument is true, it could mean that there is 'overproduction' in the regulated sector relative to the optimal level of resource utilization in the economy.

Consider now emission permits from the point of view of the firm. The conventional analysis is as follows. If the permits are grandfathered to the firm, the scarcity rent stays with the firm. Alternatively, if the permits are auctioned, the rent will be captured by the seller of permits. Thus, from a distributional point of view, auctioned permits are equivalent to taxes. From the firm's perspective it also follows that a regulatory measure is equivalent to a transferable permit. Of course, the firm can sell the permits, which will have a market value equal to the scarcity rent. This, however, forces the firm to reduce production, and the net value of this lost production will again be exactly equal to the scarcity rent.

It is convenient to think about permits in terms of separating efficiency and equity. The conventional analysis of permits rests on this assumption; the initial allocation of permits is considered to be an equity issue, the market guarantees efficiency. Because there is a ceiling on emissions, one might well argue that the separation issue is moot, as long as the market is competitive. Yet, it is for example unclear in the European system if its current shaping induces firms to re-locate their investment plans, depending on the specific allocation rules chosen in each country; see Boehringer and Lange (2005).

Individual markets

A subset of firms and households interact at a given market. A more stringent environmental policy will affect the cost of production/consumption and therefore the price households pay for the good or service they buy from the firms. At the level of a market, we need to estimate both consumer and producer surplus measures. In the conventional analysis, we typically disentangle the distribution of cost between buyers and sellers. Because firms are owned by households this distinction is somewhat peculiar, yet not without pedagogical merit.

There is some empirical evidence regarding the incidence difference between environmental policy instruments at this second stage of our analysis. Markandya (1998), in his survey of distributional issues in environmental policy, argues that permit markets in the US are beneficial for households in lower income brackets. Thus, grandfathering may well have progressive impacts. He does not make explicit the incidence assumptions made in those studies, that is how costs are shifted across markets.

In the standard analysis of environmental policy, as well as in our analysis above, markets are typically assumed to be competitive. We therefore close this section by commenting briefly on other kinds of market structures. The case is certainly empirically relevant (consider water regulation and district heating plants, both containing many examples of monopolies). If we allow the ownership structure to include publicly-owned companies, impacts of environmental policy depend on the assumed objective of the public company: profit maximization, cost minimization or some other objective (like covering average variable cost). From an efficiency perspective, prices should be set at marginal (not average) cost. When average costs are declining in the relevant market interval, marginal cost pricing means that the company makes a loss. Conversely, rising average costs imply that the company makes a profit using marginal cost pricing. Either way, the company may not be allowed to make profits and must set price to average cost. Consequently, depending on the cost structure, average cost pricing implies either lower or higher prices, compared to efficient pricing. In turn, this will have distributional consequences. It is possible to invoke a pricing rule that takes on any efficiency-equity trade-off directly, as in Feldstein (1972). His idea implies different pricing rules for necessary and luxury services.

Interrelated markets at the sector level

Environmental policy may have indirect impacts in several markets not directly affected by a policy measure. When markets adjust and the impacts cascade throughout the economy, any policy measure may generate 'winners' and 'losers' in ways not always transparent initially. Given the fact that a market economy can include millions of decision-makers and thousands of related markets, it is useful to approach the issue of connected markets by beginning at the sector level. Indeed, if it can be assumed that repercussions mostly stay within the sector, there are a number of advantages to not estimating a full general equilibrium model.

Consider augmenting the partial equilibrium analysis of the cost of an environmental policy measure at the market level, as in the previous section. To the output market, add a labor market and a market for housing and consider the question as to how the policy will affect house owners. For simplicity, assume that supply of labor and housing is given. The policy measure will decrease the demand for labor and therefore the wage. Because the labor input will be less expensive *ex post*, firms will increase their demand for making more emissions. If the wage level remains constant, as in a partial equilibrium analysis, this indirect impact does not materialize. Finally, assuming that the demand for housing depends on wages and environmental quality, we find an ambiguous effect on the price of a house from the policy. It will tend to decrease because of the income effect, but increase if consumers are willing to pay for the increase in environmental quality.

Consequently, when we analyze the distributional impact of the environmental tax, market repercussions complicate the analysis. For further discussions and empirical implementation, see for example Roback (1982). For further examples of how repercussions within a sector complicate environmental policy analysis, see for example Brännlund and Kriström (1993, 1996). A comprehensive analysis of welfare measurement in sector models is given in Just et al. (1982).

Interrelated sectors – economy-wide models
The final step of the analysis is to allow all markets of the economy to interact. In a general equilibrium model, the economy is interpreted as a system of mutually dependent markets. A change which at a first glance only seems to affect one market, can in practice affect *all* markets in the economy. This perspective has several advantages. Experience shows that many indirect and complex relationships are revealed that otherwise can be difficult to disentangle with alternative approaches. For example, the literature on the existence of 'double dividends' from tax swaps tells us that the partial equilibrium intuition can lead us astray (Bovenberg and de Mooijj, 1994). General reviews of the application of CGE models in environmental policy analysis are contained in Bergman (2003) and Conrad (2002).

What can we then learn from these models in a distributional analysis? To be specific, consider introducing a carbon tax along with a battery of tax recycling options in line with the literature on double dividends. While it is very difficult to represent non-linear tax-schedules correctly in a computable general equilibrium model (see Bergman, 2003), insights from the literature include the fact that recycling matters from a distributional point of view. Thus, if in the carbon tax example we use the labor tax as a replacement option, several studies suggest that the policy is regressive, even when taking into account all the market repercussions; see for example Harrison and Kriström (1999). If, instead, the tax proceeds are returned lump-sum, the policy may well be progressive, although more costly, because a distortionary tax is not being simultaneously reduced. Such numerical experiments highlight the equity–efficiency trade-off starkly; if we use the more efficient replacement option, the policy turns out regressive and vice versa. In Sweden, this kind of result might well explain why the government is now using lump-sum return, rather than the previously favored labor tax decrease.

Finally, Whalley (1984) shows how alternative incidence assumptions, that is how the tax burden is shifted backwards and forwards across markets 'can determine whether the tax structure appears to be progressive or regressive' (Atrostic and Nunns, 1990, p. 377).

At this point, one piece of the puzzle is surely missing, namely the links between the ecological and economic systems. For example, Dasgupta

(2001, p. 201), in a developing country context, discusses how forest concessions in the uplands of a watershed could result in damages on low-income farmers downstream (via siltation, increased incidence of flooding, and so on). If the forest merchant is not charged for the externality inflicted, one effectively subsidizes forest cutting at the expense of the potentially poor farmers and fishermen. This, and many more examples, suggests that we would like to incorporate non-market interactions in our framework.

There is yet to be developed a consensus how eco–eco interactions are to be empirically included in an intertemporal general equilibrium approach. There are, of course, many examples of how non-market values are included in models where the economy and ecological systems interact, but they typically lack distributional information. Furthermore, not many general equilibrium models include the environmental benefits in a consistent manner. One exception is Sieg et al. (2001), who study the benefits of environmental improvement in a general equilibrium framework.

A particularly attractive way forward is to use the insights from the literature on green accounting. The UN's system of environmental and resource accounting is one often implemented approach, based on social accounting matrices (SAM). In principle, such a matrix contains all relevant stocks and flows and can easily be extended to include distributional information. Yet, the UN's system is based on a Keynesian framework with welfare properties that are not completely understood; does an increase of the UN's version of 'green national product' signal a welfare change? The answer to this question is not known (Heal and Kriström, 2005b).

Mäler's (1991) SAM is explicitly based on a dynamic general equilibrium model with detailed representation of ecology–economy interactions. However, its quintessential statistic, Mäler's (1991) green NNP, has been severely critized later on by the author himself, see for example Dasgupta and Mäler (2001). For further thoughts on how to include distributional information in a SAM in our context, see Horan et al. (2003).

4. Empirics

The economic literature on the distribution of benefits and costs up to about 1985 has been summarized by Zimmerman (1986) roughly as follows:

1. Environmental damage is regressively distributed.
2. Environmental benefits are progressively distributed, in particular regarding recreation and natural parks.
3. Indirect impacts through market repercussions tend to strengthen the regressivity of environmental policy.
4. The net cost of environmental policy is regressively distributed.

While the post-1985 environmental economics literature on distributional issues is not overwhelmingly large, we might still comment on these findings. First, whether or not environmental damage is regressively distributed is a subtle issue, particularly when studying siting problems. The reason is that one must handle the 'chicken–egg' problem; see Hite (2000). Under one hypothesis, the poorer part of the population moves to a more hazardous location *because* the land prices are lower there. See Hamilton (2006) for further discussion.

Post-1985 literature on distribution and the environment challenges, to some extent, the earlier result that benefits are progressively distributed. Indeed, surveys on the income elasticity of the demand for environmental improvements report that this elasticity is less than one more often than not (see for example Kriström and Riera, 1996; Hökby and Söderquist, 2003; and the survey by Pearce, 2006). Given the fact that it is difficult to measure environmental benefits with any precision, it might well be that current methods underestimate this income elasticity. Or so some economists have argued. Yet, McFadden and Leonard's (1992, p. 22) proposition that environmental goods 'should be luxury goods' is not strongly supported by current evidence.

On the cost side, much of the available literature tends to support the pre-1985 contention that environmental policy is regressive. This is possibly so because energy issues have often been studied. In many developed countries, expenditure shares on energy increase with lower income, and the regressivity result is then almost immediate. Whether or not indirect impacts strengthen regressivity is somewhat unclear. As noted earlier, there is empirical evidence that goes either way. Yet, it is not easy to find examples where the net costs are distributed progressively, although there are policy packages that can work this way; see, for example, Bovenberg and Goulder (2001) on giving away permits.

Another more recent insight regards the regressivity of regulatory systems. It is often much more difficult to disentangle the distributional effects of regulations; after all, there are no direct payments of taxes or permits. Yet, the evidence that we do have points to regressivity and that energy support programs may well benefit the well-to-do much more than the less well-off. The empirical evidence on this issue is, we must warn, scarce. See Sutherland (1994).

5.   Discussion

Economists, not least environmental economists, are increasingly returning to a scrutiny of distributional issues. We have listed a number of challenges from the conceptual angle that will whet the appetite of many economists. While we find those conceptual issues most demanding and perhaps most interesting from a professional point of view, it may well be that the practical work of consistently shedding light on the fact that environmental policy inevitably creates winners and losers is most important in practice.

The outrage that a World Bank memo on the efficiency of exporting waste from rich to poor countries created suggests that, while an environmental policy can be logical from an efficiency point of view, this does not guarantee its acceptance.[8] There may be a lesson to learn from the calamity this memo created, if only the simple one that many of us care about who wins and who loses from any policy; there is, at any rate, a legitimate demand for detailed information.

While efficiency may well be 'first in logical order' (to paraphrase J.B. Clark) within the field of economics, it is increasingly clear that there is much to be gained from studying efficiency and equity together. This is a lesson that we have learned from recent developments in several fields of economics. We can trace the difficulties of separating efficiency and equity, in almost all cases, to underlying market failures. This should be sufficient motivation for environmental economists to pay more attention to distributional issues.

Notes

1. This chapter builds on Kriström (2006) and Heal and Kriström (2005b).
2. For example, we skip issues such as policy options to confront distributional problems arising from policy and refer to Serret and Johnstone (2006) for detailed empirical reviews.
3. Discussed for example in Heal (1998).
4. Fullerton and Rogers (1993, p. 19) suggest that the regressive impacts of taxes, in general, appear 'muted' in a lifetime context.
5. A survey of studies using lifetime income measures is in Metcalf (1999).
6. Atrostic and Nunns (1990, p. 382).
7. Helfand (1999, p. 229) argues, with some supporting empirical examples, that distributional concerns tend to favor the use of standards over taxes.
8. See *The Economist* (1992).

References

Aronsson, T. and K.G. Löfgren (1999), 'Welfare equivalent NNP under distributional objectives', *Economics Letters*, **63**(2): 239–43.

Asheim, G. (forthcoming), 'Can NNP be used for welfare comparisons?', *Environment and Development Economics*, Memorandum 24/2005, Department of Economics, Oslo University.

Atkinson, A.B. and F. Bourguignon (1998), 'Income distribution and economics', introduction to *Handbook of Income Distribution*, A.B. Atkinson and F. Bourguignon (eds), Amsterdam: North Holland.

Atrostic, B.K. and J.R. Nunns (1990), 'Measuring tax burden. A historical perspective', in E.R. Berndt and J.E. Triplett (eds), *Fifty Years of Economic Measurement*, Chicago: University of Chicago Press, pp. 343–408.

Bergman, L. (2003), 'CGE modelling of environmental policy and resource management', in J. Vincent and K.-G. Mäler (eds), *Handbook of Environmental and Resource Economics*, Amsterdam: North-Holland.

Boehringer, C. and A. Lange (2005), 'On the design of optimal grandfathering schemes for emission allowances', *European Economic Review*, **8**: 2041–55.

Bovenberg, L. and R. de Mooijj (1994), 'Environmental levies and distortionary taxation', *American Economic Review*, **84**: 1085–89.

Bovenberg, L. and L. Goulder (2001), 'Addressing industry distributional concerns in US climate change policy', http://weber.ucsd.edu/~carsonvs/papers/810.pdf.

Boyce, J.K. (2002), *The Political Economy of the Environment*, Cheltenham, UK and Northampton, MA, USA: Edward Elgar.

Brännlund, R. and B. Kriström (1993), 'Assessing the impact of environmental charges: a partial general equilibrium model of the Swedish forestry sector', *Environmental and Resource Economics*, **3**: 297–312.

Brännlund, R. and B. Kriström (1996), 'Welfare measurement in single and multi-market models: theory and application', *American Journal of Agricultural Economics*, **78**: 157–65.

Brown, D. and G. Heal (1979), 'Equity, efficiency and increasing returns to scale', *Review of Economic Studies*, **46**(4): 571–85.

Carneiro, P., K.T. Hansen and J.J. Heckman (2002), 'Removing the veil of ignorance in assessing the distributional impacts of social policies', Department of Economics, University of Chicago.

Conrad, K. (2002), 'Computable general equilibrium models in environmental and resource economics', in Mohan Munasinghe (ed.), *Macroeconomics and the Environment*, Cheltenham, UK and Northampton, MA, USA: Edward Elgar, pp. 601–23.

Dasgupta, P. (2001), *Human Well-Being and the Natural Environment*, Oxford and New York: Oxford University Press.

Dasgupta, P. and K.-G. Mäler (2001), 'Wealth as a criterion for sustainable development', *World Economics*, **2**(3): 19–44.

Dewees, D.N. (1983), 'Instrument choice in environmental policy', *Economic Inquiry*, **21**(1): 53–71.

Economist, The (1992), 'Let them eat pollution', **322**(7745): 66.

Feldstein, M. (1972), 'Distributional equity and the optimal structure of public prices', *American Economic Review*, **62**(1): 32–6.

Fullerton, D. and D.L. Rogers (1993), *Who Bears the Lifetime Tax Burden?*, Washington, DC: The Brookings Institution.

Hamilton, J. (2006), 'Environmental equity and the siting of hazardous waste facilities in OECD countries', in Y. Serret and N. Johnstone (2006), *The Distributional Effects of Environmental Policy*, Cheltenham, UK, Northampton, MA, USA and Paris: Edward Elgar Publishing and OECD, pp. 227–85.

Harrison, G.W. and B. Kriström (1999), 'General equilibrium effects of increasing carbon taxes in Sweden', in R. Brännlund and I. Gren (eds), *Green Taxes: Economic Theory and Empirical Evidence*, Cheltenham, UK and Northampton, MA, USA: Edward Elgar.

Heal, G. (1998), *Valuing the Future: Economic Theory and Sustainability*, New York: Columbia University Press.

Heal, G.M. and B. Kriström (2005a), 'Income, wealth and sustainable welfare in representative-agent economies', Working Paper, 26 July, Columbia University.

Heal, G.M. and B. Kriström (2005b), 'National income and the environment', in J. Vincent and K.-G. Mäler (eds), *Handbook of Environmental and Resource Economics*, Amsterdam: North-Holland, pp. 1147–1217.

Helfand, G. (1999), 'Standards versus taxes in pollution control', J.C.J.M. van den Bergh (ed), *Handbook of Environmental and Resource Economics*, Volume 1, Cheltenham, UK and Northampton, MA, USA: Edward Elgar, pp. 223–34.

Hite, D. (2000), 'A random utility model of environmental equity', *Growth and Change*, **31**(1).

Hochman, E. and D. Zilberman (1978), 'Examination of environmental policies using production and pollution micro-parameter distributions', *Econometrica*, **46**(4): 739–60.

Hökby, S. and T. Söderqvist (2003), 'Elasticities of demand and willingness to pay for environmental services in Sweden', *Environmental and Resource Economics*, **26**: 361–83.

Horan, R., J. Hrubovcak, J. Shortle and E. Bulte (2003), 'Accounting for the distributional impacts of policy in the green accounts', in C. Perrings and J. Vincent (eds), *Natural Resource Accounting and Economic Development: Theory and Practice*, Cheltenham, UK and Northampton, MA, USA: Edward Elgar.

Hourcade, J.-C. (2001), 'Articulating national, regional and international policy: simple signals in an Heterogeneous World', IPIECA Symposium, 15–16 October, Cambridge, Boston, USA.

Johansson, P.O. (1993), *Cost-Benefit Analysis of Environmental Change*, Cambridge, UK: Cambridge University Press.

Just, R.E., D.L. Hueth and A. Schmitz (1982), *Applied Welfare Economics and Public Policy*, New York: Prentice-Hall.

Kriström, B. (2006), 'Framework for assessing the distribution of financial effects of environmental Policies', in Y. Serret and N. Johnstone (2006), *The Distributional Effects of Environmental Policy*, Cheltenham, UK, Northampton, MA, USA and Paris: Edward Elgar and OECD, pp. 79–136.

Kriström, B. and P. Riera. (1996), 'Is the income elasticity of environmental improvements less than one?', *Environmental and Resource Economics*, 7(1): 45–55.

Mäler, K.-G. (1991), 'National accounts and environmental resources', *Environment and Resource Economics*, 1(1): 1–15.

Markandya, A. (1998), 'Poverty, income distribution and policy making', *Environmental and Resource Economics*, 11(3–4): 459–72.

Martinez-Alier, J. (2002), 'The environmentalism of the poor: a study of ecological conflicts and valuation', Cheltenham, UK and Northampton, MA, USA: Edward Elgar.

McFadden, D.L. and G.K. Leonard (1992), 'Issues in the contingent valuation of environmental goods: methodologies for data collection and analysis', in J.A. Hausman (ed.), *Contingent Valuation: A Critical Assessment*, Amsterdam: North-Holland, pp. 165–208.

McGuire, M.C. and H. Aaron (1969), 'Efficiency and equity in the optimal supply of public goods', *Review of Economics and Statistics*, LI, February: 31–9.

Metcalf, G.E. (1999), 'A distributional analysis of green tax reforms', *National Tax Journal*, 52: 655–81.

Pearce, D.W. (2006), 'Framework for assessing the distribution of environmental quality', in Y. Serret and N. Johnstone (2006), *The Distributional Effects of Environmental Policy*, Cheltenham, UK, Northampton, MA, USA and Paris: Edward Elgar and OECD, pp. 23–78.

Perotti, R. (1996), 'Growth, income distribution, and democracy: what the data say', *Journal of Economic Growth*, 1: 149–87.

Persky, J. (2001), 'Cost-benefit analysis and the classical creed', *Journal of Economic Perspectives*, 15(4): 199–208.

Poterba, J.M. (1991), 'Is the gasoline tax regressive?', *Tax Policy and the Economy*, 5: 145–64.

Roback, J. (1982), 'Wages, rents and the quality of life', *Journal of Political Economy*, 90(6): 1257–78.

Rose, A., B. Stevens and G. Davis (1998), *Natural Resources Policy and Income Distribution*, Baltimore: Johns Hopkins University Press.

Samuelson, P.A. (1961), 'The evaluation of "social income", capital formation and wealth', in F.A. Lutz and D.C. Hague (eds), *The Theory of Capital*, New York: St Martin's Press, Chapter 3, pp. 32–57.

Serret, Y. and N. Johnstone (2006), *The Distributional Effects of Environmental Policy*, Cheltenham, UK, Northampton, MA, USA and Paris: Edward Elgar and OECD.

Sieg, H., V.K. Smith and H.S. Banzhaf (2001), 'Estimating the general equilibrium benefits of large changes in spatially delineated public goods', Working Paper, Carnegie Mellon University, 20 February.

Smith, S. (1992), 'The distributional consequences of taxes on energy and the carbon content of fuels', *European Economy*, Special Edition, 1: 241–68.

Spulber, D.F. (1985), 'Effluent regulation and long run optimality', *Journal of Environmental Economics and Management*, 12: 103–16.

Stiglitz, J.E. (1995), *Whither Socialism?*, Cambridge, Massachusetts: MIT Press.

Sutherland, R.J. (1994), 'Income distribution effects of electric utility DSM Programs', *Energy Journal*, **15**(4): 103–16.

Whalley, J. (1984), 'Regression or progression: the taxing question of incidence analysis' (The Innis Lecture), *Canadian Journal of Economics*, **17**(4): 654–82.

Zimmerman, K. (1986), 'Discussion: distributional considerations and the environmental policy process', in A. Schnaiberg, N. Watts and K. Zimmerman (eds), *Distributional Conflicts in Environmental Resource Policy*, Wissenschaftzentrum, Berlin: WZB Publications.

11 Environmental justice and sustainability
Julian Agyeman

Prologue

In writing a chapter such as this, in which two essentially different political projects, paradigms and movements are to be compared and examined for their potential for rapprochement, I am reminded of two incidents, one in 2002, and the other in 2005, which showed me that although I, and increasing numbers of others see the (need for greater) linkages between environmental justice and sustainability, conceptually, movement-wise and public policy- and planning-wise, many people do not.

Before being accepted for publication by New York University Press as *Sustainable Communities and the Challenge of Environmental Justice*, from which much of this chapter is drawn, I sent the proposal to the MIT Press. In 2002, two reviewers, both very well published senior academics in environmental and sustainability policy in the US looked at my manuscript and told me in no uncertain terms 'instructors will probably want to adopt books that cover either solely environmental justice or sustainable development, and not both'.

The short-sightedness and weaknesses of this 'silo' approach to public policy and planning were cruelly and starkly exposed in August 2005, as Hurricane Katrina came ashore. For those of us in the public policy and planning world, many questions have been raised: was this the leading edge of climate change and an example of what's in store for us if we don't take action on greenhouse gases? Why were the clear warnings about the vulnerability of New Orleans not listened to? Were race and class factors in the level and speed of the response by public officials? Have the government's expenditures on wars compromised our ability to safeguard against so-called 'natural' disasters? These and countless other questions are unfortunate reminders of the desperate need for 'joined up' thinking, to look broadly across urban, social and environmental issues, and to develop just and sustainable approaches to resolve them.

1. Introduction

This chapter will briefly describe the characteristics of environmental justice and sustainability as both concepts and social movements. It will then highlight an emergent paradigm, the '*just sustainability paradigm*' (JSP), which increasingly links both environmental justice and sustainability. In order to

Table 11.1   The Just Sustainability Index

0 – No mention of equity or justice in core mission statement *or* in prominent, contemporary textual or programmatic material.
1 – No mention of equity or justice in core mission statement. Limited mention (once or twice) in prominent, contemporary textual or programmatic material.
2 – Equity and justice mentioned, but focused on inter-generational equity in core mission statement. Limited mention (once or twice) in prominent, contemporary textual or programmatic material.
3 – Core mission statement relates to intra- and inter-generational equity and justice *and/or* justice and equity occur in same sentence in prominent, contemporary textual or programmatic material.

assess US environmental organizations' commitment (or lack of) to the JSP, a *'just sustainability index'* (JSI) on a scale of 0–3 was developed (see Table 11.1). A range of leading US environmental and sustainability membership organizations were assigned JSIs (see Table 11.2). Following this, some examples of organizations operating within the JSP in US cities will be shown. Finally, routes for further research will be suggested.

2.   Environmental justice
Agyeman and Evans (2004, pp. 155/156) have argued that,

> environmental justice may be viewed as having two distinct but inter-related dimensions. It is, predominantly at the local and activist level, a vocabulary for *political opportunity, mobilization and action*. At the same time, at the government level, it is a *policy principle* that no public action will disproportionately disadvantage any particular social group.

As a vocabulary for political opportunity, mobilization and action, nowhere has environmental justice developed more 'traction' than in the USA. Here, environmental justice organizations emerged from grass-roots activism in the Civil Rights movement. Whether neighborhood-, community-, university- or regionally based, and whether they are staffed or unstaffed, they have expanded the dominant *traditional* environmental discourse based around environmental stewardship to include social justice and equity considerations. In doing this, they have redefined the term 'environment' so that the dominant wilderness, greening and natural resource focus now includes urban disinvestment, racism, homes, jobs, neighborhoods and communities. The 'environment' became discursively different; it became 'where we live, where we work and where we play' (Alston, 1991). The US environmental justice movement has been, and continues to be, very

Table 11.2   Just Sustainability Indices for US national environmental and sustainability organizations requiring membership

Organization	Just Sustainability Index
American Rivers	0
Center for Health and Environmental Justice	*3*
Center for a New American Dream	*3*
Defenders of Wildlife	0
Earth Island Institute	2
Earthjustice	2
Environmental Defense	*3*
Environmental Law Institute	1
Friends of the Earth	2
Greenpeace	1
League of Conservation Voters	0
Izaak Walton League	1
National Audubon Society	0
National Environmental Trust	0
National Parks Conservation Association	1
National Wildlife Federation	0
Natural Resources Defense Council	2
Nature Conservancy	0
North American Association for Environmental Education	2
Physicians for Social Responsibility/EnviroHealthAction	1
Redefining Progress	*3*
Resources for the Future	0
Sierra Club	2
The American Solar Energy Society	0
The Ocean Conservancy	0
The State PIRGs	0
The Wilderness Society	1
The Wildlife Society	1
The Union of Concerned Scientists	0
WWF	1

effective at addressing the issues of poor people and people of color, who are disproportionately affected by environmental 'bads' such as toxic facilities, poor transit or increased air pollution and who have restricted access to environmental 'goods' such as quality green and play spaces.

The 1987 study by the United Church of Christ, Commission on Racial Justice, 'Toxic Wastes and Race in the United States', was pivotal. It showed that certain communities, predominantly communities of color, are at disproportionate risk from commercial toxic waste. This finding was confirmed by later research (Adeola, 1994; Bryant and Mohai, 1992; Bullard, 1990a, 1990b; Mohai and Bryant, 1992; Goldman, 1993). It also led to the coining of a term by Benjamin Chavis which became the rallying cry of many: *environmental racism*. This, combined with the conclusion of Lavelle and Coyle (1992) in the *National Law Journal* that there is unequal protection and enforcement of environmental law by the EPA, has ensured that there is now a fully-fledged environmental justice movement made up of tenants' associations, religious groups, civil rights groups, farm workers, professional not-for-profits, university centers and academics and labor unions, among others.

As such, according to Pulido (1996), in the USA it is a multiracial movement which is organizing around LULUs (Locally Unwanted Land Uses) such as waste facility siting, transfer storage and disposal facilities (TSDFs) and other issues such as lead contamination, pesticides, water and air pollution, workplace safety, and transportation. More recently, issues such as sprawl and smart growth (Bullard et al., 2000), sustainability (Agyeman et al., 2003) and climate change (International Climate Justice Network, 2002; Congressional Black Caucus Foundation, 2004) have become targets for the environmental justice critique.

However, in many other countries without the peculiarities of racial dynamics typical of the USA, socio-economic factors often trump race as determinants of environmental justice discourses and activism. These 'movements' for environmental justice (if they can *strictly* be called that), are springing up worldwide, including Eastern Europe (Costi, 1998, 2003), Canada (Jerrett et al., 1997; Buzzelli and Jerrett, 2004; Gosine, 2003), the UK (Agyeman, 2000, 2002; Agyeman and Evans, 2004; Boardman et al., 1999; FoE Scotland, 1999, 2000; Dunion and Scandrett, 2003), South Africa (McDonald, 2002; Roberts, 2003), Nigeria (Agbola and Alabi, 2003), South Asia (Wickramasinghe, 2003), New Zealand (Rixecker and Tipene-Matua, 2003) and the 'developing world' (Adeola, 2000; Guha and Martinez-Alier, 1997).

In addition, because of its increasingly broad usage, especially outside the USA, environmental justice will be used in this chapter to include poor and disadvantaged groups as well. As Cutter (1995, p. 113) notes, 'environmental justice . . . moves beyond racism to include others (regardless of race or ethnicity) who are deprived of their environmental rights, such as women, children and the poor'. While there is not the space here to go into it, Agyeman (2002) has argued that access to the English countryside ('an exclusive, ecological or white space, which invokes a sense of fear, of dread', p. 38) amongst minority ethnic groups is an environmental *right*. This brings issues such as countryside access and 'rural racism' into the environmental justice debate in Britain (see also Bell, 2004, for a fuller discussion on rights and a 'Rawlsian conception of environmental justice').

As a policy principle that no public action will disproportionately disadvantage any particular racial or social group, President Clinton's Executive Order 12898 (1994) set the standard:

> each Federal agency shall make achieving environmental justice part of its mission by identifying and addressing, as appropriate, disproportionately high and adverse human health or environmental effects of its programs, policies, and activities on minority populations and low-income populations in the United States (1994, pp. 1–101)

In addition, at the sub-national level, 'more than 30 states have expressly addressed environmental justice' according to the American Bar Association (2004, p. 4). One such state is Massachusetts:

> Environmental justice is based on the principle that all people have a right to be protected from environmental pollution and to live in and enjoy a clean and healthful environment. Environmental Justice is the equal protection and meaningful involvement of all people with respect to the development, implementation and enforcement of environmental laws, regulations and policies and the equitable distribution of environmental benefits. (Commonwealth of Massachusetts, 2002, p. 2)

This definition has *procedural* justice aspects ('meaningful involvement of all people'), *substantive* justice aspects ('right to live in and enjoy a clean and healthful environment') and *distributive* justice aspects ('equitable distribution of environmental benefits'). It also makes the case that environmental justice should not only be *reactive* to environmental 'bads', important though this is, but that it should also be *proactive* in the distribution and achievement of environmental 'goods': for instance, in relation to this chapter, a sustainable community with a higher quality of life.

In order to implement the policy, the state's Executive Office of Environmental Affairs (EOEA) arrived at the following definition of what it called 'Environmental Justice Populations':

> EJ Populations are those segments of the population that EOEA has determined to be most at risk of being unaware of or unable to participate in environmental decision-making or to gain access to state environmental resources. They are defined as neighborhoods (US Census Bureau census block groups) that meet one or more of the following criteria:
>
> - The median annual household income is at or below 65 percent of the statewide median income for Massachusetts; or
> - 25 percent of the residents are minority; or
> - 25 percent of the residents are foreign born, or
> - 25 percent of the residents are lacking English language proficiency.

> (Commonwealth of Massachusetts, 2002, p. 5)

While imperfect, these criteria are a base around which to implement and evaluate the EJ policy. MASSGIS, the state's GIS service, has now mapped all EJ Populations based on currently available 2000 US Census data. The policy acknowledges that Environmental Justice Populations make up 5 per cent of the Commonwealth's land area and take in about 29 per cent of its population. Location wise and unsurprisingly 'many of these Environmental Justice Populations are located in densely populated urban neighborhoods, in and around the state's oldest industrial sites, while some are located in suburban and rural communities'. (Commonwealth of Massachusetts, 2002, p. 5)

What does the State intend to do about the environmental injustices in Massachusetts?

> it is the policy of the EOEA that environmental justice shall be an integral consideration to the extent applicable and allowable by law in the implementation of all EOEA programs, including but not limited to, the grant of financial resources, the promulgation, implementation and enforcement of laws, regulations and policies, and the provision of access to both active and passive open space. (Commonwealth of Massachusetts, 2002, p. 4)

In real terms, this means that the State intends to increase public participation and outreach through the development of strategies, training, fact sheets and regional environmental justice teams; minimize risk to Environmental Justice Populations through targeted compliance, enforcement and technical assistance; encourage investment and economic growth particularly around contaminated sites; infuse state resources by developing an inventory of underutilized commercial/industrial properties; incorporate an environmental justice criterion in the awarding of technical assistance, grants and audits in Massachusetts General Law 21E (hazardous waste and brownfield) sites in Environmental Justice Populations and promote cleaner production and the creation, restoration and maintenance of open spaces.

The final piece of the *policy principle* jigsaw is that, at the federal level, there is an Office of Environmental Justice in the Environmental Protection Agency and a National Environmental Justice Advisory Council (NEJAC) together with an inter-agency working group developed as a result of Executive Order 12898.

Taken as a whole, this 'jigsaw' of a Presidential Executive Order and its implications for federal agencies – an Office of Environmental Justice in the EPA; the NEJAC; and state-based strategies with their spatial designations of 'environmental justice populations' together with the power of the US environmental justice movement(s) – is what Agyeman and Bickerstaff (forthcoming) call the 'environmental justice infrastructure'. Taking the cue of authors such as Latour (2005), who have argued that the world is a hybrid assemblage of objects, people and ideas, Agyeman and Bickerstaff (forthcoming) build a picture of the actors, resources, relations, tactics and strategies that are (being) collectively assembled to constitute different environmental justice infrastructures.

3. Sustainability

In the late 1980s, around the same time as environmental justice was developing as a public policy issue, the ideas of 'sustainability' and 'sustainable development' were achieving prominence among local, national and international policy makers and politicians, together with policy entrepreneurs in NGOs. Since then, there has been a massive increase in published and online material dealing with *sustainability* and *sustainable development*. This has led to competing and conflicting views over what the terms mean, what is to be sustained, by whom, for whom, and what is the most desirable means of achieving this goal.

One thing that seems increasingly certain is that the 'science' of sustainability is not our greatest challenge. In almost all *'areas'* of sustainability, we know scientifically and technically what we need to do and how to do it; but we're just *not* doing it. An advertisement in the *New York Times*, paid for by outofgas.com, said the same: 'It's time to free ourselves from foreign oil, and create millions of new jobs in the process. This is no pipe dream. The research and technology exist. We have the national wealth. Do we have the will?' (*New York Times*, 2004, p. A9).

As Brulle (2000, p. 191) argues:

> with the exception of Commoner, the vast majority of ecological scientists have not examined the social and political causes of ecological degradation (Taylor, 1992, pp. 133–51). While the natural scientists may have great competence in their specific areas of expertise, their social and political thinking is 'marred by blindness and naivete' (Enzensberger, 1979, p. 389).

Similarly, Agyeman et al. (2002, p. 78) have argued elsewhere that:

> sustainability . . . cannot be simply a 'green', or 'environmental' concern, important though 'environmental' aspects of sustainability are. A truly sustainable society is one where wider questions of social needs and welfare, and economic opportunity are integrally related to environmental limits imposed by supporting ecosystems.

Building on this *socio-political*, or *'just'* approach to sustainability are Polese and Stren (2000, p. 15) who argue simply that, 'to be environmentally sustainable, cities must also be socially sustainable'. Second, that of

Middleton and O'Keefe (2001, p. 16): 'unless analyses of development [local, national, or international]. . .begin not with the symptoms, environmental or economic instability, but with the cause, social injustice, then no development can be sustainable'. Third, that of Hempel (1999, p. 43): 'the emerging sustainability ethic may be more interesting for what it implies about politics than for what it promises about ecology'. Fourth, Buhrs (2004, p. 434) is perhaps most direct: 'addressing environmental justice issues is important, if not a precondition, for the achievement of global sustainability'. Finally that of Adger (2002, p. 1716), who notes:

> I would argue that inequality in its economic, environmental, and geographical manifestations is among the most significant barriers to sustainable development. It is a barrier because of its interaction with individuals' lifestyles and because it prevents socially acceptable implementation of collective planning for sustainability.

A global example of this tension between scientific and socio-political approaches is the difference between the 'green' agenda of environmental protection, biodiversity and the protection of the ozone layer typical of countries in the North, and the 'brown' agenda of poverty alleviation, infrastructural development, health and education typical of countries in the South. Guha and Martinez-Alier (1997, p. 21), academics from the South and North respectively, have argued ' "No Humanity without Nature!" the epitaph of the Northern environmentalist, is here answered by the equally compelling slogan "No Nature without Social Justice!" ' (Kothari and Parajuli, 1993).

Sustainability is *at least* as much about politics, injustice and inequality, as it is about science, technology or the environment. If this is so, then as Prugh et al. (2000, p. 5) argue, 'sustainability will be achieved, if at all, not by engineers, agronomists, economists and biotechnicians but by citizens'. While there is not the space to examine citizenship and sustainability debates here, there is a fast-growing amount of literature in this direction (see, for example, *Environmental Politics*, Volume 14, number 4).

Sustainability is interpreted in this chapter as meaning 'the need to ensure a better quality of life for all, now and into the future, in a just and equitable manner, while living within the limits of supporting ecosystems' (Agyeman et al., 2003, p. 5). It represents an attempt to look holistically at the human condition, at human ecology, and to foster joined up or connected – rather than piecemeal – policy solutions to humanity's greatest problems. The definition focuses on four main areas of concern that are the foundations of the JSP: *quality of life, present and future generations, justice and equity* in resource allocation, and *living within ecological limits*.

4. The just sustainability paradigm in theory and practice

Despite the admonitions of MIT Press reviewers and the real historical and geographical differences in origin between *environmental justice* and *sustainability*, together with the different languages, vocabularies, resources, repertoires, educations and social locations of environmental justice and sustainability activists, there *does* exist an area of theoretical, conceptual and practical compatibility between them. Each concept has its own particular discursive frame and paradigm that can be seen as being at opposite ends of a continuum.

At one end is the *Environmental Justice Paradigm* (EJP) of Taylor (2000). It is a framework for integrating class, race, gender, environment and social justice concerns. Based around the Principles of Environmental Justice developed at the 1991 National People of Color Environmental Leadership Summit in Washington, DC, it represents the theoretical underpinning of the environmental justice project and activism. At the other end is the *New Environmental Paradigm* (NEP) of Catton and Dunlap (1978). It sets out an environmental stewardship and sustainability agenda which currently influences the work of most US and environmental and sustainability organizations in the North but, unlike the EJP, has little to say about *intragenerational* equity or justice (although it is better on *intergenerational* issues). This is the 'equity deficit' of *environmental* sustainability.

Agyeman (2005a, p. 6) notes that

> the JSP is an emerging discursive frame and paradigm. It is not, however rigid, single and universal, but links to both the EJP and NEP. In this sense, it can be seen as being both flexible and contingent, composed of overlapping discourses, which come from recognition of the validity of a variety of issues, problems and framings. . ... It prioritizes justice and equity, but does not downplay the environment, our life support system. In essence, it is malleable, acting as a 'bridge' spanning the continuum between the EJP and the NEP.

Notwithstanding the differences between the NEP and EJP, which are primarily around the issues of race and class, justice and equity, *not* about the need for greater environmental protection, there is a rich and critical nexus where facets of each paradigm are realized as *'cooperative endeavors'* (Schlosberg, 1999) around common issues such as toxics use reduction and transportation. Yet such co-operation has so far largely been based around what Gould et al. (2004, p. 90) call 'short-term marriages of convenience' rather than 'longer-term coalitions'. In this respect it currently falls well short of Cole and Foster's (2001, p. 164) concept of *'movement fusion'*: 'the coming together of two (or more) social movements in a way that expands the base of support for both movements by developing a common agenda'.

This 'just' perspective on sustainability is a view shared by most thinkers in the environmental justice movement. Typical is Edwards, former Executive Director of the Panos Institute in Washington, DC, who wrote an influential paper in the Environmental Protection Agency Journal, called 'Sustainability and People of Color', at around the time of the 1992 United Nations Conference on Environment and Development. In it, he argued that people of color *do* embrace sustainable development because it will lead to a US 'transformed by the guiding principles of freedom, justice and equality' (Edwards, 1992, p. 51).

However, crucially, the JSP *does not* supplant the EJP, but is operative alongside it, with their discourses overlapping. They are complementary. The JSP represents, in many ways, a bridge between the EJP and NEP. As such, the JSP is an acknowledgement of both the *successes* of the EJ movement in getting justice on the environmental agenda and the *failures* of the NEP to develop a realistic, justice-based political project. At this stage it is worth making two points clear. First, that the interpretive differences (that is, in core values and beliefs, environmental philosophy, political ideology, diagnostic attribution and repertoire of action) between the JSP and NEP (especially the technocentric wing) are greater than those between the JSP and the EJP. Second, and although a generalization, the *intimate* and *visceral* experience of socio-economic and race-based injustices visited upon activists in the environmental justice movement and their communities is largely not shared by those in groups representative of the JSP whose 'experience' of it is more likely to be at arm's length.

However, irrespective of whether we experience injustice first-hand, or empathize deeply with those who do, or if we take a global, US-wide or more local focus, or a moral or practical approach, inequity and injustice resulting from, among other things, racism and classism are bad for the environment and bad for sustainability. What is more, the environmental sustainability movement, typified in the USA by The National Audubon Society, WWF and Nature Conservancy, does not have an analysis or theory of change with strategies for dealing with these issues. For instance, Shellenberger and Nordhaus (2004, p. 12), in their stinging indictment of the US environmental movement, 'The Death of Environmentalism' ask: 'Why, for instance, is a human-made phenomenon like global warming – which may kill hundreds of millions of human beings over the next century – considered "environmental"? Why are poverty and war not considered environmental problems while global warming is?'

Gelobter et al. (2005:10), in their riposte to 'The Death of Environmentalism', 'The Soul of Environmentalism' argue that: 'many environmentalists of color admire the mainstream movement's goals, but they also know firsthand that social justice is routinely ignored in the mainstream movement's decision making.'

Indeed, such issues are not even on the radar. Another example, from the early 1990s, happened when a member of Greenpeace UK's human relations staff was asked if she felt that her organization's employees reflected multicultural Britain. She replied calmly, 'No, but it's not an issue for us. We're here to save the world'.

Yet research has shown how, globally, nations with a greater commitment to equity and a correspondingly more equitable society tend also to have a greater commitment to environmental quality (Torras and Boyce, 1998). Good examples here are the Nordic countries of Sweden, Denmark, Norway and Finland. In a survey of the 50 US states, Boyce et al. (1999) found that those with greater inequalities in power distribution (measured by voter participation, tax fairness, Medicaid access and educational attainment levels) had less stringent environmental policies, greater levels of environmental stress and higher rates of infant mortality and premature deaths. At a more local level, a study by Morello-Frosch (1997) of counties in California showed that highly segregated counties, in terms of income, class and race, had higher levels of hazardous air pollutants. If sustainability is to become a process with the power to *transform*, as opposed to its current *environmental, stewardship* or *reform* focus, justice and equity issues need to be incorporated to its very core.

In short, characterizing the JSP involves taking a broader frame than that on which the traditional and globally dominant US and Northern environmental sustainability agendas are predicated. It involves understanding and supporting *both* Northern *environment-based* and Southern *equity-based* agendas, *equally*. As Jacobs (1999, p. 33) argues:

> in Southern debate about sustainable development the notion of equity remains central, particularly in the demand not just that national but that global resources should be distributed in favor of poor countries and people. . ... In the North, by stark contrast, equity is much the least emphasized of the core ideas, and is often ignored altogether.

How do US environmental and sustainability organizations measure up to the JSP? Using organizational websites and the search terms '*equity*', '*justice*' and '*sustainability*', a search of *both* organizational mission statements *and* prominent, contemporary textual or programmatic material was undertaken. Derivations of equity, justice and sustainability, such as '*equitable*', '*just*' or '*sustainable*', were also used if the original terms yielded no results. In addition, and to fully ensure no organization was potentially excluded, sentiments such as 'the fundamental right of all people to have a voice in decisions', 'disproportionate environmental burdens' or mention of 'environment' instead of 'sustainability' (only if associated with '*justice*' or '*just*') were counted as having fulfilled the search terms. This Index comes with some caveats and limitations, however. If organizational '*mission*' only was examined, an argument could be made that 'aspiration' and not 'behavior' was being studied. That is why *both* 'mission' *and* 'program' issues form the JSI on the basis that most organizational websites have a wealth of up-to-date programmatic information. This, in combination with mission information, provides a *relatively* accurate picture of an organization's commitment to the JSP.

The list of organizations, it could be argued, is somewhat arbitrary. However, no 'official' list of national environmental and sustainability organizations exists. Many of the organizations in Table 11.2 were derived from SaveOurEnvironment.org, a collaborative effort of the US's most influential environmental advocacy organizations. From these groups, a 'snowball' technique was applied to gain yet more. Depressingly but not surprisingly, there are three conclusions that can be drawn.

First, among the 30 national environmental and sustainability membership organizations shown, over 30 per cent had a JSI of 0. This means that in such organizations there is '*No mention of equity or justice in core mission statement or in prominent, contemporary textual or programmatic material*'.

Second, the average JSI was 1.06. While not statistically significant, this suggests that the majority of US national environmental and sustainability membership organizations make '*no mention of equity or justice in* [their] *core mission statement [and] limited mention (once or twice) in prominent, contemporary textual or programmatic material*'. This backs up Taylor's (2000) point about the lack of social justice concerns (or *intra*-generational equity) within the NEP.

Third, only organizations with a JSI of 3 could be considered to be operating within the JSP. In other words, their '*core mission statement relates to intra and intergenerational equity and justice and/or justice and equity occur in same sentence in prominent, contemporary textual or programmatic material*'. These organizations are Center for Health and Environmental Justice, Center for a New American Dream, Environmental Defense, and Redefining Progress.

If the picture as regards big membership organizations is depressing, the JSP *is* being implemented today, in US cities, primarily by small, local, community responsive organizations often with multiracial staff who can use the overlapping discourses of the JSP (see Agyeman, 2005a and 2005b, for details of Boston's *Alternatives for Community and Environment*). Two such organizations are Urban Ecology in Oakland, California, and Bethel New Life, in Chicago, Illinois. Both are working on land use planning issues in low-income and minority neighborhoods and both espouse the principles of just sustainability.

Urban Ecology, Oakland, CA
Urban Ecology in Oakland, California, is an organization founded in 1975. As the website says:

> Urban Ecology has not focused on the traditional environmental priorities of preserving land, air and water. Neither have we had a traditional community development focus aimed at, for example, generating affordable housing. Rather, our work has integrated elements of these disciplines and others, with healthy 'human habitats' as the common denominator. We have sought to advance sustainability in the Bay Area using three main strategies – alternative visioning, education and policy advocacy, with all of our work grounded in the three Es of environment, economy and social equity. (www.urbanecology.org)

It is engaged in two primary avenues towards promoting just sustainability principles in land use planning within the San Francisco Bay Area. First, its *Community Design Program* provides planning and design services to low-income urban neighborhoods, such as the Weeks Neighborhood in East Palo Alto, to assist them with community development. They have developed a process to bring the services of city planners into communities to engage in local needs assessments and community visioning. Urban Ecology helps organizations facilitate the drafting of a community plan that addresses the immediate and long-term needs of the area, and assists the local community organizations with implementation strategies. Although the needs of the community are given first priority, Urban Ecology staff promote ideas such as transit access, pedestrian-friendly streetscapes and affordable infill housing to help revitalize neighborhoods with sustainability principles in mind.

Second, Urban Ecology's *Sustainable Cities Program* approaches municipal governments such as Berkeley, Fremont, Oakland and San Francisco and works with community groups such as San Jose's Tamien Neighborhood Association to promote more sustainable development patterns. The suburbs at the frontiers of urban sprawl are encouraged to adopt Smart Growth principles that allow for diverse housing options and alternative transportation infrastructure. Urban Ecology advocates for infill development, affordable housing, transit oriented development, reduced parking requirements and mixed-use projects. They provide information to municipalities and citizen groups about private developers who have applied these principles in their projects. Urban Ecology also runs workshops for the public on how to review new projects and advocate for sustainable land development. In the Bay Area, the issues of urban sprawl, environmental preservation and social justice are deeply linked together, and groups such as Urban Ecology are working with many communities in pursuit of more local and regional just sustainability.

Bethel New Life, Inc., Chicago, IL

Rioting and disinvestment in the late 1960s and early 1970s left this West Garfield Park community in Chicago in deep trouble. Bethel Lutheran Church members pledged to fight the despair and in 1979, they bought a three-flat apartment building which became Bethel New Life, Inc. Now with 318 employees, 893 volunteers, over 1100 affordable housing units, 7000 people in living wage jobs and $100 million invested in the community, this faith-based organization has gained, like the Dudley Street Neighborhood Initiative (DSNI) in Boston, a national reputation for cutting edge just sustainability initiatives.

The organization is a Community Development Corporation (CDC) whose strapline, 'Weaving together a healthier, sustainable community', reflects their wide-ranging asset-based community development interests through programs such as cultural arts, employment, housing and economic development, family support, seniors and community development. As their website states: 'all programs & initiatives at Bethel New Life, Inc. are conceived with sustainability in mind, and must be: wanted by the community, financially viable and mission appropriate'.

In terms of land use planning, their current major project is the Lake Pulaski Commercial Center. The Bethel New Life project team includes Farr Associates (architects), Phoenix Construction (contractor), Piper & Marbury (law firm), Matanky Realty (commercial leasing/operations), and Argonne National Laboratory (energy model and monitoring). The Center is a 23 000 square foot, two-story 'smart, green' building, a play on its 'smart growth' and 'green' qualities. With a bridge to the Lake Street El platform on the Green line, it is a Transit Oriented Development (TOD) that will enable non-motorized users quick access. Using photovoltaic cells, a 'living green roof' that will enhance energy retention, super-insulation and energy efficient windows, as well as other energy efficiencies that combine to cut energy operating costs in half, it will house a child and infant daycare center, employment services and five storefronts.

Major funding for this $4.5 million project comes from the City of Chicago Empowerment Zone, State of Illinois Department of Commerce and Economic Opportunity, City of Chicago Department of Environment, US Bank, and Commonwealth Edison. A majority of the construction contracts are with Minority Business Enterprise/Women's Business Enterprise companies, which will create much-needed jobs in the community. In addition, almost 70 new permanent jobs will be created in food services, childcare and retail. Another of the CDC's programs, Bethel Employment Services, will be housed in the Center and will try to favor local community members in its recruitment drive.

5. Next steps

The identification and characterization of the JSP is in its infancy. It is more fully developed in *Sustainable Communities and the Challenge of Environmental Justice* (Agyeman, 2005a). However, further research is needed both to assess the extent of equity and justice inputs to traditional, reform or environmental sustainability agendas in other countries, and worldwide, and to identify and help shape future scenarios. For example, the Stockholm Environment Institute (2002, p. 16) has, through its Global Scenario Group's 'Great Transition' project, begun to map four possible scenarios for the future of the planet: *Conventional Worlds, Barbarism, Great Transitions* and *Muddling Through*. Their preferred scenario, *Great Transitions*, has two variants: *Eco-Communalism*, and the preferred variant, the *New Sustainability Paradigm*, which 'validates global solidarity, cultural cross-fertilization and economic connectedness while seeking a liberatory, humanistic and ecological transition'. This *Great Transition*, through the *New Sustainability Paradigm*, is the only one of the four scenarios that sees an increase in *equity* as essential (Gallopin et al., 1997). In this, the *New Sustainability Paradigm* moves very close to the JSP.

The emergent JSP is a far bigger tent than could be filled solely by just sustainability and most environmental justice organizations. Future research could look more broadly towards initiatives such as the 'Just Transition Alliance', 'a voluntary coalition of labor, economic and environmental justice activists, Indigenous people and working-class people of color [which] has created a dialogue in local, national, and international arenas' (www.jtalliance.org/docs/aboutjta.html). Another example is the 'Apollo Alliance' which aims 'to create three million good jobs, free ourselves from imported oil, and clean up the environment' (www.apolloalliance.org/). These, and many other alliances are forming around the world which could unite under the JSP to create more just and sustainable communities.

References

Adeola, F. (1994), 'Environmental hazards, health and racial inequity in hazardous waste distribution', *Environment and Behavior*, **26**(1): 99–126.

Adeola, F. (2000), 'Cross national environmental injustice and human rights issues: a review of evidence from the developing world', *American Behavioral Scientist*, **43**(4): 686–706.

Adger, N. (2002), 'Inequality, environment and planning', *Environment and Planning A*, **34**(10): 1716–19.

Agbola, T. and M. Alabi (2003), 'Political economy of petroleum resources development, environmental injustice and selective victimization: a case study of the Niger Delta region of Nigeria', in J. Agyeman, R. Bullard and B. Evans (eds), *Just Sustainabilities: Development in an Unequal World*, London: Earthscan/MIT Press.

Agyeman, J. (2000), *Environmental Justice: from the Margins to the Mainstream?*, Town and Country Planning Association 'Tomorrow' Series, London: TCPA.

Agyeman, J. (2002), 'Constructing environmental (in)justice: transatlantic tales', *Environmental Politics*, **11**(3): 31–53.

Agyeman, J. (2005a), *Sustainable Communities and the Challenge of Environmental Justice*, New York: New York University Press.

Agyeman, J. (2005b), 'Alternatives for community and environment: where justice and sustainability meet', *Environment: Science and Policy for Sustainable Development*, **47**(6): 11–23.

Agyeman, J. and K. Bickerstaff (forthcoming), '(Dis)assumbling environmental justice: developing cross-national comparisons'.

Agyeman, J. and B. Evans (2004), ' "Just sustainability": the emerging discourse of environmental justice in Britain?', *Geographical Journal*, **170**(2): 155–64.

Agyeman, J., R. Bullard and B. Evans (2002), 'Exploring the nexus: bringing together sustainability, environmental justice and equity', *Space and Polity*, **6**(1): 70–90.

Agyeman, J., R. Bullard and B. Evans (2003), *Just Sustainabilities: Development in an Unequal World*, London: Earthscan/MIT Press.

Alston, D. (1991), Speech delivered at the First National People of Color Environmental Leadership Summit, Washington, DC, October.

American Bar Association (2004), *Environmental Justice for All: A Fifty State Survey of Legislation, Policies and Initiatives*, Chicago: American Bar Association and Hastings College of the Law.

Bell, D. (2004), 'Environmental justice and Rawls' difference principle', *Environmental Ethics*, **26**: 287–306.

Bethel New Life, Inc., www.bethelnewlife.org.

Boardman, B., S. Bullock and D. McLaren (1999), *Equity and the Environment. Guidelines for Socially Just Government*, London: Catalyst/Friends of the Earth.

Boyce, J.K., A.R. Klemer, P.H. Templet and C.E. Willis (1999), 'Power distribution, the environment, and public health: a state level analysis', *Ecological Economics*, **29**: 127–40.

Brulle, R. (2000), *Agency, Democracy and Nature. The US Environmental Movement from a Critical Theory Perspective*, Cambridge, MA: MIT Press.

Bryant, B. and P. Mohai (eds) (1992), *Race and the Incidence of Environmental Hazards*, Boulder, CO: Westview Press.

Buhrs, T. (2004), 'Sharing environmental space: the role of law, economics and politics', *Journal of Environmental Planning and Management*, **47**(3): 429–47.

Bullard, R. (1990a), *Dumping in Dixie*, Boulder, CO: Westview Press.

Bullard, R. (1990b), 'Ecological inequalities and the New South: black communities under siege', *The Journal of Ethnic Studies*, **17**(4): 101–15.

Bullard, R., G. Johnson and A. Torres (eds) (2000), *Sprawl City. Race, Politics and Planning in Atlanta*, Washington, DC: Island Press.

Buzzelli, M. and M. Jerrett (2004), 'Is there empirical evidence of environmental racism in the Canadian city? An empirical test of air pollution exposure in Hamilton, 1996', *Environment and Planning A*, **36**: 1855–76.

Catton, W. and R. Dunlap (1978), 'Environmental sociology: a new paradigm', *The American Sociologist*, **13**: 41–9.

Cole, L. and S. Foster (2001), *From the Ground Up. Environmental Racism and the Rise of the Environmental Justice Movement*, New York: NYU Press.

Commonwealth of Massachusetts (2002), *Environmental Justice Policy*, Boston: State House.

Congressional Black Caucus Foundation Inc. (2004), *African Americans and Climate Change: An Unequal Burden*, Washington DC: CBCF.

Costi, A. (1998), 'Environmental justice and sustainable development in Central and Eastern Europe', *European Environment*, **8**: 107–12.

Costi, A. (2003), 'Environmental protection, economic growth and environmental justice: are they compatible in Central and Eastern Europe?', in J. Agyeman, R. Bullard and B. Evans (eds), *Just Sustainabilities: Development in an Unequal World*, London: Earthscan/MIT Press.

Cutter, S. (1995), 'Race, class and environmental justice', *Progress in Geography*, **19**(1): 111–22.

Dunion, K. and E. Scandrett (2003), 'The campaign for environmental justice in Scotland', in J. Agyeman, R. Bullard and B. Evans (eds), *Just Sustainabilities: Development in an Unequal World*, London: Earthscan/MIT Press.

Edwards, M. (1992), 'Sustainability and people of color', *EPA Journal*, **18**(4): 50–52.

Enzensberger, H. (1979), 'A critique of political ecology', In A. Cockburn and J. Ridgeway (eds), *Political Ecology*, New York: New York Times Books.

Executive Order 12898 (1994), 'Federal Actions To Address Environmental Justice in Minority Populations and Low-Income Populations' 59 FR 7629.

Friends of the Earth Scotland (1999), 'FoE Issue Challenge to Scottish Parliament', Press Release, 23 January, Edinburgh: Friends of the Earth Scotland, www.gn.apc.org/www.foe-scotland.org.uk/media-releases/99-01-23-seraconference.html.

Friends of the Earth Scotland (2000), *The Campaign for Environmental Justice*, Edinburgh: Friends of the Earth Scotland.

Gallopin, G., A. Hammond, P. Raskin and R. Swart (1997), *Branch Points: Global Scenarios and Human Choice*, Stockholm: Stockholm Environment Institute, PoleStar Series Report No. 7.

Gelobter, M., M. Dorsey, L. Fields, T. Goldtooth, A. Mendiratta, R. Moore, R. Morello-Frosch, P. Shephered and G. Torres (2005), *The Soul of Environmentalism. Rediscovering Transformational Politics in the 21st Century*, Oakland: Redefining Progress.

Goldman, B. (1993), *Not Just Prosperity. Achieving Sustainability with Environmental Justice*, Washington, DC: National Wildlife Federation.

Gosine, A. (2003), 'Talking race', *Alternatives*, **29**(1): 3.

Gould, K., T. Lewis and T. Roberts (2004), 'Blue-green coalitions: constraints and possibilities in the post 9-11 political environment', *Journal of World-Systems Research*, **X**(1) Winter: 90–116.

Guha, R. and J. Martinez-Alier (1997), *Varieties of Environmentalism. Essays North and South*, London: Earthscan.

Hempel, L.C. (1999), 'Conceptual and analytical challenges in building sustainable communities', in D.A. Mazmanian and M.E. Kraft (eds), *Towards Sustainable Communities: Transition and Transformations in Environmental Policy*, Cambridge: MIT Press, pp. 43–74.

International Climate Justice Network (2002), Press Release, Johannesburg, 29 August.

Jacobs, M. (1999), 'Sustainable development: a contested concept', in A. Dobson (ed.) *Fairness and Futurity. Essays on Environmental Sustainability and Social Justice*, Oxford: Oxford University Press.

Jerrett, M., J. Eyles, D. Cole and S. Reader (1997), 'Environmental equity in Canada: an empirical investigation into the income distribution of pollution in Ontario', *Environment and Planning A*, **29**: 1777–1800.

Just Transition Alliance, www.jtalliance.org/docs/aboutjta.htm.

Kothari, S. and P. Parajuli (1993), 'No nature without social justice: a plea for ecological and cultural pluralism in India', in W. Sachs (ed.), *Global Ecology: A New Arena of Political Conflict*, London: Zed Books.

Labour, B. (2005), *Reassembling the Social*, Oxford: Oxford University Press.

Lavelle, M. and M. Coyle (eds) (1992), 'Unequal protection: the racial divide in environmental law' (Special Supplement), *National Law Journal*, **15**: 52–4.

McDonald, D. (ed.) (2002), *Environmental Justice in South Africa*, Athens: Ohio University Press/Cape Town, Cape Town University Press.

Middleton, N. and P. O'Keefe (2001), *Redefining Sustainable Development*, London: Pluto Press.

Mohai, P. and B. Bryant (1992), 'Environmental injustice: weighing race and class as factors in the distribution of environmental hazards', *University of Colorado Law Review*, No. 63: 921–32.

Morello-Frosch, R. (1997), 'Environmental justice and California's "Riskscape". The distribution of air toxics and associated cancer and non cancer risks among diverse communities', unpublished dissertation, Department of Health Sciences, University of California, Berkeley.

New York Times (2004), 'The Real Cost of Gas' 28 May, p. A9.

Polese, M. and R. Stren (2000), 'The new sociocultural dynamics of cities', in M. Polese and R. Stren (eds), *The Social Sustainability of Cities. Diversity and the Management of Change*, Toronto: University of Toronto Press.

Prugh, T., R. Costanza and H. Daly (2000), *The Local Politics of Global Sustainability*, Washington, DC: Island Press.

Pulido, L. (1996), *Environmentalism and Economic Justice. Two Chicano Struggles in the Southwest*, Tucson: University of Arizona Press.

Rixecker, S. and B. Tipene-Matua (2003), 'Maori Kaupapa and the inseparability of social and environmental justice: an analysis of bioprospecting and a people's resistance to (bio)cultural assimilation', in J. Agyeman, R. Bullard and B. Evans (eds), *Just Sustainabilities: Development in an Unequal World*, London: Earthscan/MIT Press.

Roberts, D. (2003), 'Sustainability and equity: reflections of a local government practitioner in South Africa', in J. Agyeman, R. Bullard and B. Evans (eds), *Just Sustainabilities: Development in an Unequal World*, London: Earthscan/MIT Press.

Schlosberg, D. (1999), *Environmental Justice and the New Pluralism: the Challenge of Difference for Environmentalism*, Oxford: Oxford University Press.

Shellenberger, M. and T. Nordhaus (2004), 'The Death of Environmentalism. Global Warming Politics in a Post-Environmental World', available at: www.thebreakthrough.org/images/Death_of_Environmentalism.pdf.

Stockholm Environment Institute – Boston (2002), *Great Transition. The Promise and Lure of the Times Ahead*, Boston: Stockholm Environment Institute.

Taylor, B. (1992), *Our Limits Transgressed: Environmental Political Thought in America*, Kansas City: University Press of Kansas.

Taylor, D. (2000), 'The rise of the environmental justice paradigm', *American Behavioural Scientist*, **43**(4): 508–80.

Torras, M. and J.K. Boyce (1998), 'Income, inequality and pollution: a reassessment of the environmental Kuznets curve', *Ecological Economics*, **25**: 147–60.

United Church of Christ Commission for Racial Justice (1987), *Toxic Wastes and Race in the United States*, New York: United Church of Christ Commission for Racial Justice.

Urban Ecology, www.urbanecology.org.

Wickramasinghe, A. (2003), 'Women and environmental justice in South Asia', in J. Agyeman, R. Bullard and B. Evans (eds), *Just Sustainabilities: Development in an Unequal World*, London: Earthscan/MIT Press.

12 Vulnerability, poverty and sustaining well-being

W. Neil Adger and Alexandra Winkels

1. Introduction

A key tenet of sustainable development is that resources and opportunities should be widely shared in society. Where this fails to occur, individuals, communities and the ecosystems on which they depend are made vulnerable to external perturbations, to failures in governance, and to social crises. Thus development, if it is to be sustainable in the broadest sense, needs to address underlying vulnerabilities in society and vulnerabilities that are created by unsustainable resource use and exploitation.

The recognition that reducing vulnerability is a legitimate normative goal of sustainable development has become apparent in the context of global change. Vulnerability is an important characteristic of individuals, social groups and of natural systems. It is a state in which the ability of people in society to cope with environmental and other stresses is in question. The vulnerability of a group or individual depends on the capacity to respond to external stresses that may come from environmental variability and change, or from social upheaval and change. Vulnerability is made up of a number of components including exposure and sensitivity to hazard or external stresses and the capacity to adapt. Thus, vulnerability does not exist in isolation from the wider political economy of resource use. It is caused by inadvertent or deliberate human action that reinforces self-interest and the distribution of power.

In this chapter we argue that recognizing the interdependencies between factors that create vulnerabilities is central to achieving sustainable development that ensures people's well-being. The concept of vulnerability is important in analysing, for example, the widely observed disparities between the rich and poor regions of the world and between the vulnerable on the one hand and those who are able to insulate themselves against shocks on the other. To this end the first section examines interdependencies of various social, economic and environmental processes that create vulnerabilities. The chapter then takes a close look at the links between vulnerability and livelihoods, recognizing that, in order to achieve well-being for most, the multi-dimensionality of people's vulnerabilities needs to be understood and confronted. Vulnerability is conceptualized in a variety of ways depending on disciplinary emphasis, ranging from the vulnerability of social and ecological systems to the vulnerability of individual livelihoods. One of the most important aspects of the influence of vulnerability on well-being is its context specificity. While measuring vulnerability should be based on commonly agreed-upon thresholds of risk, danger and harm, different approaches are needed to assess people's vulnerability in different contexts. The final section reviews some of these measurement issues and draws out future research trends.

2.   The landscape of vulnerability

Vulnerability is common currency in debates on environmental risks and human development. In the past decade vulnerability is a term used by decision-makers in designing a response to both human-made and natural disasters. In the climate change arena, for example, countries are vulnerable to the impacts of climate change; some populations are exposed to risk associated with the potential spread of vector-borne diseases; and ecosystems and species are vulnerable to degradation or extinction. Many international development agencies now frame their development assistance around concepts of sustainable livelihoods, which incorporate the assessment of vulnerability (Cannon et al., 2002).

The popularity of the term has arisen in these contexts and is underpinned by insights into risk and hazards, institutions and governance, and human well-being (Cutter, 1996; 2003; Blaikie et al., 1994; Turner et al., 2003a). Vulnerability theory explains the processes that convert the distribution of resources in a society into a state which leads to powerlessness, and risk of unsustainable outcomes (both in material terms and in terms of experience) for sections of society. A theory of vulnerability further seeks to distinguish between environmental change as a human-induced element of risk and as a natural element of perturbation, renewal and change (Adger, 2006).

Human well-being is vulnerable to disease, war and natural disaster, while economic structures promoting well-being are vulnerable to globalization, currency speculation and crises of confidence. But well-being is made up of diverse components that have been articulated (by the Millennium Ecosystem Assessment 2003, for example), as basic material needs, health, good social relations, personal security and freedom and choice. Many elements of vulnerability relate to the absence of well-being and security as well as unsustainable resource use, but equally emphasize the importance of empowerment and citizenship within well-being and sustainability.

Vulnerability thus encapsulates the susceptibility to harm of groups or individuals to stress as a result of social change and environmental hazard and change. There are social dimensions to vulnerability and physical and ecological dimensions to vulnerability related to exposure to hazards and dimensions of risk. There are many conceptualizations of vulnerability (see Alwang et al., 2001), but there is common agreement that vulnerability is made up of a number of key components including exposure and sensitivity to hazard and the capacity to adapt. For any given social and economic system, the functional attributes are:

Vulnerability $= f$(exposure, sensitivity, adaptive capacity)

The terms are elaborated in Table 12.1. Exposure encapsulates the likelihood of occurrence and the impact of a discrete event whose influence extends over a particular area with particular characteristics. The characteristics of exposure include magnitude, frequency, duration and areal extent of the hazard (Burton et al., 1993). Sensitivity is the extent to which a human or natural system can absorb impacts without suffering long-term harm or some significant state change. This concept of sensitivity, closely related to resilience, can be observed in physical, ecological and social systems. Adaptive capacity is the ability of a system to evolve in order to accommodate environmental hazards or policy change and to expand the range of variability with which it can cope.

Vulnerability is socially differentiated: virtually all natural hazards and human causes of vulnerability impact differently on different groups in

Table 12.1 Attributes of vulnerability to environmental and social change and perturbations

Element of vulnerability	Definition
Exposure	The nature and degree to which a system experiences environmental or socio-political stress.
Sensitivity	The extent to which a human or natural system can absorb the impacts without suffering long-term harm or some significant state change. This concept of sensitivity, closely related to resilience, can be observed in physical systems with impact-response models, but requires greater interpretation in ecological and social systems, where harm and state change are more contested.
Adaptive capacity	The ability of a system to evolve in order to accommodate environmental perturbations or to expand the range of variability with which it can cope.

society. Many comparative studies have noted that the poor and marginalized have historically been most at risk from natural hazards (see Chapter 11). Poorer households are forced to live in higher risk areas, exposing them to the impacts of earthquakes, landslides, flooding, tsunamis and poor air and water quality. This has particularly been shown throughout the urbanized world (Mitchell, 1999; Pelling, 2003). Women are differentially at risk from many elements of environmental hazards, including, for example, the burden of work in recovery of home and livelihood after an event (Fordham, 2003). In many studies of the impact of earthquakes (including analysis of the Asian tsunami of 2004) women and other household dependants have suffered much greater mortality. Even for volcanic eruptions, which would appear to be indiscriminate in impact in terms of social status, it is noted that significant social differentiation is important (Sidle et al., 2004). Flooding in low-lying coastal areas associated with monsoon climates or hurricane impacts, for example, are seasonal and usually short-lived, yet can have significant unexpected impacts for vulnerable sections of society. Yet river flooding is an integral part of many farming systems as it provides nutrients in fertile floodplain areas. Hence natural hazards are often a disadvantageous aspect of a phenomenon at one point in time that is predominantly, and usually beneficial. Impacts associated with geological hazards often occur without much effective warning and with a speed of onset of only a few minutes. By contrast, the HIV/AIDS epidemic is a long wave disaster with a slow onset but catastrophic impact (Barnett and Blaikie, 1994).

Vulnerabilities are becoming connected to global change in environmental and economic systems. While there is little doubt that the connections of globalization have brought about a revolution in knowledge, information and ideas, the negative consequences of capital flows and of the ability of both countries and transnational corporations to wield power at the global scale are also enormous. There are three major mechanisms of interdependence of vulnerabilities of ecosystems, people and places (see Adger et al., 2007). These are the processes of global environmental change, economic market linkages, and flows of resources, people and information.

The first of the mechanisms for interdependence is the set of physical and biological processes that constitute global environmental change. Due to the global nature of environmental change processes accelerating in particular during the past century, impacts of environmental change in one locality have increased connection to regional and global systems. Second, economic market linkages are not only linked to global environmental change, but also can in and of themselves be drivers of interdependent vulnerabilities. The processes of global environmental change are indeed amplified by the social, political and economic trends of globalization.

Global environmental change is driven in part by widening disparities between rich and poor both within and between countries. Liberalizing trade and integrating economies into world markets (see also Chapter 25) can make the incomes of the poor insecure, open to vagaries and price fluctuations, and ultimately more vulnerable when other shocks and stresses come along (O'Brien and Leichenko, 2000).

The third mechanism of interdependence of vulnerabilities across space and time is the closer connection between places in the world which has emerged through increased air travel and lower transport costs, and through movements of people and resources around the world. This has several dimensions, both positive and negative in terms of vulnerability. Demographic changes and migrations (see Chapter 8) produce new forms of sensitivity to risk, while providing some populations with new opportunities or access to resources that enable them to mitigate uncertainty. Increasing proportions of very old or very young people in a population, for example, change the nature of susceptibility to emerging diseases and pathogens. Further, the actual movement of resources for energy, food and primary production have both direct and indirect consequences. The food eaten at dinner tables across the industrialized world, for example, has increasing environmental impact due to energy and fertilizer inputs, transport, and land use changes associated with new production. Agricultural and economic policies in one part of the world have direct consequences on producers in another part of the world, and the globalization of consumer tastes is now driving commodity production in agricultural regions. The consequences of the movement of materials round the world are also increasingly apparent in bio-invasive species, demand for habitats and over-exploitation of species, and the emergence of new diseases (Adger et al., 2007).

One of the sustainability goals is to ensure a minimum level of well-being which, among other things, depends on people's ability to cope adequately with shocks and stresses that may plunge them into poverty. Ensuring people's well-being relies therefore on finding ways to reduce vulnerability by taking into account the interdependencies of global and local mechanisms as described above that create these vulnerabilities. This is particularly crucial for the poor and marginalized in many countries as they are least able to insure themselves against the ill effects of global economic fluctuations and environmental risks (Wood, 2003).

3.   Livelihoods and well-being
Over the past 50 years there have been spectacular successes in raising living standards in many parts of the world. Yet economic growth alone has not eliminated poverty anywhere. Deprivation of opportunity is still widespread, most obviously in the developing world where lack of absolute

income for large numbers of people limits their health, material well-being and their freedom (Sen, 1999). Policies to promote livelihoods and well-being of populations in the developing world have been subject to various ideological fashions and beliefs. The focus on economic growth in the 1950s and 1960s was superseded by a focus on poverty elimination through basic need strategies in the 1970s. Poor economic performance in many developing countries in the 1980s resulting from structural adjustments policies (see Chapter 14) and a sharp rise in poverty during that period led to a renewed interest in poverty and the poor themselves (Gardner and Lewis, 1996).

The Millennium Development Goals demonstrate that the livelihoods and well-being of the world's poor are now conceptualized in terms of access to opportunity and absence of insecurity and vulnerability. The goals include focus on inadequate incomes, hunger, gender inequality, environmental deterioration and lack of education, health care, and clean water (UNDP, 2003). Sen (1999) argues that the overarching goal of human development should be the ability for all people to realize their potential and that this is not fulfilled through economic means alone. In this context it is important to emphasize that poverty and vulnerability are not the same thing. Hence, while those who are poor are more likely to be vulnerable, the non-poor may also be vulnerable to a deterioration in well-being as a result of a shock.

Sustainable livelihoods and realized capabilities are the antithesis of vulnerability and poverty. Sen (1981) developed the concept of human capability to explain the causes and persistence of poverty even in times of overall positive economic growth. Poverty is the lack of capability to live a decent life (Sen, 1999). Entitlements and capabilities are the actual or potential resources available to individuals based on their own production, assets or reciprocal arrangements. Entitlements are sources of welfare or income that are realized or are latent. They are 'the set of alternative commodity bundles that a person can command in a society using the totality of rights and opportunities that he or she faces' (Sen, 1984, p. 497). Poverty, manifest for example through food insecurity, is a consequence of human activity, which can be prevented by modified behaviour and by political interventions. Thus, vulnerability is the result of processes in which humans actively engage and which they can almost always prevent. The theory of entitlements as an explanation for famine causes was developed in the early 1980s (Sen, 1981; 1984) and displaced prior notions that shortfalls in food production through drought, flood or pest were the principal cause of insecurity in agrarian societies. Essentially, vulnerability occurs when people have insufficient real income and access to resources, and when there is a breakdown in other previously-held endowments (see Chapter 14 for examples).

Analysis of entitlements, access to resources and welfare services in the face of stress and crisis is therefore a cornerstone of vulnerability theory. The need for livelihoods to be sustainable has been the focus of research and action on resource-dependent societies and economies. A widely accepted definition of so-called sustainable livelihoods is that by Robert Chambers and Gordon Conway (1992), which highlights the need for reducing vulnerability, coping with stress, and moving forward through adaptation while securing well-being into the future:

> A livelihood comprises the capabilities, assets (including both material and social resources) and activities required for a means of living. A livelihood is sustainable when it can cope with and recover from stresses and shocks and maintain or enhance its capabilities and assets both now and in the future, while not undermining the natural resource base. (Chambers and Conway, 1992)

The sustainable livelihood concept appears in many guises and is subject to a continuing debate. Discussions focus on the operationalization of these ideas and how to make both processes and outcomes relevant for policy and development practice. The sustainable livelihoods approach provides a tool for the assessment not only of micro-level conditions such as individual or households capabilities, access to assets and individual aspirations, but situates these attributes within their wider institutional, historical, environmental and economic context.

Within a particular vulnerability context (such as a combination of shifting seasonal constraints, short-term economic shocks and longer-term trends of change) individuals deploy different types of 'livelihood assets' or capital in variable combinations (Bebbington, 1999; Reardon and Vosti, 1995; Scoones, 1998; Ellis, 2000). Understanding how institutions shape, and are shaped by, livelihood processes is also important in livelihood research (Ellis, 2000). Institutions, in this context, are the formal and informal rules, norms or procedures that govern relationships within and between different organizations and between formal organizations and the civic sphere. Vulnerable communities and individuals are excluded from access and institutions to decision-making: so-called relational aspects of deprivation (Kabeer, 2000).

Economic, social, demographic, political and psychological aspects of human vulnerability gain different prominence in different disciplines (shown in Table 12.2). In the context of disaster management human vulnerability is defined with respect to discrete events in nature or associated with technological failures (such as pollution incidents). Vulnerability is usually defined as an underlying condition, undermining people's capability to respond adequately to the disaster, thus precipitating a negative outcome with respect to their well-being (Kreimer and Arnold, 2000).

Table 12.2   Examples of how vulnerability is conceptualized across different arenas and disciplines

Vulnerability area	Traditions	Objectives	Sources
Vulnerability to hazards	Vulnerability and capacities	Identification and prediction of vulnerable groups to facilitate intervention	Anderson and Woodrow (1998); Frankenberger et al., (2001)
	Pressure and release	Structural analysis of underlying causes of vulnerability to hazards and risks, linking discrete risks with political economy of resources	Blaikie et al. (1994); Pelling (2003)
Vulnerability of social- ecological systems	Vulnerability to global change	Explaining the vulnerability of coupled human–environment systems	Turner et al. (2003a; 2003b) Luers et al. (2003); O'Brien et al. (2004)
	Climate change and variability	Explaining (and predicting) social, physical or ecological system vulnerability to (primarily) future risks	Smit and Pilifosova (2001); Parry et al. (2001); Ford and Smit (2004)
Vulnerability of livelihoods and poverty	Entitlements and capabilities	Developed to explain vulnerability to famine even in the absence of shortages of food or production failures	Sen (1981); Swift (1989); Watts and Bohle (1993)
	Poverty and social exclusion	Explains why populations become or stay poor based on analysis of economic factors and social relations	Kabeer (2000); Kamanou and Morduch (2004); Morduch (1994)
	Assets and vulnerability	Explains vulnerability of populations to risks on the basis of capital assets, from physical to social	Bebbington (1999); Moser (1998); Rakodi (1999); Reardon and Vosti (1995)
	Sustainable livelihoods analysis	Explains the material outcomes and the ability to sustain these over time on the basis of capital assets	Chambers et al. (1989); Davies (1996); Ellis (2000)

There has been much work in the field of climate change that seeks to illuminate vulnerability, but this is often focused solely on a social system or on the vulnerability of a species or ecosystem damage. Research that seeks to understand the vulnerability of systems, which includes both social and natural elements, is primarily concerned with the assessment of vulnerability of that system in its various manifestations (Adger et al., 2001; Turner et al., 2003a). Research in development economics perceives vulnerability as an outcome of a process of household responses to risk. Since the measurement of vulnerability at the individual level is extremely difficult, it is often reduced to one single causal factor. Alternatively, vulnerability of livelihoods and well-being is a condition that takes into account both exposure to risks and a household's defencelessness against deprivation, that is the external and internal aspects of vulnerability (Chambers et al., 1989; Kamanou and Morduch, 2004).

4. Vulnerability as a relative measure of deprivation and susceptibility to harm

There is no straightforward way to measure vulnerability. Measurement of vulnerability inevitably needs to reflect social processes, environmental perturbations and material outcomes: it is not easily reduced to a single metric. While it is easy to recognize personally the feeling of vulnerability and perhaps to grasp the outcome of vulnerability in others in a similar situation, the translation of this complex set of parameters into a quantitative metric has been argued to reduce its impact and hide its complexity (Alwang et al., 2001). There have been significant advances in methods in vulnerability analysis towards measures that both incorporate human well-being and recognize the relative and perceptual nature of vulnerability.

In the quantitative social sciences, particularly in economics, there have been attempts to develop metrics for vulnerability that are comparable across time and location to make them more tractable (Kamanou and Morduch, 2004; Alwang et al., 2001). Much of the research is concerned with vulnerability to poverty and, in the search for tractability, often focuses on consumption as the key parameter. But since societies are vulnerable to multiple stresses and vulnerability is manifest in various outcomes (not just material), there are, in effect, different thresholds on vulnerability informed by values and social context (Alwang et al., 2001). It is important nonetheless to provide consistent frameworks for measuring vulnerability that provide complementary quantitative and qualitative insights into outcomes and perceptions of vulnerability. While quantitative measures allow comparison of relative vulnerability across circumstances, these do not substitute for the narrative richness of stakeholder-led or qualitative assessments of vulnerability in different places and contexts.

Households capable of deriving an adequate living from their assets or the transient poor can all be vulnerable to poverty as a result of shocks to those livelihoods. Households that already face capability constraints due to structural factors such as landlessness or contextual factors such as the lack of social welfare from government or community, are also vulnerable to a further decline in welfare through the exposure to shocks such as failing local markets or illness within the family. Vulnerability is, however, also the outcome of a shock and social exclusion by limiting the capability to deal with subsequent shocks. The degree to which a household is vulnerable, and continues to be so, is a function of the risk factors, both internal and external to the household, and their capability (determined by asset portfolio) to respond to these risks (Alwang et al., 2001).

Livelihoods can be exposed to risks particular to the household (idiosyncratic risks) as well as to those shared throughout the wider community (covariate risks). On the one hand, the sources of risks can be related to external shocks such as varying climatic conditions (for example floods and droughts), commodity price fluctuations, or poorly functioning input and output markets. While some droughts contribute to the development of a famine crisis, not every drought results in a famine. Table 12.3 summarizes the types of risk arising from changing environmental, social and economic conditions and how these can affect access to assets and activities, which shape livelihoods. Risk sources can also be specific to households and are often related to illness and death, or changing social relationships.

In addition to the physical and social risks in Table 12.3, there are institutional and relational sources of risk (Wood, 2003). Chronic poverty, for example, may give rise to a number of risks induced by inequality, class relations, exploitation, and social exclusion from community structures. Household vulnerability and social exclusion are therefore in themselves risk factors because they re-enforce the deeper structures that lead to deprivation and chronic poverty (Wood, 2003). Those households who already face deprivation of livelihood capability are less able to reallocate their assets to overcome other risky events.

Methods for vulnerability assessment in the context of development assistance and famine early warning systems have been developed and used across the developing world (Cannon et al., 2002; Twigg, 2001; Stephen and Downing, 2001). Local and national indicators have been developed, seeking to overcome issues of validation and triangulation of data to derive more robust measures for both policy analysis and intervention (Yohe and Tol, 2002). A common critique of indicator research, particularly focused on country-level analysis, is that it fails to account for sub-national spatial and social differentiation of vulnerability, and local conditions mediate the

Table 12.3 *Types and sources of risk to sustainable livelihood*

Sources of livelihood	Environmental risk	Social risk		Economic risk	Conflict
		Government	Community		
Human capital Labour power, education, health	Disease epidemics due to poor sanitary conditions, AIDS	Declining public health expenditures, user charges, declining education expenditures	Breakdown in community support of social services	Privatization of social services, reduction in labour opportunities	Conflict destroys social infrastructure and restricts mobility
Financial and natural capital Productive resources and capital resources	Drought, flooding, land degradation, pests, animal disease	Land confiscation, insecure tenure rights, taxes, employment policies	Appropriation and loss of common property resources, increased theft	Price shocks, rapid inflation, food shortages	Conflict leads to loss of land, assets, and theft
Social Capital Claims, kinship, networks, safety nets, common property	Recurring environmental shocks, breakdown ability to reciprocate, morbidity and mortality affect social capital	Reduction in safety net support (school feeding etc)	Breakdown of labour reciprocity, breakdown of sharing mechanisms, stricter loan requirements, lack of social cohesion	Shift to institutional forms of trust, stricter loan collateral requirements, migration for employment	Communities displaced by war, theft leads to breakdown in trust
Sources of income Productive activities, process and exchange activities, other sources of employment, seasonal migration	Seasonal climatic fluctuations affecting employment opportunities, drought, flooding, pests, animal disease, morbidity and mortality of income earners	Employment policies declining subsidies or inputs, poor investment in infrastructure, taxes		Unemployment, falling real wages, price shocks	Marketing channels disrupted by war

Source: Adapted from Frankenberger et al. (2001, p. 77).

capacity to adapt. Progress has been made, however, in the spatial mapping of elements of vulnerability (for example O'Brien et al., 2004).

The implications of the relative nature of vulnerability and its manifestations in perceptions of insecurity are that any generalized method to measure vulnerability needs to incorporate an objective material measure of vulnerability but also to capture relative vulnerability, inequality in its distribution and social status. The vulnerability of any population is not simply a matter of the number of people who are vulnerable through not having entitlements to resources or not being exposed to stresses associated with environmental change. Rather a generalized measure needs to account for the severity of the vulnerability and the measure needs also to be sensitive to redistribution of risk within vulnerable populations. Ideally a measure of vulnerability, therefore, requires certain characteristics. These necessary characteristics of a measure are familiar in micro-economics and social statistics, for example in the measurement of poverty (building on Foster et al., 1984), because they also deal with issues of well-being, relative versus absolute change and transient versus persistent states.

Luers and colleagues (2003) directly address many of the dilemmas of measuring vulnerability. Their approach represents a state-of-the-art. In recognizing many of the constraints they make a case for measuring the vulnerability of specific variables: they argue that vulnerability should shift away from quantifying critical areas or vulnerable places towards scale-neutral systematic measures. They argue for assessing the vulnerability of the most important variables in the causal chain of vulnerability to specific sets of stressors. They develop generic metrics that attempt to assess the relationship between a wide range of stressors and the outcome variables of concern (Luers et al., 2003). In their most general form:

$$\text{Vulnerability} = \frac{\text{sensitivity to stress}}{\text{state relative} \atop \text{to threshold} \times {\text{probability of} \atop \text{exposure to stress}}}$$

The parameter under scrutiny here could be a physical or social parameter. In the case of Luers et al. (2003) they investigate the vulnerability of farming systems in an irrigated area of Mexico through examining agricultural yields. But the same generalized equation could examine disease prevalence, mortality in human populations, or income of households – all of which are legitimate potential measures within vulnerability analysis.

Whatever the generalized form of vulnerability measure there is an inescapable need for a threshold of risk, danger or harm. The measures of vulnerability severity discussed above involve a measure of well-being. But this could be measured in a number of different ways. It could be objective material measures such as indicators of mortality, income, wealth or freedom from crime or access to education, depending on the nature of the vulnerability being measured. In addition vulnerability as experienced could be measured directly through indicators of perception, as used in social psychology.

The problem of course is that any meaningful threshold is likely to be highly heterogeneous. As Watts and Bohle (1993) and Cutter (2003) argue, vulnerability is manifest in specific places at specific times: hence the determination of the threshold level of well-being that constitutes the threshold is not simply a proportional measure, the same for all sections of society. In addition, the choice of thresholds is based on values and preferences and hence is both institutionally and culturally determined. The measurement of vulnerability inevitably requires external judgements and interpretations of the thresholds of acceptable risk. This characteristic of the inescapability of a vulnerability threshold needs to be both made explicit and embraced in vulnerability methods.

5. Trends and prospects for future research

There are a number of linkages between livelihoods, sustainability and vulnerability. First, due to the complexity of the future (for example trends in environmental change, technologies and other social and demographic processes), individuals and social systems are always vulnerable to surprise and susceptible to unforeseen consequences of action (Cutter, 2003; Schneider et al., 1998). While policy makers always express surprise at events, many of these are predictable or at least 'imaginable'. Yet vulnerability persists, due both to inherent unpredictability in some physical systems, but also because of ideological blocks to perceiving certain risks. Thus technological risks that create new vulnerabilities (from nuclear power to genetically-modified agricultural crops) are ignored in the name of progress. If a goal of sustainable development is to eliminate risks to the most vulnerable, then this suggests that application of the precautionary principle should be central to decision processes.

The second area of linkage between sustainability and vulnerability, and the major focus of this chapter, has been the link between widespread access to minimum levels of well-being as a sustainability goal and the implementation of this goal through vulnerability reduction. We have argued here that the distribution of income and access to resources represent fundamental determinants of capability and vulnerability. Evidence that inequality plays a role in exacerbated environmental degradation is compounded when wider conceptions of marginalization and resilience are included (see Chapter 5). The changing nature of access to resources and thus well-being and the impacts of global economic change potentially undermine social resilience and create circumstances to which the only response of the vulnerable is resistance. Social resilience is enhanced or undermined both by the formal institutions of the state and the legal framework of property rights, and by the outcomes of democratic governance. There is much rhetoric on the need to reduce vulnerability in the context of global disasters and the threats of climate change. Yet the consequences of actually implementing action that puts vulnerability centre stage are profound, and, in our view, explain why sustainable development for the marginalized and vulnerable who bear the brunt of environmental degradation is a moral and political imperative.

References

Adger, W.N. (2006), 'Vulnerability', Global Environmental Change, **16**: 268–81.
Adger, W.N., P.M. Kelly and N.H. Ninh (eds) (2001), *Living with Environmental Change: Social Vulnerability, Adaptation and Resilience in Vietnam*, London: Routledge.
Adger, W.N., H. Eakin and A. Winkels (2007), 'Nested and networked vulnerabilities in South East Asia', in L. Lebel (ed.), *Global Environmental Change and the South-east Asian Region: An Assessment of the State of the Science*, Washington, DC: Island Press (in press).
Alwang, J., P.B. Siegel and S.L. Jorgensen (2001), 'Vulnerability: a view from different disciplines', Discussion Paper Series No. 0115, Washington DC: Social Protection Unit, World Bank.
Anderson, M.B. and P.J. Woodrow (1998), *Rising from the Ashes. Development Strategies in Times of Disaster*, London: Intermediate Technology Publications.
Barnett, A. and P. Blaikie (1994), 'AIDS as a long wave disaster', in A. Varley (ed.), *Disasters, Development, and Environment*, Chichester: Wiley, pp. 139–62.
Bebbington, A. (1999), 'Capital and capabilities: a framework for analyzing peasant viability, rural livelihoods and poverty', *World Development*, **27**: 2021–44.
Blaikie, P., T. Cannon, I. Davis and B. Wisner (1994), *At Risk: Natural Hazards, People's Vulnerability and Disasters*, London: Routledge.
Burton, I., R.W. Kates and G.F. White (1993), *The Environment as Hazard*, 2nd edn, New York: Guilford Press.
Cannon, T., J. Twigg and J. Rowell (2002), *Social Vulnerability, Sustainable Livelihoods and Disasters*, London: Livelihoods and Institutions Group, Natural Resources Institutes, University of Greenwich.
Chambers, R. and G. Conway (1992), 'Sustainable rural livelihoods: Practical concepts for the 21st Century', Discussion Paper 296, Brighton: Institute of Development Studies, University of Sussex.
Chambers, R., A. Pacey and L.A. Thrupp (1989), *Farmer First: Farmer Innovation and Agricultural Research*, London: Intermediate Technology Publications.
Cutter, S.L. (1996), 'Vulnerability to environmental hazards', *Progress in Human Geography*, **20**: 529–39.
Cutter, S.L. (2003), 'The vulnerability of science and the science of vulnerability', *Annals of the Association of American Geographers*, **93**: 1–12.
Davies, S. (1996), *Adaptable Livelihoods. Coping with Food Insecurity in the Malian Sahel*, London: Macmillan.
Ellis, F. (2000), *Rural Livelihood Diversity in Developing Countries*, Oxford: Oxford University Press.
Ford, J.D. and B. Smit (2004), 'A framework for assessing the vulnerability of communities in the Canadian Arctic to risks associated with climate change', *Arctic*, **57**: 389–400.
Fordham, M. (2003), 'Gender, disaster and development: the necessity for integration', in M. Pelling (ed.), *Natural Disasters and Development in a Globalizing World*, London: Routledge, pp. 57–74.

Foster, J., J. Greer and E. Thorbecke (1984), 'A class of decomposable poverty measures', *Econometrica*, **52**: 761–6.

Frankenberger, T., M. Drinkwater and D. Maxwell (2001), 'Operationalizing household livelihood security', in FAO (ed.), *Forum on Operationalizing Participatory Ways of Applying Sustainable Livelihoods Approaches*, Rome: FAO.

Gardner, K. and D. Lewis (1996), *Anthropology, Development and the Post-modern Challenge*, London: Pluto Press.

Kabeer, N. (2000), 'Social exclusion, poverty and discrimination: Towards an analytical framework', *IDS Bulletin*, **31**.

Kamanou, G. and J. Morduch (2004), 'Measuring vulnerability to poverty', in S. Dercon (ed.), *Insurance against Poverty*, Oxford: Oxford University Press.

Kreimer, A. and M. Arnold (2000), *Managing Disaster Risk in Emerging Economies*, Washington, DC: World Bank.

Luers, A.L., D.B. Lobell, L.S. Sklar, C.L. Addams and P.A. Matson (2003), 'A method for quantifying vulnerability, applied to the agricultural system of the Yaqui Valley, Mexico', *Global Environmental Change*, **13**: 255–67.

McCarthy, J.J., O.F. Canziani, N.A. Leary, D.J. Dokken and K.S. White (eds) (2001), *Climate Change 2001: Impacts, Adaptation, and Vulnerability*, Cambridge: Cambridge University Press.

Millennium Ecosystem Assessment (2003), *Ecosystems and Human Well-being: A Framework for Assessment*, Washington, DC: Island Press.

Mitchell, J.K. (ed.) (1999), *Crucibles of Hazard: Mega-cities and Disasters in Transition*, Tokyo: UNU Press.

Morduch, J. (1994), 'Poverty and vulnerability', *American Economic Review*, **84**: 221–5.

Moser, C. (1998), 'The asset vulnerability framework: reassessing urban poverty reduction strategies', *World Development*, **26**: 1–19.

O'Brien, K.L. and R.M. Leichenko (2000), 'Double exposure: assessing the impacts of climate change within the context of economic globalisation', *Global Environmental Change*, **10**: 221–32.

O'Brien, K.L., R. Leichenko, U. Kelkarc, H. Venemad, G. Aandahl, H. Tompkins, A. Javed, S. Bhadwal, S. Barg, L. Nygaard and J. West (2004), 'Mapping vulnerability to multiple stressors: climate change and globalization in India', *Global Environmental Change*, **14**: 303–13.

Parry, M., N. Arnell, T. McMichael, R.J. Nicholls, P. Martens, S. Kovats, M. Livermore, C. Rosenzweig, A. Aglesias and G. Fischer (2001), 'Millions at risk: defining critical climate change threats and targets', *Global Environmental Change*, **11**: 181–3.

Pelling, M. (2003), *The Vulnerability of Cities: Natural Disasters and Social Resilience*, London: Earthscan.

Rakodi, C. (1999), 'A capital assets framework for analyzing household livelihood strategies', *Development Policy Review*, **17**: 315–42.

Reardon, T. and S.A. Vosti (1995), 'Links between rural poverty and the environment in developing countries: asset categories and investment poverty', *World Development*, **23**: 1495–506.

Schneider, S.H., B.L. Turner II and H.M. Garriga (1998), 'Imaginable surprise in global change science', *Journal of Risk Research*, **1**: 165–85.

Scoones, I. (1998), 'Sustainable rural livelihoods a framework for analysis', *IDS* Working Paper No. 72.

Sen, A. (1981), *Poverty and Famines: An Essay on Entitlements and Famines*, Oxford: Clarendon.

Sen, A.K. (1984), *Resources, Values and Development*, Oxford: Blackwell.

Sen, A. (1999), *Development as Freedom*, Oxford: Oxford University Press.

Sidle, R.C., D. Taylor, X.X. Lu, W.N. Adger, D.J. Lowe, W.P. de Lange, R.M. Newnham and J.R. Dodson (2004), 'Interactions of natural hazards and society in Austral-Asia: evidence in historical and recent records', *Quaternary International*, **118–119**: 181–203.

Smit, B. and O. Pilifosova (2001), 'Adaptation to climate change in the context of sustainable development and equity', in J.J. McCarthy, O. Canziani, N.A. Leary, D.J. Dokken and

K.S. White (eds), *Climate Change 2001: Impacts, Adaptation and Vulnerability. IPCC Working Group II*, Cambridge: Cambridge University Press, pp. 877–912.

Stephen, L. and T.E. Downing (2001), 'Getting the scale right: a comparison of analytical methods for vulnerability assessment and household-level targeting', *Disasters*, **25**: 113–35.

Swift, J. (1989), 'Why are rural people vulnerable to famine?', *IDS Bulletin*, **20** (2): 8–15.

Turner, B.L.II, R.E. Kasperson, P.A. Matson, J.J. McCarthy, R.W. Corell, L. Christensen, N. Eckley, J.X. Kasperson, A. Luers, M.L. Martello, C. Polsky, A. Pulsipher and A. Schiller (2003a), 'A framework for vulnerability analysis in sustainability science', *Proceedings of the National Academy of Sciences US*, **100**: 8074–79.

Turner, B.L.I., P.A. Matson, J.J. McCarthy, R.W. Corell, L. Christensen, N. Eckley, G.K. Hovelsrud-Broda, J.X. Kasperson, R.E. Kasperson, A. Luers, M.L. Martello, S. Mathiesen, R. Naylor, C. Polsky, A. Pulsipher, A. Schiller, H. Selin and N. Tyler (2003b), 'Illustrating the coupled human-environment system for vulnerability analysis: three case studies', *Proceedings of the National Academy of Sciences US*, **100**: 8080–85.

Twigg, J. (2001), 'Sustainable livelihoods and vulnerability to disasters', Benfield Greig Hazard Research Centre, University College London.

UNDP (2003), *Human Development Report 2003 Millennium Development Goals: A Compact among Nations to end Human Poverty*, Oxford: Oxford University Press.

Watts, M.J. and H.G. Bohle (1993), 'The space of vulnerability: the causal structure of hunger and famine', *Progress in Human Geography*, **17**: 43–67.

Wood, G. (2003), 'Staying secure, staying poor: the Faustian bargain', *World Development*, **31**: 455–71.

Yohe, G. and R.S.J. Tol (2002), 'Indicators for social and economic coping capacity: moving toward a working definition of adaptive capacity', *Global Environmental Change*, **12**: 25–40.

PART IV

GROWTH, CONSUMPTION AND NATURAL WEALTH

13 The resource curse and sustainable development
Richard M. Auty

1. Introduction

Resource abundance can increase the rate of investment in resource-rich economies relative to resource-poor ones and also expand the capacity of the economy to import the capital goods needed to build the infrastructure of a high-income country. Consequently, natural resource abundance can accelerate economic growth and thereby strengthen sustainable development, provided the correction of market failure curbs environmental damage. Renewable natural resources can yield the rent stream to promote this outcome indefinitely under informed and rational management. But sustainable development can also be based upon the rent from depleting finite resources. To achieve this, resource and environmental accounting shows that a sufficient fraction of the natural resource rent should be invested during the exploitation of the finite resource in order to maintain or enhance the total capital stock (see Chapter 17 and 18). In this way the income stream generated by the resource is passed on to future generations in perpetuity. This perspective assumes either that there are natural substitutes for the depleted resource or that technological substitutes will be found. In this view, conservation of the finite resource might be undesirable if new technology renders the resource obsolete.

Nevertheless, the notion that natural resource abundance can be a curse has emerged strongly since the 1980s. It is not a new idea, however. Imperial Spain provides a long-recognized example of a country that failed to prosper from the gold and silver shipped from its New World colonies. In contrast, Spain's beleaguered Dutch colonies were developing the economic dynamic that was to win them their freedom and make them the commercial model for western Europe. Subsequently, the failure of Argentina[1] and, until very recently, of Australia to sustain the successful growth that both those countries enjoyed during the second half of the nineteenth century (Lewis, 1978) has been attributed to the curse of wealth. A stark contrast has arisen since the 1960s between the rapid economic transition of the four resource-poor Asian dragons (Hong Kong, Singapore, South Korea and Taiwan) and the growth collapses experienced through the 1970s and 1980s by many resource-rich countries (Lal and Myint, 1996).

2. The incidence of the 'resource curse'

The recent growth collapses in many oil-rich economies attracted particular attention from researchers. As a group these countries received transfers from the oil consumers estimated by Chenery (1981) at 2 per cent of gross world product (GWP) annually during 1974–78 and an additional 2 per cent during 1979–81. For individual oil exporters, the oil windfalls ranged from around an extra 10–15 per cent of non-oil GDP annually for Venezuela and Indonesia, through almost 40 per cent for Trinidad and Tobago (Gelb et al., 1988), to over 100 per cent of non-oil GDP for Saudi Arabia (Auty, 1990). Yet with the exception of Indonesia, the oil exporters experienced growth collapses. Nigeria provides the most spectacular example: the country is estimated to have absorbed oil rent in excess of $300 billion during 1974–2004, averaging around an extra 23 per cent of non-oil GDP during 1974–81. These revenues transformed a dynamic and diversified economy, which grew by 7 per cent per annum during 1967–74 into a mono-product basket case with a per capita income by 2004 less than one-quarter of what it would have been if it had sustained its pre-oil boom growth rate. There is little wonder that Gelb (1988) entitled his book: *Oil Windfalls: Blessing or Curse?*

Research into the resource curse focused at first upon the mineral economies, which appeared to have performed especially poorly during the years after 1973. Gelb et al. (1988) analysed the macroeconomic response of six oil-exporting countries (Algeria, Ecuador, Indonesia, Nigeria, Trinidad and Tobago and Venezuela). They concluded that most governments found it politically difficult to resist pressure to spend the oil windfalls, so that the over-rapid domestic absorption of the oil revenues triggered patterns of consumption that sustained Dutch disease effects and proved difficult to cut back when oil prices fell. Indonesia shows, however, that a growth collapse can be avoided if sufficient oil revenue is used to diversify the economy competitively (Timmer, 2004).

Auty (1990) examined the efforts of eight oil-exporting countries to 'sow the oil' by diversifying into resource-based industrialization (RBI). He demonstrated that few oil-rich governments had the capacity to build RBI plants efficiently and that the sharp increase in production of energy-intensive products caused by such investments was sufficient to glut global markets so that the high-cost plants could not recoup their costs. In the worst cases, like the steel plants in Nigeria, Venezuela and Trinidad and Tobago, the RBI projects degenerated into sinks for public sector funds rather than yielding the expected increased capital with which to further diversify the economy. Subsequently, Auty (1993) analysed six ore-exporting countries, which also failed to make effective use of the rent from copper, bauxite and tin to achieve the required competitive diversification of their economies.

Such studies did not go unchallenged. For example, Neary and van Wijnbergen (1986) noted that some restructuring of the mineral economy was a rational response to a mineral boom, and would be self-correcting as the boom faded, provided prudent policies were followed. Elsewhere, Davies (1995) took umbrage at the alleged maladroit performance of the mineral economies, arguing that many displayed relatively high indices of social welfare, irrespective of their growth performance. It was at this stage in the debate that Sachs and Warner weighed in with a series of papers drawing upon econometric analysis of data on the performance of the developing countries as a group since 1970.

Sachs and Warner (1995a) used the average share of exports in GDP as their measure of resource dependence, and they confirmed a negative link between reliance on natural resources and economic growth. They showed that the cross-country average share of primary exports in GDP during 1970–89 was 13 per cent, but that a one unit standard deviation increase (13 per cent) in the share of primary exports reduced the growth rate of per capita GDP by almost 1 per cent. This finding appears to be insensitive to the inclusion of other variables in the analysis, or to changes in the chosen measure of resource intensity. Sachs and Warner (1997) went on to demonstrate that the underlying adverse effect of a rich natural resource endowment on per capita GDP growth is indeed robust. They showed that the finding persists after additional tests that control for institutional quality, the share of investment in GDP, the shift in exports prices compared with import prices, a dummy variable for a regional effect, the removal of outliers such as the oil-exporting countries and splitting the time period into two separate decades.

Similarly, Auty and Kiiski (2001) detected growth collapses in three out of four sub-groups of resource-rich countries during the 1973–85 years of price shocks, while growth collapsed in most oil-exporting countries, the fourth category, in the mid-1980s. In contrast, the growth rates of the resource-poor countries remained relatively high or even accelerated (see Table 13.1). The net effect of these trends was to lift the median income of the resource-poor countries significantly above that of the resource-rich countries, whereas a generation earlier it had been one-third lower.

3. Exogenous explanations for the resource curse

Explanations for the recent disappointing performance of the resource-rich countries have been sought in terms of falling commodity prices, high levels of price volatility, Dutch disease effects and the commodity production function. More recent attention has focused on endogenous explanations like policy error and rent-seeking activity.

Table 13.1   Share of rents in GDP 1994 and GDP growth 1985–97, by natural resource endowment

Resource Endowment	PCGDP growth 1985–97 (%)	Total rent (% GDP)	Pasture and cropland rent (% GDP)	Mineral rent (% GDP)
Resource Poor[1,2]				
Large	4.7	10.56	7.34	3.22
Small	2.4	9.86	5.41	4.45
Resource Rich				
Large	1.9	12.65	5.83	6.86
Small, non-mineral	0.9	15.42	12.89	2.53
Small, hard mineral	−0.4	17.51	9.62	7.89
Small, oil exporter	−0.7	21.22	2.18	19.04
All Countries		15.03	8.78	6.25

Notes:
Comprehensive data on rents available for 1994 only.
[1] Resource-poor = 1970 cropland/head < 0.3 hectares.
[2] Large = 1970 GDP > $7 billion.

Source: Derived from World Bank (2002a).

One early post-war explanation for the resource curse arises from the Prebisch terms of trade hypothesis, which argues that over the long term, prices of primary commodities decline relative to prices of manufactures (Prebisch, 1950). Consequently, over time the resource-rich countries must export more and more primary products in order to import a given volume of manufactured goods. Worse, nascent industrialization is snuffed out by competition from established manufacturers in the industrial countries, while the industrial countries use their wealth and political influence to set the rules of international trade in their favour. However, Duncan (1993) found that the successful resource-driven countries diversified out of slow-growth commodities into high-growth ones, so that the policy response appears to be more important than the actual long-term trend in primary commodity prices. Moreover, by the year 2000, some 80 per cent of developing country exports were manufactures compared with 20 per cent for primary products, the reverse of the ratios in 1980.

A second explanation is that resource-rich countries experience relatively high terms of trade *volatility*. This case garners more factual support than the Prebisch terms of trade argument. Westley (1995) measures the volatility in the terms of trade as the standard deviation of their percentage rate of change. Over the period 1960–93, the standard deviation in annual percentage price changes for 49 primary commodities was 26.4 per cent, while the standard deviation in the World Bank primary commodity price index was half that percentage. The terms-of-trade volatility of the regions with the highest primary export shares (Latin America, sub-Saharan Africa, Middle East and North Africa) was two to three times that of industrial countries during the 1970–92 period. However, several studies published in the 1960s refuted the hypothesis that export price instability constituted a significant obstacle to growth (Macbean, 1966; Michaely, 1962). For example, Macbean found that short-term export instability was not an important constraint on development, and that the relationship between domestic variables and export fluctuations was not a strong one. He examined export instability in a dozen developing countries during 1946–58 and found specific local causes of revenue changes to be more important than global prices: variations in *supplies* of exports have been more problematic than fluctuations in demand (Macbean, 1966, p. 34).

A third explanation for the resource curse is the Dutch disease effect, whereby the booming resource sector keeps the value of the currency so high that other tradables sectors cannot compete internationally. Corden and Neary (1982) explain the effects with a three-sector model comprising a resource sector, a sector of other tradables, typically manufacturing and agriculture, and a non-tradables sector. A boom in the resource sector has three effects: a spending effect; a relative price effect; and a resource move-ment effect. First, spending the increased export revenues boosts demand for tradables and non-tradables, but global competition precludes price rises on tradables so any excess demand is met by imports. Second, in the absence of complete sterilization of the rising foreign exchange income, the currency experiences a real appreciation that reduces the competitive-ness of the non-booming tradable activity. Yet domestic prices of *non*-tradables rise due to increased demand because they are unaffected by the currency appreciation or by competitive imports. As a result, prices of non-tradables rise relative to the prices of tradables, so that resources of capital and labour move from tradables into non-tradables, reducing exports and raising imports. Third, this movement of resources between sectors lowers capital accumulation if the non-tradable sector is more labour-intensive than the tradable sector. This is because movements in favour of the non-tradable sector tend to raise wages and lower returns to capital, reducing capital accumulation. Moreover, if resource booms cause manufacturing to shrink and manufacturing is favourable to growth (due, for instance, to the gains from learning-by-doing), the resource-abundant economy can experience slower long-term growth than it would if it had no resources (Matsuyama, 1992). Krugman (1987) identifies the con-ditions under which temporary resource booms can lead to an enduring loss of competitiveness.

However, strong proponents of the dominance of Dutch disease effects like Sachs (1999), neglect the fact that an export boom may not have harmful consequences if the increased primary export revenue is sustainable and/or the adjustment process is not too rapid. Moreover, as already noted, Neary and van Wijnbergen (1986: pp. 40–41) point out that some de-industrialization may be a symptom of the economy's adjustment to a new equilibrium rather than a symptom of a disease.

The fourth explanation is more selective and suggests that commodities with a capital-intensive production function, such as most mines and plantations, produce socio-economic linkages that are detrimental to growth (Engerman and Sokoloff, 1997; Woolcock et al., 2001). The capital-intensive production function of mining stunts both backward and forward productive linkages. This is because the specialized inputs required are subject to localization economies and are acquired most cheaply as imports. Moreover, the higher added value stages of mining such as fabrication tend to be market-oriented due to high freight costs. In addition, final demand linkages are also limited due to the small size of the highly productive mine workforce and the foreign ownership of capital. This pattern of linkages leaves fiscal linkage (taxation of the returns to capital and labour) as the principal stimulus to the domestic economy. Baldwin (1956) describes the growth-stunting effects of such 'point' linkages for the plantation in his comparative model of the 'West' and 'South' regions of the United States in the nineteenth century.

Engerman and Sokoloff (1997) contrast this pattern of point linkages with the diffuse linkages of commodities like peasant cash crops, whose more flexible production function offers few barriers to entry and funnels revenue through many economic agents. Baldwin (1956) clearly shows with reference to yeoman farms in nineteenth century America how the flexible production function responds to small additions to investment, which boost productivity and incomes. Consequently, final demand linkage is high and stimulates a wide range of local production to supply basic farm inputs and household consumer goods. Similarly, fiscal linkage is more likely to be expended on boosting rural infrastructure and education than in the case of enclave activities like plantations and mines. A further benefit arising from diffuse linkages comes from the low sunk costs associated with yeoman crops, like wheat and maize, which facilitate economic diversification, *pace* Duncan (1993), allowing producers to respond to falling prices by switching from low-growth to high-growth commodities.

Unfortunately for the robustness of this fourth explanation, central governments have proved all too capable of transforming diffuse linkages into point source linkages by imposing swingeing taxes through, for example, commodity marketing boards that allow the government to siphon away crop rent and more (Osei, 2001; Krueger, 1993). Moreover, the examples of Chile, Western Australia and the Witwatersrand show that mining can nurture a diversified economy, which sustains real GDP growth, while Graham and Floering (1984) demonstrate that the presence of plantation agriculture (in this case the nucleus plantation) need not be associated with disappointing economic growth.

A more recent variant of the institutional explanation for under-performance by resource-rich countries posits their institutional inheritance and specifically whether that inheritance promotes wealth extraction or wealth creation (Acemoglu et al., 2002). Basically, if the colonial settlers worked the overseas territory themselves, as in the case of Zimbabwe for example, the institutional structure tended to promote wealth creation whereas if climatic conditions were less conducive to permanent colonial settlement, the institutions tended to be aimed at wealth extraction. However, this variant of the theory also encounters criticism. For example, Glaeser et al. (2004) demonstrate that the statistical methods used by Acemoglu et al. (2002) are flawed and that their thesis underestimates the importance of human capital and policy choice.

4.   Endogenous explanations for the resource curse: rent and policy error

There seems to be no clear economic reason why natural resource abundance should cause countries to experience relatively low economic growth. By following the right policies, natural resources should be a boon and not a curse. This raises the possibility that resource-rich countries may encounter special difficulties that prevent them from implementing sound policies.

Lal (1993) analyses policy effects on the long-term growth trajectory of resource-deficient and resource-rich countries, drawing upon 21 countries. He finds that whereas eight out of ten land-abundant (resource-rich) countries pursued policies that led to growth collapses (the exceptions are Malaysia and Thailand), only three out of eight intermediate countries did so, while all three labour-abundant (that is resource-deficient) countries maintained rapid growth. Lal concludes that the labour-abundant countries follow the easiest development trajectory. The resource-poor country pursues competitive industrialization which begins with reform in favour of outward-oriented policies at a low per capita income. This is because, if the domestic market of the resource-deficient country is small, then reliance on trade is inevitable so that political opposition to trade policy reform is weaker. In contrast, the land-abundant (resource-rich) country faces a longer initial dependence on primary product exports, which retards competitive industrialization because the supply price of labour is higher than in the resource-deficient country at a similar level of per capita income. This tempts the governments of resource-rich countries to seek to 'grow' out of their difficulty by engineering a populist boom or a state co-ordinated Big Push (Sachs, 1989). This strategy triggers inflation, fiscal repression and a growth collapse so that a period of declining real wages is required to restore growth, but it elicits strong political opposition.

However, it is policies (along with basic social conditions and cultural history) and not resource composition that determine growth. This position is supported by Sachs and Warner (1995b, p. 23) who found that all developing countries following a reasonable set of political and economic policies between 1970 and 1989 achieved annual per capita growth of 2 per cent or greater. Sachs and Warner (1995b) went on to examine the effect of policy error, using trade openness as a proxy for the degree of state intervention. They note an inverted U-shaped relationship between trade policy measured on the horizontal axis and natural resource dependence. As primary product export dependence increases, trade policy first closes but then opens again at higher levels of resource dependence. The apex of this inverted U-shape occurs where primary exports reach 33 per cent of GDP, with most developing countries below this level. Sachs and Warner attribute this policy closure to fear of the employment diminishing effects of Dutch disease by governments of resource-rich countries. They hypothesize that such fear leads to stronger protectionist policies in order to sustain the fledgling manufacturing sector. Interestingly, the downswing of the inverted U-shape (that is the subsequent opening of trade policy) reflects the dominance of that section of the curve by those oil exporters with extremely large oil reserves, which therefore lack an urgent incentive to diversify away from dependence on the depleting oil asset. This may also explain the adherence to an open trade policy of the government of Botswana: some 60 per cent of the diamond revenue is estimated to be rent, so Botswana shares many characteristics with the oil exporters, but with the important bonus of experiencing far less revenue volatility because, in contrast to OPEC, the diamond cartel has held prices steady, so far at least.

Gelb et al. (1991) model the political process of trade policy distortion. They model a resource-rich country whose government creates unproductive jobs in public administration and in protected state-owned enterprises (SOEs) in order to alleviate urban unemployment. They use a Harris–Todaro migration model and assume a single urban wage in the three urban subsectors (which comprise a private sector, a productive public sector and a non-productive public sector). The model posits that an exogenous rise in the urban wage creates a wage gap that raises the premium on rural out-migration so that unemployment expands in the modern urban sector (see Chapter 14). The government responds to additional urban unemployment by increasing taxation (whose burden falls disproportionately on the private sector) in order to invest capital in the creation of additional urban jobs. But this process is self-defeating because it renders work in the unproductive public sector preferable to farming, so that more people migrate to the city where their unemployed presence intimidates the government from which the unemployed rural migrants extract still more rent. Krueger (1992) finds that the fraction of primary sector revenue extracted by the governments in sub-Saharan Africa may have reached 50 per cent.

Gelb et al. (1991) use a CGE model to estimate the potential scale and impact of the resulting rent misallocation. They test the sensitivity of the model against widely differing savings functions. The functions range from, at one extreme, forced saving by the government (which is assumed to use a tax that squeezes private consumption without reducing productive investment), through to a level of taxation at the other extreme that does not change consumption but does cut productive investment in direct proportion to the scale of the tax. Simulations using empirically plausible data over 13 time periods suggest that the consumption losses are invariably significant and that the efficiency of capital can be depressed below the level required to sustain economic growth within a decade.

Auty and Gelb (2001) formalize the impact of high rents on the political economy in terms of a two-stage process. They argue that high rents incentivize governments to capture the immediate public and personal gains from rent redistribution at the expense of promoting wealth creation, whose gains are more long-term. In addition, prolonged reliance on natural resource rent postpones competitive industrialization and heightens the risk that government rent deployment will distort the economy away from its underlying comparative advantage and lock it into a staple trap. The essence of the staple trap is a burgeoning sector of unproductive public employment and protected manufacturing whose demand for rent eventually outstrips the supply, causing governments to tax the returns to capital and labour from the primary sector as well as the rent. The net effect is to intensify the reliance of the economy upon a primary sector whose competitiveness is being eroded so that it becomes vulnerable to shocks and a growth collapse from which recovery is protracted because during a growth collapse, all forms of capital are degraded.

5. Conclusions and policy implications

It seems that fashionable post-war policies designed to increase state intervention in support of forced industrialization lie behind the recent growth collapses in resource-rich countries. This policy was invariably captured by vested interests, blocking economic reform so that economic distortions intensified and reversed the required competitive diversification of the economy. Natural resource rents sustained maladroit policies for longer, and the higher the rent relative to GDP and the more it was concentrated on the government, the greater the distortion and the less resilient the economy (see Table 13.1). Ironically, the same post-war concern for the adverse impacts of the terms of trade also encouraged the governments of commodity-dependent economies to seek to boost prices by forming cartels such as OPEC and the IBA. These producer groups were associated with heightened price volatility, which yielded economic shocks in the 1970s, both negative and positive, which triggered the growth collapses.

The global economic impact of the oil windfalls can be compared to the release of a radioactive cloud that rains destruction upon those countries that it passes over. The 1973 price shock caused many of the distorted oil-importing economies of sub-Saharan Africa to collapse, since they were not deemed sufficiently creditworthy to merit the loans urgently required to restructure their economies in order to pay for higher oil import bills. In contrast, western banks on-loaned petro-dollars to Latin American governments, which either invested them inefficiently or else found ways of channelling them via SOEs into current public consumption. Consequently, few such governments were able to service their burgeoning debt when interest rates turned sharply positive in the early-1980s, ushering in Latin America's 'lost decade'. Finally, the global recession triggered by high oil prices first softened those prices and then led to precipitous decline in 1985, triggering the collapse of most oil-exporting economies.

The implications are clear: the growth collapses result from policy failure so that a solution must recognize the constraints of governance upon policy formation in developing countries (see Table 13.2). Domestic and external political interests need to ally to find ways of strengthening the motive of governments to promote efficient wealth creation through the provision of public goods and the maintenance of incentives to invest efficiently. This in turn calls for the progressive strengthening of sanctions against anti-social governance, notably property rights and the rule of law; civic society (or voice); and political accountability for transparent public finances. More realistically, in the highly distorted political economies that are the legacy of the growth collapses in resource-rich countries, compromises are required between the International Financial Institutions (IFIs), pro-poor domestic groups and entrenched rent-seeking interests that will increasingly channel the natural resource rents away from wealth-repressing activity and towards wealth creation (Khan and Jomo, 2000).

Note

1. By 1913 land-abundant Argentina was the richest country in South America with a per capita income 10 per cent above that of the West European industrial country average (Maddison, 1995).

Table 13.2 Index of institutional quality 2002, oil-rich countries and small resource-poor countries

Country	PCGDP (US$PPP 2002)	Voice + Account-ability	Political stability	Effective governance	Regulation burden	Rule of law	Graft	Overall index
Oil-rich								
Nigeria	800	−0.70	−1.49	−1.12	−1.18	−1.35	−1.35	−7.19
Uzbekistan	1 640	−1.66	−0.94	−1.10	−1.44	−1.16	−1.03	−7.33
Angola	1 840	−1.39	−1.60	−1.16	−1.33	−1.56	−1.12	−8.16
Azerbaijan	3 010	−0.97	−1.13	−0.96	−0.82	−0.79	−1.07	−5.74
Ecuador	3 340	−0.06	−0.70	−0.96	−0.60	−0.60	−0.99	−3.91
Syria	3 470	−1.56	−0.14	−0.57	−0.97	−0.41	−0.29	−3.94
Venezuela	5 220	−0.41	−1.20	−1.14	−0.54	−1.04	−0.94	−5.27
Algeria	5 530	−0.96	−1.54	−0.59	−0.79	−0.54	−0.65	−5.05
Gabon	5 530	−0.42	0.20	−0.45	−0.19	−0.27	−0.71	−1.84
Kazakhstan	5 630	−1.05	0.52	−0.80	−0.74	−0.90	−0.87	−3.84
Trinidad + Tobago	6 440	0.56	0.03	0.47	0.66	0.34	−0.04	2.02
Saudi Arabia	12 660	−1.40	0.05	−0.05	0.08	0.44	0.57	−0.31
Small resource-poor								
Kenya	1 010	−0.58	−0.86	−0.85	−0.50	−1.04	−1.05	−4.98
Nepal	1 370	−0.52	−1.63	−0.51	−0.50	−0.50	−0.30	−3.86
Haiti	1 610	−1.11	−1.31	−1.56	−0.95	−1.76	−1.70	−8.39
Mauritania	1 790	−0.67	0.43	−0.16	0.01	−0.33	0.23	−0.49
Sri Lanka	3 510	−0.06	−0.90	0.03	0.12	0.23	−0.14	−0.72
El Salvador	4 790	0.06	0.35	−0.53	0.04	−0.46	−0.54	−1.08
Mauritius	10 820	0.80	0.99	0.53	0.56	0.89	0.53	4.30
Singapore	23 730	0.51	1.28	2.26	1.89	1.75	2.30	9.99
Hong Kong	27 490	0.15	1.08	1.44	1.50	1.30	1.52	6.99

Source: World Bank (2002b).

References

Acemoglu, D., S. Johnson and J. Robinson (2002), 'Reversal of fortune: Geography and institutions in the making of the modern world income distribution, *Quarterly Journal of Economics*, **117**(4): 1231–94.

Auty, R.M. (1990), *Resource-Based Industrialization: Sowing the Oil in Eight Exporting Countries*, Oxford: Clarendon Press.

Auty, R.M. (1993), *Sustaining Development in Mineral Economies: The Resource Curse*, London: Routledge.

Auty, R.M. (2001), *Resource Abundance and Economic Development*, Oxford: Oxford University Press.

Auty, R.M. and A.H. Gelb (2001), 'Political economy of resource-abundant states', in R.M. Auty (ed.), *Resource Abundance and Economic Development*, Oxford: Oxford University Press, pp. 126–44.

Auty, R.M. and S. Kiiski (2001), 'Natural resources, capital accumulation, structural change and welfare', in R.M. Auty (ed.), *Resource Abundance and Economic Development*, Oxford: Oxford University Press, pp. 19–35.

Baldwin, R.E. (1956), 'Patterns of development in newly settled regions', *Manchester School of Social and Economic Studies*, **24**: 161–79.

Chenery, H.B. (1981), 'Restructuring the world economy', *Foreign Affairs*, **59**: 1102–20.

Corden, M. and J.P. Neary (1982), 'Booming sector and Dutch Disease economics: a survey', *Economic Journal*, **92**: 826–44.

Davis, G. (1995), 'Learning to love the Dutch Disease: evidence from the mineral economies', *World Development*, **23**: 1765–79.

Duncan, R.O. (1993), 'Agricultural export prospects for sub-Saharan Africa', *Development Policy Review*, **11**(1): 31–45.

Engerman, S.L. and K.L. Sokoloff (1997), 'Factor endowments, institutions, and differential paths of growth among New World economies', in S. Haggard (ed.), *How Latin America Fell Behind*, Stanford, CA: Stanford University Press, pp. 260–304.

Gelb, A.H. and associates (1988), *Oil Windfalls: Blessing or Curse?*, New York: Oxford University Press, pp. 262–88.

Gelb, A.H., J. Knight and R. Sabot (1991), 'Public sector employment, rent seeking and economic growth', *The Economic Journal*, **101**: 1186–99.

Glaeser, E.L., R. La Porta, F. Lopes-de-Silanes and A. Shleifer (2004), 'Do institutions cause growth?', NBR Working Paper 10568, Cambridge, MA: National Bureau of Economic Research.

Graham, E. and I. Floering (1984), *The Modern Plantation in the Third World*, London: Croom Helm.

Khan, M.H. and K.S. Jomo (2000), *Rents, Rent-Seeking and Economic Development*, Cambridge: Cambridge University Press.

Krueger, A.O. (1993), *Political Economy of Policy Reform in Developing Countries*, Cambridge, MA: MIT Press.

Krueger, A.O. (1992), *The Political Economy of Agricultural Pricing Policy: A Synthesis of the Political Economy in Developing Countries*, Baltimore, MD: Johns Hopkins University Press.

Krugman, P.R. (1987), 'The narrow band, the Dutch disease and the competitive consequences of Mrs Thatcher', *Journal of Development Economics*, **27**: 41–55.

Lal, D. (1993), *The Repressed Economy: Causes, Consequences, Reform*, Aldershot, UK and Brookfield, US: Edward Elgar, pp. 345–62.

Lal, D. and H. Myint (1996), *The Political Economy of Poverty, Equity and Growth*, Oxford: Clarendon Press.

Lewis, W.A. (1978), *Growth and Fluctuations 1870–1913*, London: George Allen and Unwin.

Macbean, A.I. (1966), *Export Instability and Economic Development*, Cambridge, MA: Harvard University Press.

Maddison, A. (1995), *Monitoring the World Economy 1820–92*, Paris: OECD.

Matsuyama, K. (1992), 'Intercultural productivity, comparative advantage, and economic growth', *Journal of Economic Theory*, **58**: 317–34.

Michaely, M. (1962), *Concentration in International Trade*, Amsterdam: North Holland.

Neary, P.J. and S.N. Van Wijnbergen (1986), *Natural Resources and the Macro Economy*, Cambridge, MA: MIT Press.

Osei, R. (2001), 'A growth collapse with diffuse resources', in R.M. Auty (ed.), *Resource Abundance and Economic Development*, Oxford: Oxford University Press, pp. 165–78.

Prebisch, R. (1950), *The Economic Development of Latin America and its Principal Problems*, Santiago: ECLA/UN, reprinted in: *Economic Bulletin for Latin America*, 7, 1962, pp. 1–22.

Sachs, J.D. (1989), 'Social conflict and populist policies in Latin America', NBER Working Paper 2897, Cambridge, MA: National Bureau of Economic Research.

Sachs, J.D. (1999), 'Resource endowments and the real exchange rate: a comparison of Latin America and East Asia', in T. Ito and A.O. Krueger (eds), *Changes in Exchange Rates in Rapidly Developing Countries*, Chicago Ill: University of Chicago Press, pp. 133–53.

Sachs, J.D. and A. Warner (1995a), 'Economic reform and the process of global integration', *Brookings Papers on Economic Activity*, 1: 1–118.

Sachs, J.D. and A. Warner (1995b), 'Natural resources and economic growth', mimeo, Cambridge, MA: HIID.

Sachs, J.D. and A. Warner (1997), 'Natural resource abundance and economic growth', Cambridge, MA: HIID.

Timmer, C.T. (2004), 'Operationalizing pro-poor growth: Indonesia', Washington, DC: World Bank.

Westley, G. (1995), 'Economic volatility from natural resource endowments', *Development Policy*, Washington, DC: Inter-American Development Bank, September.

Woolcock, M., J. Isham and L. Pritchett (2001), 'The social foundations of poor economic growth in resource-rich countries', in R.M. Auty (ed.), *Resource Abundance and Economic Development*, Oxford: Oxford University Press, pp. 76–92.

World Bank (2002a), *World Development Indicators 2002*, Washington, DC: World Bank.

World Bank (2002b), *Governance Quality Index 2001*, Washington, DC: World Bank.

14 Structural change, poverty and natural resource degradation
Ramón López

1. Introduction

Structural change, defined as the process by which the output and employment shares of primary productive sectors decrease over time, is one of the most ubiquitous and least controversial stylized facts of modern economies.[1] Both countries that have been able to grow fast, mainly in Europe, parts of Asia and North America, and those less successful countries in Latin America and sub-Saharan Africa have experienced a process where urban activities have grown significantly faster than primary, mostly natural resource-dependent sectors.[2]

Development theorists once considered structural change to be both a key cause and also a consequence of economic growth (Lewis, 1955; Renis and Fei, 1961). Traditional activities in the rural sector were regarded as largely constrained by the fixity of certain factors of production and by the limitations of absorbing new technologies in such activities. As investment in manufacturing and other mainly urban activities is implemented, labor productivity in such industries expands, thus creating a wedge between labor returns in rural and urban areas. This wedge acts as a pull effect on the rural population, prompting rural out-migration and an increasing share of urban output in GDP and of the labor force employed in urban areas. Switching factors of production from the low productivity primary sectors to the high productivity urban sectors was seen as an engine of economic growth and as a source of concomitant real wage increases.

The above optimistic model, which can be termed *benign structural change* (BSC), was hailed enthusiastically by development theorists and practitioners alike. This was the answer to the criticisms made by many social scientists (especially from the left) during the post-second world war period of the western market economy. Provide adequate economic incentives for industrial investments, give then some time to the system to clear the backwardness of the traditional activities (at first wages would not increase much as too large a segment of the labor force was really surplus labor, with an almost zero opportunity cost) and then the miracle of ever-increasing labor earnings would follow the initially large profit rates that are needed to trigger such a miracle.

Later, however, development practitioners began to realize that though the prediction of massive out-migration from rural areas was fully confirmed, the prediction that modern activities, especially manufacturing, would grow rapidly was less clear and the prediction of continuous real wage increases was even more elusive. What is clear is that, with a handful of important exceptions mainly in Asia, rapid and persistent economic growth has not been a common feature among the countries that were considered developing or under-developed in the 1950s. Structural change has taken place at least to some degree even in the largely unsuccessful countries, but it has consisted mainly in a progressive diffusion of subsistence and poverty from the rural to the urban sector. In fact, the movement from rural labor subsistence activities has been much more toward equally backward urban subsistence service and related sectors than to the high-productivity industrial sectors. The end result: slow economic growth and poverty on a large scale. This process can be called *perverse structural change* (PSC).

It is by now clear that many of the so-called 'fixed' factors supporting primary production are not in fact fixed. These factors are mostly natural resources which, far from being fixed, are vulnerable to over-exploitation and poor management. This is especially true in tropical and sub-tropical areas where natural resources are much more fragile than in temperate areas (Sánchez, 1976; López, 1997).[3] More importantly, the propensity of natural resources to degrade plays a key role in structural change. In fact, because BSC originated in the rapid expansion of productivity in the non-primary sector, it significantly contributes to diminished pressure on natural resources by reducing rural population and allowing for a slower growth in the exploitation of natural resources. By contrast, PSC originates in the declining productivity of labor in primary sectors rather than on a more rapid expansion of productivity in the non-primary sectors. PSC, far from releasing pressure on natural resources, may be triggered precisely by the degradation of the natural resource base, which in turn causes declining labor productivity in the primary sector. Thus, PSC is likely to be associated with not only economic stagnation and worsening poverty but also with widespread natural resource degradation.

Clearly the classical development economists, perhaps influenced by the historical experience of the industrial economies at the time, focused their modeling efforts on only one type of equilibrium, the benign one. Also in consonance with the approach by most mainstream economists then and now, they ignored the fact that primary activities are supported by natural assets which have important dynamic properties. In reality, however, there are pathways that may converge to at least two fundamentally different equilibria and, moreover, the dynamics of natural resources are likely to play a key role in determining which of these pathways the economy follows. The dynamics of the system is essentially path dependent. As we shall see, history matters, as well as government policy, in a way that even relatively modest differences in these factors can cause the economy to converge to an equilibrium that has dramatically different connotations for welfare, income distribution, poverty and natural resources.

The objective of this chapter is to study the mechanics of structural change. In particular, we study the conditioning factors that are likely to determine whether a country follows a pathway that may converge to an equilibrium characterized by BSC or, alternatively, PSC. In addition we look at the consequences of these two types of equilibrium for the poor. We show that under certain conditions, both the rate of resource degradation and changes in the distribution of access to natural resources among the rural population play a key role in determining whether structural change is benign or perverse.

The orthodox response to the realization that most developing countries appear to converge to an equilibrium that resembles more closely the perverse equilibrium than the benign one was to blame it on 'inadequate' incentives (Schulz, 1968; Krueger et al., 1991; Easterly, 2001). By inadequate incentives they meant excessive government intervention, market distortions and trade protectionism. The resulting wisdom was to take the government out of the economy by privatizing state enterprises, deregulating the economy, liberalizing international trade, eliminating restrictions to foreign investment, and so on. This diagnostic was backed by a massive conceptual and empirical literature developed over the 1970s and 1980s pointing to the need for 'structural adjustment'. The concerted actions of international lending banks through structural adjustment lending caused many developing countries to adopt at least certain important components of such a program. The experience of so many countries that implemented pro-market reforms over the last two decades, however, allows us to conclude that such reforms have in many countries contributed little to spur economic growth and much less to environmentally and socially sustainable growth (World Bank, 2000; López 2003).[4]

An important feature of the policy advice from international lending institutions was their almost exclusive emphasis on removing government interventions that interfered with markets. At the same time, the policy advice largely neglected the evident biases in the allocation of public expenditures and in the way in which public revenues were raised in many countries. There is increasing empirical evidence showing that governments fail to supply public goods at an appropriate scale, preferring instead to spend public resources in largely unproductive subsidies to favor the economic elites (World Bank, 2000; López and Toman, 2006). At the same time, government revenues greatly rely on indirect taxes instead of income and property taxes, mainly as a consequence of the lack of political will by governments to control rampant tax evasion by the economic elites (IMF, 2003; de Ferranti et al., 2004). Even today there is reluctance among mainstream economists and international institutions to recognize that such government spending and revenue-raising biases are likely to cause large economic distortions, which in turn induce slower growth, worsening poverty and damaging the environment.[5] We argue below that, whether an economy follows a pathway closer to BSC or, alternatively, to PSC in significant part depends on the way in which governments allocate expenditures and raise revenues. The greater the pro-elite bias of governments, the more likely it is that a perverse path will be followed.

2. Sources of structural change

Structural change means at least a relative, if not an absolute, compression of the primary or natural resource-dependent sectors *vis-à-vis* the industrial and service sectors. Clearly, this process is triggered by changes in the relative productivity of the primary and non-primary sectors. BSC is mostly originated in a continuous increase of labor demand by the modern sector as a consequence of increased (usually private) investment and labor productivity in non-primary sectors. The non-primary sector exerts a strong pulling effect on the labor force linked to natural resource-intensive activities thus inducing a continuous reallocation of the labor force from primary to non-primary activities *despite* the fact that the primary sector may maintain or even expand its productivity as well. The 'despite' is very important because it conveys the idea that BSC is not associated with a loss of productivity of the primary sectors due to, for example, degradation of the natural resources and lack of technical change. That is, the primary sector continues to allow a high marginal productivity of labor which supports the opportunity cost of labor. Thus, BSC is likely to result in continuously increasing real wages, especially for the unskilled workers which often have the primary sector as their main alternative employment source.

PSC, by contrast, is mainly triggered by two factors: (1) the stagnation or even loss of productivity of the primary sectors due to, for example, the degradation of soils, water sources, forest biomass, fisheries and other natural resources; (2) the disenfranchising of part of the rural poor from their natural resources even if there is no or little resource depletion. Degradation of natural capital, a key factor of production in the primary sectors, causes a fall of the marginal product of labor employed in such sectors. This, in turn, reduces labor income in the primary, mainly rural, activities leading to a progressive migration of the labor force toward the non-primary, usually urban sectors. More importantly, the opportunity cost of the migrant workers is thus lower as a consequence of the diminished labor productivity in the primary sectors. That is, in sharp contrast with BSC, in this case real wages often fall or at least remain stagnant. That is, PSC is associated with a labor 'push' from the primary sectors instead of the 'pull' effect from the non-primary sector that occurs in the case of BSC. Given that the non-primary sector is not particularly dynamic in this case, an important segment of the migrating workers become sub-employed and have to take refuge in the informal or subsistence urban sector.[6]

Factor (2) above is related to *distributional changes* in access to natural resources among the rural population. Certain politico-economy processes all too common in history are also important factors that cause the push effect in primary sectors. 'Enclosure' episodes, where subsistence producers have been disenfranchised from their lands, have not been unique to the European experience during the early phases of the industrial revolution. Under various different forms a similar process of forced expulsion of important segments of rural communities has often been repeated in modern times in Latin America, Africa and Asia.[7] The usurpation of the land resources belonging to rural, usually subsistence, communities by large commercial interests is facilitated by: (i) the existence of poorly defined or even a lack of legal property rights of poor communities upon their resources; (ii) the tacit or even explicit complicity of governments which do little to protect the interests of the poor *vis-à-vis* those of commercial interests.

When the use of the expropriated resources is shifted from traditional usually labor-intensive activities to more capital-intensive (and less labor-demanding) ones, the net demand for labor falls. A 'labor surplus' situation occurs.[8] This causes increased migration to urban areas of workers that have a very small opportunity cost. The net effect is of course downward pressure on real wages with the consequent increases of profits and expansion of the non-primary sectors. In addition, part of the increased flow of displaced labor is not able to find employment in the formal sector and simply engrosses the subsistence informal service sector.

In addition to the outright usurpation of land and other resources of rural households, there are other, more subtle, forms of usurpation which are even more common. Large investments in mining, logging, hydroelectric and other energy projects, and irrigation infrastructure have also led to the displacement of large, often poor, populations. Significant segments of the rural population become environmental refugees as their vital natural resources including land and water are curtailed with little if any compensation. Entire rural communities have been left with little option but to migrate into urban areas as a consequence of massive scarcity of vital environmental services. This has been triggered not by environmental damage caused by the subsistence communities themselves, but by spill-overs and overuse of water and other resources vital for the survival of local communities, caused by big extractive investments subject to little effective regulation (World Bank, 2000).

A related process is caused by violence associated with social strife and civil wars that tend to affect rural areas more intensively than urban ones. Outright violence, as per its close relative 'non-market pressures' by economic elites on the poor, also forces the loss of entitlement of the rural poor to their resources, which, in turn, causes their out-migration, often toward urban areas.

In summary, in sharp contrast with the conventional view, which regards low productivity in rural areas as a 'technical' problem linked to excessive population growth and limited resources, we consider it largely the result of unbalanced political power.

The almost unchecked political power of the elites means that they face few restraints from governments. They thus have the power to disenfranchise the poor from their resources when such resources become valuable to them, and face few environmental regulations which can control the externalities arising from their extractive investments affecting the rural poor. The net result of this is that the poor end up with progressively less access to the natural resources and/or a more degraded natural resource and environmental base to support their labor productivity and even their survival.

In summary, there are three major push factors affecting the rural population: (i) outright usurpation of the resources belonging to subsistence rural households by commercial interests; (ii) scarcity of environmental resources that are vital for the survival of poor households caused by unrestrained large-scale extraction of natural resources; (iii) violence caused by civil wars and other conflicts. Factors (i) and (ii) both are associated with environmental degradation and/or natural resource redistribution from many poor individuals to a few wealthy ones. Also, both factors entail tacit or explicit government policies that fail to protect the environment and the poor in favor of promoting the benefits of commercial interests instead.

The central implication of the previous discussion is the following: government failure to protect the property rights of the rural poor upon their natural resources and to prevent massive negative environmental externalities from the commercial exploitation of natural resources increases the likelihood of perverse structural change.

3. Public expenditures: an analytical taxonomy

The loss of entitlement of the rural poor to natural resources, be it through outright usurpation of part of their resources or through environmental externalities caused by uncontrolled exploitation of natural resources by commercial interests, is caused by government policy failures. These government failures include lack of delimitation and public enforcement of property rights as well as direct incentives to large commercial interests to expropriate resources of the rural poor often in the name of 'progress'. But broader public policies have other more indirect effects on the pathways to structural change which are perhaps even more important than policies which directly concern the rural sector. In particular, the allocation of public revenues (normally 20 per cent of GDP or more) is a key determinant of the nature of structural change and through this of the evolution of poverty and the environment. Of course governments spend public revenues on a great variety of items. But a fundamental analytical taxonomy of public expenditures simply divides them between two types:

(i)   *Type A*. Expenditures on public and semi-public goods. These include pure public goods (e.g. goods which at least approximately satisfy the two classical criteria used to define a public good: non-excludable and non-rival) as well as public expenditures directed to palliate the effects of market failure.
(ii) *Type F*. Expenditures in subsidies to private firms not affected by market failure (often referred to as 'corporate welfare').

The role of Type A expenditures in supplying (pure) public goods is clear. Certain institutions and infrastructure can only be supplied by the state (either directly or indirectly via concessionary investments). In addition, government expenditures to palliate market failure or their effects can also be regarded as public goods, or, better, semi-public goods. Capital, environmental and knowledge/intellectual rights failures are among the most pervasive and important market failures facing most developing country economies.

Capital market failures. Capital market failures are responsible for preventing or restricting socially profitable investments available to individuals or firms that have no or restricted access to capital markets. Below we show that under certain commonly assumed conditions capital market failure does not affect the efficiency and level of aggregate investment in physical and financial capital but it does limit the efficiency and the level of aggregate investment in human capital.

Under constant returns to scale the distribution of physical and financial capital among firms has no effect on the productivity of these assets. The reason for this is clear: under constant returns to scale the marginal value product of physical capital is constant and independent of the firm's level of capital.[9] Therefore, credit market failure which limits the ability of certain firms (that is those that have more restricted market access) to invest in such assets will simply imply that the investment will be concentrated in those firms that have an advantage in the credit market. This reallocation of investment, however, has no effect on either efficiency or on aggregate industry output.

While the assumption of constant returns to scale for firms is not only plausible but also follows from commonly accepted behavioral assumptions, such an assumption is utterly unreasonable for individuals as producers. Individual workers can be regarded as producers of an intermediate output, labor productivity. Production of labor productivity by individuals occurs through a production function where the main variable or semi-variable input is human capital (education, skills, and so on) which is combined with the worker's fixed factor, his/her own life span and natural ability to absorb knowledge. Thus, given the existence of these important fixed factors, it is clear that the marginal productivity of human capital in the production of labor productivity for an individual rapidly declines beyond a certain point.[10] Assume that there are two types of workers, those that face credit market constraints to finance investments in human capital (which also have little or no accumulated savings) and those that can make the human capital investment unconstrained by financial restrictions. The latter group will choose the investment level at the point where the present value of the marginal value product of human capital equals its marginal cost. The financially constrained individuals, however, will have to invest less, only up to the level that their availability of financial resources allows them.

The implication of this observation for the impact of capital market failure is obvious: if a segment of individuals face capital markets restrictions, those that do not face them will not make up for the shortfall of investment in human capital that the capital-constrained individuals cause. Individuals not facing credit constraints will quickly reach a rapidly declining marginal productivity of human capital which eventually will limit their ability to invest further. That is, credit market imperfections affect not only the distribution of human capital among individuals but also the total level of investment in human capital and, therefore, the aggregate level of productivity 'produced' by individuals. This is in sharp contrast with the case of physical capital discussed earlier, where credit market failure is likely to affect the distribution of capital across firms but not efficiency or output levels.

Thus, if the rationale for government intervention is to promote economic efficiency and growth, there is ample justification for intervening in financing human capital investment for the segments of society that have imperfect access to capital markets (generally the poor) but there is little justification for public intervention in subsidizing investment in other forms of capital unless the distribution of capital among firms is a goal by itself. In addition, given that human capital investments are much harder to use as collateral than physical or financial assets, it is likely that the impact of capital market failure will be much more intense for investments in human assets than in physical or financial ones. This reinforces the importance of public interventions in financing human capital investment *vis-à-vis* interventions to subsidize non-human assets.

One important observation: it appears that capital market failures of one form or another are universal and extremely difficult to eradicate. They are almost a natural structural feature in a market economy (Stiglitz, 2000). This practically rules out the possibility of first best intervention, which would consist of creating policies and/or institutions that remove the market failure at source; thus the importance of relying on second best instruments consisting of publicly financing investment in human capital for those that suffer the consequences of capital market failures. Thus, we classify public outlays in human capital (including education and health) as Type A expenditures, and corporate subsidies as Type F.

Other market failures. Environmental externalities as well as externalities affecting the incentives to knowledge creation cause inefficiency and slower welfare growth and, ultimately, more poverty. Therefore, public investments to mitigate such externalities can be considered semi-public goods. Unlike capital market failures, it appears that these failures can be dealt with via first best instruments. There is a degree of consensus among environmental economists that environmental regulation and the development of adequate institutions, including property rights and others, for the sake of monitoring and enforcement of environmental regulation, can go a long way in preventing at least the most pernicious impacts of lack or failure of environmental markets. The need for environmental (corporate) subsidies once such first best policies and institutions exist is questionable. In any case, studies have shown the significant drawbacks of using environmental subsidies instead of taxes or even quotas as instruments to control negative environmental externalities (Oates, 1996).

The same may be true for market failures leading to under-investment in knowledge or R&D; it seems that there are institutional arrangements, mainly intellectual property rights and institutions for their enforcement, that can considerably mitigate the key externality associated with the free diffusion of certain forms of knowledge that discourage private investments in R&D. Whether or not subsidies to knowledge creation are needed when such institutions exist is debatable, but in any case there is some agreement that efficient corporate subsidies, if at all needed, should be targeted directly to R&D.

The implication of this analysis is the following: there are conceptual reasons to include certain public expenditures directed to mitigate market failures or to mitigate the effects of market failure as Type A public goods. Public financing of human capital, expenditures in environmental regulation and enforcement of such regulations, property right institutions and intellectual property right regulations and their enforcement can all be considered Type A semi-public goods. Targeted public investment in environmental protection as well as in R&D may also fall within the Type A expenditures. All other corporate subsidies should be considered Type F.

4.   The composition of public expenditures and structural change

In this section we first present an analysis of the key economic distortions caused by Type F expenditures; next we illustrate the large rates of return of Type A public investment, and the under-investment in certain important public assets despite high rates of return. Finally we evaluate the implications of this for structural change.

Type F expenditures and economic distortions

The literature on public subsidies has traditionally emphasized the market distortions caused by such subsidies. That is, the emphasis has been on the fact that subsidies generally prevent prices from being 'right'. Without denying the importance of the price distortion effect, we here focus on the distortions caused by the crowding out of Type A expenditures caused by Type F (subsidy) expenditures within the public budget. The crowding out distortion is dynamic rather than purely static. Such distortion directly affects economic growth, poverty and natural resource dynamics through a variety of mechanisms.

Empirical studies show that governments in developing countries spend a large share of the public budget in Type F expenditures.[11] The budget crowding out of Type A expenditures has serious consequences for structural change and may significantly affect the potential for economic growth. As discussed earlier, Type A investments are vital to assure an adequate supply of human capital, R&D, key infrastructure and institutions, and to prevent excessive damage to the environment and the natural resources. That is, Type A investments are critical to provide the economy with human, institutional and environmental assets that in general are highly complementary with private investment in physical, financial and knowledge assets. The best way of providing incentives to the private sector to invest at sufficiently high levels is by providing the right public assets that will support the profitability of private assets at high levels, not subsidies. High levels of Type F expenditures means that governments have either to provide fewer public goods and/or that they need to raise taxes further. As we shall see, the under-supply of public goods has serious effects on growth and structural change. We focus here on the reduction of Type A investment caused by too much Type F expenditure.[12]

Corporate subsidies and other forms of Type F expenditures contribute to creating privileges and promote increased consumption by the wealthy (the usual recipients of public subsidies) but they do not give durable incentives to productive private investment. The low effectiveness of corporate subsidies as an instrument to promote investment and productivity has been shown by empirical studies in many countries around the world. Empirical studies using detailed firm-level data by Bregman et al. (1999) for Israel, Fakin (1995) for Poland, Lee (1996) for Korea, Bergstrom (1998) for Sweden, Estache and Gaspar (1995) for Brazil, Harris (1991) for Ireland, and several others have shown that subsidies and corporate tax concessions targeted to specific firms are at best ineffective in promoting investment and technological adoption and, in some instances, even counterproductive.

A large share of Type F expenditures does stimulate one type of investment within the private sector: lobbying. When half of the public budget is up for grabs the incentives to 'invest' in lobbying are indeed large. Unproductive lobbying expenditures by the private sector can reach enormous proportions especially in countries where governments are most open to corporate welfare, up to 10 per cent of GDP, according to certain studies. A key signal that triggers the private sector to spend so many resources in lobbying is of course the fact that a sizable share of public expenditures is devoted to Type F expenditures. Thus, Type F expenditures not only crowd out the productive Type A public investment but also induce crowding out of productive investment in favor of unproductive investments within the private sector.

The economic returns to type A expenditures
Empirical studies show extraordinarily high rates of return to investments provided mainly through Type A expenditures including human and environmental public goods. The literature reports such high returns with an amazing degree of consensus for many countries around the world. Investments in formal education (especially in secondary education), health, R&D (both in agriculture as well as in other sectors), agricultural extension, air and water pollution abatement, and investments in the management of certain natural resources are reported to have very high rates of return. The permanence of such high returns per se does not necessarily reflect under-investment, mainly given the possible existence of significant non-convexities. Non-convexities may imply that the marginal returns to these assets do not necessarily fall, or decrease only very slowly with their accumulation. Thus, if this is the case, even a rapid accumulation of the assets would do little to reduce their rates of return. However, given such

high returns, one would expect a great emphasis of governments on invest-ing in such assets. Yet, as we shall see, this is not the case. In fact, in the over-whelming majority of developing countries, investment in human and environmental assets has not even kept up with population growth. That is, per capita human and environmental wealth appears to be declining.

Returns to education   Two recent surveys, one by Psacharopoulos (1994) and another one, an update of the first survey by Psacharopoulos and Patrinos (2002), report findings of hundreds of studies around the world that have used a great variety of methodologies and diverse types of data and time periods over the last three decades or so. Despite this variability in data, countries and methodology, there is a high degree of homogeneity of results for most countries. In fact, the calculated rates of return found in the great majority of the countries analyzed are extremely high. The average private rate of return for investment in primary education is about 20 per cent, while the average social rate of return is about 30 per cent.[13] Only in a handful of countries are the returns to primary and secondary education both below 15 per cent. In addition, from the evidence for coun-tries that have more than one study, it follows that in the vast majority of them the rates of return to education have not declined over time.

It is hard to imagine discount rates even near these rates as shown by the large number of projects that are implemented with much lower *ex-ante* rates of return in developing and developed countries alike. Despite these large rates of return, in most developing countries one encounters massive school drop-out rates, especially at the late primary and high school levels. Even in middle-income countries such as Chile, Brazil and Mexico, high school drop-out rates reach 40 per cent to 50 per cent (World Bank, 2000). Even primary school drop-out rates were also high in the 1990s: Chile, 23 per cent; Mexico, 28 per cent; Indonesia, 23 per cent; Philippines, 30 per cent. Similarly, public expenditure per student as a percentage of GDP per capita was extremely low. According to the World Bank (2003) public expenditure per student in primary school was about 8 per cent of per capita GDP in Argentina, 9 per cent in Chile, 7 per cent in Mexico and 2 per cent in Venezuela. This compared to 23 per cent in Korea or the United States.

The high rates of return of schooling and the high rates of school deser-tion may be mutually consistent if liquidity constraints prevent parents from affording child education even if it is 'freely' provided by the state. This issue becomes more acute when children have an opportunity cost in the child labor market or in subsistence family operations. In fact, certain government programs that reduce the opportunity cost of children attend-ing school at working age (above 10 or 11 years old) and that reduce commuting time to school by increasing public school density especially in rural areas, have been quite successful in increasing school attendance. Making parents more aware of the value of education and increasing their participation in their children's education is another effective mechanism to promote more school enrollment. All this, however, requires a greater allocation of government resources to education, including not only public financial resources, but also human and institutional resources. In a context of a usually tight availability of such resources, this additional allocation of government resources to education obviously needs hard choices in terms of cutting other expenditures or increasing public revenues. Based on the available data on government expenditures per student as a proportion of per capita income, governments in developing countries are not opting for such choices. They seem to have other priorities.

R&D and farm extension   A survey by Alston et al. (2000) reviewed almost 300 studies that evaluated private and social rates of return to agriculture R&D and farm extension (both of them mostly done through public institutions) in about 95 countries. The methodologies and data used varied dramatically across the many studies. The simple mean (social) rate of return for agricultural research among all studies in developing countries was over 50 per cent while the mean rate of return for public expenditures in agricultural extension was even higher, of the order of 80 per cent! In most countries these rates rarely fall below 30 per cent, still obviously a fantastic pay-off. Exploiting the fact that there are many countries for which there is more than one comparable study available, the authors concluded that, as in the case of returns to education, there is no evidence to support the view that the rates of return have declined over time. Despite this great social profitability, studies often report that with few exceptions countries are not expanding agricultural R&D and many have indeed drastically cut them back.[14]

R&D in non-agricultural contexts, especially those that emphasize research on the adaptation of foreign technologies also seems to yield very large returns. Countries that are able to incorporate new industrial technologies more rapidly into the productive system have been shown to grow faster than countries that are slower to do so. Although, unlike agricultural research, much industrial R&D is often directly done by the private sector itself, the large positive externalities of such research are by now well documented. Yet well structured and systematic public programs to support industrial R&D by the private sector are seldom encountered in developing countries.

Returns to environmental investments   Pearce (2005) carefully evaluates a large number of empirical studies measuring the rate of return to environmental investments. The rates of return of course show significant variability across the various assets and regions, but in general he found high rates of return especially to investments in water and sanitation, energy, anti-desertification, wetlands conservation, fisheries conservation, and several others. World Bank (2000) examines a great number of studies that report the health benefits of reducing air and water pollution in developing countries. As with the case of the other public goods discussed above, the dollar value of pollution reduction *vis-à-vis* its cost is highly favorable even if one uses a relatively high time discount rate. Cost–benefit analyses for controlling air pollution in many large cities in Asia and Latin America have sometimes yielded extremely high rates of return to such investments (World Bank, 2000; O'Ryan, 2001). The same is true for investments in decreasing water contamination including sewage treatment plants and related investments. For example, according to various World Bank studies cited in World Bank (2000), in China a $40 billion investment in clean water within a 10-year period would yield a present value benefit of $80 to $100 billion. In Indonesia, a $12 billion investment would give benefits of the order of $25 to $30 billion in terms of present value. Some studies for investment in air pollution control in various countries provide estimates even more favorable than the clean water investment. In China, for example, according to the World Bank, a $50 billion investment for selected cities could return benefits of the order of $200 billion in reduced illness and death.

Despite the high rates of return to investments in urban water and air pollution abatement, such investments do not seem to have received a high priority as shown by available indicators for cities in developing countries. For example, according to a sample of cities with per capita income below $2500 for the year 1998, less than 40 per cent treated their waste water, and less than 60 per cent of the population had water or sewage connections (World Bank, 2002).

High returns but low investment in human and environmental assets
The emerging literature on genuine savings is providing a clearer picture of the real changes in various wealth components over time (see Chapters 3 and 18). The World Bank has provided estimates of *genuine* investment for many countries by adding net investment in human and natural capital to estimates of net investments in physical capital (Hamilton, 2000). Apart from extending the analysis to more than 110 countries, an important modification over previous estimates of genuine savings done by the World Bank is that now measures of change of net wealth are expressed on a per capita basis. Per capita rather than total wealth change is an adequate and consistent measure of welfare change (Dasgupta and Mäler, 2002). The measure of per capita genuine savings as defined by Hamilton in his

country estimates equals net investment in manufactured or physical capital minus depletion of natural resources plus net investment in education, health and R&D.

The estimates for the year 1997 show that out of 90 low and middle income countries in Asia, Africa and Latin America, 71 (or about 80 per cent of them) exhibit *negative* per capita changes in wealth. While these estimates cover a large sample of countries, the fact that they refer only to one year raises the question of how representative this year might be. An analysis using the same definition of wealth as Hamilton but that covered a 20-year period is reported by Dasgupta (2005). Five Asian countries (Bangladesh, India, China, Nepal and Pakistan) and many sub-Saharan countries over the period 1973–93 were considered. This analysis shows similar results to Hamilton's. Not only has sub-Saharan Africa experienced decreased per capita net wealth, rather four of the five Asian countries also show negative per capita wealth changes. The only exception is China, which, as in Hamilton's analysis, has managed to accumulate wealth in advance of its population growth.

The overwhelming majority of the countries considered by these two studies show positive per capita growth rates for physical capital, implying that the reason for the negative growth rates of total wealth is that human, knowledge and environmental assets are growing at a rate below that of population. As a minimum, 80 per cent of the countries considered are experiencing reductions in their per capita human and environmental wealth. Since at least some countries may be compensating the declines of human and environmental assets with positive per capita growth of physical assets, the number of countries experiencing declines in human-environmental assets may be even larger.

We thus have an important paradox. Despite the apparently large rates of return to human, knowledge and environmental assets, the emerging literature on genuine savings is showing that the overwhelming majority of the developing countries are reducing the per capita availability of such assets. Given the semi-public good nature of these assets and the fact that their accumulation is seriously affected by market failures, their growing scarcity has to be traced back to the misallocation of public expenditures discussed earlier. Governments are spending too much in Type F goods and too little in Type A goods.

The development consequences of public expenditure misallocation
Public expenditure policies biased in favor of Type F expenditures and the consequent crowding out of Type A expenditures cause scarcity of public and semi-public assets, including human capital and knowledge. This over time means that the economy's endowment of human capital and knowl-

edge grows too slowly relative to that of countries where the government spends more in Type A goods. Human capital and knowledge becomes relatively scarce (and expensive). At the same time, the fact that the government spends too little in regulating and protecting the use of natural capital implies that the economy develops an artificial abundance of natural capital available to be exploited. Thus, the type F biases in public allocation create (false) comparative advantages in primary production and in industries that require little knowledge and human capital. Low skill industries often use technologies that are prone to remain stagnant with relatively slow productivity growth and are often 'dirty' or environmentally demanding. The net effect of this model is a slow increase of labor productivity in the non-primary sectors, insufficient to exert a large pull effect on the labor force. At the same time, the natural capital degrades as a consequence of the scarcity of environmental institutions, regulations and investment in the protection of the natural capital associated with the public expenditure policies. This triggers the push forces on the labor force employed in the primary sectors in a context of a falling opportunity cost of unskilled labor. These are the key factors causing perverse structural change.

An opposite effect takes place in countries where governments emphasize Type A public policies. In this case the factor endowments progressively change toward a greater abundance of human capital and knowledge. This creates the conditions for developing comparative advantages in the knowledge-intensive industries where productivity often grows fast, thus permitting a strong pull effect upon the labor force initially employed in the primary sectors. At the same time, the development of property right institutions and policies that regulate and protect the natural capital is likely to prevent both the usurpation of the resources owned by subsistence households as well as the destruction of ecosystems vital for the survival of the rural poor caused by large resource extraction projects. This is likely to help support the opportunity cost of unskilled workers in primary activities, thus permitting a slower process of out-migration from primary activities of workers that retain a relatively high opportunity cost. That is, this model of development promotes strong pull forces in non-primary activities while it ameliorates the push forces in primary sectors. These are of course conditions that increase the likelihood of benign structural change.

One can thus summarize and generalize the previous analysis as follows: PSC is in part the result of the misallocation of public revenues. Moreover, the greater the share of Type F public expenditures, the more likely it is that the economy will follow a perverse structural change pathway.

5. Conclusions

Structural change can be an important source of sustainable development and poverty reduction. The change of the structure of production and employment from primary, resource-dependent sectors towards non-resource sectors may considerably alleviate the pressures upon the natural capital that economic growth tends to impose. At the same time it can provide new opportunities to the poor to increase their productivity and hence their income. However, structural change can follow a completely different path if the change in the composition of the economy is forced as a consequence of the degradation of natural capital and/or the disenfranchisement of the rural poor instead of faster productivity growth in the non-primary sector. The labor force migrating from primary activities often finds that the productivity of the so-called modern sector is stagnant and provides limited employment opportunities, forcing a portion of them to depend on urban subsistence activities. Unfortunately it appears that this form of perverse structural change is more common than the benign form of structural change.

The two central results discussed in this chapter show that PSC is the product of misguided public environmental and natural resource policies, as well as also misguided allocations of public revenues. Clearly, behind these policy 'mistakes' there are powerful political economy forces, corruption and ideological biases often fomented by economists ('corporate subsidies are good because they contribute to creating jobs'). To a large extent the real origin of the problem is the weak countervailing power of the poor to face the great lobbying capacity of the elites and their intellectual allies. This weakness inclines the balance toward public policies which systematically favor the most powerful segments of the economic elites, but that in the end contribute to causing economic stagnation, environmental destruction and poverty. Which are the political failures that prevent the emergence of adequate countervailing powers among the vast majority of the population in developing countries that are poor or semi-poor even in democratic regimes? This is certainly a key question that deserves much more research.

Notes

1. This phenomenon was already documented in the late 1950s by prominent economists of the time such as Kuznets (1966) and Chenery (1960). More recently, several authors have further characterized and provided explanations for this process (Baumol et al., 1985; Echevarria (1997); Kongsamut et al., 2001).
2. An illustration of the high speed of structural change is provided by the following data: in just a decade (1990–2000) the share of the rural population in total population in Latin America fell from almost 29 per cent to just over 24 per cent (de Ferranti et al., 2004).
3. Also, it is in tropical and sub-tropical regions where most of the developing countries are located.

4. Examples of countries that 'did everything right' by strictly adhering to the orthodox policy prescription but that registered economic, social and environmental performance as bad as the pre-reform period are numerous: Bolivia and Argentina are dramatic examples of countries that implemented drastic pro-market reforms. Today, 15 to 20 years later, many of their welfare indicators are worse than in the pre-reform period (de Ferranti et al., 2004). Several countries in Sub-Saharan Africa have followed a similar experience.

5. Interestingly, the mounting empirical evidence on these issues is almost systematically ignored by mainstream economists; rarely have these studies been able to make their way into 'reputable' economic journals and they have mostly been ignored in the policy debate. The following are a small sample of the many studies showing that subsidies to the elites and large corporations are counterproductive as a development tool: Bergstrom (1998); Bregman et al. (1999); Estache and Gaspar (1995); Harris (1991); and Van Beers and de Moor (2001).

6. Despite the increased urban sub-employment caused by the lack of dynamism of the modern sector, out-migration from the rural areas may continue if the expected wage of potential migrants is still above the labor income obtained in the rural sector. As in the Harris–Todaro mechanism, a static equilibrium defining wage and (urban) unemployment may exist. In our case, however, such equilibrium would occur if migration reduced pressures on natural capital, eventually leading to a stationary level of the stock of natural capital in rural areas, at which point labor productivity in primary activities would stop falling.

7. Kates and Haarman (1992), López (1997) and Stonich (1989) review a great number of large-scale enclosure episodes that have taken place in modern times around the world.

8. Several enclosures events in Latin America have been caused by certain commodity booms, which have suddenly made land resources belonging to rural communities much more enticing. Particularly important have been land usurpations triggered by beef booms which have induced a drastic reallocation of the land from labor-intensive subsistence production to land-intensive cattle operations. See Heath and Binswanger (1996) and López (1997) for an account of such processes and their economic consequences.

9. If the production function is linearly homogenous, firm i's variable profit function can be written as: $\Pi^i = k^i \pi(p,w)$, where k^i is the stock of capital of firm i and p is the output price, w is a vector of input prices, and $\pi(\ )$ is a unit profit function (Diewert, 1973). Also, by Hotelling's lemma, the level of output of firm i is $q^i = k^i \partial \pi(p,w)/\partial p$. Thus aggregate output $Q = \Sigma_i q^i = \partial \pi(p,w)/\partial p \Sigma_i k^i$ is not affected by the distribution of k across firms if all firms face the same output and input prices and if they have access to the same technology. Output will be determined by the total level of capital but not by how it is distributed across firms.

10. There is so much that an individual can learn given his/her natural cognitive and life span limitations.

11. In Brazil, for example, more than 50 per cent of total government expenditures by the federal government were Type F in the late 1990s (Calmon, 2004). In a sample of 10 Latin American countries over the period 1985–2000, it was found that on average 53 per cent of government expenditures in rural areas were Type F (López, 2005). See also Van Beers and de Moor (2001) and World Bank (2000) for evidence for other countries.

12. Governments may opt to raise taxes to make a large volume of type F expenditures still compatible with an adequate supply of Type A investment. However, raising taxes, especially in the context of most developing countries, is subject to significant political constraints and is also costly. Still another way of providing sufficient public goods while still keeping a large volume of Type F expenditures is to resort to increasing public deficits and consequently, to more debt. Obviously this mechanism is available only in the short run. The dramatically negative consequences of uncontrolled public deficits and increasing debt are well known.

13. Examples of most recent studies: Brazil, 35.6 per cent for primary and 21 per cent for higher education; Uganda, 66 per cent for primary and 28.6 per cent for secondary; Morocco, 50 per cent for primary and 10 per cent for secondary; Taiwan, 27.7 per cent

for primary and 17.7 per cent for higher; India, 17.6 per cent for primary and 18.2 per cent for higher. These are social rates of return, with the exception of India. Private rates are even higher.
14. The case of Peru is illustrative. In the mid-1990s the government decided to privatize agricultural research. The government sold 21 agricultural experiment farms where most of the agricultural research in the country was performed. The result: by the year 2000 20 of the 21 experiment stations had been transformed into commercial farm operations. Only one remained as an experimental farm. Agricultural research in Peru practically became extinct.

References

Alston, J., M. Marra, P. Pardey and P. Wyatt (2000), 'Research return redux: a meta-analysis and the returns of R&D', *Australian Journal of Agricultural Economics*, **44**: 1364–85.
Baumol, W.J., S.A.B. Blackman and E.N. Wolff (1985), 'Unbalanced growth revisited: asymptotic stagnancy and new evidence,' *American Economic Review*, **75**(4): 806–17.
Bergstrom, F. (1998), 'Capital subsidies and the performance of firms', Stockholm School of Economics, Working Paper No. 285.
Bregman, A., M. Fuss and H. Regev (1999), 'Effects of capital subsidization on productivity in Israeli industry', *Bank of Israel Economic Review*, **72**(1): 77–101.
Calmon, P. (2004), 'Evaluation of subsidies in Brazil', unpublished, Washington, DC: The World Bank.
Chenery, Hollis B. (1960), 'Patterns of industrial growth', *American Economic Review*, **50**(4): 624–54.
Dasgupta, P. (2005), 'Sustainable economic development on the world of today's poor', in D. Simpson, M. Toman and R. Ayres (eds), *Scarcity and Growth Revisited*, Washington, DC: Resources for the Future Press.
Dasgupta, P. and K.-G. Mäler (2002), 'Decentralization schemes, cost–benefit analysis, and net national products as a measure of social well-being', Development Economics Discussion Papers No. 12, London School of Economics, STICERD.
De Ferranti, D., G. Perry, F. Ferreira and M. Walton (2004), *Inequality in Latin America: Breaking with History?*, Latin American and Caribbean Studies, Washington, DC: The World Bank.
Diewert, W.E. (1973), 'Functional forms for profit and transformation functions', *Journal of Economic Theory*, **6**(3): 284–316.
Easterly, W. (2001), *The Elusive Quest for Growth*, Cambridge, Mass: MIT Press.
Echevarria, C. (1997), 'Changes in sectoral composition associated with economic growth', *International Economic Review*, **38**(2): 431–52.
Estache, A. and V. Gaspar (1995), 'Why tax incentives do not promote investment in Brazil', in A. Shah (ed.), *Fiscal Incentives for Investment and Innovation*, Baltimore: Oxford University Press.
Fakin, B. (1995), 'Investment subsidies during transition', *Eastern European Economics*, **33**(5): 62–75.
Hamilton, K. (2000), 'Sustaining economic welfare: estimating changes in per capita wealth', World Bank Policy Research Working Paper No. 2498, Washington, DC: The World Bank.
Harris, R. (1991), 'The employment creation effects of factor subsidies: some estimates for Northern Ireland', *Journal of Regional Science*, **31**: 49–64.
Heath, J. and H. Binswanger (1996), 'Natural resource degradation effects of poverty and population growth are largely policy-induced: the case of Colombia', *Environment and Development Economics*, **1**(1): 65–84.
IMF, Independent Evaluation Office (2003), *Fiscal Adjustment in IMF-Supported Programs*, Washington, DC: International Monetary Fund.
Kates, R. and V. Haarmann (1992), 'Where the poor live: are the assumptions correct?', *Environment*, **34**: 4–28.
Kongsamut P., S. Rebelo and D. Xie (2001), 'Beyond balanced growth', *Review of Economic Studies*, **68**(4): 869–82.

Krueger, A., M. Schiff and A. Valdés (eds) (1991), 'Political economy of agricultural pricing policy', Baltimore: Johns Hopkins University Press.

Kuznets, S. (1966), *Modern Economic Growth: Rate, Structure, and Spread*, New Haven: Yale University Press.

Lee, J. (1996), 'Government interventions and productivity growth in Korean manufacturing industries', *Journal of Economic Growth*, **1**(3): 392–415.

Lewis, A. (1955), *The Theory of Economic Growth*, Homewood, IL: Richard D. Irwin.

López, R. (1997), 'Where development can or cannot go: the role of poverty–environment linkages', in B. Pleskovic and J. Stiglitz (eds), *Annual World Bank Conference on Development Economics 1997*, Washington, DC: The World Bank.

López, R. (2003), 'The policy roots of socioeconomic stagnation and environmental implosion: Latin America 1950–2000', *World Development*, **31**(2): 259–80.

López, R. (2005), 'Why governments should stop non-social subsidies: measuring their consequences for rural Latin America', World Bank Policy Research Working Paper No. 3609.

López, R. and M. Toman (2006), *Economic Development and Environmental Sustainability*, Oxford: Oxford University Press.

O'Ryan, R.E. (2001), 'Cost-effective policies to improve urban air quality in Santiago, Chile,' in T. Tietenberg (ed.), *Emissions Trading Programs: Implementation and Evolution, Volume 1*, International Library of Environmental Economics and Policy, Aldershot, UK; Burlington, VT and Sydney: Ashgate, pp. 53–64.

Oates, W.E. (1996), *The Economics of Environmental Regulation. Economists of the Twentieth Century Series*, Cheltenham, UK and Brookfield, USA: Edward Elgar, distributed by Ashgate, Brookfield, Vt., pp. xvi, 452.

Pearce, D. (2005), 'Managing environmental wealth for poverty reduction', Poverty and Environment Partnership MDG7 Initiative.

Psacharopoulos, G. (1994), 'Returns to investment in education: a global update', *World Development*, **22**(9): 1325–43.

Psacharopoulos, G. and H. Patrinos (2002), 'Returns to investment in education: a further update', World Bank Policy Research Working Paper No. 2881, Washington, DC.

Renis, G. and J.C.H. Fei (1961), 'A theory of economic development', *American Economic Review*, **51**: 533–65.

Sánchez, P. (1976), *Properties and Management of Soils in the Tropics*, New York: J. Wiley.

Schulz, T.W. (1968), *Economic Growth and Agriculture*, New York: MacGraw-Hill.

Stiglitz, J.E. (2000), 'Capital market liberalization, economic growth, and instability', *World Development*, **28**(6): 1075–86.

Stonich, S. (1989), 'The dynamics of social processes and environmental destruction: a Central American case study', *Population and Development Review*, **15**(2): 269–96.

Van Beers, C. and A. de Moor (2001), *Public Subsidies and Policy Failure*, Cheltenham, UK and Northampton, MA, USA: Edward Elgar.

The World Bank (2000), *The Quality of Growth*, Oxford University Press and World Bank.

The World Bank (2002), 'World development report 2002: Building institutions for markets', Oxford and New York: Oxford University Press for the World Bank, pp. xii, 249.

The World Bank (2003), *World Development Indicators*, World Bank, vol. 1, no. 2, pp. 1–392.

15 Economic growth and the environment
Matthew A. Cole

1. Introduction

The complex relationship between economic growth and the environment has been a focus of academic attention since the 1970s. During the 1970s opinion was polarized between the pro-growth 'technological optimists' on the one hand and the anti-growth 'technological pessimists' on the other. The former placed great faith in our ability to find technological solutions to environmental problems, to change the composition of output and to find substitutes for scarce resources, thereby removing potential environmental limits. Technological pessimists argued that such benefits were likely to be short term and stressed the irreversibility of fossil fuel exhaustion. The advent of sustainable development saw the emphasis move from resource scarcity towards sink limits, but differing opinions regarding the impact of economic growth on the environment remained, largely a result of differing views of the capital stock that is to be maintained over time.

More recently, quantitative analyses, such as the estimation of environmental Kuznets curves and the decomposition of emissions into scale, technique and composition effects, have illuminated the debate to an extent. These studies suggest that economic growth does not have to be damaging to the environment and can co-exist alongside reductions in environmental pollution. Emissions of local air pollutants appear to have benefited from new technology and increased energy efficiency which, particularly in slow-growing (for example developed) countries, more than compensates for increased emissions resulting from the pure scale effect. The evidence also suggests that changes to the output mix (the composition effect) have only a minor impact on emissions. However, it increasingly appears that the relationship between emissions and income, even if an inverted U-shape, is likely to be country-specific. Much uncertainty still surrounds the precise conditions under which emissions, and other environmental indicators, can improve in the face of economic growth.

This chapter reviews the debate on economic growth and the environment, starting with a historical account of the so-called 'limits to growth' debate of the 1970s. The rise of sustainable development and its influence on this debate will also be considered, before attention turns to a critical review of the environmental Kuznets curve hypothesis and pollution decomposition studies. Conclusions are then provided.

2. The 'limits to growth' debate

With a few notable exceptions, the relationship between economic growth and the environment received little attention prior to the 1960s.[1] The publication of Rachel Carson's *Silent Spring* in 1962, however, increased public awareness considerably by examining the impact of man's indiscriminate use of chemicals in the form of pesticides and insecticides. Perhaps as a result of *Silent Spring*, environmental issues received growing attention throughout the 1960s. In 1966, Kenneth Boulding produced his seminal article 'The Economics of the Coming Spaceship Earth' in which he highlighted the danger of steadily increasing production levels, both in terms of reducing finite resource stocks and in terms of environmental pollution.

With these concerns in mind, in 1972 Donella and Dennis Meadows and a team from the Massachusetts Institute of Technology produced a report for the Club of Rome's Project for the Predicament of Mankind entitled *The Limits to Growth*. A world model was constructed to estimate the future impact of continuous exponential growth under a number of different assumptions. The 'standard' world model assumed that the physical, economic or social relationships that have historically governed the development of the world system would remain effectively unchanged. Additionally, this model assumed that population and industrial capital would continue to grow exponentially, leading to a similar growth in pollution and in demand for food and non-renewable resources. The supply of both food and non-renewable resources was assumed to be fixed. Not surprisingly given the assumptions, the model predicted collapse due to non-renewable resource depletion.

The radical nature of the report attracted much attention, not only in academic circles, but also in society at large. As a result, *The Limits to Growth* fuelled a debate which continued throughout the 1970s. The contrasting viewpoints in this debate stem from differing opinions concerning three factors: the rate of technical progress; future changes in the composition of output and the possibilities of substitution (Lecomber, 1975). 'If these three effects add up to a shift away from the limiting resource or pollutant equal to or greater than the rate of growth, then the limits to growth are put back indefinitely.' (Ekins, 1993, p. 271). However, for Lecomber (1975, p. 42) the point to be stressed is that 'this establishes the *logical* conceivability, not the certainty, probability or even the possibility in practice, of growth continuing indefinitely.'

3. The rise of sustainable development

The advent of the 1980s saw attention turn from the limits to growth arguments of the 1970s towards the notion of sustainable development. The term 'sustainable development' appears to have been first advanced in 1980 by the International Union for the Conservation of Nature and Natural Resources (Ruttan, 1994) although it was the Brundtland Commission Report (WCED, 1987) which brought the concept to the top of the agenda of institutions like the United Nations and the World Bank. Since the Brundtland Report the goal of sustainable development has been adopted by an ever-increasing number of organizations and bodies.

The popularity of sustainable development would seem to belie, or is perhaps indicative of, the vagueness of the term. Countless definitions of sustainable development now exist, each typically reflecting the academic discipline in which the author has expertise. Economists tend to emphasize the need to maintain living standards (see especially chapters 3 and 18); ecologists are more concerned with biodiversity and resilience (Chapters 4 and 5) and sociologists prioritize the need to maintain sociological bonds and interrelationships within communities. The amorphous nature of the concept means that it is impossible to state the precise relationship between sustainable development and economic growth although, as shall be seen below, certain general viewpoints may be defined. Opponents of sustainable development use its ambiguity as ammunition, however, claiming such a vague concept to be meaningless. Wilfred Beckerman, continuing his pro-growth stance adopted in the 1970s clearly holds such a view and believes sustainable development to be 'devoid of operational value' (Beckerman, 1992, p. 491). Others are critical of the 'watered down' interpretation of sustainable development that has been adopted by the political main-stream, believing it to provide little scope for environmental improvement.

Despite the countless definitions, it is generally agreed that the most appropriate mechanism for ensuring the well-being of future generations is to ensure that the next generation has access to a stock of capital at least as large as the current stock. However, two viewpoints emerge regarding the precise nature of the capital stock which is to be maintained. These differing viewpoints allow a distinction to be drawn between 'weak' and 'strong' forms of sustainable development (see, for example, Pearce, 1993 and Chapter 4 of this volume).

The capital stock consists of man-made capital (such as the means of production, infrastructure, human capital) together with natural capital (such as fossil fuels, habitat, clean water). Proponents of 'weak' sustainable development simply require that the *aggregate* capital stock is maintained and thus believe that a fall in natural capital can be compensated by an increase in man-made capital. In contrast, the strong sustainability school questions the substitutability between these two forms of capital and hence believes it insufficient simply to maintain the aggregate capital stock irrespective of the relative size of its constituents.

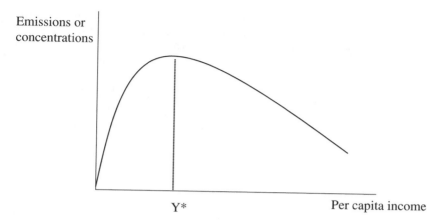

Emissions or
concentrations

Y*

Per capita income

Figure 15.1   A hypothetical environmental Kuznets curve

With regard to the relationship between economic growth and the environment, the two viewpoints again differ. Typically, the 'weak' sustainable development position is that economic growth and environmental health are often complementary. By this definition, the recommendations of the Brundtland Report would fall into the weak sustainability category since it actually called for 'more rapid economic growth in both industrial and developing countries.' (WCED, 1987, p. 89). Indeed, most governments and global institutions also see no conflict between economic growth and the environment and place great faith in future technological advance and in our ability to find substitutes for scarce resources. Many believe there to be an inverted U- shaped relationship between pollution and production, as illustrated in Figure 15.1, and use this as evidence of our ability to decouple pollution from production. This inverted-U relationship is also known as the environmental Kuznets curve (EKC) relationship and will be examined in detail below.[2]

The 'strong' sustainability school believes that the only way to achieve reductions in the scale of materials and energy throughput is to reduce the scale of economic output. Concentrating on sink-limits rather than resource exhaustion, supporters of this viewpoint (for example Daly and Cobb, 1989) are therefore sceptical of the potential for decoupling and point to the risk of irreversibility associated with damage to the natural environment.

4.   The environmental Kuznets curve

The advent of the 1990s saw a significant increase in the availability of environmental data, particularly measuring concentrations or emissions of air and water pollution. This data has enabled econometric analyses of the relationship between per capita income and environmental indicators which were previously impossible. The first such studies by Grossman and Krueger (1991; 1995) and Shafik (1994) found evidence of an inverted U-shaped relationship between pollution and per capita income (again, as illustrated in Figure 15.1) which has typically been explained in terms of the interaction of scale, composition and technique effects. A country's total emissions of a pollutant (X_t) can be defined in the following way;

$$X_t = \sum_{i=1}^{n} a_{it} s_{it} Y_t \qquad (15.1)$$

where Y_t denotes GDP at time t, a_{it} denotes the amount of pollution generated per unit of output in sector i at time t, and s_{it} represents the share of output deriving from sector i at time t. The first term, a, can be referred to as the technique effect, the second term, s, as the composition effect and the third term, Y, as the scale effect. As an economy develops we would expect the scale of the economy to increase, which, *ceteris paribus*, is likely to increase emissions. However, a growing economy is also likely to devote more resources to the regulation of environmental damage and may increasingly benefit from new technology. These changes are likely to affect the techniques of production resulting in reductions in emissions. Finally, as an economy develops, its composition is likely to change from an emphasis on agriculture, to heavy industry, to light manufacturing and services. The contraction of heavy industry and the movement towards light manufacturing and services is likely, *ceteris paribus*, to reduce emissions. It has therefore been argued that the inverted U-shaped relationship results from a dominance of scale effects over composition and technique effects in the early stages of development, with a reversal of this dominance in later stages of development.

Typically, the basic EKC equation that has been estimated is of the following form, estimated in either logs or levels:

$$X_{it} = (\alpha + \beta_i F_i) + \delta Y_{it} + \phi (Y_{it})^2 + \varepsilon_{it} \qquad (15.2)$$

Where X denotes the environmental indicator, either in per capita form or in the form of concentrations, Y denotes per capita income, F denotes country-specific effects and i and t refer to country and year, respectively. Note that some studies include a cubic income term.

In equation (15.2), if $\delta > 1$ and $\phi < 1$ then the estimated curve has a maximum turning point per capita income level, calculated as $Y^* = (-\delta/2\phi)$. Table 15.1 summarizes the results of those EKC studies that have

Table 15.1 Estimated turning points from EKC studies (all in 1985 US dollars)

Media	Environmental indicator	Shafik (1994)	S&S[2] (1994)	G&K[3] (1995)	Cole *et al.* (1997)	Cole (2003)
Air[1]	Nitrogen Oxides		$12 041		$14 700	$19 626
	Sulphur Dioxide	$3 670	$8 916	$4 053	$6 900	$11 168
	Carbon Monoxide		$6 241		$9 900	
	SPM[4]	$3 280	$9 811	$6 151	$7 300	
	Carbon Dioxide[5]	⇑			$62 700	$38 624
Water	Nitrates			$10 524	$25 000	
	Faecal Coliform			$7 955		
	Lead			$1 887		
	Mercury			$5 047		
	Arsenic			$4 900		
General	Municipal waste	⇑			⇑	

Notes:
1. Air pollution is measured as per capita emissions, except Shafik (1994) and G&K (1995) who use concentrations data.
2. S&S refers to Selden and Song (1994).
3. G&K refers to Grossman and Krueger (1995).
4. SPM = suspended particulate matter.
5. The ⇑ symbol indicates that the indicator was estimated to increase monotonically with per capita income.

covered a range of environmental indicators. Table 15.1 indicates a reasonable degree of compatibility across studies. For local air pollutants, turning points are estimated at reasonably low levels of per capita income indicating that emissions/concentrations are now falling in most developed economies. Pollution concentrations in river water also tend to have relatively low estimated turning points, with the exception of nitrates from Cole et al. (1997). Municipal waste is estimated to increase monotonically with per capita income in the two studies to have examined it.

Many other studies have included additional variables in the EKC relationship, or considered different pollutants (see for example, Cole, 2003; Cole and Elliott, 2003; Hilton and Levinson, 1998; Torras and Boyce, 1998). There are, however, several studies that find very different results to those summarized in Table 15.1. Dijkgraaf and Vollebergh (1998) estimate EKCs for carbon dioxide emissions using both an OECD panel and individual time-series regressions for each country. Interestingly, for the panel as a whole they find an inverted U-shaped relationship between per capita income and emissions, with a turning point level of income well within the sample income range. This is in stark contrast to the CO_2 results from other

EKC studies (for example Cole et al., 1997; Holtz-Eakin and Selden, 1995). For their individual country time-series regressions, Dijkgraaf and Vollebergh find very varied results thereby questioning the existence of a meaningful global EKC for CO_2 emissions.

Harbaugh et al. (2002) also question whether there is a systematic relationship between per capita income and pollution. They estimate the relationship between per capita income and concentrations of sulphur dioxide, total suspended particulates and smoke and find their results to be highly sensitive to choice of functional form, to additional covariates and to changes in the countries, cities and years included in their sample. A plausible reason for this, as suggested by the authors, is the noisy nature of concentrations data which requires the use of dummies to control for a number of site-specific determinants. Stern and Common (2001), however, consider SO_2 *emissions* and also question the traditional EKC methodology (and its results). This study is briefly discussed below.

Criticisms of the EKC
Criticisms of the EKC fall into two categories, firstly those aimed at the EKC methodology and secondly those concerned with the interpretation of EKC results. The following are criticisms of the EKC methodology:

- The basic EKC is determined by changing trade patterns rather than growth-induced pollution abatement, and these trade patterns have typically been neglected by EKC studies. The North's declining share of manufacturing in GNP, in part resulting from its more stringent environmental regulations relative to the South, indicates that the North is simply exporting its pollution to the South. The EKC inverted U therefore merely represents a redistribution of pollution from North to South. Stern (1998) and Stern et al. (1996) both cite this as a criticism of the EKC relationship.
- The EKC assumes unidirectional causality from GNP to emissions and allows no mechanism through which environmental degradation can affect income levels. Least squares estimation in the presence of such simultaneity will provide biased and inconsistent estimates.
- Econometric issues. The most fundamental econometric criticisms are provided by Stern and Common (2001) and Perman and Stern (2003). These papers raise two key issues; (a) Studies that use only OECD data will typically estimate turning points at lower per capita income levels than those using data for the world as a whole. This arises because the developing countries are experiencing increasing emissions of even local air pollutants such as SO_2. (b) Per capita income and emissions are typically non-stationary variables and EKC

regressions do not appear to co-integrate. It is also likely that there are omitted non-stationary variables. Standard EKC estimation in the presence of these features is likely to generate spurious results.

- Other econometric criticisms have also been raised in the literature. Stern et al. (1996) are concerned that many EKC studies ignore the issue of heteroscedasticity which is likely to be present in cross-section data. Furthermore, most EKC studies estimate a quadratic relationship between pollution and income and therefore fail to allow for the possibility of emissions beginning to increase again at high income levels. Finally, Harbaugh et al. (2002) and Ekins (1997) argue that different datasets, functional forms (for example logs versus levels) and estimation techniques all provide different results, suggesting that the EKC relationship is fragile.
- Stern (1998) criticizes EKC regressions that allow levels of pollution to become zero or negative as being incompatible with the laws of thermodynamics, since all resource use inevitably produces waste.

In addition to these, a number of concerns have been raised regarding the interpretation of EKCs:

- Arrow et al. (1995) argue that although EKCs have been estimated for some local air pollutants it is dangerous to assume that similar relationships will exist for all other environmental indicators.
- EKCs do not indicate that economic growth automatically solves environmental problems. Emissions reductions have only been attained through investment and regulations, neither of which are automatic consequences of economic growth.
- Mean versus median income. Although many EKCs estimate turning points around the current world mean per capita income level, this does not mean that, globally, emissions are about to decline. Global income distribution is skewed with far more people below the mean than above it. If median income levels are considered rather than mean, EKCs indicate that emissions will continue to increase for many years to come.

5. Economic growth and the environment: beyond the EKC

Clearly, the reliability and accuracy of the EKC framework remains questionable. To an extent, differing opinions of the EKC reflect semantic differences in how EKCs are actually defined. Many economists would agree that the majority of developed countries have experienced an inverted U-shaped relationship between income and local air emissions, determined by the interaction of scale, composition and technique effects. Since emissions

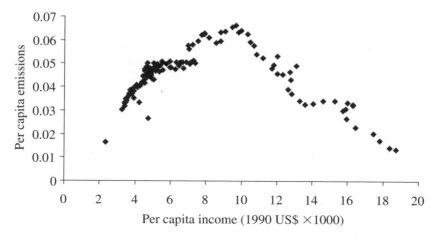

Source: Income data from Maddison (2001). Sulphur Dioxide data from Stern (2005).

Figure 15.2   *The relationship between per capita income and per capita sulphur dioxide emissions, UK 1850–1998*

of most local air pollutants are falling in developed countries they must once have risen, thereby providing an inverted U. Figure 15.2 provides the example of sulphur dioxide emissions in the UK over the period 1850–1998. However, disagreement arises over whether turning points have differed across countries due to differing economic, social, political and cultural conditions. Hence, whilst many would agree that country-specific EKCs are likely to exist, the existence of a universal 'one size fits all' systematic relationship between income and emissions receives far less support.

The growing perception that the EKC framework is too simplistic has led to a number of attempts to provide a more detailed understanding of the factors influencing pollution emissions by decomposing emissions into their constituent parts. A relatively simple decomposition of carbon dioxide emissions is provided by Hamilton and Turton (2002) for OECD countries and Zhang (2000) for China, as outlined in equation (15.3);

$$X_{it} = \frac{X_{it}}{FE_{it}} \frac{FE_{it}}{TE_{it}} \frac{TE_{it}}{GDP_{it}} \frac{GDP_{it}}{P_{it}} P_{it} \qquad (15.3)$$

where X refers to emissions, FE is fossil fuel use, TE is total energy use (fossil and non-fossil) and P is total population. These studies both find scale effects (population and GDP per capita) to be the main factors increasing emissions, whilst the technique effect in the form of energy intensity (TE/GDP) is the main factor reducing emissions.[3]

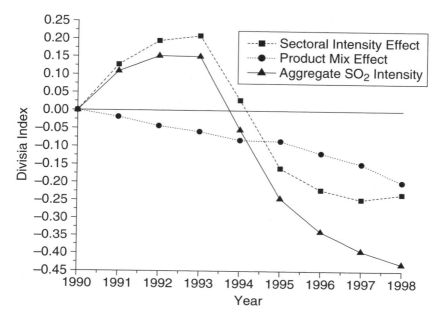

Source: Cole et al. (2005).

Figure 15.3 *A decomposition of aggregate sulphur dioxide intensity in the UK*

Cole et al. (2005) utilize a divisia index approach to decompose aggregate intensities of sulphur dioxide, nitrogen oxides and carbon dioxide into a composition (product mix) effect and a technique (sectoral intensity) effect.[4] This analysis is undertaken for Austria, France, the Netherlands and the UK using industry-specific emissions data for the 1990s. For Austria, France and the Netherlands the technique effect alone was found to be the main factor explaining declining aggregate emissions intensities. For the UK, the composition effect was also found to play a role. Figure 15.3 presents the results for sulphur dioxide in the UK and illustrates the joint role played by technique and composition effects in reducing aggregate pollution intensity.

Stern (2002) provides a more complex decomposition for sulphur dioxide, as given by equation (15.4), and applies this to 64 countries for the period 1973–90;

$$\frac{X_{it}}{P_{it}} = \gamma_i \frac{Y_{it}}{P_{it}} A_t \frac{E_{it}}{Y_{it}} \prod_{j=1}^{J} \left(\frac{y_{jit}}{Y_{it}}\right)^{\alpha_j} \sum_{k=1}^{K} \frac{e_{kit}}{E_{it}} \varepsilon_{it} \qquad (15.4)$$

Equation (15.4) decomposes per capita sulphur dioxide emissions into five effects:

$\dfrac{Y_{it}}{P_{it}}$ GDP per capita (the scale effect)

A_t a global time trend representing technological progress

$\dfrac{E_{it}}{Y_{it}}$ energy intensity (energy use per unit of output)

$\dfrac{y_{1it}}{Y_{it}}....\dfrac{y_{Jit}}{Y_{it}}$ product mix (shares of the output of different industries, y, in total Y)

$\dfrac{e_{1it}}{E_{it}}....\dfrac{e_{Jit}}{E_{it}}$ fuel mix (shares of different energy sources, e, in total energy use E)

Stern's findings are summarized in Table 15.2. Again, the main factors reducing emissions are technological change and energy intensity (which combine to form the technique effect), although it is notable that, for this 'global' sample, the sum of these does not exceed the scale effect.

These decomposition studies therefore suggest that, for local air pollutants at least, the impact of technological change and increased energy efficiency is likely to outweigh the increased emissions resulting from the scale effect. Whilst a global pollutant is also likely to benefit from these technique effects, they are likely to be dominated by the scale effect, resulting in a net increase in emissions.

6. Conclusions

Whilst the limits to growth debate has yet to be fully resolved, it is clear that many of the predictions made by opponents to economic growth in the 1970s have proved to be wide of the mark. This failure to convince society

Table 15.2   Decomposing global sulphur dioxide emissions

	Weighted logarithmic % change
Scale effect	53.78
Technological change	−19.86
Energy intensity	−10.20
Product mix	3.77
Fuel mix	−0.13

Source: Stern (2002).

at large of the need to replace economic growth as a key policy objective is illustrated by the fact that the Brundtland Report still interpreted growth as being compatible, even complementary, to environmental well-being. Indeed, this viewpoint is held by most mainstream advocates of sustainable development.

The profusion of quantitative analyses that began in the 1990s have enlightened the debate to an extent. Although the EKC methodology has been criticized for being too simplistic, one broad conclusion which stems from EKC and other quantitative studies is that economic growth can be compatible with reductions in emissions of some pollutants. Whilst a pollution-income path that is common to all countries is questionable, it seems probable that all countries can benefit from technique effects resulting from technological advance and increased energy efficiency. For local air pollutants, these technique effects are likely to dominate scale effects, resulting in a reduction in pollution. This is particularly likely to occur in relatively slow-growing, developed economies. However, the relative size of scale, composition and technique effects is likely to be influenced by the economic, political, cultural and environmental characteristics of individual countries. The role played by governance may also be critical. Countries with identical income levels yet significantly different levels of political governance are unlikely to share similar emissions levels.

Although environmental improvement can occur alongside economic growth, it is important to stress that this is not an automatic procedure. Growth does not reduce pollution. Rather, the evidence suggests that growth *may* facilitate the required legislation and investment to help reduce *per capita* emissions of *some* pollutants. This carefully worded statement illustrates the great care that is needed when examining the relationship between growth and the environment. It also suggests that future research within this area should increasingly focus on the precise conditions under which pollution can be reduced. This is likely to require highly detailed studies of individual countries, an examination of the role played by governance and environmental regulations, and increasingly detailed decomposition studies. As the availability of environmental data continues to improve, particularly industry-specific emissions data and pollution abatement expenditure data, so too should our ability to further increase our understanding of the complex relationship between economic growth and the environment.

Notes

1. One such exception is the classical economist John Stuart Mill. Writing in 1848, Mill comments 'Nor is there much satisfaction in contemplating the world with nothing left to the spontaneous activity of nature; with every rood of land brought into cultivation . . . every flowery waste or natural pasture ploughed up, all quadrupeds and birds . . . exterminated and scarcely a place left where a wild shrub or flower could grow' (Mill, 1871, p. 331).

2. The environmental Kuznets curve is named after the original Kuznets curve which postulated an inverted U-shaped relationship between per capita income and income inequality (Kuznets, 1955).
3. Similar findings are made by Bruvoll and Medin (2003) and Selden, Forrest and Lockhart (1999).
4. Since the variable being decomposed is expressed as an intensity (that is emissions scaled by output) the scale effect is removed.

References

Arrow, K., B. Bolin, R. Costanza, P. Dasgupta, C. Folke, C.S. Holling, B.-O. Jansson, S. Levin, K.-G. Maler, C. Perrings and D. Pimental (1995), 'Economic growth, carrying capacity and the environment', *Ecological Economics*, 15(2): 91–5.
Beckerman, W. (1992), 'Economic growth and the environment: whose growth? Whose environment?', *World Development*, 20(4): 481–96.
Boulding, K.E. (1966), 'The Economics of the Coming Spaceship Earth', in H. Jawett (ed.), *Environmental Quality in a Growing Economy*, Baltimore: Johns Hopkins Press.
Bruvoll, A. and H. Medin (2003), 'Factors behind the environmental Kuznets curve: a decomposition of changes in air pollution', *Environmental and Resource Economics*, 24: 27–48.
Carson, R. (1962), *Silent Spring*, Penguin.
Cole, M.A. (2003), 'Development, trade and the environment: how robust is the environmental Kuznets curve?', *Environment and Development Economics*, 8: 557–80.
Cole, M.A. and R.J.R. Elliott (2003), 'Determining the trade–environment composition effect: the role of capital, labour and environmental regulations', *Journal of Environmental Economics and Management*, 46(3): 363–83.
Cole, M.A., R.J.R. Elliott and K. Shimamoto (2005), 'A note on trends in European industrial pollution intensities: a divisia index approach', *Energy Journal*, 26(3).
Cole, M.A., A.J. Rayner and J.M. Bates (1997), 'The environmental Kuznets curve: an empirical analysis', *Environment and Development Economics*, 2(4): 401–16.
Daly, H.E. and J.B. Cobb (1989), *For the Common Good: Redirecting the Economy Towards Community, the Environment and a Sustainable Future*, London: Green Print.
Dijkgraaf, E. and H.R.J. Vollebergh (1998), 'Growth and/or (?) environment: is there a Kuznets curve for carbon emissions?', presented at the 2nd biennial meeting of the European Society of Ecological Economics, Geneva, 4–7 March.
Ekins, P. (1993), ' "Limits to growth" and "sustainable development": grappling with ecological realities', *Ecological Economics*, 8: 269–88.
Ekins, P. (1997), 'The Kuznets curve for the environment and economic growth: examining the evidence', *Environment and Planning A*, 29: 805–30.
Grossman, G.M. and A.B. Krueger (1991), 'Environmental impacts of a North American free trade agreement', National Bureau of Economic Research working paper 3914, NBER, Cambridge, MA.
Grossman, G.M. and A.B. Krueger (1995), 'Economic growth and the environment', *Quarterly Journal of Economics*, May, pp. 353–7.
Hamilton, C. and H. Turton (2002), 'Determinants of emissions growth in OECD countries', *Energy Policy*, 30: 63–71.
Harbaugh, B., A. Levinson and D. Wilson (2002), 'Re-examining the empirical evidence for an environmental Kuznets curve', *Review of Economics and Statistics*, 84(3): 541–51.
Hilton, F.G. and A. Levinson (1998), 'Factoring the environmental Kuznets curve: evidence from automotive lead emissions', *Journal of Environmental Economics and Management*, 35(2).
Holtz-Eakin, D. and T.M. Selden (1995), 'Stoking the fires? CO_2 emissions and economic growth', *Journal of Public Economics*, 57: 85–101.
Kuznets, S. (1955), 'Economic growth and income inequality', *American Economic Review*, 45(1), March.
Lecomber, R. (1975), *Economic Growth Versus the Environment*, London: Macmillan.
Maddison, A. (2001), *The World Economy: A Millennial Perspective*, Paris: OECD.

Meadows, D.H., D.L. Meadows, J. Randers and W.W. Behrens (1972), *The Limits to Growth: A Report for the Club of Rome's Project on the Predicament of Mankind*, Washington, DC: Universe Books.

Mill, J.S. (1871), *Principles of Political Economy*, Longman.

Pearce, D.W. (1993), *Blueprint Three: Measuring Sustainable Development*, London: Earthscan.

Perman, R. and D.I. Stern (2003), 'Evidence from panel unit root and cointegration tests that the environmental Kuznets curve does not exist', *Australian Journal of Agricultural and Resource Economics*, **47**: 325–47.

Ruttan, V.W. (1994), 'Constraints on the design of sustainable systems of agricultural production', *Ecological Economics*, **10**: 209–19.

Selden, T.M. and D. Song (1994), 'Environmental quality and development: is there a Kuznets curve for air pollution emissions?', *Journal of Environmental Economics and Management*, **27**(2): 147–62.

Selden, T.M., A.S. Forrest and J.E. Lockhart (1999), 'Analyzing reductions in US air pollution emissions: 1970–1990', *Land Economics*, **75**: 1–21.

Shafik, N. (1994), 'Economic development and environmental quality: an econometric analysis', *Oxford Economic Papers*, **46**: 757–73.

Stern, D.I. (1998), 'Progress on the environmental Kuznets curve?', *Environment and Development Economics*, **3**(2): 173–96.

Stern, D.I. (2002), 'Explaining changes in global sulfur emissions: an econometric decomposition approach', *Ecological Economics*, **42**: 201–20.

Stern, D.I. (2005), 'Global sulfur emissions from 1850 to 2000', *Chemosphere*, **58**: 163–75.

Stern, D.I. and M.S. Common (2001), 'Is there an environmental Kuznets curve for sulfur?', *Journal of Environmental Economics and Management*, **41**: 162–78.

Stern, D.I., M.S. Common and E.B. Barbier (1996), 'Economic growth and environmental degradation: the environmental Kuznets curve and sustainable development', *World Development*, **24**(7): 1151–60.

Torras, M. and J.K. Boyce (1998), 'Income, inequality and pollution: a reassessment of the environmental Kuznets curve', *Ecological Economics*, **25**(2): 147–60.

WCED (World Commission on Environment and Development) (1987), *Our Common Future (The Brundtland Report)*, Oxford: Oxford University Press.

Zhang, Z. (2000), 'Decoupling China's carbon emissions increase from economic growth: an economic analysis and policy implications', *World Development*, **28**: 739–52.

16 Sustainable consumption
Tim Jackson

1. Introduction

There is an emerging recognition of the importance of consumption within international debates about sustainable development. The actions people take and the choices they make – to consume certain products and services rather than others or to live in certain ways rather than others – all have direct and indirect impacts on the environment, on social equity and on personal (and collective) well-being.

Quite recently and somewhat hesitantly, therefore, policy makers have begun to engage with the question of whether and how it may be possible to intervene in consumption patterns and to influence people's behaviours and lifestyles in pursuit of sustainable development. The UK, for example, has taken a (perhaps surprising) lead in this area. In 2003, in the wake of the Johannesburg Summit, the UK Government was amongst the first to launch a national strategy on sustainable consumption and production. This strategy initiated a continuing and wide-ranging process of consultation, evidence review and policy formation that has already had significant impact and offers the potential for some quite radical policy innovations in the next few years. Amongst the activities fostered under this umbrella were the UK Round Table on Sustainable Consumption, a new 'evidence base' on sustainable consumption and production, a set of public engagement forums on sustainable living, and a sustainable consumption action plan to be launched in 2006 (DTI, 2003a, p. 32; DEFRA, 2005a). These kinds of activities may not yet be convincing evidence that the UK as a whole has embraced sustainability. But they certainly offer an indication of the importance placed by policy makers on the relevance of lifestyle and consumption in delivering sustainable development.

The purpose of this chapter is broadly twofold. In the first part of the chapter I present a very brief policy history of the concept of sustainable consumption, and describe some of the political and ideological tensions that underlie the concept. In the second part of the chapter, I discuss some of the key features of the sustainable consumption debate, and place these in the contexts of wider and deeper discussions about consumer behaviour and the nature of modern consumer society. Finally, I will offer some tentative suggestions concerning the extent to which these broader understandings of consumption might be regarded as enhancing or hindering the prospect of sustainable development.

2. Sustainable consumption – a brief policy history

Evidence of concern about the consumption and overconsumption of material resources can be traced to (at least) the second or third century BC (Bloch, 1950). Early modern critics of the level of resource consumption witnessed by industrial society have included Henry Thoreau (1854), William Morris (1891) and Thorstein Veblen (1899). Overconsumption of resources first registered in the international policy arena in 1949 when the newly-formed United Nations held an international Scientific Conference on the Conservation and Use of Resources. The issue was revisited at the United Nations Conference on the Human Environment in Stockholm in 1972.

In the same year, the Club of Rome published one of the first and most influential documents to bring attention to the impact that rising levels of affluence could have in terms of resource depletion and environmental degradation (Meadows et al., 1972; see also Chapter 15). Falling commodity prices and new discoveries undermined many of the authors' worst predictions about resource scarcity. But the relevance of consumption patterns to pressing environmental problems (such as climate change, ozone depletion and the management of hazardous waste) proved a more robust element of the Club of Rome critique, and by the early 1990s, consumption had become a vital element in the debate about 'sustainable development' (WCED, 1987).

The terminology of sustainable consumption itself can be dated more or less to Agenda 21 – the main policy document to emerge from the United Nations Conference on Environment and Development (the first Earth Summit) held in Rio de Janeiro in 1992. Chapter 4 of Agenda 21 was entitled 'Changing consumption patterns' and it called for 'new concepts of wealth and prosperity which allow higher standards of living through changed lifestyles and are less dependent on the Earth's finite resources'. In so doing, it provided a potentially far-reaching mandate for examining, questioning and revising consumption patterns – and, by implication, consumer behaviours, choices, expectations and lifestyles.

This mandate was initially taken up with some enthusiasm by the international policy community. In 1994, the Norwegian government hosted a roundtable on sustainable consumption in Oslo involving business, NGO and government representatives (Ofstad, 1994). The United Nations Commission on Sustainable Development (CSD) launched an international work programme on changing production and consumption patterns in 1995. At the 'Rio plus 5' conference in 1997, governments had identified sustainable consumption as an 'over-riding issue' and a 'cross-cutting theme' in the sustainable development debate. By the late 1990s, initiatives on sustainable consumption were in full flood. The 1998 Human Development Report focused explicitly on the topic of consumption (UNDP, 1998). In the same year, the Norwegian government organized a further workshop in Kabelvåg (IIED, 1998). The government of South Korea hosted a follow-up conference in 1999. The United Nations Environment Programme (UNEP) launched a sustainable consumption network, integrated sustainable consumption policies into the Consumer Protection Guidelines, and in 2001 published a strategic document emphasizing the opportunities afforded by the new sustainable consumption focus (UNEP, 2001).

By the time the World Summit on Sustainable Development (WSSD) convened in Johannesburg in 2002, the concept of 'sustainable consumption' had been placed firmly on the policy map and 'changing consumption and production patterns' had been identified as one of three 'overarching objectives' for sustainable development (UN, 2002). But consensus on what sustainable consumption actually is or should be about had proved remarkably difficult to negotiate (Manoochehri, 2002; Jackson and Michaelis, 2003; Seyfang, 2003). The Appendix to this chapter illustrates that there is still no clear agreement either on a precise definition of sustainable consumption or even on the domain of application of the concept.

Two specific points are worth noting about this range of definitions. The first is that they take a variety of positions in relation to extent to which sustainable consumption actually addresses the issues of consumer behaviour, lifestyle and 'consumerism'. Some definitions are very much more explicit that the domain of interest is the activity of consuming and the behaviour of consumers. Other definitions, however, seem to favour an approach that concentrates on production processes and consumer products, suggesting that the route to sustainable consumption lies mainly in the more efficient production of more sustainable products. Others seem to want, almost deliberately, to conflate these two issues.

A second, related point of variation between these definitions lies in the extent to which they imply consuming more efficiently, consuming more responsibly, or quite simply consuming less. While some definitions insist that sustainable consumption implies consuming less, others assert that it means consuming differently, and that it categorically does not mean consuming less.

The dominant institutional consensus has tended to settle for a position in which sustainable consumption means (more) consumption of more sustainable products and this is achieved primarily through improvements in the productivity with which resources are converted into economic goods. This position is typified by a speech given by the former UK Trade and Industry Secretary, Patricia Hewitt, in 2003 in which she argued (DTI, 2003b) that:

[t]here is nothing wrong with rising consumption, indeed it is to be welcomed as symptomatic of rising living standards in our communities. And it is quite right that the poorest in the world aspire to escape poverty and enjoy those standards. But we need to make sure the products and services we consume are designed not to harm our environment. We can enjoy more comfort, more enjoyment and more security without automatically increasing harmful and costly impacts on the environment. But it requires a re-thinking of business models to make more productive use of natural resources.

Even on the world stage, at the second Earth summit in Johannesburg, the WSSD Plan of Implementation (UN, 2002) appeared to retreat from the idea of lifestyle change advanced in Agenda 21 ten years earlier. Instead, the focus was placed firmly on improvements in technology and the supply of more eco-efficient products, services and infrastructures – that is to say on resource productivity improvements of one kind and another.

Reasons for the institutional reticence to engage with thorny issues of consumer behaviour and lifestyle are not particularly hard to grasp. In particular, addressing them would involve questioning fundamental assumptions about the way modern society functions. Intervening in consumer behaviour would contradict the much-vaunted 'sovereignty' of consumer choice. Reducing consumption would threaten a variety of vested interests and undermine the key structural role that consumption plays in economic growth. Questioning consumption and consumer behaviour quickly becomes reflexive, demanding often uncomfortable attention to both personal and social change. To make matters worse, arguments to reduce consumption appear to undermine legitimate efforts by poorer countries to improve their quality of life.

Nonetheless, the fall-back position adopted by conventional institutions is also problematic for a number of reasons. In the first place it tends to collapse any distinction between sustainable consumption and sustainable production. Secondly, the concentration on efficiency and productivity tends to obscure important questions about the *scale* of resource consumption patterns. In fact, it would be entirely possible, under this framing of the problem, to have a growing number of ethical and green consumers buying more and more 'sustainable' products produced by increasingly efficient production processes, and yet for the absolute scale of resource consumption – and the associated environmental impacts – to continue to grow. Finally, and perhaps most importantly, by focusing on what are broadly technological avenues of change, this version of sustainable consumption ignores vitally important issues related to consumer behaviour, lifestyle and the culture of consumption – key underlying factors that play a vital role in determining the overall scale of resource consumption.

In summary, it may well prove impossible to negotiate a common consensus on what sustainable consumption is or to agree a clear definition of it. But this does not mean that the current institutional position is adequate to the challenge of sustainability. In fact, a growing body of literature with a very long pedigree suggests an increasingly urgent need for policy and public debate to reach the parts of consumption that institutional initiatives on sustainable consumption (narrowly conceived) have so far signally failed to reach.

3. Dimensions of sustainable consumption

One of the many confusing tensions underlying the sustainable consumption debate is the question of what, precisely, is being or should be (or should not be) consumed in the consumer society. There is, for example, an important (although not always very clearly articulated) difference between material resource consumption and economic consumption. Material resource consumption – with its attendant implications for resource scarcity and environmental degradation – has been the principal focus of many of the policy debates on sustainable development. But economic consumers do not only buy and consume material resources. In fact, so-called 'final consumers' (households, for example) rarely buy materials per se at all. Rather they consume a variety of goods and services, which employ a variety of different kinds of material inputs and give rise to a range of different material and environmental impacts. Resources are consumed in the course of economic consumption; but the two processes are not identical or even congruent. Some forms of resource consumption take place outside of the economic framework. Some forms of economic consumption involve virtually no resource consumption at all.

This lack of congruence is, in one sense, precisely what has allowed the institutional position on sustainable consumption to retain a degree of credibility. Continued economic growth is perhaps the most deeply entrenched political imperative of post-war modern governments. Without a continuing rise in household consumption levels, economic growth would stall, giving way to the spectre of recession and the fear of unemployment, undermining the political credibility of the government that presides over these. Thus, any attack on levels of economic consumption is anathema to modern governments. But what if economic consumption can be decoupled from material resource consumption? What if consumers can be persuaded more and more to buy less and less materially-intensive products? So long as the decoupling of economic expenditure from material resources occurs faster than the growth in economic consumption, then surely it should be possible to preserve the sanctity of economic growth and at the same time achieve important environmental goals?

This position is the one implicit in the UK's sustainable consumption and production framework, which sets out a variety of 'decoupling indicators' showing that economic growth is faster than the growth in material inputs and waste outputs (DTI, 2003c; DEFRA, 2005b). In spite of this evidence, however, there is little doubt that economic consumption has historically relied heavily on the consumption of material resources; that improvements in resource productivity have generally been offset by increases in scale (see Chapter 15 for evidence for and against); and that the goods and services that people actually buy continue to be inherently material in nature (Princen et al., 2002; Jackson and Marks, 1999). Thus, simplistic appeals to reduce material consumption whilst maintaining economic growth risk charges of naivity or even disingenuity.

At the very least, a realistic programme for achieving such a 'decoupling' requires a robust examination of the complex relationships between economic value and material inputs and outputs. In fact, this 'mapping' of consumer demand and lifestyle choice onto resource requirements and environmental impacts represents one of the most prolific and important avenues of current and future research in sustainable consumption (for example, Barrett et al., 2005; Druckman et al., 2005; Tukker, 2005; Hertwich, 2005).[1]

But the 'decoupling' arguments also require a sophisticated understanding of consumer motivations and behaviours, and in particular of the relationship between consumer desires and the materiality of products. Why do we consume? Why do we consume material products? What factors shape and constrain our choice of material products? What do we expect to gain from consuming material goods? How successful are we in meeting those expectations?

All these questions become vitally important in the attempt to reduce the aggregate material impact of society's consumption patterns. Strangely, however, they have not yet been asked – or have only recently been asked – explicitly within the sustainable consumption debate itself. Rather, the literature directly relating consumer motivation to sustainability has tended to fall into two main camps. On the one hand, there is a fairly recent, empirically-based literature which attempts to identify the psychological parameters of 'environmentally-responsible' or 'environmentally-friendly' behaviour (de Young, 1996; Thøgersen and Ölander, 2002). On the other hand there is much more extensive literature with a very long pedigree which attacks (over-)consumption as a form of social pathology (Galbraith, 1958; Fromm, 1976; Durning, 1992; Frank, 1999).

The first literature set strives to identify existing behavioural types and patterns which, if replicated and extended, might lead to sustainable consumption at the macro level (Thøgerson, 1999). The second literature set highlights the social and psychological disbenefits of material consumption (Kasser, 2002). Often based implicitly or explicitly on humanistic psychology and couched in the (problematic) language of 'human needs', one of the interesting aspects of this literature is that it suggest the existence of a kind of double dividend for sustainable consumption. Specifically, a corollary of the thesis that material (over-)consumption has social and psychological disbenefits is that reducing consumption has social and psychological benefits; that it may be possible to live better by consuming less (Jackson, 2005a). This implication has provided the basis for the emergence of a clear – if not clearly significant – movement towards voluntary simplicity and downshifting (Schor, 1998; Elgin, 1993).

Both of these sets of literature have some potential value in forwarding the debate about consumption and sustainability. Nonetheless, they barely scratch the surface of the broader set of questions about consumer motivations indicated above. Ironically, of course, some at least of these broader questions have been addressed extensively and for several decades outside the sustainable consumption debate. For this reason, it is worth examining that broader literature in more detail.

4.   Understanding 'unsustainable' consumption

The problem for those engaged in sustainable consumption lies not so much in a dearth of theories to work from as in a superabundance of possible answers, hailing from disciplines as diverse as economics, psychology, anthropology, biology, sociology and marketing. In fact the contemporary and historical science and social science literature is replete with different models of consumer behaviour, each offering a variety of different versions of the nature and role of the 'modern consumer'. These roles include, for example: the satisfaction of functional needs, the construction of identity, the pursuit of status and social distinction, the maintenance of social cohesion, social and/or sexual selection, negotiation of the boundary between the sacred and the profane, and the pursuit of personal and collective meaning.[2]

This multiplicity of roles for consumption is what led Gabriel and Lang (1995) to refer to the consumer as 'unmanageable' and inspired Miller (1995) to talk about consumption as 'the vanguard of history'. Our consumption patterns offer a complex, yet telling picture of the kind of society we have become and of our relationship to material goods. Getting to grips with this complexity is challenging. But two or three key lessons emerge from the vast literature on modern consumption.

The first of these is that no purely functional account of material commodities can provide a robust basis for analysing consumer behaviour or for negotiating more sustainable consumption patterns. Rather material artefacts must be seen as playing important symbolic roles in our lives (Baudrillard, 1968; 1970; Dittmar, 1992; McCracken, 1990). This symbolic role of consumer goods allows us to engage in vital 'social conversations' about status, identity, social cohesion, and the pursuit of personal and cultural meaning.[3] In short it allows us to use the 'language of goods' (Douglas and Isherwood, 1979) to 'help create the social world and to find a credible place in it' (Douglas, 1976, p. 27).

Another hugely important lesson from the literature is that, far from being able to exercise free choice about what to consume and what not to consume, people often find themselves locked in to unsustainable consumption patterns by factors outside their control (Sanne, 2002; Shove, 2003; Warde, 2003). 'Lock-in' occurs in part through 'perverse' incentive structures – economic constraints, institutional barriers, or inequalities in access that actively encourage unsustainable behaviours. It also occurs because of social expectations or from sheer habit. At one level, consumer behaviour is simply the manifestation of everyday routine 'social practices' (Spaargaren and van Vliet, 2000) which are themselves the product of a 'creeping evolution of social norms'.

These lessons emphasize the difficulty associated with negotiating sustainable consumption patterns. But they also highlight another key feature in the literature: namely, the social and institutional context of consumer action. We are fundamentally social creatures. We learn by example and model our behaviours on those we see around us. Our everyday behaviour is guided by two kinds of social norms (Cialdini et al., 1991). 'Descriptive norms' teach us how most people around us behave. They allow us to moderate our own behaviour. I know what kind of clothes to wear and when to put out my recycling partly by observing continually what others around me do. 'Injunctive norms' alert us to what is sanctioned or punished in society. Driving outside the speed limit, polluting the water supply and (perhaps) failing to separate our recyclables from the rubbish are all examples of behaviours which carry varying degrees of moral sanction.

In both cases, there is lot at stake. Our ability to observe social norms influences the way we are perceived in our peer group and is important to our personal success. My ability to find a mate, keep my friends and stay in a good job are all mediated by my success in following social norms. Descriptive and injunctive norms can sometimes point in opposite directions. Most people agree that breaking the speed limit is wrong; but many people do it. The same is true for other environmentally unsustainable behaviours.

Some social theories suggest that our behaviours, our attitudes, and even our concepts of self are (at best) socially constructed (Mead, 1934) and (at worst) helplessly mired in a complex 'social logic' (Baudrillard, 1970).

Social identity theory, for example, regards key aspects of our behaviour as being motivated by the particular social groups that we belong to (Tajfel, 1982, for example). Certain behaviours are more or less ruled in or ruled out for me, simply because I perceive myself as belonging to a particular social group. The roots of these 'normal behaviours' have very little to do with individual choice.

5.   Policies for sustainable consumption
The policy implications of all this are potentially profound. Until quite recently, consumer policy has been influenced heavily by concerns for 'consumer sovereignty' and by an allegiance to the rational choice model (Jackson, 2005b). From this perspective, the role of policy appears to be straightforward, namely to ensure that the market allows people to make efficient choices about their own actions. For the most part, this has been seen as the need to correct for 'market failures'. These failures occur, for example, if consumers have insufficient information to make proper choices. In this perspective, policy should therefore seek to improve access to information. In addition, private decisions do not always take account of social costs. Policy intervention is therefore needed to 'internalize' these external costs and make them more 'visible' to private choice.

Unfortunately, the evidence suggests that policies based on information and price signals have had only limited success in changing unsustainable behaviours. In one extreme case, a California utility spent more money on advertising the benefits of home insulation than it would have cost to install the insulation itself in the targeted homes.[4] Price signals too are often insufficient to overcome the barriers to more sustainable behaviour. In some cases, more sustainable choices are already cost-effective, but are not taken up for a variety of reasons.

The rhetoric of 'consumer sovereignty' and 'hands-off' governance does not help much here because it regards choice as individualistic and fails to unravel the social, psychological and institutional influences on private behaviours. Some behaviours are motivated by rational, self-interested, and individualistic concerns. But conventional responses neither do justice to the complexity of consumer behaviour nor exhaust the possibilities for policy intervention in pursuit of behavioural change.

It is clear that sustainable consumption demands a more sophisticated policy approach aimed at removing perverse incentive structures and making sustainable consumption behaviours easy (Darnton, 2004; Jackson, 2005b; DEFRA, 2005a). It is beyond the scope of this chapter to outline in detail the components of such a strategy. But the considerations of the previous section suggest that it must have, at the very least, the following crucial dimensions:

- it must enable and facilitate access to more sustainable choices;
- it must ensure that incentive (and penalty) structures support rather than hinder the desired changes;
- it must engage people in community initiatives to help themselves re-negotiate unsustainable behaviours and practices and develop more sustainable lifestyles; and
- it must exemplify the desired changes in Government policies and practices.

6. A 'double dividend' in sustainable consumption?

In closing, it is worth returning briefly to the argument that sustainable consumption offers a kind of double dividend. If the consumer way of life is – as critics have suggested – both ecologically damaging and psychologically flawed, then the possibility remains that we could live better by consuming less, and reduce our impact on the environment at the same time (Jackson, 2005a). But how realistic is this perspective, in the light of the discussion above? Is it consistent with fundamental understandings about consumer behaviour and human motivation? Does it reflect socially achievable and culturally relevant ambitions? Or is it simply a delusion based on utopian understandings of human nature?

These are important and as yet unexplored questions, which perhaps, more than any other, characterize both the promise and the challenge of sustainable consumption. A more detailed pursuit of this issue is beyond the scope of this chapter. In closing, however, I make three specific observations about the promise embodied in this perspective.

In the first place, the insight that material commodities play symbolic roles and that these symbolic roles serve important social and psychological functions is perhaps the clearest message yet that simplistic appeals to consumers to forego material consumption will be unsuccessful. Such an appeal is tantamount to demanding that we give up certain key capabilities and freedoms as social beings. Far from being irrational to resist such demands, it would be irrational not to, in such a society. A sophisticated understanding of this very real social constraint must inform the otherwise naive appeal for a decoupling of economic and material activity.

Secondly, and despite the fact that our present consumer society is inherently material in its choice of symbolic goods, symbolic value is not solely embodied in material artefacts. A variety of other social and cultural constructs have – over history – played vital roles in the construction, negotiation and exchange of symbolic meaning. These include processes of ritual, myth, and narrative and institutions such as the family, the community and the church (Campbell, 1959; Berger, 1969; Taylor, 1989). Though the tide of cultural change may have swept some of these institutions away, it does not seem impossible – in theory at least – to conceive of futures in which some of the symbolic functions of material commodities are once again taken back by other kinds of institutions with lower resource 'footprints'.

Finally, however, it is abundantly clear that cultural change at this level is not immediately or easily negotiable. As Baudrillard (1970) was keen to point out, symbolic meaning is negotiated through a complex 'social logic' that lies beyond individual choice and appears to defy conventional policy prescriptions and interventions. Perhaps the biggest challenge for sustainability policy therefore lies in identifying the myriad ways in which governments currently intervene in and could potentially influence this social logic.

In the final analysis, these remarks should serve to warn us against simplistic prescriptions for change. Material goods and services are deeply embedded in the cultural fabric of our lives. Through them we not only satisfy our needs and desires, we also communicate with each other, negotiate important social relationships, and pursue personal and cultural meaning. In this context, motivating sustainable consumption may be as much about building supportive communities, promoting inclusive societies, providing meaningful work and encouraging purposeful lives as it is about awareness-raising, fiscal policy or persuasion.

Appendix: definitions of sustainable consumption

The use of goods and services that respond to basic needs and bring a better quality of life, while minimizing the use of natural resources, toxic materials and emissions of waste and pollutants over the lifecycle, so as not to jeopardize the needs of future generations (Ofstad, 1994).

The special focus of sustainable consumption is on the economic activity of choosing, using, and disposing of goods and services and how this can be changed to bring social and environmental benefit (IIED, 1998).

Sustainable consumption means we have to use resources to meet our basic needs and not use resources in excess of what we need (Participant definition, Kabelvåg, IIED, 1998).

Sustainable consumption is not about consuming less, it is about consuming differently, consuming efficiently, and having an improved quality of life (UNEP, 1999).

Sustainable consumption is consumption that supports the ability of current and future generations to meet their material and other needs, without causing irreversible damage to the environment or loss of function in natural systems (OCSC, 2000).

Sustainable consumption is an umbrella term that brings together a number of key issues, such as meeting needs, enhancing quality of life, improving efficiency, minimising waste, taking a lifecycle perspective and taking into account the equity dimension; integrating these components parts in the central question of how to provide the same or better services to meet the basic requirements of life and the aspiration for improvement, for both current and future generations, while continually reducing environmental damage and the risk to human health (UNEP, 2001).

Sustainable consumption and production is continuous economic and social progress that respects the limits of the Earth's ecosystems, and meets the needs and aspirations of everyone for a better quality of life, now and for future generations to come (DTI, 2003a).

Sustainable consumption is a balancing act. It is about consuming in such a way as to protect the environment, use natural resources wisely and promote quality of life now, while not spoiling the lives of future consumers (NCC, 2003).

Notes

1. That I have less to say specifically about this avenue of research is a potential limitation of this chapter. However, this kind of work has a long pedigree in environmental economics and is in part covered by other chapters in this volume.
2. See Jackson (2003; 2004; 2005a; 2005b), Jackson and Michaelis (2003), Princen et al. (2002), Sanne (2002), Michaelis (2000), Røpke (1999), Jackson and Marks (1999), Crocker and Linden (1998), Gabriel and Lang (1995) for reviews and overviews of some of this literature.
3. The use of the term 'social conversations' in this context draws on the early work of G.H. Mead (1934).
4. Cited in McKenzie Mohr (2000).

References

Barrett, J., R. Birch, N. Cherrett and T. Wiedmann (2005), *Reducing Wales' Ecological Footprint. A resource accounting tool for sustainable consumption*, Cardiff/York: WWF Cymru/SEI York.

Baudrillard, J. (1968), 'The system of objects', extracted in *Selected Writings*, 1988, Polity Press, Cambridge, pp. 24–5.

Baudrillard, J. (1970), *The Consumer Society – myths and structures*, (reprinted 1998), London: Sage Publications.

Berger, P. (1969), *The Sacred Canopy – Elements of a Sociological Theory of Religion*, New York: Anchor Books.

Bloch, J. (1950), *Les Inscriptions d'Asoka*, Paris: Belles Lettres.

Campbell, J. (1959), *The Masks of God: Primitive Mythology*, Volume 1 of 4, New York, NY: Arkana, Penguin Group.

Cialdini, R., C. Kallgren and R. Reno (1991), 'A focus theory of normative conduct: a theoretical refinement and re-evaluation of the role of norms in human behaviour', *Advances in Experimental Social Psychology*, **24**: 201–34.

Crocker, D. and T. Linden (eds) (1998), *The Ethics of Consumption*, New York: Rowman and Littlefield.

Darnton, A. (2004), 'Driving public behaviours for sustainable lifestyles', London: Department for Environment, Food and Rural Affairs.

DEFRA (2005a), 'Securing the future – delivering UK sustainable development strategy', London: HMSO.

DEFRA (2005b), 'Sustainable development indicators', London: HMSO.

de Young, R. (1996), 'Some psychological aspects of reduced consumption behaviour', *Environment and Behaviour*, **28**(3): 358–409.

Dittmar, H.E. (1992), *The Social Psychology of Material Possessions – to have is to be*, New York: St Martin's Press.

Douglas, M. (1976), 'Relative poverty, relative communication', in A. Halsey (ed.), *Traditions of Social Policy*, Oxford: Basil Blackwell.

Douglas, M. and B. Isherwood (1979), *The World of Goods – Towards an Anthropology of Consumption*, London: Penguin Books.

Druckman, A., P. Sinclair and T. Jackson (2005), 'A geographically and socio-economically disaggregated local household consumption model for the UK', paper presented to the 10th European Round Table on Sustainable Consumption and Production, Antwerp, October.

DTI (2003a), 'Changing patterns – UK government framework for sustainable consumption and production', London: Department of Trade and Industry.

DTI (2003b), Speech to the Green Alliance Environment Forum, Right Hon. Patricia Hewitt, Department of Trade and Industry. www.dti.gov.uk/ministers/speeches/hewitt140703.html.

DTI (2003c), 'Sustainable consumption and production indicators' a joint DEFRA/DTI consultation paper, London: Department of Trade and Industry.

Durning, A. (1992), *How Much is Enough?*, New York: W.W. Norton.

Elgin, D. (1993), *Voluntary Simplicity*, New York: William Morrow.

Frank, R. (1999), *Luxury Fever – Money and Happiness in an Era of Excess*, Princeton: Princeton University Press.

Fromm, E. (1976), *To Have or to Be?*, London: Jonathon Cape.

Gabriel, Y. and T. Lang (1995), *The Unmanageable Consumer*, London: Sage.

Galbraith, J.K. (1958), *The Affluent Society*, Harmondsworth: Penguin Books.

Hertwich, E. (2005), 'Consumption and industrial ecology', *Journal of Industrial Ecology*, **9**(1): 1–6.

IIED (1998), 'Consumption in a sustainable world', Report of the Workshop held in Kabelvåg, Norway, 2–4 June, Ministry of the Environment, Oslo and International Institute of Environment and Development, London.

Jackson, T. (2003), 'Models of Mammon – a cross-disciplinary survey in pursuit of the sustainable consumer', paper presented to the UK Environmental Psychology conference, Aberdeen, 23–25 June.

Jackson, T. (2004), 'Consuming paradise? Unsustainable consumption in cultural and social-psychological context', in Klaus Hubacek, Atsushi Inaba and Sigrid Stagl (eds), *Driving Forces of and Barriers to Sustainable Consumption*, Proceedings of an International Conference, University of Leeds, 5–6 March.

Jackson, T. (2005a), 'Live better by consuming less? Is there a double dividend in sustainable consumption?', *Journal of Industrial Ecology*, **9**(1–2): 19–36.

Jackson, T. (2005b), 'Motivating sustainable consumption – a review of evidence on consumer behaviour and behavioural change', a report to the Sustainable Development Research Network, London: Policy Studies Institute.

Jackson, T. and N. Marks (1999), 'Consumption, sustainable welfare and human needs – with reference to UK expenditure patterns 1954–1994', *Ecological Economics*, **28**(3): 421–42.

Jackson, T. and L. Michaelis (2003), *Policies for Sustainable Consumption*, London: Sustainable Development Commission.

Kasser, T. (2002), *The High Price of Materialism*, Cambridge, Mass: MIT Press.

Manoochehri, J. (2002), 'Post-Rio sustainable consumption: establishing coherence and a common platform', *Development*, **45**(3): 51–7.

McCracken, G. (1990), *Culture and Consumption*, Bloomington and Indianapolis: Indiana University Press.

McKenzie Mohr, D. (2000), 'Promoting sustainable behavior: an introduction to community-based social marketing', *Journal of Social Issues*, **56**(3): 543–54.

Mead, G. (1934), *Mind, Self and Society*, Chicago: University of Chicago Press.

Meadows, D.H., D.L. Meadows, J. Randers and W.W. Behrens III (1972), *The Limits to Growth: A Report to the Club of Rome*, New York: Signet.

Michaelis, L. (2000), *Ethics of Consumption*, Oxford: Oxford Centre for the Environment, Ethics and Society, Mansfield College.

Miller, D. (1995), *Acknowledging Consumption – a review of new studies*, London: Routledge.

Morris, W. (1891), *News from Nowhere; or an Epoch of Rest: being some Chapters from a Utopian Romance*, reprinted 1970, London: Routledge.

NCC (2003), 'Green choice: what choice?', summary of NCC research into consumer attitudes to sustainable consumption, London: National Consumer Council.

OCSC (Oxford Commission on Sustainable Consumption) (2000), 'Report on the Second Session of the Oxford Commission on Sustainable Consumption', OCSC 2.8, Oxford: Oxford Centre for the Environment, Ethics and Society.

Ofstad, S. (ed.) (1994), *Symposium: Sustainable Consumption*, Oslo: Ministry of Environment.

Princen, T., M. Maniates and K. Conca (2002), *Confronting Consumption*, Boston, Mass: MIT Press.

Røpke, I. (1999), 'The dynamics of willingness to consume', *Ecological Economics*, **28**(3): 399–420.

Sanne, C. (2002), 'Willing consumers – or locked in? Policies for a sustainable consumption', *Ecological Economics*, **42**: 273–87.

Schor, J. (1998), *The Overspent American – Upscaling, Downshifting and the New Consumer*, New York: Basic Books.

Seyfang, G. (2003), 'Organics, fair trade and Frankenstein foods: sustainable consumption from the boardroom to the breakfast table', paper presented to the RGS-IBG Conference 3 September.

Shove, E. (2003), *Comfort, Cleanliness and Convenience*, London: Berg.

Spaargaren, G. and B. van Vliet (2000), 'Lifestyle, consumption and the environment: the ecological modernisation of domestic consumption', *Society and Natural Resources*, **9**: 50–76.

Tajfel, H. (ed.) (1982), *Social Identity and Intergroup Relations*, Cambridge: Cambridge University Press.

Taylor, C. (1989), *Sources of the Self: The Making of the Modern Identity*, Cambridge, MA: Cambridge University Press.

Thøgersen, J. (1999), 'Spillover processes in the development of a sustainable consumption pattern', *Journal of Economic Psychology*, **20**: 53–81.

Thøgersen, J. and Ölander, F. (2002), 'Human values and the emergence of a sustainable consumption pattern: A panel study', *Journal of Economic Psychology*, **23**: 605–30.

Thoreau, H. (1854), *Walden (and resistance to civil government)*, reprinted 1992, New York and London: W.W. Norton.

Tukker, A. et al. (2005), 'Environmental impact of products (EIPRO): Analysis of the life cycle environmental impacts related to the total final consumption of the EU25', European Science and Technology Observatory / Institute for Prospective Technological Studies.

UN (2002), 'Johannesburg plan of implementation', New York: United Nations.

UNDP (1998), *Human Development Report 1998*, Oxford and New York: Oxford University Press.

UNEP (1999), 'Changing consumption patterns', *Industry and Environment*, **22**(4), special issue, October–December.

UNEP (2001), 'Consumption opportunities: strategies for change', Paris: United Nations Environment Programme.

Veblen, T. (1899), *The Theory of the Leisure Class*, 1998 edn, Great Minds Series, London: Prometheus Books.

Warde, A. (2003), 'Consumption as social practice', paper presented to the ESRC/AHRB workshop on New Theoretical Approaches to Consumption, Birkbeck College, October.

WCED (1987), *Our Common Future*, The Brundtland Report, Oxford: Oxford University Press.

PART V

PROGRESS IN MEASURING SUSTAINABLE DEVELOPMENT

17 Environmental and resource accounting
Glenn-Marie Lange

1. Overview of environmental accounts

Sustainable development is the stated objective of many countries and the search for operationalizing this concept has focused in part on the system of national income accounts (SNA) (UN et al., 1993). The SNA is crucial because it constitutes the primary source of information about the economy and is widely used for assessment of economic performance and policy analysis throughout the world. However, the SNA has a number of well-known shortcomings regarding the treatment of the environment. For example, while the income from extracting minerals is recorded in the national accounts, the simultaneous depletion of mineral reserves is not. Uncultivated fisheries and forests receive similar treatment. This can result in quite misleading economic signals about sustainable national income. Indeed, one of the primary motivations for the early environmental accounting efforts in the mid-1980s was concern that rapid economic growth in some developing countries was achieved through liquidation of natural capital, a practice that appears to boost GDP in the short run, but is not sustainable in the long run.

Equally important, ecosystems provide non-marketed goods and services that are often not fully included in national accounts, or are wrongly attributed to other sectors of the economy. For example, the harvest for own use of firewood and wild foods, so critical to livelihoods in many developing countries, is often underestimated. Forests provide recreation and tourism services, which are not attributed to the forest industry. Forests may also provide watershed protection benefiting agriculture, hydroelectric power, municipal water supply and so on, but the value of these services is not recognized and, hence, not attributed to the forestry sector. Thus the total benefits from sustainable forestry are underestimated, and other sectors of the economy are not fully aware of their dependence on the health of this natural resource.

Over the past few decades, many natural scientists and social scientists have worked to develop environmental accounts as a tool to promote sustainable development. This effort resulted first in the publication of an interim handbook in 1993, the *System of Environmental and Economic Accounting* (SEEA), under the aegis of the UN's Statistical Commission (UN, 1993), followed by a substantially revised and expanded SEEA

Handbook in 2003 based on more than a decade of additional conceptual work and empirical applications by national and international agencies, academics and NGOs (UN et al., 2003).

The SEEA provides a comprehensive and broadly accepted framework for incorporating the role of the environment and natural capital in the economy through a system of satellite accounts to the SNA. As satellite accounts, the SEEA has a similar structure to the SNA, consisting of both stocks and flows of environmental goods and services. The SEEA has four major components, which are constructed, wherever possible, in both physical and monetary units:

- Asset accounts, which record the volume and economic value of stocks and changes in stocks of natural resources.
- Flow accounts for materials, energy and pollution, which provide information at the industry level about the use of energy and materials as inputs to production and final demand, and the generation of pollutants and solid waste. The flow accounts also make explicit the input of non-market environmental services to production and final consumption that may be implicitly included in the production values of other sectors.
- Environmental protection and resource management expenditure accounts, and other environmentally related transactions. These accounts reorganize information already in the SNA to make more explicit 1) expenditures incurred to protect the environment and manage natural resources and 2) taxes, fees and other charges, and property rights related to the environment.
- Environmentally-adjusted indicators of macroeconomic performance, which include indicators of sustainability such as environmentally-adjusted GDP and NDP, Adjusted Net Savings (genuine savings: see Chapter 18), and a broader measure of national wealth that includes natural capital in addition to manufactured capital.

Environmental accounts are now constructed regularly by many developed countries and some developing countries (Table 17.1). Of course, environmental accounts are a broad undertaking and countries have implemented them on an incremental basis, compiling the parts of the accounts that are most useful for their environmental priorities. Environmental accounts improve policy making by providing aggregate indicators for monitoring environmental–economic performance, as well as a detailed set of statistics to guide resource managers toward policy decisions that will improve environmental–economic performance in the future.

Table 17.1   Countries with environmental accounting programs

	1. Assets (physical & monetary)	2. Flow Accounts for Pollutants & Materials		3. Environmental protection & Resource Management Expenditures	4. Macro-economic indicators
		Physical	Monetary		
INDUSTRIALIZED COUNTRIES					
Australia	X	X		X	X-monetary
Austria	X			X	
Canada	X	X		X	
Denmark	X	X		X	
Finland	X	X		X	
France	X	X		X	
Germany	X	X	X	X	
Italy	X	X		X	
Netherlands	X	X			X-physical
New Zealand	X	X	X		
Norway	X	X			
Sweden	X	X	X	X	
UK	X	X		X	
DEVELOPING COUNTRIES					
Botswana	X	X	X[a]		
Chile	X		X[a]	X	
China	X	X			
Indonesia	X				
Korea	X	X	X	X	X-monetary
Mexico	X	X	X	X	X-monetary
Moldova		X[a]			
Namibia	X	X	X[a]		
Philippines	X	X	X	X	X-monetary
South Africa	X	X	X[a]		
Thailand	X				
OCCASIONAL STUDIES					
Colombia		X	X	X	
Costa Rica				X	
Eu-15	X	X	X	X	
Japan	X	X	X	X	X-monetary
Swaziland	X				

Notes:
[a] Accounts for water only.
An extensive range of environmental accounting case studies are available for many other countries, but mainly as an experimental or one-time study rather than on-going work by a government agency.

This chapter describes some of the policy applications for each component of the environmental accounts; a more detailed review of applications can be found in (Lange, 2003a; 2004a; Lange et al., 2003; World Bank, forthcoming 2005). For technical aspects of the environmental accounts, the reader is referred to (UN et al., 2003).

2.   Asset accounts: monitoring total wealth

Theoretical work (by for example Arrow et al., 2003a; Dasgupta and Mäler, 2000; Heal and Kristrom, 2005; Kunte et al., 1998; see also Chapter 18) has demonstrated that sustainable development requires non-declining per capita wealth, where wealth is defined in the broadest sense to include produced, natural and human (including social) capital. This implies that economic development can be viewed as a process of 'portfolio management' seeking to optimize the management of each asset and the distribution of wealth among different kinds of assets (World Bank, 2002). The particular challenge for resource-rich economies is to transform natural capital into other forms of productive wealth, a process that requires good policy in three critical areas: 1) promotion of efficient resource extraction that maximizes resource rent, 2) recovery of the rent by an agency capable of reinvesting rent and 3) efficient reinvestment of rent.

Environmental accounts provide information to monitor sustainable development by measuring total wealth (produced + natural capital)[1] over time, which indicates whether depletion of resources is compensated for by investment in other assets; for example is development sustainable or not? The environmental accounts also provide more detailed information to assess the environmental and natural resource policies guiding this process: the amount of resource rent being generated from each resource, the amount of rent recovered by various agencies, and the share of that rent, if any, that is invested in other assets.

The SEEA asset accounts *in physical units* provide indicators of ecological sustainability and information for resource management. The volume of mineral reserves, for example, is needed to plan extraction paths and indicates how long a country can rely on its minerals. A more complete assessment of sustainability requires calculation of the *monetary value* of a resource stock as well. From the monetary accounts, trends in per capita national wealth – a measure of sustainable development – can be derived. These trends can also be analyzed to assess characteristics important to economic development, such as the diversity of wealth, ownership distribution, and volatility due to price fluctuations, an important feature for economies dependent on primary commodities (see Lange, 2003a, for a discussion of this issue and some examples).

Among the developed countries, only Australia (ABS, 2004a) and Canada (Smith and Simard, 2001) regularly include natural capital in the balance sheets of their annual national income accounts, and a number of other countries calculate the value of some assets, particularly subsoil assets. In the developing countries, figures for total wealth including natural capital have been compiled for Botswana and Namibia (Lange, 2004b), and are shown in Table 17.2 and Figure 17.1.[2]

Both Botswana and Namibia have significant natural capital: diamond mining accounts for roughly a third of Botswana's GDP; mining and fishing account for over 20 per cent of Namibia's GDP. But only Botswana has been successful in using its natural capital to increase national wealth, pushing it into the ranks of upper middle-income countries. Namibia has not used its natural capital to build wealth.

The rapid growth of national wealth in Botswana is consistent with its development policy, which set a goal of improving living standards and reducing poverty based on investment of mineral revenues (see Lange and Wright, 2004). Botswana has recovered much of the resource rent generated by its minerals and has consistently reinvested virtually all of it (see below). Namibia, occupied by South Africa until 1990, has not based its development strategy on reinvestment of resource rent. Namibia has not recovered as much of the resource rent, partly due to external factors such as the lack of control over its marine fisheries before 1990, but partly due to domestic policy decisions even after independence. Not surprisingly, Namibia has failed to build national wealth. The effect is significant: Botswana's per capita, real GDP has grown at an annual rate of 5 per cent, while Namibia's per capita, real GDP has stagnated, declining at an annual rate of –0.025 per cent (Lange, 2004b).

Table 17.2 shows the breakdown of wealth by asset type. For a small country like Botswana with limited capacity to absorb capital quickly, the importance of net foreign financial assets has been particularly important.

Recovery of resource rent and reinvesting it in alternative assets is key to sustainable development. Regarding recovery of resource rent, Botswana has been rather successful, recovering on average 76 per cent of rent. Namibia has had much more volatile rent in both mining and fishing. The Namibian mining industry, dominated by diamonds, uranium and gold, has paid on average at least 50 per cent of the rent in taxes. By contrast, government has not recovered much rent from fisheries, partly because rent taxes (fishing quota levies) were set rather low and not adjusted for inflation, but also because of poor enforcement of rent collection.

As long as fisheries are not being depleted, recovery and reinvestment of resources is not necessary for sustainable development. When managed sustainably, fisheries will continue to generate income and employment for

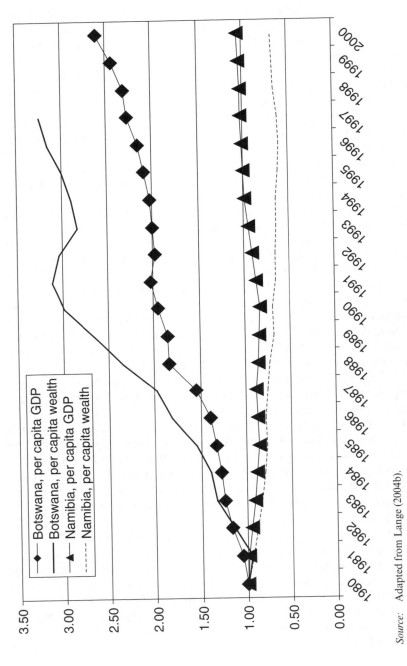

Source: Adapted from Lange (2004b).

Figure 17.1   Growth of real per capita wealth and national income in Botswana and Namibia (1980 = 1.00)

Table 17.2 Total real, per capita wealth of Botswana and Namibia, 1980 to 1998 (pula per person in 1993 prices)

	Botswana					Namibia					
	Produced capital			Net foreign financial assets	Total	Produced capital		Natural capital		Net foreign financial assets	Total
	Public	Private	Minerals			Public	Private	Minerals	Fisheries		
1980	2063	4695	6472	253	13483	7483	9253	6839	–	NA	23575
1981	2233	4953	5143	406	12735	8687	10289	4972	–	NA	23948
1982	2369	4972	7477	439	15257	8796	10149	3830	–	NA	22776
1983	2461	4996	9583	789	17830	9170	10239	3195	–	NA	22604
1984	2652	5257	9851	987	18747	8753	9386	2625	–	NA	20765
1985	2809	5253	10164	2680	20906	7843	8211	2688	–	NA	18742
1986	3068	5304	12577	3442	24392	8215	8502	3313	–	NA	20030
1987	3632	5466	13465	4177	26741	8429	8410	3322	–	NA	20161
1988	4071	6184	16962	4472	31689	7878	7694	3108	–	NA	18680
1989	4333	7191	19232	5038	35794	7715	7624	2841	–	−655	17526
1990	4726	7891	22068	5539	40224	8188	8072	2355	1035	−500	19150
1991	5122	8424	22058	6449	42054	8565	8319	2020	786	−299	19391
1992	5531	8761	20239	6392	40924	8357	8182	1606	1070	−305	18910
1993	5988	8885	16704	6643	38221	7950	8011	1061	1519	188	18729
1994	6253	9122	16868	6903	39145	7158	7474	820	1861	160	17471
1995	6633	9251	17698	6855	40437	7093	7720	648	1703	3	17167
1996	7083	9348	17738	8274	42442	6682	7622	784	795	−85	15798
1997	7559	9659	21346	8526	47090	6543	7634	895	1187	256	16515
1998	NA	NA	NA	NA	NA	6203	7657	678	2298	246	17082

Notes: Exchange rate of Namibia dollars for Botswana pula in 1993 was P0.74. The Botswana pula in 1993 was P0.74. The Botswana pula was worth US$0.41.

Source: Adapted from Lange (2004b).

future generations. However, exploitation of fisheries cannot be sustainably increased as the human population grows. For a country with a growing population and aspirations for higher standards of living, failure to rein-vest resource rent represents a lost opportunity to build national wealth. Furthermore, the recent collapse of the pilchard industry calls into ques-tion whether the fisheries are being managed sustainably.

Regarding the final requirement for using natural capital to build national wealth – reinvestment of resource rent – the policies of Botswana and Namibia are quite different. Botswana developed an explicit policy of reinvestment of all resource rent from mining and an indicator to monitor this policy, the Sustainable Budget Index (SBI). (See Lange and Wright, 2004, for discussion of the SBI). Namibia has had no explicit policy regard-ing reinvestment of revenues from natural capital.

3.   Flow accounts for materials, services and pollution

The flow accounts of the environmental accounts are compiled and used for economic analysis much more extensively than the asset accounts. They provide macroeconomic indicators of sustainability as well as more detailed information to support economic analysis of sources of environmental pressure and options for change that can be used to improve sustainability. The aggregate indicators provide an overview of the relationship between economic development and the environment; the more detailed accounts help explain the overview.

The flow accounts consist of three components: use of material and energy resources, resource degradation and emission of pollutants, and pro-duction and use of ecosystem services. The flow accounts are compiled in both physical and monetary units. The physical accounts help set priorities for policy based on the *volume* of resource use, pollution and so on while the monetary accounts identify the relative *costs and benefits* of reducing pollu-tion, resource use and so on. The flow accounts are also used in economic models to evaluate options for development and specific policy instruments for implementing a given development strategy, such as green taxes.

Physical accounts
At their simplest, the flow accounts are used to monitor the trend over time of environmental goods and services, and pollution emissions, both total and by industry. An example for wastewater and water pollution from the Netherlands' accounts is shown in Figure 17.2.

The construction of environmental–economic profiles, or 'eco-efficiency' indicators has become a common way of monitoring sustainability, and is also used for benchmarking industry performance. These descriptive statistics provide a first approach to identifying major users of resources

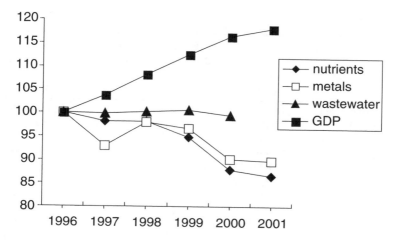

Source: Van der Veeren et al. (2004, Figure 25).

Figure 17.2 Index of growth of GDP, wastewater and emissions of nutrients and metals into water in the Netherlands, 1996 to 2001 (1996 = 1.00)

and sources of emissions, and provide a comparison of each sector's relative environmental burden and economic contribution. Typically, eco-efficiency indicators report an industry's percentage contribution to the national economy (value-added, employment) alongside its environment impact such as emissions of various pollutants. A similar sector-level indicator is the 'resource productivity indicator' calculated as materials (energy, water and so on) or pollution per unit of value-added. (See example from the water accounts for Australia in Table 17.3 and a more extensive example for two industries in Sweden in Figure 17.3.)

While the eco-efficiency indicators report the *direct* generation of pollution associated with production, it is useful for policy makers to understand the *driving forces* that result in such levels of pollution. The driving forces for economic production are the final users. Input–output analysis has been used to measure the total impact (direct + indirect) of a given final use. This approach is especially useful in understanding the effects of different patterns of household consumption or trade on the environment. An example for SO_2 air pollution in Sweden is given in Figure 17.4.

Monetary accounts
Effective environmental management is based not only on an understanding of the *volume* of environmental goods and services and pollution, but

Table 17.3   Water profile and water productivity in Australia, 2000–2001

	Water consumption (ML)	Percent distribution of water consumption	Percent of industry gross value-added	A$ VA/L water consumption
Agriculture, total	16 660 381	66.9%	1.8%	$ 0.0006
Livestock	5 568 474	22.4%	0.3%	$ 0.0003
Dairy farming	2 834 418	11.4%	0.3%	$ 0.0005
Vegetables	555 711	2.2%	0.3%	$ 0.0033
Fruit	802 632	3.2%	0.3%	$ 0.0020
Grapes	729 137	2.9%	0.3%	$ 0.0019
Sugar	1 310 671	5.3%	0.1%	$ 0.0002
Cotton	2 908 178	11.7%	0.2%	$ 0.0004
Rice	1 951 160	7.8%	0.1%	$ 0.0002
Forestry & fishing	26 924	0.1%	0.3%	$ 0.0574
Mining	400 622	1.6%	6.3%	$ 0.0848
Manufacturing	866 061	3.5%	13.6%	$ 0.0847
Electricity and gas supply	1 687 778	6.8%	2.1%	$ 0.0066
Water supply	1 793 953	7.2%	0.8%	$ 0.0024
Other industries	832 100	3.3%	75.2%	$ 0.4877
Households	2 181 447	8.8%	NA	NA
Environment	459 393	1.8%	NA	NA
Total	24 908 659	100.0%	100.0%	

Note: NA: not applicable.

Source: Based on ABS (2004b, Tables 1.3 and 5.11).

also an understanding of the *economic* implications. Policy makers need to know, for example, what the welfare loss of pollution is (damage costs) and where limited financial resources will be most effective in reducing environmental pressure, that is, the relative benefits and costs of reducing different forms of environmental degradation from different sources. Similarly they need to know the value of damages from deforestation in terms of reduced productivity or increased production costs in other sectors of the economy.

One of the most important applications of environmental accounting in developing countries has been to identify goods and services from ecosystems such as forests that are not adequately represented in the SNA. Many non-market forest goods for example, (fuelwood, wild foods, medicines, construction materials and so on) are, in principle, included in the SNA,

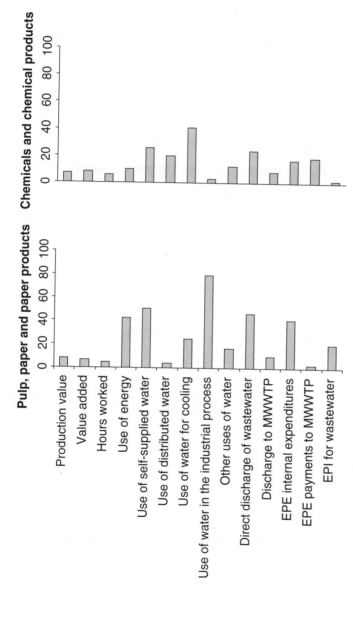

Notes: The values are percentages of the total for manufacturing enterprises recorded against each variable.
EPE = Environmental protection expenditure; EPI = Environmental protection investment.

Source: Based on Sjölin and Wadeskog (2000).

Figure 17.3   Environmental–economic profiles for some Swedish industries, 1995

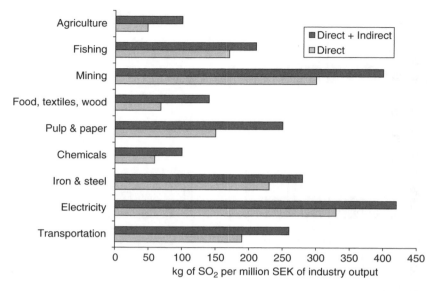

Source: Based on Hellsten et al. (1999).

Figure 17.4   *Direct and total emissions of sulfur dioxide per unit of industrial output delivered to final users in Sweden, 1991*

Table 17.4   *Goods and services provided by forests in Sweden and South Africa*

	Sweden, 1999 (million euros)	South Africa, 1998 (million rands)
Commercial timber harvest	2 370	1 856
Non-market timber and non-timber goods	225	2 692
Recreation	2 370	29
Livestock grazing	–	1 021
Pollination services	–	786
Protection from noise	20	–
Carbon storage	810	480
Total	5 795	6 864

Source: Adapted from Lange (2004a).

but due to measurement problems countries may underestimate the harvest of these goods. In South Africa, for example, the value of non-market forest goods, timber and non-timber, is greater than the commercial timber harvest, but it is not included in the national accounts of South Africa (Table 17.4).

In addition, forests provide environmental services that are often not recognized explicitly in the SNA. In Sweden, the value of recreation services from forests is equal to the value of the timber harvest, but this service is not attributed to forests. Similarly, forests in South Africa contribute substantially to agriculture (providing livestock grazing services and habitat for wild bees that provide pollination services): a conservative estimate is 1907 million Rands in 1998; again, greater than the commercial timber harvest, which is the only explicit value for forests in the national accounts. In the case of these forest services, the value is included in the national accounts, but as part of the livestock and crop activities, not as forest input to those activities.

The issue of ecosystem services and undercounted non-market goods is particularly important for many developing countries that may be overexploiting their forests (or other natural resources, for example fisheries and marine resources, wildlife and so on) for short-term economic growth. They may have calculated that the revenues received compensate for the deforestation. But if the cost–benefit calculation does not also take into account the loss of forest services to other sectors, such as tourism, agriculture, hydroelectric power, fisheries, municipal water supply and so on, it is quite possible that the losses from deforestation may outweigh the benefits.

The monetary flow accounts have also been used to address other policy issues that are important for resource management, for example the subsidy for water or wastewater treatment. The monetary accounts for water report both the cost of delivery and the market price charged for water and wastewater; the difference between the two is the subsidy. Figure 17.5 shows figures for wastewater treatment in the Netherlands at a national level. Calculation of subsidies from the monetary accounts for water have been compiled at the industry level for three southern African countries; Botswana, Namibia and South Africa (Lange and Hassan, forthcoming 2006). The accounts for all three countries show extensive cross-subsidization, especially of agriculture.

In many other countries, developed and developing, the cost of air and water pollution is a major concern. After some initial experimentation with valuation of pollution, many countries have not continued efforts to incorporate these into their environmental accounts. In large part, this is because of a lack of consensus over alternative methods of valuation, and partly because accurate valuation is quite difficult. There are two broad approaches

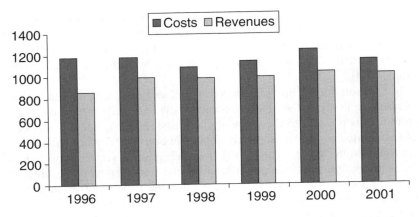

Note: Data are compiled only for households and companies connected to municipal sewer systems.

Source: Van der Veeren et al. (2004, Figure 34).

Figure 17.5   Costs and revenues for wastewater treatment services in the Netherlands, 1996 to 2001 (in million euros)

to valuation recommended in the SEEA: the *cost* of actions to prevent or remediate degradation, and the *benefit* of actions to reduce pollution measured in terms of the value of the damages prevented.

In the absence of efficient markets, the cost and benefit measures are likely to be quite different. The damage cost is the theoretically correct approach for measuring changes in economic well-being and adjusting macroeconomic aggregates, although both measures provide useful information for environmental management. Until the SEEA provides more concrete guidelines about valuation, most countries are unlikely to include them in their environmental accounts. An example of monetary accounts for air pollution in Sweden, based on the damage cost approach, is shown in Figure 17.6.

Economic modeling with environmental accounts
Assessment of trade-offs in a partial equilibrium framework is a first step towards understanding the policy impacts on the environment. But understanding the impact of broader changes, such as trade liberalization, population growth, agricultural and industrial policy, energy pricing and so on usually requires an economy-wide environmental–economic model.

One of the most important applications of the flow accounts is for economic planning. Planning for sustainable development requires an integration of environmental and economic modeling. In the past, it was difficult

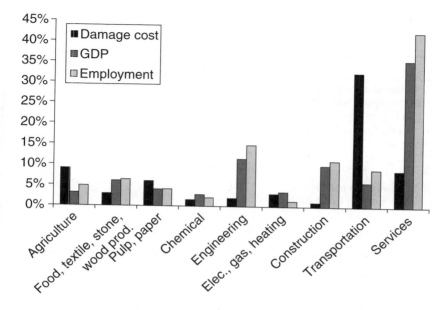

Source: Ahlroth (2000).

Figure 17.6 Economic contribution and environmental burden from domestic pollution by selected industries in Sweden, 1991

to integrate environmental and economic planning because the underlying database for such models did not exist. The contribution of environmental accounting is to provide the economist with a consistent, systematic, and reliable set of accounts that are linked to the economic accounts. While this topic is too broad to review in detail here, examples of widespread modeling applications include: modeling of environmental taxes and resource user fees, modeling trade and the environment, modeling environmental impacts of long-term development strategies, energy modeling.

4. Environmental protection and resource management expenditure accounts

This component of the environmental accounts takes figures that are already included in the SNA and rearranges them to make them more useful for policy. There are three major parts: accounts for environmental protection expenditure, accounts for natural resource management, and environmental taxes and related fees. Two examples are provided here that are both relevant to all countries, developed and developing.

Table 17.5   Resource management costs and taxes paid by the fishing industry in Namibia, 1994–1999

	1994	1995	1996	1997	1998	1999
A. Resource management costs incurred by government						
Total management costs (millions of Namibian dollars)	52.1	54.3	69.3	73.9	82.4	66
Monitoring, control, surveillance	47%	58%	65%	59%	59%	52%
Research	44%	31%	25%	31%	29%	34%
Other	9%	10%	10%	10%	12%	14%
Total	100%	100%	100%	100%	100%	100%
B. Taxes and fees paid by fishing industry (millions of Namibian dollars)	131.8	111.1	72	91	97.3	119.6
C. Management costs as % of taxes and fees paid	40%	49%	96%	81%	85%	55%

Source: Adapted from Lange (2003b).

Table 17.5 presents information needed to assess a common situation: is a resource that is commercially exploited paying at least enough in taxes to cover the costs of its management? In this case, only taxes and fees directly related to the resource are included, not any corporate business income taxes, which all companies may pay, regardless of what industry they are in. In the Namibian fishing industry, the taxes contributed have always covered the costs to government of managing the industry.

In the second example, Sweden has compared the share of carbon emissions by industry to the share of carbon taxes that a given industry pays (Figure 17.7). If a carbon tax is administered equally, on the basis of CO_2 emitted, the two shares should be the same for an industry. Surprisingly, there seems to be little relationship between the two. Households pay a much greater share than the share of CO_2 they are directly responsible for, while manufacturing pays much less.

5.   Economy-wide indicators of sustainable development

A wide range of macroeconomic indicators can be derived from the asset and flow accounts of the SEEA; the major ones are listed in Table 17.6. The role of economic valuation in accounting, and the border between accounting and economic analysis are unresolved issues in the SEEA. Consequently, the SEEA does not make a recommendation for any particular indicators and presents both physical and monetary macroeconomic indicators. The Netherlands has been the major proponent of phys-

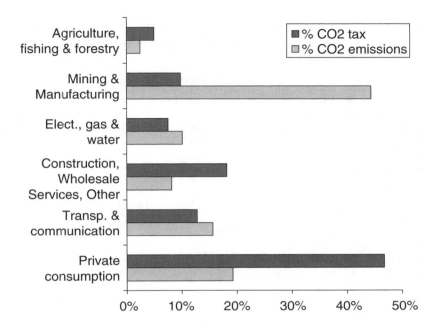

Source: Based on data from Sjölin and Wadeskog (2000).

Figure 17.7 *Carbon taxes and carbon emissions by industry in Sweden, 1997 (percentage of total)*

ical NAMEA indicators for main environmental 'themes' determined by national emission targets.

Within the monetary macro-indicators, there is further controversy over whether sustainability is more accurately monitored from a national income approach (for example environmentally adjusted GDP) or from a wealth approach (for example genuine savings). These issues are addressed in more detail in Chapter 18. There is also a view reported in the SEEA that hypothetical national income calculated through modeling exercises should also be included in the environmental accounts. However, most practitioners recognize that such indicators, while quite useful, belong firmly in the realm of economic analysis rather than statistics.

6. The future of environmental accounting

Environmental accounts make a great contribution to further integrating environmental and economic analysis by providing a single database that is consistent for both sets of information. The SEEA, as an official handbook endorsed by the UN Statistics Committee, provides the basis for viewing

Table 17.6   Environmental macroeconomic indicators, physical and monetary

A. Physical Aggregates

Indicators	Basis
NAMEA Theme Indicators developed by Statistics Netherlands for composites of ● greenhouse gas emissions, ● acidification ● eutrophication ● solid waste	Derived from the NAMEA system (National Accounts Matrix including Environmental Accounts), embedded in the SEEA flow accounts
Indicators associated with Material Flow Accounts ● TMR: Total Material Requirements ● DMI: Direct Material Input ● NAS: Net Additions to Stock ● TDO: Total Domestic Output ● DPO: Domestic Processed Output	Derived from SEEA

B. Monetary Aggregates

Indicators	Basis
1. Measures that revise existing macroeconomic indicators	
Depletion adjusted product and income measures: daGDP, daNDP, daGNI, daNNI	Subtract depletion of natural capital assets from macroeconomic aggregates
Environmentally adjusted product and income: eaNDP, eaNNI	Subtract depletion of natural capital and environmental degradation based on maintenance cost from macroeconomic aggregates In some implementations, parts of environmental protection expenditures are also subtracted.
Genuine income (gY) NNI (Net national income) less damage costs	Subtract depletion of natural capital and environmental degradation based on damage cost from macroeconomic aggregates
Total wealth, Inclusive Wealth ● Value of total wealth over time ● Change in wealth over time (see Genuine Savings below) ● Change in composition of wealth, ownership distribution etc.	Adds to balance sheet for assets and liabilities of produced assets, natural capital assets and human capital (experimental; not included in national balance sheets at this time)

Table 17.6 (continued)

B. Monetary Aggregates	
Indicators	Basis
Genuine Savings, Adjusted Net Savings (ANS)	Revise conventional measure of Net Savings for net change in natural capital and human capital
2. Measures that estimate new, hypothetical macroeconomic aggregates	
Sustainable National Income (SNI) as developed by R. Hueting	Modeling hypothetical GDP, GNI if economy was forced to meet environmental standards using currently available technology
Other forms of sustainable GDP, NDP, GNI, NNI	Modeling of hypothetical GDP from a range of either short- and medium-term options (e.g. carbon tax) to long-term strategic analysis of alternatives for sustainable development

Source: Adapted from Lange (2003a).

environmental accounting as simply a more thorough way of doing national accounts. However, the SEEA is far from a complete handbook providing clear standards on all issues, and the problem is both conceptual and empirical. The three most urgent issues are the following:

Asset valuation, depletion and degradation. At this time, the SEEA presents several alternative approaches to measuring the value of assets and depletion/degradation but makes no recommendation for which approach to use, even though the approaches can give widely differing results. The issue of constant price asset values is not even discussed in the SEEA. This situation is not one that will encourage countries to implement the asset accounts.

Macroeconomic indicators (monetary). Ministries of Finance need to know whether their development strategy is laying the basis for long-term economic growth or not. In developing countries, PRSPs (Poverty Reduction Strategy Programs) have been widely adopted as a planning technique to promote *sustainable* economic growth and poverty reduction. However, PRSPs use GDP and other conventional macro indicators in their monitoring framework; consequently, policy makers receive information about only half of the objective, short-term economic growth, but not sustainability of that growth. The long-term cost of soil erosion, for example, is enormous in many countries and may undermine any short-term gains in

GDP. There is a great need for a complementary indicator of sustainability, such as Genuine Savings, that can be used in PRSPs. The SEEA does not make clear whether countries should be monitoring stocks (wealth and changes in wealth/savings) or flows (national income).

Ecosystem accounting. Some ecosystem values, notably for forests, have been incorporated in environmental accounts, but much of this work has not yet been systematically incorporated in the SEEA. Accounting for ecosystem services is especially important for developing countries for several reasons. Developing countries contain most of the world's biodiversity; biodiversity protection services benefit not only local communities but also the global community. Ecosystem services, such as water and soil protection, are often under greatest threat in developing countries, but these countries often have fewer resources to cope with loss of ecosystem services (flood control, water purification, increased health care and so on). In addition, the well-being of developing countries may be more vulnerable to loss of these services as a majority of people depend directly on ecosystem health (for example soil stability for subsistence farming, fisheries habitat and so on), and often have limited alternative sources of livelihood. Noting that the poor are often those most vulnerable to deterioration of natural systems, the *Millennium Ecosystem Assessment* states that 'development policies aimed at reducing poverty that ignore the impact of our current behavior on the natural environment may well be doomed to failure' (Millennium Assessment Board, 2005).

Notes

1. There is no consensus yet about how to measure human capital.
2. The most important natural capital is included here: minerals for both countries and fisheries for Namibia. The value of other important natural capital, notably land and water, has not yet been estimated, but this is not expected to seriously affect the trends in per capita wealth. This is discussed further in (Lange, 2004b).

References

Ahlroth, S. (2000), 'Correcting NDP for SO$_2$ and NOx emissions: implementation of a theoretical model in practice', National Institute for Economic Research (NIER): Stockholm.
Arrow, K., P. Dasgupta and K. Mäler (2003a), 'Evaluating projects and assessing sustainable development in imperfect economies', *Environmental and Resource Economics*, **26**: 647–85.
Arrow, K., P. Dasgupta and K. Mäler (2003b), 'The genuine saving criterion and the value of population', *Economic Theory*, **21**: 217–25.
Australian Bureau of Statistics (ABS) (2004a), *Australian System of National Accounts*, Consolidated Balance Sheet, Canberra: ABS.
Australian Bureau of Statistics (ABS) (2004b), 'Water Accounts Australia 2001–2001', Canberra: ABS.
Dasgupta, P. and K. Mäler (2000), 'Net national product, wealth, and social well-being', *Environment and Development Economics*, **5**: 69–94.
Hamilton, K. and M. Clemens (1999), 'Genuine savings rates in developing countries', *World Bank Economic Review*, **13**(2): 333–56.

Heal, G. and B. Kriström (2005), 'National income and the environment', in K. Mäler and J. Vincent (eds), *Handbook of Environmental Economics, Volume 3*, Amsterdam: North-Holland.

Hellsten, E., S. Ribacke and G. Wickbom (1999), 'SWEEA – Swedish environmental and economic accounts', *Structural Change and Economic Dynamics*, **10**(1): 39–72.

Kunte, A., K. Hamilton, J. Dixon, and M. Clemens (1998), 'Estimating national wealth: methodology and results', Environment Department Papers, Environmental Economics Series No. 57, Washington: The World Bank.

Lange, G. (2002), 'Trade and the environment in Southern Africa: impact of the user pays principle for water on exports of Botswana, Namibia, and South Africa', paper presented at the Conference of the International Input–Output Association, 10–15 October, Montreal, Canada.

Lange, G. (2003a), 'Environmental accounts: uses and policy applications', Environment Department Paper No. 87, Washington, DC: World Bank.

Lange, G. (2003b), 'Fisheries accounts; management of a recovering fishery', in G. Lange et al., *Environmental Accounting in Action: Case Studies from Southern Africa*, Cheltenham, UK and Northampton, MA, USA: Edward Elgar.

Lange, G. (2004a), 'Manual for environmental and economic accounts for forestry: a tool for cross-sectoral policy analysis', FAO Forestry Department Working Paper, March.

Lange, G. (2004b), 'Wealth, natural capital, and sustainable development: the contrasting examples of Botswana and Namibia', *Environment and Resource Economics*, November, **29**(3): 257–83.

Lange, G. (2005), 'Introducing environmental sustainability into the Ugandan national accounts', report to IUCN and the Environment and Natural Resources Sector Working Group, Kampala, Uganda, March.

Lange, G. and R. Hassan (forthcoming, 2006), *The Economics of Water Management in Southern Africa: An Environmental Accounting Approach*, Cheltenham, UK and Northampton, MA, USA: Edward Elgar.

Lange, G. and M. Wright (2004), 'Sustainable development in mineral economies: the example of Botswana', *Environment and Development Economics*, August, **9**(4).

Lange, G., R. Hassan and K. Hamilton (2003), *Environmental Accounting in Action: Case Studies from Southern Africa*, Cheltenham, UK and Northampton, MA, USA: Edward Elgar.

Millennium Assessment Board (2005), 'Millennium Ecosystem Assessment', available from www.millenniumassessment.org.

Sjölin, M. and A. Wadeskog (2000), *Environmental Taxes and Environmentally Harmful Subsidies*, Report prepared for DG Environment and Eurostat, available at http://www.scb.se/mi1301.

Smith, R. and C. Simard (2001), 'A proposed approach to sustainable development indicators based on capital', paper presented by Statistics Canada at the National Conference of Sustainable Development Indicators, 27 March, Ottawa, Canada.

United Nations (1993), *Operational Manual for the System of Integrated Environmental and Economic Accounts*, New York: UN.

United Nations, European Commission, International Monetary Fund, Organization for Economic Cooperation and Development and World Bank (1993), *System of National Accounts*, New York: UN.

United Nations, European Commission, International Monetary Fund, Organization for Economic Cooperation and Development and World Bank (2003), *Integrated Environmental and Economic Accounting 2003*, New York: UN.

Van der Veeren, R., R. Brouwer, S. Schenau and R. van der Stegen (2004), 'NAMWA: a new integrated river basin information system', Voorburg, The Netherlands: Central Bureau of Statistics.

World Bank (2002), *World Development Report*, Washington, DC: World Bank.

World Bank (forthcoming, 2005), *Where is the Wealth of Nations?*, Washington, DC: World Bank.

18 Genuine saving as an indicator of sustainability

Kirk Hamilton and Katharine Bolt

1. Introduction

Choosing sustainable development is an ethical position adopted by society, reflecting a desire to ensure that future generations enjoy at least as much welfare as the current generation. Because sustainability is inherently about the future, measuring it has been a challenge. Without indicators, promises to achieve sustainability risk being largely empty.

A common thread in the literature on sustainable development concerns the treatment of the environment and natural resources within the System of National Accounts (SNA). This is important because the SNA has an incomplete treatment of resource issues. To give one example, commercial natural resource stocks are supposed to be measured in the national balance sheet accounts of the SNA, but there is no corresponding adjustment to net national income or net saving to reflect the consumption of capital that occurs when these stocks are exploited. Similarly, there is no explicit accounting in the SNA for the damages to economic assets that result from pollution emissions. The consequence is that SNA measures of income and saving are overstated, substantially so for the most resource-dependent economies. In many countries finance ministries are simply working with the wrong figures.

If depletion of the environment is ignored in the most common and powerful set of indicators used to guide economic development, then the threat to sustainability is obvious. Decisions to exploit natural resources now may harm future generations if the depletion of one asset is not offset by investment in another – the fact that this depletion is occurring would be completely invisible in standard national accounting.

To correct this flaw in the national accounts, measures of 'genuine' saving account for the change in real wealth in an economy after due account is taken of the depreciation and depletion of the full range of assets in the economy. Pearce and Atkinson (1993) laid the conceptual foundation for such an extended measure of saving, as well as presenting some of the first empirical estimates using results from the green national accounting literature.

In a series of papers, Hamilton and Clemens (1999), Dasgupta and Mäler (2000) and Asheim and Weitzman (2001) have established the growth theoretic basis for the linkage between saving and sustainability. While the main result from this literature will be presented below, the intuition is straightforward. If we conceive of wealth – the value of all assets in an economy – as the basis of future welfare, then current changes in wealth must have future welfare consequences. It is at least conceivable that a decline in wealth now will lead to falls in future levels of welfare – such an economy would not be sustainable by Pezzey's (1989) definition. Growth theory makes this connection concrete.

The focus in the sustainable development literature is on genuine saving rather than 'genuine income' (that is consumption plus genuine saving) for good reason – adjusting the level of income to reflect the depreciation of a wider array of assets does not in itself indicate whether an economy is on a sustainable path. However, the fact that genuine income would typically be lower than the standard measure of Net National Income does send an important message – that we should not be treating asset consumption as income.

Genuine saving is more than a theoretical construct. In addition to the empirical results in Pearce and Atkinson (1993) and Hamilton and Clemens (1999), the World Bank has been publishing estimates of 'adjusted net' saving (the formal name for genuine saving at the Bank) for 140 countries since 1999 in the *World Development Indicators* (World Bank, 2005).

The plan of the chapter is the following. The next section will lay out the theoretical basis and measurement issues for genuine saving. This will be followed by presentation of some of the published saving estimates from the World Bank. Recent extensions of the saving analysis in the literature will be presented. Finally, the chapter concludes with some thoughts on current challenges.

2. Theory and measurement

Pearce and Atkinson (1993) made a first attack on the problem of measuring sustainable development by employing basic intuitions concerning assets and sustainability. They argued that sustainability can be equated to non-declining values of all assets, including natural resources. The consequence of this conceptualization is that changes in asset values, measured by net saving, should signal whether an economy is on a sustainable path. Pearce and Atkinson presented empirical results on net saving for a range of developed and developing countries using values published in the green accounting literature.

More recent theoretical work on savings has firmly established the linkage between net savings, social welfare and sustainable development. Hamilton and Clemens (1999) tackle the problem for an optimal economy, and Dasgupta and Mäler (2000) for non-optimal economies (with suitable definition of shadow prices). Asheim and Weitzman (2001) show that growth in real NNP (where prices are deflated by a Divisia index of consumption prices) indicates the change in social welfare in the economy.

Genuine saving is defined as,

$$G = \sum_{i=1}^{N} p_i \dot{K}_i \qquad (18.1)$$

Here the K_i are the stocks of assets in the economy, and the p_i are their shadow prices. The expression says that genuine saving is measured as the change in real wealth. To measure sustainability it is important that genuine saving span as wide a range of assets as possible, including assets with negative shadow prices such as pollution stocks. In principle changes in the stocks of produced, human, natural, social and institutional capital should all be measured in saving – in practice there are data and conceptual problems associated with the measurement of assets like social capital.

The basic theoretical insight of Hamilton and Clemens (1999) is to show that genuine saving G, utility U, social welfare V, marginal utility of consumption λ, and pure rate of time preference ρ are related as follows:

$$V = \int_{T}^{\infty} U(C,...) \cdot e^{-\rho(s-t)} ds \qquad (18.2)$$

$$G = \lambda^{-1} \frac{dV}{dt} \qquad (18.3)$$

This says that social welfare is equal to the present value of utility, and that genuine saving is equal to the instantaneous change in social welfare measured in dollars.[1] The utility function can include consumption C and any other set of goods and bads to which people attribute value.

Hamilton and Clemens (1999) go on to show that negative levels of genuine saving must imply that future levels of utility over some period of time are lower than current levels – that is negative genuine saving implies unsustainability. Similar implications hold for the approaches of Dasgupta and Mäler (2000) and Asheim and Weitzman (2001).

These approaches to greening the accounts, and the models that underpin them, are agnostic on the question of the degree of substitutability between different assets, in particular between produced and natural assets. An important strand of the sustainability literature, dating back to Pearce et al. (1989), looks at the question of *strong* versus *weak* sustainability (see also Chapter 4). Weak sustainability assumes that there are no fundamental constraints on substitutability. If, however, some amount of nature must be conserved in order to sustain utility – the strong sustainability assumption – then these saving models need to be modified to incorporate the shadow price of the sustainability constraint.

A formal approach to the strong vs weak sustainability problem has been explored in the 'Hartwick rule'[2] literature. Dasgupta and Heal (1979) and Hamilton (1995) show that if the elasticity of substitution between produced capital and natural resources is less than 1, then the Hartwick rule is not feasible – eventually production and consumption must fall, implying that the economy is not sustainable under the rule.

The question of ecological thresholds is potentially important in measuring sustainable development. Crossing certain boundaries may produce catastrophic results, such as the re-routing of the Gulf Stream as a result of global warming, or the death of most plankton in the ocean as a result of ozone layer destruction. In environmental economic terms we may think of a threshold as a point where the marginal damage curve is unbounded. As long as marginal damages are smooth as a threshold is approached, the saving approach will give correct signals concerning sustainability, since approaching the threshold will eventually result in negative savings. If the marginal damage curve is not smooth and becomes vertical at the threshold, then the saving rule may not indicate unsustainability as the threshold is approached. There is clearly an important question of the science of threshold problems, since we do not know a priori what the shape of the marginal damage curve is for many important problems.[3]

Pezzey (2004) makes the point that genuine saving provides a *one-sided* sustainability test: if saving is negative, then there must be future declines in utility. The opposite is not true in general – positive saving at a point in time does not indicate that future utility is everywhere non-declining. However, Hamilton and Hartwick (2005) show that making positive genuine saving an element of a policy rule can yield sustainability – this result is described below.

3. Empirical experience

Each year the World Bank publishes genuine saving estimates in the *World Development Indicators* (World Bank, 2005).[4] The following summarizes how the saving estimates are constructed:

Genuine saving =   Gross national saving
                   +   Education expenditure
                   −   Consumption of fixed capital
                   −   Depletion of energy resources
                   −   Depletion of minerals

- Net depletion of forests
- CO$_2$ damages
- Particulate pollution damages

There are a number of points to note about the calculation. First, genuine saving as published by the World Bank is not just a 'green' indicator – it includes investment in human capital (as proxied by education expenditure) as a part of saving. Carbon dioxide damages, a global issue representing damages inflicted on other countries, are included in national savings on the assumption that a certain property right holds: that countries have the right not to be polluted by their neighbours. Finally, damages from particulate matter in air are based on the value of damage to health – healthfulness is treated as an asset, part of human capital.

In any given year 10–30 countries actually have negative genuine saving. As Figure 18.1 shows, aggregate savings for the developing regions of the world show distinctive levels and trends.

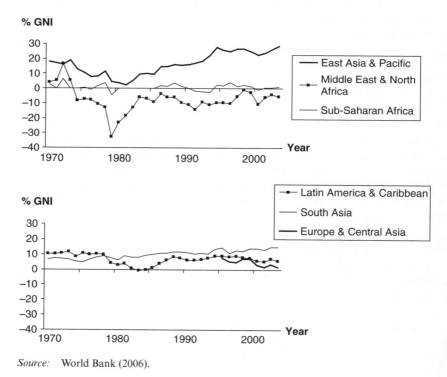

Source: World Bank (2006).

Figure 18.1   Trends in genuine saving by region

The main features of the regional saving rates are as follows:

- The Middle East and North Africa stands out for its consistently negative saving rate, reflecting high dependence on petroleum extraction. Regional genuine saving rates are highly sensitive to changes in world oil prices. This is clearly shown in Figure 18.1 – genuine saving rates dropped in 1979, largely owing to the consumption of sharply increased oil rents following the Iranian revolution.

- East Asia and Pacific stands in stark contrast, with recent aggregate genuine saving figures nearing 30 per cent, driven largely by China. The boom in economic performance from the second half of the 1980s until the Asian financial crisis in 1997 is reflected in the genuine saving numbers, largely driven by increases in gross national saving.

- Genuine saving rates have been hovering around zero in sub-Saharan Africa. Positive saving in countries such as Kenya, Tanzania and South Africa is offset by strongly negative genuine saving rates in resource-dependent countries such as Nigeria and Angola, which have genuine saving rates of −30 per cent in 2003.

- South Asia displays consistently strong genuine saving rates, fluctuating between 10 and 15 per cent since 1985, with India dominating the aggregate figure.

- Latin American genuine saving rates have remained fairly constant throughout the 1990s. The large economies in the region, Mexico and Brazil, have positive genuine saving rates in excess of 5 per cent. However, like many oil producers, Venezuela's genuine saving rate has been persistently negative since the late 1970s.

- Genuine saving data for Eastern Europe and Central Asia are only available from 1995. Saving rates have fallen from over 7.7 per cent in 1995 to 1.7 per cent in 2003, largely driven by dissaving in the oil states of Azerbaijan, Kazakhstan, Uzbekistan, Turkmenistan, and the Russian Federation.

One of the themes that suggests itself in the analysis of regional trends in saving is the link between high resource dependence (typically on oil) and genuine saving rates. Figure 18.2 looks more specifically at this question by scattering genuine saving rates against rates of dependence on exhaustible resources in 2003 (only mineral and energy rent shares greater than 1 per cent of GNI are shown).

The tendency in Figure 18.2 is clear. If mineral- and energy-dependent economies were diligently investing their rents in other types of capital, as the Hartwick rule suggests, then there should be no apparent link between resource dependence and genuine saving. Instead we see a clear downward

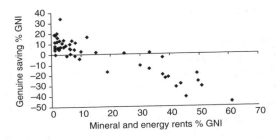

Source: World Bank (2006).

Figure 18.2   Genuine saving vs exhaustible resource dependence, 2003

trend, which suggests a tendency to consume rents that increases with resource dependence.

Genuine saving lends itself to a variety of empirical applications beyond the analysis of sustainability. Recent examples include Atkinson and Hamilton (2003) who explore the extent to which genuine saving can explain the 'resource curse', while de Soysa and Neumayer (2005) look at the impact of trade openness and other liberalization measures on genuine saving.

4.   Extensions

Reference was made above to the Hartwick rule, a rule for achieving sustainability that is built around genuine saving. Under this rule an economy will achieve maximal constant consumption forever (or constant utility in a more general formulation) if genuine saving is set to zero at each point in time. This holds even in the canonical exhaustible resource economy of Dasgupta and Heal (1979) with fixed technology, a single produced capital stock and a finite resource stock that is essential for production – in this economy the rule reduces to 'invest resource rents'.

Hamilton and Hartwick (2005) point toward a generalization of the Hartwick rule by deriving the following relationship between consumption, saving and the interest rate for an optimizing Dasgupta–Heal economy:

$$\dot{C} = G\left(r - \frac{\dot{G}}{G}\right) \tag{18.4}$$

Here C is consumption and r the (time-varying) interest rate. This expression relates growth in consumption to the sign of genuine saving and the difference between the interest rate and the growth rate of genuine saving.

Dixit et al. (1980) showed that a slightly generalized version of the Hartwick rule holds in any economy that is competitive – an economy where producers maximize profits and households maximize utility. A competitive economy is not necessarily PV-optimal (the path defined by solving the growth problem where the present value (PV) of utility is maximized), so a variety of policy rules can potentially be applied. Hamilton and Withagen (2007) show that expression (18.4) holds in competitive economies, which means that it is possible to define a more general rule for sustainability: in a competitive economy, maintaining genuine saving rates that are (i) positive and (ii) growing at a rate less than the interest rate, will lead to increasing consumption at each point in time.

Ferreira and Vincent (2005) use World Bank historical data on consumption and genuine saving to test a basic proposition linking current saving to future welfare. They start with a result from Weitzman (1976): if the economy is PV-optimal and the interest rate is constant then,

$$G(t) = r \int_t^\infty C(s)e^{-r(s-t)}ds - C(t) \tag{18.5}$$

Genuine saving is equal to the difference between a particular weighted average of future consumption and current consumption. This relationship is tested econometrically using per capita data from 1970 to 2000. Ferreira and Vincent find that the relationship holds best for non-OECD countries, and that there is a better fit as more stringent measures of saving are tested, that is when going from gross saving to net saving to genuine saving (but excluding the adjustment for education expenditure, which performs very badly).

Hamilton and Hartwick (2005) note that expression (18.4) can be integrated to yield,[5]

$$G = \int_t^\infty \dot{C}(s) \cdot exp\left(-\int_t^s r(\tau)d\tau \right) ds \tag{18.6}$$

So genuine saving is equal to the present value of changes in future consumption. Hamilton (2005) uses historical data to test whether this expression holds. Figure 18.3 displays the right-hand side of expression (18.6) scattered against genuine saving in 1980. The broad conclusion is similar to Ferreira and Vincent (2005) – using data for all countries, genuine saving fits expression (18.5) better than other measures of saving, while the fit is extremely poor in OECD countries.

Hamilton et al. (2006) show that a particularly simple saving rule yields sustainability in a competitive Dasgupta–Heal economy: if genuine saving is positive and constant then consumption will rise without bound. This rule and the standard Hartwick rule are then used to test the counterfactual: how rich would countries be if from 1970 to 2000 they had followed either the standard Hartwick rule or had maintained genuine saving at

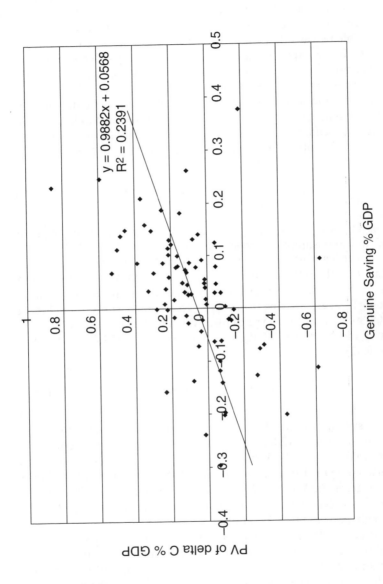

Source: Hamilton (2005).

Figure 18.3 PV of change in consumption vs genuine saving, 1980

a constant value equal to 5 per cent of 1987 GDP? Figure 18.4 compares the two counterfactual estimates of fixed capital (it is assumed that all savings are invested in produced assets) with the observed level of fixed capital in 2000 for selected countries.

The results of following either policy rule are dramatic for the oil producers: Venezuela, Trinidad and Tobago and Gabon would all be as rich as South Korea if they had followed the constant genuine saving rule. Nigeria would not be rich, but it would be five times richer than it is today. It is no simple matter for a resource-dependent developing country to maintain positive savings through financial crises, civil unrest and natural disasters – but the payoffs are potentially huge.

Finally, World Bank (2006, ch. 5) extends the empirical work on genuine saving to examine the effects of population growth. The net change in wealth per capita G_N is calculated as

$$G_N = \frac{G}{N} - g\frac{W}{N}.$$ (18.7)

For population N, this says that the net change in wealth per capita is equal to total genuine saving per person minus a Malthusian term, the population growth rate g times total tangible wealth W per person. Dasgupta (2001) shows that this expression measures the change in social welfare when (i) the population growth rate is constant, (ii) per capital consumption is independent of population size, and (iii) production exhibits constant returns to scale.

Figure 18.5 scatters the net change in wealth per capita against GNI per capita (logarithmic scale) in 2000. The upward trend and the fact that most low income countries (GNI of less than \$750 per capita) face net declines in wealth per capita means, roughly speaking, that the rich are getting richer while the poor are getting poorer. However, Hamilton (2005) presents evidence that the Malthusian adjustment tends to overstate the impact of population growth on future changes in consumption.

World Bank (2006) also calculates the saving gap – the increase in saving that would be required to bring a country's net change in wealth per capita back to zero. For many African countries in particular this gap is huge, from 10–70 per cent of GNI, suggesting that economic and environmental policy alone will not suffice to bring sustainability in per capita terms to these economies.

5. Challenges for the future

A conceptual challenge for the work on genuine saving concerns the question of optimality. Hamilton and Clemens (1999) derive expression (18.3)

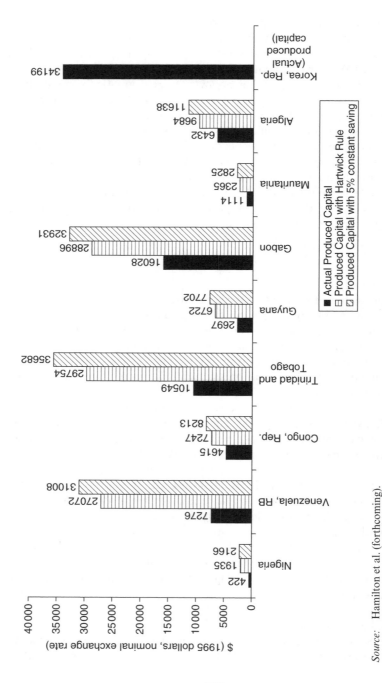

Source: Hamilton et al. (forthcoming).

Figure 18.4 Actual and counterfactual produced capital under alternative policies, 2000 ($ per capita)

302

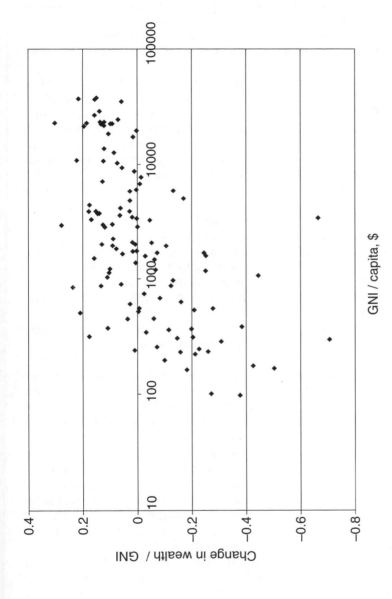

Source: World Bank (2006).

Figure 18.5 Net change in wealth per capita vs GNI per capita, 2000

in an optimal economy, so the application of the theory to the real world becomes an important question. Dasgupta and Mäler's (2000) solution is to derive the parallel expression for a non-optimal economy, but they are required to use accounting prices that are defined as the partial derivatives of the value function V for the non-optimal path – to define the prices it is therefore necessary to define the path. Arrow et al. (2003) explore this question in some depth.

If we assume that world prices for resources do reflect scarcities and are therefore relatively undistorted, then the derived shadow prices should be a reasonable reflection of the user costs associated with resource extraction. Whether genuine saving measured using these prices truly reflects the change in social welfare is still an open question, although there is a huge amount of literature on cost–benefit analysis of projects which would suggest using precisely these prices. More work on this topic is required.

The new results on saving rules in competitive economies offer promise in this regard – there is no underlying assumption of optimality, and it is at least a reasonable proposition that many economies are competitive. One obvious conclusion follows from expression (18.4): if genuine saving is negative and constant then the economy is on an unsustainable path. The general rule for sustainability was stated above: maintain positive saving and ensure that it does not grow faster than the interest rate. These saving rules for competitive economies offer scope for actually using the concept of genuine saving in designing policies for sustainability.

There is no shortage of empirical questions when it comes to measuring genuine saving. Among the challenges that appear the most urgent are:

- Identifying non-linearities in the natural world that may not be captured in any simple way in measures of genuine saving. We do not want to be assuring ministers that all is well because saving is positive, only to discover that a major flip in natural systems has severe consequences for human welfare.
- Valuing truly difficult assets such as biodiversity.
- Inventorying and valuing the environmental services that underpin so much economic activity, whether it is pollination or regulation of flow in a watershed. While many of these values are captured indirectly in other asset values – the value of farmland, for example – the fact that there is no explicit valuation means that there are opportunities for unpleasant policy surprises.
- Estimating elasticities of substitution for resources. The availability of databases of natural resource stocks and flows, in quantity and value terms, means that there should be more scope for exploring this important question – World Bank (2006, Chapter 8) estimates the

elasticity of substitution between land and fixed capital to be close to one, an important result.

The policy challenges involved in increasing genuine saving are closely linked to the components of saving. The 'bottom line', genuine saving, will be affected by fiscal and monetary policies that influence gross saving effort. In addition, increasing human capital investments and making them more effective will boost the bottom line. Achieving efficient levels of resource extraction and pollution emissions will also increase genuine saving – note, however, that this does not imply reducing resource extraction or pollution emissions to zero.

While the focus of this chapter has been on saving, the profitability of investments financed by this saving is of paramount importance. If governments invest in 'showcase' projects with low or negligible social returns, then savings have in effect been consumed, with consequent effects on future welfare.

Finally, for the poorest economies, increasing saving could be taken to imply decreasing consumption, not a palatable policy option in countries where consumption is already at subsistence levels. For these countries a better alternative will be to focus on boosting the efficiency of the economy through economic reforms, raising growth and potentially leading to a virtuous cycle of increasing saving and consumption.

Notes

1. This result is foreshadowed in Aronsson et al. (1997, expression 6.18) who show that net saving measured in utility units is equal to the present value of changes in utility for a general (possibly time-varying) pure rate of time preference.
2. Hartwick (1977) showed that consumption is sustainable (in fact constant) in a fixed technology economy with an essential exhaustible resource if: (i) net saving is everywhere 0; (ii) the elasticity of substitution between resources and produced capital is 1; and (iii) the elasticity of output with respect to produced capital is greater than the corresponding elasticity for the resource.
3. See also Pearce et al. (1996).
4. The formal name of the saving indicator is 'adjusted net saving'. Genuine saving is the informal name.
5. This is also proved, in a more general framework, in Dasgupta (2001) Ch. 9, appendix A.7.

References

Aronsson, T., P.-O. Johansson and K.-G. Löfgren (1997), *Welfare Measurement, Sustainabiliy and Green National Accounting: A growth theoretical approach*, Cheltenham, UK and Northampton, MA, USA: Edward Elgar.

Arrow, K.J., P. Dasgupta and K.-G. Mäler (2003), 'Evaluating projects and assessing sustainable development in imperfect economies', *Environmental and Resource Economics*, 26(4): 647–85.

Asheim, G.B. and M.L. Weitzman (2001), 'Does NNP growth indicate welfare improvement?', *Economics Letters*, 73(2): 233–9.

Atkinson, G. and K. Hamilton (2003), 'Savings, growth and the resource curse hypothesis', *World Development*, 31(11): 1793–807.

Dasgupta, P. (2001), *Human Well-being and the Natural Environment*, Oxford: Oxford University Press.

Dasgupta, P. and G. Heal (1979), *Economic Theory and Exhaustible Resources*, Cambridge: Cambridge University Press.

Dasgupta, P. and K.-G. Mäler (2000), 'Net national product, wealth, and social well-being', *Environment and Development Economics*, **5**, Parts 1&2: 69–93, February and May.

de Soysa, I. and E. Neumayer (2005), 'False prophet, or genuine savior? Assessing the effects of economic openness on sustainable development, 1980–99', *International Organization*, **59**(3): 731–72.

Dixit, A., P. Hammond and M. Hoel (1980), 'On Hartwick's rule for Regular Maximin Paths of Capital Accumulation and Resource Depletion', *Review of Economic Studies*, **XLVII**: 551–6.

Ferreira, S. and J. Vincent (2005), 'Genuine savings: leading indicator of sustainable development?', *Economic Development and Cultural Change*, **53**(3): 737–54.

Hamilton, K. (1995), 'Sustainable development, the Hartwick rule and optimal growth', *Environmental and Resource Economics*, **5**(4): 393–411.

Hamilton, K. (2005), 'Testing genuine saving', Policy research Working Paper no. 3577, Washington: The World Bank.

Hamilton, K. and M. Clemens (1999), 'Genuine savings rates in developing countries', *The World Bank Economic Review*, **13**(2): 333–56.

Hamilton, K. and J.M. Hartwick (2005), 'Investing exhaustible resource rents and the path of consumption', *Canadian Journal of Economics*, **38**(2): 615–21.

Hamilton, K. and C. Withagen (2007), 'Savings growth and the path of utility', *Canadian Journal of Economics*, **40**(2), forthcoming.

Hamilton, K., G. Ruta and L. Tajibaeva (2006), 'Capital accumulation and resource depletion: a Hartwick rule counterfactual', *Environmental and Resource Economics*, **34**: 517–33.

Hartwick, J.M. (1977), 'Intergenerational equity and the investing of rents from exhaustible resources', *American Economic Review*, **67**(5): 972–4.

Pearce, D.W. and G. Atkinson (1993), 'Capital theory and the measurement of sustainable development: an indicator of weak sustainability', *Ecological Economics*, **8**: 103–8.

Pearce, D.W., K. Hamilton and G. Atkinson (1996), 'Measuring sustainable development: progress on indicators', *Environment and Development Economics*, **1**: 85–101.

Pearce, D.W., A. Markandya and E.B. Barbier (1989), 'Blueprint for a green economy', London: Earthscan.

Pezzey, J. (1989), 'Economic analysis of sustainable growth and sustainable development', Environment Dept Working Paper No. 15, The World Bank.

Pezzey, J. (2004), 'One-sided sustainability tests with amenities and changes in technology, trade and population', *Journal of Environmental Economics and Management*, **48**(1): 613–31.

Weitzman, M. (1976), 'On the welfare significance of national product in a dynamic economy', *Quarterly Journal of Economics*, **90**(1): 156–62.

World Bank (2005), *World Development Indicators*, Washington: The World Bank.

World Bank (2006), *Where is the Wealth of Nations? Measuring Capital for the 21st Century*, Washington: The World Bank.

19 Measuring sustainable economic welfare
Clive Hamilton

1. Introduction[1]

It has long been recognized that, above a threshold, GDP growth does not correlate well with changes in national well-being (for example Layard, 2005 and Chapter 16 of this volume). That threshold has been well and truly passed by OECD countries. The principal shortcomings of GDP as a measure of changes in national well-being are: the failure to account for how increases in output are distributed within the community; the failure to account for the contribution of household work; the incorrect counting of defensive expenditures as positive contributions to well-being; and the failure to account for changes in the stocks of both built and natural capital.

There have been several attempts to construct indicators of changes in well-being that are more comprehensive than GDP. A well-known earlier index was built by Nordhaus and Tobin (1972). In more recent years Daly and Cobb have constructed the Index of Sustainable Economic Welfare (ISEW) in an influential appendix to their book, *For the Common Good* (1990). The Daly and Cobb index has led to a lively debate on a series of methodological and measurement issues (much of which was presented in Cobb and Cobb, 1994), and construction of similar indexes for several other countries.[2]

These later efforts have placed a particular emphasis on accounting for environmental costs in the new measure of welfare. The initial Daly and Cobb index for the USA has been refined and developed by Cobb, Halstead and Rowe (1995) and renamed the Genuine Progress Indicator (GPI), the name that has increasingly replaced ISEW and that will be used here.

2. Welfare and sustainability

The key to understanding the attempts to develop the GPI lies in the notion of sustainability. The best starting point is John Hicks' 1939 definition of income. 'Hicksian income' is defined as the maximum amount that a person or a nation could consume over some time period and still be as well off at the end of the period as at the beginning (Hicks, 1946: 172).[3] Thus income is maximum *sustainable* consumption. Sustaining consumption over a given period depends on maintaining the productive potential of the capital stocks that are needed to generate the flow of goods and services that are consumed.

The GPI takes this idea and sets itself two tasks:

1. to define and measure 'consumption' in a way that provides a better approximation of actual well-being than the simple measure of marketed goods and services that appears in the national accounts; and
2. to account for the sustainability of consumption by incorporating measures of changes in the value of capital stocks.

Taking account of these two classes of influence on welfare over time, we may end up with a situation in which GDP is increasing while consumption (more broadly defined) is rising or falling, and while capital stocks are growing or declining.

The GPI combines changes in the value of stocks and the values of flows of current consumption. Consistent with the definition of Hicksian income, capital stocks perform two functions in the GPI method of measuring changes in welfare – they yield an annual flow of services and they contribute to the sustainability or otherwise of levels of consumption in the future. In order to prevent the depreciation or depletion of capital stocks, a portion of current consumption needs to be 'set aside' to replenish the stocks. The implication of this is that, unlike the way in which changes in GDP are used, year-on-year changes in the GPI are not very meaningful. The purpose of the GPI is to illustrate trends over time.

We now look more closely at the two tasks that the GPI sets itself and then consider some of the further methodological issues it gives rise to.

3.   Measuring 'consumption' comprehensively

For individuals or households, consumption may be defined as annual flows of marketed and non-marketed goods and services. Perhaps the biggest category of non-marketed goods and services comprises those produced in the home by unpaid household work. Non-marketed goods and services also include services provided by the natural environment, such as the aesthetic and recreational services of old-growth forests and the health-sustaining properties of clean air.

A more comprehensive definition of consumption that takes account of non-marketed goods and services is particularly important because measured GDP growth may reflect nothing more than the transfer of activity from the non-market to the market sector, a problem long recognized in the development literature. This is most apparent in the case of household work, but applies equally to any other 'free' service. Just as, in the well-known observation, GDP declines 'if a man marries his housekeeper', GDP rises if an entrance fee is levied on visits to a national park or a family decides to eat out more often.

Consumption includes negative flows or 'bads'. Some monetary expenditures by final consumers – which are therefore included as expenditures in GDP – represent not additions to welfare but attempts to offset some change in social, environmental or individual circumstances which is causing a decline in welfare. These are known as defensive expenditures and are deducted from the value of personal consumption expenditure, which provides the starting point of the GPI.

These observations apply to consumption by individuals. At a national level it is important to take account of differences in the welfare impact of consumption between households or individuals. One of the most frequently heard criticisms of the use of GDP growth as a measure of national welfare is that it assumes that an extra $1 million of consumption by wealthy households has the same impact on national welfare as an extra $1 million of consumption by impoverished households. The GPI rejects this assumption and adjusts consumption flows by a measure of income distribution.

The GPI assumes that personal consumption spending by individuals on marketed goods and services is the major component of welfare and that an increase in this spending represents, *ceteris paribus*, a corresponding increase in welfare. There is a large amount of literature critical of the assumption that there is a close relationship between changes in consumption spending and changes in individual welfare (see for example Layard, 2005; Frey and Stutzer, 2002). Many studies have shown that, above a certain level of income, perceived well-being depends more on the level of one's income relative to other people's incomes, or to previous or expected levels, than on absolute levels.[4] But the purpose of the GPI is to demonstrate that, even using conventional economic methods, a more comprehensive attempt to account for changes in welfare may show large deviations from GDP over time. Consequently, we adopt the assumption that increases in personal consumption (adjusted for the distribution of income) reflect increases in welfare. It is important to keep this 'consumption framework' in mind because, if it is accepted, many of the criticisms of the GPI and ISEW are neutralized.

4. Accounting for changes in the value of capital stocks

Sustaining levels of consumption requires that the productive potential of capital stocks be maintained. Capital stocks can be divided into five forms, which we discuss in turn. While GDP accounts for changes in none of them, the GPI attempts to incorporate changes in the value of the first three.

Built capital This covers the stocks of physical machinery, buildings and infrastructure that are essential to sustaining levels of GDP. These stocks deteriorate and a portion of income must be set aside each year to invest in them to maintain and improve their productive potential. This is a long-recognized problem and has led periodically to attempts by statistical agencies to construct measures of net national product (NNP). The GPI adjusts consumption spending to take account of net capital growth which, if positive, adds to sustainable economic welfare. (In principle, it should take account of changes in annual flows of services from the stock of built capital.)

Financial assets   A nation's ability to sustain investment in built capital assets is diminished if it is accumulating foreign debts, since some part of future income must be devoted to repaying the debts.[5] But if those loans are being invested productively then future income will be higher and it will be possible to repay the debts without additional burden. To the extent that foreign debt has been invested productively in the past, current consumption will be higher. But if foreign borrowing is dissipated on consumption goods it represents a drain on future consumption. The GPI adjusts consumption spending to account for net foreign liabilities.

Natural capital   Maintaining the stocks of natural capital is essential to sustaining consumption in the future, especially when consumption is defined more broadly. These stocks take two forms. The first are stocks of renewable and non-renewable resources used as inputs in production, such as minerals, fossil fuels and soils. The second take the form of waste sinks that are provided by the natural environment and are essential for dissipating waste products so that they do not represent a danger to humans. The GPI takes account of the depletion of both types of natural capital. However there are some difficult methodological issues concerning the substitutability of built for natural capital that are discussed in the next section.

Human capital   This represents the accumulation of health, skills, knowledge and experience in humans that makes them more productive than brute labourers. Technology is partly embodied in humans. The GPI does not account for human capital because of the conceptual and measurement difficulties involved. If it did, the GPI would ideally be adjusted to account not for annual investments in human capital but for the annual services provided by the stock of human capital. This is an area for future work.

Social capital   A nation that possesses sound and stable political, legal and commercial institutions and cohesive, supportive and trusting communities will be in a better position to generate flows of goods and services than one that does not. However, this form of 'capital' is difficult to define precisely and to measure and is for that reason excluded from the GPI.

Substitutability among capital assets
The depletion of one form of capital does not represent a decline in sustainable consumption if other forms of capital are accumulating and can be substituted for the disappearing asset. Thus the issue of substitutability

within and between these classes of assets is critical. For instance, the run-down in physical capital is not necessarily a problem if financial wealth that could be used to rebuild it (or could be used to invest in assets in other countries) is being accumulated outside of the country.

More controversially, the run-down of one type of natural asset will not necessarily impose a cost if built capital or another type of natural asset can perform, at the same or similar cost, the same functions. The question of the degree of substitutability of built for natural capital is perhaps the most strongly contested issue in the economics of the environment (see Chapters 3, 4 and 6 in this volume and, for example, Neumayer, 2003). We have taken the view that for three classes of natural assets complete substitutability between built and natural assets is not a valid assumption. These classes are:

1. Certain natural resources that are irreplaceable and form essential inputs to continued productive activity – soils and supplies of fresh water are examples;
2. Waste sinks, that is those components of the natural environment that absorb or process wastes and render them benign, particularly the atmosphere (covering the climate system and the ozone layer) and the oceans; and
3. Assets whose services are consumed directly by final consumers and which are valuable because of their unique natural features – old-growth forests and coral reefs are examples.

In addition to these, there may be some natural resources for which there are, or probably will be, substitutes, but for which the substitutes are likely to be significantly more expensive. Fossil fuel-based energy is the most pertinent category here. Energy is essential for economic activity, yet the evidence suggests that the market for energy may not adequately reflect the likely scarcity of fossil fuels (especially oil and natural gas).

Neumayer (2000) has argued that the fact that changes in the value of these 'non-substitutable' assets are added in the GPI to other consumption goods makes them substitutable, so that the GPI is an indicator of weak sustainability only. But adding the value of haircuts to the value of oranges in calculating GDP does not make them substitutes for each other. He also argues, correctly, that some ISEWs or GPIs use an erroneous method to value the depletion of natural resource stocks, which tends to exaggerate the difference between GDP and the adjusted welfare measure.

Defensive expenditures
Whereas GDP counts them as additions to output, the GPI deducts defensive expenditures undertaken by consumers and governments because, by

definition, they are undertaken to offset some decline in social welfare. In principle, most defensive expenditures are reactions to a decline in the value of the stock of social, human or natural capital, as long as they are broadly defined. This applies to private defensive expenditures on health and personal security and public defensive expenditure on social welfare. If we could adequately account for changes in stocks of human and social capital then it would not be necessary to deduct defensive spending.

A more difficult question is that of how much of a given expenditure is defensive and how much makes a net contribution to welfare (Neumayer, 1999). This is particularly relevant to some public expenditures, on social security and law and order for instance. An increase in spending on policing, courts and prisons due to a crime wave is clearly defensive, yet some basic level of spending on crime prevention and punishment is essential and makes a large contribution to national well-being. Ultimately judgements about how much spending is defensive and how much makes a positive contribution to welfare will be somewhat arbitrary.

Time accounting
The GPI attempts a systematic approach to valuing time.[6] The value of time is a very important aspect of various components of the GPI, including the value of household and community work and the costs of unemployment and of overwork. In the Australian GPI we have adopted the principle that the value of time devoted to voluntary activities counts as a positive in the GPI and the value of time engaged in involuntary activities counts as a negative. The following voluntary activities contribute to our welfare:

- paid work (except the involuntary component referred to below as 'overwork');
- household work;
- community work; and
- leisure activities.

The following activities diminish welfare and, as such, impose costs on the community:

- involuntary leisure,[7] that is the times when we are unemployed but want to be employed; and
- involuntary work, that is the times when we are doing paid work but would prefer not to be.

The distribution of these activities varies between different groups inside and outside the labour force, partly by choice and partly involuntarily. The hours devoted to each type of activity must be valued and added or subtracted from the GPI.

Temporal relevance of the GPI

The GPI is a measure of sustainable consumption. Thus in addition to measures of currently consumed goods and bads – including the costs of crime, the costs of commuting, the benefits of household work, and the distribution of income – it considers the future implications of present consumption (and production) activities. Thus it incorporates an estimate of the unsustainability of foreign debt, indicated by the proportion of total foreign borrowing that finances consumption rather than investments that can generate revenues to be used to repay the debt. It also considers the long-term impact of economic activities on the stocks of irreplaceable natural capital assets. In this way, future costs are in a sense brought forward.

As a result, while graphing GPI per person over time illustrates the direction of change, caution must be exercised in interpreting the GPI measure in any one year as a measure of national welfare in that year. Just as a consumer can increase their consumption levels and thus 'welfare' by spending up on a credit card, credit binges must be paid for by lower consumption in future years. Neumayer (1999) has observed that the GPI/ISEW cannot function simultaneously as an indicator of current welfare and as an indicator of sustainability. While there is some confusion in the GPI literature about what it does measure, it seems agreed that the GPI does not function as an indicator of current welfare and of sustainable income but as an indicator of sustainable welfare. In other words, it measures what we might call 'Hicksian welfare', the maximum amount of welfare that a nation can enjoy over some time period and still be as well off at the end of the period as at the beginning.

The GPI therefore engages in a type of smoothing process. As a result, we take the view that it may be misleading to construct the GPI on an annual basis (and even more misleading to do so on a quarterly basis) if the impression were given that an increase, say, in the GPI from one year to the next indicated that national well-being had risen by that amount. On the other hand, many of the items included in the GPI are current rather than capital items and do indicate year-on-year changes in well-being.

The results of three GPI/ISEW calculations are shown in Figure 19.1.

5.   Conceptual problems in the GPI

While many people have welcomed the GPI, others have raised objections.[8] There are four objections to the GPI that have been raised, the first three of which are misconceived.

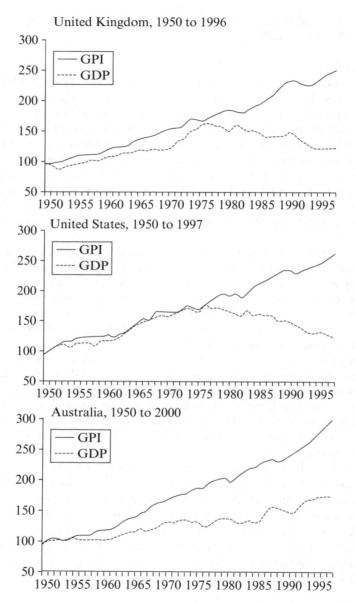

Sources: Jackson et al. (1997); Anielski and Rowe (1999); Hamilton and Denniss (2000).

Figure 19.1   GPI and GDP per person: United Kingdom, United States and Australia (1950–2000)

'Subjective weighting'

It is often claimed that the 'weighting' of various components in the GPI is subjective. In fact, the GPI uses a range of techniques to attach dollar values to the various components, thus converting every component into a common unit of measurement. For instance, the value of household labour is arrived at by multiplying the number of hours worked in the household by the hourly wage rate of a housekeeper. The value of the loss of ozone is arrived at by assessing the health costs of the damage caused. These are not subjective 'weights' but are dollar values generated in markets of one sort or another – actual markets, related markets or hypothetical markets. Everything is expressed in dollar values via prices generated in markets, so that the weights look after themselves.

Arbitrariness of components

Some critics argue that the GPI lacks a sound theoretical foundation; as a result the inclusion of various components is arbitrary (Neumayer, 1999). While the rationale has not always been clearly stated in previous GPIs and ISEWs, the selection of components is not arbitrary but follows some rules. The process begins by identifying the deficiencies of GDP as a measure of welfare and asks how it would need to be changed to make it a better measure. In so doing, it builds a framework for measuring sustainable consumption.

Thus the GPI is not 'arbitrary' in the sense that its authors simply add in components at random. In each case, there is an identified problem with GDP as a measure of welfare, and an attempt is made to fix it so far as is permitted by availability of data. When statisticians calculate NNP by subtracting an estimate of the depreciation of built capital from GNP and say that it is a better measure of changes in output, we do not accuse them of being arbitrary; they are correcting for a known problem.

Quality of goods

It is sometimes argued that the GPI fails as a measure of changes in national well-being because it does not account for the improvement in the quality of goods. Thus real consumption spending may double over a given period, but the utility derived from that spending may more than double because the quality of goods has improved. For example, in real terms we may pay the same amount for a TV today as we did 20 years ago, yet the benefit we derive is much higher because the set has a bigger and flatter screen, and the quality of picture and sound are better.

This is true; however, exactly the same criticism applies to the use of GDP as a measure of national well-being, so it should be no surprise that since the GPI begins with the final consumption component of GDP, all of the problems in it will be carried over to the GPI. Arguably, the quality problem 'cancels out', so that if we focus our attention on the gap between GDP and GPI then it is perfectly feasible to maintain that the GPI is a better measure of changes in economic well-being. This does, however, temper the usefulness of conclusions drawn on the basis of changes in the GPI over time.

Ethical versus *economic* values

There is one serious problem with the GPI as a measure of national wellbeing that should be acknowledged. Aggregating all of the factors into a single monetary index strikes many people as being invalid. By converting everything into dollars, doesn't the GPI fall into the same trap as GDP, that of reducing well-being to economics? This is perhaps the major flaw in the GPI. The problems with the approach become apparent when we attempt, for example, to estimate the costs of climate change, since the greatest costs will be associated with loss of life, which must be given a dollar value if it is to be included. Should the life of a person in a poor country be worth less than the life of someone in a rich country? Placing dollar values on many things converts ethical values into economic ones, a process that for many people actually devalues the environment and human life (see Chapter 2 on this issue). These profound problems with the GPI are acknowledged. For some, constructing the GPI is the most effective way of pointing to the failings of current systems of measurement. Moreover, refusing to value some things means they must be left out of the GPI, even though it is generally agreed they affect our well-being.

6.   Areas for future refinement of the GPI

There are a number of areas of future work that will help refine and resolve difficulties in the GPI method. They include:

- Employing better measurement of changes in income distribution over time, including more robust estimates of the social preference for equality, or aversion to inequality;
- Development of a more comprehensive natural resource accounting framework for incorporating environmental and resource use impacts in to the GPI;
- Securing the collaboration of various government agencies in providing the best and most consistent data on a number of variables (for example those components affected by transport including urban air pollution, costs of noise, costs of accidents); and
- Using a full capital depreciation framework for the GPI components, that is evaluation of the elements of human and social capital and valuing changes in these stocks.

Notes

1. I would like to thank the editors for very helpful comments on an earlier draft of this chapter.
2. Including the UK (Jackson and Marks, 1994; New Economics Foundation, 2004), Canada (Coleman, 1998), Germany (Diefenbacher, 1994), Sweden (Jackson and Stymne, 1996) and Australia (Hamilton, 1997; Hamilton and Denniss, 2000).
3. Hicks also wrote that 'the practical purpose of income is to serve as a guide for prudent conduct' (Hicks, 1946: 172), a comment that has particular relevance for today's concern with ecological sustainability.
4. For a formal treatment of the roles of relative incomes, aspirations and environmental quality in welfare see Ng and Wang (1993).
5. In the case of debts owed to domestic creditors, increased consumption now by the debtor is offset by a decline in consumption now by the creditor, a situation that is later reversed.
6. The most systematic attempt to sort out the problem of time valuation in the GPI appears in Hamilton and Denniss (2000).
7. Some GPIs include the cost of (lost) leisure. Others include the costs of overwork instead.
8. See for example Castles (1997) and Neumayer (1999, 2000).

References

Anielski, M. and J. Rowe (1999), *The Genuine Progress Indicator – 1999 update*, San Francisco: Redefining Progress.

Castles, I. (1997), 'Measuring wealth and welfare: why HDI and GPI fail', paper to a symposium on Wealth, Work and Well-being, Academy of the Social Sciences in Australia (10 November).

Cobb, C. and J. Cobb (1994), *The Green National Product: A Proposed Index of Sustainable Economic Welfare*, Maryland: University Press of America.

Cobb, C., T. Halstead and J. Rowe (1995), *The Genuine Progress Indicator: Summary of Data and Methodology*, San Francisco: Redefining Progress.

Coleman, R. (1998), 'Measuring sustainable development: the Nova Scotia genuine progress indicator', report published by GPI Atlantic, Nova Scotia, Canada.

Daly, H. and J. Cobb (1990), *For the Common Good*, Boston: Beacon Press.

Diefenbacher, H. (1994), 'The index of sustainable economic welfare in Germany', in C. Cobb and J. Cobb (eds), *The Green National Product*, Lanham, MD: University of Americas Press.

Frey, B. and A. Stutzer (2002), *Happiness and Economics*, Princeton: Princeton University Press.

Hamilton, C. (1997), 'The genuine progress indicator: a new index of changes in well-being in Australia', Australia Institute Discussion Paper No. 14 (October) (with contributions from Hugh Saddler).

Hamilton, C. (1999), 'The genuine progress indicator: methodological developments and results from Australia', *Ecological Economics*, **30**: 13–28.

Hamilton, C. and R. Denniss (2000), 'Tracking well-being in Australia: the genuine progress indicator 2000', Australia Institute Discussion Paper No. 25 (December).

Hicks, J. (1946), *Value and Capital*, 2nd edn, London: Oxford University Press.

Jackson, T. and N. Marks (1994), *Measuring Sustainable Economic Welfare – A Pilot Index: 1950–1990*, Stockholm: Stockholm Environment Institute.

Jackson, T. and S. Stymne (1996), *Sustainable Economic Welfare in Sweden: A Pilot Index 1950–1992*, Stockholm: Stockholm Environment Institute.

Jackson, T., N. Marks, J. Ralls and S. Stymne (1997), *Sustainable Economic Welfare in the UK 1950–1996*, Guildford, Surrey: Centre for Environmental Strategy, University of Surrey.

Layard, Richard (2005), *Happiness: Lessons from a new science*, New York: Penguin.

Neumayer, E. (1999), 'The ISEW: not an index of sustainable economic welfare', *Social Indicators Research*, **48**: 77–101.

Neumayer, E. (2000), 'On the methodology or ISEW, GPI and related measures: some constructive suggestions and some doubt on the "threshold" hypothesis', *Ecological Economics*, **34**(3): 1–34.

Neumayer, E. (2003), *Weak versus Strong Sustainability: Exploring the Limits of Two Opposing Paradigms*, Cheltenham, UK and Northampton, MA, USA: Edward Elgar.

New Economics Foundation (2000), 'Chasing Progress: Beyond measuring economic growth', London: www.neweconomics.org.au.

Ng, Yew-Kwang and Jianguo Wang (1993), 'Relative income, aspiration, environmental quality, individual and political myopia', *Mathematical Social Sciences*, **26**: 3–23.

Nordhaus, W. and J. Tobin (1972), 'Is growth obsolete?', in National Bureau of Economic Research, *Economic Growth: Fifth Anniversary Colloquium*, New York: NEBR.

Pannozzo, L. and R. Colman (2004), 'Working time and the future of work in Canada: a Nova Scotia GPI case study', Report published by GPI Atlantic Nova Scotia, Canada.

20 Environmental space, material flow analysis and ecological footprinting
Ian Moffatt

1. Introduction

The terms 'sustainability' and 'sustainable development' are often used interchangeably in both academic research and policy making. They are, however, different, and should be defined clearly and used carefully. To sustain an activity or process is to ensure that the system runs for a long time. In environmental and ecological economics a sustainable resource is a potentially renewable resource which can be used indefinitely. The word 'sustain' is often used in the context of maximum sustainable yield (MSY) and has been used for understanding and contributing to resource policy in areas such as multi-species forestry and fisheries management (Clark, 1976; Christensen, 1995). Sustainable development is a broader concept than sustainability and stresses both the idea of sustaining activity for a long time for current and future generations as well as linking such activity to development rather than economic growth per se. It is also vital for development to be sustainable that the life support systems of the planet are protected (WCED, 1987). One thing is certain, you cannot have continuous growth of economies, population, resource consumption and pollution generation on a planet with finite biophysical stocks and limited assimilative processes (Daly, 1972). This was noted over three decades ago at the Stockholm conference on the Human Environment (Ward and Dubos, 1972) and at the summits in Rio de Janeiro (1992) and in Johannesburg (2002). Sustainable development is an on-going process integrating ecological, economic, equity and ethical considerations for current and future generations of people and other living creatures, without endangering the life support systems of the planet upon which ultimately all life depends (Moffatt, 1996a).

This chapter examines environmental space, material flow analysis and ecological footprints as contributions to the processes of achieving the goal of sustainable development. The next section discusses weak and strong sustainable development issues and resource use. Sections 3 to 5 examine environmental space, material flow analysis and ecological footprinting respectively. Each section defines the concept, briefly describes the methodology including for brevity a 'master equation' for the concept, and illustrates its application with examples. Section 6 then subjects the three methods to a critical assessment with regard to contemporary research problems and policy relevance. The final section provides a summary of the positive findings.

2.   Weak and strong sustainable development and resource use

The three approaches described in this chapter are all based on the idea of strong as opposed to weak sustainable development. Whilst we accept that if a country is unable to pass a weak test for sustainable development then it is unlikely to pass a stronger test (Pearce and Atkinson, 1993; Atkinson et al, 1997; Neumayer, 2003) – the weak test is underpinned by very questionable and debatable assumptions of resource use (Beckerman, 1998; Daly and Cobb, 1989). These include the assumption of perfect substitutability between man-made (Km) and natural capital (Kn); setting the correct price for specific resource use which is often not included in the market and the role of technical change in areas where there may be no technical solutions. Weak sustainable development is generally based on neo-classically derived marginal analysis at the resource frontier rather than on absolute limits (Mirowski, 1990). Furthermore, it could be argued that the weak sustainability argument assumes that the ecology is subservient to economics. If, however, we are to assume that economics is a subset of ecology then we must consider strong sustainability.

Strong sustainability is based on several principles of classical science. These recognize the fact that we only have one earth and that for sustainable living we have to live within its absolute biophysical limits. From the principles of conservation of matter we cannot make matter but we can change its form. From the laws of thermodynamics we cannot get any more energy from a machine than we put into it. The earth ecosystems derive the bulk of their energy from solar radiation, and in open living systems energy consumption is hierarchically organized to maintain higher-level organisms in ecosystems. From ecology we cannot expect a receiving environment to exceed its assimilative capacity without increasing levels of pollution above a natural level. The proximity and precautionary principles are also included in strong sustainability arguments. The differences between the weak and strong perspectives are shown in Table 20.1.

Resources are a term of cultural appraisal (Kirk, 1963) and depend in part on a society's technology and on the political choices to use resources or leave them untouched as part of nature. The indigenous Aboriginal peoples of North Australia, for example, did not use metal as mining the earth was seen by some tribes as desecrating the land in which their God resides. They feared that such activity could result in divine retribution. During the Roman occupation of Britain (AD 120) coal, formed in the Carboniferous period about 350 million years ago, was used for making

Table 20.1   Fundamental differences between weak and strong sustainable development

Problem	Weak	Strong
Theoretical basis	Marginal economic analysis absolute scale is of little relevance	Matter and energy throughput in a finite, absolute space
Units of measurement	Monetary valuation including natural capital	Various units used but money downplayed
Prices	Provide crucial signals of relative scarcity in a perfect market	Imperfect market so prices unreliable, widespread externalities and control from multinational companies
Dynamics	Steady state equilibrium	Multiple steady states and thresholds
Future	Discounting and present values are central	Discounting discouraged focus on justice
Valuation	Utilitarian valuation	Rights based approach and energy valuation
Property	Private property supported by government to protect rights	Government and supra governmental organisation to protect diverse property rights
Individual behaviour	Maximizing social welfare	Restrictions on individuals' and organizations' behaviour to manage the scale of economic and environmental impacts
Nature Environment	Current generations pass on undiminished stock of aggregate capital	Current generations to safeguard stock of natural capital for the future
Technology	Major factor to permit growth over time	Unpredictable and increases risks to life support systems. Proximity and Precautionary principle
Business	Maximize profits	Triple bottom line
Justice	Pareto optimum solution	Social and environmental justice

jewellery. Later in the Industrial Revolution (circa 1790) the Carboniferous capitalists used coal to fuel industrial production (Rees, 1985). In this sense natural resources are neutral stuff which may become useful for different purposes (Zimmermann, 1951).

When examining sustainable development it is conventional to describe resources as a stock (that is a physical quantity) or as a flow (that is rate of use). It is also essential to note that the use of any resource leads to waste which, in the earth's closed and inter-related biogeochemical cycles, generally impacts on other ecological cycles. Most of the potentially living resources – the life support systems of the planet – depend on incoming radiation from the sun and matter from the earth. If we are to use potentially renewable resources in a sustainable manner then we must ensure that the rate of harvesting (or fishing or hunting) is much less than the natural rate of reproduction. Next, that the rate of pollution and waste generation is less than the natural assimilative capacity of the receiving environment. For strong sustainable development we need to ensure that the man-made capital resulting from the use of the non-renewable resources (for example minerals, fossil fuels) are set aside to fund renewable alternatives (Daly, 1990). We should also strive to minimize the damage to the environment which always accompanies resource use. The methods underpinning environmental space, material flows and ecological footprints assume that these ideas are well understood.

3.   Environmental space

Environmental space is defined as a share of the planet and its resources that the human race can sustainably take without depriving future generations of the resources they would need. The idea of environmental space was first put forward in 1994 (Opschoor and Weterings, 1994). It describes the quantity of energy, non-renewable (for example minerals) and potentially renewable resources (for example water, food, wood, farmland) that we can use in a sustainable fashion without exceeding environmental limits (McLaren et al., 1998, p. 6). It was argued that at the current rates of use non-renewable resources would have a short life, that the use of potentially renewable resources would result in overexploitation and that the assimilative capacity for waste would be exceeded unless reductions in resource use occur. The second major assumption underpinning environmental space is the idea of equity for current and future generations. This was, of course, noted in the Brundtland definition of sustainable development (WCED, 1987). In environmental space equity is defined as an equal per capita share of resources.

Environmental space was used in both national and European-wide studies. The original Netherlands study defines environmental space as estimating the global resource (such as wood energy, water, raw materials, arable land) and dividing it by the number of world citizens, to produce an average figure for each resource per capita for a given date. By comparing the global average per capita figure for a given resource with the total of that resource consumed in a particular country then the amount of environmental space consumed by a nation can be observed. The test for sustainable development using environmental space is 'the use of resources and pollution of that country can be compared to the environmental space belonging to that country' (Buitenkamp et al., 1991, p. 18). The calculation for environmental space is simple and is given in equations 20.1 and 20.2.

$$\text{Environmental Space } (ES)_{x,t} = (GR_{x,t}/GP_t) \qquad (20.1)$$

where: $ES_{x,t}$ = environmental space for resource x at time t
$GR_{x,t}$ = global resource (or assimilative capacity) of type x at time t
GP_t = global population at time t.

The amount of a resource and pollution generated by that nation is then compared to the actual amount (Q) of resource (or pollutant) of type x used (or released) in country i at time t:

$$\text{Environmental space for country } i\text{: } ES_{i,x,t} = Q_{i,x,t}/P_{i,t} \qquad (20.2)$$

where: $ES_{i,x,t}$ = environmental space for country i using resource x at time t
$Q_{i,x,t}$ = country i's use of resource x at time t
$P_{i,t}$ = population of the ith country at time t.

The environmental space for country i is the amount (Q) of consumption of resource x per capita. Then a country's consumption of one resource ($ES_{i,x,t}$) can be compared to the environmental space of global resource use ($ES_{x,t}$). The policy prescriptions which follow from the calculations of environmental space are based on a comparison of one nation's resource use of type x with the global average. Naively, if $ES_{i,x,t} > ES_{x,t}$ then policies should be implemented to reduce resource use of type x in country i. If $ES_{i,x,t} = ES_{x,t}$ then presumably no reductions are necessary. If $ES_{i,x,t} < ES_{x,t}$ do policy makers increase resource consumption in country i?

The environmental space concept was actively pursued by Friends of the Earth groups across Europe (Friends of the Earth, 1995a, 1995b). In a series of national reports the environmental space required for countries in a sustainable Europe as described (Buitenkamp et al., 1991; McLaren et al., 1998). By 1996 reports on sustainable Europe and some nations within Europe had been published (Tables 20.2 and 20.3). Generally, these studies argued that Europeans are consuming more than our fair earth share of environmental space and that we would have to undertake massive cuts in resource use by 2050. To achieve these large cuts a per capita reduction

Table 20.2   Summary of Environmental Space, actual consumption and targets for 2010 for the European Union

Resource	Present use per capita/year	Environmental Space per capita/year	Change needed (%)	Target 2010 per capita per year	Target 2010 (%)
CO₂ emissions[1]	7.3 t	1.7 t	77	5.4 t	26
Primary energy use	123 GJ	60 GJ	50	98 GJ	21
Fossil fuels	100 GJ	25 GJ	75	78 GJ	22
Nuclear	16 GJ	0 GJ	100	0 EJ	22
Renewables	7 GJ	35 GJ	+400	20 GJ	+74
Non-renewable raw materials[2]					
Cement	536 kg	80 kg	85	423 kg	21
Pig iron	273 kg	36 kg	87	213 kg	22
Aluminium	12 kg	1.2 kg	90	9.2 kg	23
Chlorine	23 kg	0 kg	100	17.2 kg	25
Land use (EU12)	0.726 ha	–	–	0.64 ha	12
Arable	0.237 ha	0.10 ha	58	0.15 ha	37
Pasture	0.167 ha	0.09 ha	47	0.113 ha	32
Net import of agricultural land	0.037 ha	0 ha	100	0.0185 ha	50
'Unused' agricultural area	0 ha	–	–	0.047 ha	–
Unprotected woodland	0.164 ha	0.138 ha	16	0.138 ha	16
Protected area	0.003 ha	0.061 ha	+1933	0.064 ha	+2000
Urban area	0.053 ha	0.0513 ha	3.2	0.0513 ha	3.2
Wood[3]	0.66 m³	0.56 m³	15	0.56 m³	15
Water[4]	768 m³	n/a	n/a	n/a	n/a

Notes:
1: Present use for Europe-NIS, Environmental Space and target for Europe;
2: Present use for EU12, Environmental Space and target for Europe;
3: EU + EFTA + CEE;
4: The Environmental Space of water cannot be calculated on a European level.

Source: Friends of the Earth (1995b, p. 14).

Table 20.3   *Estimates of the changes required to produce a sustainable Scotland and the United Kingdom*

Resource	Scotland			UK		
	1990	2010	%	1990	2010	%
CO_2	9.63	5.4	−44	10.1	5.4	−47
Water	165 m³	165 m³	0	243.1 m³	243.1 m³	0
Cement	257 kg	80 kg	−69	282 kg	177 kg	−37
Pig iron	85 kg	36 kg	−58	213 kg	163 kg	−24
Aluminium	5.27 kg	1.2 kg	−77	7.9 kg	6.2 kg	−22
Chlorine	16 kg	12 kg	−25	16 kg	12 kg	−25
Wood	0.22 ha/*cap*	0.2 ha/*cap*	−9	0.041 ha/*cap*	0.036 ha/*cap*	−12
Arable	0.13 ha/*cap*	0.24 ha/*cap*	+85	0.078 ha/*cap*	0.082 ha/*cap*	+5
Pasture	0.99 ha/*cap*	0.27 ha/*cap*	−73	0.12 ha/*cap*	0.007 ha/*cap*	−94
Built-up	0.045 ha/*cap*	0.045 ha/*cap*	0	0.031 ha/*cap*	0.051 ha/*cap*	+65
Nuclear	phase out	phase out		phase out	phase out	

Source: Friends of the Earth Scotland (1996) and Friends of the Earth England, Wales and Northern Ireland (1996).

target was established for each resource for 2010. Whilst such ideas are useful as a guide to policy they are only useful if the underlying basis for such proposed cuts is sound; alas, even in the important example of atmospheric carbon dioxide reductions, this was not the case (see section 6).

It will be observed that in both the European-wide and national studies most of the resources have to be drastically reduced. In one sense this research effort by numerous groups was to be welcomed as a bold statement of the degree of unsustainability different European countries exhibited. The original Netherlands study was set up to encourage debate over sustainable development. This debate must not, however, ignore the technical details in the methods used. It is wrong to assume that these technical details 'should in no case to be allowed to delay the debate on the consequences of the concept of limited and finite environmental space for daily life in society' (Buitenkamp et al., 1991, p. 181). This is methodologically unacceptable because if the method is wrong then the policy prescriptions offered would carry very little or no conviction. Quite simply if you divide the resource consumption by the global population you obtain 'environmental space per capita' for a given time. As the global population grows, the 'environmental space per capita' share is reduced and, on this basis, it could be argued that countries need to control global population growth as well as reduce resource consumption. We will return to criticisms of the environmental space method in section 6. Finally, whilst the idea of environmental space was poorly conceived, it did point the way to more rigorous methods such as material flow analysis and ecological footprinting.

4. Material flow analysis

The purpose of material flow analysis is to track and quantify the flow of materials including energy in a defined area over a set time period. It is obvious that any economy takes in raw materials from the environment including imports from foreign nations, for further processing, manufacturing, production and consumption (Linstead and Ekins, 2001). Some materials such as the construction of buildings and infrastructure add to the stock of man-made capital. Eventually, the products become waste and may be recycled, but finally have to be disposed via landfill or incineration. Since any resource input sooner or later becomes an output, it is possible to account for resource flows and use them in material balance modelling (Figure 20.1).

The mass balance equations used in material flow analysis (MFA) can be written as follows:

$$MF_i = A_i + B_i - C_i + / - D_i \qquad (20.3)$$

where: MF_i = the material flow analysis for country i
$\quad\quad\ A_i$ = resource flows into area i (material imports + product imports + water consumption)
$\quad\quad\ B_i$ = material production in area i
$\quad\quad\ C_i$ = resource flows from area i (material exports + product exports + waste production + waste water + water output)
$\quad\quad\ D_i$ = the change to the stock in area i.

Obviously, collecting all the relevant data for each of items A, B, C and D is a difficult and time-consuming task. Fortunately, the Statistical Office of the European Communities has developed national economy-wide material flow accounts (Eurostat, 2001). These accounts exclude water and air but include energy flows through the national economy. Several studies have been undertaken at the national scale to give an empirical account of resource use (Linstead et al., 2004). In the United Kingdom, for example, a material flow analysis using resource use in agriculture, forestry and fishing together with mining of minerals, fossil fuels and other aggregates was undertaken in 2002. The calculation also includes 'hidden' flows of materials such as mining wastes which are moved during extraction but are not used directly in the economy. In the UK for the period 1970–2000 it was shown that the total resource use rose during the 1970s as oil and gas production from the North Sea reserves started to flow, but eased off during the early 1980s. Generally, there has been an increase in material flows, in line with economic growth, in the latter part of the 1980s, but from 1990 onwards resource use has stabilized despite a considerable increase in the size of the UK economy (Sheerin, 2002). From 1990–2001 GDP in the UK

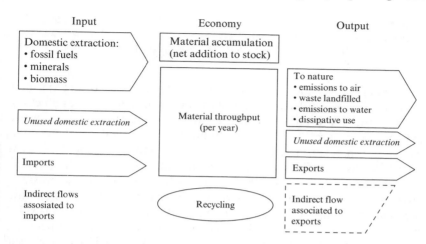

Notes: TMR = domestic extraction (fossil fuels, minerals, biomass) + unused domestic extraction + imports + indirect flows associated with imports; DMI = domestic extraction (fossil fuels, minerals, biomass) + imports; DMC = DMI minus exports.

Source: Eurostat (2001).

Figure 20.1   A material balance model

has increased by 28 per cent yet the Total Material Requirement (TMR) increased by 7 per cent, the Direct Material Input (DMI) remained constant and the Direct Material Consumption (DMC) fell by 10 per cent (DEFRA, 2003).

Material flow accounting can also be used at sub-national scales at either the level of individual business enterprises, or at specific sectors of the economy such as mineral resource use in North-West England (NCBS, undated) or at the city and regional scales (Ravetz, 2000). In 2002 a study of material flow analysis and ecological footprint (see later) in York was published (Barrett et al., 2002). Although the researchers acknowledge that both the fossil fuel carriers and hidden flows (such as the overburden left at the site where minerals are mined) may have been underestimated (30 per cent and 35 per cent less than the UK average respectively) they give a good account of the material flow in the urban economy. In 2000 the total material requirement of York was 3 387 000 tonnes; an average of 18.8 tonnes per person for each York resident.

Just under half of this was material that entered the city, the rest being either energy carriers (579 000 tonnes) or hidden flows (1 231 000 tonnes). The majority of the material flows into York are due to the construction of houses and roads (approximately 67 per cent). The stock of materials in York increased by over 1 million tonnes. On the output side, over 250 000 tonnes of materials left York or were deposited in landfill sites and nearly 70 000 tonnes were recycled. Over 4.5 million tonnes of greenhouse gases were produced (Barrett et al., 2002, p. xiv).

An imaginative study of South-East England has used material flow analysis to explore different scenarios of development and waste reduction. In 2000 the South-East region generated 36.8 million tonnes of waste (53 per cent construction and demolition, 19 per cent industrial and commercial, 16 per cent agricultural, 11 per cent household and 1 per cent other). Whilst the different sectors do use the waste hierarchy (recycle, recover and reuse some of the resources) it is estimated that waste is growing at 1–3 per cent per year and could double in 25 years. This growing problem was examined by a material flow analysis combined with an exploration of four different scenarios. The four scenarios of waste generation were: a high growth of 3 per cent per year; a Business as Usual 2 per cent per year, a zero growth and a 'factor four' rapid minimization scenario beginning with 3 per cent growth and tapering to −3 per cent, giving a net decline in waste of −14 per cent by 2020.

Unsurprisingly, the waste minimization scenario results in less waste but implementing such a strategy is a major task especially as economic and demographic growth is forecast for the South-East region of the UK (Anon, undated).

One of the policy drivers in material flow analysis is the idea of 'Factor Four' reductions in resource use to half resource use and double output (Ayres, 1978; Weizsacker et al., 1997). The scientific basis for this factor X (where X is any positive real number) argument is very suspect (Robert et al., 2000). It will be noted that Figure 20.2 simply shows a hypothetical monotonically declining function for resource use. Obviously, if you increase non-renewable resource consumption by any amount then the quantity of resources will decline. In a series of papers Schmidt-Bleek asserts, without any proof, that we need to make a 50 per cent cut in materials inputs advanced economies (or more if population growth is taken into account) (Schmidt-Bleek, 1992; 1993a; 1993b). It is this assertion, coupled with the view that technical solutions to resource efficiencies can be implemented, that colour the thinking in this area of material flow analysis. As a policy instrument this untested idea has had some support in the advanced industrial nations. Whilst it is good to see innovative ideas being produced to address the problems of unsustainable consumption of commodity production we must, however, temper this enthusiasm for every new idea with careful criticisms (see section 6 below).

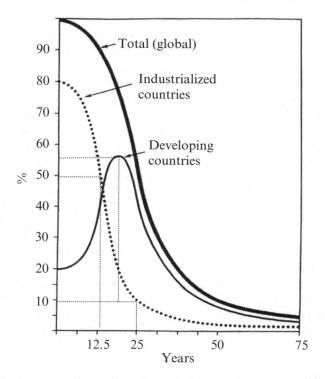

Figure 20.2 A hypothetical decline in material flows

5. Ecological footprint

The ecological footprint concept has captured the imagination of academics, decision-makers and the public because it can be measured, is easy to understand and it has a resonance with different scientists, policy makers and other members of the public. There is a large and rapidly growing literature concerned with ecological footprinting. It has been the focus of academic scrutiny (Ayres, 2000; Haberl et al., 2004); the basis for many empirical studies as an indicator of strong sustainability (Wackernagel and Rees, 1994) and is being examined by both governments in Europe and businesses as a sustainability indicator (Chambers and Lewis, 2001). The question for academics and policy makers is not just whether the footprint is attractive but whether it is internally consistent and whether it helps as an input into policies which are designed to make development sustainable in the early years of this century.

The ecological footprint concept can be defined as the total area required to indefinitely sustain a given population at the current standard of living and at an average per capita consumption rate. The original idea of ecological footrpinting was proposed by Rees in a study of cities which consume vast amounts of resources (Rees, 1992). In 1994 this concept was developed and illustrated from work in Canada (Wackernagel and Rees, 1994). Over the last ten years the early methodology of ecological footprinting has been substantially altered partly in response to well intentioned criticisms (see *Ecological Economics*, 2000, Vol. 32). Essentially it is a measure of land per person – not a density – but an expression of how much of the earth's surface is required to support an average person in a specific area. More precisely, ecological footprint accounts measure the amount of the earth's biological productivity that a human population – global population, a country, a city or an individual – occupies in a given year using prevailing technology no matter where that land is located. This methodology has now been established by setting up a global forum so that standard methods can be used in substantive studies. The National Footprint Accounts (NFA) constitute the underlying methodology with which ecological footprints have been calculated for 149 countries of the world (WWF, 2004). A detailed description of the NFA methodology has been presented in 2004 (Monfreda et al., 2004) and also from the Global Footprint Network (Wackernagel et al., 2004a). The unit of measurement is the biologically productive area, termed the global hectare (gha), which represents an equal amount of biological productivity. The gha is normalized so that the number of actual hectares of bioproductive land and sea on the earth is equal to the number of global hectares on this planet. To calculate the biocapacity of a nation, each of six different types of bioproductive areas within a nation are multiplied by both an equivalence and yield factor for that land type. The six bioproductive areas are:

- Crop land for food and animal feed, fibre oil crops and rubber;
- Grazing land for animals for meat, hides, wool and milk;
- Forest area for harvesting timber or wood fibre for paper;
- Fishing grounds for catching fish;
- Built-up areas for accommodating infrastructure for housing, transport and industrial production;
- Land for sequestering the excess CO_2 from burning fossil fuels to replace it with biomass, for harvesting fuelwood, for nuclear energy and for hydropower (Wackernagel et al., 1999).

The hectares for each type of bioproductive area are converted into global hectares (gha) by multiplying an equivalence factor (to represent the world's average potential productivity of a given bioproductive area or land cover type) with yield factors (to capture the difference among local and global average productivity). The biocapacity for an area constitutes the supply side of the equation and the aggregate human demand (ecological footprint) can then be compared. Whilst an individual nation's area demand can exceed supply it is obvious that to live ecologically sustainably on the earth we must live within the earth's biocapacity. If we exceed this limit then we do so by depletion of natural capital (Kn). An individual nation can also exceed its biocapacity by depletion of Kn and by imports (ecological trade deficit). Obviously all nations cannot continue to live in ecological deficit and be ecologically sustainable.

Essentially the ecological footprint 'master equations' for ecological footprinting can be written as a supply and demand identity .The supply is given as:

$$\text{Biocapacity (gha)} = \Sigma[A(\text{ha}) \times EQV(\text{gha/ha}) \times Y] \qquad (20.4)$$

where: A = area in hectares
       EQV = equivalence factor
       Y = yield.

The demand can be given as:

$$EF_{i,x,t} = \Sigma[A_{i,x,t} \times EQV_{i,x,t} \times ((Ps_{i,x,t} + I_{i,x,t} - E_{i,x,t})/Y_{x,t})] \qquad (20.5)$$

where: A_i = area of land cover x in country i at time t
    $EF_{i,x,t}$ = ecological footprint for country i using resource x at time t in gha
    $EQV_{i,x,t}$ = equivalence factor for country i using resource x at time t
P_i, I_i and E_i = production, imports and exports of country i of resource x at time t
     $Y_{x,t}$ = global yield of resource x at time t.

The right-hand side of equation (20.4) is the summation of each area in hectares multiplied by the equivalence factor multiplied by the yield for each land cover class. Equation (20.5) represents the ecological footprint or demand side of the identity. Again in a general form the area given to a land cover type is multiplied by the equivalence factor divided by yield per ha and then summed for all six bioproductive areas. The equivalence factor represents the world average potential productivity of a given bioproductive area relative to the world average potential productivity of all bioproductive areas (Wackernagel et al., 2004b, p. 262; For full details of the method see Wackernagel et al, 2004a).

Once the ecological footprint is calculated by summing all the resources used in a country or area it can be compared to the demand with the actual country or area also expressed in global hectares. Three policy prescriptions follow from an ecological footprint analysis. First, if a country's footprint is greater than its area measured in global hectares then some reductions in resource consumption are required. If the ecological footprint demand is equal to or less than the supply, then one condition for ecological sustainability is being met and presumably the socio-economic practices are within the ecological footprint and are therefore contributing to sustainable development.

Currently, ecological footprints can be calculated using an aggregate or compound approach or alternatively a component approach using an index. The compound approach uses national data to determine the average person annual consumption (national data /total size of population) whilst the component approach builds up the economy by different sectors using an index (Simmons et al., 2000) and can be more useful for a range of policies. These two approaches are complementary and have been used in many studies (Wackernagel and Rees, 1994; Chambers et al., 2000; Haberl et al., 2004). Studies have been undertaken including global scale with the Living Planet Index (Loh, 2002; WWF, 2004; Wackernagel et al., 2002). National studies of the economy of Australia (Lentzen and Murray, 2001), Austria (Haberl et al., 2004), UK (Barrett and Simmons, 2003) Canada, Chile, Italy, the Philippines and South Korea (Wackernagel et al., 2004b), Scotland (Best Foot Forward, 2004) and Wales (Best Foot Forward, 2002b; WWF, 2005a) as well as Benin, Bhutan, Costa Ricas and the Netherlands (van Vuuren and Smeets, 2000) have been completed. Urban studies including London (Best Foot Forward, 2002a), Liverpool (Barrett and Scott, 2001), as well as regional studies of Guernsey (Barrett, 1998), Isle of Wight (Best Foot Forward, 2000c), the South-East England (Anon., undated) and Tuscany (WWF, Italia, 2004) have been published. The redesigned ecological footprints methodology now consists of a 2000 rows by 100 columns spreadsheet for each country. The integration of ecological footprinting accounting into standard economic models allows systematic evaluation of policy options as extensive scenario analysis becomes possible. It opens up possible links with UN National Statistical accounting which offers a consistent time series from 1970 for all UN member states and all other countries in the world. The relevant data can be found at (http://unstats.un.org/unsd/snaama/Introduction.asp). This permits the integration of ecological footprinting with input–output analysis to allocate ecological footprints and material flows to final consumption (Wiedmann et al., 2005; Moffatt et al., 2005). It also opens up the prospect of integrating input–output and dynamic modelling to explore future scenarios at different geographical and hierarchical scales (Moffatt et al., 2001; Kratena, 2004; Faucheux and O'Connor, 1998; and Faucheux et al., 1999).

The original ecological footprint was a one-shot or static review but it is important to explore scenarios of different development paths in a dynamic context. This approach has been used in the study of North America using the ecological footprint scenario model (EFSM). The researchers note that if North Americans want to maintain their lifestyles and their corresponding levels of consumption while avoiding ecological deficits, then the productive capacity of all ecosystems would have to at least double and be coupled with a reduction in economic growth or its accompanying spending (Senbel et al., 2003, p. 90). The summary results from their work indicate that reducing consumption has the most significant impact on the ecological footprint. Without such changes in reduced consumption and increased resource productivity, then 'North Americans will increasingly live in a continent of ecological deficits' (Senbel et al., 2003, p. 92). Given that natural and agricultural ecosystems can not continue to double their productivity, the future looks dismal. A second study using the IMAGES model to examine responses to global warming has indicated that the global ecological footprint will not exceed 15 billion gha in 2050. This scenario assumes that there are changes to production and reduced consumption in the rich nations and economic growth in low-income areas even with population growth (van Vuuren and Bouwman, 2005). Unfortunately, the planet has only 11.3 billion gha, which means that even if this scenario is followed we are still overshooting the ecological limit by approximately 33 per cent (WWF, 2005a). The message from these recent ecological footprint studies is clear: we must reduce resource consumption if we are to live within the ecological limits of this earth.

6. A constructive critique of the methods

The three methods described in this chapter are being developed by a variety of individuals and groups and are being promoted as contributions to measuring sustainable development. This is an important aspect of research, as measurement can help avoid self-deception and can contribute to policy. Indeed the UK sustainable development strategy notes the need for innovative ways to measure sustainable development as well as for ways of contributing to policy initiatives (Cm 6467, 2005). Ideally, these methods should be applicable at different spatial scales and through different organizations, for example Governmental, businesses and local communities so that we can all contribute to the process of making development sustainable. Given the importance of the issues we are involved in, such as maintaining the life support systems and improving the quality of life for all inhabitants on the planet, it is essential that we develop robust methods. This section offers some constructive criticisms of each of the methods and then some more general comments on how we can make progress in this area of research.

Environmental space

There are numerous criticisms that can be made of the environmental space concept (Moffatt, 1996b). First, from a scientific perspective it is difficult to know with any precision the amount of non-renewable resources available at current technologies and prices. Next, it is generally agreed that human economic activity is putting strains on many environmental systems. It would therefore seem sensible to reduce resource consumption but Friends of the Earth Europe have relied on a weak argument for environmental space to propose draconian reductions in resource use. Third, environmental space assumed greater certainty about waste assimilation processes than is currently scientifically known. It is exceedingly difficult to establish such limits in an accurate manner. The major exception is the atmospheric assimilation of carbon dioxide (CO_2). In this case it can be shown scientifically that anthropogenic emissions to the stock of atmospheric CO_2 have grown from 276 ppmv in 1790 to over 360 ppmv by 2000 (Gorshkov, 1995). Yet, applying the environmental space concept to this major problem yields misleading results and, if accepted, could give rise to misguided policies. In 2000, for example, some environmentalists suggested that

> assuming a global target of 11.1 gigatonnes CO_2 emissions is required to maintain global stability by 2050, and assuming the global population in 2050 is 9.8 billion, the per capita 'environmental space' for energy is 1.1 tonnes per year. UK per capita production of CO_2 is in the region of 9 tonnes, thus implying a reduction in UK emissions by about 85%'. (Chambers et al., 2000, p. 21)

Fourth, statistically environmental space is simply an average number, but no standard deviations around the mean are given. Obviously if you divide a finite resource by a large (and growing) number of people then year on year the 'fair share per capita' becomes smaller. Hence, the policy to reduce resource use in one country simply because the global population has grown is naive and best ignored. Fifth, the idea of a fair share of environmental space is ethically naive as it confuses inequality with inequity (Le Grand, 1991, p. 11) this vitally important issue will be discussed below. So what should be done?

With regard to the serious problem of humanly induced global climate change the scientific community would like a reduction of 60 per cent put in place by 2050 (IPCC, 1992). The reductions are based on good science and accurate measurements and not on the poor methodology underpinning environmental space. The good science refers to identifying the correct causal processes such as burning fossil fuels and land use change as part of the feedback loops which contribute substantially to the complex processes known as global climate change (Moffatt, 1991; Moffatt, 2004). The accurate measurement of atmospheric CO_2 concentrations establishes a time series of data from the pre-industrial to today. Given the processes and the measurements, then it is possible to calculate the reductions in CO_2 required by each country (Moffatt, 2004; Owen and Hanley, 2004). In the case of the UK, and using the figure presented by Friends of the Earth (McLaren et al., 1998), a 60 per cent reduction would mean a reduction from its current 9 tonnes to 3.6 tonnes per capita by 2050 and not the 1.1 tonnes per capita required from environmental space arguments. It could be argued that larger reductions should be preferred on the basis of inter-national equity. So how would such reductions come about? There are at least two strategies: the first is to reduce emissions by some international agreement and the second is not to produce them in the first place! The Kyoto agreement, signed by 141 nations in 2005, has started the process of CO_2 reductions. It could be argued that the Kyoto reductions are a small step in the right direction, but from a scientific perspective they are, in themselves, insufficient to prevent a further global warming phenomenon. The reductions proposed at the Kyoto meetings are a first step towards 60 per cent reductions. In the political arena the ideals of CO_2 reductions have not gone far enough. Obviously, given the small nature of the proposed reductions at Kyoto, there is much more to do politically and diplomati-cally to get all nations (especially the USA) to agree to the proposals.

The second approach to reduce greenhouse gas emissions is to introduce new technologies and refine older ones. The new technologies would include hydrogen power, and more efficient electrically driven engines. The energy for the latter would come from the use of older technologies – the so-called alternative technologies of waves, wind and solar power. The use of these potentially renewable resources could maintain the quality of life and improve conditions for many of the poorer nations without causing further damage to the earth's life support systems. These developments would need to be encouraged both by changes to the macroeconomics of the global economy and by ensuring, if necessary by international law, that large companies do not prevent these developments.

Material flow analysis

We can all agree that reductions in resource use are a good thing so that environmental waste is all but eliminated (Jacobs, 1991). It is, however, difficult to ensure that if resource productivity is raised, this will be enough to offset extra demands on the environment arising from economic and population growth. Pearce has conducted a 'thought experiment' to show that resource productivity would have to increase by 1.8 per cent per annum to offset the potential rising environmental impact from economic and demographic growth, 1975–1998. If past trends in resource productivity occur, rather than Factor Four or greater resource efficiencies, then the world 'will be worse off environmentally in 50 years' time' (Pearce, 2001, p. 12). Recent research has also reported on a rebound effect in resource efficiencies. The rebound effect occurs when an improvement in energy or material use is offset by an increase in the number of units consumed (for example video recorders, washing machines, new cars) (DEFRA, 2003). Even if a nation apparently achieves some resource efficiencies one must, however, be very wary of assuming such elimination has been accomplished by increases in efficiency in resource use (that is dematerialization), and by restructuring (that is decoupling) the economy.

It is acknowledged that business has caused major ecological damage and that this cannot continue if we are to safeguard the environment for current and future generations as well as for other life forms. In the UK, for example, indices of TMR alongside GDP and population all increased between 1970–1999. While GDP grew by a large amount there was only a relatively modest increase in material flows through the economy. Some might argue that these results show an increase in resource productivity (dematerialization) and a de-coupling of the economy from resource requirements (DEFRA, 2002). Similarly, in the OECD nations the energy intensity (the amount of energy used to generate 1 unit of GDP) has fallen, but the total energy consumption has increased by over 30 per cent in 20 years. This would indicate that resource efficiencies are taking place. The argument over dematerialization of the economy of the OECD countries needs to be set in context. Relative dematerialization has occurred in certain sectors of the OECD economies. Yet to a significant degree this has been brought about 'by the net transfer of energy and resource intensive industries to the developing world, in effect displacing rather than solving the environmental problems of production' (Robins and Trisoglio, 1995, p. 164).

Apart from the debatable scientific basis for Factor X reductions, material flow accounting does permit detailed analysis of resource use and pollution generation at different geographical scales and over time. Obviously, when using MFA there is a need to be clear about whether or not the reductions proposed are an important contribution to reducing our ecological footprint or, alternatively, they are simply applied as fine tuning to reductions in the emissions of waste to the receiving environment. Currently, MFA is used in both contexts. The MFA approach has its limitations and its merits. The major limitation in MFA is that the materials flowing from the 'cradle to the grave' are simply measured as a mass. The impact of one tonne of arsenic on a receiving environment such as a river system would be more lethal than one tonne of sewage. Yet the differential impacts of the resource flows into the receiving environment are rarely stated – simply adding up the total mass moved is insufficient from an ecological perspective. Clearly, the determination of MFA in an economy is a good first step towards monitoring the links between the economy and ecology. It should, however, be noted that a blanket reduction in MFA is 'not guaranteed to be ecologically effective, but is guaranteed to be highly economically ineffective with respect to whatever reduction in environmental damage that might be achieved' (Neumayer, 2003, p. 181). Neumayer also doubts that MFA can be used as a strong sustainability measure. Others, however, see MFA as one way to demonstrate the ways in which increases in efficiency as well as reductions in material and energy flows (sufficiency) can be modelled (Barrett et al., 2002). Furthermore, MFA does allow decision-makers to examine scenarios to assist in choosing the best options to encourage reductions in both resource consumption and waste generation and to consider the appropriate technical changes as a contribution to sustainable development.

Ecological footprinting
As the ecological footprint concept evolved it has been subjected to many criticisms (Ecological Economics, 2000). First, the unit of measure 'global hectares' has been criticised as too crude an indicator for detailed policy proposals. Initially this was true, but recent developments have integrated footprints with more conventional national accounts. Next, the idea of trade flows being difficult to account in ecological footprinting has been raised, but this has also been partially answered by integrating ecological footprinting with material flows and input–output analyses (Moffatt et al., 2005; Wiedmann and Barret; 2005; Wiedmann et al., 2005). Clearly, it is physically impossible for every country to be a net importer of biocapacity as this will lead to global overshoot of resource use (Wackernagel et al., 2002). It should, however, be noted that the ecological footprint does not address all environmental issues involved with pollution and species loss. It should also be realized that the earth-share of ecological footprinting is open to the same criticism of environmental space. To argue for a fair earth share by simply dividing the amount of land expressed as global hectares (gha) by the total global population is meaningless as it again confuses equity with equality (Le Grand, 1991). If, however, emphasis is placed on absolute limits and not per capita ratios then the footprint can still be a useful indicator of environmental sustainability. As noted in the previous section we cannot live beyond the 11.3 gha of this planet. We need therefore to encourage each nation to reduce conspicuous consumption, control population growth and introduce ecologically friendly technology. It should, however, be noted that the variations in the ecological footprint in different countries may be due to socio-economic rather than ecological processes (Kooten and Bulte, 2000).

There is, however, a partial solution to the problem of living ecologically sustainably on the earth. Numerous ecological footprinting studies have shown that waste, food and energy make up a large portion of the footprint. In the case of Scotland, for example, these three components make up 38 per cent, 29 per cent and 18 per cent respectively (Best Foot Forward, 2004). Clearly, these are sensitive parameters in the ecological footprinting methodology and each one could be reduced. In the case of energy, ignoring the nuclear option as too high a risk and potentially very damaging, then the use of renewable resources for energy production can be an effective way of reducing the footprint. Assuming that we move to renewable energy sources we could, in theory, have reduced the size of the ecological footprint of anthropogenic CO_2 emissions by over 50 per cent for the period 1961–99. This was technically and practically possible but would have to overcome the vested interests of the powerful energy lobby. It would also require some alterations to macroeconomic policy to encourage both the development and market for renewable energy sources. Nevertheless, this simple example illustrates that if energy were obtained from non-carbon resources then the ecological footprint would drop automatically and substantially (Ayres, 2000). Similarly, if waste could be substantially reduced then this would also have a major impact on reducing the size of the footprint. If policies were pursued to increase renewable energy supplies and reduce waste substantially then this would substantially reduce the ecological footprint well below the biocapacity limit.

If the global adoption of alternative energy has the potential of reducing the ecological footprint to well below the biocapacity limits, does this then mean we are living sustainably? Clearly the answer to this question is a qualified 'yes'. If policies are implemented to promote reductions to zero in nuclear and fossil fuel energy over, say, ten years, and simultaneously increase the input from renewable energy sources to meet demand, then we have the *necessary* conditions for sustainable living. In order to attain the *necessary* and *sufficient* conditions for sustainable development we need also to address other environmental problems (such as different pollutants and biodiversity loss) as well as economic and social justice issues. This inevitably raises ideological and ethical problems concerning contemporary globalization with its use and abuse of the earth's environment and its inhabitants. Harvey suggests that a globalized world is one of 'class oppression, state domination, unnecessary material deprivation, war and human denial and that we should strive to create our environments in a state of liberty and mutual respect of opposed interests' (Harvey, 2001, p. 120). He suggests that we need to adopt a holistic, dialectical approach to understanding the dynamics of the current trajectory that we are locked into in order to break free from the present situation. Alternatively, those in favour of natural capitalism argue that, 'natural capitalism is not about fomenting social upheaval. On the contrary that is the consequence that will surely arise if fundamental social and environmental problems are not addressed' (Hawken et al., 1999, p. 322). Clearly, there are ideological differences underpinning these diametrically opposed perspectives. The current generations have a difficult choice because making the wrong decisions can result in universal misery and the collapse of civilizations (Diamond, 2005). Closely associated with this vital issue is the related question of a just distribution of resources. We have suggested that the fair share approach (equal resources per capita) confuses equality with equity. This is an important normative issue with major environmental, economic and social policy implications. It should, however, be noted that, 'Policies should be equitable and that distributional consequences of policies should, so far as possible, be just or fair. These are considerations that policy makers ignore at their peril' (Le Grand, 1991, p. 175). Policy making should be transparent, accountable, just and based on sound methodologies. It is the integration of multi-disciplinary research into ecological, economic and equity issues that poses the fundamental methodological challenge for making development sustainable.

7. Conclusions

Environmental space, material flow analysis and ecological footprinting are discussed in the literature on sustainability and sustainable development. From its inception environmental space was based on some very suspect scientific premises. We do not know the amount of non-renewable resources remaining in the earth's crust nor, with the exception of atmospheric CO_2, do we know the global assimilative capacity of the earth's receiving environments. In order to contribute to sustainable development Friends of the Earth proposed the use of environmental space as a blunt policy tool. This method is very suspect and has resulted in the environmental space concept being ignored by both the scientific community and most policy makers.

Material flow analysis is based on sound concepts of the conservation of matter and the laws of thermodynamics. This sophisticated form of analysis allows researchers and others to explore different ways in which materials and energy flow through a system. The systems under investigation can be at different geographical scales including natural and man-made ecosystems such as factories and businesses, cities, regional and national economies, and globally. Ideally it would be interesting to tie these models of material flow analysis with similar models of ecosystems but this has rarely happened (Odum and Odum, 1976). The problem of using material balances (MFA) and conventional neo-classical economics still remains. Nevertheless, the development of material flow analysis including the use of scenarios has the potential to contribute to action leading to sustainable development at different geographical scales.

The ecological footprint concept has developed a large and rapidly growing amount of literature. As noted earlier this methodology has now been standardized and this also has been applied at different spatial scales. It has also been argued that by committing to alternative energy supplies it is possible to reduce the ecological footprint substantially. Furthermore, recent work on integrating ecological footprinting with material flow analysis and input–output analysis shows that the allocation of resource use sector by sector can be achieved. Despite this progress it should be noted that the problem of linking masses with monetary measures still remains – although some attempts to bridge this gap are being made but a firmer theoretical basis for combining mass and monetary measures is required. At present the integration of MFA with ecological footprinting via input–output analysis is a step along the way to a more formal solution to this ecological–economic problem. Current work permits the examination of scenarios and allows policies to be targeted at different sectors of the economy as a contribution to do more with less. It would also assist in sustainable consumption.

If we are to live within the ecological possible, as proponents of strong sustainable development urge, then it can be seen that many nations are currently living well beyond what the world's ecosystems can withstand. At a global level, we are exhausting the earth's renewable and non-renewable resources on the untenable assumption that current economic and demographic growth and resource consumption processes, together with waste generation, can continue indefinitely on a planet of finite size. The measures described in this chapter are beginning to address these problems. This raises issues over the radical restructuring to our economic system so that individuals and their organizations can begin to live as part of the ecology of the planet rather than trying in a futile manner to live apart from it. These changes are not impossible to achieve, and there are signs of hope as outlined in the UK Government Sustainable Development Strategy (Cm 6467, 2005). The challenge is up to the political will and determination of our elected leaders to encourage business and individuals to behave as *citizens* rather than consumers (Dobson, 2003). In this sense, individuals, as citizens of a global community, can contribute to the creation of an ecologically sound and socially just economy and it is through the collective political processes that sustainable development will be achieved.

References

Anon (undated), 'Taking stock managing our impact an ecological footprint of the South East Region', www.takingstock.org, accessed 25 February 2005.
Atkinson, G., R. Dubourg, K. Hamilton, M. Munasinghe, D. Pearce and C. Young (1997), *Measuring Sustainable Development: Macroeconomics and the Environment*, Cheltenham, UK and Northampton, MA, USA: Edward Elgar.

Ayres, R.U. (1978), *Resources, Environment and Economics: Applications of the Materials/Energy Balance Principle*, New York: Wiley.

Ayres, R.U. (2000), 'Commentary on the utility of the ecological footprint concept', *Ecological Economics*, **32**: 347–9 (special issue on ecological footprinting).

Barrett, J. (1998), *Sustainability Indicators and Ecological Footprints: The case of Guernsey School of Built Environment*, Liverpool: Liverpool John Moores University.

Barrett, J. and A. Scott (2001), 'An ecological footprint of Liverpool: developing sustainable scenarios', Sweden: Stockholm Environment Institute.

Barrett, J. and C. Simmons (2003), 'An ecological footprint of the UK: Providing a tool to measure the sustainability of local authorities', York: Stockholm Environment Institute, University of York.

Barrett, J., H. Vallack, A. Jones and G. Haq (2002), 'A material flow analysis and ecological footprint of York: technical report', Sweden: Stockholm Environment Institute.

Beckermann, W. (1998), 'Sustainable Development: Is it a useful concept?', *Environmental Values*, **3**: 191–209.

Best Foot Forward (2002a), 'City limits: a resource and ecological footprint analysis of Greater London', Oxford: Best Foot Forward.

Best Foot Forward (2002b), 'Ol-troed Cymru: the footprint of Wales', Oxford: Best Foot Forward.

Best Foot Forward (2004), 'Scotland's footprint a resource flow and ecological analysis of Scotland', Oxford: Best Foot Forward.

Best Foot Forward and Imperial College London (2000c), 'Island state an ecological footprint analysis of the Isle of Wight', Oxford: Best Foot Forward.

Buitenkamp, M., H. Verner and T. Wams (eds) (1991), 'Action plan: sustainable Netherlands', Netherlands: Friends of the Earth.

Chambers, N. and K. Lewis (2001), *Ecological Footprint Analysis: Towards a Sustainability Indicator for Business*, Certified Accountants Educational Trust, Research Report No. 65, London.

Chambers, N., C. Simmons and M. Wackernagel (2000), *Sharing Nature's Interest*, London: Earthscan.

Christensen, V. (1995), 'A model of the trophic interactions in the North Sea in 1981, the year of the stomach', *Dana*, **11**(1): 1–28.

Clark, C.W. (1976), *Mathematical Bioeconomics: the Optimal Management of Renewable Resources*, London: Wiley.

Cm 6467 (2005), 'The UK Government sustainable development strategy', London: HM Government.

Daly, H.E. (1972), *Steady State Economics: The Economics of Biophysical and Moral Growth*, San Francisco: W.H. Freeman.

Daly, H.E. (1990), 'Towards some operational principles for sustainable development', *Ecological Economics*, **2**(1): 1–6.

Daly, H.E. and J.B. Cobb (1989), 'On Wilfred Beckerman's critique of sustainable development', *Environmental Values*, **4**(1): 49–55.

DEFRA (2002), 'Changing patterns: UK Government framework for sustainable consumption and production', London: Department of Environment Food and Rural Affairs.

DEFRA (2003), 'Sustainable consumption and production indicators: Joint DEFRA/DTI consultation paper on a set of "decoupling" indicators of sustainable development', London: Department of Environment Food and Rural Affairs.

Diamond, J. (2005), *Collapse: how Societies Choose to Fail or Survive*, London: Allen Lane.

Dobson, A. (2003), *Environmental Citizenship*, Oxford: Oxford University Press.

Ecological Economics (2000), 'Commentary forum: the ecological footprint', *Ecological Economics*, **32**(3): 341–94.

Eurostat (2001), 'Economy-wide material flow accounts and derived indicators', Luxembourg: Eurostat.

Faucheux, S. and M. O'Connor (eds) (1998), *Valuation for Sustainable Development*, Cheltenham, UK and Northampton, MA, USA: Edward Elgar.

Faucheux, S., D. Pearce and J. Proops (1999), *Models of Sustainable Development*, Cheltenham, UK and Northampton, MA, USA: Edward Elgar.

Friends of the Earth (FoE) (1995a), *Towards Sustainable Europe: The Study*, Brussels: Friends of the Earth.

Friends of the Earth (FoE) (1995b), *Towards Sustainable Europe: A Summary*, Brussels: Friends of the Earth.

Friends of the Earth Scotland (1996), *Towards a Sustainable Scotland*, Scotland: Friends of the Earth.

Friends of the Earth England, Wales and Northern Ireland (1996), 'Draft report on sustainable UK', London: Friends of the Earth.

Gorshkov, V.G. (1995), *Physical and Biological Bases of Life Stability*, Berlin: Verlag.

Haberl, H., M. Wackernagel and T. Wrbka (2004), 'Land use and sustainability indicators', *Land Use and Policy*, **21**(3): 194–320, (Guest Co-editor Ian Moffatt).

Harvey, D. (2001), *Spaces of Capital Towards a Critical Geography*, Edinburgh: Edinburgh University Press.

Hawken, P., A.B. Lovin and L.H. Loven (1999), *Natural Capital: the next Industrial Revolution*, London: Earthscan.

IPCC (Intergovernmental Panel on Climate Change) (1990), *Climate Change – The IPCC Scientific Assessment World Meteorological Organisation and the United Nations Environmental Program*, Cambridge: Cambridge University Press.

IPCC (Intergovernmental Panel on Climate Change) (1992), *The Supplementary Report to the IPCC Scientific Assessment*, edited by J.T. Houghton, B.A. Callander and S.K. Varney, Cambridge: Cambridge Univesity Press.

Jacobs, M. (1991), *The Green Economy: Environment, Sustainable Development and the Politics of the Future*, London: Pluto.

Kirk, W. (1963), 'Problems in geography', *Geography*, **48**: 357–71.

Kooten, Van, G.C. and E.H. Bulte (2000), 'The ecological footprint: useful science or politics?', *Ecological Economics*, **32**: 385–9.

Kratena, K. (2004), ' "Ecological value added" in an integrated ecosystem–economy model – an indicator for sustainability', *Ecological Economics*, **48**(2): 189–200.

Le Grand, J. (1991), *Equity and Choice: An Essay in Economics and applied Philosophy*, London: Harper Collins.

Lenzen, M. and S.A. Murray (2001), 'A modified ecological footprint method and its application to Australia', *Ecological Economics*, **37**(2): 262–71.

Linstead, C. and P. Ekins (2001), 'Mass balance UK: mapping UK resource and material flows', London: Forum for the Future.

Linstead, C., C. Gervais and P. Ekins (2004), 'Mass balance: an essential tool for understanding resource flows', London: The Royal Society for the Conservation of Nature.

Loh, J. (2002), 'Living Planet Index', Gland, Switzerland: WWF International.

McLaren, D., S. Bullock and N. Yousef (1998), *Tomorrow's World: Britain's Share in a Sustainable Future*, London: Earthscan.

Mirowski, P. (1990), 'Smooth operator: how Marshall's demand and supply curves made neo-classicism safe for public consumption but unfit for science', in R.M. Tullbeg (ed.), *Alfred Marshall in Retrospect*, Edward Elgar, Aldershot, UK and Brookfield, US: pp. 61–90.

Moffatt, I. (1991), *The Greenhouse Effect: Science and Policy, in the Northern Territory*, Darwin: Australia Australian National University, NARU.

Moffatt, I. (1996a), *Sustainable Development Principles, Analysis and Policy*, Carnforth and New York: Parthenon Press.

Moffatt, I. (1996b), 'An evaluation of environmental space as the basis for sustainable Europe', *International Journal Of Sustainable Development and World Ecology*, **3**: 49–69.

Moffatt, I. (2004), 'Global warming and its relationship to the economic dimensions of policy', in A.D. Owen and N. Hanley (eds), *The Economics of Climate Change*, London: Routledge, pp. 6–34.

Moffatt, I., N. Hanley and M.D. Wilson (2001), *Measuring and Modelling Sustainable Development*, Carnforth and New York: Parthenon Press.

Moffatt, I., T. Wiedmann and J. Barrett (2005), 'The impact of Scotland's economy on the environment: a note on input–output and Ecological Footprint analysis', *Quarterly Economic Commentary*, Fraser of Allende Institute, University of Strathclyde, **30**(3): 37–44.

Monfreda C., M. Wackernagel and D. Deumling (2004), 'Establishing national natural capital accounts based on detailed ecological footprint and biological capacity assessments', *Land Use Policy*, **21**(3): 231–46.

NCBS (National Centre for Business and Sustainability) (undated), 'Rocks to rubble: Building a Sustainable Region', National Centre for Business and Sustainability, Manchester (http://www.thencbs.co.uk), accessed 22 February, 2005.

Neumayer, E. (2003), *Weak versus Strong Sustainability*, Cheltenham, UK and Northampton, MA, USA: Edward Elgar.

Odum, H.T. and E.C. Odum (1976), *Energy Basis for Man and Nature*, New York: McGraw-Hill.

Opschoor, J.B. and R. Weterings (1994), 'Towards environmental performance indicators based on the notion of Environmental space' Rijswijk, Netherlands: Advisory Council for Research on Nature and Environment (RMNO).

Owen, A.D. and N. Hanley (eds) (2004), *The Economics of Climate Change*, London: Routledge.

Pearce, D. (2001), *Measuring Resource Productivity*, London: DTI and Green Alliance.

Pearce, D. and G. Atkinson (1993), 'Capital theory and the measurement of sustainable development: an indicator of weak sustainability', *Ecological Economics*, **8**(2): 103–8.

Ravetz, J. (2000), *City Region 2020: Integrated Planning for a Sustainable Environment*, London: Earthscan.

Rees, J. (1985), *Natural Resources Allocation, Economics and Policy*, London: Methuen.

Rees, P. (1992), 'Ecological footprint and appropriate carrying capacity: what urban economics leaves out', *Environment and Urbanisation*, **4**: 121–30.

Robert, K.-H., J. Holmberg and E.U. von Weizsacker (2000), 'Factor X for subtle policy-making', *Green Management International*, **31**(Autumn): 25–37.

Robins, N. and A. Trisoglio (1995), 'Restructuring industry for sustainable development', in J. Kirkby, P. O'Keefe and L. Timberlake (eds), *The Earthscan reader in Sustainable Development*, London: Earthscan, pp. 161–73.

Schmidt-Bleek, F. (1992), 'Materials flow and eco-restructuring', *Fresenius Environmental Bulletin*, **1**: 529–34.

Schmidt-Bleek, F. (1993a), 'MIPS – a universal ecological measure', *Fresenius Environmental Bulletin*, **2**: 306–11.

Schmidt-Bleek, F. (1993b), 'Towards universal ecology disturbance measures', *Journal of Regulatory Toxicology and Pharmacology*, **18**: 456–62.

Senbel, M., T. McDaniels and H. Dowlatabadi (2003), 'The ecological footprint: a non monetary metric of human consumption applied to North America', *Global Environmental Change*, **13**: 83–100.

Sheerin, C. (2002), 'UK material flow accounting economic trends 583', Office of National Statistics, London, www.statistics.gov.uk/article.asp?id=140, accessed 25 February 2005.

Simmons, C., K. Lewis and J. Barrett (2000), 'Two Feet – two approaches: a component based model of ecological footprinting', *Ecological Economics*, **32**: 375–80.

Vuuren, D.P. van and E.M. Smeets (2000), 'Ecological footprints of Benin, Bhutan, Costa Rica and the Netherlands', *Ecological Economics*, **34**(1): 115–30.

Vuuren, D.P. van and L.F. Bouwman (2005), 'Exploring past and future changes in the ecological footprint of world regions', *Ecological Economics*, **52**(1): 43–62.

Wackernagel, M. and W. Rees (1994), 'Ecological Footprints and Appropriated Carrying Capacity', in A.-M. Jansson, M. Hammer, C. Folke and R. Costanza (eds), *Investing in Natural Capital: the Ecological Economics Approach to Sustainability*, Washington: Island Press, pp. 362–90.

Wackernagel, M., L. Lewan and C.B. Hansson (1999), 'Evaluating the use of natural capital with the ecological footprint', *Ambio*, **28**(7): 604–12.

Wackernagel, M., C. Monfreda, D. Moran, S. Goldfinger, D. Deumling and M. Murray (2004a), 'National footprinting and biocapacity accounts, 2004: the underlying calculation method', Global Footprint network, Oakland California, USA, pp. 1–32, www.footprintnetwork.org, accessed 5 April 2005.

Wackernagel, M., C. Monfreda, K.-H. Erb, H. Haberl and N.B. Schulz (2004b), 'Ecological footprint time series of Austria, the Philippines, and South Korea for 1961–1999: comparing the conventional approach to an "actual land" approach', *Land Use Policy*, **21**: 261–9.

Wackernagel, M., N.B. Schulz, D. Deumling, A.C. Linares, M. Jenkins, V. Kapor, C. Monfreda, J. Loh, N. Myers, R. Noorgaard and J. Randers (2002), 'Tracking the ecological overshoot of the human economy', Proceedings of the National Academy of Science, **99**(14): 9266–71.

Ward, R. and R. Dubos (1972), *Only One Earth*, Harmondsworth: Penguin.

WCED (1987), *Our Common Future*, Oxford: Oxford University Press.

Weizsacker, E.V., A.B. Lovins, and L.H. Lovins (1997), *Factor Four: Doubling Wealth, Halving Resource Use*, London: Earthscan.

Wiedmann, T. and J. Barrett (2005), 'The use of input–output analysis in REAP to allocate ecological footprints and material flows to final consumption categories', REAP Report number 2, Stockholm Environment Institute, University of York.

Wiedmann, T., J. Minx, J. Barrett and M. Wackernagel (2005), 'Allocating ecological footprints to final consumption with input output categories', *Ecological Economics*, **56**(1): 28–48.

WWF (2004), 'Living Planet Index', World Wide Fund for Nature International (WWF), Global Footprint Network, UNEP World Conservation Monitoring Centre, WWF, Gland, Switzerland, www.panda.org/livingplanet.

WWF (2005a), 'Living Planet Report 2004', Gland, Switzerland: WWF.

WWF (2005b), 'Reducing Wales' ecological footprint', Report Summary, Cardiff: WWF Cymru.

WWF, Italia (2004), *Ecological Footprint of the Tuscany Region*, Rome: WWF.

Zimmerman, E.W. (1951), *World Resources and Industries*, California: University of California Press.

PART VI

SUSTAINABLE DEVELOPMENT AT DIFFERENT SCALES

21 Sustainable cities and local sustainability
Yvonne Rydin

1. Introduction

The local level has been fertile ground for the sustainable development agenda. And within an increasingly urbanized world – currently some 3 billion people, roughly half of the world's population, live in urban centres – this means cities taking on the concept of urban sustainability (Satterthwaite, 2002). In this chapter we shall review the arguments for pursuing sustainable development at the local, urbanized level. While local action for sustainability cannot on its own achieve sustainable development, it is argued that such local action is both a necessary element and can make a substantial contribution in its own right. However, as at national levels, conflicts between environmental, economic and social goals mean that there are inevitable choices involved in setting a local sustainability agenda. The chapter suggests some alternative visions for sustainable cities and discusses the importance of urban politics. Finally it critically assesses the implications of globalization for a focus on urban sustainability and how this affects the potential for local action to address sustainable development.

2. Local action for sustainable development

5 June is United Nations World Environment Day and for 2005 the theme was Green Cities. In London a whole series of local events took place to celebrate London Sustainability Weeks, some hundreds in total. This is but one example of the mass of individual activities that have been occurring for some time now in cities and locations worldwide under the banner of sustainable development (see Gilbert et al., 1996, for a review prepared for the UN Habitat Conference 1996). Such local action is based on a distinctive view of the sustainable development agenda and, in particular, the Brundtland process.

The 1992 Rio Summit on Environment and Development, which followed on the publication of the Brundtland Report (WCED, 1987), was marked by the tabling of conventions on climate change and biodiversity, a statement on forestry and Agenda 21, a manifesto for sustainable development put together by a coalition of governmental and non-governmental actors (Lafferty and Meadowcroft, 2000). Within Agenda 21, Chapter 28 argued the case for the importance of local level action and in particular for

Local Agenda 21 initiatives in support of Agenda 21 (the document is available at www.un.org/esa/sustdev/documents/agenda21). Since Agenda 21 was adopted (although without any force of law behind it) by all governments at Rio, this chapter has come to have considerable significance in the local sustainable development movement. There are two distinct sides to the arguments made for the importance of local level action to sustainable development. The first can be called the 'ends' argument, the second the 'means' argument.

The 'ends' argument can be summed up in terms of the environmentalist adage 'think global, act local'. Proponents of this view argue that the majority of the actions required to deliver sustainable development can only happen at the local level. As the first paragraph of Chapter 28 puts it: 'Because so many of the problems and solutions being addressed by Agenda 21 have their roots in local activities, the participation and cooperation of local authorities will be a determining factor in fulfilling its objectives.' In one sense it could be argued that 100 per cent of the change needed has to occur at some local site: in this household, that factory, this green space. However, this does not mean that the policy action is best located in the locality. The conventional view is that behavioural change can most effectively be generated through national policy frameworks, themselves often a response to international pressure. Such national frameworks may comprise fiscal measures (taxes, subsidies, and so on) or systems of regulation or a combination.

For example, in the arena of climate change, carbon taxes and related market-based instruments such as carbon permits are seen by environmental economists as a direct way to change behaviour through raising the relative costs of environmentally unfriendly decisions. International frameworks such as the Kyoto Protocol are intended to encourage, even require national governments to introduce such schemes. However, as the recent history of the Kyoto Protocol has demonstrated, there are dangers in relying on such national and international action and there is considerable potential in using local action. In the USA, frustrated by the refusal of the Bush Government to ratify the Kyoto Protocol, cities across the country have formed an alliance to commit themselves collectively to meeting Kyoto Protocol targets (www.ci.seattle.wa.us/mayor/ climate).

This example emphasizes that there are actions that local governments can take to advance sustainable development. Chapter 28 was written by local government representatives and particularly argued for action by this tier of government: 'Local authorities construct, operate and maintain economic, social and environmental infrastructure, oversee planning processes, establish local environmental policies and regulations, and assist in implementing national and subnational environmental policies' (Section 28.1). The extent and impact of these activities depends of course on the power and resources that are available to such local governments. In some countries a wide range of resources and powers fall to the local level – Sweden is one such example with considerable income from a local income tax as well as a specific Local Agenda 21 fund from central government (Bjørnæs et al., 2005). Many localities, such as those in the USA, are able to set taxes to induce behavioural change and most local government has a range of regulatory powers that it can use.

But advocates of local action for sustainable development go beyond this. They argue that regardless of the resources and powers at the local level, this scale has a great capacity to induce behavioural change through 'softer' means than regulation or fiscal means. Thus much of the emphasis of local sustainability action is based on the greater engagement with local communities that is possible within specific localities and hence the greater scope for instilling sustainability values within those communities. A mix of persuasion, building partnerships and networks is seen as part of the policy brew for creating a local sustainable development culture, a brew that only really works at this local scale.

At this stage, the 'ends' argument finds common cause with the 'means' argument. While a focus on ends involves thinking about the best way to deliver sustainable development outcomes, the focus on means emphasizes those aspects of the Brundtland process that looked for a radically different way to make policy. The Brundtland process itself has been noted for its participatory way of operating, with visits to local communities to gather views, information and examples. This theme runs through its recommendations as well with repeated calls for a more participatory mode of policy making, and hence a shift towards more participatory as opposed to representative democracy in general (WCED, 1987).

The emphasis on participatory policy making has particular resonance at the local level. Here, it is argued, people can feel closer to government, including both its political and administrative aspects. Local government is more accessible, not just in terms of distance but often also socially; local political representatives and officials are less likely to come from an entirely different social category than can be the case with national governments. And if local government is easier for local people to reach, the reverse is also held to be true. Local events, campaigns and initiatives designed to promote sustainable development are more likely to reach local people. Completing the quotation of the opening paragraph of Chapter 28 of Agenda 21: 'As the level of governance closest to the people, they [local governments] play a vital role in educating, mobilizing and responding to the public to promote sustainable development.'

For these reasons, the local arena has proved a particularly fruitful one for bringing Chapter 28 of Agenda 21 to life. Local Agenda 21 (LA21) has blossomed as a series of local approaches to taking the sustainable development agenda forward on a worldwide scale. The 2002 World Summit on Sustainable Development held in Johannesburg confirmed a general commitment to local level action as part of the implementation of Agenda 21. One of the objectives of the implementation plan issued at the Summit was 'Strengthening capacities for sustainable development at all levels, including the local level, in particular those of developing countries' (WSSD, 2002, p. 48). Certainly the statement by the 'local government of the world' to the Summit emphasized the role they could play and, while the WSSD Implementation Plan did not refer to LA21 by name, this statement concluded with the words: 'Local Governments will reinforce their commitment to Local Agenda 21 and its implementation throughout the next decade of Local Action 21', their terminology emphasizing the growing importance of action as opposed to just agenda-setting (statement available at www.dfa.gov.za/docs/2002/wssd0830.htm).

Approaches to LA21 vary, as is appropriate to fit local circumstances (Lafferty, 2001; Lafferty and Eckerberg, 1997; LASALA, 2001). Some countries, such as Germany, where there has been a strong, established tradition of local environmental management, have seen LA21 as an opportunity to extend this role and seek to draw local populations into their municipal agenda. In other countries, such as the UK, where local government has fewer powers and autonomy and perhaps less of a track record in environmental policy, then LA21 has been more of an opportunity to develop civil action for sustainability. The meaning of 'bottom-up' action is here taken to mean action within communities and civil society more broadly rather than just at the lowest level of government.

Thus LA21 comprises a whole range of initiatives from local government public transport schemes, to community-led recycling projects, local time-banks and management of local nature reserves, to awareness-raising events such as Green Fairs involving local NGOs. This mix is intended not only to deliver sustainable development outcomes but also to create new forms of local democracy with active citizenship and partnerships of local government, NGOs and community organizations. In countries with a developed local government sector, this is seen as a way of redressing imbalances and making local government more accountable; in countries with failing local government – inefficient, ineffective, even corrupt – this can provide some potential for local communities achieving outcomes to their benefit. Either way community empowerment becomes synonymous with the sustainable development agenda. As Mitra puts it: 'a general consensus that urban sustainability should be uniquely defined by each jurisdiction. It cannot be defined or achieved behind closed doors. Rather, experience has shown that it is critical to have the buy-in of the affected population.' (2003, p. 5).

There has been some debate over whether there is a tight connection between the means and ends aspects of local sustainability. Portney, looking at the USA, states that it is 'difficult to find cases where there is evidence that sustainable initiatives' participatory processes have successfully transformed the values of city officials or residents' (2003, p. 155). Yet, in a European research project, a connection was found between the pursuit of participatory environmental governance by local municipalities and progress in substantive terms of sustainable outcomes (Evans et al., 2005). Since process change does not logically or automatically result in different outcomes, this is an issue that clearly deserves further attention.

3. Local and urban sustainability as a substantive concept

While the emphasis on the process dimension of the sustainable development agenda has seemed to many to be an exciting way to revitalize local governance, and such local action can promise new ways to deliver sustainable development, this still leaves unexplained what the substantive content of sustainable development is or should be at the local level. Most local policy statements on sustainable development reiterate the Brundtland definition in some version (Rydin, 2003, Ch. 9). Other chapters in the current volume have explored alternative interpretations of this Brundtland definition that are possible (see also Baker et al., 1997). Ambiguity and competing interpretations also characterize the concept of local or urban sustainability. Sustainable development is not simply about raising the priority accorded to the environmental or ecological; the Brundtland report and subsequent debates have also emphasized the importance of the social or equity agenda, as well as the necessary reliance on economic processes to deliver outcomes, albeit a reformed and reinvigorated set of economic processes. Therefore alternative combinations, balances and trade-offs between the environmental, social and economic dimensions can be identified, producing the variety of definitions of sustainable development and explaining some of the ambiguity of the concept.

These alternatives are also reflected at the local scale, providing very different agendas for local sustainability. These can be recast as different visions for a sustainable city. Figure 21.1 provides an outline of these alternatives: (see also Haughton, 1999, where he applies his fourfold typology of sustainable cities to the case of Adelaide, South Australia). The nirvana of local sustainability would be achieving social, environmental and economic objectives simultaneously. The WSSD statement by local government saw this as comprising 'viable local economies, just and peaceful communities, eco-efficient cities, and secure resilient communities able to respond to change, while ensuring safe and accessible water supplies and protecting our climate, soil, biodiversity and human health' (WSSD, 2002).

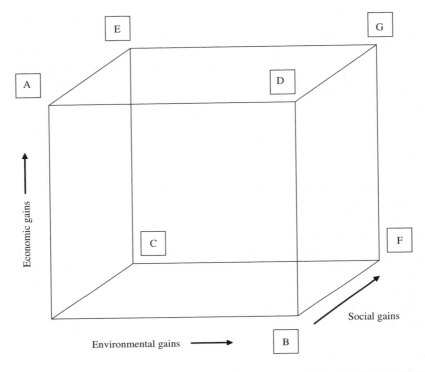

Figure 21.1   Conceptualizing the sustainable city

Vision of the City	Urban policy emphasis on . . .
A – The Green City	visual amenities, green spaces, reducing local pollution and reclaiming derelict land
B – The Limited City	reducing resource inputs, increasing recycling and aiming towards self-sufficiency
C – The Just City	social equity and social inclusion from urban regeneration
D – The Ecologically Modernized City	identifying win–win scenarios for environmentally-friendly local business
E – Socially Responsible Local Economic Development	ensuring urban economic development provides social benefits
F – The Environmentally Just City	reducing inequalities in the impact of environmental burdens and risks
G – The Sustainable City	finding win–win–win scenarios

In practice, in any specific timescale and within any specific policy or pro-gramme, it is not always possible to pursue win–win–win scenarios and real choices have to be made as to what to prioritize and what to downplay. For example, the UK Government's *Sustainable Communities Plan* for building new residential development to meet predicted demographic change has chosen to emphasize economic and social concerns rather than prioritize environmental ones (ODPM, 2003). The focus is on creating viable local economic development and socially inclusive communities. While there are some environmental initiatives (such as requiring an element of renewable energy sources), concerns remain about the standard of eco-efficiency of the housing, the flood risks and the impact on water security.

The inevitability of choice within the local sustainability agenda means that local politics is brought to the forefront in determining the final balance between objectives (Hamm and Muttagi, 1998, p. 2). While LA21 processes may seek to empower local communities this has to be seen against the backdrop of existing political structures and power balances. These remain deeply significant in framing the local sustainable development debate and hence the kind of sustainable locality or city that is envisaged. For this reason, the prevailing power of economic interests, of their corporate discretion and of societal economic discourses remains a key influence on how local possibilities for sustainable development are seen (Rydin, 2003).

This is not to deny the possibility of environmental and social goals being promoted by local political coalitions. Some commentators argue strongly for cities acting as 'sustainability heroes'. For example, Satterthwaite argues that 'There is no reason why well-governed cities should not achieve the highest standards in terms of quality of life, efficient resource use, low waste volumes and low greenhouse gas emissions per person' (2002, p. 3). Indeed urban areas can be highly efficient sites of resource use, being more energy-efficient in terms of both space heating and transport per unit than rural areas. Even in the developing world's megacities, conditions 'may appear chaotic and out-of-control but most have life expectancies and provision for piped water, sanitation, schools and health care that are well above their national average' (Satterthwaite, 2002, p. 4).

However, such pressures for sustainable development in cities have to contend with existing structural preferences for the economic status quo, which in many cases has shaped aspirations. Win–win options based on expanding the economic base of an area and using this to provide social and environmental gains remain a key theme of many sustainable city agendas. London is a key example here (Rydin et al., 2004). In a paper by one of the Mayor's key advisors, Ross makes it clear that the Mayoral strategy is based on promoting London as a world city and attracting inward investment (2001). The aim is to pursue conventional economic growth in London and then use this to achieve supplementary social and environmental gains. It is the approach that lies behind the growth machine and urban regime politics (Stone, 1989; Harding, 1994) and is clearly part of the logic by which it has been decided that London should bid for the 2012 Olympic Games, a 'sustainable Games'. In the USA, this approach is given expression at the urban level through the 'smart growth' movement (Portney, 2003, Ch. 4; but see also Holcombe and Staley, 2001).

Cox et al. (2002, p. 5) point out that this is the

> emerging 'mainstream' consensus on sustainable development that is being adopted by powerful stakeholders (government and business especially) . . . It is a particular view of sustainability that takes on board elements of the 'green' critique of modern market economies to expose hidden environmental and social costs, but retains an attachment to economic sustainability.

The hope is that sufficient leverage can be generated to deliver real environmental and social gains with a framework of expanded local economic development. Thus the Greater London Authority is pursuing ambitious renewable energy and recycling initiatives within its world city perspective for London, aiming for a lower environmental impact world city (see www.london.gov.uk).

While commentators such as Low et al. urge city governments to resist this emphasis on local economic development and the harnessing of environmental concerns as a means to this end (2000, pp. 301–2), this is a difficult path for cities to follow given their dependency on local economies for finance and competition with other cities for development. Rethinking the kind of local economic development that should be pursued, working against conventional market-led approaches is a path that tends only to be adopted in two circumstances: in areas that have already been bypassed by contemporary economic activity and where there is no hope of inward investment; or where a local community is trying to take a stand against the impacts of such inward investment, say in the form of major infrastructure or other developments.

4. The limits of local and urban sustainability
This issue of how localities and cities relate to prevailing economic processes also throws the spotlight on a distinctive feature of the local sustainable development agenda: how far can sustainable development be conceived of as a feature of a locality in an era characterized by globalization? This has been a particular issue in sustainable city debates, due to the fundamental nature of cities as characterized by their relationship to their hinterlands (Jacobs, 1970).

Cities only developed historically because they could rely on food inputs from an agricultural hinterland, usually in the immediate vicinity of the city borders. In the earliest stages of urbanization, this was combined with the sewage waste from cities being used as fertilizer for the surrounding farmland. As cities have grown, they have usually gone through a stage when it has proved increasingly difficult to get rid of waste products from urban consumption and production, producing pollution to all media (air, water and land) and a solid waste disposal problem. City and national governments have tended to react to the negative effects of such urban environmental externalities with a degree of regulation in order to safeguard public health to at least some extent and prevent the collapse of urban systems (Button, 2002). Both historically in the case of long urbanized countries and currently in the case of newly urbanizing ones, the poor have borne the brunt of such externalities and have generally been last in the queue for being protected from them.

However, with the advent of evidence on climate change, the negative environmental externalities associated with urban living patterns have been shown to impact beyond the city itself, beyond the immediate rural hinterland, and to affect the global ecosystems and, as a result, far-distant communities. The urban environmental agenda becomes transformed into an urban sustainability agenda: protecting urban environments (and associated communities) and limiting the pollution and waste exported out of cities, both to specific ex-urban locations *and* into global and regional pollution sinks (Capello et al., 1999). The climate change agenda also highlights the importance of cities being adapted to deal with impacts that cannot be mitigated.

At the same time, cities have increased the quantity of resources that they have drawn upon to sustain urban consumption, production and exchange activities. These include renewable resources (like food), non-renewable resources (such as mined aggregates for construction) and – centrally – energy resources for a variety of uses, notably space heating and transport. A key aspect of urban sustainability is, therefore, also about reducing the need for such inputs, through demand management and increased efficiency, and switching from non-renewable to renewable sources. Renewable resources (such as water) also have to be used within their capacity to renew themselves.

Tools such as ecological footprints (see also Chapter 20 in this volume) have been applied at the city level to present in a highly visible form the extent to which urban living takes up a disproportionate share of the world's environmental resources. The 2002 calculation of London's ecological footprint (to be found at www.citylimitslondon.org) estimated that the city's ecological impact was 293 times its geographical area and 42 times its biocapacity. In per capita terms, London residents had a footprint of 6.63 global hectares per capita, while an equal share of the measured earth's resources would have been 2.18 gha per cap. While it is recognized that the global share of a city can never be reduced to its own physical area because of its inherent nature as dependent on a hinterland (Haughton and Hunter, 1994, Ch. 1), this view of urban sustainability has led to calls for a move towards greater self-sufficiency, towards reducing the resource inputs into the city and reducing the pollution and waste exported (Portney, 2003).

The idea of an unlimited and increasing throughput of resources through an urban area (see Table 21.1) is supposed to be transformed under sustainable development to the idea of a recycling city, with much diminished throughput; this parallels Jacobs' arguments for a similar switch at the level of the national economy (1991). So more waste is recycled within the city, water and energy efficiency enhanced and urban agriculture promoted. If some resources can be generated from within the city's own capacities (for example, with demolition waste being used for construction landfill) then others should be brought in from less far afield, so saving on transport, associated energy use and CO_2 emissions. Thus local farmers' markets and local sourcing are favoured over supermarket produce that has travelled long distances (often by air freight) and embodies substantial quantities of 'food miles'.

This localist message has a strong resonance within much of the environmentalist literature. Dobson (1995) provides a survey and Smith et al. (1998) a selection of examples encompassing the ideas that not only should

Table 21.1   Environmental input–output analysis for cities

Environmental system	Inputs to cities	Outputs from cities
Lithosphere	Food production sites Minerals and aggregates Hydrocarbons Habitat sites Land for development Landscape settings	Site contamination Landfill for waste disposal Land development
Atmosphere	Clean air Climate control functions	Air pollution at local, regional and global scales
Aquasphere	Water supply Water-based habitat sites Sites for water-based economic and social activities	Sewage disposal Polluted water Land drainage
Biosphere	Food Flora and fauna Habitats Living landscapes	Species change Species spread

waste be dealt with locally and resources sourced locally, but local economies should prioritize local goods and services over imported ones and even seek to delink from non-local financial systems through means such as local exchange and trading schemes (LETs). In addition there should be local political autonomy based on delegation within political systems to the lowest community level, a celebration of local and 'indigenous' cultures, resisting the influence of the mass media. Marvin and Guy (1997) have argued that a new ideology of 'new localism' can be identified which encompasses the idea that 'environmental policy initiatives at the local level will effectively deal with the ecological chaos of today by creating a more rational future with local government leading to development of more sustainable communities, life and work styles' (1997, p. 311). Central to this ideology is the argument that environmental problems *need* to be tackled at the local level and that local government is *best* suited to tackle these problems. This takes the argument beyond the recognition that local action has a role to play.

One difficulty with this perspective is that it can be seen as trying to ignore the nature of cities within contemporary globalization. The OECD (1997) defines globalization as 'a process in which the structure of economic markets, technologies, and communication patterns become progressively more international over time'. By the mid-1990s it was apparent that the growth in transnational investment and of actors operating on a global scale in production, services, investment and property development was accelerating, and for a period in the 1990s some argued that global forces were in danger of annihilating space altogether, reducing the differences between localities, homogenizing the local (Castells, 1998).

Without accepting this, it seems clear that there is evidence for the acceleration of trends towards more rapid and extensive interaction on a global scale and even, perhaps, that distinctive contemporary urban patterns are emerging (see Newman and Thornley, 2002, for a review). This means that cities and localities need to be seen as nodes within global flows of capital, people, knowledge, cultural resources, and so on; flows occurring across space with increasing speed and complexity. For Appadurai, the locality is not scalar or spatial but relational and contextual (1996, p. 178). Hence the environmental and social impacts of cities and their sustainability need to be considered in terms of city-based urban activities having an influence along the lines of flows that connect every city and locality to myriad other ones across the world. We need to see urban sustainability within the context of globalized product and resource flows, where the economic and social impacts of those flows are spread across the globe (see Table 21.2).

Table 21.2 sets out criteria by which the social and environmental impact of economic activity occurring in a city (or any locality) can be judged,

Table 21.2   A sustainable development agenda for assessing urban economic activity

	Location of impact		
	In the city	Elsewhere in the region/country	Elsewhere globally
Social benefits	Local community benefits for the most disadvantaged sectors	Similar benefits generated elsewhere along the production chains	Similar benefits generated along international production chains
Environmental benefits	Enhancing air quality, urban amenities, habitats, land decontamination	Air quality measures, waste management, water conservation, pollution control, increased resource efficiency, carbon fixing	Increased resource efficiency (minerals, aggregates, hydrocarbons), carbon fixing

taking into account the social and environmental impacts at different geographical distances from that activity: in the city, in the region or country, and globally. Looking at urban and local sustainability in this way throws up dilemmas. Above it was suggested that part of the 'localist' message was the potential to mitigate climate change through reducing consumption of 'food miles', that is the transport embodied in food consumed within cities. This would favour locally sourced food over that freighted in over long distances. Yet such a localist approach ignores the social impact of such a shift in purchasing patterns, where local communities at the other end of global food chains are dependent on exporting their produce. Clearly there are complex issues over terms of trade, the locally-retained benefits of producing food for export and even the environmental impact of export-based production. But in a globalized world these complexities require attention rather than ignoring them through an emphasis on the purely local when considering local or urban sustainability.

Such an approach lays an additional requirement on LA21, to contribute to local understanding of the multi-faceted nature of the impacts arising from urban activities (Low et al., 2000). Many LA21s are already contributing to this through the trans-global links that are being formed between local communities. Hobbs (1994) has shown how there is a history to such trans-global links in the context of human rights and peace campaigns. Bulkeley and Betsell (2003) review the growth of such transnational networks of sub-national government, challenging hierarchical interpretations of global environmental governance. This is clearly a substantial challenge, comprising the attempt to build international social capital for collective action towards sustainable development. But in this way, local and urban sustainability could be recast as 'thinking locally, acting globally'.

There is evidence that local government at the WSSD understood the importance of combining a global with a local perspective on sustainable development. Their statement said that 'We are deeply concerned about the impact of globalisation at local level (sic), especially within the developing world and countries with economies in transition. We have witnessed first-hand the devastating effects of aspects of our international system on local communities and our local spaces.' They go on to call for action at the level of international relations, while also seeing local government institutions as having a role to play. It must be recognized that rethinking the local sustainability perspective in globalized terms will not be easy. While there remains considerable activity on the LA21 front, there is some evidence that the rate of growth may be slowing and even turned into decline. The collective action problem bedevils attempts to maintain high levels of participation (Rydin and Pennington, 2000). The costs of participating inhibit civil society actors from high and sustained levels of involvement; self-interest can inhibit local economic actors from any other than token involvement. Some LA21s are being taken over by local government precisely because of this difficulty of sustaining community activism.

Therefore, trying to extend that collective action from the city and neighbourhood towards global concerns in the name of international social capital is to multiply any difficulties. Distance and heterogeneity can inhibit the building of such connections, although there are a mass of small 'twinning' initiatives between cities, communities and schools that are seeking to make such connections real. The activities of communities with antecedents in far-distant countries can also help build such connections; ethnic minority communities can be substantial assets in this task. Often the exact linkage between local consumption activities in one place and their social and environmental impact in another can be difficult to trace. Therefore the linkage may be best mediated through Fair Trade campaigns, perhaps supplementing specific spatial linkages. New York – one of the world's largest consumers of coffee – could benefit both from drinking more Fair Trade coffee but also having some specific twinning arrangements with coffee-producing regions.

To return to the key theme of this chapter – the need to make choices within the urban sustainability agenda – it may be that we need to decide on short-term and long-term goals. Given the urgency for action implied by current climate change scenarios, perhaps the short-term goal should be to prioritize local level action to mitigate climate change, looking to win–win options where economic activity can increase the eco-efficiency of our cities. But in the longer term, we will need an understanding of the global interconnectedness of our cities and local communities in broader terms if sustainable development, as envisaged by the Brundtland Commission over 25 years ago, is to become a reality.

References

Appadurai, A. (1996), *Modernity at Large*, Minneapolis: University of Minnesota Press.
Baker, S., M. Kousis, D. Richardson and S. Young (1997), 'Introduction: the theory and practice of sustainable development in EU perspective' in S. Baker, M. Kousis, D. Richardson and S. Young (eds), *The Politics of Sustainable Development*, London: Routledge.
Bjørnæs, T., K. Eckerberg, J. Holm and M. Joas (2005), 'Sector and vertical administrative coordination by local environmental governance', paper to 10th Nordic Environmental Social Sciences Conference, Gothenburg, Sweden 15–17 June.
Bulkeley, H. and M. Betsill (2003), *Cities and Climate Change*, London: Routledge.
Button, K. (2002), 'City management and urban environmental indicators', *Ecological Economics*, **40**(2): 217–33.
Capello, R., P. Nijkamp and G. Pepping (1999), *Sustainable Cities and Energy Policies*, Berlin: Springer-Verlag.
Castells, M. (1998), *End of Millennium*, Oxford: Blackwells.
Cox, J., D. Fell and M. Thurstain-Goodwin (2002), *Red Man, Green Man*, London: RICS Foundation.
Dobson, A. (1995), *Green Political Thought*, 2nd edn, London: Routledge.
Evans, B., M. Joas, S. Sundback and K. Theobald (2005), *Governing Sustainable Cities*, London: Earthscan.
Gilbert, R., D. Stevenson, H. Girardet and R. Stren (1996), *Making Cities Work: the role of Local Authorities in the Urban Environment*, London: Earthscan.
Hamm, B. and P. Muttagi (eds) (1998), *Sustainable Development and the Future of Cities*, London: Intermediate Technology Publications.
Harding, A. (1994), 'Urban regimes and growth machines', *Urban Affairs Quarterly*, **29**: 356–82.
Haughton, G. (1999), 'Searching for the sustainable city', *Urban Studies*, **36**(11): 1891–906.
Haughton, G. and C. Hunter (1994), *Sustainable Cities*, London: Jessica Kingsley Publishers with Regional Studies Association.
Hobbs, H. (1994), *City Hall Goes Abroad: the Foreign Policy of Local Politics*, London: Sage Publications.
Holcombe, R. and S. Staley (eds) (2001), *Smarter Growth*, Westport, CT: Greenwood Press.
Jacobs, J. (1970), *The Economy of Cities*, Harmondsworth: Penguin.
Jacobs, M. (1991), *The Green Economy*, London: Pluto.
Lafferty, W. (ed.) (2001), *Sustainable Communities in Europe*, London: Earthscan.
Lafferty, W. and K. Eckerberg (1997), *From Earth Summit to Local Forum: studies of Local Agenda 21 in Europe*, Oslo, Norway: PROSUS.
Lafferty, W. and J. Meadowcroft (2000), *Implementing Sustainable Development: Strategies and Initiatives in High Consumption Societies*, Oxford: Oxford University Press.
LASALA Project Team (2001), *Accelerating Local Sustainability – evaluating European Local Agenda 21 Processes*, Freiburg, Germany: Volume 1 ICLEI.
Low, N., B. Gleeson, I. Erlander and R. Lidskog (eds) (2000), *Consuming Cities: the Urban Environment in the Global Economy after the Rio Declaration*, London: Routledge.
Marvin, S. and S. Guy (1997), 'Creating myths rather than sustainability: the transition fallacies of the new localism', *Local Environment*, **2**(3): 311–8.
Mitra, A. (2003), *Painting the Town Green: the use of Urban Sustainability Indicators in the United States of America*, London: RICS Foundation.

Newman, P. and A. Thornley (2002), 'Globalisation, world cities and urban planning; developing a conceptual framework' in A. Thornley and Y. Rydin (eds), *Planning in a Global Era*, Aldershot, UK: Gower, pp. 27–46.

OECD (1997), *Economic Globalisation and the Environment*, Paris: OECD.

Office of the Deputy Prime Minister (ODPM) (2003), *Sustainable Communities: Building for the Future*, London: ODPM.

Portney, K. (2003), *Taking Sustainable Cities Seriously*, Cambridge, MS: MIT Press.

Ross, J. (2001), 'Management philosophy of the Greater London Authority', *Public Money and Management*, October–December, pp. 35–41.

Rydin, Y. (2003), *Conflict, Consensus and Rationality in Environmental Planning: an Institutional Discourse Approach*, Oxford: Oxford University Press.

Rydin, Y. and M. Pennington (2000), 'Public participation and local environmental planning: the collective action problem and the potential of social capital', *Local Environment*, **5**(2): 153–69.

Rydin, Y., A. Thornley, K. Scanlon and K. West (2004), 'The Greater London Authority – a case of conflict of cultures? Evidence from the planning and environmental policy domains', *Environment and Planning C*, **22**: 55–76.

Satterthwaite, D. (2002), *Coping with Rapid Urban Growth*, RICS Leader Edge Series London: RICS.

Smith, M., J. Whitelegg and N. Williams (1998), *Greening the Built Environment*, London: Earthscan.

Stone, C. (1989), *Regime Politics: Governing Atlanta*, Lawrence, KS: University Press of Kansas.

World Commission on Environment and Development (WCED) (1987), *Our Common Future*, Oxford: Oxford University Press.

World Summit on Sustainable Development (WSSD) (2002), *Plan of Implementation*, paper tabled at WSSD, Johannesburg, 4 September.

22 Sustainable agriculture
Clement A. Tisdell

1. Introduction[1]

Humans today are mostly dependent on agriculture for food, a necessity for their survival. This may explain why so much recent attention has been given to the question of whether agriculture, particularly modern agriculture, can maintain its current levels of production and those predicted for the near future. Furthermore, in the broader debate about conditions needed for sustainable development, there are concerns that the negative environmental spillovers arising from agriculture, especially modern or industrialized agriculture, will result in economic growth that cannot last (cf. Robertson and Swinton, 2005). Agricultural development has also changed and is altering the global pool of genetic resources in objectionable ways to many (for example loss of valued wildlife) and in a manner that may eventually undermine the sustainability of agricultural production itself.

Concerns about the ability of agriculture to provide sustainably for the needs of human populations are by no means new. For example, T.R. Malthus (1798) argued that, because of the law of diminishing marginal productivity, agriculture would be limited in its ability to feed an ever-increasing population. Later writers, such as David Ricardo (1817), argued that, with technical or scientific progress and sufficient capital investment in agriculture, the Malthusian problem would not be a real issue. Engels (1959) dismissed the Malthusian view, passionately saying that 'nothing is impossible to science'. However, in recent times, doubts have arisen about whether intensive agriculture based on high inputs of capital and high use of resources external to farms, and relying on 'modern' science, is really sustainable. It is claimed that application of modern industrialized methods that have produced much agricultural growth are bringing about environmental changes (and in some instances, social changes) that will undermine that growth eventually and depress that level of agricultural production (Conway, 1998; Altieri, 2000; 2004).

There are many different views of what constitutes agricultural sustainability and about the necessary conditions to attain it. Therefore, in this chapter, a brief outline and discussion of contemporary concepts of agricultural sustainability follows and the concepts mainly used in this chapter are stated. The sustainability of modern (industrialized) agriculture compared to traditional agriculture is then examined and this is followed by a discussion of whether organic agriculture is likely to be more sustainable than non-organic agriculture. This leads on to a discussion of the relationship between agricultural development and wild biodiversity conservation, examination of the broad issues raised in this essay, and conclusions.

2. Concepts of sustainable agriculture

Consideration of concepts is important because they determine the focus of scientific enquiry. In relation to sustainable agriculture, we need to consider the following questions: what constitutes sustainable agriculture? Can it be achieved? If so, how can it be achieved? Is it desirable?

Several concepts of sustainable agriculture exist in the literature, most of which have been reviewed by Christen (1996). Christen (1996) claims, as a result of his review, that sustainable agriculture should have the following attributes: (1) ensure inter-generational equity; (2) preserve the resource base of agriculture and obviate adverse environmental externalities; (3) protect biological diversity; (4) guarantee the economic viability of agriculture, enhance job opportunities in farming and preserve local rural communities; (5) produce sufficient quality food for society; and (6) contribute to globally sustainable development.

Whether or not it is desirable for agriculture to possess all these attributes can certainly be debated. Few of these objectives may be absolutely desirable. For example, should rural communities be sustained at any cost? Furthermore, it may be impossible to fulfil all these desired objectives simultaneously. Consequently, some formulations of the desired sustainability attributes of agriculture may constitute little more than a pipe dream.

In this chapter, the main focus will be on the maintenance or sustainability of agricultural product (or yields) as an indicator of sustainable agriculture, and particular attention will be given to whether modern industrial-type agricultural systems are less sustainable than traditional agricultural systems.

At the outset, it should be recognized that sustainability of yields is only one valued attribute of the performance of agricultural systems. In comparing systems, many other attributes can also count, such as the level of the yields or returns and the income distributional consequences of the farming system (cf. Conway, 1998, p. 174). Furthermore, whether a particular agricultural system continues to be adopted can be expected to depend not only on biophysical factors but also on its social consequences.

Even if differences in the sustainability of yields is the sole basis for choosing one agricultural system rather than another, anomalies can arise, as illustrated in Figure 22.1, and as discussed more generally by Tisdell (1999a) in relation to sustainable development. In Figure 22.1, the curves

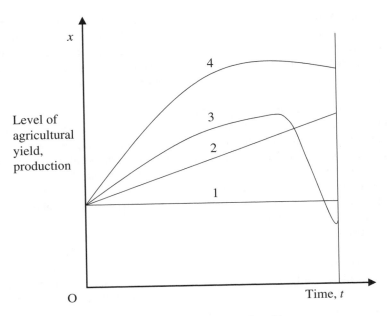

Figure 22.1   Comparisons of some agricultural yield patterns –
agricultural sustainability is not an absolute virtue

marked 1, 2, 3 and 4 show the performance of four alternative agricultural
techniques over time for a finite relevant time period. Only systems 1 and 2
exhibit sustainability of yields. However, system 4 is superior to both of
these because it results in greater yields in every period. From some perspectives, it is even possible that system 3 is socially preferable to systems
1 or 2 (Tisdell, 1999a).

Figure 22.1 makes it clear that sustainability of agricultural yields or
production is not an absolute virtue. However, that does not mean that sustainability is unimportant. It can be a private and social folly to obtain considerable short-term benefit while ignoring or inadequately considering the
long-term consequences of current actions. There is a danger that modern
economies will do just that for reasons outlined in the literature about sustainable development that has evolved in recent times.

3.   Sustainability of modern industrialized agriculture versus traditional agriculture

Conway (1985, 1987) and Altieri (1995) have argued that traditional agricultural systems are likely to be more sustainable than modern industrialized
agricultural systems. However, both modern and 'traditional' systems can be

diverse, and agricultural systems are still evolving. Therefore, while the above observation seems to hold broadly, it needs some qualification as, for example, pointed out by Pretty (1998). For instance, although slash-and-burn or shifting agriculture (and early forms of agriculture) can be relatively sustainable, when rotation cycles are sufficiently shortened, yields decline and it no longer remains sustainable (Ramakrishnan, 1992).

Methods for undertaking modern agriculture can vary. Technologies are available that can increase the sustainability of yields in modern agriculture compared to widely used methods. These include intercropping, appropriate crop rotations, agroforestry, sylvo-pastures, green manuring, conservation tillage (low or no tillage), biological control of pests rather than by the use of pesticides, and integrated pest management (Conway, 1998, p. 170; Conway and Barbier, 1990). These technologies, however, are not dominant in modern agriculture and do not replicate traditional agroecosystems.

Altieri (2004, p. 35) estimates that 10–15 per cent of all land under cultivation in the developing world is still cultivated using traditional cultivation methods. These are a result of a complex co-evolutionary process between natural and social systems. They are usually place-specific and well adapted to local conditions. Altieri's estimates also indicate that a very low percentage of cultivated land globally is cultivated using traditional methods.

On the whole, most modern industrialized agricultural systems differ significantly from those adopted in traditional agriculture. Traditional agroecosystems are, as a rule, characterized by several features that help maintain yields. These include high species numbers (considerable biodiversity); use of local varieties of crops of wild plants and animals well adapted to local conditions; maintenance of closed cycles of materials and little waste because of effective recycling practices; pest control through natural levels of external inputs; pest control through natural biological interdependencies; high structural diversity in space (intercropping) and in time (crop rotations) and a high degree of adaptation to local micro-environments (cf. Altieri, 2004; Gliessman, 1998). They tend also to be labour-intensive and have evolved as a result of local knowledge.

Modern industrialized agrosystems usually lack most of the attributes associated by Altieri (2004) and others with traditional agrosystems. They are characterized by use of few species on the farm (often only one farmed species); use of varieties of crops not developed locally to suit local conditions (for example, varieties developed by companies, often multinational ones, specializing in plant breeding), the presence of monoculture, and relatively open cycles resulting in considerable imports of materials to farms as well as substantial exports of materials from them in the form of products and wastes.

The openness of most modern industrialized agricultural systems compared to the relatively closed cycles of most traditional agricultural systems creates sustainability problems for modern agriculture. Potential obstacles to sustaining yields from modern agriculture include the following.

- Possible lack of future availability of many external inputs, such as fossil fuels and some types of fertilizer, because global stocks are finite and they are exhaustible and non-renewable (Ewel, 1999).
- Reduced soil fertility due to long-term use of chemical fertilizers, for example increased acidity of the soil, and impoverishment of soil structure due to frequent cultivation and lack of return of organic matter to the soil to provide humus (Ewel et al., 1991). Frequent cultivation and lack of intercropping may also encourage soil erosion, eventually reducing soil depth so much that yields fall.
- The widespread use of chemical pesticides and herbicides in modern agriculture can create sustainability problems. For example, resistance of pests to pesticides tends to develop in the long term. Furthermore, some pesticides and weedicides have adverse impacts on soil flora and fauna, which can negatively impact on farm productivity.
- Given the urbanized structure of modern societies (and the fact that the degree of urbanization is continuing to rise, especially in developing countries) large amounts of produce sent by farms to urban areas deplete or 'mine' soils on farms. Little of the wastes from off-farm consumption is recycled to farms, mainly because of the high transport and collection costs involved in their return to agricultural land. This large exported surplus of modern agriculture entices agriculture into the high use of artificial external inputs. Therefore, growing urbanization may create a major barrier to the development of sustainable agriculture in modern times and makes it difficult, if not impossible, to return to traditional agro-ecosystems.
- Modern agriculture is often a source of unfavourable environmental externalities or spillovers. This is because of its open-cycle character and the type of cultivation and husbandry practices adopted. It can pollute shared water bodies, cause salting or waterlogging of soils over extensive areas and seriously disrupt hydrological cycles. Furthermore, the uncoordinated use of shared water bodies by agriculturalists can threaten the maintenance of their production. This can happen, for instance, if farmers initially use water from underground aquifers at a rate faster than their rate of recharge.

Modern agriculture is associated with a global reduction in crop varieties and breeds of livestock. This is a result of: (1) growing globalization (the extension of free market systems geographically and easier access to knowledge globally); and (2) the development of food production technologies and methods that allow increased artificial manipulation of micro-environments in primary food production; and (3) more widespread trade that reduces dependence of local agriculture on local material inputs (Tisdell, 2003). Market extension encourages greater specialization in agricultural production by farmers and the adoption of specialized breeds of livestock or varieties of crops and results in path dependence, as pointed out by Tisdell (2003). Consequently, agricultural production systems become more specialized. This reduces the scope for their co-evolution at the local rural level, and agricultural innovations have primarily become dependent on large specialist corporations supplying inputs to farms and/or marketing farm produce (Heffernan, 2000).

The change in the organizational structure of agriculture involving greater dependence on external inputs supplied by large corporations tends to reinforce the dependence pattern. Sellers of agricultural inputs focus their efforts and research on ways to sell greater external inputs to agriculturalists. Scientific research on non-traded inputs and products is liable to be neglected. Local knowledge of farmers may be lost and local development of agro-ecological systems may cease or be curtailed. These factors, as well as advertisements and other means of marketing, may bias the agricultural development path in favour of open-cycles. In addition, urban 'bias' (Lipton, 1977) in agricultural production to serve urban areas grows as urbanization gains momentum. Government policies may encourage agricultural production for sale to urban areas (or even international export) rather than for subsistence (cf. Kiriti and Tisdell, 2003).

Table 22.1 summarizes those attributes of modern agriculture that are liable to make it less sustainable than traditional agriculture. It is based on the representative typology adopted, for example, by Altieri (2004). It raises the question of why there has been such a swing to modern industrialized agriculture even though it lacks many sustainability properties.

However, before discussing this, let us briefly consider the sustainability of organic agriculture compared to non-organic agriculture.

4.   The sustainability of organic versus non-organic agriculture

The demand for organic agricultural produce has increased in more developed countries (Lampkin and Padel, 1994). Reasons for this include the following: (a) organic produce is widely believed to be healthier than food produced by non-organic agricultural systems; (b) a high degree of sustainability is attributed to organic agriculture compared with agro-ecosystems that extensively use chemicals, such as pesticides and artificial

Table 22.1   Typical attributes of modern industrialized agriculture and of traditional subsistence agriculture

Modern Agriculture	Traditional Agriculture
1. High level of external inputs. Low level of self-sufficiency	1. Low level or no external inputs. High degree of self-sufficiency
2. Open-cycle agrosystems. Encouraged by market extension and urbanization	2. Closed cycle agro-systems. No or little marketing
3. Loss of agricultural biodiversity. Loss of co-evolution	3. Retention of agricultural biodiversity. Evolution of genetic material by co-evolution
4. High degree of export of wastes resulting in adverse externalities – pollution.	4. Low degree of export of wastes. Low external impacts
5. Significant reduction in on-farm natural resources due to export of products and 'wastes'	5. Little reduction in on-farm natural resources
6. Dominance of monocultures and specialized forms of agricultural production	6. Mixed systems of agriculture production e.g. polyculture.
7. Market-dominated. Increasingly dominated by global markets	7. Subsistence or semi-subsistence use dominates

fertilizers; (c) Organic agriculture is believed to be more environmentally friendly than modern agriculture, including less threatening to wildlife.

However, varied organic agro-ecosystems are possible and not all replicate traditional farming systems. For example, organic agriculture can depend on fossil fuels for energy and on high import of organic material to farms. There may be a high degree of specialization in farm production and significant agricultural biodiversity loss. The use of some organic materials can pose health risks unless appropriate care is taken; for example, the use of human excreta as fertilizer. Wildlife may be threatened by habitat change, although the degree of change may be less than with industrialized modern agriculture.

Some forms of organic agriculture, for example, cattle and sheep grazing in parts of Australia, involve extensive land use. Nevertheless, such land uses have been implicated in loss of wild species and significant habitat changes (Tisdell, 2002, p. 91).

While organic farming is likely to be more favourable to the conservation of wildlife than non-organic farming (for example, because it does not use chemical pesticides), that does not mean that organic farming is favourable to biodiversity in the wild. Organic agriculture usually involves major changes in natural habitat or, in the terminology of Swanson (1994, 1995), much land conversion. This is an important factor in reducing biodiversity in the wild. Furthermore, not all organic farmers are favourably disposed towards wildlife (McNeely and Scherr, 2003, p. 91).

5. Agriculture and the conservation of wild biodiversity

Many conservationists favour protection of wild biodiversity as an ingredient of sustainability. Unfortunately, the development of agriculture, particularly modern agriculture, has reduced this biodiversity and threatens to reduce it even further (McNeely and Scherr, 2003, Ch.4; Pretty, 1998, pp. 62–5; Tisdell, 1997).

The mechanisms by which agricultural expansion (especially of modern agriculture) does this are varied and complex. They include: land clearing and conversion which results in loss of habitat for many wild species (cf. Swanson, 1994; 1995); greater uniformity of habitat with loss of diversity in niches and loss of niches for wild species (Tisdell, 1999c, Ch. 4); increased competition of agriculturalists with wild species for natural resources resulting in less availability of these resources to wild animals and/or the destruction of wild species by agriculturalists as pests; poisoning of wildlife as a side effect of agricultural pesticide use; and the release of pollutants from farms that poison wildlife or alter their natural environments in an unfavourable way. For example, eutrophication of water bodies as a result of farm run-off of nutrients can lead to the demise of some wild species.

In addition, hydrological changes brought about by modern farming can seriously affect wild biodiversity. For example, farm irrigation schemes can greatly reduce the level of flows and cyclical patterns of river flows and this can adversely affect species dependent on the previously natural rhythms, for example their breeding, and lead to loss of seasonal wetlands, and even permanent wetlands. Regeneration of the red river gum on the Murray River basin in Australia, for instance, is threatened by the fact that this river is heavily utilized for human use (mostly agricultural) and the variability of its flows has been much reduced. Red river gums are important for the survival of several Australian wildlife species. In addition, the breeding of several species of wild duck is hampered by reduced frequency of flooding. Or to give another example, removal of trees with the aim of increasing agricultural productivity (an aim not always realized in this case) often leads to the death of other trees and vegetation in areas subject to dryland salinity. Furthermore, streams and other water bodies in the area may become very saline. This can result in loss of native species as has occurred in parts of Western Australia.

Because agriculture (broadly defined) accounts for the use of such a large area of land globally (McNeely and Scherr, 2003, p. 32; Tisdell, 2004) and, politically at least, large increases in protected areas are unlikely, maintenance of wild biodiversity is highly dependent on conservation of wildlife outside protected areas. With this in mind, McNeely and Scherr (2003, Ch. 5) have advocated the development of eco-agriculture, this is the development of agriculture that is more favourable than currently to the protection of wild biodiversity and natural ecosystems. They outline policies that might be adopted to promote eco-agriculture. However, some of these policies may require more in-depth consideration. For example, they recommend increasing farm productivity as a means to reduce land conversion to agriculture and give a favourable impression of Green Revolution technology saying that it 'almost certainly helped to slow land conversion in the developing world' (McNeely and Scherr, 2003, p. 136). However, while it certainly helped to provide more food for people, it is by no means clear that it had positive consequences for wild biodiversity conservation.

In fact, a difference in views appears to exist among conservationists about which forms of agriculture are most favourable to nature conservation. Some conservationists favour intensive agriculture and silviculture on the basis that this is highly productive compared to extensive agriculture or silviculture (FAO, 2003), whereas others favour the opposite policy.

Those favouring intensive agriculture or silviculture believe that, although major habitat change would occur in the farmed or plantation area, this will enable a larger land area to remain in a natural state than if extensive agriculture and silviculture is practised, and that this will conserve more biodiversity in the wild than otherwise. However, the situation appears to be quite complex and needs more intensive evaluation before coming to a firm policy conclusion.

6. Discussion

If the productivity of modern industrialized agriculture is unsustainable, why have such agro-ecosystems been so widely adopted and why do they continue to be adopted given private and social misgivings about them? Let us consider such a choice from the viewpoint of an individual agriculturalist and from a social perspective.

Agriculturalists may adopt modern industrialized agro-ecosystems for the following reasons:

- They may be unaware of the degree to which these systems lack sustainability. Sellers of external agricultural inputs that contribute to this lack of sustainability have no incentive to inform potential buyers about this aspect.

- High levels of present returns available in the short- to medium-term from modern agriculture may be attractive to farmers. They may, for example, discount their future returns at a high rate. The aim of many is to obtain funds to educate their children so they can earn higher incomes by leaving agriculture. Furthermore, if a higher return on funds can be obtained from investment of the capital tied up in an agricultural property by investing it elsewhere in the economy, there is an economic incentive to realize the capital (for example, by mining farm resources) and invest the capital elsewhere (Clark, 1976).

- Modern economies are cash-based economies. Farmers need to obtain cash to educate their children, obtain health services, obtain other non-agricultural commodities and pay government taxes. To do this, farmers must market produce. When market transaction costs and other factors are taken into account, the costs of using traditional methods of production to supply agricultural produce to markets may exceed that from the use of modern agricultural techniques. Market competition may make it uneconomical for farmers to use traditional techniques, even if modern techniques result in higher costs in the long-term (Tisdell, 1999b, pp. 48–53). The market itself becomes a barrier to the retention of traditional agricultural technologies.

- Government policies appear to encourage the development of commercial agriculture via the nature of their extension services, information provision, the direction of agricultural research and, in some cases, subsidies for external inputs. This may partly reflect urban bias (Lipton, 1977) since urban populations depend on the agricultural surplus supplied by commercial agriculture.

- In some societies, power relationships and entitlements in families may bias agricultural development in favour of commercial crops produced from modern agro-ecosystems. For instance, in some parts of Africa, husbands have control of cash earned from cash crops, and control of crops by women is mostly restricted to subsistence crops (Kiriti and Tisdell, 2003; 2004).

- Environmental spillovers from modern farming practices will be ignored by farmers in their private decisions unless their costs or benefits are internalized. Farm costs still do not reflect many of these externalities.

A second pertinent question is why do modern agrosystems have so much social support if they are unsustainable? Reasons may include the following: current generations may not be as much concerned about the fate of future generations as is sometimes imagined; their practical concern may extend to only two or three future generations. Or again, it may be widely believed that scientific advances will be able to address any agricultural sustainability problems that may arise in the future. Furthermore, special interest groups and governments may be myopic in their outlook.

The increasing dominance of economic liberalism based on market operations is likely to reinforce the dominant position of modern industrialized agriculture. Increasingly governments have vacated the area of agricultural R&D in favour of private corporations and have passed property rights legislation covering new plant varieties and transgenic material. These provide incentives to private industry to develop and market new genetic material. This is likely to increase the dependence of agriculture on external inputs and may further reduce agricultural biodiversity (Altieri, 1999). In a market system, suppliers of agricultural materials are interested in promoting open agricultural systems rather than closed ones. This is because the more closed an agricultural system, the fewer are the sales of agricultural suppliers.

7.   Concluding remarks

Modern industrialized agricultural systems have produced considerable farm surpluses and have enabled large urban populations to be sustained at relatively high standards of living. Doubts, however, have arisen about how well these modern systems can sustain their productivity in the long run given their high level of dependence on external inputs, their open cycles, their degradation of their natural resource base and their erosion of genetic assets. Nevertheless, there seems little prospect of a return to traditional agro-ecosystems in the near future. It is difficult to see how they would be able to support the degree of global urbanization that currently exists and which is growing, especially in developing countries.

At the same time, there is a case for greater government intervention in modern agriculture to increase its sustainability. For instance, there is a case for public policies, such as taxes on unfavourable agricultural externalities or subsidies on favourable externalities, that ensure externalities are taken into account by farmers (cf. Robertson and Swinton, 2005). However, lack of agricultural sustainability does not arise solely from lack of consideration of environmental spillovers, as should be clear from the above discussion.

Market systems can encourage the use of unsustainable productive practices. Policy makers should, therefore, be more guarded in their support for market extension, particularly in developing areas where subsistence and semi-subsistence agriculture still prevails. Increased government support for agro-ecological research (Dalgaard et al., 2003; Pretty, 2003) may also be justified. This is because its benefits are mostly internal to farms, and property rights in its research results are difficult or impossible to establish and enforce. In a market system, researchers have little economic incentive to engage in such research because they can appropriate few gains by marketing commodities based on results from it.

The market system, the driving force of modern agriculture, appears to be a two-edged sword. On the one hand, market extension promotes the division of labour and specialization in agricultural production (as well as other types of production), and as Adam Smith (1910) pointed out, these are forces for raising productivity in any economy. But, on the other hand, will this increase in agricultural productivity be sustained? Market extension brings into play forces (identified in this chapter) that at the very least make it difficult to sustain the productivity of market-based agriculture. This needs to be more widely recognized than at present. In addition, the view expressed by White et al. (1993, p. 236) that 'on balance, markets probably promote sustainability more than they hurt [it]' is not proven. Furthermore, even if this statement by White et al. is false, current societies do not appear to be in a mood, nor in a position, to alter radically their market systems in the foreseeable future. We may now be locked into market systems.

Note

1. I wish to thank Hemanath Swarna Nantha for research assistance. Portions of this work have indirectly benefited from an Australian Research Council grant for the study of the economics of conserving wildlife.

References

Altieri, M.A. (1995), *Agroecology the Science of Sustainable Agriculture*, Boulder: Westview Press.

Altieri, M.A. (1999), 'The environmental risk of transgenic crops on agroecological assessment', in I. Serageldin and W. Collins (eds), *Biotechnology and Biosafety*, Washington, DC: World Bank, pp. 31–38.

Altieri, M.A. (2000), 'Ecological impacts of industrial agriculture and the possibilities for truly sustainable farming', in F. Magdoff, J.B. Foster and F.H. Buttel (eds), *Hungry for Profit: The Agribusinesses Threat to Farmers, Food and the Environment*, New York: Monthly Review Press, pp. 77–92.

Altieri, M.A. (2004), 'Linking ecologists and traditional farmers in the search for sustainable agriculture', *Frontiers in Ecology and the Environment*, 3(1): 35–42.

Christen, O. (1996), 'Sustainable agriculture – history, concept and consequences for research, education and extension', *Berichte Uber Landwirtschaft*, **74**(1): 66–86.

Clark, C.W. (1976), *Mathematical Bioeconomics: The Optimal Management of Renewable Resources*, New York: John Wiley.

Conway, G.R. (1985), 'Agroecosystems analysis', *Agricultural Administration*, **20**: 31–5.

Conway, G.R. (1987), 'The properties of agroecosystems', *Agricultural Systems*, **24**: 95–117.

Conway, G.R. (1998), *The Doubly Green Revolution: Food for All in the Twenty-First Century*, Ithaca: Cornell University Press.

Conway, G.R. and E.B. Barbier (1990), *After the Green Revolution: Sustainable Agriculture for Development*, London: Earthscan.

Dalgaard, T., N.J. Hutchings and J.R. Porter (2003), 'Agroecology, scaling and interdisciplinarity', *Agriculture, Ecosystems and Environment*, **100**: 39–51.

Engels, F. (1959), 'Outlines of a critique of political economy', in K. Marx (ed.), *Economic and Philosophic Manuscript of 1844*, Moscow: Foreign Languages Publishing House.

Ewel, J.J. (1999), 'Natural systems as models for the design of sustainable systems of land use', *Agroforestry Systems*, **45**: 1–21.

Ewel, J.J., M.J. Mazzarino and C.W. Berish (1991), 'Tropical soil fertility changes under mono-cultures and successional communities of different structure', *Ecological Applications*, **1**: 289–302.

FAO (2003), *State of the World's Forests 2003*, Rome: Food and Agriculture Organization.

Gliessman, S.R. (1998), *Agroecology: Ecological Process in Sustainable Agriculture*, Ann Arbor, MI: Ann Arbor Press.

Heffernan, W.D. (2000), 'Concentration of ownership and control of agriculture', in F. Magdoff, J.B. Foster and F.H. Buttel (eds), *Hungry for Profit: The Agribusiness Threat to Farmers, Food and the Environment*, New York: Monthly Review Press, pp. 61–75.

Kiriti, T.W. and C.A. Tisdell (2003), 'Commercialisation of agriculture in Kenya: a case study of policy bias and food purchases by farm households', *Quarterly Journal of International Agriculture*, **42**: 439–57.

Kiriti, T.W. and C.A. Tisdell (2004), 'Marital status, farmsize and other influences on the extent of cash cropping in Kenya: a household case study', *Indian Development Review*, **2**: 185–204.

Lampkin, N.H. and S. Padel (1994), *The Economics of Organic Farming: An International Perspective*, Wallingford, UK: CABI.

Lipton, M. (1977), *Why Poor People Stay Poor: A study of Urban Bias in World Development*, London: Temple Smith.

Malthus, T.R. (1798), *An Essay on the Principle of Population as it Affects the Future Improvement of Mankind*, London: J. Johnson.

McNeely, J.A. and J.J. Scherr (2003), *Ecoagriculture: Strategies to Feed the World and Save Wild Biodiversity*, Washington, DC: Island Press.

Pretty, J. (1998), *The Living Land*, London: Earthscan.

Pretty, J. (2003), 'Agroecology in developing countries. The promise of a sustainable harvest', *Environment*, **45**(9): 9–20.

Ramakrishnan, P.S. (1992), *Shifting Agriculture and Sustainable Development*, Paris: UNESCO and Carnforth, UK: The Parthenon Publishing Group.

Ricardo, D. (1817), *The Principles of Political Economy and Taxation*, London: J. Murray.

Robertson, G.P. and S.M. Swinton (2005), 'Reconciling agricultural productivity and environmental integrity: a grand challenge for agriculture', *Frontiers in Ecology and the Environment*, **3**(1): 38–46.

Smith, A. (1910), *The Wealth of Nations*, London: J.M. Dent and Sons, first edn, 1776.

Swanson, T.M. (1994), *The International Regulation of Extinction*, New York: New York University Press.

Swanson, T.M. (1995), 'Why does biodiversity decline? The analysis of forces for global change', in T.M. Swanson (ed.), *The Economics and Ecology of Biodiversity Decline: The Forces Driving Global Change*, Cambridge, UK: Cambridge University Press.

Tisdell, C.A. (1997), 'Agricultural sustainability and conservation of biodiversity: competing policies and paradigms', in A.K. Dragun and K.M. Jakobsson (eds), *Sustainability and Global Environmental Policy: New Perspectives*, Cheltenham, UK and Northampton, MA, USA: Edward Elgar, pp. 97–118.

Tisdell, C.A. (1999a), 'Conditions for sustainable development: weak and strong', in A.K. Dragun and C. Tisdell (eds), *Sustainable Agriculture and Environment*, Cheltenham, UK and Northampton, MA, USA: Edward Elgar, pp. 23–36.

Tisdell, C.A. (1999b), 'Ecological aspects of ecology and sustainable agriculture production', in A.K. Dragun and C.A. Tisdell (eds), *Sustainable Agriculture and Environment*, Cheltenham, UK and Northampton, MA, USA: Edward Elgar, pp. 37–56.

Tisdell, C.A. (1999c), *Biodiversity, Conservation and Sustainable Development*, Cheltenham, UK and Northampton, MA, USA: Edward Elgar.

Tisdell, C.A. (2002), *The Economics of Conserving Wildlife and Natural Areas*, Cheltenham, UK and Northampton, MA, USA: Edward Elgar.

Tisdell, C.A. (2003), 'Socioeconomic causes of loss of animal genetic diversity: analysis and assessment', *Ecological Economics*, **45**: 365–76.

Tisdell, C.A. (2004), 'Economic incentives to conserve wildlife on private lands: analysis and policy', *The Environmentalist*, **24**: 153–63.
White, D.C., J.B. Braden and R.H. Hornbaker (1993), 'Economics of sustainable agriculture', in J.L. Hatfield and D.L. Karlen (eds), *Sustainable Agriculture Systems*, Boca Raton, Florida: Lewis Publications, pp. 229–60.

23 Corporate sustainability: accountability or impossible dream?
Rob Gray and Jan Bebbington

1. Introduction

Corporations are, at the risk of over-simplification, the engines of the economy. They are the key means through which economic activity takes place (and, under the neo-liberal agenda, they will be so increasingly). Corporations are so often the seat of innovation through which growth is sought and, apparently, achieved. They are, indubitably, the site of increasing economic and political power (see, for example, Korten, 1995). It seems incontrovertible that, in the absence of a fundamental change in the political will of governments (especially those of the developed world), any serious examination of sustainability and how it might be achieved must have the corporation at its heart. (For more detail, see, for example, Hawken et al., 1999; Gladwin et al., 1995; Kovel, 2002.)

And yet that is precisely what the Rio Earth Summit, through the good offices of the International Chamber of Commerce (ICC) and (what became known as) the World Business Council for Sustainable Development (WBCSD), managed to avoid. The Earth Summit explicitly excluded the corporate world from its analysis and recommendations on the apparently sober grounds that the sustainable development agenda was safe in the hands of business and that business would deliver sustainability to the people (see especially Mayhew, 1997). However implausible – even impossible – such a claim might seem, many leading corporations have adopted the language of sustainable development as their own and have, if anything, stepped up the level of claims for the sustainability of their companies' operations (see, for example, SustainAbility/UNEP, 2001, p. 10). To what extent are such assurances valid? The truth of the matter is that no one can know for certain. As we shall see below, the business community seems strangely reluctant to produce convincing evidence to support its claims of sustainability. At the same time, the prima facie case is that the primary engine of economic development is, in all probability, a major *source* of the unsustainability – not its cure. This is a conclusion drawn in the light of much of the evidence of planetary sustainability continuing to go in the wrong direction (see, especially, Meadows et al., 2005).

It is this crucial matter that we will try and unpick in this chapter. The following section explores a number of the key systemic elements of the relationship between corporations and sustainability and then section 3 examines whether or not there is a 'business case' for the adoption of sustainability. Section 4 looks at the potential of eco-efficiencies and social responsibility in the move towards sustainability whilst section 5 looks at a selection of the new accounting systems that try and measure (aspects of) sustainability at the corporate level. Section 6 of the chapter explores reporting for and about sustainability whilst section 7 provides some brief conclusions.

2. Corporations and approaches to sustainability

'Corporate sustainability' has more than a little of the oxymoron about it. Corporations – at least large, modern, western corporations relentlessly guided by the irresistible exigencies of financial markets – are driven to seek out growth in the name of profitability. Only in the most unlikely of circumstances can such (relatively single-minded pursuit of) growth be seen as 'sustainable'. Perhaps the growth might succeed, through impressive (and typically elusory) eco-efficiencies, to *reduce* the ecological footprint of the organization or even the industry. Perhaps single-mindedly ensuring that the shareholders receive at least the level of increase in returns that they expect really *does* increase the welfare and well-being of all the communities that the organization touches. But it is not especially likely – and any conscious steps taken by the corporation towards greater social justice and/or reduced ecological footprint are only bi-products of a fairly relentless searching out of cost reductions, risk reductions and income opportunities.

So if one were seeking to move away from unsustainability, it is not so very obvious that the corporation would be the place to start. What is more, the larger corporations – and, most especially, business representative groups – do seem to be pathologically[1] opposed to any form of 'tinkering with the market' (what most people would call regulation) that might offer any kind of perceived restriction on corporate wealth-creation opportunities (sic). To avoid any such constraints, businesses lobby in many overt – and increasingly subtle – ways,[2] thus ensuring that any attempts to, for example, mandate formal accountability over sustainability; develop taxation regimes that might (for example) internalize externalities and thus significantly reduce the production of waste; or move towards massive reductions in energy use; are stifled by business for a range of very obvious reasons. (This was so clearly demonstrated at the Rio Earth Summit; see, for example, Welford, 1997; Mayhew, 1997; Eden, 1996.) There was a time when it was popular to think that a major purpose of the state was to monitor and regulate business – a risible notion it now seems when a major task of business appears to be to monitor and regulate the state (see, for example, Bakan, 2004).

There is another compelling reason to think that if we wish to get there (sustainability) one would be advised not to start from here (the corporation in advanced global financial capitalism). That is, sustainability itself is primarily a global concept. Whilst it can be developed to sit comfortably at regional and eco-systems levels and it might, at a stretch, make some oblique sense at a factory or site level, to equate a spatial concept like 'sustainability' with a financial concept like 'corporation' involves a considerable intellectual leap of faith. That is, it is not clear what one would need to demand of each economic unit in order for a region or an industry or a planet to be itself sustainable – clearly there is no absolute requirement that each unit or entity must be fully sustainable of and by itself. So it is perhaps less difficult – although still very testing – to imagine a sustainable world in which groups of economic activity are collectively sustainable. We must, therefore, tread carefully then when trying to attempting to translate sustainability to the level of the organization.

And yet the current system of economic organization means that the primary locus of power, decision-making, privilege and economic (as well as social and environmental) impact in the economy is at the level of the organization. This disjunction must be addressed in some way. And whilst we can never, by definition, know whether a global or regional position of 'sustainability' has been reached by a focus exclusively on organizational performance, we may well be able to gain a more detailed and analytical understanding of the situation we face and bring the 'engines of the economy' formally back into the reckoning by examining the degree of *unsustainability* of the corporate sector.[3]

Such a strategy would operate on the principle that whilst we may never know what a 'sustainable' corporation looked like, we could certainly identify unsustainable organizations. That is, an organization which is demonstrably using non-renewable natural capital and/or failing to replenish or substitute for other forms of natural capital and which can be shown to be exploiting and advancing social inequity and/or other manifestations of social injustice is clearly, in itself, unsustainable. This does not, of course, mean that the whole system is therefore unsustainable. But if such a description could be made of even a substantial minority of major economic units then one might begin to argue that an a priori case of unsustainability needs to be considered. Further, if all (or most) economic organizations could be seen to be significantly unsustainable then we may conclude that our economic system is, itself, unsustainable. On the available evidence this would appear – to us at least – to be the current case.

There are, quite obviously, a range of different assumptions about the components of this abstract state of unsustainability.[4] Each set of assumptions offers a different basis on which to begin to assess the likely size of the sustainability mountain that mankind will have to climb if it is to survive. For ourselves, whilst we could offer nothing more substantial than acts of imagination about what a sustainable world might look like if we set off in its pursuit now, we are entirely convinced that the unsustainability we currently face is deep, systemic and only, barely, recoverable. We subscribe therefore to a 'deep green' view bordering on ecologism. In line with, for example, the recent *Limits to Growth: the 30-year Update* (Meadows et al., 2005) we are unable to imagine substantial reductions in unsustainability without profound structural and systemic change – and soon.

Although few authors examining the business–sustainability interface are explicit about their own conception of the size of the 'problem', most manage to work successfully with an indistinct 'we know unsustainability when we see it' approach – (which has the advantage of not scaring or alienating corporate clients too greatly). Some authors have sought, with varying degrees of success, to imagine what corporations in a sustainable world might look like (Hawken et al., 1999; Willums, 1998). A particularly insightful approach has been taken by the widely acclaimed *Factor Four* in which are outlined a number of the technological solutions from which a sustainable economy might be built.[5] This analysis then leads to an examination of what the current impediments are in the present economy which stop these possibilities being realized and, conversely, what major surgery is needed on the *corpus economicus* to permit innovative and sustainable solutions to emerge and become the norm. Further work has also been initiated which seeks to examine how groups of organizations in a particular *locale* might mutually support each other in the development of 'sustainability parks' (see, for example, Clayton et al., 1999). But perhaps the greatest effort in this, still emerging, area has been directed at what organizations *can* (as opposed to should) do (the art of the possible) that may take them closer to a position of sustainability. Broadly, this effort has led to initiatives concerned with eco-efficiencies and social responsibility, (in this the WBCSD has perhaps been the most prominent); initiatives concerned to develop new metrics and information systems for organizations; and, thirdly, initiatives concerned with developing wider and more detailed accountability. It is on these three that the rest of the chapter will concentrate.

3. The business case for sustainability?
Before proceeding with an, inevitably, brief examination of efforts and initiatives in the field, it is necessary to try and spell out a central tenet – and, indeed, a central source of conflict – in the development of the notion of

the sustainable corporation. That is: is it, or can it ever be, in businesses' own self-interest to pursue sustainability? To read much business literature (most notably Corporate Annual Reports and Sustainability Reports – see below) and, more particularly, to listen to business commentators and representative groups (SustainAbility/UNEP, 2001; Schmidheiny, 1992) one would be left with the impression that a business pursuing the maximization of shareholder wealth (or whatever analogue of maximizing profits is currently in fashion) faces little or no conflict when asked to seek out sustainability. That is 'the business case' for a corporation to pursue sustainability is frequently offered as self-evident.[6] Unfortunately, little or no evidence is offered for this contention,[7] rather it seems as though the corollary – that business might not be sustainable – is quite simply unthinkable and is, therefore, treated as if no such possibility could exist.

The problem here is threefold. First, one is left questioning, if the case for sustainable development at the corporate level is so self-evident, why are most companies not more obviously pursuing it? (And why, indeed, do companies so actively resist any suggestion that business might move in this direction?) Second, one is also left wondering, if corporations are so clearly either sustainable or on the path to sustainability why are they so patently unwilling to share the evidence to this effect in their reporting? (We examine this issue more fully below.) Finally, it seems to us (and we are far from alone in this view) that the prima facie case must be that business is actually unsustainable and is likely to remain so under present economic and legal arrangements. Consider the following.

At its simplest, the standard definition of sustainability (from the Brundtland Commission, WCED, 1987) requires that the needs of present generations and the needs of future generations are met and that this involves both environmental and social justice for both the present and the future generations. The WBCSD (Schmidheiny, 1992) coined the notion of 'eco-efficiency' (which they define as 'doing more with less') to capture the issues of 'environmental justice' and environmental stewardship in terms which business can understand. However, whilst eco-efficiency may well capture the reduction in use of environmental resources *per unit* it fails to capture increases in *total* environmental resources through material growth in consumption and production. To capture this latter notion we have coined the phrase *eco-effectiveness* (in order to capture the difference indicated by the notion of the ecological footprint). So, for a condition of sustainability to obtain, there must be fairly reliable evidence that a total of six conditions (as represented by the six cells shown in Table 23.1) are being satisfied. Our judgement of the evidence is that there is *no* evidence to suggest that more than one or two of the least important are currently being satisfied – even under the most rose-tinted of interpretations.[8]

Table 23.1   Are the conditions of sustainability being satisfied?

Elements of sustainability	The needs of the present generation	The needs of future generations
Social justice	×	×
Eco-efficiency	× (?)	✓ (??)
Eco-effectiveness	×	×

Source: Adapted from Gray and Bebbington (2001).

The importance of this argument is that, if it is indeed the case that there are a number of substantial conflicts between the pursuit of conventional profit and the pursuit of sustainability, then (i) business will struggle to deliver sustainability and (ii) experiments and initiatives by organizations should, if they are of substance, reveal the conflict. (Such experiments should also show how and why the conflicts arise and the difficulties they present to the corporation.) Initiatives vary considerably in this regard.

4.   Towards the triple bottom line? Eco-efficiencies and social responsibility

The first step towards a more sustainable organization is often assumed to be thinking about what John Elkington (Elkington, 1997) termed businesses' 'triple bottom line' (TBL). The TBL comprises an economic, a social and an environmental element and, it is argued, the balancing of these three may well move organizations in more potentially sustainable directions. Whilst the economic element of the TBL might be approximated by the profit figure,[9] many businesses and business commentators have assumed that eco-efficiency might approximate the environmental 'bottom line' whilst social responsibility might approximate the social element.

There seems little question that corporations the world over have made significant strides in the direction of eco-efficiency. The reasons are simple: the natural ability of organizations to innovate has been combined with the firm's primary motivator – profitability – in the form of a potential source of income and/or cost reduction. Energy efficiency, waste reduction and initiatives such as design for the environment all offer direct potential financial benefits to the company whilst offering the prospect of a lower environmental impact. These are the so-called 'win–win' situations (Walley and Whitehead, 1994) that business (and its dominant measurement system, accounting) is well-equipped to seek out and exploit.

To the natural efficiencies that organizations can exploit has been added a range of additional potentials as a result of governmental initiative. Changing the taxation of certain resources; offering grants and other financial incentives for the adoption of (say) pollution-reducing technology; increasing the policing of environmental performance and the associated fines; trading in emission permits and so on, all go towards offering responsive organizations new opportunities for income or opportunities for the reduction of costs. Carefully chosen, such initiatives significantly enhance the win–win possibilities facing the firm.

If these win–win situations sound mostly like 'carrots', there has also been a simultaneous increase in the 'sticks' of liability and risk. Liabilities that corporations might face come in many forms – fines, loss of contracts, increases in costs and so on – but the most striking has tended to be with the liabilities for contaminated land. This has been exemplified, (again most strikingly), in the US where one of an organization's most valuable assets – land – can be discovered to be contaminated and a source of immense potential clean-up costs.[10]

Such potential liabilities (with their legal overtones) merge into a more general area of 'environmental risk' where an organization might be concerned by, for example, the loss of customers, disenchantment of employees, mistrust by governments, loss of reputation and so on as a result of its (actual or perceived) environmental performance.[11] No organization wishes to be systematically subject to such negative affects and is, thereby, motivated to manage and reduce those risks.

It is risks such as these which lead to the adoption of (at least the rhetoric of) social responsibility. Again, here, there are win–win situations for the firm to exploit (customer and employee loyalty, reputation in the employment market, trust with regulators and so on), but there is also an increasing array of sources of encouragement and/or legislation for the enterprise to adopt practices that are understood to be more socially responsible. Indeed, it is the prospect of public embarrassment as much as any other single other thing that seems to have encouraged a wider spread of such things as Fairtrade products, product stewardship 'councils' (such as the Marine Stewardship Council and the Forestry Stewardship Council) and the careful examination of child labour practices.

Whilst, on the surface at least, all of these initiatives appear to be potentially commensurate with moves towards sustainability, this is not necessarily so. There seem to be three principal reasons for this. First, the TBL is not a necessarily reliable indicator of sustainability unless, at a minimum, the three elements can be seen to be derived directly from a formal understanding of sustainability in the first place. This is quite obviously not the case here. Second, it is exceptionally unlikely that eco-efficiency can deliver a reduced ecological footprint or that the adoption of a number of risk-driven social responsibility policies can ever begin to deliver any notion of social justice – however defined. Finally, each of the initiatives voluntarily adopted by corporations (or, more generally, introduced by government with the support and advice of business) can be said to go with the 'grain of market'. That is, such initiatives, by definition, must offer no challenge to any of the systemic structural issues that might give rise to the concerns that one may have about unsustainability. Consequently, such initiatives must fail to offer any challenge to the notion of an economic activity justified through a neo-classical economics and guided by an economic-based profit measure which themselves have little or no explicit capacity for social or environmental concerns. So, again by definition, such initiatives cannot be conceptually consonant with any notion that it might be impossible for a profit-seeking entity driven by an unforgiving financial market (that is shareholders of quoted companies) to do other than maximize consumption, maximize pollution, maximize wastefulness, and maximize externalities as a result of the relentless pursuit of profit, (see, for example, Kovel, 2002; Bakan, 2004).

As a result, we need to tread carefully around any notions (like eco-efficiency and social responsibility) that appear to sit so comfortably with business. That is, however worthy and benign these notions might appear to be and however attractive some slightly anodyne notion of TBL might appear, the chance of an approach based on these notions ever delivering anything vaguely in tune with sustainability seems diminishingly small. (For more detail, see Henriques and Richardson, 2004).

5.   Beyond the triple bottom line: developing new metrics

In an attempt to get beyond the 'comfort zone' offered by environmental management and stakeholder management (the more formal terms for what we have described above) there have been a series of experiments which have sought to explore that interface of conflict between the traditional pursuit of business goals and the exigencies of sustainability. These experiments have tended to be located around the development (or exploration) of various metrics through which an organization might address its unsustainability[12] and an illustrative selection of these will indicate their potential.

One line of approach can be particularly well illustrated by a strand of work undertaken by the World Resources Institute (WRI). This approach is based on the derivation, development and application of performance indicators[13] of less unsustainable practices that can be used in – and about – businesses. For instance, one of the WRI publications – *Sustainability Rulers* (Ranganathan, 1998) – synthesizes over 50 studies concerned with the derivation (and, less frequently, the integration) of social and environmental indicators that can be used as adjuncts to the more traditional financial performance measurement. Perhaps the paper's primary contribution (in addition to providing an accessible digest of this material) lies in the difficulties that it highlights: key amongst these are the near impossibility of getting any acceptance (and hence use) of indicators which are not fully integrated with the financial performance measurement systems; and the continuing difficulty of developing any sensible integration between the economic, the social and the environmental in the derivation of meta-indicators. These are problems that have dogged performance indicators for almost as long as they have been used, and the resistance to their adoption almost certainly says more about the system than it does about the indicators.

A different approach to identifying the (un-)sustainable organization can be found in the related approaches of 'sustainable cost analysis' and 'sustainability gap analysis'.[14]

The 'sustainable cost analysis' has a number of variants. At its simplest it is the application of the concept of the maintenance of man-made, renewable/substitutable and critical natural capital at the level of the organization. The sustainable organization would be one which maintained these three capitals over an 'accounting' period allowing for expenditure on man-made and renewable capital to repair or remediate or substitute for capital usage. As no organization currently behaves like this, the 'sustainable cost' is the amount that the organization *would have had to spend* if it *had been* sustainable. The figures that result from this tend to be enormous given that, *inter alia*, critical natural capital is, by definition, often irreplaceable and therefore of infinite cost, (see, for example, Gray, 1992). Although this approach demonstrated that few, if any, corporations are sustainable, it hit a series of significant practical problems – not least amongst which is that 'sustainable options' are not available to organizations and those that are available would involve quite enormous quantities of other resources – including staff time (see, for example, Bebbington and Gray, 2001). As a consequence, the approach mellowed into an examination of *remediation –* what would it cost to repair the damage caused by organizational activity? (The most obvious example of this is the sequestration of carbon dioxide.) It is here that Forum for the Future (an independent think-tank based in Britain) took up the story and has continued working on ways to produce useable metrics at the level of business. Whilst the work continues to show that businesses are not environmentally sustainable, in its adoption of weaker forms of sustainability as the underlying principle, the potential costs involved seem less frightening to the corporate mind (see, for example, Howes, 2004).[15]

A very different approach has been developed by BP working in conjunction with academic and consultancy partners (see, for example, Baxter et al., 2004). The 'Sustainability Assessment Model' (SAM) is, in its initial incarnation at least, a project-based system of analysis which produces a *signature* of the project's economic, social, environmental and resource impacts over its life. The resultant signature gives managers a handle on where the 'positives' and 'negatives' of the project may lie; how that signature compares with other competing possible projects and, indeed, in an ideal world, how that signature conforms to a standard set by the company concerned. The undoubted value of the 'tool' lies in its making the impacts tangible in a way which managers can then address directly and seek to reduce where appropriate. And, although the signature is not the sustainability of the project as such and any simple quantification owes as much to its assumptions as to its calculations, the approach has enjoyed a widespread practical application in organizations which are seeking to formally identify how far from their 'zone of comfort' the demands of sustainable development actually lie.

Key to all of the foregoing examples is that they systematically – albeit in a different way – demonstrate the unsustainability of the organization. The data which then emerges from these experiments offers managers of integrity the possibility of seeking to reduce that unsustainability of operations. What seems increasingly evident, however, is that the discretion over the unsustainability/sustainability of the organization's activities available to any manager, regardless of their individual commitment, is fairly slight. Therefore, few, if any, corporations can successfully become sustainable without considerable outside help and systemic adjustment. But, to listen to most businesses and business commentators (see, for example, KPMG, 2002, p. 26), it seems obvious that this message is not getting through – the majority, if they think about it at all, continue to blithely assume that their organization is sustainable.[16] The place where these assumptions are at their most crass – but, ironically, the place where the greatest strides towards a more sustainable business community could realistically be made – is in external reporting of sustainability. It is to that that we now turn.

6. Admitting defeat? – Reporting on sustainability

Since 1990, there has been a steady and impressive growth in reporting on social and environmental issues by corporations. The vast majority of this reporting has been voluntary – and therein lies its strengths and its weaknesses. Its strengths are that such reporting has been undertaken with the enthusiastic backing of business; it has not been stifled by minimal regulatory compliance and (at its best) it has been experimental and developmental. The down-side, however, is substantial. First, relatively few corporations undertake such reporting (estimates suggest a maximum of 2000 of the world's 50 000 MNCs undertake such reporting). As a result of the voluntary nature, reporting tends to follow fashion (first it was environmental reporting; then it was social reporting; and now, increasingly, the fashion is for 'sustainability reporting' or 'corporate responsibility' reporting). The application of reporting standards and the *completeness* of that reporting are, at best, uneven. Therefore the widespread upbeat claims about the quality, diversity and incidence of 'reporting on sustainability' that are not carefully qualified might be thought to be, at best, misleading. Equally, any report which only covers selected elements of an organization's activity around a concept that it blatantly fails to define might, and not entirely unkindly, be thought a trifle dishonest, perhaps?

Detailed surveys by organizations as diverse as KPMG (1999; 2002); Corporate Register (2004); PIRC (2000) and Trucost (2004) paint a consistent but disturbing picture. Throughout the developed world, there has been a steady rise in reporting by the larger companies but only in a few countries, (notably, Japan, UK, USA, Netherlands and Germany) is this consistently more that a third of the largest 100 companies. When one turns to look at other nations or to look at slightly smaller companies in even the high-reporting countries, the proportions drop to trivial levels very quickly indeed. Reporting also varies considerably by sector. The traditionally leading sectors are pharmaceuticals, chemicals and electronics, whilst retail and financial services can normally be relied upon to bring up the rear. So, here we have the first (predictable) result of a voluntary reporting regime – most companies (predictably) ignore it.

However, such a result may not be a relevant source of depression in our quest to understand the sustainability of the corporation because, it transpires, the quality of the reports is almost universally trivial. Environmental reporting is relatively widespread but it is the very rarest of companies indeed which provide eco-balances by which a reader can judge whether all environmental interactions are covered. That is, it is not possible to assess the *completeness* of the reporting: no companies – as far as we are aware – have provided an ecological footprint so that they might comment on its increase and how that might be commensurate with environmental stewardship. Social reporting is less extensive but no report in the KPMG 2002 survey addresses the corporation's impact on social justice, and most concentrate on important, but partial, matters to do with employees and community giving. It is a rare company which provides data on the full range of its stakeholders – preferring to selectively report on interactions with a favoured few.

Within those reports identified as 'sustainability reports' the situation is no better and even those that are 'in conformance with' the *Global Reporting Initiative Sustainability Reporting Guidelines*[17] provide only the most superficial data on the extent of the organization's sustainability or otherwise. Indeed, sustainability is much more likely to be entirely ignored; it is rare to see any corporation address it all. No reasonable person could make any sensible judgement on the basis of an organization's reporting in their 'Sustainability Reports' on whether or not the organization was unsustainable.[18]

Unfortunately, the traditional sources of 'monitoring' of such reports provide only the very slightest of control over these reports. The monitoring 'in the market place' through, for example, awards schemes and surveys has steadily struggled to steer between acting as an encouragement for the leading companies (who are after all doing things voluntarily) and acting as a firm assessor of standards (and thereby risk undermining voluntary efforts).[19] The more formal route of 'audit' – which is also a voluntary undertaking in this field – has also shown itself unable to challenge its (voluntary) clients. Research has shown that the attestation or assurance statements which attach to these reports are, at best, useless and, at worst, highly misleading. They certainly do not tell us that the 'sustainability report' that they are assuring us about actually tells us nothing about sustainability.[20] Accountability over sustainability it certainly is not. The danger, of course, is that (just as happened with partial environmental reports and even more partial social reports) the very concept on which the future of the planet depends – sustainability – will be emasculated, appropriated and destroyed by (at best, well-meaning) assertions in the interests of corporations. As things currently stand, we believe we must treat the current crop of 'sustainability reports' with the profoundest mistrust as one of the most dangerous trends working *against* any possibility of a sustainable future.

The tragedy is not just that such extensive resources are used to mislead and deceive society. The real tragedy is that if sustainable business organization is ever to be achieved, then societies, individually and collectively, need to know the extent to which corporations, with the very best will in the world, are *not* capable of delivering sustainability. It is this – accountability for the extent to which a corporation *cannot* be sustainable, socially responsible and/or environmental benign – that is the real potential of corporate reporting. Only then can societies learn whether or not (a) it is necessary to reform the corporation and/or (b) it is possible for the corporation to reform itself and/or (c) the incentives and penalty systems of the society need substantial adjustment and/or (d), as we reluctantly suspect, we face a systemic problem, and unsustainability lies at the very heart of our current advanced form of international financial capitalism. Our failure to develop substantive sustainability reporting prevents us from addressing these entirely crucial matters.

7. Conclusions

In retrospect it might seem strange that anybody ever thought that the modern, large corporation driven by unforgiving financial markets could ever deliver anything but more and more consumption and, consequently, more waste, more destruction and more externalities in the name of profit. The nature of the corporation – especially when it is owned by distant shareholders whose (legal and personal) interests in the entity typically amount to little more than increasing their risk-adjusted financial returns – is an avaricious one. As Bakan (2004) so eloquently and persuasively shows, it is not in the nature of the corporation to deliver compassion, consideration, care and restraint. It is in the nature of the corporation (as Friedman so eloquently argues) to maximize financial returns whilst playing within the rules of the game. The current rules of the game do not only not encourage those activities which we might think were essential for a more sustainable world but actually make them impossible and often illegal. The corporation, unless society is able to substantially change the rules of the game cannot possibly deliver sustainability and we are somewhat crazy to think that it ever can. A different sort of enterprise, garnered around with rules, incentives and entirely different performance measurement and rewards structures may very well be able to deliver a less unsustainable world. Corporations as we currently know them surely cannot.

Notes

1. The term 'pathological' here is partly intended to stimulate thought about why those who most benefit from regulation would be most likely to oppose it and partly as an oblique reference to Bakan (2004) who is both eloquent and persuasive on this issue.
2. See, for example, SustainAbility/WWF (2005).
3. Unsustainability is a useful concept (and most importantly developed by Paul Ekins: see, for example, Ekins, 1992; Ekins et al., 2003).
4. See Bebbington and Thomson (1996) for a discussion of the assumptions underlying different conceptions of sustainability from 'strong' to 'weak' sustainability.
5. Weizsäcker et al. (1997); Elkington (1995).
6. Consequently the public statements from Ray Anderson, CEO of Interface (the world's largest carpet manufacturer) and during the 1990s from Body Shop executives to the effect that they, and probably no large corporation, is or can be sustainable are very valuable and important.
7. A significant exception to this is represented by a SustainAbility/UNEP (2001) publication, *Buried Treasure*, in which a more careful attempt to suggest that corporations as we understand them can deliver sustainability is offered. Despite SustainAbility's other work (perhaps most notably, *Who needs it?*, Elkington, 1995) the systemic challenges offered by sustainability; the lack of any evidence that a shift from our present system to a less-unsustainable one would be linear; plus the absence of *any* evidence on how ecological footprints might be controlled and reduced and how social justice might be re-empowered in the face of global corporations is left, disturbingly unaddressed.
8. Relatively recent research suggests (see Gray and Bebbington, 2000) that even environmentally leading companies have little understanding of sustainability.

9. It is now recognized that the economic impacts – both positive and negative – are greater than the profit figure as that figure ignores the economic multiplier effects from the organization's financial interactions.

10. The US legislation, known as the 'Superfund' legislation holds 'responsible parties' liable for cleaning up contaminated land. Such liabilities can be greater than the original value of the land itself. For more detail see, for example, Gray and Bebbington (2001).

11. These risks are now often collectively called 'reputation risk'.

12. These initiatives have also for a variety of reasons – mostly of a pragmatic and /or political nature – given more emphasis to environmental sustainability than social sustainability.

13. It should perhaps be noted that very many efforts in this area are driven by business and/or consultancy and, it seems as a consequence, do not pay particular attention to prior historical attempts in the relevant field. Thus whilst the work explicitly addressing sustainability is relatively recent, there have been experiments and initiative with social indicators, environmental indictors and other business-based attempts to develop social and environmental metrics for well over half a century. (See, for example, Gray et al., 1996 and Gray and Bebbington, 2001 for an introduction to a number of these historic areas.)

14. Both of these have within them the influence of the work of Paul Ekins and draw, to varying degrees, from the development of environmental (and later ecological) economics and owe a direct intellectual debt to, for example, David Pearce and Kerry Turner. And see Bebbington et al. (2001) for an introduction to the issues arising with the attempt to introduce full cost accounting at the entity level.

15. One particularly striking example of a company trying to approach such metrics within their own reporting is that of BSO Origin in the early 1990s.

16. Evidence of this assertion abounds: in the casual use of the term in corporate communications and annual reports; in the mushrooming number of conferences and books seeking to define and encourage the 'sustainable corporation'; in the adoption of the term(s) with no analysis or recognition of *any* potential for conflict with conventional business pursuit. It is at its most manifest, in our view, in two (quite breathtaking) quotations: 'The performance of companies implementing sustainability principles is superior because sustainability is a catalyst for enlightened and disciplined management' and 'The concept of corporate sustainability has long been very attractive to investors because of its aim to increase long term shareholder value' Dow Jones Sustainability Group Indexes Report Quarterly 3/99. Neither of these statements is even vaguely true or, if you prefer, there is no evidence in support of them, whilst the evidence against is potentially overwhelming.

17. www.globalreporting.org/. The Global Reporting Initiative (GRI) is a multi-stakeholder initiative which has led the field in the development of guidelines that companies wishing to approach the elusive notion of sustainability reporting may follow.

18. Imagine a conclusion that one could make no assessment of the corporation's financial position from its financial report. I think we would be justified in those circumstances in adjudging that the reports were, at best, an expensive waste of time.

19. This is an assertion based on extensive personal experience involved in just such activities. More detailed criticism of such important activities would seem churlish and simply bad manners.

20. For more detail see, for example, Ball et al. (2000); Owen et al. (2000).

References

Bakan, J. (2004), *The Corporation: the Pathological Pursuit of Profit and Power*, London: Constable and Roinson.

Ball, A., D.L. Owen and R.H. Gray (2000), 'External transparency or internal capture? The role of third party statements in adding value to corporate environmental reports', *Business Strategy and the Environment*, **9**(1): 1–23.

Baxter, T., J. Bebbington and D. Cutteridge (2004), 'Sustainability assessment model: modelling economic, resource, environmental and social flows of a project', in A. Henriques and J. Richardson (eds), *The Triple Bottom Line: does it all add up?*, London: Earthscan, pp. 113–20.

Bebbington, K.J. and R.H. Gray (2001), 'An account of sustainability: failure, success and a reconception', *Critical Perspectives on Accounting*, **12**(5): 557–87.

Bebbington, K.J. and I. Thomson (1996), *Business Conceptions of Sustainability and the Implications for Accountancy*, London: ACCA.

Bebbington, K.J., R.H. Gray, C. Hibbitt and E. Kirk (2001), *Full Cost Accounting: An Agenda for Action*, London: ACCA.

Clayton, A., G. Spinardi and R. Williams (eds) (1999), *Policies for Cleaner Technologies: A New Agenda for Government and Industry*, London: Earthscan.

Corporate Register (2004), *Towards Transparency: Progress on Global Sustainability Reporting 2004*, London: ACCA, available at http://www.accaglobal.com/pdfs/environment/towards_trans_2004.pdf.

Eden, S. (1996), *Environmental Issues and Business: Implications of a Changing Agenda*, Chichester: John Wiley.

Ekins, P. (1992), *Wealth beyond Measure: An Atlas of New Economics*, London: Gaia.

Ekins, P., S. Simon, L. Deutsch, C. Folke and R. De Groot (2003), 'A framework for the practical application of the concepts of critical natural capital and strong sustainability', *Ecological Economics*, **44**(2/3): 165–85.

Elkington, J. (1995), *Who Needs it? Market Implications of Sustainable Lifestyles*, London: SustainAbility.

Elkington, J. (1997), *Cannibals with Forks: the Triple Bottom Line of 21st century Business*, Oxford: Capstone Publishing.

Gladwin, T.N., T.-S. Krause and J.J. Kennelly (1995), 'Beyond eco-efficiency: towards socially sustainable business', *Sustainable Development*, **3**: 35–43.

Gray R.H. (1992), 'Accounting and environmentalism: an exploration of the challenge of gently accounting for accountability, transparency and sustainability', *Accounting Organisations and Society*, **17**(5): 399–426.

Gray, R.H. and K.J. Bebbington (2000), 'Environmental accounting, managerialism and sustainability: Is the planet safe in the hands of business and accounting?', *Advances in Environmental Accounting and Management*, **1**: 1–44.

Gray, R.H. and K.J. Bebbington (2001), *Accounting for the Environment*, 2nd edn, London: Sage.

Gray, R.H., D.L. Owen and C. Adams (1996), *Accounting and Accountability: Changes and Challenges in Corporate Social and Environmental Reporting*, London: Prentice Hall.

Hawken, P., A.B. Lovins and L.H. Lovins (1999), *Natural Capitalism: The Next Industrial Revolution*, London: Earthscan.

Henriques, A. and J. Richardson (2004), *The Triple Bottom Line: Does it All Add Up?* London: Earthscan.

Howes, R. (2004), 'Environmental cost accounting: Coming of age? Tracking organisation performance towards environmental sustainability', in A. Henriques and J. Richardson (eds), *The Triple Bottom Line: Does it All Add Up?*, London: Earthscan, pp. 99–112.

Korten, D.C. (1995), *When Corporations Rule the World*, West Hatford/San Francisco: Kumarian/Berrett-Koehler.

Kovel, J. (2002), *The Enemy Of Nature: The End of Capitalism or the End of the World?*, London: Zed Books.

KPMG (1999), *KPMG International Survey of Environmental Reporting 1999*, Netherlands: KPMG/WIMM.

KPMG (2002), *KPMG 4th International Survey of Corporate Sustainability Reporting*, Netherlands: KPMG/WIMM.

Mayhew, N. (1997), 'Fading to grey: the use and abuse of corporate executives' "representational power"', in R. Welford (ed.), *Hijacking Environmentalism: Corporate Response to Sustainable Development*, London: Earthscan, pp. 63–95.

Meadows, D.H., J. Randers and D.L. Meadows (2005), *Limits to Growth: the 30–year Update*, London: Earthscan.

Owen, D.L., T. Swift, M. Bowerman and C. Humphreys (2000), 'The new social audits: accountability, managerial capture or the agenda of social champions?', *European Accounting Review*, **9**(1): 81–98.

Pension & Investment Research Consultants Ltd (2000), *Environmental Reporting 2000: The PIRC Survey of the FTSE All-Share Index*, London PIRC.

Ranganathan, J. (1998), *Sustainability Rulers: Measuring Corporate Environmental and Social Performance: Sustainable Enterprises Perspectives Series*, Washington, DC: World Resources Institute.

Schmidheiny, S. (1992), *Changing Course*, New York: MIT Press.

SustainAbility (2000), *The Global Reporters: the First International Benchmark Survey of Corporate Sustainability Reporting*, London: SustainAbility/UNEP.

SustainAbility (2002), *Trust Us: The 2002 Global Reporters Survey of Corporate Sustainability Reporting*, London: SustainAbility/UNEP.

SustainAbility/UNEP (2001), *Buried Treasure: Uncovering the Business Case for Corporate Sustainability*, London: SustainAbility/UNEP.

SustainAbility/WWF (2005), *Influencing Power: Reviewing the Conduct and Content of Corporate Lobbying*, London: SustainAbility, available at http://www.sustainability.com.

Trucost (2004), *Environmental Disclosure in the Annual Report and Accounts of Companies in FTSE All-share*, Bristol: Environment Agency.

Walley, N. and B. Whitehead (1994), 'It's not easy being green', *Harvard Business Review*, May/June, pp. 46–52.

WCED (World Commission on Environment and Development) (1987), *Our Common Future (The Brundtland Report)*, Oxford: Oxford University Press.

Weizsäcker E. Von, A.B. Lovins and L.H. Lovins (1997), *Factor Four: Doubling Wealth, Halving Resource Use*, London: Earthscan.

Welford R. (ed.) (1997), *Hijacking Environmentalism: Corporate Response to Sustainable Development*, London: Earthscan.

Willums, Jan-Olaf (1998), *The Sustainable Business Challenge: A Briefing Agenda for Tomorrow's Business Leaders*, with WBCSD, Sheffield: Greenleaf Publishing.

PART VII

THE INTERNATIONAL DIMENSION

24 International environmental cooperation: the role of political feasibility
Camilla Bretteville Froyn

1. Introduction[1]

Why is it so difficult to establish effective institutions for the provision of global public goods? This chapter draws on contributions from game theory and public choice theory to explore the obstacles to creating effective institutions for the provision of public goods and how they might be overcome. In particular, it focuses on how international and domestic factors influence a country's choice regarding co-operation and compliance in international environmental agreements (IEAs).[2]

The chapter argues that the bottom line in international environmental cooperation will always be determined by what is politically feasible. Furthermore, since shared resources are prone to overuse when countries pursue unilateral policies, and since the provision of global public goods will have to rely on volunteerism, the aim of any IEA should be to ensure participation and compliance. It argues further that this can best be achieved by restructuring the relationships among countries in a mutually preferred way, taking into account the complexity of a country's negotiating position that results from the influence of different domestic constituencies with a stake in environmental policy.

Game theory is concerned with the strategic actions of different players (consumers, firms, governments, and so on) where these actions are in some way interlinked. This could for example be firms interacting in an emissions permit market or governments negotiating reductions in greenhouse gas emissions. The fundamental assumption is that players choose their strategies based on the beliefs they have regarding the choices of other players. Game theory provides tools for increased understanding of what drives the results in international co-operation.[3] The public choice literature analyzes how decisions are made by governments, focusing on how political agents motivated by self-interest seek to sway public policies. Public choice theory suggests that a proper understanding of institutional settings allows relatively straightforward net-benefit maximizing models to account for a rich and complex range of policy outcomes (Congleton, 2004), including government negotiating positions in international forums.[4, 5]

The next section provides a brief explanation for the need for IEAs, while section 3 gives a theoretical argument for why optimal levels of co-operation are so hard to achieve. The following three sections focus on ways to increase co-operation: the prevention of free-riding (section 4); a closer look at self-enforcing environmental agreements (section 5); and multiple agreements (section 6). Section 7 argues that it is important to take into account that a country's negotiating position is a result of bargains struck among different domestic interest groups. Concluding remarks are offered in the last section.

2.   The need for international environmental agreements

IEAs offer issue-specific remedies for almost every kind of international environmental problem (Barrett, 2003). They establish institutions for conserving threatened species, unique ecosystems, and sites of cultural heritage; for controlling pests and plagues; for reducing pollution; for safeguarding workers from toxic substances; for protecting animals from inhumane farming practices; for promoting the conservation of tropical forests; for controlling desertification; for banning nuclear weapons testing; and much more.[6] Some IEAs work quite effectively, such as the Montreal Protocol, which regulates emissions of substances that deplete the ozone layer, but many are weak and ineffectual.

The need for international environmental co-operation is linked to market failures in which participants' self-interested actions do not achieve an efficient outcome so that it is possible to increase the welfare of one or more individuals without harming the welfare of someone else. When market failures exist, social welfare may be increased by intervening in the market.[7] Market failures can result from externalities, which are inter-dependencies among two or more countries not taken into account by market transactions.[8] One example is transborder pollution: if the emitting country is not required to compensate the downwind country (or countries), then the emitter would have no incentive to curb its polluting activity. From a social welfare perspective, too much production is taking place unless the externality-imposed costs are included in the producer's production costs. When market failures are of an international character there is no world government that can intervene, but agreements constitute an alternative form of 'intervention'. At the international level, externalities require bilateral or multilateral agreements.

Another source of market failure is public goods. For international public goods, the benefits are shared by countries in a non-exclusive and non-rival manner. This means that the benefits from the public good can be received by payers and non-payers alike, and that one country's consumption of the good does not affect the consumption possibilities of other countries. Thus each country would be better off if all countries contribute to the provision of the public good, but each country is still better off if it can free-ride on the other country's contributions.[9] International public goods can be bilateral (for example, reducing mercury discharges that affect two countries), regional (for example, reducing sulfur dioxide emissions in Europe), or global (for example, protection of the ozone shield, protection of biodiversity, or the reduction of greenhouse gases to prevent global warming). This chapter focuses mainly on international co-operation for the provision of global environmental public goods.[10]

The characteristics of global public goods give rise to collective provision issues that are difficult to overcome, and make the need for international institutions substantial. For the purposes of this chapter, an institution is defined as a persistent and connected set of rules that prescribe behavioral roles, constrain activity, and shape expectations.[11] The rules of any institution, however, will reflect the relative position of its actual and potential members (Keohane, 1989). Rules also determine the type of institution that will develop, who will benefit, and how effective it will be. In the development of such international institutions, countries are like game players that must choose their strategies based on their beliefs about the likely choices of others. The existence of international regimes will, thus, not ensure optimal levels of cooperation. Failure to solve the problem of providing international public goods is well known, and an institution's level of success will depend on the different country's response to the agreed-upon set of rules (the design).

3. The law of the least ambitious program

The law of the least ambitious program: *Where international management can be established only through agreement among all significant parties involved, and where such a regulation is considered only on its own merits, collective action will be limited to those measures acceptable to the least enthusiastic party* (Underdal, 1980, p. 36).

The public goods problem of under-provision is particularly challenging on a global scale because there is no supranational authority to enforce an agreement. In the absence of such an authority, alternative arrangements are needed. The process of treaty-making, however, is complex and determines the quality of the outcome. A number of problems with global environmental protection have not been satisfactorily resolved through international institutions. One well-known example is fisheries, which experts for years have said have been over-fished because they have not been sufficiently regulated through international agreements. Another example is the lack of protection of tropical forests that provide public goods to the global economy through benefits from biodiversity, ecosystem linkages and carbon sequestration. The law of the least ambitious program blames this shortcoming on the unanimity rule by pointing out that it invariably places the final word with the parties who are dragging their feet.[12]

The law of the least ambitious program has a strong intuitive appeal, and offers some very basic and important insights in international cooperation (Hovi and Sprinz, 2006). What it basically says is that as long as all parties involved have to agree on the sets of rules that form the institution, the prescription of behavioral roles and constraints on activity will not be stricter than what is acceptable to the least ambitious.[13] The reason is simply that the least ambitious will suffer the smallest loss should the negotiations break down. This gives them bargaining power, and they will thus tend not to give in. The other countries, on the other hand, could choose to dump the least enthusiastic party, rather than to give in, but at a price: they could then negotiate a more potent, but incomplete, treaty.[14]

The most well-known example might be the international climate negotiations. The Kyoto Protocol, as agreed to in 1997,[15] was merely a sketch of an institution, and it took several years of tough negotiations to agree on the specific rules of conduct.[16] Compared to the original expectations of the Kyoto Protocol, the final climate treaty was a compromise and significantly watered down. The main reason for this is the minimum participation rule.[17] The US withdrawal from the climate negotiations in March 2001 gave the supporters of soft rules additional bargaining power. These parties clearly held the most rigid positions in the negotiating process, not willing to give much to reach agreement. However, the parties supporting strict rules, that is, the most ambitious, seemed to want the Kyoto Protocol to survive badly enough to place the final word with the ones in favor of soft rules (Froyn, 2001). In the end they had to give in on all areas in order to save the Kyoto Protocol,[18] which entered into force on 16 February, 2005, after 81 countries had ratified the treaty.[19]

As this example points out, the existence of international regimes will not ensure that countries will be able to achieve optimal levels of cooperation. For global public goods provision, the incentive for nations to free-ride and the costs of detecting and punishing such behavior will be greater the larger the number of countries.[20] Institutions must therefore be designed to reduce these incentives.

4. Preventing free-riding in international environmental co-operation

IEAs are established in an attempt to provide international public goods and resolve environmental externalities among government jurisdictions. The political and institutional problems that have to be overcome are therefore complex. Even if policy-making authority is delegated to an international commission, or a treaty provides incentives to participate, state sovereignty implies that domestic legislation remains the method by which such international environmental policies are implemented. Multilateral solutions to environmental problems are therefore clearly more challenging to achieve than solutions to domestic environmental problems.[21] Those challenges seem likely to linger as long as nations remain sovereign (Congleton, 2001). Since a country is likely to participate in institutions – such as the Kyoto Protocol – only when co-operation is associated with an individual net gain (Svendsen, 2003; Underdal, 1998),[22] the provision of global public goods must rely on some kind of volunteerism. The only way to deal with the free-rider problem is thus to restructure the underlying incentives, such that it is in the countries' best interest to both participate and comply, and this should be the primary aim of any environmental treaty (Barrett, 2003; Barrett and Stavins, 2003). How this can be done is discussed below.

Enforcement

In the considerable body of literature that addresses the under-provision of global public goods, a main problem analyzed is free-riding. When potential ratifiers are uncertain about the actions of others, each country must anticipate the probability of other countries not cooperating.[23] Distrust is relevant whenever some parties have, or might have, an incentive to free-ride. There are two types of incentives for free-riding: the incentive for a country not to sign an IEA and thus benefit from the signatories' abatement efforts (non-participation), and the incentive for a signatory to violate its commitments in an agreement (non-compliance) (Finus, 2001). Participation and compliance are joint problems, but they have often been analyzed separately.[24] A country can avoid complying with a treaty by simply not participating in the first place, and non-participation is the biggest credible deviation a single country can carry out. Indeed, to the extent that abiding by the commitments of an international treaty will result in a net loss, a rational decision-maker will avoid implementing a policy to comply (Underdal, 1998). Deterring free-rider behavior, however, requires sacrifices by others, and larger sacrifices are less credible because they are more self-damaging (Barrett, 2003; Barrett and Stavins, 2003). The creation of incentive mechanisms to ensure participation and compliance is thus a major challenge for parties in negotiations on IEAs.

Nevertheless, a remarkably small number of treaties include enforcement mechanisms (Barrett, 2003). The current climate regime, as specified by the final version of the Kyoto Protocol,[25] however, is an exception. But even though the Marrakesh Accords provide details for a compliance mechanism,[26] it has been pointed out that the current design suffers from a number of weaknesses (cf, Barrett, 2002; 2003; Hagem et al., 2005; Hagen and Westskog, 2005).[27] It is therefore not likely that the Kyoto Protocol's enforcement mechanism will be able to ensure that ratifying countries fulfill their obligations. Hence, external means of enforcement are potentially required as an alternative – or a supplement – to the provisions of the Marrakesh Accords.[28] This can be achieved, for example, by linking environmental negotiations to other economic issues.

Issue linkage
One suggested solution to offset countries' free-riding incentives is the linkage of environmental negotiations to other economic issues (issue linkage). The idea is to link an issue with excludable benefits (a club good) to the public good provision. Compared to the stand-alone environmental agreement, an agreement with this type of issue linkage ensures that the benefit–cost ratio for accession is increased, and participation is thus more attractive (Barrett, 2003). Suggestions include linking the climate change regime with the international trade regime (Barrett, 1997; 2003) by, for example, incorporating trade sanctions as a means of enforcement; or with research and development (R&D) cooperation, by excluding non-parties from enjoying the fruits of cooperative R&D (Barrett, 2003; Carraro and Siniscalco, 1995; 1997).[29]

It is not always the case, however, that issue linkage helps international cooperation. The effect depends on the issues that are linked and on how they are linked. Murdoch et al. (1997) argues for instance that, had the Convention on Long-Range Transboundary Air Pollution (CLRTAP) not provided for separate protocols to be negotiated for each of the different pollutants, the outcome of the negotiations would have given smaller reductions in sulfur emissions.[30] Thus, issue linkage can hinder as well as aid co-operation.

Side payments
Another theoretic solution to the free-rider problem is international transfers or side payments. Transfers may be needed to make co-operation individually attractive in asymmetric settings, that is, when the benefits from and/or costs of co-operation differ across countries. The basic idea is to redistribute the surplus to be gained from co-operation to compensate the countries that would otherwise have chosen the non-co-operative outcome.[31] Some countries are affected more than others (in absolute or relative terms) by an environmental problem. The asymmetries often dominate negotiations, and are often perceived to be a main reason for why agreement is so hard to achieve. Barrett (2003), however, shows that side payments (or carrots) *can* promote co-operation, but only when countries are sufficiently asymmetric, and when the side payments are combined with credible threats of punishment (sticks).

The side payment solution might be difficult to implement in the case of a long-term problem like climate change. Simulation models for climate change mitigation have shown that, in the long run, the gains from co-operation will more than compensate for the initial losses due to abatement efforts. However, the fact that the expected break-even date lies very far into the future complicates the side payment solution because the countries cannot borrow against future gains in order to compensate for early losses, although these kinds of distribution problems might be solvable through some kind of banking system.[32] Side payments are not often observed, at least not in monetary terms, but one recent example is that the EU promised to support Russia for membership in the WTO in order to persuade the Russian government to ratify the Kyoto treaty.

5. Self-enforcing environmental agreements: a closer look

The structure and characteristics of IEAs will have a significant influence on the effectiveness as well as the costs and benefits of mitigation. The effectiveness and the costs and benefits of an international regime (such as the Kyoto Protocol or other possible future environmental agreements) depend on the number of signatories to the agreement and their abatement targets and/or policy commitments (IPCC, 2001).

A main strand of the literature on international environmental co-operation focuses on the conditions for the formation of multilateral agreements (or coalitions) in game theoretic settings. The fundamental assumption is that international agreements must be *self-enforcing* since there is no supranational authority that can enforce compliance. Notable examples are Asheim et al. (2006), Barrett (1994; 1997; 1999), Carraro and Siniscalco (1992; 1993), Hoel (1992), and Tulkens (1979). The assumption of self-enforcement implies that optimal co-operation can only be sustained by an international treaty if no country can gain by not being a party to it, and no party can gain by not implementing it. An agreement must therefore specify a strategy that, if obeyed, must succeed in deterring free-riding and enforcing compliance. A strategy is credible if no country is worse off accepting the agreement (*individual rationality*) and no sub-coalition of two or more countries can achieve a higher joint payoff by concluding a partial agreement (*collective rationality*). Furthermore, collective rationality implies that an equilibrium agreement must be renegotiation proof, meaning that it must be in the (collective) best interest of other countries to insist that a non-compliant country be punished before co-operation can be resumed (Barrett, 1999; 2003; Finus, 2001).

International environmental agreement models differ with respect to the specification of the utility functions of governments and the stability concept they employ. However, they can roughly be divided into two groups – dynamic game models and reduced-stage game models (Finus and Rundshagen, 2003).

The *dynamic game models* typically assume an infinitely repeated game where governments agree on a contract in the first period that has to be enforced in subsequent periods by using credible threats (for example Barrett, 1994; 1999). Studies using these models have found that a global treaty typically will achieve very little and at worst not enter into force, and that an incomplete treaty (a sub-coalition) may achieve more than the global treaty. The reason for these results is that the larger the number of parties to an agreement (k), the greater the harm suffered by the (k-1) other countries when they impose the punishment needed to deter a unilateral deviation, and consequently the less credible the threat.

Barrett (2002), shows that a single treaty can be broadened to incorporate all countries (a consensus treaty), but at the cost of limiting the per-country level (the 'depth') of co-operation. He shows that countries can reach agreement around a weak treaty, or they can negotiate a more potent but incomplete treaty. Thus, when the constraint of self-enforcement binds, we cannot have it both ways. Something has to give. Either participation must be less than full, or signatories must choose abatement levels that fall short of maximizing their collective payoff (Barrett, 2003). Allowing the depth of cooperation to vary, Barrett (2002) demonstrates that countries might prefer a 'broad but shallow' treaty over one that is 'narrow but deep'.

Reduced-stage game models depict coalition (or treaty) formation as a two-stage game. In the first stage, countries decide on the coalition formation. In the second stage, they choose abatement levels and how the gains from co-operation will be distributed (for example Chandler and Tulkens, 1992; Carraro and Siniscalco, 1993; Hoel, 1992). Some of these models define equilibria with both internal stability, meaning that no signatory has an incentive to leave the coalition, and external stability, meaning that no non-signatory wants to accede to the agreement. A key result is that the number of signatories generally falls short of the complete coalition (the global treaty): often, the equilibrium coalition is rather small. A second result is that the coalition typically achieves results far from the social optimum.[33, 34]

There are several important lessons to be learned from these game theoretic models. One is that if an international treaty, like the Kyoto Protocol, sustains full compliance, the reason is that the agreement achieves very little. Another is that even though the Kyoto Protocol is only a first step, if the subsequent stages in the process replicate the Kyoto formula, the outcome is likely to continue to be very close to 'business as usual'. A third is that a more ambitious future version of the current climate regime would, on the other hand, most likely either fail to enter into force or fail to sustain full compliance. Moreover, since many of the proposals for alternatives to the Kyoto Protocol also do not address the fundamental issues of enforcement and participation, they too are likely to fail (Barrett, 2001). This does not, however, imply that negotiation is a hopeless waste of time, but rather that the current design of the Kyoto Protocol does not restructure the game of climate change mitigation in a way that provides the supporting incentives needed to effect a change in behavior over time.[35]

6. Multiple agreements

In an effort to increase participation, a few contributions have addressed the possibility of giving countries the freedom to negotiate more than one agreement. Bloch (1997), Carraro (1998; 1999; 2000), and Carraro and Siniscalco (1998) provide examples with the use of reduced-stage game models. A two-stage coalition game is used to show that when more than one coalition is possible, the equilibrium coalition structure that endogenously emerges from the negotiation process is characterized by several coalitions. It has also been shown, in this setting, that social welfare can be higher with multiple agreements than with a single global accord due to increased total abatement (Carraro, 2000).

The question of more than one agreement is analyzed in an infinitely repeated game framework in Asheim et al. (2006). Using a simple dynamic model, with weak renegotiation-proofness as solution concept,[36] they demonstrate that two agreements can sustain a larger number of co-operating parties than a single global treaty. They also show that a regime based on multiple agreements can Pareto dominate a single agreement regime. The results support the conclusions reached by Carraro and others (for example Carraro, 1999; 2000 and Carraro and Siniscalco, 1998) using a reduced-stage game framework.

An important driving force in infinitely repeated games is the way in which the agreements are enforced. In the global treaty regime of Barrett (1999) and Asheim et al. (2006), a single deviation triggers punishment by all other parties. This drives the number of participating countries down via the renegotiation-proofness requirement.[37] If not all participating countries punish a deviator, then more than one country will cooperate in the punishment phase, and the renegotiation-proofness requirement is less strict. This admits a larger number of participating countries. In the two treaty regime in Asheim et al. (2006), participation is broadened because a deviation triggers punishment by all parties in the deviator's treaty, but not by the countries that are parties to the other treaty.[38, 39]

If a regime with multiple treaties is to be negotiated, one would need a criterion to decide what countries to include in which agreement. One appealing criterion might be geographical region, although other criteria are certainly also conceivable. A regime with regional agreements may, for example, facilitate external enforcement better than a regime with one global agreement, because countries in the same region tend to be highly integrated. A high level of interdependence implies that a host of options are available (via issue linkages) for providing responses to non-compliance in any one particular issue area. In addition, countries that are in close geographic proximity also tend to be culturally close, have similar economic and political systems, and therefore have similar preferences.[40] All of this might lower the costs of reaching agreement in the first place. Countries may thus both be more likely to comply with a regional agreement and more inclined to join a regional agreement in the first place (Asheim et al., 2006). All of these features represent a potential rationale for regional agreements, and could make such a regime an attractive option for example in the negotiations on future commitment periods under the Kyoto Protocol.

7. Interest group influence

Environmental policies influence a country's economy in a number of different ways, and the design of such policies is thus of great concern to a number of groups. The influence of interest groups is therefore a reoccurring theme in the study of environmental politics. One of the early classics in the public choice literature is Mancur Olson's (1965) *The Logic of Collective Action*. In this book he applies public choice reasoning to the analysis of various collective-action problems involving interest groups. Interest groups have been a focal point within the public choice literature ever since.

When arguing that government intervention is needed to correct market failures when public goods, externalities and other sorts of market failures are present, the economics literature often makes the implicit assumption that these failures can be corrected at zero cost. The government is seen as an omniscient, benevolent institution that dictates policies in order to achieve a Pareto-optimal allocation of resources. The public choice literature challenges this utopia model of government by examining not how governments *may* or *ought to* behave, but how they *do* behave. It reveals that governments, too, can fail in certain ways.

Public choice argues that if the state exists in part to provide public goods and eliminate externalities, then it must accomplish the same preference revelation task for these public goods as the market achieves for private goods. The public choice approach to non-market decision-making has been (1) to make the same behavioral assumptions as general economics (rational, utilitarian individuals), (2) often to depict the preference revelation process as analogous to the market (voters engage in exchange, individuals reveal their demand schedules via voting, citizens exit and enter clubs), and (3) to ask the same questions as traditional price theory: Do equilibria exist? Are they stable? Are they Pareto efficient? How are they obtained? (Müller, 2003).

Formally, public choice can be defined as the economic study of non-market decision-making, or simply the application of economics to political science. The subject matter of public choice is that of political science: the theory of the state, voting rules, voter behavior, party politics, the bureaucracy, public goods, and so on. The basic behavioral postulate of public choice, however, is as for economics: that people are egoistic, rational, utility-maximizers (Müller, 2003). It is assumed that each agent acts optimally towards his preferences. However, the preferences regarding, for example, environmental policies differ according to who or what the agent is. While a firm strives to maximize profit, for example, politicians seek to maximize influence and power (Svendsen, 1998). With this rational behavioral assumption, the public choice approach is able to deliver clear-cut predictions and simplicity, which makes it very user-friendly. However, preferences might not be as stable as the theory predicts, making it less applicable in practice. Norms and values, which are changeable, could influence the cost–benefit analyses behind decisions (Krogstrup and Svendsen, 2004).[41]

In an open society, environmentalist groups and their opponents, generally the corporations and businesses that resist the costs involved in complying with environmental regulation, are presumed to spend resources on trying to influence policy makers. The policy makers need the votes, the money, the moral approbation, and the publicity these groups might provide in exchange for policy stances that gain approval and avoid disapproval. Environmental policy is thus a function of the different pressures emanating from these (and other) interest groups, and hence seldom fully reflects the interests of any one of them (Barkdull and Harris, 2002). In public choice theory, it is assumed that the direction in which these interest groups will try to push the policy choice will depend on the distribution of costs and benefits from regulation (Müller, 2003; Svendsen, 1998). A proper understanding of institutional settings thus allows relatively straightforward net-benefit maximizing models to account for a rich and complex range of policy outcomes (Congleton, 2004), including government negotiating positions in international forums.

A country's environmental foreign policy is presumed to be the outcome of bargains struck among different constituencies with a stake in environmental policy (Barkdull and Harris, 2002). Somehow the preferences of a country's citizens must be consolidated into a unitary negotiating position. At the federal government level in the United States, for example, this requires resolution of conflicting positions taken by different executive branch departments by means of inter-agency bargaining. For wide-ranging issues like global warming, a dozen or more government agencies may be involved that, in turn, represent a variety of interests. Each agency's negotiating position is thus influenced by lobby groups such as trade associations, industries, and environmental and other non-governmental organizations. The internal negotiations are thus very complex, and after finally agreeing on what the country's interests are, the official delegation must negotiate with delegations from other countries.

Explaining a given environmental foreign policy, a county's position in international negotiations, or the overall character of a country's policy direction therefore requires identifying the groups that participate, their relative influence, and the strategy and tactics they employ. Because of the economic implications of environmental policy, elites take a strong interest in this issue area and usually attempt to direct the government towards policies compatible with corporate freedom and economic growth (Bang, 2004; Barkdull and Harris, 2002).[42]

8.   Concluding remarks

The bottom line in international environmental cooperation will always be determined by what is politically feasible. Because of the multiplicity of decision-makers, ranging from the international governmental level down to the micro level of firms and individuals, it is very hard to find strategies for global environmental protection that are acceptable to all. Therefore, it is also hard for a country's government to choose a position in international negotiations. In combination with the fact that environmental policies cannot be isolated from other socio-economic goals, this multiplicity makes negotiations on international environmental cooperation particularly complicated. Domestic interest conflicts are thus among the biggest obstacles to achieving a common political strategy for the protection of the global environment. Another is the free-rider issue.

The economics literature has focused very much on optimal solutions and cost-effectiveness. These are important issues, but optimal solutions are less appealing if they are not politically feasible. The primary concern for international environmental protection should rather lie with increasing cooperation. The level of co-operation is to a large degree defined by participation and compliance. Although countries might be less likely to participate in and comply with treaties that are excessively costly, cost-effectiveness is neither a necessary nor a sufficient condition for participation and compliance (Barrett, 2003).

The world's level of protection of the global environment plays for all intents and purposes no small part in determining whether the world is on a sustainable path, since shared resources are prone to overuse when countries pursue unilateral policies. Because the provision of global public goods relies on volunteerism, the only way to beat the free-rider issue is to restructure the underlying incentives. A central challenge of international co-operation is thus to figure out how the relationships among countries can be restructured in a mutually preferred way. According to Barrett (2003), five tasks are necessary to achieve this: first, to create an aggregated gain, that is, a reason for all countries to come to the bargaining table; second, to distribute this gain such that all countries would prefer that the agreement succeed; third, to ensure that each country would lose by not participating, given that all the others agree to participate; fourth, to provide incentives for all parties to comply with the treaty; and fifth, to deter entry by third parties.

The outcome of an institution will always depend on the responses of the different countries to the agreed-upon set of rules. A sixth task that should be added is therefore the necessity of taking into account the complexity of a country's negotiating position resulting from different domestic constituencies with a stake in environmental policy. Thus, to achieve higher levels of provision of global environmental public goods, incentive restructuring to achieve political feasibility, not optimality or cost-effectiveness, should be the primary focus in the negotiations on any international environmental treaty.

Notes

1. This chapter has benefited from comments on earlier drafts by Guri Bang, Scott Barrett, Jon Hovi, Fredric C. Menz and Lynn Nygaard. Financial support from the Research Council of Norway is also gratefully acknowledged. Responsibility for errors and opinions is my own.
2. For an overview of historic and existing IEAs and an excellent in-depth discussion of what determines success or failure in international environmental cooperation, see Barrett (2003).
3. For an introduction to how game theory can be useful in situations that require international cooperation, see for example Sandler (1997). For introductions to game theory in general, see Binmore (1992) or Gibbons (1992).
4. See Müller (2003) for an extensive review of this literature. For examples of issues addressed in the public choice tradition, see Buchanan and Tollison (eds) (1984).
5. Both theories use the rational choice paradigm which sheds light on a wide variety of political choice settings. The general idea is that both individual choices and political outcomes are the result of the same fundamental forces and materials: self interest, scarcity and conflict. Fairly narrow self-interest can account for a wide range of human behavior once individual interests are identified for the institutional settings of interest. Thus, a good deal of human behavior, perhaps most, can be understood using the rational choice model of behavior, once the particular costs and benefits of actions for a given institutional setting are recognized. What is unique about this approach to political economy is the willingness to identify costs and benefits in essentially all choice settings, including many where more orthodox economists and political scientists fear to tread (Congleton, 2004).
6. See Barrett (2003) for a comprehensive review of existing IEAs.

7.   See for example Hanley et al. (1997) for a discussion of market failures and possible policy options for market intervention in an environmental economics context.
8.   For an elaborate discussion of the theory of externalities; see for example Baumol and Oates (1988); for early contributions, see for example Coase (1960) and Meade (1952).
9.   See for example Müller (2003) for an extensive discussion of collective choice problems and public goods. See for example Hanley et al. (1997) or Sandler (1997) for treatments of public goods in an environmental setting.
10. See also Peterson and Wesley (2000).
11. See Keohane (1989) for a discussion of this definition.
12. Metaphors that have been used to describe such situations are for example 'marching in step with the slowest' and 'it is the slowest ship that sets the pace of the convoy'.
13. See Hovi and Sprinz (2006) for a thorough discussion of the law.
14. This trade-off between depth and breadth is discussed further in section 5.
15. The Kyoto Protocol, signed in Kyoto, Japan, at the Third Conference of the Parties (COP3) of the UN Framework Convention on Climate Change (UNFCCC) in 1997 sets limits on greenhouse gas emissions for industrialized countries.
16. Not until 2001, in Marrakesh, did the parties agree on these rules. See UNFCCC (2001).
17. Countries representing at least 55 per cent of the 1990 CO_2 emissions from industrialized countries had to ratify the Kyoto Protocol for it to enter into force. The USA alone represents 36.1 per cent of these emissions and needed therefore support from countries representing only an additional 9 per cent to block the ratification.
18. Canada and Russia were, for instance, credited with considerably more carbon binding in their forests than what was offered in earlier rounds of negotiations, and the supplementarity demand on the flexibility mechanisms was considerably relaxed.
19. These 81 countries accounted for 61.6 per cent of Annex 1 CO_2 emissions (unfccc. nt/files/essential_background/kyoto_protocol/application/pdf/kpstats.pdf). Accessed 19 April, 2005.
20. Hagem et al. (2005) and Hagem and Westskog (2005) show how sanctioning can be a double-edged sword; that is the compliance mechanism in the Kyoto Protocol is such that the punishment not only hurts the non-complying party, but also others, thus giving an incentive not to punish.
21. This problem was pointed out in a general setting already in Mancur Olson's seminal contribution where he states that reliance on voluntary compliance in large groups leads to free-riding and under- or non-provision of the public good (Olson, 1965).
22. It is a widely held notion that the United States left the Kyoto negotiations because it perceived ratification to be too costly for the American economy (see for example Grubb and Yamin, 2001; and Svendsen, 2003).
23. See Sandler and Sargent (1995) for a discussion of different *coordination games* where potential ratifiers are uncertain about the actions of others. This is a different type of game, however, than discussed here.
24. For example Chayes and Chayes (1995).
25. This definition of the climate regime will apply to the rest of the chapter.
26. See UNFCCC (2001). For an elaborate discussion of this compliance mechanism see for example Ulfstein and Werksman (2005).
27. The main objections to the compliance mechanism are that (i) the punishment might be forever delayed; (ii) the anticipation of being punished is likely to induce countries to hold out for a generous allowance for the second period; (iii) there are no provisions for enforcement of failure by a non-compliant country to accept the punishment; (iv) a country that is being punished might choose to withdraw from the Kyoto Protocol; (v) the compliance mechanism is not legally binding, and can be made so only through an amendment that must be ratified by the member countries, and (vi) the punishment produces negative welfare effects for all countries, not only the non-complier, thus giving incentives not to punish (see also n. 20).
28. See Hovi (2005) and Stokke (2005) for discussions of the potential relevance and effectiveness of external enforcement in relation to the international climate regime.

29. It has also been suggested linking climate agreements with other public goods like existing air pollution regimes by for example including tropospheric ozone precursors and aerosols among the regulated species (Rypdal et al., 2004).
30. Note that reduction of sulfur emissions is generally a regional public good.
31. For contributions on this issue see for example Barrett (1994; 1999; 2003), Carraro (1999), Carraro and Siniscalco (1993), Eykmans and Tulkens (2001), and Finus (2001).
32. For instance, Eyckmans and Tulkens (2001) point out that the transfers in their simulation model are single numbers representing the present value of consumption flows over 320 years, and that these cannot realistically be conceived of as being paid as lump sum transfers today.
33. Other models apply the concept of *the core* to determine the equilibrium coalition structure. This concept is, however, fundamentally different from the one discussed here. The core is a cooperative game theoretic concept, and cooperative game theory assumes binding agreements. A key result of these models is that by choosing a cleverly designed transfer scheme, the complete coalition establishing the social optimal emission vector *can* under special circumstances be an equilibrium, depending on the number of countries and on the degree of farsightedness.
34. See Finus and Rundshagen (2003) for a review of these models. For overviews of the coalition literature, see Bloch (1997) and Finus (2001).
35. See Barrett and Stavins (2003) for a discussion of alternatives to the Kyoto Protocol design.
36. In order to be a weakly renegotiation-proof equilibrium in the sense of Farrell and Maskin (1989, pp. 330–31), strategy profile must satisfy two requirements. First, it must be a subgame perfect equilibrium. The second requirement is that two continuation equilibria must not exist such that all players are better off in one continuation equilibrium than the other (Asheim et al., 2006).
37. See Asheim et al. (2006).
38. In the appendix to Barrett (1999) a similar regime is examined, but rejected on the grounds that it fails to be strongly collectively rational. In order for a treaty to be strongly collectively rational, the countries called upon to punish the deviating country also would collectively prefer to impose the prescribed punishments than revert to cooperation or impose an alternative, feasible punishment (Barrett, 2003).
39. Thus, compared to Barrett (1999), Barrett (2002), the consensus treaty paper mentioned in the previous section, changes both the equilibrium concept *and* the model. By contrast, Asheim et al. (2006) show that overall participation can be increased with multiple treaties even *without* changing the model, using weakly renegotiation-proof equilibrium as solution concept.
40. Of course, this is not always the case. In the Middle East, for instance, some neighboring countries are likely to have very different preferences.
41. With regards to climate change mitigation, this problem is obvious. The costs are very tangible and easy to measure in the form of for example loss of jobs, whereas benefits are more arbitrary because they are destined for the future (Portney, 1998).
42. For discussions of the factors that have shaped climate strategies and policies in, for example, the United States, see for example Bang (2004), Bang et al. (2007), Christiansen (2003), and Fisher (2004).

References

Asheim, G.B., C.B. Froyn, J. Hovi and F.C. Menz (2006), 'Regional versus global cooperation for climate control', *Journal of Environmental Economics and Management*, **51**(1): 93–109.

Bang, G. (2004), 'Sources of influence in climate change policymaking: a comparative analysis of Norway, Germany, and the United States', Ph.D., Department of Political Science, University of Oslo, Norway.

Bang, G., C.B. Froyn, J. Hovi and F.C. Menz (2007), 'The United States and international climate cooperation: international "pull" versus domestic "push"', *Energy Policy*, **35**(2): 1282–91.

Barkdull, J. and P.G. Harris (2002), 'Environmental change and foreign policy: a survey of theory', *Global Environmental Politics*, **2**(2): 63–89.

Barrett, S. (1994), 'Self enforcing international environmental agreements', *Oxford Economic Papers*, **46**: 804–78.

Barrett, S. (1997), 'The strategy of trade sanctions in international environmental agreements', *Resource and Energy Economics*, **19**: 345–61.

Barrett, S. (1999), 'A theory of international cooperation', *Journal of Theoretical Politics*, **11**: 519–41.

Barrett, S. (2001), 'International cooperation for sale', *European Economic Review*, **45**: 1835–50.

Barrett, S. (2002), 'Consensus treaties', *Journal of Institutional and Theoretical Economics*, **158**: 529–47.

Barrett, S. (2003), *Environment & Statecraft: the Strategy of Environmental Treaty-Making*, New York: Oxford University Press.

Barrett, S. and R. Stavins (2003), 'Increasing participation and compliance in international climate change agreements', *International Environmental Agreements: Politics, Law, and Economics*, **3**: 349–76.

Baumol, W.J. and W.E. Oates (1988), *The Theory of Environmental Policy*, 2nd edn, Cambridge: Cambridge University Press.

Binmore, K. (1992), *Fun and Games – A text on Game Theory*, Lexington, MA: D.C. Heath and Company.

Bloch, F. (1997), 'Non-cooperative models of coalition formation in games with spillovers', Chapter 10 in C. Carraro and D. Siniscalco (eds), *New Directions in the Economic Theory of the Environment*, Cambridge: Cambridge University Press.

Buchanan, J.M. and R.D. Tollison (eds) (1984), *The Theory of Public Choice – II*, Ann Arbor: The University of Michigan Press.

Carraro, C. (1998), 'Beyond Kyoto, a game theoretic perspective', in the Proceedings of the OECD Workshop on Climate Change and Economic Modeling, Background Analysis for the Kyoto Protocol, Paris, 17–18 September.

Carraro, C. (1999), 'The structure of international agreements on climate change', in C. Carraro (ed.), *International Environmental Agreements on Climate Change*, Dordrecht: Kluwer Academic Publishers.

Carraro, C. (2000), 'The economics of coalition formation', in J. Gupta and M. Grubb (eds), *Climate Change and European Leadership*, Dordrecht: Kluwer Academic Publishers.

Carraro, C. and D. Siniscalco (1992), 'The international dimension of the environmental policy', *European Economic Review*, **26**: 379–87.

Carraro, C. and D. Siniscalco (1993), 'Strategies for the international protection of the environment', *Journal of Public Economics*, **52**: 309–28.

Carraro, C. and D. Siniscalco (1995), 'Policy coordination for sustainability: commitments, transfers, and linked negotiations', in I. Godin and A. Winters (eds), *The Economics of Sustainable Development*, Cambridge: Cambridge University Press.

Carraro, C. and D. Siniscalco (1997), 'R&D cooperation and the stability of international environmental agreements', in C. Carraro (ed.), *International Environmental Agreements: Strategic Policy Issues*, Cheltenham, UK and Northampton, MA, USA: Edward Elgar.

Carraro, C. and D. Siniscalco (1998), 'International environmental agreements: incentives and political economy', *Journal of Public Economics*, **42**: 561–72.

Chandler, P. and H. Tulkens (1992), 'Theoretical foundations of negotiations and cost sharing in transfrontier pollution problems', *European Economic Review*, **36**, 388–98.

Chayes, A. and A.H. Chayes (1995), *The New Sovereignty. Compliance with International Regulatory Agreements*, Cambridge, Mass.: Harvard University Press.

Christiansen, A.C. (2003), 'Convergence or divergence? Status and prospects for US climate strategy', *Climate Policy*, **3**, 343–58.

Coase, R. (1960), 'The problem of social cost', *Journal of Law and Economics*, **3**: 1–44.

Congleton, R.D. (2001), 'Governing the global environmental commons: the political economy of international environmental treaties and institutions', in G.G. Shultze and H.W. Ursprung (eds), *Globalization and the Environment*, New York: Oxford University Press.

Congleton, R.D. (2004), 'The political economy of Gordon Tullock', *Public Choice*, **121**: 213–38.

Eyckmans, J. and H. Tulkens (2001), 'Simulating coalition stable burden sharing agreements for the climate change problem', FEEM Working Paper No. 75.

Farrell, J. and E. Maskin (1989), 'Renegotiation in repeated games', *Games and Economic Behavior*, **1**: 327–60.

Finus, M. (2001), *Game Theory and International Environmental Cooperation*, Cheltenham, UK and Northampton, MA, USA: Edward Elgar.

Finus, M. and B. Rundshagen (2003), 'Endogenous coalition formation in global pollution control: a partition function approach', in C. Carraro (ed.), *Endogenous Formation of Economic Coalitions*, Cheltenham, UK and Northampton, MA, USA, Edward Elgar, pp. 199–243.

Fisher, D.R. (2004), *National Governance and the Global Climate Change Regime*, Maryland: Rowman & Littlefield Publishers.

Froyn, C.B. (2001), 'The slowest sets the pace', *Cicerone*, 6/2001, www.cicero.uio.no/media/1657.pdf.

Gibbons, R. (1992), *A Primer in Game Theory*, New York: Harvester Wheatsheaf.

Grubb, M. and F. Yamin (2001), 'Climate collapse at The Hague: what happened, why, and where do we go from here?', *Internal Affairs*, **77**(2): 261–76.

Hagem, C. and H. Westskog (2005), 'Effective enforcement and double-edged deterrents', in O.S. Stokke, J. Hovi and G. Ulfstein (eds), *Implementing the Climate regime: International Compliance*, London: Earthscan.

Hagem, C., S. Kallbekken, O. Mæstad and H. Westskog (2005), 'Enforcing the Kyoto Protocol: sanctions and strategic behavior', *Energy Policy*, **33**(16): 2112–22.

Hanley, N., J.F. Shogren and B. White (1997), *Environmental Economics in Theory and Practice*, Oxford and New York: Oxford University Press.

Hoel, M. (1992), 'International environmental conventions: the case of uniform reductions of emissions', *Environmental and Resource Economics*, **2**: 141–59.

Hovi, J. (2005), 'The pros and cons of external enforcement', in O.S. Stokke, J. Hovi and G. Ulfstein (eds), *Implementing the Climate Regime: International Compliance*, London: Earthscan.

Hovi, J. and D.F. Sprinz (2006), 'The limits of the Law of the Least Ambitious Program', *Global Environmental Politics*, **6**(3): 28–42.

IPCC (2001), 'Climate change 2001: synthesis report. Contribution of Working Groups I, II, and III to the Third Assessment Report of the Intergovernmental Panel on Climate Change', R.T. Watson and the Core Writing Team (eds), Cambridge: Cambridge University Press.

Keohane, R.O. (1989), *International Institutions and State Power*, Colorado: Westview Press.

Krogstrup, J. and G.T. Svendsen (2004), 'Can the EU persuade the US to rejoin the Kyoto Agreement?', *Energy & Environment*, **15**(3): 427–35.

Meade, J.E. (1952), 'External economies and diseconomies in a competitive situation', *Economic Journal*, **62**(2): 54–67.

Müller, D.C. (2003), *Public Choice III*, Cambridge: Cambridge University Press.

Murdoch, J.C., T. Sandler and K. Sargent (1997), 'A tale of two collectives: sulphur versus nitrogen emissions', *Economica*, **64**: 281–301.

Olson, M. (1965), *The Logic of Collective Action*, Cambridge, MA: Harvard University Press.

Peterson, W. and F. Wesley (2000), 'The design of supranational organizations for the provision of international public goods: the case of global environmental protection', *Review of Agricultural Economics*, **22**(2): 352–66.

Portney, P.R. (1998), 'Applicability of cost–benefit analysis to climate change', in Willian D. Nordhaus (ed.), *Economics and Policy Issues in Climate Change*, Washington: Resources for the Future.

Rypdal, K., T. Berntsen, J.S. Fuglestvedt, A. Torvanger, K. Aunan, F. Stordal and L.P. Nygaard (2004), 'Tropospheric ozone and aerosols in climate agreements: scientific and political challenges', *Environmental Science and Policy*, **8**(1): 29–43.

Sandler, T. (1997), *Global Challenges – An Approach to Environmental, Political, and Economic Problems*, Cambridge: Cambridge University Press.

Sandler, T. (1998), 'Global and regional public goods: a prognosis for collective action', *Fiscal Studies*, **19**: 221–47.

Sandler, T. and K. Sargent (1995), 'Management of transnational commons: coordination, publicness, and treaty formation', *Land Economics*, **71**: 145–62.

Stokke, O.S. (2005), 'Trade measures, WTO and climate compliance: the interplay of international regimes', in O.S. Stokke, J. Hovi and G. Ulfstein (eds), *International Compliance: Implementing the Climate Regime*, London: Earthscan.

Svendsen, G.T. (1998), *Public Choice and Environmental Regulation*, Cheltenham, UK and Northampton, MA, USA: Edward Elgar.

Svendsen, G.T. (2003), *The Political Economy of the European Union*, Cheltenham, UK and Northampton, MA, USA: Edward Elgar.

Tulkens, H. (1979), 'An economic model of international negotiations relating to transfrontier pollution', in K. Krippendorff (ed.), *Communication and Control in Society*, New York: Gordon & Breach.

Ulfstein, G. and J. Werksman (2005), 'Hard enforcement and due process', in O.S. Stokke, J. Hovi and G. Ulfstein (eds), *International Compliance: Implementing the Climate Regime*, London: Earthscan.

Underdal, A. (1980), *The Politics of International Fisheries Management: The Case of the North-East Atlantic*, Scandinavian University Press, Oslo, Norway.

Underdal, A. (1998), 'Explaining compliance and defection: three models', *European Journal of International Relations*, **4**(1): 5–30.

UNFCCC (2001), 'The Marrakesh Accords & the Marrakesh Declaration', http://unfccc.int/cop 7/accords_draft.pdf.

25 Trade and sustainable development
Kevin P. Gallagher

1. Introduction

The world community faces the enormous challenge of the need to increase the well-being of more than half its inhabitants without jeopardizing the ability of the natural environment to function now and into the future – the challenge of sustainable development. The recent wave of globalization in the world offers an opportunity to meet that challenge. However, there is increasing concern that the current form of globalization is at odds with sustainable development.

Although the last decades of the twentieth century ushered an unprecedented level of international trade and investment, poverty and inequality remain key characteristics of the global economy in the twenty-first century. The World Bank defines poverty as those persons who earn less than $2 per day (1999 purchasing power parity) and extreme poverty as those who earn less than $1. Using this definition, about half of the world's population are poor, almost 3 billion people. Close to half of the poor live in extreme poverty, 1.4 billion (Cline, 2004).

The world's ecosystems fare no better. According to the recent Millennium Ecosystem report conducted by 1300 experts from 95 countries, '60 percent of the ecosystem services that support life on Earth – such as fresh water, capture fisheries, air and water regulation, and the regulation of regional climate, natural hazards and pests – are being degraded or used unsustainably' (UNDP, 2005). Such degradation is proving to be costly in economic terms. The World Bank and other international agencies estimate that the economic costs of environmental degradation range from 6 to 10 per cent of GDP on an annual basis (Gallagher, 2004).

The speed and distribution of these changes are too fast for many people to comprehend and accept. An escalating series of protests is occurring at nearly every major meeting surrounding global economic affairs: the WTO meeting in Seattle in 1999, the Washington IMF/World Bank meetings in the spring of 2000, the July 2001 G-8 meeting in Geneva, the Summit of the Americas meeting in Quebec in April 2001, the WTO meetings in Cancun in 2003 and so forth. These events are paralleled by similar protests in capitals across the globe. The protests outside the meetings, and the increasing levels of disagreement among nations themselves, illustrate the breadth and depth of concerns of a growing but ill-defined constituency about the potential impacts of an unfettered global marketplace.

With this concern in mind the world community has reasserted the need for development through the Millennium Development Goals and the global commitment to sustainable development signed at the World Summit for Sustainable Development. At the same time, most of the world's nations have also embarked on a new round of global trade negotiations – the so-called Doha Round under the World Trade Organization (WTO). The Doha Declaration makes explicit reference to sustainable development:

> We strongly reaffirm our commitment to the objective of sustainable development, as stated in the Preamble to the Marrakesh Agreement. We are convinced that the aims of upholding and safeguarding an open and non-discriminatory multilateral trading system, and acting for the protection of the environment and the promotion of sustainable development can and must be mutually supportive. (WTO, 2001)

This chapter outlines the relationship between international trade and sustainable development. It is organized into three parts. The first discusses the theoretical relationships between these two phenomena, the second examines the empirical evidence, and policy considerations conclude the chapter.

2. Trade and sustainable development: theory

In theory international trade and sustainable development can be mutually compatible, and perhaps even reinforcing. According to independent theories of international trade on the one hand, and environmental economics on the other, trade liberalization can bring economic benefits that can be distributed in a manner to reduce poverty and protect the environment.

The economist David Ricardo showed that because countries face different costs to produce the same product, if each country produces, and then exports, the goods for which it has comparatively lower costs, then all parties benefit. The effects of comparative advantage (as Ricardo's notion became called) on factors of production were developed in the 'Heckscher–Ohlin' model. This model assumes that in all countries there is perfect competition, technology is constant and readily available, there is the same mix of goods and services, and that factors of production (such as capital and labor) can freely move between industries.

Within this rubric, the Stolper–Samuelson theorem adds that international trade can increase the price of products (and therefore the welfare) in which a country has a comparative advantage. In terms of foreign direct investment (FDI), FDI can contribute to development by increasing employment and by human capital and technological 'spillovers' where foreign presence crowds in new technology and investment. In theory, the gains from trade accruing to 'winning' sectors freed to exploit their comparative advantages have the (Pareto) possibility to compensate the 'losers' of trade liberalization. Moreover, if the net gains from trade are positive there are more funds available to stimulate growth and reduce poverty. In a perfect world then, free trade and increasing exports could indeed be unequivocally beneficial to all parties.

These theories have been extended to conceptualize the trade and environment relationship. A useful framework for thinking about trade and the environment has been proposed by Gene Grossman and Alan Krueger (1993). They identify three mechanisms by which trade and investment liberalization affect the environment: scale, composition, and technique effects (see also Chapter 15). Scale effects occur when liberalization causes an expansion of economic activity. If the nature of that activity is unchanged but the scale is growing, then pollution and resource depletion will increase along with output. Composition effects occur when increased trade leads nations to specialize in the sectors where they enjoy a comparative advantage.

When comparative advantage is derived from differences in environmental stringency then the composition effect of trade will exacerbate existing environmental problems in the countries with relatively lax regulations. Race-to-the-bottom discussions are perfectly plausible in economic theory. The Hecksher–Ohlin (H–O) theory in trade economics postulates that nations will gain a comparative advantage in those industries where they are factor-abundant. Applying the H–O theory to pollution then, it could be argued that a country with less stringent environmental standards would be factor-abundant in the ability to pollute. Therefore, trade liberalization between a developed and a developing nation where the developed nation has more stringent regulations may lead to an expansion in pollution-intensive economic activity in the developing country with the lesser regulations. The developing country with the less stringent regulations becomes a 'pollution haven' for pollution-intensive economic activity (Copeland and Taylor, 2003).

Technique effects, or changes in resource extraction and production technologies, can potentially lead to a decline in pollution per unit of output for two reasons. First, the liberalization of trade and investment may encourage multinational corporations to transfer cleaner technologies to developing countries. Second, if economic liberalization increases income levels, the newly affluent citizens may demand a cleaner environment.

The economic and environmental dimensions of trade and sustainable development are outlined in Table 25.1. The first column exhibits the 'winners' and 'losers' of trade liberalization. The second column outlines the economic dimensions, the third outlines the environmental dimensions.

Table 25.1   Stolper–Samuelson and sustainable development

	Economic	Environmental
Winners	export sectors	export sectors pollution haloes composition effects
Losers	import sectors	export sector scale and composition effects worker health and safety
		import sector liabilities genetic diversity

From an economic perspective, when liberalization occurs and nations trade where they have a comparative advantage the 'winners' are those sectors which can now export more of their goods or services. Theoretically this will not only cause expansion of exports but also of employment and wages in such sectors as well. The 'losers' of the liberalization are those sectors that will find it harder to face an inflow of newly competitive imports. In those sectors one would expect a contraction of that sector, layoffs, and wages decreases. If the gains to the export sector outweigh the losses to the import sector the net gains are positive. This leaves the 'possibility' that the winners can compensate the losers or that the gains from trade may be used to stimulate pro-poor growth.

Drawing on the framework on trade and environment outlined above, the third column in Table 25.1 outlines potential environmental winners and losers. There can possibly be environmental benefits from being an economic winner as well. First, this can occur if trade liberalization causes a compositional shift toward less environmentally degrading forms of economic activity. Second, there is also the possibility of environmental improvements in relatively environmentally destructive sectors if those sectors attract large amounts of investment from firms that transfer state-of-the-art environmental technologies to the exporting sector.

Trade liberalization can also have negative effects. Of course, trade liberalization can cause a composition effect where the economy moves toward more pollution-intensive industry. One example of this is Brazil, which liberalized trade in the 1990s and subsequently its exports became more pollution-intensive (Young, 2004). Scale effects can also adversely impact the environment, and the health and safety of the workers in economically expanding plants that may have to handle increasing amounts of pollution-intensive inputs.

It is often overlooked that there can also be adverse environmental effects of being a trade policy 'loser'. Some analysts argue that the shrinking of a sector that is environmentally degrading is beneficial for an economy because by definition less economic activity will equal less pollution. On the other hand, a shrinking sector can bring with it environmental liabilities that may cost taxpayers increased funds. Moreover, from a political economy perspective, shrinking sectors may put pressure on governments to turn a blind eye to environmental performance in order to maintain an economic presence (in other words causing a worsening technique effect).

Losing economic comparative advantages can also hurt the environment when losing sectors are those related to positive externalities. In Mexico, small holder maize growers are finding it hard to compete with a flood of US corn imports after the North American Free Trade Agreement (NAFTA) was signed. Mexico is the center of origin for maize and the cradle of maize crop genetic diversity. Thus, pressure to leave the land or convert it to other crops is threatening such diversity and global food security (Nadal and Wise, 2004). Smallholders cultivating maize are generating positive externalities of protecting a global public good and maintaining diversity. Yet, such prices are not reflected in their goods. Similar examples are with jute production in Bangladesh (Boyce, 2002).

In theory then, trade liberalization can benefit the environment but only if winners compensate the social and environmental losers with the gains from trade in the form of institution building for sustainable development. This is very difficult in developing countries for political, cultural and economic reasons. On the political level, trade liberalization costs a great deal of political capital to begin with. It is then very difficult to get the winners of a trade policy to agree to give away a portion of their gains. What's more, many in developing countries may not accept compensation for losing. Indigenous groups see themselves as having ancient rights to land and resources and may not be willing to be 'bought off' (Kanbur, 2001). Even if they could be bought off, at what price? The fields of ecological and environmental economics have made great strides in recognizing that there are values for the environment that need to be incorporated into the price scheme to allocate resources in a more socially optimal manner. However, the methodologies for identifying the exact prices for those values are very much in their infancy, controversial, and many times inappropriate – especially in developing country contexts (Ackerman and Heinzerling, 2004).

3. Trade and sustainable development: evidence

The evidence on the effects of the recent wave of trade liberalization on sustainable development is mixed. Trade liberalization has not been linked to economic growth and therefore has not brought many opportunities for developing the necessary institutions to make trade work for development.

It is estimated that the annual gains from the Uruguay Round were approximately $200 billion annually. However, it has also been shown that 70 per cent of those gains have gone to the developed countries and most of the rest has gone to a small handful of developing countries. Indeed, in the first six years following the Uruguay Round, it is estimated that the 48 LDCs were worse off by $600 million per year (Stiglitz and Clayton, 2004). Thus, when the developed world proposed another round of global trade talks in 2001 in Doha, Qatar, the developing countries accepted on condition that development form a core part of the negotiations.

In a comprehensive review of the literature, Rodriquez and Rodrik (2001) have shown that there is no systematic relationship between a nation's average level of tariff and non-tariff barriers and its economic growth rate. An assessment of the literature on FDI and development came to similar conclusions; FDI alone was not correlated with local spillovers in developing countries (Gallagher and Zarsky, 2005). Whereas developing country per capita income growth was 3 per cent on an annual basis between 1960 to 1980 – a period of considerable levels of state management of developing economies – the more integrated period from 1980 to 2000 yielded average annual growth rates of 1.5 per cent in the developing world. The latter rate is less than 1 per cent per annum if India and China (two interventionist countries) are taken out (Chang, 2003).

More recent work has shown that trade liberalization alone is not a sufficient condition for economic growth. Institutional innovation coupled with macroeconomic and political stability are key to the growth process (Wacziarg and Welch, 2003). Indeed, there is now fairly widespread agreement among growth economists that institutional quality is the strongest driver of economic growth, more so than trade or geographical contexts (Rodrik, 2004). Whereas traditional trade theory emphasizes obtaining welfare gains through specialization, institutional approaches emphasize obtaining welfare gains from increasing productivity by means not necessarily based on specialization.

The evidence on the environmental effects of trade is mixed as well. Economic integration is contributing to worldwide environmental degradation, but not so much because the developing world is serving as a 'pollution haven' for developed world pollution. In 1992, the World Bank's *World Development Report* made the case that while trade-led growth may cause sharp increases in environmental degradation during the early stages of economic development, such degradation would begin to taper off as nations reached 'turning points' ranging between $3000 to $5000 GDP per capita (World Bank, 1992). The Bank was generalizing from a landmark

1991 paper by economists Gene Grossman and Alan Krueger. Working with a cross-sectional database of largely developed and some developing countries, this article examined the relationship between ambient concentrations of criteria air pollutants and GDP per capita. When they plotted their regression results they found that lower income nations had higher rates of pollution per capita where the reverse occurred for higher income nations (Grossman and Krueger, 1993).

This relationship became known as the environmental Kuznets curve (EKC: see Chapter 15), borrowing its name from the landmark article by Simon Kuznets that found a similar relationship between income inequality and GDP per capita in a cross-section of countries in the 1950s (Kuznets, 1955). For the developed countries, the three factors described earlier (scale, composition and technique effects) are seen to be interacting – as income has grown the composition of industry has shifted toward relatively less pollution-intensive economic activity while at the same time improvements in technology and environmental regulation have occurred. Although overall levels of growth (scale) have vastly increased, they have been offset by composition and technique effects.

To this day, generalizations of these findings have been used to make the claim that nations should grow now through trade liberalization and worry

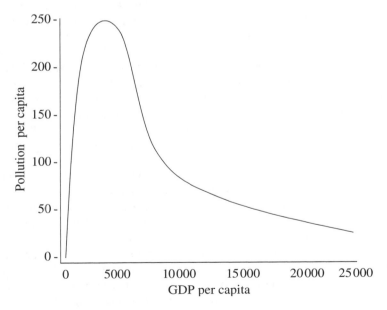

Figure 25.1 The environmental Kuznets curve

about the environment later (Bhagwhati, 1993). EKC studies have become a cottage industry, with close to a hundred articles published since the original 1991 piece (see Panayatou, 2000; Stern, 1998). What is ironic is the fact that, as the policy community has rushed to generalize the EKC in the political realm, the consensus in the peer-reviewed academic literature on the EKC has become much more cautious. Most importantly, the literature shows that the empirical evidence for the EKC is relatively weak and limited. While a thorough review of that literature is beyond the scope of this chapter, the following limits can be outlined (for a good review see Stern, 1998, and Chapter 15 of this volume):

- EKCs are limited to a small number of pollutants.
- EKC studies have relatively small representation from developing countries.
- EKC turning points are much higher than original estimates.[1]
- Income isn't the only factor contributing to an EKC. Later studies have shown that factors such as the degree of political freedom and democracy in a nation, population density, economic structure, and historical events (such as the oil price shocks of the 1970s) correlate with reductions in pollution.
- Limited evidence for the EKC in single-country trajectories. The majority of early EKC studies utilize cross-sectional or panel data of largely developed countries to estimate the relationship between income and pollution.

Yet, opponents of free trade often claim that trade liberalization will result in a mass migration of pollution-intensive industry from developed countries with stringent environmental regulations to developing countries with lax environmental standards. Not only will such migration cause increases in pollution in developing countries, they argue that pressure will then be exerted on developed country standards in the name of competition – effectively creating a 'race-to-the-bottom' in standards.

Like the EKC literature, it is also ironic that the majority of the peer-reviewed literature has found very limited evidence for pollution havens but that the policy community continues to cite it as a dire consequence of trade liberalization. Very recently however, a small handful of papers have found evidence for pollution havens. Again, a full review of the literature is beyond the scope of this chapter. However, extensive studies have been conducted at the global and regional level. There have been a number of widely cited studies on international trade flows and environmental regulations. Many have identified and studied a set of 'dirty' industries, where regulations might be expected to have the greatest effect. Although the definitions of dirty industries vary, many of the same industries tend to show up on everyone's lists.

James Tobey looked at the behavior of 23 nations in 1977, testing whether environmental policy affected the patterns of trade in commodities produced by dirty industries (Tobey, 1990). He defined a dirty, or pollution-intensive, industry as one where pollution abatement costs in the United States were 1.85 per cent or more of total costs. Industries meeting this standard were pulp and paper, mining, iron and steel, primary non-ferrous metals, and chemicals. For international comparisons Tobey created an ordinal variable ranging from 1 to 7 to measure the level of stringency of a country's environmental policies. He then regressed net exports of each country's dirty industries on their factor inputs (land, labor, capital and natural resources) and on environmental stringency. In no case did he find that environmental stringency was a statistically significant determinant of net exports.

World Bank researchers Patrick Low and Alexander Yeats tested whether developing countries gained a comparative advantage in pollution-intensive products during the period 1965–88 (Low and Yeats, 1992). Their model relies on calculation of revealed comparative advantage (RCA), defined as the share of an industry in a country's total exports, relative to the industry's share of total world exports of manufactures. Low and Yeats looked at RCAs of 109 countries for pollution-intensive industries. Their list of pollution-intensive industries, selected on the basis of pollution abatement costs in the US, consists of iron and steel, non-ferrous metals, petroleum refining, metal manufacturing, and pulp and paper. Low and Yeats found that for these industries the RCAs of developing countries were growing relative to those of industrial countries. They observed decreases in dirty industry RCAs in the developed world and increases in Eastern Europe, Latin America and West Asia.

Results along the same lines were found in a study by Mani and Wheeler (1998). They found that from 1960 to 1995, pollution-intensive output as a percentage of total manufacturing fell in the OECD and rose steadily in the developing world as a whole. However, the location of pollution havens has changed over time because economic growth in any one country brings 'countervailing pressure to bear on polluters through increased regulation, technical expertise, and clean sector production' (Mani and Wheeler, 1998, p. 244).

Using a different methodology, another World Bank team looked at trade liberalization and the toxic intensity of manufacturing in 80 countries between 1960 and 1988 (Lucas et al. 1992). Analyzing aggregate toxic releases per unit of output, they identified metals, cement, pulp and paper, and chemicals as the dirtiest industries. Lucas et al. found that the dirty (toxic-intensive) industries grew faster in the developing countries as a whole, but this growth was concentrated in relatively closed, fast growing economies, rather than in the countries that were most open to trade. Regional work on Latin America has generated similar results (Birdsall and Wheeler, 1993).

Very recently however, a handful of studies have indeed found evidence of pollution havens in the world economy. A study by Cole (2004) examines North–South trade flows for ten air and water pollutants. Cole finds evidence of pollution haven effects, but finds that such effects are quite small relative to other explanatory variables. Another study, by Kahn and Yoshino (2004) looks at bilateral trade data over the years 1980 to 1997 for 128 nations for 34 manufacturing industries, and examines how low-, middle-, and high-income nations differ regarding their income elasticity in exporting pollution-intensive products. They find that among nations outside of regional trade blocs there is general support for the pollution haven hypothesis. As national incomes rise, exports of pollution-intensive products decrease relative to exports of 'cleaner' goods. Nations participating in regional trading arrangements have slightly weaker pollution haven effects than those observed outside of regional trading blocs.

The reason why so many of these studies fail to find evidence for pollution havens (or find small effects) in developing countries is that the economic costs of environmental degradation are relatively much smaller than many other factors of production – especially those that determine comparative advantage. In general, the developing world is factor abundant in unskilled labor that takes the form of manufacturing assembly plants. On average, such manufacturing activity is relatively less pollution-intensive than more capital laden manufacturing activities such as cement, pulp and paper, and base metals production. A full review of this literature is beyond the scope of this chapter (see Jaffe, 1995 and Neumayer, 2001, for comprehensive reviews of this literature).

A snapshot of the record on trade and sustainable development in Latin America is useful. Perhaps no region of the world has experimented with economic integration more that Latin America. Since the late 1980s, many Latin American nations have introduced a deep package of reforms including: reducing tariffs and other protectionist measures; reducing barriers to foreign investment; restoring 'fiscal discipline' by reducing government spending; and promoting the export sector of the economy. According to a sweeping assessment of the impacts of the reforms conducted by the Economic Commission for Latin America and the Caribbean (ECLAC), the region's economies grew at an annual rate of less than 2 per cent between 1980 and 2000, compared to a rate of 5.5 per cent between 1960 and 1980. Growth was faster during the 1990s than in the 1980s, but it still did not compare to the period previous to the reforms. Chile is an exception where growth rates almost doubled over the past 20 years compared to the 1960 to 1980 period (Stallings and Peres, 2000). The ECLAC report concludes that the reforms contributed to an increase in poverty and inequality in the region.[2] As a result, there has been widespread popular resistance, which is putting added pressure on governments to question both the Washington Consensus and free-trade agreements.

The United Nations Environment Program (UNEP) and ECLAC report that environmental trends in the region continue to worsen (ECLAC/UNEP, 2003). Increasing urbanization and the modernization of agriculture are leading to increases in air, soil and water pollution and subsequent adverse human health effects. The report notes that the health problems associated with deteriorating air quality and toxic substances are as serious as the health problems previously caused by underdevelopment. Finally, although on average industrial manufacturing has shifted toward relatively 'cleaner' sectors, increasing rates of pollution are occurring because of 'serious shortcomings' in environmental management.

Specific to the EKC and pollution haven theories, on average, countries in Latin America and the Caribbean experienced positive composition effects, meaning that the composition of industry shifted toward 'cleaner' production. However, pollution in Latin American industry is increasing because nations in the hemisphere lack the proper policies to stem the environmental consequences of trade-led growth in those sectors. In addition, many firms lack the will or ability to adhere to the environmental ramifications of their operations, and non-governmental organizations have not always been there to apply appropriate pressure. Of the case studies conducted here, Brazil has actually experienced a general increase in pollution-intensive activity, whereas Mexico follows the general trend (WGDEA, 2004).

4. Trade and sustainable development: policy and institutions

The evidence just summarized underscores the need to couple any economic integration with social and environmental policy at the local, national and international level. The fact that there is only mixed evidence that trade liberalization is associated with growth shows that trade must be coupled with institution building. The fact that there is limited evidence for the EKC shows that economic integration cannot be relied on for automatic environmental improvements. Indeed, the evidence shows that the lack of effective institutions in the presence of economic integration has exacerbated longstanding problems in the developing world.

However, a silver lining lies in the fact that there is little evidence of pollution havens. Such evidence suggests that strengthening environmental institutions and standards in developing and developed countries alike will not deter foreign and domestic investments. Because the abatement costs of pollution are so small relative to other key costs, firms will not move to or from developing countries as regulations rise (at least to US levels). Michael Porter's hypothesis (Porter and van der Linde, 2002), that regulation-inspired innovation to decrease environmental degradation can lead to reduced costs and therefore increased competitiveness, also deserves to be spelled out. Environmental regulation can lure firms to seek ways of increasing resource productivity and therefore reduce the costs of inputs. Such 'innovation offsets' can exceed the costs of environmental compliance. Therefore, the firm that leads in introducing cleaner technologies into the production process may enjoy a 'first-mover advantage' over those industries in the world economy that continue to use more traditional, dirtier production methods. (For a critical rebuttal see Palmer et al., 1995.)

Rhys Jenkins (1998) has offered a synthesis of the Porter hypothesis, arguing that regulation is more likely to lead to 'innovation offsets' under three conditions. Note that each condition requires that a firm has substantial market power in an industry in which there is substantial innovative activity. First, because cost reductions are more likely to occur where new clean technologies are developed rather than in industries that adopt end-of-pipe solutions, the level of R&D is likely to be a factor in determining the impact on competitiveness. Second, innovation offsets are more likely in industries or firms that have the ability to absorb environmental costs, which is most often determined by profit margins and firm size. Finally, they are more likely in firms that have the ability to pass increased costs on to consumers in the form of higher prices.

Creative policy does not have to be designed by government. Conroy (2002) analyzes how advocacy organizations have used certification processes to reward firms that produce and trade goods that use high social and environmental standards in their production processes. Through such efforts, the Forest Stewardship Council has certified 60 million acres of forest between 1995 and 2001, accounting for more than 5 per cent of the world's working forests. Working on the demand side of the equation, advocacy groups set up market campaigns to pressure firms to buy these products. Indeed, some retail giants are now actually *seeking* to participate in these processes. When governments or citizens' groups recognize more sustainable practices in the developing world, there are avenues to gain market access for production processes that would be deemed inefficient by an unfettered marketplace.

Although developing countries agreed to enter a new round of trade negotiations only on the condition that development would be the centerpiece, there are growing concerns that this promise will go unfulfilled. Key among those concerns is the notion that a new trade agreement will not give the developing world the 'policy space' to use the very instruments and tools that many industrialized nations took advantage of to reach their current levels of environmental protection and development. The verdict is still out on this, but new agreements must give countries the space to establish the necessary institutions to steer growth toward development. If that doesn't occur, the world trading system will continue to confuse the means of increasing trade and investment with their ends of sustainable development.

Besides preserving the space for national efforts, three models of institutions have emerged that deal with trade and sustainable development linkages at the regional and global levels. On the one hand the European Union (EU) has a very deep set of linkages between integration and sustainable development, whereas the WTO has quite limited linkages. Trade arrangements negotiated by the United States are somewhere in the middle.

The EU has made decreasing economic, social and environmental disparities a cornerstone of its regional integration strategies. According to Anderson and Cavanagh (2004) the EU made $324 billion in development grants to this end between 1961 and 2001. Annual aid for a new member of the EU can be as high as 4 per cent of GDP. As a result, the relatively less well-off European countries have improved their social and environmental situations as well as having benefited economically from integration. Coupled with development funds the EU has established regional social and environmental ministries that establish independent standards and allow for civil society participation and monitoring as well.

In its regional arrangements, the US allows for a much more limited level of linkages between trade and sustainable development. The majority of regional trade arrangements (such as the US agreements with Chile, Jordan, Morocco, Singapore, Central America and others) have text concerning environmental matters but leave out social concerns completely, set up no institutions, and have very limited avenues for civil society participation. Indeed, according to Anderson and Cavanagh (2004) EU development funds are approximately ten times the amount of US economic assistance grants to all of Latin America. In the largest US regional arrangement, the North American Free Trade Agreement (NAFTA), a parallel agreement set up an environmental institution called the Commission for Environmental Cooperation. With an annual budget of $9 million the institution can do little more than provide technical assistance to the parties involved, but it does allow interesting levels of civil society participation. NAFTA does not include any mechanism to address regional inequality. Thus, the experience of Ireland, Spain and Greece with EU development funds has resulted in increasing standards of living as well as social and environmental improvements, Mexico has become worse off since NAFTA – incomes have grown a mere 1 per cent annually and poverty and inequality have worsened. What's more, the economic costs of environmental degradation have reached 10 per cent of GDP annually (Gallagher, 2004; Gallagher and Zarsky, 2005).

On the world stage, the WTO has limited formal linkage between sustainable development and trade, though that may be changing. On the social end, the WTO (and the GATT before it) have allowed for 'special and differentiated treatment' for developing countries – allowing them to deploy many of the development policies that were used in the developed world in the past but are now not allowed. However, successive rounds of WTO negotiations are shrinking the policy space for such policies. Agreements on intellectual property rights, investment rules, and services have all made it much more difficult for developing nations to deploy the development policies used by middle and high income nations in the twentieth century (Gallagher, 2005).

On the environmental front, there has been a longstanding controversy regarding the extent to which WTO laws restrict the ability of nations and the world community to establish effective environmental policy. At the national level, numerous cases have gone before the WTO claiming that national environmental policies have served as unfair trade barriers to member nations. Two famous cases involving tuna and shrimp respectively occurred when developing country governments challenged US laws that restricted imports of these fish when they were caught by using techniques that also killed dolphins or sea turtles. Developing countries saw such laws as unfair trade barriers. The WTO has ruled that it does not object to environmental policy per se, but to environmental policies that are trade restrictive. The US has since amended these laws (Neumayer, 2001).

Although there has never been a WTO case to this effect, at the multilateral level there is growing concern that Multilateral Environmental Agreements (MEAs) will be overridden by WTO laws. Many MEAs use trade restrictions as an enforcement mechanism and the fear is that such mechanisms would be deemed WTO illegal and thus reduce the effectiveness of MEAs and 'chill' the negotiations of future MEAs (Neumayer, 2001). In response to this the Doha Round of WTO negotiations (2001 – present) is charged with examining the relationship between MEAs and the WTO.

Some scholars and policy makers argue that more needs to be done, that indeed a 'World Environmental Organization' should be established in order to serve as a counterweight to the WTO (Esty, 1997; Speth, 2004). Indeed, such an institution has also been proposed by none other than former WTO head Renalto Ruggerio: 'I would suggest that we need a similar multi-lateral rules-based system for the environment – a World

Environment Organization to also be the institutional or legal counterpart to the WTO' (Ruggiero, 1999).

Discussion of a World Environmental Organization has become quite controversial, with many in the environmental community arguing against it on numerous grounds. Some say that the existing global environmental regime (surrounding such bodies as the United Nations Environment Program) has not been able to fulfil its mandate and the focus should be reforming the existing architecture, not creating new institutions that could become plagued with the same problems (Najam, 2003).

Notes

1. A number of articles have found turning points ranging from $7500 GDP per capita to $15 000 and higher. Indeed, 28 per cent of the more than 100 EKC tests found no turning points and the average turning point for those that did find an inverted-U is $12 749. Such evidence implies that pollution per capita may continue for decades before 'turning' around.
2. See Chapter 14 for another perspective on poverty and inequality in the developing world.

References

Ackerman, Frank and Lisa Heinzerling (2004), *Priceless: On Knowing the Price of Everything and the Value of Nothing*, New York: New Press.

Anderson, Sarah and John Cavanagh (2004), *Lessons of European Integration for the Americas*, Washington: Institute for Policy Studies.

Bhagwati, Jagdish (1993), 'The case for free trade', *Scientific American*, November.

Birdsall, Nancy and David Wheeler (1993), 'Trade policy and industrial pollution in Latin America: where are the pollution havens?', *Journal of Environment and Development*, **2**(1).

Boyce, James K. (2002), 'The globalization of market failure', in Kevin P. Gallagher and Jacob Werksman (eds), *International Trade and Sustainable Development*, London: Earthscan.

Chang, Ha-Joon (2003), *Rethinking Development Economics*, London: Anthem Press.

Cline, William (2004), *Trade Policy and Global Poverty*, Washington: Institute for International Economics.

Cole, Matthew A. (2004), 'Trade, the pollution haven hypothesis and the EKC', *Ecological Economics*, **48**(71).

Conroy, Michael (2002), 'Can advocacy-led certification systems transform global corporate practices? Evidence, and some theory, PERI Working Paper No. 21.

Copeland, Brian and Scott Taylor (2003), *Trade and Environment*, Princeton, NJ: Princeton University Press.

Economic Commission for Latin America and the Caribbean and United Nations Environment Program (ECLAC/UNEP) (2003), *The Sustainability of Development in Latin America and the Caribbean: Challenges and Opportunities*, Santiago: ECLAC/UNEP.

Esty, Daniel (1997), *Greening the GATT*, Washington: Institute for International Economics.

Frankel, J.A. and D. Romer (1999), 'Does trade cause growth?', *American Economic Review*, **89**(3): 379–99.

Gallagher, Kevin P. (2004), *Free Trade and the Environment: Mexico, NAFTA, and Beyond*, Palo Alto, CA: Stanford University Press.

Gallagher, Kevin P. (ed.) (2005), *Putting Development First: The Importance of Policy Space in the WTO and IFIs*, London: Zed Books.

Gallagher, Kevin P. and Lyuba Zarsky (2005), 'No miracle drug – foreign direct investment and sustainable development', in Lyuba Zarsky (ed.), *International Investment for Sustainable Development: Balancing Rights and Rewards*, London: Earthscan Books.

Grossman, Gene and Alan Krueger (1993), 'Environmental impacts of a North American free

Trade agreement', in Peter Garber (ed.), *The US–Mexico Free Trade Agreement*, Cambridge: MIT Press.

Jaffe, Adam (1995), 'Environmental regulation and the competitiveness of US manufacturing', *Journal of Economic Literature*, **33**: 132–63.

Jenkins, Rhys (1998), 'Environmental regulation and international competitiveness: a review of the literature', INTECH Working Paper #9801, Maastricht, United Nations University.

Kahn, Mathew E. and Yutaka Yoshino (2004), 'Testing for pollution havens inside and outside of regional trading blocs', *Advances in Economic Analysis & Policy*, **4**(2), Article 4.

Kanbur, Ravi (2001), 'Economic policy, distribution, and poverty: the nature of disagreements', http://people.cornell.edu/pages/sk145/papers/Disagreements.pdf.

Kuznets, Simon (1955), 'Economic growth and income inequality', *American Economic Review*, **1**: 1–28.

Low, Patrick and Alexander Yeats (1992), 'Do "Dirty" industries migrate?', in Patrick Low (ed.), *International Trade and the Environment*, Washington, DC: World Bank.

Lucas, Robert, David Wheeler and Humala Hettige (1992), 'Economic development, environmental regulation, and the international migration of toxic industrial pollution', in Patrick Low (ed.), *International Trade and the Environment*, Washington, DC: World Bank.

Mani, Muthukumara and David Wheeler (1998), 'In search of pollution havens? Dirty industry in the world economy, 1960–1995', *Journal of Environment and Development*, **7**(3): 215–47.

Nadal, Alejandro and Timothy Wise (2004), 'The environmental costs of agricultural trade liberalization: Mexico–US maize trade under NAFTA', Working Group Discussion Paper DP04, June 2004.

Najam, Adil (2003), 'The case against a new international environmental organization', *Global Governance*, **9**: 367–84.

Neumayer, Eric (2001), *Greening Trade and Investment*, London: Earthscan.

Palmer, Karen, Wallace Oates and Paul Portney (1995), 'Tightening environmental standards: the benefit cost or the no cost paradigm', *Journal of Economic Perspectives*, **9**(4): 119–32.

Panayotou, Theodore (2000), *Economic Growth and the Environment*, Cambridge, MA: Center for International Development, Harvard University.

Porter, Michael E. and Claas van der Linde (2002), 'Toward a new conception of the environment–competitiveness relationship', *Journal of Economic Perspectives*, **16**: 125–46.

Rodrik, Dani (2004), 'How to make the trade regime work for development', mimeo, Harvard University.

Rodriquez, Francisco and Dani Rodrik (2001), 'Trade policy and economic growth: a skeptic's guide to the cross-national evidence', NBER Working Paper 7081.

Ruggerio, Renalto (1999), address to the World Trade Organization, March.

Sachs, J.D. and A. Warner (1995), 'Economic reform and the process of global integration', *Brookings Papers on Economic Activity*, **1**: 1–95.

Speth, Gustave (2004), Red Sky at Morning: America and the Crisis of the Global Environment, New Haven, CT: Yale University Press.

Stallings, Barbara and Wilson Peres (2000), *Growth, Employment, and Equity: The Impact of the Economic Reforms in Latin America and the Caribbean*, Washington: ECLAC/Brookings.

Stern, David (1998), 'Progress on the environmental Kuznets curve', *Environment and Development Economics*, **3**: 173–6.

Stern, David (2004), 'The rise and fall of the environmental Kuznets curve', *World Development*, **32**(8): 1419–39.

Stiglitz, Joseph and Andrew Charlton (2004), *An Agenda for the Development Round of Trade Negotiations in the Aftermath of Cancun*, London: Commonwealth Secretariat.

Tobey, James (1990), 'The effects of domestic environmental policies on patterns of world trade', *Kyklos*, **43**(2): 191–209.

UNDP (2000), *Millennium Development Goals*, New York: United Nations.

UNDP (2005), *Millennium Ecosystem Assessment*, New York: United Nations.

Wacziarg, R. and K.H. Welch (2003), 'Trade liberalization and growth: new evidence', NBER Working Paper 10152, Cambridge, MA, December.

Working Group on Environment and Development in the Americas (WGDEA) (2004), *Globalization and the Environment: Lessons from the Americas*, Washington: Heinrich Boel.

World Bank (1992), *World Development Report*, Washington, DC: World Bank.

World Trade Organization (WTO) (2001), *Doha Ministerial Declaration*, www.wto.org.

Young, Carlos (1999), *Trade Liberalization and Industrial Pollution in Brazil*, Santiago: CEPAL.

Young, Carlos (2004), 'Trade, foreign investment, and the environment in Brazil', Medford, MA: Global Development and Environment Institute Discussion Paper, Tufts University.

26 The international politics of sustainable development
John Vogler

1. Introduction

There are many definitions of sustainable development, but few betray its political nature. One exception is to be found in a 1992 statement by Maurice Strong, the moving force behind the United Nations Conference on Environment and Development (UNCED) held in that year.

> Sustainable development involves a process of deep and profound change in the political, social, economic, institutional and technological order, including redefinition of relations between developing and more developed countries.[1]

From the perspective of international politics, the critical part is the 'redefinition of relations between developing and more developed countries'. Sustainable development represented a political construct designed to facilitate a bargain across the deep structural divide between North and South. This would allow global negotiation on the environmental concerns voiced by developed states through the necessary accommodation of the economic and political demands of the developing countries. In the much changed and highly differentiated circumstances of the early twenty-first century international system, it continues to serve this function. This article seeks to outline the way in which the concept has been moulded by international politics, how it reflects not only the balance between the G77/China and the OECD countries but other significant changes in the world system as well.

The concept has always been associated with the United Nations organization and landmarks in its evolution are provided by three great UN conferences held over the 30 years from 1972 to 2002; at Stockholm, Rio and Johannesburg. In this period there has been a discernible shift from a near exclusive concern with the environmental predicament, to an integrated conception of environmental, economic and social determinants of the human future, in which the former is by no means dominant.

A conventional survey of these developments might regard sustainable development as a new arena for the expression of the national interests of a widening range of states, at various levels of economic development, with their own political and commercial agendas to pursue. However, the concept was not just the rhetorical plaything of self-interested states. As it became institutionalized within the UN system, it began to take on a life of its own, to spawn new commissions and meetings and to re-shape the way in which other organizations defined their missions. It came to be closely associated with the growing significance of non-state actors and particularly the NGOs that populate what has come to be termed 'global civil society'. It may also be argued that, as well as reflecting the prevailing political and economic order, sustainable development, or more accurately the forces that it represents, is inherently subversive of that order.

2.   Stockholm and the origins of sustainable development

The emergence of the sustainable development concept can be understood in terms of the changing structure of the international political system after 1945 and more specifically, the evolution of the United Nations organization. In 1945, at its foundation, the UN comprised 51 members – the overwhelming majority being developed states. European colonial empires survived, although mortally damaged by the events of the Second World War. In 1947 India and Pakistan were granted their independence and in the ensuing 20 years the old colonial empires in Africa and South and South-East Asia were almost entirely liquidated. This surge of new independent states transformed the membership of the United Nations. By 1965 total membership was 114, of which more than 80 were newly independent developing states. Developing countries, courted by both camps in the Cold War, had since the Bandung meeting in 1955 attempted to proclaim their 'non-alignment'.

Although sometimes divided by their allegiances and indeed lack of allegiance in the Cold War, the newly independent states were able to unite around a number of other issues such as opposition to continued colonialism and to the Apartheid regime in South Africa. Above all, they shared a consciousness of their relative weakness in the international economy, of their dependence on their former colonial masters and of the need to promote development. By the early 1960s demands for action on the inequities on trade and development and for increased aid funding had become insistent in the UN General Assembly leading to the formation in 1964 of UNCTAD (The United Nations Conference on Trade and Development). It was in this context, on 15 June 1964, that the caucus of developing world states, the G77 (Group of 77) was founded. It now has some 132 member states including China (it is quite usual to refer to the G77/China). G77 Chapters will now be found at all major multilateral organizations and conferences but the heart of its activity remains the United Nations General Assembly, and the G77's primary decision-making body is its Ministerial Meeting, held annually at the beginning of the regular session of the UN General Assembly in New York.

The G77 caucus was able to command a significant majority in the General Assembly and although its resolutions do not have the binding character of those of the Security Council, they can and do serve to set the international agenda and to direct the work of the organization. Thus, although militarily and economically weak, in relation to the developed countries, the G77 could deploy an organizational weapon. This they proceeded to do in a number of contexts with the general aim of advancing their own economic development and addressing the structural inequities of the existing international system. In 1967, the General Assembly held a Special Session on development followed by its adoption, in October 1970, of the 0.7 per cent of GNI aid target for the developed countries.[2]

Thus, by the early 1970s, the development agenda was well established within the UN General Assembly. By contrast, environmental concerns had achieved very little international profile and were only just beginning, during the 1960s, to enter the politics of developed states, as issues such as nuclear contamination and transboundary sulphur deposition (acid rain) began to register. There was sufficient interest, however, to stimulate calls for UN action on international environmental issues and a conference was proposed by the Swedish government in early 1968. By December of that year the UN General Assembly had agreed to convene the United Nations Conference on the Human Environment (UNCHE) at Stockholm in 1972. The vote was unanimous even though there were misgivings amongst the G77 that international discussions of the environment might be used as an excuse to restrict development and curtail flows of aid (Engfeldt, 1973). It was important to enlist the continuing support of a General Assembly majority by establishing connections with the development agenda. This landmark meeting, sponsored by the UNCHE Preparatory Committee (Prep Com) and held in a motel in the Swiss village of Founex in June 1971, first gave political definition to what later became sustainable development (Caldwell, 1990, p. 52). There, a group of 27 experts articulated the links between environment and development stating that: 'although in individual instances there were conflicts between environmental and economic priorities, they were intrinsically two sides of the same coin' (*Founex Report*, 1971: 1.5, 2). While in advanced countries economic development might be identified as the cause of environmental degradation, for the developing countries development was the only solution to the linked problems of poverty and degradation. Many of what were to become the perennial themes of UN debates about sustainability were clearly foreseen at Founex. The Report stressed that the 'extent to which developing countries pursue a style of development that is responsive to social and environmental goals must be determined by the resources available to them' and that this must reinforce the advanced countries' commitment to providing development aid (ibid., 1.15: 6). This aid should be additional to that already provided (ibid., 4.17: 29). Environmental issues were recognized as being 'relatively marginal' to countries with pressing development concerns (ibid., 3.12: 21) and their social and economic policy fell 'entirely and exclusively within the sovereign competence of developing countries' (ibid., 3.1: 15). Finally, the Report sees, albeit 'dimly', some of the trade consequences of the environmental agenda in the developing world: concern that raised standards of environmental protection would become a form of disguised protectionism to lock them out of developed world markets and that ecological dumping might occur (ibid., 4.5: 22–3).

There were many important outcomes of the 1972 Stockholm UNCHE. They included the creation of the UN Environment Programme (UNEP) and the setting up of government departments of the environment across the world.[3] At the conference itself the Prime Minister of India, Indira Gandhi, who was the only other head of government to attend alongside the sponsor Olaf Palme, attracted much attention with her statement that 'poverty is the greatest polluter'.[4] The conference proceedings were also free of the Cold War confrontation that tended to impair other international gatherings at the time because the Soviet Union and its allies operated a boycott to protest at the non-admission of East Germany. The Stockholm Declaration, with its 26 Principles, became a significant source for the development of 'soft' environmental law, some of which reflected the Founex discussions by laying down some essential connections between environment and development, although the term 'sustainable development' does not appear in the conference records.[5]

3.   Rio and the sustainable development bargain

While Stockholm provided the bases, in all but name, for international discussions of sustainable development it was almost immediately eclipsed by the gathering crisis in the world economy, the 1973 war in the Middle East and by a new G77 strategy. Dramatic rises in the price of oil in the early 1970s and the willingness of the oil-producing states, gathered in OPEC, to exert pressure upon the West over the plight of the Palestinian people, provided the context for a sustained G77 campaign for economic justice and the structural reform of the international economic system. What became known as the New International Economic Order (NIEO) was launched by a 1974 General Assembly Resolution on the Economic Rights and Duties of states, which called for a major increase in aid transfers and the restructuring of the international commodities system. The demands for NIEO spread well beyond this and can be traced in G77 positions at a range of other negotiations. The important third Law of the Sea Conference, which went on throughout the 1970s, included a central Southern demand for equitable sharing of the supposed mineral riches of the deep seabed and its declaration as the 'Common Heritage of Mankind'. Similar ideas appeared in discussions within that previously apolitical and technical body, the International Telecommunication Union. Here the demand from the G77 was for 'equity in orbit'; to change the rules for the allocation of the right to use the geostationary orbit (GSO) such that developing countries such as India could benefit from the new satellite technology. In the struggle at the UN over the NIEO, and over the creation of a Common Fund for Commodities in particular, the link between underdevelopment and environmental conservation was relegated to the sidelines. The Coyococ meeting organized by UNCTAD and UNEP in 1974 is reflective of the times:

> The quadrupling of oil prices through the combined action of the oil producers sharply alters the balance of power in world markets and redistributes resources massively to some third world countries. Its effect has been to reverse decisively the balance of advantage in the oil trade and to place close to $100 billions a year at the disposal of some third world nations. Moreover, in an area critical to the economies of industrialized states, a profound reversal of power exposes them to a condition long familiar in the third world – a lack of control over vital economic decisions. (Coyococ Declaration, 1974: 3)

There is very little in the Declaration on environmental interdependence but a great deal about resource-based power, the need for third world self reliance and the failure of market mechanisms. What was proposed (in line with what was being negotiated for the deep seabed in the Law of the Sea Convention) were 'strong international regimes for the exploitation of common resources' and the 'management of resources and environment on a global scale' (ibid., p. 8). North–South negotiations proceeded within the UN context and responses from the developed world, notably the Brandt Report (Independent Commission on Development Issues, 1980) tended to focus upon the economic interdependence between the developing countries of the South and inflation and recession afflicted economies of Western Europe and the United States.[6]

The campaign for a NIEO exploited a period of economic turmoil and political and military retreat by the United States and its allies – the debacle in Saigon and the rest of Indochina in 1975 followed by the humiliation of the seizure of its Teheran embassy in 1979. It was soon to be replaced by a much more strident approach in the West involving an active pursuit of the Second Cold War against the Soviet Union and a rejection of the politics of interdependence, replaced by a vigorous pursuit of free market solutions. Amongst the first casualties were the North–South dialogue which essentially collapsed at the Cancun Conference of 1981 and the Law of the Sea

Convention (signed but not ratified by the US and her allies in 1982). The interesting question is how and why the seeds of the Brundtland Report (WCED, 1987) came to be sown and nurtured in these rather unpromising circumstances. The Commission itself was set up by the General Assembly in 1983 and reported in 1987. Its analysis is well known, it built upon what had been achieved at Stockholm and provided the most politically significant of all definitions of 'sustainable development'. By 1987 political conditions were much more receptive. The Second Cold War was drawing to a close with the Intermediate Nuclear Forces (INF) agreement of that year. In December 1989 Resolution 44/228 of the General Assembly agreed to convene a second great conference – UNCED – in 1992.

The concept of sustainable development acquired political impetus through rising public concern in the developed countries over the new and alarming phenomenon of global environmental change. In some ways it replaced fears of nuclear Armageddon that had prevailed in the early 1980s. Preparations for the conference ran alongside the intergovernmental negotiations for Climate and Biodiversity Conventions. For the G77 it provided a new opportunity to restore some of the negotiating credibility that had been lost with the collapse of the NIEO. According to one British diplomatic participant:

> The Brundtland Report shows a hard headedness uncharacteristic of such exercises in the emphasis it gives institutional factors. But the genius of the piece lies in its adoption and promulgation of the concept of 'sustainable development'. In one neat formula, Mrs Brundtland provided a slogan behind which first world politicians with green electorates to appease, and third world politicians with economic deprivation to tackle, could unite. The formula was of course vague, but the details could be left for later. (Benton, 1994: p. 129)

Rio was preceded by a series of Prep Coms which developed key conference texts, *Agenda 21* and the *Rio Declaration*, along with the separate intense negotiations for Climate and Biodiversity which were scheduled to provide completed texts for formal signature at Rio. The UN Framework Convention on Climate Change (UNFCCC), like the other Conventions, had to grapple with North–South issues and questions of responsibility. To do so the Convention includes the important principle of 'common but differentiated responsibilities' under which only the developed Annex I countries are obligated to make emissions reductions commitments in the first instance.[7] Financial assistance in terms of 'capability building' is provided for the developing countries to fulfil their responsibilities in terms of providing national reports. North–South difficulties were more evident in the bad-tempered negotiations for the Convention on Biodiversity (CBD), involving arguments about the extent of developed world finance that would support the preservation of biodiversity resources mainly located in the South and the sharing of economic benefits from the utilization of 'sovereign' biodiverse resources by developed world biotechnology firms.[8] There was also an attempt to follow up Western public and NGO concerns over the fate of tropical forests with a convention to conserve them, but this foundered on developing country suspicions of violation of economic sovereignty. It was replaced at Rio with a non-binding statement of forest principles.

The conference itself proved to be an international event on an unprecedented scale as heads of government vied to make their mark on what was dubbed the Rio 'Earth Summit'. Its very title, connecting Environment *and* Development, was indicative of North–South bargaining at the UN, in which demands for international action on the environment were set against claims for additional development aid and technology transfer.[9] At the Conference itself the most serious argument concerned the extent to which developed nations would 'pay' for the implementation of UNCED decisions on sustainable development with additional aid contributions. Major aid donors re-packaged their existing programmes and promised new funds, but the net results appear to have been minimal and the oft-repeated UN target of 0.7 per cent of GNI is still far short of fulfilment.[10] The key outputs of the Conference (as opposed to the FCCC and the CBD) are to be found in the *Rio Declaration*, *Agenda 21* and the Commission on Sustainable Development (CSD). All are quite explicitly concerned with sustainable development and it is thus, at the conclusion of the Earth Summit, that the concept truly arrives on the international scene.

Agenda 21, doubtless the most enduring product of the Prep Coms and the conference, is a vast (over 500 pages) compendium of agreed good practice and advice for achieving sustainable development in almost every conceivable area, except the Antarctic. It has no legal authority but has proved to be widely influential even down to the level of the many local *Agenda 21*s that were created in the aftermath of Rio. Ten years later the next great UN conference at Johannesburg pledged itself to discuss how the contents of Agenda 21 might be better implemented. *The Rio Declaration on Environment and Development* also mentions the achievement of sustainable development in ten of its 27 clauses. What had been intended as a visionary, brief and inspiring *Earth Charter* was, when put into the hands of the Prep Com, turned into an example of how the sustainability concept can be transformed by international politics into a portmanteau of special interests, contradictory approaches and inoffensive platitudes. Thus a right to development, national resource sovereignty, free market economic systems, the precautionary approach and common but differentiated responsibilities are all present alongside clauses such as Principle 25: 'Peace, development and environmental protection are interdependent and indivisible'. As one commentary describes it: 'Far from a timeless ethic, it was now a snapshot of history' (Grubb et al., 1993, p. 85).[11] As such, the *Declaration* provides a useful indicator of how far the new concept of sustainable development had moved on from the discussions of environment and development 20 years previously (it itself consciously sought to build upon the Stockholm Principles). A comparison of the two reveals some enduring themes. The famous Stockholm Principle 21 is repeated verbatim as Rio Principle 2 and there are many new concerns, legal innovations and the rights of women and indigenous people that figure in the later document. However, the bulk of the Stockholm conclusions were concerned with strictly environmental matters while acknowledging development issues, whereas at Rio the balance is noticeably shifted towards a range of socio-economic concerns. This change is certainly reflected in subsequent, generally accepted, UN conceptualizations in terms of three 'pillars' designed '. . . to ensure a balance between economic development, social development and environmental protection as interdependent and mutually reinforcing components of sustainable development' (United Nations General Assembly, A/57/532/add.1, 12 December 2002).

4. Johannesburg: sustainable development under globalization

Rio institutionalized a process of continuing dialogue on sustainable development and spread the concept across the UN system and beyond. An important consequence was its still incomplete influence on other organizations such as the World Bank, which had been traditionally prone to funding decisions based upon narrow considerations of economic welfare. Other bodies, such as the EU where it achieved Treaty status as an objective of the Union, came to use the concept as a means of attempting to integrate disparate areas of policy and resolve contradictions between them. A similar move, from environmental policy to the governance of sustainability, was observable in the academic literature from Vogler and Jordan (2003). In terms of the core politics of the UN, the creation of the Commission on Sustainable Development, set up by the General Assembly at the instigation of the UNCED, served to keep the Rio agenda alive by institutionalizing the formal review of the implementation of *Agenda 21* by states and 'major groups'. The CSD works under the auspices of the Economic and Social Council which elects its 53 state members on a regional basis. In 1997 a full-scale consideration of Rio 'plus 5' was held by a General Assembly Special Session to be followed by the convening of a new summit level UN conference, the 2002 World Summit on Sustainable Development (WSSD) to be held at Johannesburg.

Rio occurred in the immediate aftermath of the Cold War, the Soviet Union having finally collapsed in 1991. In the ensuing ten years the United States occupied a hegemonic position and many of the old boundaries and economic divisions in the system were obliterated in a process, hardly noticed at Rio, of globalization. An integral role was played by the creation of a new trade regime under the World Trade Organization (WTO), set up in 1995 as a consequence of the previous GATT Uruguay Round. Although deep and abiding inequalities remained, particularly between the mass consumption societies of the OECD and parts of Africa, the landscape of North–South relations was subject to radical alteration. Membership or impending membership of the WTO and increasingly full participation in the global economy meant that some key members of the G77, such as China, India and Brazil, achieved such high rates of growth that they came to be regarded as future economic superpowers.[12] This inevitably raised the question of the environmental consequences and sustainability of such growth and of the justification for 'common but differentiated responsibilities' in such radically altered circumstances. At the same time the inclusion of agriculture in trade negotiations and the increasing presence of powerful Southern economies at the WTO led to a new site of North–South confrontation in what was optimistically termed the Doha Development Round.[13] One potential casualty was any attempt to introduce environmental standards into international trade practices, viewed (as had been predicted at Founex) with immense suspicion by developing countries as a form of covert protection for developed world markets. These developments placed further strain on the G77 coalition, opening up gaps between oil producers, middle income and fast growing economies and the wretchedly poor Highly Indebted and Poor Countries (HIPC). At the same time the North was hardly monolithic as significant differences, traceable across most of the environmental negotiations of the 1990s, opened up between the United States and the European Union.

Within this political context the Johannesburg Conference confirmed a trend, evident since Rio, of the increasing importance of the socio-economic pillars of sustainable development. The environmental agenda at the two previous UN conferences had been sustained by peaks in the public 'attention cycle' of major developed countries. Public concern at environmental degradation had motivated governments in the late 1960s, and the Rio meeting had been driven on by the 'discovery' of stratospheric ozone depletion and the enhanced greenhouse effect at a time when Cold War fears had rapidly subsided. Johannesburg occurred amidst mounting developed world preoccupation with terrorism and stability in Central Asia and the Middle East. At the same time, the plight of much of the African continent, ravaged by AIDS, warfare and under-development, was justifiably prominent in the minds of governments and the public. The Rio agenda reflected the underlying power relations between North and South, with the South being reduced to obstruction over particular agreements (such as that proposed for forestry), while attempting, unsuccessfully, to obtain some compensatory leverage to increase aid flows and technology transfer. The WSSD occurred under changed circumstances. Held in South Africa, it highlighted a common international concern with the urgency of poverty alleviation alongside the increasing strength of some developing world economies under conditions of rapid globalization.

WSSD incorporated the concept of sustainable development throughout its deliberations and was initially dubbed 'the implementation summit'. Inevitably demands for additional financial resources and technology transfer continued but much of the debate had already been pre-empted by the establishment of the Millennium Development Goals in 2000 and by the March 2002 meeting of finance ministers which set out the 'Monterrey Consensus' on development funding.[14] These, as well as the WTO's Doha Round, were frequently referred to at the Conference. Pride of place in the Johannesburg 'Plan of Implementation' (UN, 2002), which formed the principal output of the Conference and the plenary sessions of the WSSD, was given to poverty eradication. It was described as 'the greatest global challenge facing the world today and an indispensable requirement for sustainable development' (ibid., p. 7), in effect confirming Indira Gandhi's statement, 30 years before, that 'poverty was the greatest polluter'. Closely associated were a range of so-called 'WEHAB' issues on water and sanitation, energy, health, agriculture and biodiversity, highlighted by the UN Secretary General as having been inadequately pursued at Rio and where, for some at least, 'time-bound targets' were established. However, it would be a mistake to conclude that strictly environmental questions were completely neglected, for a substantial part of the *Plan of Implementation* covers 'Protecting and managing the natural resource base of economic and social development' (Paras 24–46). What is also noticeable, in comparison to previous summit texts, is that there is a genuine attempt at conceptual integration:

> Unlike Agenda 21, the Plan of Implementation recognizes poverty as a running theme, linked to its multiple dimensions from access to energy, water and sanitation, to the equitable sharing of the benefits of biodiversity. This reflects a shift from a uni-dimensional income focus on poverty to a multidimensional approach that embraces a vision of 'sustainable livelihoods'. (ENB, 2002, p. 170)

Other elements emphasize the magnitude of change since the heady days of the New International Economic Order debates of the 1970s. The new context was globalization, which had its own section (V) of the Plan and there was at the Conference extensive stress upon the opportunities provided by Type II partnerships between developing world governments and the private sector (UN, 2002, p. 50). Nonetheless, some underlying North–South problems continue to be identifiable in much the same form as during the 1970s – declining and unstable developed world incomes from commodity exports (ibid., p. 95) – and the 1980s – the unsustainable indebtedness of many developing countries (ibid., p. 89). Following the Millennium Development Goals and the Monterrey Consensus, WSSD provided yet another opportunity to urge the developed states to meet the 0.7 per cent GNI aid commitment first established two years before the Stockholm conference (ibid., p. 85).

In common with its predecessor, the WSSD relied on extensive Prep Com discussion. There were four in all, producing a lengthy document comprising an uneasy alignment of differing interests to be handled with the greatest of care if the various underlying compromises were not to come unstitched. A controversy emerging from Rio, and the long debates over climate change, involved the principle of 'common but differentiated responsibilities'. This had become increasingly unacceptable to the United States, whose delegates sought first to remove and then to limit in application (to narrowly defined environmental issues).[15] A number of new issues spilled over from recent WTO and other meetings. They were fought over not because binding financial and other commitments were at stake, for the WSSD produced hardly any; but because of their symbolic importance for the future and the sense in which they set the terms of an emerging global bargain between North and South. At the North's insistence references to 'good governance' in the developing countries and the full incorporation of developing countries in a reformed international financial architecture pervade the WSSD text where they are regarded as the basis for additional assistance. Closely related is the need for the South to adopt 'sound' macroeconomic policies and to open their markets, particularly in the services sector. The G77 inserted text on common but differentiated responsibilities; the crucial matter of the removal of the developed world's agricultural subsidies and tariffs and its continuing obligations in terms of aid, debt relief and technology transfer.[16] One important environmental issue, arising in relation to the global trade regime, had already been central to the long-disputed negotiations for a Biosafety Protocol to the Convention on Biodiversity. This was the fundamental question of the subordination of MEAs (multilateral environmental agreements) to WTO rules. Not directly a North–South issue, it was still one that greatly exercised environmental campaigners who feared the hegemony of neo-liberal ideas and trade promotion over the protection of the environment. In the end textual compromises were achieved to the extent that the two should be 'mutually supportive' (ENB, 2002, p. 13).

5.   The international politics of sustainability and the sustainability of international politics

At first sight, much of the foregoing can be understood in classic power-political terms. Sustainable development provided a new arena for the pursuit and accommodation of state interests. Most of the compromises reveal such factors at work, including the central one of the North's interest in environmental quality and the South's development demands. At a national level, a close study of any of the negotiations will reveal the working of particularistic national and corporate interests. The G77, for example, has had difficulty in reconciling the imminent peril of the small island developing states (SIDS), in the face of climate change, with the refusal of the energy exporters even to recognize the problem. At Johannesburg the interests of energy producers on both sides of the North–South divide prevented the emergence of any clear targets for renewable energy (ENB, 2002, p. 7). The desire of Northern states to open up Southern markets, often for GMOs, while protecting their own agricultural producers and avoiding further public expenditure in aid commitments was also evident. There was also more than a touch of national commercial interest in the enthusiasm for Type II partnerships, which would allow corporations to acquire Southern business in the provision of water and sanitation.

Many of the interests pursued were not even remotely connected to issues of sustainable development. The withdrawal of the Eastern bloc from UNCHE in 1972 turned on the question of the status accorded to the German Democratic Republic. At Rio there were difficulties with reference to Israel's occupation of Palestine, and at Johannesburg, the conflict between the Zimbabwean and British governments.[17] Organizations with budgets and personnel to protect also have interests and the rivalries within the thicket of UN bodies and specialized agencies are particularly intense. Thus UNEP continues to have the rather lowly status of a programme rather than becoming a fully-fledged organization like the FAO or the World Bank.

It would, however, be wrong to leave it at that. Perhaps the central insight of International Relations scholarship on international environmental co-operation has been the significance of institutionalization that may serve to tame and redirect the interests of states. Sustainable development has become increasingly institutionalized in the international system. It began with the creation of UNEP and a range of other initiatives stemming from the Stockholm conference. At Rio, *Agenda 21* called for the creation of the

CSD under the UN's Economic and Social Committee and its annual work programme at the centre of a wider process of reviewing progress since UNCED.[18] Such institutionalization serves to keep the interplay between economic and social development and environmental questions on the international agenda. Thus whereas both Stockholm and Rio can be attributed to the stimulus of external events, Johannesburg was more the programmed outcome of an embedded process. Operating within a highly institutionalized setting involving a great deal of organizational politics has some other important consequences, which are central to an understanding of the events described in this article and which must contradict any simple 'realist' power politics account. The latter would predict that outcomes would be determined by the relative military and economic strength of state participants. While this may be part of an explanation of the situation at Johannesburg, where we might portray US hegemony challenged by the rising economies of the South, this cannot fully account for the Rio process. A common thread runs through the campaigns led by the G77 caucus that relied for their success upon an ability to mobilize voting majorities in international organizations and to exploit perceived interdependencies between North and South (Vogler, 2000, pp. 193–5).

How far does sustainable development actually subvert rather than reflect normal international politics? There are two prominent questions here for theorists of international relations. First there is a challenge to the primacy of the sovereign state, most obviously represented in the enormous encouragement given by the Rio process to what has been termed global civil society. The structures that have been developed to deal with sustainability issues, notably NGO participation and the Major Group system at UNCED, certainly introduce a new element of functional representation into the international system.[19] NGO activity has been very significant in changing agendas, in monitoring the behaviour of governments and in operating inside government delegations (Princen and Finger, 1994; Willetts, 1996; Newell, 2000). There is most certainly now a 'mixed actor situation', but this does not necessarily amount to a fundamental subversion of the system where sovereignty over natural resources continues to be jealously guarded and where state participants in the Rio process are careful to insert 'intergovernmental' into the title of many of the key organizations. A salient characteristic of the Johannesburg WSSD was not only the number of NGOs involved but their rising alarm at the prominence of another, more powerful, type of non-state actor – the transnational business corporation. The extent to which states can regulate the activities of the corporate sector is just one part of a lively debate about the possibility and desirability of state action for sustainability under conditions of globalization (Barry and Eckersley, 2005).

Rather than considering how the international political system, as presently constituted, can manage the problems of sustainability, some analysts have taken a more radical stance. For them, the sustainable development agenda is indicative of a deeper crisis in global social ecology which must prompt questions that are inherently subversive of the current political order (Sachs, 1993; Saurin, 1996; Paterson, 2001). It challenges the 'issue hierarchy', the dominance of the international trade regime and indeed the whole apparatus of globalization that serves the interests of capital accumulation and mass consumption societies. Since the failure of the NIEO, North–South dialogue on environment and development has essentially failed to engage the underlying pathologies of the global system as both Northern and Southern states pursue their short-sighted interests within a neo-liberal consensus. Thus the international politics of sustainable development represents at best a distraction and at worst an obstacle to human survival. Endless conferences and diplomacy (which themselves have major ecological costs in terms of air-miles travelled and paper consumed) merely give the impression that something is being done, while reinforcing the underlying structures of the global political economy. From this perspective the urgent question does not concern the international politics of sustainable development, but the sustainability of international politics itself.

Notes

1. This definition by Maurice Strong is one of 57 listed by Susan Murcott, AAAS Annual Conference IIASA 'Sustainability Indicators Symposium, Seattle,WA2/16/97, www.sustainableliving.org/appen-a.htm.

2. By Resolution 2626 (XXV) of 24 October 1970. The target was established by the 1969 Report of the Pearson Commission *Partners in Development*. Most developed world aid donors have officially endorsed the target, but few have achieved it. It is worth mentioning in the light of controversies at Rio and Johannesburg that the United States, although a large donor in absolute terms, has never been committed to the 0.7 per cent target.

3. There was also the *Stockholm Plan of Action* with 109 recommendations including a moratorium on whaling.

4. According to Conference Chair, Maurice Strong, 'she played a key role in elevating the concerns of the developing world at the Stockholm conference, and re-fashioning its agenda around developing countries' concerns and interests . . . thanks to her leadership, never more could the environment issue be considered in the narrow context of the pollution problems of the rich' (Strong, 1999, p. 2).

5. Principle 5 notes that 'non-renewable resources of the earth must be employed in such a way as to guard against the danger of their future exhaustion and to ensure that benefits from such employment are shared by all mankind'. Principle 8, 'Economic and social development is essential for ensuring a favourable living and working environment for man and for creating conditions on earth that are necessary for the improvement of the quality of life'. Principle 9, 'Environmental deficiencies generated by the conditions of under-development and natural disasters pose grave problems and can best be remedied by accelerated development through the transfer of substantial quantities of financial and technological assistance as a supplement to the domestic effort of the developing

countries and such timely assistance as may be required'. Principle 10 calls for price stability and adequate earnings for commodities. Principle 11, 'The environmental policies of all states should enhance and not adversely affect the present or future development potential of developing countries, nor should they hamper the attainment of better living conditions. . .' Principle 12 covers the need for additional aid and technical assistance to developing countries to cover the costs they may incur in meeting environmental standards. Principle 21 has become the most widely quoted, 'States have in accordance with the Charter of the United Nations and the principles of international law, the sovereign right to exploit their own resources pursuant to their own environmental policies, and the responsibility to ensure that activities within their jurisdiction or control do not cause damage to the environment of other states or areas beyond the limits of national jurisdiction'. None of these principles are binding, they merely express the 'common conviction' of the Stockholm participants (Declaration of the UN Conference on the Human Environment, 1972).

6. 'Above all, we believe that a large-scale transfer of resources to the South can make a major impact on growth in both the South and the North and help revive the flagging world economy' (Independent Commission on International Development Issues, 1980, p.. 36). Environmental issues figure alongside population growth and migration although there is a reference to the danger associated with global warming and deforestation and sustainable development is briefly foreshadowed, 'It is clear to us that the growth and development of the world economy must in future be less destructive to natural resources and the environment so that the rights of future generations are protected' (ibid., p. 115).

7. The concept also appears as Principle 7 of the Rio Declaration. It has since proved to be a source of enormous difficulty in achieving US adherence to the Kyoto Protocol to the agreement. The 1997 Byrd–Hagel Resolution of the US Senate forbids a US government to enter into an agreement that has differential and advantageous terms for US industrial competitors such as China.

8. The Bush administration refused to sign the CBD, but Clinton acceded. For an account of the negotiations in Nairobi see Benton (1994, pp. 197–206).

9. Resolution 44/228 was carefully crafted to ensure Southern participation and promised that the Conference would 'examine with a view to recommending effective modalities for favourable access to, and transfer of technologies . . . including on preferential terms'.

10. There is analysis of the financial commitments that supports the view that very little additional assistance resulted from Rio: (Grubb et al., 1993, Appendix I: pp. 169–77).

11. An example of a directly political insertion is no.23 'the environment and natural resources of people under oppression, domination and occupation shall be protected'. The reference is to Israeli occupation of Palestinian land.

12. In 2005 the WTO had 148 members, the great majority of which could be classified as 'developing countries'. The GATT/WTO system had been run by a 'Quad' of developed economies, the US, EU, Canada and Japan often through 'green room' informal negotiating procedures excluding most of the developing world. Now the system began to alter in the same way as the UN itself had been transformed in the 1960s.

13. The major developing WTO members began to organize themselves in the context of agricultural negotiations during the Doha Round to form the G20, involving Brazil, China and India amongst others.

14. The Millennium Development Goals (MDGs) were established by the General Assembly in its September 2000 'Millennium Declaration' (A/RES/55/2). They comprised a set of targets, usually to be achieved by 2015 and including a reduction by 50 per cent of people living on less than $1 a day, universal primary education, and a 75 per cent reduction in child mortality. Goal 7 is to ensure environmental sustainability by integrating SD principles into national decision-making, reducing by 50 per cent people without access to safe drinking water and achieving a 'significant improvement' in the lives of 100 million slum dwellers by 2020. The final Goal 8 was to develop a global partnership for development, based on an open trade and financial system but providing

special treatment for the most disadvantaged. The 2002 'Monterrey Consensus' emerged from an international meeting of finance ministers in Mexico preceding WSSD. Seen by the World Bank as the foundation of a future development partnership it comprised a collection of non-binding declarations on good governance, economic and social reform, stability oriented macroeconomic policies alongside generally non-specific ODA promises (the USA and EU made actual increased aid commitments at that time) and trade reform. UN 2002, *International Conference on Financing for Development*, Monterrey, Mexico 18–22 March, A/CONF.198/11.

15.   This was an argument fought out over numerous references to CBDR in the draft text which pitted the US against all the other participants including the EU, champion of the Kyoto Protocol. Another Rio principle involving US–EU disagreement was the latter's enthusiasm to include wording on the 'precautionary principle' as opposed to the existing 'precautionary approach' which eventually remained in the WSSD text. The point is that a 'principle' and one that takes into account developments in international law in the 1990s and indeed the EU Treaties themselves, is regarded as more binding than an 'approach'. On the details of the negotiations see ENB (2002, pp. 4–5).

16.   Para 131 states that 'Good governance is essential for sustainable development' and then adds a long list of other mutually reinforcing essentials including, democracy, peace, women's rights, poverty eradication, human rights, the right to development, the rule of law and market-oriented societies. Para 141 brings other key components of the compromise together in addressing the problems of international good governance involving 'the international finance, trade, technology and investment patterns that have an impact on the development of developing countries'. Measures shall include 'ensuring support for structural and macro-economic reform, a comprehensive solution to the external debt problem and increasing market access for developing countries'. The reform of the international financial architecture will become more transparent and developing countries will have more effective participation in decision-making processes. All this will be within 'A universal, rules-based, open and non-discriminatory and equitable world trading system as well as meaningful trade liberalization.'

17.   Steven Krasner (1985) has provided a realist account of Southern strategy during the 1970s in which the objectives of advocates of the NIEO were driven by the need for new and weak states to assert their sovereignty in the international system.

18.   The CSD was initiated in Chapter 38 of *Agenda 21* as an international mechanism to monitor its implementation. The General Assembly responded by setting up the Commission in 1992 (Res. 47/191). Commencing in 1993 the CSD has held annual meetings. As an ECOSOC body it is composed of 53 states, elected on a regional basis and representatives of 'major groups' also participate in its sessions. Up until the UN General Assembly Special Session on Rio plus 5 in 1997 it reviewed *Agenda 21* chapter by chapter. Subsequently it was tasked by UNGASS to adopt a more clustered and thematic approach. In 2003 CSD 11 agreed in future to adopt a two-year cycle of meetings within a multiyear work programme stretching to 2017. Each two-year implementation cycle would involve a Review Session and a Policy Session to consider 'a thematic cluster of issues and a suite of cross cutting issues' (ENB, 2005, p. 2). An example would be water and sanitation questions which are not handled coherently elsewhere in the UN system.

19.   At Stockholm 113 countries were represented, only two at head of government level. There were 400 IGOs and NGOs (Grubb et al., 1993, p. 4). At Rio, 178 countries, 117 at head of state or government level, 1400 NGOs and 35000 accredited participants (Benton, 1994, pp. 223–4). At WSSD, 191 governments, 82 heads of government and 21 340 participants (ENB, 2002, pp. 1–4).

References

Barry, J. and R. Eckersley (eds) (2005), *The State and the Global Ecological Crisis*, Cambridge MA: MIT Press.

Benton, T. (1994), *The Greening of Machiavelli: The Evolution of International Environmental Politics*, London: Royal Institute of International Affairs/Earthscan.

Caldwell, L.C. (1990), *International Environmental Policy: Emergence and Dimensions*, Durham: Duke University Press.

Earth Negotiations Bulletin (ENB) (2002), 'Summary of the World Summit on Sustainable Development: 26 August–4 September 2002', **22**(51).

Earth Negotiations Bulletin (ENB) (2005), 'Summary of the Intergovernmental Preparatory Meeting for the 13th Session of the Commission on Sustainable Development 28 February–4 March 2005', **5**(217).

Engfeldt, L.G. (1973), 'The United Nations and the human environment – some experiences', *International Organization*, **27**: 393–412.

The Founex Report on Development and Environment (1971), available at http://www.southcentre.org/publications/conundrum/conundrum-04.htm-91k.

Grubb, M. et al. (1993), *The Earth Summit Agreements: A Guide and Assessment*, London: Royal Institute of International Affairs/Earthscan.

Independent Commission on International Development Issues (1980), *North–South: A Programme for Survival: Report of the Independent Commission on International Development Issues under the Chairmanship of Willy Brandt*, London: Pan Books.

Krasner, S.D. (1985), *Structural Conflict: The Third World Against Global Liberalism*, Berkeley: University of California Press.

Meyer, J.W. et al. (1997), 'The structuring of a world environmental regime', *International Organization*, **51**: 623–51.

Newell, P. (2000), *Climate for Change: Non-State Actors and the Global Politics of the Greenhouse*, Cambridge: Cambridge University Press.

Paterson, M. (2001), *Understanding Global Environmental Politics: Domination, Accumulation, Resistance*, London: Routledge.

Princen, M. and M. Finger (1994), *Environmental NGOs in World Politics: Linking the Global and the Local*, London: Routledge.

Sachs, W. (ed). (1993), *Global Ecology*, London: Zed Books.

Saurin, J. (1996), 'International relations, social ecology and the globalisation of environmental change', in J. Vogler and M.F. Imber (eds), *The Environment and International Relations*, London: Routledge, pp. 77–98.

Strong, M. (1999), 'Hunger, poverty, population and environment', The Hunger project Millennium Lecture, Madras India, 7 April, www.thp.org/reports/strong 499.htm.

United Nations (1972), *Declaration of the United Nations Conference on the Human Environment*, www.unep.org/Documents.Multilingual/Default.Print.asp?DocumentD= 97andAR.

United Nations (2002), 'Plan of implementation of the world summit on sustainable development', in *Report of the World Summit on Sustainable Development, Johannesburg, South Africa, 26 August–4 September 2002*, A/CONF.199/20.

Vogler, J. (2000), *The Global Commons: Environmental and Technological Governance*, Chichester: John Wiley.

Vogler, J. and A. Jordan (2003), 'Governance and the environment' in F. Berkhout et al. (eds), *Negotiating Environmental Change: New Perspectives from Social Science*, Cheltenham, UK and Northampton, MA, USA: Edward Elgar, pp. 137–58.

Willetts, P. (1996), 'From Stockholm to Rio and beyond: the impact of environmental movements on the UN consultative arrangements', *Review of International Studies*, **22**(1): 57–81.

World Commission on Environment and Development (1987), *Our Common Future*, Oxford: Oxford University Press.

27 Financing for sustainable development
David Pearce

1. The issue

Does the pursuit of sustainable development require special financing? Achieving sustainable development is about policy measures that alter human behaviour towards the environment and towards society in general. Behavioural change could be achieved in various ways and some of those do not necessarily involve any financial flows. For example, moral suasion – the process of awareness raising and encouraging moral behaviour – need not involve any finance, although it may involve non-monetary costs to those changing their behaviour. The argument from moral suasion is self-fulfilling: if we all behaved 'sustainably' the world would have a better chance of being sustainable. The problem, as is well known, is that humans are complex mixtures of selfish and altruistic behaviour and simply appealing to the altruistic aspects of behaviour frequently fails to achieve goals that might be considered to be consistent with sustainability. Simply put, humans are not altruistic enough. In other cases, for example in its part in combating racism, suasion has arguably worked quite well. But acknowledgement of the difficulties of suasion leads to the second approach to sustainability, one based on coercive laws which ban or regulate adverse behaviour and perhaps reward good behaviour. Such laws also need not have any financial flows associated with them. By and large, this approach to sustainability characterizes most environmental and social policy. Such laws have worked fairly well in many cases. But economists and political scientists have repeatedly warned of the dangers in the direct regulatory approach.

First, regulations, and especially bans, frequently create economic rents which result in rent-seeking, rent capture and corruption, essentially unproductive activities which detract from potential human well-being. Activity shifts from creating human well-being to securing as large a part as possible of the financial gains associated with restrictions. Second, regulation can be expensive, with the result that coalitions are formed to prevent or water down further regulations. Third, regulations, especially those formed at the international level, frequently achieve no more than would have happened without the regulation: they lack 'additionality' (Barrett, 2003). This is because of the essentially game-theoretic nature of such agreements whereby no one agent is going to agree to harm themselves for the overall common good. Hence what they agree to is what they would have done anyway, with their participation and agreement being hailed in rhetorical terms. Regulations can of course be associated with some financial flows: fines for non-compliance would be an obvious example. But, by and large, regulation works, when it does work, by threat, where the threat is criminal or civil liability.

No one suggests that suasion and direct regulation have no role to play in the pursuit of sustainability, but there is an increasing interest in policy mechanisms that do involve financial flows. In the market place for private goods the role of finance is obvious. The seller of a good (or service) parts with that good to a buyer in return for a cash flow from the buyer to the seller. Finance for publicly provided (public) goods is more indirect. Public goods are goods which when provided to one person tend to be provided to a larger group, with few prospects of excluding any individual in that group. In the same vein, public goods are difficult to appropriate, that is to charge prices according to use. The provider or supplier of public goods is usually the government or the agent of the government, and beneficiaries do not pay directly for the good but indirectly via their taxation. The taxes paid may not be linked directly to the benefits – that is the financing of the public good comes out of general taxation. More recently, there has been a growing interest in linking tax payments more directly to the public good through 'hypothecation' or 'earmarking'. One justification for hypothecation comes from the public choice literature which argues that taxpayers will be more content to pay for public goods if they can trace the ways in which their payments translate into public good provision.

All of this is familiar. The problem is what to do with the very large variety of non-market goods, many of which have public good characteristics, for which there are no markets and for which public provision may not exist or, if it exists, may not work efficiently. It is this class of goods and services that we focus on in this chapter. Examples are well known: reduced global warming, avoided biodiversity loss, cleaner water and air, protected areas where public finance is insufficient, and so on.

2. Financial flows and the Coase theorem
A financial flow involves an exchange of cash or in-kind benefits between three agents in the economy: the individual, corporation or agency generating environmental and/or social harm; the agent suffering the harm; and the regulator or government. For simplicity, let us call these agents 'the polluter', 'the sufferer' and 'the regulator'. By definition, the sufferer becomes a beneficiary if the polluter ceases to pollute. Hence we will also speak of 'beneficiaries'. As Coase (1960) made clear, polluters or sufferers/beneficiaries may hold the property rights. If polluters hold the

rights then sufferers should be able to pay polluters not to pollute and it will be in their self-interest to do this so long as the marginal damage they suffer exceeds the payment they make for a marginal reduction in pollution. In turn, the polluter's self-interest is served if the received payment exceeds the marginal benefit he/she would have made from the damaging activity. If the sufferer holds the property rights, then the polluter cannot pollute unless he/she pays the sufferer compensation that exceeds the damage done. Figure 27.1 shows the familiar Coasian bargain diagram.

The horizontal axis shows pollution (for which read resource degradation, social harm and so on). $MNPB$ measures the marginal net private benefits to the polluter from the activity creating the pollution. To fix ideas, it is simplest to construe $MNPB$ as marginal profits. Then, if the polluter holds the property rights, he/she will operate at Q_{priv} where total profits $A + B + C$ are maximized, unless induced to do otherwise. MD shows the marginal damage suffered by the sufferer. MD can also be defined as the marginal external cost arising from the polluter's activity. At Q_{priv} the sufferer bears a cost of $B + C + D$. It is immediately obvious that there are gains to be made by some sort of bargain. Total social welfare at Q_{priv} is the difference between profits and suffering, that is $A - D$. But if a move to Q^* could be engineered, net social welfare would be $A + B - B = A$. Given the property rights rest with the polluter, the sufferer can pay any sum less than $C + D$ to induce the polluter to surrender profits associated with activity level Q_{priv}. Exactly what is paid depends on the relative bargaining strengths of the parties in question.

The reader can determine that exactly the same result holds if the sufferer has the property rights. In this case, the starting point is the origin and

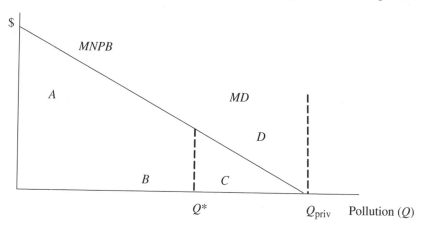

Figure 27.1   The Coase theorem

payments less than $A + B$, but more than B, will compensate the sufferer for tolerating pollution. Either way, the optimum Q^* is achieved and the achievement comes about without the interference of the third agent, the regulator. For those who believe in the optimality of free markets, the Coase theorem is a justification for the minimal role of regulation and the government. Note that the problem of the optimal provision of non-market goods has been solved with a flow of finance: either compensation flows from polluter to sufferer, or payment (sometimes misleadingly called a 'bribe' in the literature) flows from sufferer to polluter. It is this financial flow that secures optimality in the sense of economic efficiency.

Economic efficiency is not necessarily the same thing as sustainability, since that depends on the notion of sustainability adhered to (see Chapters 4 and 6 for a discussion). If it is weak sustainability, in which there is substitution at the margin between environmental, social and man-made assets, then economic efficiency is sustainability. If it is strong sustainability, which subsumes weak sustainability but has the added constraint that environmental assets must not (in some sense) decline, then this goal appears to be achieved if the polluter has the property rights, but not if the sufferer has the property rights. The reason for this is that pollution is reduced (which is the same as saying environmental assets increase) in the former case, but it is increased in the latter case. The starting point matters. But since strong sustainability denies the substitutability of compensation and environmental assets, it would effectively rule out the polluter paying compensation to the sufferer for an increase in pollution. (There would have to be some form of regulation that would deny the polluter paying compensation. In practice, such payments are not uncommon, for example with airport noise compensation.) Strong sustainability therefore involves an efficiency loss equal to area A in Figure 27.1. This is not surprising since it involves an added constraint on the maximization of social welfare. But the nature and existence of this efficiency loss is not always made clear in the sustainability literature.

The Coase theorem generates financial flows which act to secure sustainability in the weak sense. The theorem simply does not operate with strong sustainability and if sufferers have property rights to zero pollution – no bargain involving compensation for suffering would be permitted. If polluters have the property rights, then strong sustainability would presumably still sanction a move like the one from Q_{priv} to Q^* in Figure 27.1 since it is (a) efficient and (b) reduces pollution.

While theoretically elegant, the Coase theorem is in fact very problematic when efforts are made to transfer it to the real world. As such, the financial flows likely to be involved in actual bargains over non-market goods will be more complex than simple 'polluter pays sufferer' or 'beneficiary pays polluter'.

First, the trades involve transactions costs. Indeed, many regard the most restrictive condition in the Coase theorem to be that bargaining is costless. In reality, we know that transactions costs are very important in actual bargains. This immediately suggests a role for the regulator (government), provided regulatory costs do not outweigh the gains from trade, something that cannot be guaranteed. Regulation here would typically mean 'facilitating' the bargain by actions which directly reduce transactions costs (for example regulators may have more access to information about polluters or sufferers than do the parties themselves – an obverse of the usual assumption about asymmetric information), or by the regulator taking over the bargain on behalf of one of the parties.

Second, Coasian bargains are indifferent to equity concerns – the theorem is about efficiency alone. But governments and regulators are highly likely to have equity concerns. Interestingly, these concerns are not confined to contexts in which the sufferer is poor. They may arise where either the sufferer is poor or the polluter is poor. In the former case, government may take on the role of acting for the poor sufferer. This is the case with the Costa Rican ecosystem service payments whereby government pays upland forest owners not to deforest because of the otherwise detrimental effect on poor downstream farmers (for a discussion, see Pearce, 2004). The government effectively acts for downstream beneficiaries of upstream forest conservation and the presumption is that many of these beneficiaries are relatively poor and could not pay for beneficial conservation. The limitation of the Coase theorem in this context is that it assumes the availability of a financial fund in the hands of the sufferer. However economically rational payment to the polluter would be, if the financial resources are not there payment cannot be made. The standard response to this issue is that inability to pay is the same thing as unwillingness to pay, since willingness to pay is always constrained by income. True as that may be, the issue of unfairness remains. In such contexts, governments may well become the agents for the poorer party. The flow of finance thus becomes more complex. In the Costa Rican case, for example, the financial flows arise from a tax on vehicle pollution, the flows then being used to finance payments to upland forest owners, without any form of financial flow affecting the sufferer.

The case where the polluter is poor is less obvious, but a striking example is the technical and financial assistance given by Scandinavian countries to Baltic countries to switch energy-generating technologies away from high polluting to less polluting ones. The benefit to Scandinavia is the reduced transboundary acid rain deposition that results. As long as Scandinavian payments are less than the value of the avoided damage, Scandinavia is better off. As long as the incremental cost of the cleaner technology is zero or negative to the Baltic States, they are better off. Here the sufferer is paying the polluter. Nakada and Pearce (1999) have shown that the same principle would be efficient for transboundary pollution from China to Japan.

Third, non-market goods tend to have the features of public goods. As such, in the case of pollution control there tend to be many beneficiaries ranging from a local population to the world as a whole. The Coasian solution would be for these populations to form a coalition to bargain with the polluter. This is exactly what does happen in a number of cases, notably with the Global Environment Facility (GEF) which bargains with developing and transition countries to change polluting technologies to less polluting ones or to conserve biodiversity that might not be preserved in the local national interest. As a United Nations agency, the GEF receives finance from individual subscriber nations so that taxpayers in those countries first pay the GEF for onward payments to recipient nations to change their technology and conservation choices. Theoretically, the payments equal or just exceed the 'incremental cost' to the host nation of making the switch to the globally beneficial technology or policy. The GEF is a prime example of 'market creation' whereby beneficiaries pay polluters who hold the (in this case, sovereign nation) property rights.

The fourth problem with the Coase theorem is that it assumes one of the two bargaining parties already has the property rights. In practice, many environmental problems involve ill-defined or even non-existent property rights. In the extreme, the case of no property rights is equivalent to 'open access' conditions. As is well known from the bioeconomics literature, open access produces an equilibrium in which all rents are dissipated. The equilibrium may be stable but is easily perturbed to produce situations of total resource loss (extinction). This will happen if technological change in resource harvesting (guns as opposed to spears in the case of large mammals, refrigerated ships and industrial trawl methods in the case of fish, and so on) reduces the cost of harvesting to the point where the equilibrium goes beyond some sustainability threshold. The massive problem of global over-fishing arises precisely from open access combined with new technology and rising demand.

The Coasian response to open access contexts is, correctly, to establish property rights. In many respects this is how the institutions related to natural resources and the environment are developing. The UN Framework Convention on Climate Change and the Convention on Biological Diversity are examples of attempts to establish either global communal rights to the atmosphere (global warming) or some form of attenuation of existing sovereign rights to biodiversity, but these rights mask the effective open-access nature of the resources within those sovereign states. Notably, in both cases, global beneficiaries pay the poorer parties to reduce pollution or resource loss. In the global warming case this is effected through two of the 'flexibility mechanisms' of the Kyoto Protocol – the Clean Development Mechanism and Joint Implementation. In the biodiversity case, richer countries are supposed to pay poorer countries for access to their resources and to share the benefits. In both cases, finance flows from rich to poor or poorer.

Overall, then, the Coasian paradigm is a useful starting point for analysing financial flows. When the theorem works in its original form, the financial flows are from beneficiary to polluter or from polluter to beneficiary, depending on which owns the property rights. Once it is accepted that the kinds of goods and services in the environmental context are public goods, then the way is open for a significant modification of the theorem whereby governments or regulators act as intermediaries. In this case they may collect pollution taxes or charges for onwards payment to sufferers, or they may retain the proceeds in general funds. Where polluters have the property rights, governments may act to finance the necessary payments to polluters. Finally, no flows of finance occur in the open access case where no one has defined property rights. Indeed, it is precisely because there are no financial flows that open access risks securing equilibria that are easily 'tipped' into states of extinction, as the examples of over-fishing show. The Coasian solution is to establish property rights in order to facilitate some form of bargaining or exclusion. Another way of viewing this is that the establishment of property rights permits flows of finance to occur, with all the relevant incentives for securing optimality now being enabled.

3.   Financial flows: a review of the issues

Focusing financial flows on developing countries
Recent advances in wealth accounting indicate that the conditions for sustainability centre round the notion of increasing stocks of overall per capita wealth (see Chapter 19). In turn, wealth comprises a broad spectrum of assets – conventional man-made capital, human capital, social capital and environmental (natural) capital. Preliminary wealth accounts indicate that it cannot be taken for granted that rich countries pursue paths of development that obey the fundamental 'rising per capita wealth' rule (Hamilton, 2000; Hamilton and Clemens, 1999). Nonetheless, by far the largest proportion of countries that fail to meet the rule are developing economies. In what follows we assume that the focus should be on correcting non-sustainability in the developing world, and hence the focus should also be on financial flows to developing countries, or on changing financial flows that currently harm poor countries' prospects for sustainability.

Reducing damaging financial flows: subsidies

One approach to financing sustainability that commands wide assent, and which appears to be 'win–win', is the redirection of existing financial flows that are both inimical to economic efficiency, narrowly construed, and to environmental progress. Subsidies to inputs and outputs both appear in this category and a substantial literature has grown up on the issue (for example van Beers and de Moor, 2001; Porter, 2002; Michaelis, 1996; OECD, 1996; 1997; 1998; Milazzo, 1998). The basic argument is that subsidies involve deadweight losses of well-being regardless of any environmental effects. Once the latter are brought into consideration, the scale of the combined inefficiency can be substantial. Moreover, a growing part of the subsidy literature draws attention to the fact that subsidies often do not, contrary to initial expectations, benefit the poor. Even when targeted at the poor, middle income groups tend to manipulate the subsidy system so that it benefits them. This should hardly occasion surprise once it is recognized that, like many regulations, subsidies create rents and hence a whole 'industry' emerges which seeks to capture the rents (see also Chapters 13 and 14). It is more likely that the powerful will capture the rents, further marginalizing the poor. Subsidies therefore have an equity dimension as well as an efficiency dimension.

Van Beers and de Moor suggest that, globally, subsidies to inputs and outputs, especially in agriculture, energy, water and fisheries may amount to just over $1 trillion annually. Nearly 70 per cent of these subsidies are in OECD countries. Perhaps the most startling figure is that agricultural subsidies in OECD countries account for over 30 per cent of entire world subsidies. From the standpoint of sustainability these subsidies can be thought of as highly damaging financial flows that finance non-sustainability. Not only do subsidies in OECD countries harm the environment in OECD countries, but Anderson et al. (2000) have simulated the effects of removing rich countries' tariff and non-tariff barriers to developing country exports. While it is true that developing countries face even larger barriers from protectionist policies in other *developing* countries, rich country protection costs the developing world over $100 billion annually.

It is hardly surprising therefore that those seeking finance for sustainable development should target subsidies since they appear to damage rich country environments and also damage the growth potential of poor countries by restricting and denying them markets. Subsidies within developing countries can often absorb significant fractions of public expenditure, further precluding the provision of genuine public goods in those countries. Subsidies also deny the ability of public utilities any chance to finance their own investment programmes since revenues systematically tend to fall short of costs of provision. Pearce (2002) also notes hitherto neglected effects, for example subsidies in the rich and poor world encourage resource depletion and environmental damage that harms the well-being of the poor by depleting their human capital through ill-health. Water shortages, water pollution, deforestation are all examples of this indirect link. Some idea of the potential for financing is that current annual subsidies are some 16–17 times the annual flow of official development aid to developing countries.

But how realistic is it to expect diversion of existing subsidies into projects and policies consistent with sustainability? The truth is that removing subsidies involves losers, and hence such policies cannot be described as 'win–win'. The problem is that the losers are those with the vested interest in the subsidy regime continuing and even expanding. Since those interests are, *ex hypothesi*, those with the power to capture the rents arising from subsidy regimes, it follows that removing subsidies is far from easy. Pearce and Finck von Finckenstein (1999) survey the various conditions under which subsidy regimes might be radically altered. These include careful timing of announcements to avoid likely political coalitions objecting to the changes and even undertaking the changes during periods of major political upheaval. But many of the efforts have been quite subtle, for example retaining a subsidy on a good that is purchased by rich and poor alike but differentiating the product so that the rich come to perceive it as inferior.

Reducing damaging financial flows: debt repayments
Forgiving debt repayments has become an integral part of overseas aid regimes in the last decade or so. The links to sustainable development are twofold. First, debt repayments come from public funds that could otherwise be used for the provision of public goods in the indebted country. Hence investment in for example education and health suffers. Second, debt repayments have to be in hard currencies, which means that the indebted country has to earn foreign exchange. This it may do by focusing on exporting natural resources, such as timber, in an unsustainable manner. As far as deforestation is concerned, the second of these linkages has been investigated in two major meta studies, Kaimowitz and Angelsen (1998) and Geist and Lambin (2001). Neither finds an unambiguous link between debt and deforestation, while Geist and Lambin regard the link as being very weak. This suggests that debt-forgiveness is unlikely to have any significant effect. Strand (1995) sets out a theoretical model in which exactly this result emerges when debt forgiveness is not backed up by conditionality. Whatever the benefits of debt forgiveness, they are likely to show up more in the increased flexibility of public expenditures generally rather than in natural resource damage.

Increasing financial flows: official foreign aid

Whereas direct private investment flows from rich to poor countries will generally be guided by market rates of return, and therefore have their justification in terms of conventional commercial criteria, official aid flows are more directed at the provision of public goods and services. As noted above, these public goods are integral to sustainability, including as they do infrastructure, water, education, health, power generation and the environment. Calls for increased foreign aid from donor countries (the OECD 'Development Assistance Committee' (DAC) countries) have been long-standing. Currently, only five nations exceed the United Nation's target of 0.7 per cent of donor GNP. Net Overseas Development Assistance (ODA) has risen in real absolute terms to some US$60 billion in 2002–03 (2002 prices), but compared to 1992–93 shows only a 5 per cent increase. The United States' share of ODA has fallen from 30 per cent in 1982–83 to 23 per cent in 2002–03, the absolute real amount of US aid being approximately constant over that 20-year period (www.oecd.org/dataoecd). The 0.7 per cent target, if it was met overnight, would increase flows from some $69 billion in 2003 to over $190 billion. Note that the implied increased scale ($130 billion) is similar to the $100 billion *adverse* flows arising from rich country protection policies.

Apart from moral arguments, increasing official aid has its justification in the potential role of official aid in increasing the provision of public goods in developing countries. The caveat is that the aid should be effective and here there is a further debate with claims and counter-claims about the extent to which even existing aid flows, let alone increased ones, contribute to development goals. Collier and Dollar (2001) conclude that aid may well be ineffective if it is not accompanied by 'good' policies. Once the appropriate policies are in place, however, both the rate of return to those policies and the effectiveness of aid is increased. The policy reforms involved in this assessment are those that tend not to be supported by the NGO community: macroeconomic stability and trade openness, but few would argue that the rule of law strongly influences development potential.

Increasing financial flows: looking for deep pockets

Whereas the debate over official aid focuses on both the donor ability to pay and the recipient's ability to utilize funds, the NGO community has targeted what might be called the 'supply side only' approach by looking for sources of 'mega-funds'. The object here is to find a tax base that could be subject to a very modest tax rate but with the capability to yield potentially large revenues. Currency dealings have been targeted, invoking, perhaps somewhat unfortunately, Nobel prize-winner James Tobin's name in the form of a 'Tobin tax'. Tobin was concerned with a tax to assist currency market instability. The NGO Tobin tax proposal is simply a source of revenue. To make the tax palatable to the financial markets, the suggestion by the Stamp Out Poverty campaign, an alliance of NGOs formed in 2005, is for a very modest tax rate per currency transaction. Since annual foreign exchange transactions are of the order of $250 trillion per annum, it is easy to see that even small tax rates would raise large sums of money. The problems with these kinds of financing proposals are many. Apart from the low likelihood of implementation and the high transactions costs, the tax is divorced from activities that contribute to non-sustainability. Currency transactions are either counterparts to real transactions which are likely already to attract an element of externality tax, or they are designed for arbitrage and a smooth functioning of financial markets. There is no obvious link to activities detrimental to sustainability and hence no link to the polluter pays principle. In short, it is hard to argue that foreign exchange transactions contribute to non-sustainability. Indeed, the opposite would appear to be the case. If so, the 'Tobin tax' becomes a tax on sustainable development, not a tax to deliver sustainability.

4.   Market creation: paying for environmental services

The start of this chapter indicated that the creation of markets in currently non-market goods and services generates a flow of finance that mimics the financial flows for market goods. The differences are likely to be that the goods and services provided will have significant public good characteristics. Those paying for the services are therefore going to be governments or government agencies, or organizations with altruistic goals. This indeed is how this form of market creation has evolved. Since there is now a huge number of such initiatives, only a few of the more important examples can be provided. Reviews of many of the transactions can be found in Daily (1997), Pagiola et al. (2002), Swingeland (2003), Pearce (2004) and Scherr et al. (2004).

Debt-for-nature swaps

'Debt-for-nature' swaps (DfNSs) began in the late 1980s and continue to this day, although the parties involved tend to have changed over the years. They are essentially Coasian, in that an agent concerned to secure environmental conservation or some form of human capital investment buys secondary international debt denominated in hard currencies and offers to cancel or convert it in exchange for the good or service in question. Thus, an NGO or a government might convert debt from a forested country in return for conservation of the forests. Other swaps have related to education and health initiatives, but most are linked to environmental products and services.

All swaps are confined to commercial debt – debts owed to private lenders such as commercial banks – and official bilateral debt, that is debt owed to foreign governments. No multilateral debt (for example World Bank loans) is involved in the swaps, which has limited the prospects for developing this instrument. Bilateral debt deals tend to operate through the Paris Club, a group of bilateral lenders dedicated to reducing and converting debt that threatens poor country development. In 1990, the Paris Club agreed to allow a considerable portion of international debt to be dealt with via debt-for-development swaps. In the event, only a limited number of creditor countries have operated such schemes.

Some of the most celebrated debt swaps involving governments and NGOs are those under the Enterprise for the Americas Initiative (EfAI), established in 1990. The debt in question is owed by Latin American and Caribbean countries to the USA. The US Tropical Forest Conservation Act (TFCA) of 1998 enabled further expansions of the EfAI, permitting debt reductions against forest conservation. From 1991 to 1993 EfAI conversions amounted to $875 million face value, creating local trust funds in seven Latin American/Caribbean countries of $154 million. The TFCA has provision for $325 million of funding. Another significant government player in DFNSs is Switzerland, which set up a Swiss Debt Reduction Facility in 1991. The Swiss programme involves several forms of conditionality: there must be economic reform in the indebted country, there must be rule of law, and there must be a general debt reduction programme in the country in question. The Swiss deals have involved some $460 million face value debt or over $160 million of redemption value and investment funds (leverage appears to be zero on the Swiss deals).

Pearce (2004) shows that, to 2003, DfNSs amounted to some $5 billion when measured in terms of the face value of the debt, and just over $1 billion when measured at the purchase price. These figures are heavily influenced by one 'package deal' with Poland with a discounted value of nearly $600 million. But the sums are also leveraged as other investors piggy-back on the DfNSs. This raises the total value by some $2 billion. DfNSs are attractive to the indebted country since they reduce foreign exchange commitments, albeit for attenuated sovereignty over some natural resources. They are attractive to NGOs since they involve modest costs for potentially large scale conservation – costs per hectare of land conserved appear to be no more than a few dollars – and because they meet NGO goals of providing public environmental goods at the global level. They are also attractive to donor governments who are faced with pressures for debt forgiveness. DfNSs permit a kind of 'forgiveness with conditions', but with the conditions being generally benevolent.

The Global Environment Facility

The Global Environment Facility (GEF) was established in 1990 in a 'Pilot Phase', or GEF I, which lasted from 1991 to 1994. It is a United Nations Agency which functions by donations from OECD countries and a few non-OECD countries. Its initial activities were unrelated to any international environmental conventions other than the Montreal Protocol on ozone layer depletion. Its coverage was biodiversity, climate change, ozone layer depletion and, curiously, 'international waters' – seas and lakes shared by two or more nations. But the GEF soon took on the official role of being the financing mechanism for the Framework Convention on Climate Change (1992), the Convention on Biological Diversity (1992), the Stockholm Treaty on Persistent Organic Pollutants and the Convention to Combat Desertification. The implementing agencies were initially the World Bank (WB), United Nations Environment Programme (UNEP) and the United Nations Development Programme (UNDP), with various other agencies being given similar powers later on.

The basic idea of the GEF is that it should assist in financing activities in the developing countries and the economies in transition that would be of benefit to the global community but which the relevant countries would not undertake as part of their normal development activities. Put another way, the GEF seeks to internalize the 'global externality' arising from development activity. An example might be a coal-fired power plant that a developing country considers the cheapest option for meeting extra power demand. Coal has a high carbon content so contributes significantly to global warming. The role of the GEF would be to investigate alternatives to coal – for example natural gas, energy efficiency, or even renewable energy. Since, *ex hypothesi*, coal is the cheapest option, the developing country needs an inducement to take on the additional or 'incremental' cost. By paying this incremental cost, the GEF secures the global benefit it was set up to secure. While the notion of incremental cost is meaningful for climate change, it is less obvious how it would be calculated in the context of biodiversity conservation. Incremental cost would have to be compared to a hypothetical baseline of what the host country would have done without the GEF's intervention. Host countries have an incentive to say they would have done nothing so that the full cost of conservation is met by the GEF.

The parallel with a Coasian bargain is obvious. Developing countries have sovereign rights to use their natural resources as they see fit, but the world as a whole has an interest in, and would benefit from, their conservation. The 'polluter pays' principle fails because of the global pervasiveness of the externalities, sovereign rights, and the poverty of the polluters. Hence, the 'beneficiary pays' principle is invoked. It can be seen that the

GEF is 'Coasian' in style, but because it seeks to provide global public goods, beneficiaries do not bargain with those who own the property rights. Rather, an international agency representing governments bargains on their behalf. As with DfNSs, various forms of co-financing occur, with the ratio being approximately 2:1 in favour of the other forms of finance. The extent to which this co-finance is 'additional', that is is not taken from financial flows for other development or conservation purposes can only be guessed at.

Table 27.1 suggests that GEF expenditures have been running at about $1 billion p.a. across all target areas, with around 60 per cent of expenditures being for climate change control.

The GEF and DfNSs exemplify the 'beneficiary pays' market creation approach. How far the associated financial flows are additional is unknown – there is some suspicion that some part of the official DfNSs and some part of the GEF expenditure is being met by diverting other overseas development assistance. However, both are examples of innovative global market creation. Both also operate in a 'bottom up' mode with outcomes being determined on a project-by-project basis. Moreover, the skills and experience generated by these deals has direct application to the development of other financial instruments for sustainable development, as we see shortly. These global examples are matched by a multitude of one-off deals in which, say, a conservation agency in the USA or Europe will pay for conservation in an area of a developing country. In some cases, notably in Costa Rica, an imaginative package of deals has been developed ranging from payments for forest conservation, through to carbon offsets and bio-prospecting (paying for genetic information from forests for example). The Costa Rican experience has attracted extensive

Table 27.1   GEF allocated funds and co-financing 1991–2002 ($ million)

	Climate change	Bio-diversity	International waters	Ozone depletion	POPs	MFAs	Total
GEF	1409	1486	551	170	21	210	3847
Co-financing	5000	2000	n.a.	67	n.a.	n.a.	7067
Total	6409	3486	551	237	21	210	10914

Notes: MFAs = multi-focal areas such as land degradation. In 2002 land degradation was recognized as a separate focal area. POPs = persistent organic pollutants, approved as a focal area in 2001 and linked to the Stockholm Convention. Co-financing estimates for biodiversity and climate change are approximate and include expected sums.
n.a. = not available but assumed to be zero or close to zero.

Source: GEF allocations from GEF (2002a). Co-financing estimates from GEF (2002b).

commentary – see for example Chomitz et al. (1998) and Rojas and Aylward (2003).

5.   Market creation: new financial instruments

One of the most interesting developments in sustainability financing has come with the development of new financial instruments to cover environmental risks or environment-related risks. These risks can be 'natural', for example changes in the weather, or they can be induced by regulation. An example of the latter would be a limit, or 'cap', set on greenhouse gas emissions in the name of global warming control. Such aggregate caps are then assigned in some way to those who emit the greenhouse gases. What is needed then is a market in the emission credits or debits that arise from, respectively, over-achieving and under-achieving an emission target. A secondary market arises which trades claims in emission reduction.

A variant on regulation-induced markets are self-regulatory markets where the emission reduction is self-imposed either out of altruism or, more generally, because corporate performance is socially rated according to some environmental and social performance index. It may pay corporations to adopt 'corporate social responsibility' (CSR) targets in order to have a higher social profile consistent with long term profits and the general avoidance of bad publicity. Legal liability for environmental pollution obviously does have an impact on corporate asset values. It is less obvious that legal pollution has such an impact, the literature being ambiguous because of poorly designed studies and advocacy rather than rigorous analysis. A study by Konar and Cohen (2001) for the USA does suggest that legal pollution may impose an intangible asset liability of around 10 per cent of the replacement value of tangible assets.

Weather derivatives and 'catastrophe (CAT) bonds' are examples of financial instruments that emerged in the 1990s to cope with natural climate variability. Weather derivatives began in 1997 in the USA and are financial contracts for protection of revenues in face of uncertainty about the weather. They are akin to insurance but with the difference that payout is triggered by the weather condition rather than by any proof of loss on the part of the insured. Self-evidently, weather derivatives began life mainly in the context of the energy sector where seasonal peaks and troughs of demand have considerable impacts on energy providers. But demand from recreational activities such as sports has also grown.

CAT bonds have a similar function, but in this case to insure against natural disasters such as earthquakes, storms, hurricanes and so on. Where this was once the province of insurance and reinsurance, some catastrophes in the late 1990s produced financial losses that outstripped the capacity of the insurance market. Insurers turned to the capital market. CAT bonds attract investors who are keen to act like reinsurers, securing returns well above money-market yields against a default risk (the risk that the catastrophic event will happen) several times lower than this. By buying bonds diversified across risks that are uncorrelated, the investor obtains considerable security. Moreover, CAT bonds are unaffected by the normal variations in financial markets – only the natural event risks matter. A secondary market has also begun to emerge, that is the bonds themselves are traded.

The relevance of these financial instruments to sustainable development may appear limited. But what these instruments are demonstrating is that financial markets can and do adapt to the changing nature of risks. In so far as disasters are threats to sustainability, these financial instruments have a role to play in ensuring that catastrophes do not bring about social collapse in the face of no insurance. Moreover, some catastrophes of the kind covered by the CAT bond market may increase with global warming, so that the market effectively adapts to the variable damage that warming is likely to bring.

The development of a derivatives market in greenhouse gas emission reduction is better known outside as well as inside financial market circles. The first carbon offsets or 'joint implementation' (JI) projects began in the USA in the late 1980s. Those deals were voluntary, that is they did not reflect any requirement to comply with a regulation, national or international. In the very first deal, Applied Energy Services invested in carbon sequestration in Guatemala, and there was no regulatory requirement to offset its own carbon emissions. The deal involved sequestering or reducing emissions of carbon dioxide outside of the own source of emissions. If there is a regulatory obligation to cut emissions the motivation for the trade would be that it is cheaper to cut emissions or sequester carbon through the trade rather than 'at home'. In a voluntary context, the motivations were primarily good corporate image and learning how the market would operate. Later trades in the 1990s were undertaken with the aim of anticipating Kyoto Protocol targets, but there was also some effort to 'capture' the regulatory process by showing forward commitment.

Joint implementation involves bilateral trades: the investor pays for reductions in emissions compared to some baseline in another location, but secures the credit for emissions reduction. 'Activities Implemented Jointly' was initiated in 1995 by Conference of Parties to the Framework Convention on Climate Change with the explicit aim of learning how joint implementation would work. Joint implementation between rich and poor countries was enabled in the 1992 Framework Convention on Climate Change but projects could not secure credits against the 2008/10 Kyoto Protocol targets. A significant number of the joint implementation projects came from the US 'Initiative on Joint Implementation' (USIJI) begun by the Clinton Administration in 1993. USIJI was originally designed to help the USA secure its Rio voluntary target of returning to 1990 emissions by 2000. The US had ratified the Framework Convention in 1994. The USIJI projects range across energy conservation, energy production (mainly switching to lower carbon energy sources in power generation), and carbon sequestration in biomass.

Notable host countries included Costa Rica, where the benefits of being a carbon trade host were recognized early on, Russia and Mexico. Various other initiatives were announced. Notable among the leaders were the Dutch Government's ERUPT programme (Emission Reduction Unit Procurement Tender), some programmes in Canada, Oregon, and the World Bank's Prototype Carbon Fund.

With the advent of the Kyoto Protocol, negotiated in 1997 and brought into force in 2005, three forms of greenhouse gas trading, or 'flexibility mechanisms', emerged:

(a)   Article 6 of the Protocol enables Annex 1 countries (basically OECD plus transition countries) to trade among themselves to secure emission reduction units (ERUs). Trades cover emission sources, such as burning fossil fuels, and so-called 'sinks'. Sinks refer to the growing of biomass (trees and other vegetation) which absorbs, or 'fixes', carbon dioxide from the atmosphere at a faster rate than it emits it. These trades must be *additional*, that is over and above what would have happened without the project, and must be *supplemental* to domestic actions, implying that, despite trading, the emphasis must be on domestic reduction activities. Article 6 carbon trading is known as 'joint implementation' and is project-based. The private sector may participate in such trades if approved by the relevant government.

(b)   Article 17 states that Parties listed in Annex B (that is countries with mandatory quantitative targets under the Protocol) 'may participate in emissions trading' but, again, such trading shall be 'supplemental to domestic actions' to meet stated targets. The units of this trade are assigned amount units (AAUs). Several proposals emerged for the establishment of an allowance trading system – for example by the governments of Australia, Canada, Iceland, Japan, New Zealand, Norway, Russia and the USA (before withdrawal). Article 17 carbon trading is known as 'emissions trading' or allowance trading.

(c)   Article 12 defines a *Clean Development Mechanism* (CDM) which involves Annex 1 countries (who have legally binding obligations) trading with non-Annex 1 countries, that is those without any obligations. Whilst virtually identical with joint implementation, the CDM establishes a principle of self-interest from the developing countries' point of view, namely that trades must contribute to their sustainable development. The Protocol is silent on the meaning of the term 'sustainable development'. The units of credit under the CDM are 'certified emission reductions' (CERs). The CDM is project-based.

A fourth form of trading arises for collective targets of which the prime example is the European Union (EU) collective target. The EU emissions trading scheme sets a 'bubble' over the Europen Union such that EU member states can trade within that bubble to achieve their goals under the EU burden sharing agreement.

Allowance-based trading of kind (b) is a cap and trade scheme. Central authorities designate an emission limit for the country, and each source has an emission limit given to it in a national allocation plan. The permits are freely tradable but each source must not, at some designated date, emit more pollutants than it has permits for. The US acid rain programme is the best example of such a scheme, but the EU Emissions Trading Scheme (EU ETS) also has such features. Schemes of kind (c) and (a) are baseline and credit schemes and tend to be project-based, that is trades are confined to a single or small set of projects. A baseline level of emissions is specified and the difference between actual and baseline emissions is credited, and credited amounts can be traded. The sources producing the emissions do not (necessarily) have a total emissions cap as in the cap and trade schemes.

The scale of the existing carbon trade market is not easy to gauge (as of 2005). Lecocq and Capoor (2003) summarized the market (other than AIJ) as comprising: (a) allowance trading currently about 4 per cent by *volume* of total trades (excluding AIJ), but (b) about 70 per cent of *transactions* are AAU. The main motives for trades are legal compliance, anticipatory legal compliance with Kyoto, voluntary compliance, and 'retail schemes' (good image projects). Between 1996 and 2003 project-based trades amounted to 220 mtCO_2e with the annual volume doubling each year from 2001. Since then most trades are Kyoto 'pre-compliance' projects, these trades having been delayed during the period when the rules of trading were not clear. The main players have been the World Bank's Prototype Carbon Fund, the Netherlands, and increasingly Japanese private buyers anticipating difficulties with complying with Japan's Kyoto target. Latin America has been the largest host for projects in volume terms. Initial prices have been lower than anticipated (the same phenomenon was witnessed with the US sulphur trading market), but the market remains thin.

The major regional market is the EU ETS which started operations in 2005 as part of the EU's commitments under the Kyoto Protocol.

The EU ETS covers 12 000 installations and has two initial phases: 2005–07 as the start-up phase and 2008–12 as the first five-year phase, 2012 coinciding with the end of the Kyoto commitment period (the time at which targets must be met). The system is akin to a cap-and-trade with each member State producing a National Allocation Plan (NAP) that has to be agreed by the European Commission. There is no overall EU 'cap'; however, each Member State determines the total allowances in combination with the Commission. Permits are initially grandfathered (allocated according to some formula related to past emissions or politically determined, but simply 'given' to emitters). There is however a facility for 5 per cent of permits to be auctioned in the set-up period, and 10 per cent in the first period. This is designed to make allowance for new entrants who might otherwise be excluded by permit holders. To all intents and purposes the currency of the EU ETS is the Kyoto AAU. Penalties for non-compliance, that is for emissions that exceed allowances held at the end of an accounting period, are fairly severe at 50 euros per tonne CO_2 in 2005–07 and 100 euros in 2008–12. It is anticipated that some 6 billion allowances will be issued between 2005 and 2007 with an asset value of over 60 billion euros (Hartridge, 2005). In early 2005, allowances were trading at around 10 euros per tonne CO_2 (about 37 euros per tonne carbon).

Critics of emissions trading in the EU point to the complex way in which the EU ETS links to national Member State policies. For example, installations covered by a domestic regulatory scheme can be exempted from the EU scheme, provided this is agreed with the Commission. This may limit the market. There is a linkage to the other Kyoto mechanisms, but CDM trades can be integrated into the EU ETS only in a limited way. The problem of 'hot air' remains. Hot air refers to allowances that are held by some Eastern European countries, Russia and the Ukraine because their Kyoto targets are actually below 'business as usual' emissions. They thus have allowances that do not relate to any real emissions. If hot air is traded, then buyers (for example EU countries) could count the allowances against their own targets but there would be no corresponding real emission reductions in the seller countries. Finally, there has been considerable suspicion that the National Allocation Plans have been very generous and in alignment with 'business as usual' levels of emissions. Against this, the Commission is known to have forced the revision of several NAPs so that the national cap was lowered, and if allowances have been so generous it would be hard to explain the volume of daily trades (over 500 000 per day in 2005). Further, the 2005–07 phase is deliberately designed for 'learning', and experience with other trading schemes suggests that trades will grow and prices will be firmer as the Kyoto commitment period approaches.

6.   Conclusions

Overall, carbon finance demonstrates to the full the ability of markets to respond to regulations with government intervention being minimized. It is easy to criticize features of all the market creation developments in this chapter – each could no doubt be better designed and more comprehensive in coverage. But the significant fact is that these innovative solutions have emerged in a remarkably short space of time. If we mark the beginning of beneficiary-pays solutions with Coase's essay of 1960, then those markets developed within just 40 years. The carbon finance story is even more remarkable. The notion of tradable permits was introduced by J.H. Dales in 1968 (Dales, 1968), and within a decade forms of sulphur oxide trading were being practised in the USA. Sustainable development clearly is a major challenge, and some would say an unachievable one. But one thing is sure – economists and finance experts have shown all the imagination and resolve necessary to develop financial markets to respond to the challenge. In the end it may not be enough, but there seem to be no limits to options for financing sustainability.

References

Anderson, K., J. Francois, T. Hertel, B. Hoekman and W. Martin (2000), *Potential Gains from Trade Reform in the New Millennium*, Washington, DC: World Bank.

Barrett, S. (2003), *Environment and Statecraft: the Strategy of Environmental Treaty Making*, Oxford: Oxford University Press.

Chomitz, K., E. Brenes and L. Constantino (1998), *Financing Environmental Services: The Costa Rican Experience and its Implications*, Washington, DC: World Bank, mimeo.

Coase, R. (1960), 'The problem of social cost', *Journal of Law and Economics*, 3: 1–44.

Collier, P. and D. Dollar (2001), 'Can the world cut poverty in half? How policy reform and effective aid can meet international development goals', *World Development*, 29(11): 1787–802.

Daily, G. (ed.) (1997), *Nature's Services*, Washington, DC: Island Press.

Dales, J.H. (1968), *Pollution, Property and Prices: An Essay in Policy-making and Economics*, Toronto: University of Toronto Press, reissued in 2002 by Edward Elgar Publishing, Cheltenham, UK.

Geist, H. and E. Lambin (2001), 'What Drives Tropical Deforestation?, Land Use Change Center Report Series No. 4, Department of Geography, University of Louvain, Belgium.

Hamilton, K. (2000), *Sustaining Economic Welfare: Estimating Changes in Wealth per Capita*, Policy Research Working Paper 2498, Washington, DC: World Bank.

Hamilton, K. and M. Clemens (1999), 'Genuine saving in developing countries', *World Bank Economic Review*, 13(2): 33–56.

Hartridge, O. (2005), 'EU ETS – From Textbook to Creation of a Multi-billion Euro Market', Brussels: DG XI, European Commission, Mimeo.

Kaimowitz, D. and A. Angelsen (1998), *Economic Models of Tropical Deforestation: a Review*, Bogor, Indonesia: Center for International Forestry Research.

Konar, S. and M. Cohen (2001), 'Does the market value environmental performance?', *Review of Economics and Statistics*, 83(2): 281–9.

Lecocq, F. and K. Capoor (2003), *State and Trends of the Carbon Market 2003*, Prototype Carbon Fund, Washington, DC: World Bank.

Michaelis, L. (1996), 'The environmental implications of energy and transport subsidies', in OECD, *Subsidies and the Environment: Exploring the Linkages*, Paris: OECD, pp. 175–92.

Milazzo, M. (1998), *Subsidies in World Fisheries: a Re-examination*, Technical Paper 406, Washington, DC: World Bank.

Nakada, M. and D.W. Pearce (1999), 'The economics of acid rain in East Asia', *Energy and Environment*, **10**(6): 705–20.

OECD (1996), *Subsidies and the Environment: Exploring the Linkages*, Paris: OECD.

OECD (1997), *Reforming Energy and Transport Subsidies: Environmental and Economic Implications*, Paris: OECD.

OECD (1998), *Improving the Environment through Reducing Subsidies*, Paris: OECD, 2 volumes.

Pagiola, S., J. Bishop and N. Landell-Mills (eds) (2002), *Selling Forest Environmental Services: Market-based Mechanisms for Conservation and Development*, London: Earthscan.

Pearce, D.W. (2002), 'Environmentally harmful subsidies: barriers to sustainable development', keynote address to OECD Workshop on Environmentally Harmful Subsidies, Paris 7–8 November.

Pearce, D.W. (2004), 'Environmental market creation: saviour or oversell?', *Portuguese Economic Journal*, **3**(2): 115–44.

Pearce, D.W and D. Finck von Finckenstein (1999), *Advancing Subsidy Reforms: Towards a Viable Policy Package*, paper prepared for UNEP: Fifth Expert Group Meeting on Financial Issues of Agenda 21, Nairobi, December.

Porter, G. (2002), *Subsidies and the Environment: an Overview of the State of Knowledge*, COM/ENV/TD(2002)59, Paris: OECD.

Rojas, M. and B. Aylward (2003), *What are we Learning from Experiences with Markets for Environmental Services in Costa Rica?*, London: International Institute for Environment and Development.

Scherr, S., A. White and D. Kaimowitz (2004), *A New Agenda for Forest Conservation and Poverty Reduction: Making Markets Work for Low-Income Producers*, Washington, DC: Forest Trends, www.forest-trends.org.

Strand, J. (1995), 'Lending terms, debt concessions and developing countries' resource extraction', *Resource and Energy Economics*, **17**: 99–117.

Swingeland, I. (ed.) (2003), *Capturing Carbon and Conserving Biodiversity: the Market Approach*, London: Earthscan.

van Beers, C. and A. de Moor (2001), *Public Subsidies and Policy Failures*, Cheltenham, UK and Northampton, MA, USA: Edward Elgar.

Index